REFERENCE BOOKS BULLETIN 1984-1985

A compilation of evaluations appearing in *Reference Books Bulletin*, September 1, 1984– August 1985

Prepared by the
American Library Association,
Reference Books Bulletin
Editorial Board
Edited by Helen K. Wright
Compiled by Mary E. Gabel

AMERICAN LIBRARY ASSOCIATION

Chicago and London 1986

Cover design by Ellen Pettengell

Composed by Precision Typographers
in Century Schoolbook and Helvetica.
Display type, Bodoni Book, composed
by Pearson Typographers.

Printed on 50-pound Warren's 1854, a
pH-neutral stock, and bound in
10-point Carolina cover stock by
the University of Chicago Printing Department

Copyright © 1984, 1985 by the
American Library Association

Permission to quote any review in full
or in part must be obtained from the
Office of Rights and Permissions of the
American Library Association.

Permission to quote a review in full
will be granted only to the publisher
of the work reviewed.

Library of Congress Catalog Card
Number 73-159565

International Standard Book Number
0-8389-3329-7
International Standard Serial Number
8755-0962

Printed in the United States of America.

To Helen K. Wright

CONTENTS

Foreword vii
Preface ix
Reference Books Bulletin Editorial Board xi
Alumni xiii
Omnibus Articles 1
  Biographical Reference Sources 1
  Children's Home Reference Library 3
  General Consumer Health Reference Books: A Selected Annotated List 5
  Home Reference Books for Junior and Senior High School Students 7
  1984 Annual Encyclopedia Roundup 10
  Science and Technology Reference Sources for High School and Undergraduate Libraries 15
Reviews and Notes 23
Databases 119
Microforms 119
News and Comments 121
Index to Subjects in Reviews and Notes 143
Index to Type of Material 153

FOREWORD

This reprint of reviews from *Reference Books Bulletin* is the first to include a foreword. And it is right and proper that it should pay tribute to the Helen K. Wright Era, her 27 memorable years as Editor ending Sept. 1, 1985. A procession of *RBB* Board chairpersons has gratefully acknowledged her guidance, citing her energy and good sense, her sustaining devotion, diplomacy, and unwavering advocacy of Board policies. To all these encomiums we heartily subscribe.

Since the first publication of these reprints for the years 1956–60, the number of reviews has increased from about 40 titles a year to three times that number. Shorter notes have been added, with more than 400 published in 1977–78, a bumper year. Omnibus articles, covering such basic works as dictionaries, encyclopedias, yearbooks, and biographical sources, have increased in number. A table of contents by type of reference and a subject index first appeared in the 1983–84 volume, adding to ease of location.

The number of reviewers has varied through the years. They now number 25, with about the same number of alumni. They are librarians and library educators who are willing to spend hours writing heavily documented reviews and shorter notes, as well as reading the efforts of their fellow reviewers and offering helpful criticism. This process assures the balanced judgment for which the reviews have been distinguished.

RBB reviewers are also willing for their work to remain anonymous, being, for the most part, just "mad" about reviewing. As one of them remarked, "It is so good to write a review which you know will be carefully read and criticized by your peers." But they are not anonymous to Helen K. Wright, who has so carefully edited their work. She has been the balance wheel for 27 years. Not for nothing is she named Helen, the face that launched a thousand reviews—or more. She has taught a generation of would-be critics how to follow guidelines which have been refined over the years. It hasn't been easy. Her sound judgment is equalled only by her tact and patience. And when we remember how much food for thought she has given us we can only say the brief blessing:

> For every cup and plateful
> God make us truly grateful.

FRANCES NEEL CHENEY

PREFACE

After the Sept. 1, 1956 merger of *Subscription Books Bulletin* with *Booklist,* the American Library Association began to publish handy cumulations of the evaluations prepared by the Subscription Books Committee and its successors. The 1984–85 volume is the seventeenth such gathering; the cumulations have come out annually since 1980. *RBB* (as the magazine is now called) appears twice monthly from September through June and monthly in July and August within the covers of *Booklist,* a general review periodical also published by the American Library Association.

The evaluations cumulated here result from the Board's unique methodology. Titles are assigned to individual Board members, who draft evaluations. These evaluations are then critiqued by other Board members and subsequently are revised by the journal's editor under the direction of the chairperson of the Board.

The universe of reference works within the Board's scope is extensive: general books, microforms, and databases produced in English that are of potential usefulness in answering specific questions in home, school, public or academic libraries. As a rule, the Board excludes or gives low priority to: (1) non-English language works; (2) titles of local or parochial interest; (3) highly technical or specialized sources; (4) works about individuals who are not included in secondary school or college curricula; and (5) craft, hobby, or collector guides and handbooks.

During the 1960s, omnibus reviews became special features of the journal, and a major strength. Beginning in September 1984, the Board began presenting bibliographical essays on subjects of interest to its subscribers. This 1984–85 cumulation contains five such added attractions: "Science and Technology Reference Sources for High School and Undergraduate Libraries"; "Home Reference Books for Junior and Senior High School Students"; "Children's Home Reference Library"; "General Consumer Health Reference Books: A Selected Annotated List"; and "Biographical Reference Sources." Also reprinted here is the Board's first annual Encyclopedia Roundup.

In September 1985, Helen K. Wright, the *RBB* Editor for 27 years, became Assistant Director of New Product Development for ALA Publishing Services. This, then, is the last cumulation to be edited by her, and it is eminently appropriate that the *Reference Books Bulletin* Editorial Board dedicate this volume to her. Ms. Wright's contributions to the journal have been far above and beyond the call of duty—they have been extraordinary. All members of the *RBB* Editorial Board, past and present, salute Helen K. Wright and wish her all the best in her future endeavors.

STUART W. MILLER
Chairperson
Reference Books Bulletin
Editorial Board
1984–85

REFERENCE BOOKS BULLETIN EDITORIAL BOARD

STUART W. MILLER, Librarian, International Association of Assessing Officers, Chicago, Illinois, Chairperson

DOUGLAS G. BIRDSALL, Head of Public Services, North Dakota State University, Fargo, North Dakota

PAMELA S. BRADIGAN, Assistant Professor and Reference Librarian, Main Library, Ohio State University, Columbus, Ohio

FRANCES NEEL CHENEY, Professor Emeritus, George Peabody College for Teachers, Vanderbilt University, Nashville, Tennessee

FRANCES EVELYN CORCORAN, IMC Coordinator, Des Plaines School District 62, Des Plaines, Illinois

WINIFRED F. DEAN, Reference/Bibliographer, Social Sciences, Cleveland State University Library, Cleveland, Ohio

ALICE A. DUPUIS, Head, Reference Department, Miami-Dade Public Library System, Miami, Florida

RUTH M. HADLOW, Head, Children's Literature Department, Cleveland Public Library, Cleveland, Ohio

VIRA C. HINDS, Professor and Director, Affirmative Action, City College of New York, New York, New York

DONALD J. KENNEY, Head, General Reference Division, Newman Library, Virginia Polytechnic Institute and State University, Blacksburg, Virginia

JOHN C. LARSEN, Associate Professor, School of Library Science, Northern Illinois University, De Kalb, Illinois

MONA MCCORMICK, Associate Librarian, Reference Department, University Research Library, University of California at Los Angeles, California

RACHEL S. MARTIN, Retired Reference Librarian, Furman University, Greenville, South Carolina

RUTH J. PERSON, Associate Dean, School of Library and Information Science, Catholic University of America, Washington, D.C.

MARGARET POWER, Reference Librarian, DePaul University Library, Chicago, Illinois

LOIS L. REILLY, Retired Performing Arts Librarian, Performing Arts Library, Oakland University, Rochester, Michigan

ROGER SUTTON, Head Librarian, North Pulaski Branch, Chicago Public Library, Chicago, Illinois

DAVID A. TYCKOSON, Reference Department, Iowa State University Library, Ames, Iowa

J. LINDA WILLIAMS, Library Media Specialist, White Marsh School, Mechanicsville, Maryland

ALUMNI

Rao Aluri, Assistant Professor, Division of Librarianship, Emory University, Atlanta, Georgia

James D. Anderson, Associate Dean, School of Communication, Information and Library Studies, Rutgers University, New Brunswick, New Jersey

Bruce D. Bonta, Head, General Reference Section, Pattee Library, Pennsylvania State University, University Park, Pennsylvania

Jennifer S. Cargill, Associate Director of Libraries for Technical Processing, Texas Tech University Library, Lubbock, Texas

Raymond Carpenter, Professor, School of Library Science, University of North Carolina, Chapel Hill, North Carolina

Marianna Tax Choldin, Head, Slavic and East European Library, Russian and East European Center, University of Illinois, Urbana, Illinois

Mary E. Collins, Reference Librarian, HSSE Library, Purdue University, West Lafayette, Indiana

Milton H. Crouch, Assistant Director for Reader Services, Bailey Library, University of Vermont, Burlington, Vermont

Donald G. Davis, Jr., Associate Professor, Graduate School of Library and Information Science, University of Texas, Austin, Texas

Paul Z. Du Bois, Director of Library Services, Roscoe West Library, Trenton State College, Trenton, New Jersey

Jack Forman, Mesa Community College Library, San Diego, California

Norman Frankel, Editor, American Medical Association, Chicago, Illinois

John T. Gillespie, Dean, School of Library Science, Palmer Graduate Library School, C. W. Post Center, Long Island University, Greenvale, New York

Charles L. Gilreath, Head, Central Reference Department, University of Arizona Library, Tucson, Arizona

Barbara W. Guptill, Municipal Reference Librarian, Seattle Public Library, Seattle, Washington

Judith H. Higgins, Director, Learning Resource Center, Valhalla High School, Valhalla, New York

Patricia M. Hogan, Administrative Librarian, Itasca Community Library, Itasca, Illinois

Norman Horrocks, Director, School of Library Service, Dalhousie University, Halifax, Nova Scotia, Canada

Vincent J. Jennings, Documents & Map Librarian, Hofstra University Library, Hempstead, New York

Martin A. Kesselman, Coles Science Center, Bobst Library, New York University, New York, New York

Donald Krummel, Professor, Graduate School of Library & Information Science, University of Illinois, Urbana, Illinois

Ruth McConnell, Assistant Head, Young People's Department, San Antonio Public Library, San Antonio, Texas

Sharon D. McFarland, Head, Library Services, National Rehabilitation Information Center, Washington, D.C.

JOSEPHINE MCSWEENEY, Professor & Reference Librarian, Pratt Institute Library, Brooklyn, New York

H. ROBERT MALINOWSKY, Associate Professor, University of Illinois, Chicago, Illinois

A. P. MARSHALL, Ypsilanti, Michigan

LAURA L. MASON, Shelbyville, Missouri

ARTHUR S. MEYERS, Director, Muncie Public Library, Muncie, Indiana

JEANETTE E. MITCHELL, Librarian, Iolani School, Honolulu, Hawaii

HUGH PRITCHARD, Reference Librarian, Dimond Library, University of New Hampshire, Durham, New Hampshire

JAMES R. RETTIG, Reference Librarian, University Library, University of Illinois, Chicago, Illinois

JANE A. ROSENBERG, Council on Library Resources, Washington, D.C.

STEWART P. SCHNEIDER, Graduate Library School, University of Rhode Island, Kingston, Rhode Island

ALAN E. SCHORR, University Librarian, California State University, Fullerton, California

SUZY M. SLAVIN, Reference Department, McLennan Library, McGill University, Montreal, Quebec, Canada

PAULINE M. VAILLANCOURT, School of Library and Information Science, State University of New York at Albany, Albany, New York

SIGRID M. WASHINGTON, Regional Branch Librarian, District of Columbia Public Library, Woodridge Regional Branch, Washington, D.C.

LUCILLE M. WERT, Professor of Library Administration & Chemistry Librarian, University of Illinois, Urbana, Illinois

JOHN T. WILLIAMS, Visiting Scholar, University of Michigan, Ann Arbor, Michigan

WILEY J. WILLIAMS, Professor, School of Library Science, Kent State University, Kent, Ohio

A. VIRGINIA WITUCKE, Evanston, Illinois

RAYMUND F. WOOD, Encino, California

RICHARD D. WOODS, Associate Professor, Department of Foreign Languages, Trinity University, San Antonio, Texas

OMNIBUS ARTICLES

BIOGRAPHICAL REFERENCE SOURCES

American autobiography 1945–1980: a bibliography. Mary Louise Briscoe, editor. Madison, Univ. of Wisconsin Pr. [1982]. xiv, 365p. 29cm. cloth $30; to schools and libraries, 10 percent discount (0-299-09090-6).
016.92´0073 U.S.—Biography—Bibliography | Autobiography—Bibliography [CIP]   82-70547

Louis Kaplan's *Bibliography of American Autobiographies* (Univ. of Wisconsin Pr., 1962) listed and very briefly described 6,377 autobiographies by Americans published before 1945. This successor to Kaplan's bibliography lists 5,008 autobiographies published in the succeeding 35 years. The editor and her associates scoured *Biography Index* (H. W. Wilson, 1946–   ), relevant bibliographies, MARC records, and recent reviews. They have defined *autobiography* liberally to include memoirs, diaries, collections of letters, and ghostwritten works—and defined *American* to include books by foreigners long resident in the U.S. They also include earlier works omitted from the previous volume. They exclude "autobiographies published in books of genealogy, manuscripts, newspapers, or periodicals" as well as spurious works. A useful addition to public and academic libraries.

Author biographies master index. 2d ed. 2v. Detroit, Gale, 1984. xxxiv, 1,597p. 28cm. cloth $195 (0-8103-0662-X).
809 Authors—Biography—Indexes [CIP]   76-27212

Indexing many biographical dictionaries and directories of writers, this compilation contains hundreds of thousands of citations to writers. Information in each entry includes birth and death dates and references to biographical sources. A basic reference source for general research collections and a useful tool for collections with strong biographical reference holdings.

Biographical books 1876–1949. Bowker, New York, 1983. lviii, 1,768p. 29cm. cloth $110 + shipping and handling (0-8352-1603-9).
016.92´002 Biography—Bibliography [OCLC]   83-167356

Biographical books 1950–1980. Bowker, New York, 1980. xlix, 1,557p. 28cm. cloth $85 + shipping and handling (0-8352-1315-3).
016.92´002 Biography—Bibliography [OCLC]   80-149017

Reproduced from magnetic tape records used in Bowker's *American Book Publishing Record*, the more than 40,000 entries in each volume include biographies, autobiographies, letters, diaries, journals, and biographical references arranged by subject and surname of biographee. Data in each entry include basic bibliographic information, subject headings, and LC/Dewey classifications. Additional features in both volumes consist of an Author Index and a Vocation Index, providing subject access to some 10,000 personal names in each book. (The 1950–80 edition has a special Biographical Books in Index by title.) Valuable as retrospective bibliographies in biography.

Biographical dictionaries and related works. By Robert B. Slocum. Detroit, Gale, 1967. xxiii, 1,056p. 24cm. cloth $64 (0-8103-0972-6).
016.92 Biography—Dictionaries—Bibliography [CIP]   67-27789

Biographical dictionaries and related works: first supplement. By Robert B. Slocum. Detroit, Gale, 1972. xiv, 852p. 24cm. cloth $76 (0-8103-0973-4).
016.92 Biography—Dictionaries—Bibliography [CIP]   67-27789

Biographical dictionaries and related works: second supplement. By Robert B. Slocum. Detroit, Gale, 1978. xviii, 922p. 24cm. cloth $76 (0-8103-0974-2).
016.92 Biography—Bibliography [CIP]   67-27789

This comprehensive bibliography of biographical dictionaries, collective biographies, epitaphs, biobibliographies, bibliographic indexes, and biographical material in government manuals and portrait catalogs has some 7,300 entries in the supplements and 4,800 in the parent work. Each is divided into three sections: Universal Biography (collective biography not related to geographic areas or vocations), National or Area Biography, and Vocational Biography (13 major occupations). Three indexes at the end of the volumes provide readers with Author, Title, and Subject access to the material. Primarily of use in large academic and public library research collections.

Biographical dictionary of southern authors: originally published as Library of Southern Literature, v.XV. Atlanta, Martin & Hoyt Co., 1929; republished by Gale, 1978. xii, 487p. 23cm. cloth $70 (0-8103-4269-3).
810´.9´975 American literature—Southern States—Bio-bibliography [OCLC]   75-26631

Reprinted from a 1907 volume of *The Library of Southern Literature*, this biographical dictionary includes 3,800 sketches of both famous and obscure persons in a variety of fields. Most biographees lived in the South during the nineteenth century. Occasional entries have cross-references to other volumes of *The Library of Southern Literature*, making this volume somewhat less valuable than it would be if it were entirely self-contained. However, its eclectic coverage of lesser-known persons living in a geographic area and time largely ignored in retrospective biographical reference sources makes this a useful dictionary for large research collections emphasizing American literature and regional studies.

Biography almanac. 2v. 2d ed. Edited by Susan L. Stetler. Detroit, Gale, 1983. 1,600p. $85/set; $48 each (0-8103-1634-X).
016.92 Biography—Indexes [OCLC]

Organized in two volumes, this second edition has enhanced the value of this well-known biographical reference source appreciably. It is both current and retrospective and covers (in v.1) more than 23,000 names, an increase of over 500 from the first edition; citations picked up from the 1981 first edition have been updated. Entries include field(s) of expertise, nationality, nicknames and pseudonyms, date and place of birth and death, and which, of some 350 reference sources, cite the biographee and provide further information. The big improvement is in the second volume: a Chronological Index by year, a separate Index by birthdays, and a Geographic Index. A minor weakness, which could lead to some confusion, especially in the Geographic Index, is the lack of guide dates or words on each Index page. This source is less comprehensive than Gale's *Biography and Genealogy Master Index* (see below), but it is a more than adequate and far cheaper alternative for most public libraries.

Biography and genealogy master index: a consolidated index to more than 3,200,000 biographical sketches in over 350 current and retrospective biographical dictionaries. 2d ed. 8v. Edited by Miranda C. Herbert and Barbara McNeil. Detroit, Gale [c1975, 1980]. (Gale Biographical Index series, no.1) 28cm. cloth $900/set (0-8103-1094-5).
920´.073 U.S.—Biography—Indexes | Biography—Indexes | U.S.—Genealogy—Indexes | Genealogy—Indexes [OCLC]   81-06706

Biography and genealogy master index: 1983 supplement. 2v. 2d ed. Edited by Miranda C. Herbert and Barbara McNeil. Detroit, Gale, 1983. 784p. (Gale Biographical Index series, no.1) 28cm. cloth $170 (0-8103-1509-2).
920′.073 U.S.—Biography—Indexes ∥ Biography—Indexes ∥ U.S.—Genealogy—Indexes ∥ Genealogy—Indexes [CIP] 82-15700

Biography and genealogy master index: 1981–82 supplement. 2d ed. 3v. Edited by Miranda C. Herbert and Barbara McNeil. Detroit, Gale, 1982. xxiii, 641; 1,328; 2,052p. (Gale Biographical Index Series, no.1) 28cm. cloth $325/set (0-8103-1095-3; ISSN 0730-1316).
920′.073 U.S.—Biography—Indexes ∥ Biography—Indexes ∥ U.S.—Genealogy—Indexes ∥ Genealogy—Indexes [CIP] 82-15700

This invaluable index contains references to approximately 3,250,000 persons in more than 350 biographical dictionaries. It is supplemented annually (the 1981–82 supplement contains three volumes with an additional 1,000,000 entries, and the 1983 supplement has 630,000 new entries in two volumes). In addition to directing readers to biographical reference sources, the index cites birth and death dates for each biographee. The *Master Index* is by far the most comprehensive index to biographical information available, and it is indispensable for large research collections in the humanities and social sciences. Its various spin-offs in the publication series are obvious choices for subject reference collections.

Children's authors and illustrators: an index to biographical dictionaries. 3d rev. ed. Adele Sarkissian, editor. Detroit, Gale, 1981. xxxv, 667p. (Gale Biographical Index series, no.2) 28cm. cloth $130 (0-8103-1084-8).
016.809 Authors—Biography—Index ∥ Illustrators—Biography—Indexes [CIP] 81-1044

Covering 275 sources, this is truly as comprehensive an index of biographical information on children's authors and illustrators as there is in print. Covering authors and illustrators of exclusively children's books, authors of young adult books, and authors and illustrators "whose writings for adults have been adopted by children (like Mark Twain)," there are about 20,000 separate entries. Also included are such authors as John Steinbeck whose works are often required reading for class assignments. Each entry cites birth/death dates. A basic biographical source for research and specialized collections dealing with juvenile literature, elementary and secondary education, and librarianship.

Eponyms dictionaries index. Edited by James A. Ruffner et al. Detroit, Gale, 1977. xxviii, 730p. 29cm. cloth $125 (0-8103-0688-3).
423′.1 English language—Eponyms—Dictionaries ∥ Biography ∥ Eponyms—Indexes ∥ Eponyms—Dictionaries [OCLC] 76-20341

More than 500 biographical references were searched and more than 100 sources were checked for information in this alphabetical listing of names of persons and things named after them. The more than 13,000 names include dates of birth and death, nationality, occupation, source of biographical information, and a listing of eponyms. The 20,000 eponyms include the name of the person for which the thing was named, the subject or field of study (more than 60 are listed), and titles of sources of additional information. A unique source of trivia and brief biographical data valuable for public and academic library reference collections of all sizes.

Historical biographical dictionaries master index. 1st ed. Edited by Barbara McNeil and Miranda C. Herbert. Detroit, Gale, 1980. x, 1,003p. (Gale Biographical Index series, no.7) 29cm. cloth $230 (0-8103-1089-9).
920′.073′016 U.S.—Biography—Indexes [CIP] 80-10719

Using the first edition of the *Biography and Genealogy Master Index* as its parent base, this culling of more than 304,000 citations to deceased "historical personages" in 42 retrospective biographical sources cites birth and death dates and the abbreviations of sources in which biographical information can be found. Because it includes persons from all time periods and from all over the world, research collections specializing in world history and the history of particular nations will find this useful. Essential for general research collections.

Index to Spanish American collective biography: Mexico. v.2. By Sara de Mundo Lo. Boston, G. K. Hall, 1982. xxix, 373p. 28cm. cloth $68 (0-8161-8529-8).
016.92′008 Latin America—Biography—Bibliography—Union lists ∥ Catalogs, Union—U.S. ∥ Catalogs, Union—Canada [CIP] 81-4570

This second of four planned volumes of this valuable index to Spanish American collective biographies covers Mexico while volume 1 was concerned with Bolivia, Colombia, Chile, Ecuador, Peru, and Venezuela. Annotated entries are arranged alphabetically within each subject section of each volume and include not only collective biographies but also such biographical sources as *Who's Who* (*Quien es quien*) and reprints of articles published as monographs. Most of the writings are in Spanish and thus have Spanish-language bibliographical information; the descriptive annotations, however, are written in English. An abbreviation at the end of each entry indicates where the book can be found—all being in at least one U.S. or Canadian academic library. An Author Index, a short Title Index, an Index of Biographees, and a Geographic Index add important access for users. An unusually thorough and well-organized biobibliography and a must for Hispanic research collections.

The New York Times obituaries index. 2v. v.I, 1858–1968; v.II, 1969–1978. New York, Microfilming Corp., 1970; 1980. 196p., 131p. 28cm. cloth (v.I/$95: 0-667-00599-4; V.II/$85: 0-667-00598-6).
920′.02 (B) Obituaries—Indexes ∥ New York Times—Indexes [OCLC] 72-113422

In a single alphabetical listing, these two volumes cite obituaries (not the ones paid for) which appeared in *The New York Times* (353,000 in v.I; 36,000 in v.II). The latter volume also reprints verbatim 50 obituaries. Entries include name, assumed name, year, date, section, page, and column in *The New York Times*. Libraries with back issues of *The New York Times* will find this a necessary and very useful source because *The New York Times Index* does not adequately index persons as subjects.

Obituaries from The London Times: including an index to all obituaries and tributes appearing in The Times during the years 1971–1975. Comp. by Frank C. Roberts. Newspaper Archive Developments Limited, 1978; dist. by Meckler. 647p. 31cm. cloth $75 (0-930466-05-5).
920′.02 Obituaries ∥ Biography—20th century ∥ Obituaries—Indexes ∥ The Times, London—Indexes [OCLC] 77-22500

Obituaries from The London Times, 1961–1970. Comp. by Frank C. Roberts. Newspaper Archive Developments Limited, 1977; dist. by Meckler. 952p. 31cm. cloth $85 (0-930466-08-X).
920′.009′04 Obituaries ∥ Biography—20th century ∥ Obituaries—Indexes ∥ The Times, London—Indexes [OCLC] 76-362909

Obituaries from The London Times, 1951–1960. Comp. by Frank C. Roberts. Newspaper Archive Developments Limited, 1979; dist. by Meckler. 896p. 31cm. $85 (0-930466-16-0).
920′.02 Obituaries [OCLC] 79-12743

The Times of London obituaries of men and women from all over the world (about 60 percent British) are reprinted here just as they appeared in the newspaper. A Subject Index follows the main text. An index to the newspaper listing all the obituaries appearing in the paper during the period concludes each volume. Because of the unusually well written portraits, this volume has biographical reference value which newspaper obituaries do not usually have. However, only libraries without *Who Was Who* and updated biographical dictionaries need it.

Performing arts biography master index. 2d ed. Edited by Barbara McNeil and Miranda C. Herbert. Detroit, Gale, 1979, 1981. xxiv, 701p. (Gale Biographical Index series, no.5) 28cm. cloth $160 (0-8103-1097-X).
016.7902′092′2 (B) Performing arts—Biography—Dictionaries—Indexes [CIP] 81-20145

This second edition of what was originally titled *Theatre, Film, and Television Biographies Master Index Guide* covers more than 270,000 citations to more than 100 biographical sources in the performing arts. In addition to theater, film, and television, this volume also covers music, dance, puppetry, and magic. Each citation includes birth and death dates and the initials of the biographical source in which the information can be located. An essential index for general research collections and specialized performing-arts collections.

Pseudonyms and nicknames dictionary. 2d ed. Jennifer Mossman, editor. Detroit, Gale, 1982. 995p. 29cm. cloth $190 (0-8103-0547-X; ISSN 0277-0350).
920.02 Biography—20th century ∥ Anonyms and pseudonyms ∥ Nicknames [OCLC] 80-13274

New pseudonyms and nicknames: an inter-edition supplement to pseudonyms and nicknames dictionary. 2d ed. Issue 1, Jan. 1983. Jennifer Mossman, editor. Detroit, Gale [c1983]. 184p. 28cm. cloth $95 (0-8103-0548-8).
920'.009'04 Biography—20th century ‖ Anonyms and pseudonyms ‖ Nicknames [OCLC]   82-24158

Greatly expanded from the book's first edition, this very comprehensive dictionary identifies the real names of more than 40,000 people and of 50,000 historical and contemporary assumed names cited in 200 sources. The people listed have often been better known publicly by a variety of pseudonyms, nicknames, stage names, and aliases. Information includes date of birth and death, source(s) of information, nationality, occupation, and assumed names. A supplement (the first of two) adds more than 5,800 new persons (and 7,800 assumed names) to those appearing in the parent work; the supplement emphasizes the nineteenth-century American gunfighters and twentieth-century cult leaders. Because *Pseudonyms and Nicknames Dictionary* is a biographical dictionary as well as an index, it has broader use than other Gale biographical sources and therefore is appropriate in medium-sized and large academic and public library reference collections.

Through a woman's I: an annotated bibliography of American women's autobiographical writings, 1946–1976. By Patricia K. Addis. N.J. & London, Scarecrow, 1983. xiv, 607p. 22cm. cloth $37.50 (0-8108-1588-5).
016.92072'0973 Women—U.S.—Biography—Bibliography ‖ U.S.—Biography—Bibliography ‖ Autobiographies—Bibliography [CIP]   82-10813

Addis has compiled an unusually successful annotated bibliography covering 2,217 titles (autobiographies, letters, diaries, journals, memoirs, reminiscences, and travel accounts) written by American women in the 30-year period immediately succeeding Louis Kaplan's *Bibliography of American Autobiographies*. Entries are arranged alphabetically by author and include basic bibliographical information, birth/death dates, and accurate, succinct annotations. Persons listed in *Notable American Women* or *NAM: The Modern Period* are so cited. Three very helpful Indexes providing excellent access follow the text: an Index by "profession or salient characteristics"; an Index by subject matter; and one by title. A second volume is planned for the period before 1946. A must for academic, research, and large public library collections. Complements the coverage provided in Kaplan's successor, *American Autobiography 1945–1980* (see above).

Twentieth-century author biographies master index: a consolidated index to more than 17,000 biographical sketches concerning modern day authors as they appear in a selection of the principal biographical dictionaries devoted to authors, poets, journalists, and other literary figures. 1st ed. Edited by Barbara McNeil. Detroit, Gale, 1984. xix, 519p. (Gale Biographical Index series, no.8) 29cm. hardcover $60 (0-8103-2095-9); paper $25 (0-8103-2096-7); ISSN 0747-7279.
809'.04 Authors—20th century—Biography—Indexes [CIP]   84-10349

Users familiar with the publisher's *Author Biographies Master Index* will appreciate the value of this latest addition to the Gale Biographical Index series. Derived in part from the master work, this index includes approximately 171,000 citations to an estimated 90,000 persons contained in 55 biographical dictionaries (210 volumes)—many of which emanate from the publisher as well. This complements similar efforts dealing with journalists, performing artists, and writers for children and young adults. For persons needing access to sketches of modern authors in a wide array of biographical sources, this index will be most useful. For public and academic libraries.

Who was when? A dictionary of contemporaries. 3d ed. [By] Miriam Allen DeFord and Joan S. Jackson. New York, Wilson, 1976. n.p. [184p.] 26x35cm. cloth $38 (0-8242-0532-4).
902'.02 Biography—Chronology, Historical—Tables [CIP]   76-2404

Covering the period from 500 B.C. to 1974, this chronological yearly chart lists deceased famous persons and identifies their field(s) of contribution. It points out who was doing what at a specified time or during another famous person's lifetime. An alphabetical Name Index with birth and death dates completes the book. Limited in biographical detail, but useful as a chronology.

Writers for young adults: biographies master index. 2d ed. Adele Sarkissian, editor. Detroit, Gale, 1984. lix, 354p. 24cm. cloth $85 (0-8103-1473-8).
016.809'Authors—Biography—Indexes [CIP]   79-13228

This list of more than 15,000 writers of literature read by young adults indexes more than 500 biographical sources (largely the same sources as those indexed in Gale's *Children's Authors and Illustrators*, see above). The format of the two works is similar. Although many well-known authors such as Richard Peck and Judy Blume appear in both indexes, this index also includes songwriters and screenwriters and related media writers. This is a unique reference, particularly useful in collections supporting studies in education, librarianship, and juvenile/young adult literature.

CHILDREN'S HOME REFERENCE LIBRARY

Who? What? Where? When? How? Why? A child's ever-fresh curiosity becomes apparent at a very early age, and answers do not always come forth readily from adult minds. Such times, therefore, offer opportunities for parents to say, "Let's look it up together." Certainly, some checking can be done at local public libraries; however, it is often advisable to seek the answer when the query is still fresh. In this way, the reference book "habit" can be started even with preschoolers. After the initial information needs are satisfied, the family can then consider more in-depth coverage at a library. The immediate information needs of a child can be met through a basic home reference library which includes an encyclopedia, a dictionary, an atlas, and an almanac.

ENCYCLOPEDIAS

An encyclopedia is undoubtedly a major investment. Usually arranged in alphabetical order, encyclopedias are works which contain informational articles on a broad range of subjects. Generally, they are designed to stimulate or launch further exploration of a subject.

Following are five multivolume children's encyclopedias that are suitable for home purchase:

Britannica junior encyclopedia for boys and girls. Prepared under the supervision of the editors of Encyclopaedia Britannica. 15v. Chicago, Encyclopaedia Britannica, Inc., 1984. $279 plus shipping and handling.

This is not a junior version of the hefty adult set; rather it is specially designed to meet the curriculum needs of children, grades four through eight.

Coverage of continents, U.S. states, and foreign countries is especially good. There is some unevenness in the coverage of other subjects; however, the articles are, on the whole, generally accurate and usually free of bias. Currentness is spotty. While the text is readable and suitable for the intended audience, the style of writing is not especially lively. A special feature is the Ready Reference Index in volume 1, which contains about 15,000 brief facts and definitions. The format is serviceable but not distinguished.

Compton's encyclopedia and fact-index. 26v. Chicago, F. E. Compton Co., Division of Encyclopaedia Britannica, 1984. $499 to homes.

Coverage of subjects of interest to children in grades 6 through 12 is good. The material is written in a variety of styles—in addition to the articles, the set contains stories, poems, puzzles, and things to do. Since a controlled vocabulary is not used, some articles may prove too difficult for elementary school children. With its emphasis on practical and curriculum-related information. *Compton's* is, on the whole, an attractive set for children and young people.

Merit students encyclopedia. 20v. New York, Macmillan Educational Corp., 1984. $1,099.50 (home price); $1,299.50 (Merit Students Home Educational Program—the 1984 copyright of *MSE* along with other educational books and products); $449 + $16/shipping (school and library price); $414/shipping for two or more sets.

Created for children from fifth grade through high school, this set maintains a high degree of accuracy and has well-balanced, objective coverage of a broad range of subjects. Major emphasis is on social studies, science, and language arts. Generally *Merit* is more comprehensive in its coverage than *New Book of Knowledge, Britannica Junior*, and *Compton's*.

New book of knowledge. 21v. Danbury, Conn., Grolier, 1984. $650 home price plus shipping and handling.

The interest and curricular needs of children from preschool through junior high are covered in this set, which places particular emphasis on social studies, geography, and science. Many of the literary articles have "story contents"—poetry, stories, or excerpts from well-known books. There are also articles on games, hobbies, and leisure activities. Illustrative material, mostly in color, is very good. The *New Book of Knowledge* provides broad, accurate coverage of general information in an attractive format with high-quality writing.

World book encyclopedia. 22v. Chicago, World Book–Childcraft International, 1984. Home bindings: classical $599; aristocrat $549; standard $499 plus $29 for shipping & handling; school and library binding $404.

With many years of proven success in meeting the reference and informational needs and interests of children from grade four through high school, *World Book* entries are up-to-date, accurate, readable, and balanced. The set contains excellent graphics.

(For in-depth reviews of these multivolume children's encyclopedias see *Reference and Subscription Books Reviews*, May 15, 1983, p.1233–43.)

A comparatively inexpensive alternative to the encyclopedias listed above is *Funk & Wagnalls New Encyclopedia*, 29v. New York, Funk & Wagnalls, 1983, $125.81, (sold to home consumers only through supermarket, one volume at a time), $199.50 (to schools and libraries); licensed distributor: Proteus Enterprises, Inc., 2210 Camden Court, Oakbrook, IL 60521. This is a straightforward, easy-to-use, attractive, alphabetically arranged encyclopedia which offers excellent value for its price. It is useful for older children.

Although not sold or represented as an encyclopedia, *Childcraft—The How and Why Library* (Chicago, World Book–Childcraft International, 1984, $199 heritage binding) is especially designed for preschool and primary-grade children. This is an attractive, clearly presented "resource library" geared to the interests and curiosities of young children. Its 15 volumes are arranged by subject; for example, v.1 *Poems and Rhymes*; v.4, *World and Space*; v.7, *How Things Work*; v.15, *Guide for Parents*.

DICTIONARIES

As soon as children can read, they should have their own dictionary. For those not ready to read, there are even picture dictionaries designed to stimulate an interest in words and their meanings. Some factors to be considered in selecting dictionaries are *Authority*: Does the publisher have a long-term commitment to dictionary publishing? *Vocabulary*: Pick out some words that interest you and compare their definitions in several different dictionaries. *Entry Format*: Dictionaries for very young children should have a simple basic format—the main word, a short definition, a sentence using the word, and an illustration. For older readers, the entries should be more complex and include pronunciation, synonyms, word histories, and usage. *Special Features*: These can include instructions for use; history of the English language; information on abbreviations, signs, and symbols; tables of weights and measures; metric conversion tables. While such miscellanea are sometimes attractive, always consider the word list as the most important part of a dictionary, particularly if you have a general encyclopedia. *Format*: Check for sturdy binding, clear type, accurate and appealing illustrations, attractive page design, and opaque, nonglare paper.

The following children's dictionaries can be considered for home purchase:

Primary Level

Macmillan very first dictionary: magic world of words. New York, Macmillan, 1983. $10.95.

My first dictionary. Boston, Houghton Mifflin, 1980. $9.95.

Elementary Level

Children's dictionary. Boston, Houghton Mifflin, 1979. $11.95.
Macmillan dictionary for children. New York, Macmillan, 1982. $12.95.
Scott, Foresman beginning dictionary. Glenview, Ill., Scott, Foresman, 1983. $13.89.
Webster's elementary dictionary. Springfield, Mass., Merriam, 1980. $9.95.

Junior High Level

Webster's new world dictionary for young readers. New York, Simon and Schuster, 1983. $14.95.
American Heritage school dictionary. Boston, Houghton Mifflin, 1977. $10.95.

All in all, dictionaries for children should be attractive as well as informative and should be adapted to the specific needs and abilities of the intended audience. Parents may wish to check with their school districts to find out whether a particular dictionary is required or recommended for assignments.

(For fuller consideration, see *Dictionaries for Children and Young Adults* prepared by the Reference Books Bulletin Editorial Board and available from the American Library Association for $2.)

ATLASES

With global changes occurring so rapidly and with television bringing world events to the child's doorstep, it is good to have an atlas at hand to locate areas under discussion. Vacation trips, too, can be more exciting and meaningful with the use of maps.

An atlas contains a collection of maps, and many include physical maps which show landforms; political maps, which indicate national/local boundaries; route maps, which highlight roads, bridges, railways, etc.; and thematic maps, which cover specific information such as population, animals, plants, and products.

In selecting an atlas for children's use, it is wise to consider the following points: What is the reputation of the publisher, the editorial staff, and special contributors? What is the intended scope and purpose? Is the atlas all-purpose? What kinds of maps are included? Is it intended to meet the needs of a particular interest? Is the material current? Does it reflect the latest census figures (for the U.S., 1980)? In what order are the maps arranged? Is supportive text included? If so, is it placed logically with reference to the maps? Is the lettering legible? Are the colors varied and attractive? Is there a general index for the whole atlas?

The following atlases can be considered for home purchase:

For Younger Children

Big blue marble children's atlas. Milwaukee, Wis., Ideals, 1980. $9.95.
Intermediate world atlas. Maplewood, N.J., Hammond, 1984. $4.67.

Rand McNally picture atlas of the world. Chicago, Rand McNally, 1979. $7.95.

For Older Children

Ambassador world atlas. Maplewood, N.J., Hammond, 1983. $34.95.
Citation world atlas. Maplewood, N.J., Hammond, 1983. $19.95 (hardcover), $15.95 (softcover).
Goode's world atlas. Chicago, Rand McNally, 1982. cloth $19.95, paper $10.95.
National Geographic atlas of the world. Washington, D.C., National Geographic Society, 1981. $44.95.
Rand McNally cosmopolitan world atlas. Chicago, Rand McNally, 1981. $45.
Rand McNally family world atlas. Chicago, Rand McNally, 1981. $16.95.

(Some of the above atlases and others are reviewed in detail in "World Atlas Survey"—*Reference Books Bulletin*, September 1, 1983, p.40–50.)

ALMANACS

General almanacs, usually published annually, cover essential facts about a wide range of subjects: countries, events, personalities, politics, sports, economics, etc. An almanac not only provides quick reference but also invites browsing. Children, as well as adults, should find one of the following almanacs packed with interesting facts.

Information please almanac. Boston, Houghton Mifflin, 1984. cloth $9.95; paper $5.95
World almanac and book of facts. New York, Newspaper Enterprise Assn., 1984. cloth $11.95; paper $4.95.

OTHER SOURCES

Other reference materials can be added to a child's home reference library as special interests and money dictate. For example, a thesaurus such as Andrew Schiller's *In Other Words: A Beginning Thesaurus* (Lathrop, 1978, $11.95) and *Junior Thesaurus: In Other Words II* (Lathrop, 1978, $12.68) can help in the search for the right word; the *Guinness Book of World Records*, available in hardcover and in paperback, deals with superlatives of all kinds; the "Golden Nature and Science Guides" are inexpensive, attractive introductions to natural and physical sciences. The six-volume set entitled *New Book of Popular Science* (Grolier, 1984, $245), written by eminent scientists, offers very readable, timely information on all phases of science. The generously illustrated *Lands and Peoples* (6v., Grolier, 1983, $245), provides a wealth of information about the geography, history, economy, and culture of peoples around the world.

Where economy necessitates very prudent spending, a child's reference library can be provided in paperback format. A sampling of such purchases might be *The Columbia-Viking Desk Encyclopedia*, *Webster's New World Dictionary for Young Readers*, *Rand McNally World-master World Atlas*, and *World Almanac*.—*Ruth M. Hadlow, Reference Books Bulletin Editorial Board, 1984–1985.*

GENERAL CONSUMER HEALTH REFERENCE BOOKS: A SELECTED ANNOTATED LIST

Health information is perennially in great demand in libraries. Information on specific disorders, symptoms, drugs, doctors, surgical procedures, and laboratory tests are examples of the variety of requests that come across reference desks, especially those in public libraries. In response to this demand, publishers have produced a wealth of health-related materials which provide consumers with a wide choice. Listed below are my recommendations for relatively recent, general consumer-health reference guides; most of them include information on symptoms, disorders, and therapies, as well as general advice on maintaining good health. Also included are some standard medical reference sources that, on occasion, can also be used by laypersons. For the most part, I have omitted clinical texts, directories, medical dictionaries, first-aid manuals, nutrition and diet books, drug manuals, and books that deal with specific populations or with special disorders; each of these categories could easily have a list of its own.

Given the enormous number of titles in this field, there is no way this list can be comprehensive. It presents a sampling of what this reviewer felt to be suitable for library reference collections.

The alternative health guide. By Brian Inglis and Ruth West. New York, Knopf, 1983. 352p. illus. $19.95 (0-394-52789-5).

A guide to "natural" therapies including those that are physical, psychological, or paranormal in nature. Each therapy is explained, and its history, development, procedures, research evidence, and suitability are explored.

American Medical Association family medical guide. Editor in chief, Jeffrey R. M. Kunz. New York, Random House, 1983. 831p. illus. tables. charts. diagrs. 24cm. cloth $29.95 (0-394-51015-1).

This guide is divided into four sections: part I, The Healthy Body, consists of several self-tests with general information on such topics as keeping physically and mentally fit and controlling stress; part II, Symptoms and Self-Diagnosis, consists of 99 flow charts to help readers determine the significance and seriousness of particular symptoms. Most of the charts refer readers to more detailed information in part III, Diseases and Other Disorders and Problems, which includes several illustrated articles on specific disorders; part IV, Caring for the Sick, covers topics of general medical practice such as choosing a physician or caring for the sick at home.

Better Homes and Gardens new family medical guide. Edited by Edwin Kiester, Jr.; illus. by Kelly Solis-Navarro and Evanell Towne. Des Moines, Iowa, Meredith, 1982. 896p. illus. 29cm. hardbound $29.95 (0-696-00344-9).

This well-illustrated and fairly complete guide includes information on preventive medicine, specific organ systems, and disorders. It also advises on first aid, taking care of children, and caring for the ill at home.

Common symptom guide: a guide to the evaluation of 100 common adult and pediatric symptoms. By John Wasson, et al. 2d ed. New York, McGraw-Hill, 1984. xiii, 353p. 18cm. paper $13.95 (0-07-068435-9).

Approximately 100 symptoms are included in this guide written primarily for clinicians. Included for each is information on associated symptoms, medical and family histories, medications, physical examinations, and other general considerations.

Complete illustrated medical handbook. Edited by Mervyn Lloyd and Joan Gomez. New York, Book Thrift, 1981. 224p. illus. $14.98 (0-89673-096-4).

With more than 500 illustrations, most in color, this attractive guide provides clear information on medical ailments arranged by major organ systems of the body. There is also a glossary of medical terms and symptoms.

Conn's current therapy, 1984: latest approved methods of treatment for the practicing physician. Edited by Robert E. Rakel. Philadelphia, W. B. Saunders, 1984. xxxix, 982p. 27cm. cloth $42 (0-7216-2712-0; ISSN 0070-2102).

Written for physicians, *Conn's Current Therapy* provides information on the newest drugs and treatment methods available. Sections on methods are written by medical specialists who actually practice these procedures.

Current medical diagnosis & treatment, 1984. Edited by Marcus A. Krupp and Milton J. Chatton. Los Altos, Calif., Lange Medical, 1984. 1,153p. 26cm. paper $24 (0-87041-254-X).

Although intended primarily for health practitioners, this guide will give information on currently accepted methods of diagnosis and treatment for various medical disorders. Lists of recent references for further study are provided.

A doctor's guide to home medical care: the A to Z handbook of common symptoms, illnesses, and emergencies. By Trevor Weston. Chicago, Contemporary Books, 1982. 230p. illus. 23cm. paper $12.50 (0-8092-5970-2).

An alphabetical list of ailments with timetables of what to do. Also tells when one should see a doctor or if a self-help measure may be appropriate. There are chapters on how to stay healthy, avoid trouble, seek medical care, and maintain fitness.

Fishbein's illustrated medical and health encyclopedia. 4v. Morris Fishbein, medical editor. Westport, Conn., Stuttman, 1983. illus. 24cm. hardcover $39.95 (0-87475-245-0).

Probably the best-known consumer health guide, *Fishbein's* provides entries on health disorders, surgical procedures, and human anatomy and physiology. Many entries include accompanying photographs or illustrations, and many also cite research reports on new medical breakthroughs and developments.

Harvard medical school health letter book. Edited by G. Timothy Johnson and Stephen E. Goldfinger. New York, Warner, 1982. 544p. illus. paper $3.95 (0-446-30104-3).

An updated compilation of material that appeared in the *Harvard Medical School Health Letter,* a monthly publication devoted to consumer health issues. Articles are divided into sections on staying healthy, hazards of living, reproduction and child care, diseases of adulthood, problems of aging, and you and the doctor.

Health and medical horizons, 1982, 1983, 1984. New York, Macmillan Educational Co., 1982, 1983, 1984. 28cm. hardcover $19.95 (1982 & 1983); $25 (1984).

These handy and authoritative annuals consist of two parts: (1) a number of signed, clearly written, up-to-date feature articles with clear illustrations and photographs on all aspects of medicine that would be of concern to laypersons and (2) an encyclopedic section of topics from *Aging and the Aged* to *Teeth and Gums.* A Glossary of medical terms and a good index complete each year's output. Especially good for home, school, and public libraries.

Jane Brody's The New York Times guide to personal health. By Jane Brody; illus. by Karen Karlsson. New York, Avon, 1982, 1983. 724p. 23cm. paper $12.95 (0-380-64121-6).

Based on Jane Brody's "Personal Health" columns that appeared in the *New York Times* since 1976, this guide includes topics on nutrition, exercise, emotional health, sexuality and reproduction, abused substances, dental health, environmental health, safety, common health problems, and serious illnesses.

The Marshall Cavendish illustrated encyclopedia of family health: doctor's answers. 24v. New York, Marshall Cavendish, 1983. 2,692p. illus. 28cm. $299.95 (0-86307-127-9).

This extremely well-illustrated, -designed, and -organized compendium of health-related facts presents several patients' questions and physicians' answers and then proceeds to present accurate information and diagrams explaining medical views of the subject. For example, *Abortion* has eight queries and replies; then the discussion covers reasons for an abortion, counseling, how abortions are carried out, aftereffects, and reassurance—all this with four pertinent diagrams, including one showing the dilation and evacuation method. The books are easy to read, and easily comprehended language is used to explain medical procedures and concepts.

Merck manual of diagnosis and therapy. 14th ed. Rahway, N.J., Merck, 1982. 2,578p. 21cm. hardcover $19.75 (0-911910-03-4; ISSN 0076-6526).

A great deal of information in one volume, mostly dealing with various medical disorders and their symptoms, diagnosis, laboratory tests, prognosis, and treatment. Medical equipment is also described, and there are sections on special subjects such as radiology, biostatistics, and poisoning.

The New American medical dictionary and health manual. 4th rev. ed. By Robert E. Rothenberg; illus. by Sylvia and Lester V. Bergman. Bergenfield, N.J., New American Library, 1982. 530p. illus. 18cm. paper $4.50 (0-451-12027-2).

Rothenberg is a surgeon who teaches at New York Medical College. In this compact, handy manual, he defines in clear, easily understood language, thousands of medical terms. The health manual portion gives data under 27 headings such as anatomy tables, contagious diseases, temperature, first aid, and health insurance. This is an inexpensive, compact, and handy compilation.

Nutrition and health encyclopedia. By David F. Tver and Percy Russell. New York, Van Nostrand, 1981. 569p. 24cm. hardcover $29.50 (0-442-24859-8).

A one-volume encyclopedia of terms from the disciplines of nutrition, physiology, biochemistry, and general medicine. Bodily functions, body organs and systems, drugs, toxic substances, food additives, and trace elements are covered. Several tables with nutritional and dietary information are included.

One thousand one health tips and guides. By Lawrence Galton. New York, Simon & Schuster, 1984. 301p. 23cm. hardcover $17.95 (0-671-47689-0); paper, $7.95 (0-671-50935-7).

This conveniently organized medical dictionary covers everything from sweaty palms to suggesting relief of nasal stuffiness by drinking caffeinated coffee. It even verifies the latest scientific findings on the value of chicken soup for colds. The A to Z coverage is in part I (Health Tips); the briefer second section (Guidelines) gives helpful information on such topics as salt content of foods, drug side effects, and caloric value of foods. A concise medical dictionary, a guide to metric weights, measures, and equivalents, a list of the beginnings and endings of commonly used medical terms, and a guide to medical specialists complete this handy compilation.

The people's survival manual: health risks and what you can do about them. By William N. Meshel. East Norwalk, Conn., Appleton-Century-Crofts, 1982. 256p. illus. 20cm. hardcover $13.95 (0-8385-7822-5); paper $6.95 (0-8385-7821-7).

A collection of essays on major "killers" such as heart attacks, strokes, and cancer and on major risk factors such as smoking, obesity, and stress. Extensive bibliographies are included for each essay.

Preventions's new encyclopedia of common diseases. By the editors of Prevention magazine. Emmaus, Penn., Rodale, 1984. 1,048p. 22cm. hardcover $21.95 (0-87857-496-4).

This *A–Z* health planning guide carries an apt caveat: "intended as a reference volume only, not as a medical manual or guide to self treatment. If you suspect that you have a medical problem, we urge you to seek competent medical help . . . to help you make informed decisions about your health, not as a substitute for any treatment that may have been prescribed by your doctor." The encyclopedia covers aging, backache, headache, hemorrhoids, skin problems, and stress, as well as a number of allied ailments. Sources are generally cited.

Where does it hurt? A guide to symptoms and illnesses. By Susan C. Pescar and Christine A. Nelson. New York, Facts On File, 1983. 313p. 24cm. hardcover $15.95 (0-87196-741-3).

Includes a section on diseases with information on symptoms, cause, severity of the problem, whether the disease is contagious, and treatment and prevention. A quick-reference symptoms guide is appended. Each symptom is described and interpreted. Related symptoms are also listed. Cross-references are extensive, and there is a bibliography.

World Book illustrated home medical encyclopedia. 4v. Chicago, World Book, 1984. 25cm. $32.95 + $2.45 shipping and handling (0-7166-2060-X).

Volume 1 begins with a general section on how your body works; this is followed by an Index of Symptoms. The rest of volume 1 and volume 2 are devoted to short articles on various medical topics using a question-and-answer format. Volume 3 deals with first aid and the care of the sick, and volume 4 is a guide to health and fitness and includes the Index for the set.—*Martin A. Kesselman.*

HOME REFERENCE BOOKS FOR JUNIOR AND SENIOR HIGH SCHOOL STUDENTS

There are some good, attractive, even relatively inexpensive books currently available that make fine home reference sources for junior and senior high school students. Some of these are compiled with students in mind; others are adapted or condensed from comprehensive treatments—and some may be superficial or inadequate. From time to time, excellent articles and books that "comparison shop" among such reference titles (some of which will be noted later) are issued. Such guides can save time and narrow down the choices. However, personal examination of titles in libraries or bookstores is the ultimate selection procedure in choosing what is appropriate for the individual concerned. The purpose of this piece is—with junior and senior high school students in mind—to point out those reference works that are frequently recommended as good home references. Criteria for selection are given. Five categories will be considered: dictionaries, almanacs, atlases, encyclopedias, and miscellaneous. Sources of broader coverage for each area (which give greater ranges in price and scholarship and which may point out not recommended titles as well) will be noted for each pertinent category. This article, however, will consider only a minimum selection of recommended titles in the five areas. The moderate price range will be emphasized.

DICTIONARIES

Since words and their good usage are essential to communication of any subject, a dictionary is one of the most basic tools for any student. There is a dictionary for nearly every taste and more than one for lovers of words. Those chosen here supplement one another in number and nature of word entries, but all can be used by at least junior high ages, and they can be utilized for general home reference. All contain clearly written definitions; identify parts of speech; indicate pronunciation, stress, and word division; point out variant meanings; and give usage notes. Most include word derivations—etymologies—which, while not essential, are intriguing and helpful in understanding word meanings. Verbal and pictorial illustrations are also an aid. The most recent in-depth comparison of good English-language desk dictionaries appeared in *Reference Books Bulletin*, Dec. 1, 1983, and most of the titles listed below appear there, where they are considered in greater detail.

In general, dictionaries are conceived and perceived either as arbiters of what is standard and acceptable language through informed consensus or as recorders and reflectors of language as currently used and drawn from collective examples. In practice, most dictionaries are a combination of the two, though treatments and scope vary. *The American Heritage Dictionary* editors believe good usage should be clearly pointed out ("ain't" is labeled nonstandard), yet declare "No word is omitted from the *Dictionary* merely because of taboo" (p.xlvi); while *Webster's New World* dictionaries exclude obscenities and label "ain't" colloquial. Illiteracies such as "irregardless" are omitted in the *Student Dictionary* and labeled nonstandard in *Random House Dictionary*, with a usage note as to why. *The New York Times Everyday Dictionary* includes it, as nonstandard for regardless, as does *The American Heritage*—with the succinct: "irregardless, a double negative, is never acceptable except when the intent is clearly humorous." *Webster's New World* says something similar, and stars "irregardless" as an Americanism. As guides to standard English, then, no student could be led astray by any of these dictionaries.

The American heritage dictionary of the English language. larger format ed. Boston, Houghton Mifflin, 1980. (ENTRIES: 15,500, PAGES: 1,600, ILLUS.: 4,000, SIZE: 11¼ x 8½ x 2½ inches, PRICE: $21.95).

This oversize volume has large, clear type, lies flat, and looks and feels good. Its wide outer margins contain illustrations, an aid that attracts junior students. Directions to good synonym notes and running guides to pronunciation aid in reference use. There are 10,000 geographic and biographical entries; included are characters from mythology. These appear in one alphabet with other entries. *AHDEL* makes a good family dictionary and lends itself to browsing, especially where there is table space to invite its ready use.

Webster's new world dictionary of the American language. Student's ed. New York, Simon & Schuster, 1981. (ENTRIES: 108,000, PAGES: 1,130, ILLUS.: 1,500, SIZE: 9¾ x 7¾ x 1½ inches, PRICE: $13.95).

Webster's new world dictionary of the American language. 2d college ed. New York, Simon & Schuster, 1984. (ENTRIES: 160,000, PAGES: 1,692, ILLUS.: 1,123, SIZE: 7¼ x 9⅞ x 2¼ inches, PRICE: $15.95; $16.95 thumb index).

As their titles imply, these dictionaries emphasize Americanisms (student's edition, 10,000 entries; college edition, 14,000 entries, identified by a small outline star), and new words (20,000, according to the publisher). Some of these starred entries seem almost for the record (e.g., hiring hall; Paul Bunyan; tunesmith), but are not found in the other dictionaries. Obscenities and most slurs have been excluded. As the Dec. 1 *Reference Books Bulletin* review points out, this is surprising for a college edition, but such exclusions may make the dictionaries more acceptable for high school use. The college edition contains "a heavier proportion of terms from the sciences" than in its first edition.

The student edition is designed for secondary schools, with entries that reflect words most likely to be met in "classroom reading, newspapers, magazines, and novels." These include slang terms not found in other dictionaries, e.g., "humongous." Print is larger than in the college edition, and there are such other helps as word-finder charts of possible spellings for sounds to aid in looking up words one cannot spell.

USEFUL PAPERBACK EDITIONS

The Random house dictionary. Based on the Random House Dictionary of the English-Language, the Unabridged ed., 1979, and The Random House College Dictionary, 1980. New York, Ballantine Books, 1983. (ENTRIES: +74,000, PAGES: 1,070, SIZE: 7 x 4¼ x 1⅝ inches, PRICE: $3.50 paper).

Almost anyone can afford paperbacks such as *The Random House Dictionary*, with its generous 74,000 entries drawn from the unabridged edition. It does not lie flat, but its convenient size, clear type, and low cost offset its chunky, compact format. It includes biographical and geographic entries, gives some word derivations, and appends tables and a brief style manual.

The New York Times everyday dictionary. New York, Times Books, 1982. (ENTRIES: +85,000, PAGES: 808, SIZE: 8⅛ x 5½ x 1½ inches, PRICE: $7.95 paper).

The New York Times Everyday Dictionary is a good buy in paperback form; a hardback edition is also available. An original work (not an abridgment of a larger edition), its 85,000 entries are based on *The New York Times* word files and reflect current terms (e.g., *bar code, acid rain*) in addition to standard fare. Derivations are not included, but its succinct definitions, bold type, and useful, keyless pronunciation (which assumes familiarity with standard English) make this an easy-access dictionary for students—or a good supplementary one.

Student dictionary. New York, Longman, 1983; dist. by Caroline House, Aurora, Ill. (ENTRIES: 38,000, PAGES: 792, ILLUS.: 15p., SIZE: 8½ x 5¼ x 1/18 inches, PRICE: $9.50 paper).

The *Student Dictionary* is an example of a special dictionary—in this instance, for foreign students or those needing help with standard English. Its workbook-preface explains symbols used to alert students to such pitfalls as verbs that do not take objects, nouns that do not take objects, and nouns that do not form plurals. It has labeled captions for illustrations—car interior, supermarket—but its main help is textual, with irregular verb form lists, usage notes, and spelling tips. Pronunciation keys are based on the International Phonetic Alphabet—with which foreign students will be more familiar than will remedial-level-English-speaking Americans. Its basic emphasis is on correct everyday usage, and it is very good for that.

ALMANACS

These annual compilations of facts, statistics, and assorted information update other reference books, albeit with a built-in time lag. Their chronologies, award lists, and sports records make for handy reference when the odd item is needed and the library is closed, but their wide variety and range make them fascinating to browse through as well. Though similar, their contents differ, and purchase of more than one would not be unnecessarily duplicative. Although their newsprint-type paper is not meant to be lasting, some families keep files of back issues for annual records. Some states and cities publish local almanacs which can be useful school references, though not comparable to the more inclusive almanacs noted here.

Information please almanac. 1985 ed. Boston, Houghton Mifflin, 1984. (PAGES: 960, ILLUS.: 16p. of maps, tables, and charts, PRICE: $5.95 paper).

Major events of the year are summarized in the Current Events section by such subject areas as business, religion, and sports. Facts are organized into roughly 40 divisions, Astronomy to Writer's Guide, including 1 giving names and addresses for selected U.S. societies and associations. Fact summaries precede the historic and political essays on each country and for each state of the U.S. There are survey essays on such items as U.S. space projects, economic trends, and special features for each annual issue. First published in 1947, it missed publication for 1984 but resumes with the 1985 issue.

World almanac and book of facts. New York, Newspaper Enterprise Assn., 1983. (PAGES: 928, ILLUS.: 5p. color, world flags, 11p. world maps, PRICE: $4.95 paper).

Published annually in November, its chronologies begin with the preceding December. Sources and dates are recorded for its wealth of statistical lists: these should be noted in order to avoid discrepancies among them, e.g., names of incumbent state officials compiled midyear and the lists of governors that reflect the November elections. "Facts" include such varied items as food values; a census of U.S. religious bodies; orders of mammals; lists of endangered species; biographical identities; and wind-chill and heat-stress index tables. First published in 1868, this is the best known almanac.

Reader's digest almanac and yearbook, 1984. Pleasantville, N.Y., Reader's Digest Assn., Inc., 1984; dist. by Random House. (PAGES: 1,024, ILLUS.: throughout, PRICE: $7.50 hardcover).

First published in 1966, this newer almanac has a less crammed, more inviting look than the older almanacs. It features news photographs and shaded lines for ease in following columns across tables. It surveys the preceding year under topics—from Accidents and Disasters to Women's Rights. Some useful types of information carried are lists of kings and dynasties (under History); notes on new words, e.g., *floppy disc, hacker* (under Language); locator maps and flags in black and white with their color descriptions (under Nations of the World); and pictures of each U.S. president.

ATLASES

Recent tests revealed that students even at the high school level had trouble locating Chicago or assigning north or south to Florida. Having a globe in the home while children are small would help them become familiar with continents and geographic relationships. For formal homework, however, a good atlas is a boon. Some paperback references sold as boxed sets for students will include an atlas—but with so small a scale and with detail so lost that reference use is minimal. Reviewers point out that while publishers of atlases for the general American public usually emphasize North American areas (as do their European counterparts—such as Philip—for Europe), a good atlas will also give detailed world coverage. Convenient, consolidated indexes, clarity and size of map reproduction, kinds of maps (physical? political? thematic?) and their scale (adequate and suitable to student needs) are some of the things to be considered, along with price. An excellent and detailed survey of world atlases appeared in *Reference Books Bulletin,* Sept. 1, 1983, p.40–50, and some idea of the numbers of atlases available—as well as a useful appraisal of each—can be gained by examining *Kister's Atlas Buying Guide* (Oryx, 1984), which reviews 105. Both surveys have been consulted in choosing the following six atlases for student home reference—good buys in a moderate price range or serviceable paperbacks in the inexpensive class.

Goode's world atlas, 16th ed. Chicago, Rand McNally, 1982 (formerly called Goode's School Atlas). (TOTAL PAGES: 384, PAGES OF MAPS: 234, SIZE: 9 x 11¼ x 26 inches, PRICE: $19.95).

Most frequently cited by standard catalogs for its outstanding features, *Goode's* is noted for balanced coverage and clear combination physical-political maps (including 18 pages of worldwide metropolitan area maps). It has numerous special maps that indicate language distribution, world religions, climate, regional landforms, etc., and a section of maps of the ocean floor. Its one-alphabet index gives longitudes and latitudes for closer location of places and gives pronunciations. Various projections are demonstrated, and application of Landsat sensing devices to mapmaking is described. Overall, this atlas is the best buy for the money.

Hammond headline world atlas. Maplewood, N.J., Hammond, 1983. (TOTAL PAGES: 48, PAGES OF MAPS: 45, SIZE: 10⅞ x 8⅜ inches, PRICE: $2.95 paper).

With "World Statistics" on the back cover and a gazetteer-index up front, almost all pages are given to full-color political, product, and physical maps for regions; locator maps; and national flags. Small, clear, and simple, with good space, the double-spread maps are given a border so no map detail is lost to center staples.

Hammond international world atlas. Maplewood, N.J., Hammond, 1983. (TOTAL PAGES: 200, PAGES OF MAPS: 191, SIZE: 12½ x 9½ inches, PRICE: $14.95).

Based on Hammond's larger atlases, the maps in this work emphasize world areas outside the U.S., for which there are no individual state maps. For regions and countries there are topographic, political, geographic, and topical maps—also a few historic ones—and flags for each country. County and city indexes appear with the map of the country rather than in a general index, so users need to know country of location in order to locate cities. Apart from this inconvenience, it is noted by *American Reference Book Annual* 1982 as a "good introductory world atlas for its price."

Rand McNally family world atlas. Census edition. Chicago, Rand McNally, 1983. (TOTAL PAGES: 320, PAGES OF MAPS: 138, SIZE: 8¾ x 11 inches, PRICE: $12.95 hardcover).

Another good medium-sized and -priced atlas. Though it emphasizes North America, it is worldwide in content. It includes world metropolitan area maps (from *Goode's*) and a selection of maps from the publisher's Cosmopolitan edition, reduced in size—which, though clear, may necessitate use of a hand lens for some. There is also a section on U.S. travel and landform maps accompanying an essay on implications of world population, called "Human Patterns and Imprints." Population figures for world areas and the U.S. are given in 56 pages.

Scott, Foresman world atlas. Glenview, Ill., Scott, Foresman & Co., 1985. (PAGES: 128, PAGES OF MAPS: 69, SIZE: 8¾ x 11 inches, PRICE: $7.48; $5.46 school price).

The British map-making firm of G. Philip & Son produced these beautiful maps, with regional ones for the U.S. Statistical tables and thematic charts and maps are included for countries and regions and for such items as climate, language, population, and trade. The clear, keyed index gives longitude and latitude. *School Library Journal* (May 1983, p.23) calls this atlas "excellent for junior high students."

World atlas. (Random House Library of Knowledge) Maps by Hammond. New York, Random House, 1982. (TOTAL PAGES: 112, PAGES OF MAPS: 89, SIZE: 9½ x 11 inches, PRICE: $7.99; $6.95 paper).

Colorful and popular with younger users, this atlas features political maps, including some metropolitan areas. It includes seven global views of land masses and oceans and discusses map projection. A physical map for each continental area is paired with a same-scale political map preceding individual maps for those areas. Each map is also located as a shaded area on a small juxtaposed globe—along with a similar shaded area superimposed on a map of the U.S., for a graphic idea of its size.

ENCYCLOPEDIAS

The range in cost and content of encyclopedias makes them a major purchase for home reference and involves considerations beyond the scope of this article. Detailed evaluations and comparisons are periodically made by reviewing media; those in *Library Journal, Wilson Library Bulletin, American Reference Books Annual,* and the yearly compilations of *Reference and Subscription Books Reviews* can be consulted in most libraries. Authority, revision policies, arangement, and ease of access to information are some considerations—i.e., *Who puts it out? When was it last revised? Is it intended for inquisitive search or ready reference? Is the index useful? Are there cross-references to other subjects or entries?* In examining a set before purchase, reviewers recommend looking up some topic on which you have knowledge to see how it is handled and to compare the topic's handling in other sets. One's potential use of a set should be considered: if judged infrequent, perhaps a good one-volume encyclopedia plus an almanac will suffice. If a used set is considered, reviewers suggest it not be more than five years old.

An omnibus review of six adult and multivolume encyclopedias appeared in *Reference and Subscription Books Reviews* Dec. 1, 1982, p.515–32, with updating for several individual ones since then. (The earlier survey of 20 encyclopedias, *Purchasing an Encyclopedia: 12 Points to Consider,* published by ALA in 1979, is out of print, and the particulars are dated though the principles are still valid.) Brief mention will be made of the most frequently recommended sets for high school and home reference. All encyclopedias cited below will be reviewed by the *Reference Books Bulletin* Editorial Board Dec. 15, 1984.

Academic American encyclopedia. 21v. Danbury, Conn., Grolier, 1984. $689 plus shipping and handling.

Well received when it first appeared in 1980, its Preface states "for students in junior high school, high school or college, and for the inquisitive adult." (See *RSBR,* Dec. 1, 1982, also *Wilson Library Bulletin,* Feb. 1982, p.459, for reviews of the 1981 edition.) Currentness, brevity, excellent graphics, and a good Index are mentioned as strong points. It is also strong in biographies with many articles on authors and individual works. Some reviewers think that these strengths make the set more suitable for ready reference than in-depth inquiry.

Collier's encyclopedia. 24v. New York, Macmillan Educational Corp., 1984. $1,099.50; $649 plus shipping and handling to schools and libraries.

For high school, college, and home use (advanced junior high students can use), *Collier's* has "strongest coverage in the humanities and social sciences," with especially good geographic coverage. It has in-depth articles and a Study Guide and subject bibliographies in the Index volume for self-help. How-to articles are included. Some color illustrations and overlays are used.

Funk & Wagnalls new encyclopedia. 29v. New York, Funk & Wagnalls, 1983. $199.50.

For junior high and up (though some of the science and other articles might give younger students trouble), this set "offers excellent value for its price." Most of its articles are on people and places, though it offers global coverage of all fields of knowledge. A bibliographic section includes "How to Write a Term Paper." (Cf. *Reference Books Bulletin,* Dec. 15, 1983.)

World Book encyclopedia. 22v. Chicago, World Book–Childcraft, 1984. $499 blue standard binding; $549 aristocrat; $599 classical plus $29 shipping/handling; $433 to schools and libraries.

Widely recommended for grade-school ages through adult, this set is noted for clear, current, reliable, general articles. These are mostly all signed, are tied in with curriculum guides, and include many how-to articles and bibliographies. There is a balance between overviews and particular information, and very good graphics. (See also *RSBR,* Dec. 1, 1982, and *Reference Books Bulletin,* Feb. 1, 1984, p.791–94.)

SINGLE-VOLUME ENCYCLOPEDIAS

While they do not attempt to substitute for multivolume encyclopedias, single-volume ones give wide-ranging coverage in useful detail for ready reference. These are useful for high school and up, though they tend to be more for general adult reference than for any in-depth school needs. Two that might be considered for junior and senior high school students follow.

The concise Columbia encyclopedia. New York, Columbia Univ. Pr., 1983. 943p. $29.95 (Avon Books, $14.95 paper).

Rewritten and condensed from the *New Columbia Encyclopedia,* this is termed "current and objective" and "a reasonably priced reference tool...for home use" by the *Reference Books Bulletin* review, Mar. 1, 1984, p.951–52. In dictionary arrangement, entries are mostly for geographic and biographic subjects. Some of the information is given in table form; there are extensive cross-references. While high schoolers could use, reviewers have noted that the technical language in some articles could prove difficult. A color section of maps is not included in the paperback edition.

The Random House encyclopedia. New rev. ed. New York, Random House, 1983. 2,918p. $99.95.

Developed more for home than library use, this oversize volume has a color-picture section arranged by themes (e.g., "History and Culture"; "Universe"), and a section of alphabetically arranged information called the Alphapedia. There is indexing from the briefer entries to topics in the Colorpedia section, and cross-references, the number of which *Wilson Library Bulletin* (Mar. 1984, p.518) notes have increased from the previous edition, but which *Reference Books Bulletin* (July 1984, p.1536) notes contain faulty paging for the Atlas section (to be corrected in later printing, according to the publisher). Still, *RBB* says that this book "remains a useful guide to general knowledge for older children and adults."

MISCELLANEOUS

For special interests, there are atlases, dictionaries, and encyclopedias for particular geographic areas, historic periods, languages, and subjects. (See F. N. Cheney and W. J. Williams, *Fundamental Reference Sources,* 2d ed. ALA, 1980, and *Reference Sources for Small and Medium-sized Libraries,* ALA, 1984.) For family interest, whether in crafts, science, sports, or the arts, there is a wealth of how-to books, field guides, special information, and record books available. Dictionaries of music or dinosaurs, handbooks of fossils or gardening, manuals on geology or wildflowers—all these and more can be located in libraries and bookstores. A favorite field guide to reptiles/birds/rocks that is never in the library when a student wants it might be purchased for a birthday or just bought as a needed home reference book. Popular library items such as the *Guinness Book of World Records* or "trivia" books are fun to have available at home—or a Hoyle games rule book to settle a point. A whole world of reference books leads beyond homework requirements to encourage latent enthusiasm and foster awareness of the greater world. Help in finding out about these is available to students and their parents at your nearest public library or state library agency.—*Ruth M. McConnell.*

1984 ANNUAL ENCYCLOPEDIA ROUNDUP

The reviewing group responsible for the contents of these pages has, throughout the 55 years of its existence, assigned highest priority to the evaluation of encyclopedias. In the past, the Board has followed a policy of fully reevaluating each general English-language encyclopedia every five years (assuming that libraries will want to replace them at five-year intervals) and of publishing omnibus reviews—surveys—from time to time (most recently at three-year intervals). Since more than 90 percent of the general encyclopedias sold in the U.S. end up in homes, the Board decided that it must provide up-to-date information on the latest editions more frequently. In January 1984 the Board therefore decided to continue to do evaluations at five-year intervals and to do an annual feature on encyclopedias focusing on changes since the Board's last comprehensive (usually five-year) reevaluations.

Our purpose here is not to repeat the report on each encyclopedia presented in our last reevaluation of it. Our goal is rather to examine each set for additions and/or deletions since its last edition reviewed, to comment on its success and/or failure to maintain acceptable levels of currentness, and to report significant shifts in its purpose, content, style, or overall quality. For a set whose latest edition has merely reinforced the Board's previously stated opinion of it, the note hereunder may be little more than a statement to that effect and a list of additions to the set, indicating the Board's overall opinion that the set is unchanged. Where we observe considerable improvement or deterioration, we comment more extensively.

Libraries contemplating replacement of older editions of encyclopedias should be helped by these comments, but perusal of our last full evaluation is advised. Consulting the latter is also recommended for anyone considering purchase of a particular set for the first time.

Encyclopaedia Britannica and *Britannica Junior Encyclopedia* did not participate in this year's survey. We expect to cover them and the nine analyzed below (*Academic American Encyclopedia, Collier's Encyclopedia, Compton's Encyclopedia and Fact Index, Encyclopedia Americana, Funk & Wagnalls New Encyclopedia, Merit Students Encyclopedia, The New Book of Knowledge, New Standard Encyclopedia,* and *World Book Encyclopedia*) in our 1985 roundup. A quantitative summary of next year's statistics appears at the end of this article. The Board hopes that this first update will prove useful to home consumers and librarians.

Academic American encyclopedia. 21v. Bernard S. Cayne, editorial director; K. Anne Ranson, editor in chief. Danbury, Conn., Grolier, Inc., 1984. illus. 26cm. retail: $750 plus shipping and handling; $600 plus shipping and handling, to schools and libraries.

Academic American Encyclopedia (*AAE*) was created in 1980 by Arête, an American subsidiary of VNU (Verenigde Nederlanse Uitgeversbedkijven)—a major Dutch publishing conglomerate. The premier edition was favorably reviewed (*RSBR,* July 1, 1981) as was the 1981 edition—the latter within an omnibus article on adult encyclopedias (*RSBR,* Dec. 1, 1982). In 1982, rights were sold to Grolier, a major and reputable encyclopedia publisher (*Encyclopedia Americana, New Book of Knowledge,* etc.). Some staff, most of the Advisory Board of Editors, and more than 2,000 contributors were retained and 140 were added, all primarily drawn (as shown in volume 1) from the professional ranks of American universities. Seventy-five percent of the articles are signed.

The set is intended to meet the reference needs of nonspecialist adults and of students from the upper elementary grades through college. It is a specific-entry encyclopedia with some extended survey articles on broad topics. According to the Preface (and verified by a random sample of the contents), the allocation of space among disciplines is unchanged from previous editions: 36 percent to the humanities and the arts; 35 percent to science and technology; 14 percent to social science; 13 percent to place-names; and 2 percent to sports and contemporary life.

AAE has maintained the impressive degree of accuracy, objectivity, and currentness noted in earlier reviews. Political, racial, and sexist bias is absent. Controversial and sensitive topics are treated dispassionately and forthrightly. Currentness is assured, not only because the set is new but also because of evident and extensive updating. According to the publisher, from 1981 through 1984 more than 250 articles on new subjects were added, 190 articles were replaced, and a further 4,400 articles updated or otherwise revised. The edition here described covers events through the fall of 1983.

AAE continues to devote considerable attention to U.S. states, Canadian provinces, and foreign countries. Articles on countries that have dominated the headlines, e.g., *Argentina, Lebanon, Grenada,* and the *Falkland Islands,* have been updated. Fact boxes for U.S. states and Canadian provinces have been expanded and revised. The policies of President Reagan's administration are recorded in various articles, e.g., *Human Rights, Arms Control, Poverty,* and *Pollution Control.*

Interest in science and technology, including health and medicine, and the rapid changes in these fields are evident in dozens of rewritten articles (e.g., *Genetic Engineering; Stereochemistry; Artificial Intelligence; Software, Computer; Hyperactive Children; Saturn*) and many new entries (e.g., *AIDS, Alzheimer's Disease, Element 109, Synchrotron Radiation, Database, Microcomputer, Videotext*).

Commendable coverage in anthropology, sociology, law, business, and economics has been expanded by the addition of well-researched, interesting articles on *Criminal Justice, Feminism, Sex Roles, Inheritance, Monetary Theory,* and *Shipping* and rewritten entries on *Crime, Drug Abuse, Marriage, Rape, Advertising, Banking Systems,* and *Retailing.*

AAE's extensive and exemplary coverage of art and architecture has been augmented by replacement articles on *Folk Art* and *Interior Design.*

AAE continues to provide impressive coverage of the lives and achievements of outstanding persons. Thirty-five percent of the set consists of personal-name entries, although the total length of the articles in question is much less, their average length being 150 words. Among new articles are ones on Mario Cuomo, Sandra Day O'Connor, Konstantin Chernenko, Yitzhak Shamir, Barbara McClintock, Sally Ride, Lane Kirkland, Stephen King, Meryl Streep, Philip Glass, and Wayne Gretzky.

In earlier reviews the Board noted that library users and staff appreciated the bibliographies appended to more than 40 percent of the articles and most of the biographical entries. Updating is evident here from the numerous books and periodical articles published since 1980 which are cited. Many 1983 imprints were noted.

AAE continues to excel in the profusion and quality of its illustrative matter. The publisher uses more than 16,000 photographs, historical prints, maps, charts, tables, diagrams, schematics, and commissioned pieces of artwork—most in full color. They occupy a third of the space. Updating is evidenced by the photographs of the Vietnam Veterans' Memorial, France's new high-speed train, and the 1983 space shuttle missions. Maps reflect, for example, the independence of Saint Kitts–Nevis and Israel's return of the Sinai to Egypt. Librarians will be pleased to learn that dates have been appended to many maps. The Index volume continues to be one of *AAE*'s real strengths. Advanced elementary and junior high school students will find it useful, particularly because of its splendid graphics and short entry style.

The Board finds that a conscientious, systematic, and extensive revision program has been implemented and that *AAE* continues to present a broad spectrum of up-to-date information that adults and high school students need—and presents it accurately, objectively and concisely.

Collier's encyclopedia. 24v. Emanuel Friedman, editor in chief. New York, Macmillan Educational Corp., 1984. illus. maps. plates. tables. 28cm. buckram $1,099.50; retail, $1,299.50 (including Collier's Educational Home Program); $699 + $20 shipping; $664 + shipping per set for two or more sets, to schools and libraries.

Since the Board's September 1, 1983 review of the 1981 edition and a 1982 update there have been no radical changes in *Collier's Encyclopedia*. However, through its continuous revision program, approximately 40 new (mainly brief) articles are added each year, and an equal number of longer articles are completely rewritten. In addition, there are, each year, minor revisions in more than 500 other articles. This adds up to a revision of about 1,700 pages per year or the equivalent of two volumes. This evaluation will concentrate on changes in *Collier's* in its 1983 and 1984 editions.

The list of contributors remains basically the same except for the addition of new names resulting from revision: several previous contributors were responsible for some of these revisions and additions and, therefore, the new contributors are relatively few, but these few appear to maintain the high standard of authority established in the past by this set, e.g., the new article *Amides* was written by the head of the chemistry department of Barnard College, and the article on the British painter David Hockney is by the editor of *Arts Magazine*.

Balance of coverage remains approximately the same: regional studies, 35 percent; humanities, 20 percent; social sciences, 20 percent; mathematics and physical sciences, 15 percent; and life sciences, 10 percent. Of articles added within the past two years, about 75 percent are biographical. Most of these are on personalities currently in the news, chiefly from world affairs (e.g., Yuri Andropov and Lech Walesa) or the arts (e.g., Nadine Gordimer, Henry Fonda), while a few fill in gaps in previous coverage (e.g., articles on the nineteenth-century American lithographers Currier and Ives and John F. Peto). Other new articles are also mainly on subjects of current importance and interest (e.g., *AIDS, Alzheimer's Disease*, and *Rastafarianism*). These articles average less than a half-page each; therefore, the total space for new entries, per year, is about 20 pages of text.

Of the approximately 40 rewritten articles in the 1984 edition, *Information Storage and Retrieval* and *Business Machines and Equipment* are of particular pertinence. *Computer* has been completely reworked—a long overdue improvement: although it is the same length as formerly (19 pages), the new article is much less technical and is more accessible to average readers—while still describing in an interesting fashion many recent developments in the field (including personal computers and their uses).

About half of the articles or parts of articles rewritten each year involve regional studies. For example, in 1984, sections of articles on several countries, e.g., Iran, Cuba, Argentina, and China, were revised, and entire articles on London, Paris, and Berlin were redone.

Other articles rewritten in the past two years include several in science (*Solar System, Automation*) and the social sciences (*Public Opinion, Banking Systems*) but only a few in the humanities: many articles in such areas as archaeology, ancient history, and mythology have remained untouched for almost 20 years. The results of the 1981 Canadian census appeared first in the 1983 edition.

Of the approximately 500 articles given spot revisions in the 1984 edition, most changes are minimal, involving only a few lines of text, e.g., the inclusion of information on a biographee's death or a brief reference to recent developments within a country (e.g., *Grenada* adds a few lines covering the regime of Maurice Bishop and the American invasion of 1983). The 1984 edition covers, sometimes only by brief references, major news events of 1983.

In its review of the 1981 set, the Board noted that the illustrations need more color. Since then, just over 600 new full-color illustrations have been added (averaging 200 per year). Articles that have been improved substantially by more extensive use of color include *American Painting, Dogs, American Revolutionary Period*, and *Photography*.

One unusual aspect of *Collier's* is its Bibliography section, in the last volume, which lists approximately 12,000 books under 31 broad subjects. This section is updated and revised on a schedule that included scrutiny of every listing during the past four-year period. Most entries are fairly up-to-date and include publications as late as 1980.

The major strengths of *Collier's* still remain intact: a readable and authoritative text geared to nonspecialists, a high level of excellence for accuracy and objectivity, relatively up-to-date coverage of topics (although improvement here is always possible), an excellent Index with more than 400,000 entries (particularly necessary because of the number of long omnibus articles), and an attractive, readable format. However, libraries with older sets must decide whether the revisions in the past two years are extensive enough to warrant purchase of new sets.

Compton's encyclopedia and fact index. 26v. Michael Reed, editor. Chicago, F. E. Compton Co., Division of Encyclopaedia Britannica, 1984. illus. diagrs. maps. 26cm. retail, $599: less $100 for teachers; $449: $419 per two or more, to schools and libraries.

The editors of *Compton's* informed the Board that "extent of revision varies from year to year in that during some years the major thrust is toward planning and during others, toward execution of the plans." Clearly, 1983 and 1984 were years of execution: the 1984 edition contains 289 new articles and 233 rewritten or extensively revised articles, about the same as the 1983 edition. This is in sharp contrast to the situation in 1980 to 1982, when almost no new or extensively revised articles showed up. Continuity of staff, editorial consultants, and contributors have been maintained except that Dale Good, an experienced encyclopedia editor, joined *Compton's* as a senior editor with the 1983 edition. There have been considerable changes in the indexing and cartographic staffs. Signed articles by qualified contributors have increased, with a number of newly signed articles on foreign countries and other subjects as noted below.

Subject coverage has been expanded in a number of geographical, biographical, and other entries. The publisher's aim for increased international coverage is achieved in the geographical articles, with *French Guiana, Fujian* (Chinese province), *Fortaleza* (Brazil), *Ibadan, Iberian Plain, Istanbul*, and *Izmir* among the newly added. Among signed articles on foreign countries rewritten by authorities and with new illustrations are *China; China, Republic of; India; Indonesia; Iran; Iraq;* and *Ireland*.

Further evidence of wider international scope is found in the choice of new biographical subjects, selected as "people who exemplify a particular style and people who have exerted a special influence." Russian artist Fabergé, German physicist Fahrenheit, Belgian-born French composer César Franck, and the Fujiwara family of Japanese statesmen are only a few of those newly represented, along with such Americans as Buckminster Fuller, Marshall Field, Bobby Jones, and Mother Jones. Some of these were covered earlier in abbreviated form in the Fact-Index.

Other new entries embrace a wide range of subjects. Literature of foreign countries is covered in articles for Indian, Islamic, Japanese, and Korean literature. In the social sciences *Foreign Aid, Frontier, Kansas-Nebraska Act, Liberalism, Literacy and Illiteracy*, and *Lobbying* are new.

Science and industry receive attention in new articles: *Folk Medicine, Food and Drug Laws, Food Supply, Forest Products, Immune System, Industrial Medicine, Inorganic Chemistry, Invertebrates, Liquor Industry*, and *Living Things*. Articles of current interest include *Fast Food* and *Jogging*.

Many extensively revised or totally rewritten articles have been signed for the first time. These include *Family; Farming; Fire Fighting; Food Processing; Fruit Growing; Furniture; Insurance; Interior Design; Knife, Fork and Spoon; Laundry; Leisure;* and *Lizard,* all by authorities.

Career information has been added in *Food and Nutrition, Forests and Forestry,* and *Insurance. Foundations and Charities* has an added list of foreign foundations.

Following the editor's policy of providing more "umbrella" articles, a number of articles in earlier editions on narrow subjects have been deleted and their content incorporated into broader topical articles, e.g., *January, February,* and *July,* now covered in *Festivals and Holidays; Flounder* and *Fluke,* now covered in *Flatfish; Flying Dragon,* now covered in *Lizard.* Rather than detracting from reference value, these and many other revisions add value to the set—and reinforce the wisdom of always consulting the Fact-Index first. One negative change is the deletion of pronunciation (except for difficult terms listed in glossaries in some articles, e.g., *Law*). This editorial decision is hard to justify, especially for difficult proper names, since coverage of foreign persons and places has increased. The editors "still try to include as many of the creative lead paragraphs ... but our newest ones (in *Frontier* or *Industrial Design,* for example) are more sophisticated than some of the older, more childish examples." This is quite noticeable in new or rewritten articles, e.g., *Leningrad,* which drops the subtitle "Russia's Window to the West," is more tightly organized, and includes color photographs.

Many bibliographies have been revised and fewer are divided into titles for younger and older readers.

References to the Master Fact-Index, which have long appeared throughout the text, have been deleted in volumes 8 and 11 to 13. The Fact-Index still remains indispensable for intelligent use of the set. The Index itself is necessarily revised annually, with 691 pages for 1984, 44 less than in the 1983 volume. Symbols for subentries have been omitted: they are now indicated by indentation. Also deleted are instructions for use previously inserted here and there throughout the Index. Prefatory information on use of the set (including quizzes, etc.) has been reorganized. All tables of data in the 1983 Fact-Index have been retained, and new ones on baseball, football, and fraternities/sororities were added. These will be of especial interest to young people.

Revision in content has been augmented by an improved format, most noticeable being deletion of flowery subtitles, *Camping,* for "The Sport of Outdoor Living." Selection of 1,300 new illustrations is discriminating, with a number of added color photographs, especially for foreign countries.

In summary, if *Compton's* continues to revise heavily at least four volumes a year, the encyclopedia will have a new look in a few years. In the past, the Board has been critical of *Compton's* because of insufficient currentness. It is apparent that in the 1984 edition the publishers are continuing recent progress in correcting this inadequacy. *Compton's* emphasis on practical and curriculum-related information makes it an attractive set for children and young people.

The encyclopedia Americana. 30v. Bernard S. Cayne, editorial director; Alan H. Smith, editor in chief. Danbury, Conn., Grolier, Inc. [c1918–1984]. illus. maps. plates. 26cm. lexotone $960 retail + shipping & handling; to schools and libraries $760 + shipping & handling.

Externally, the 1984 edition of *Encyclopedia Americana* appears to be identical to that of 1983. Its publisher has retained for its library edition the handsome tan-colored lexotone II binding, with gold stamping on the spine and front cover, which was adopted in 1983 in imitation of the original leather binding of 1833. Internally, however, there are a considerable number of changes—more than 300 articles were added; more than 600 replaced; and more than 1,000 were updated and revised. In addition, over 100 new cross-references were added according to the publisher.

Most of the new articles are timely—sketches of Jesse Jackson and Gary Hart, for example; medical articles on *AIDS* and *Alzheimer's Disease;* and, among articles on entertainment figures, articles on Dustin Hoffman and Glenda Jackson. Rewritten articles cover a wide variety of topics. Understandably enough, the biography of George Orwell has been revised from an article 6 inches long to one 20 inches; a portrait has also been added. Other rewritten articles include *Orthodox Churches* (from 4 columns, unillustrated, to 14 columns, with seven black-and-white illustrations), *Williams, Tennessee* (from 9 inches to about 18 inches, and with an updated bibliography), and *Otto I* (from an unsigned 6-inch article to a signed 17-inch article). In the 1983 edition the article *Painting* contained 28 black-and-white and 6 color illustrations of famous paintings. The 1984 edition has a completely rewritten article, more than double in length, with 95 color illustrations, of which only 1 is a repeat from 1983.

To accommodate these and other new, rewritten, or enlarged articles, other articles were shortened or, more frequently, deleted—a common practice employed by encyclopedia publishers. For example, in 1984, in order to accommodate the new *AIDS* article (as well as two other new articles beginning with *Aid to* . . .), requiring a total of nearly 12 inches, the articles *Ahrens, Ahriman, Ahuachapan, Ahura Mazda, Aibonito,* and *Aigrette* were deleted. This allowed the insertion of the three articles mentioned above and a slightly updated biography for the article on Conrad Aiken to be placed about where it was in 1983, thereby effecting minimal changes in indexing.

Accepting then, after extensive verification, the publisher's figures of more than 2,000 new or revised textual articles, nearly 500 new photographs, and some 400 new or revised artwork pages and maps throughout the set, for a total of nearly 2,500 reset and revised pages, the Editorial Board of *RBB* recommends the 1984 edition of *Encyclopedia Americana.* The Board endorses its December 1, 1983, assessment: "Highly recommended for homes and libraries, for all readers from upper-elementary grades upwards and for any readership which needs an up-to-date, general purpose, high-quality American encyclopedia."

Funk & Wagnalls new encyclopedia. 29v. Leon L. Bram, editorial director, Robert S. Phillips, editor in chief; Norma H. Dickey, special products editor in chief. New York, Funk & Wagnalls, 1983, 1984. illus. maps. tables. 24cm. kivar $125.81 to homes (available only from supermarkets); $199.50 suggested price for schools and libraries (available from regional sales organizations only).

Funk & Wagnalls has been publishing encyclopedias since 1912; in 1971 it brought out its *New Encyclopedia,* which since has been under continuous revision. For its spring 1983 printing, *F&WNE* underwent a complete rewriting and revision; the Board reviewed the set favorably December 15, 1983. The spring 1984 printing, while still showing a 1983 copyright date (because of its supermarket selling strategies, the copyright entry is renewed only every four years although revisions are made twice yearly), maintains the improvements previously cited by the Board and includes a number of revisions to articles to update information and to correct errors. The publisher states that 774 pages have been revised.

In its sampling the Board found such revisions as notation in three articles (*Yachting, Rhode Island,* and *Newport*) as well as in the article on the U.S. loss of the America's Cup Race to Australia in 1983. The table of winners has also been updated. *Arms Control, International* has been updated to include 1983 events. Whereas the spring 1983 printing mentioned Andropov's succession in the *Union of Soviet Socialist Republics* and *Andropov* articles, the article on *Brezhnev* did not mention his death; this has now been added. The article on *Lebanon* has been updated to include the assassination of Bashir Gemayel and the election of his brother Amin to replace him, but it does not include the recent terrorist bombings at the U.S. Embassy and Marine barracks in 1983; however, the U.S. and the Grenada articles have been updated to include the October bombings and also the invasion of Grenada a few days later. (The discrepancy is probably due to the fact that the publisher states that no page has been handled twice—evidently *Lebanon* was revised for the fall 1983 printing and *Grenada* and the *United States* for that of spring 1984.)

Surprisingly, the tables of Nobel Prizes, Academy Awards, Kentucky Derby winners, baseball, basketball, and football champions, etc., have not been updated; they still end with 1981 or 1982. The list of Important Manned Space Flights still covers happenings only through April 12, 1981. The Board notes with regret that Sally Ride, the first American woman to fly in space (June 1983), has yet to be mentioned.

F&WNE continues to be a good, straightforward provider of facts on people, places, and things. Articles range from brief identifications to very long treatments of more than 100 pages. *Funk & Wagnalls* makes excellent use of illustrations to amplify the text. Although the use of nonglossy paper somewhat softens the impact of the illustrations, the graphics are clear, sharp, and pertinent. Good bibliographies for further reading and suitable instructions on using the set are provided.

The 1984 printing maintains the qualities of the 1983 revision and includes a quantity of updated material. The Board's December 1983 evaluation remains valid for this printing: designed to be sold to a home audience through supermarkets (rather than door-to-door) *Funk & Wagnalls New Encyclopedia* is unique among encyclopedias. It offers excellent value for its price. While certainly not as scholarly and detailed as the largest English-language encyclopedias, it offers global coverage of all fields of knowledge. *Funk & Wagnalls* is an excellent encyclopedia for homes, useful for both adults and older children. It is also a practical purchase for libraries.

Merit students encyclopedia. 20v. Emanuel Friedman, editor in chief. New York, Macmillan Educational Co., 1984. illus. maps. diagrs. 28cm. hardcover retail $1,099.50; $1,299.50 (with other educational books and products); $475 + $20 shipping, to schools and libraries, $440 + shipping per set for two or more.

In its September 15, 1983, review of the 1982 edition of *Merit Students Encyclopedia*, the Board noted that it was accurate, objective, and current: "Significant events seem to be added promptly." The 1984 edition also deserves this praise. It includes (since the 1983 edition) 51 new articles, and more than 800 entries have been revised or updated. New articles include *Acquired Immune Deficiency Syndrome, Videodisc,* and brief biographies of Lane Kirkland and Sally Ride. Other articles are kept current: events in El Salvador are covered through 1983 and Reagan's presidency is covered through February of 1984.

Accuracy and objectivity are exemplary. *Evolution* is not only accurate and objective, but it is also clear, comprehensive, and interesting to read, including a good explanation of post-Darwinian thought. It should be noted that "objectivity" can go too far; this article makes no mention of the social and religious controversy surrounding evolution and "creationism."

Merit Students has a number of great strengths. Uniform articles on U.S. states and Canadian provinces are well organized, broader in scope, and more detailed than is usual in sets intended for a broad range of readers beginning with fifth-grade youngsters. The same is true of the lengthy biographies of U.S. presidents. Maps (produced by Rand McNally) are excellent; diagrams and charts are very helpful, well placed, and executed with style. Color illustration and photography have been reproduced exceptionally well in this edition. The Index is in the last volume, along with coverage of *X, Y,* and *Z*.

Bibliographies emphasize adult titles, although many (not all) of the juveniles listed are suggested "for younger readers." The lack of current bibliographies is a serious problem—one that the Board has noted before. In some briefer articles, e.g., *Helsinki* and *Sutherland, Joan,* suggested readings would be of little use or value, others, such as *Satellite, Artificial; Dolphin; Glacier; Skin;* and *Wave* (all popular term-paper topics) should provide direction for further study. The latest reference on *Puerto Rico* is to Kal Wagenheim's *Puerto Rico: A Profile,* published in 1971; the latest for *Cryptography* was published in 1967. Another continuing problem is the relative lack of cross-references (as the Board has also noted before). *Glacier,* for example, does not explain that there are 12 more items related to glaciers cited to in the Index.

There is, as the Board has concluded in earlier analyses, much useful information in *Merit Students Encyclopedia*. The lack of hyperbole, cuteness, or condescension deserves praise: still, many articles are beyond the comprehension of children at the upper elementary school level. *Merit Students* is a useful and attractive set, and the Board recommends it for advanced junior and senior high school students and adults. While *Merit Students* has been significantly updated in the past two years, it has not undergone any fundamental changes.

The new book of knowledge. 21v. Bernard S. Cayne, editorial director; Jean E. Reynolds, editor in chief. Danbury, Conn., Grolier, Inc., 1984. illus. maps. charts. diagrs. 26cm. lexotone $650 + shipping and handling, retail; $449.50 + shipping and handling, schools and libraries.

Basic information concerning *The New Book of Knowledge* (publishing history, scope, arrangement, treatment, special features, etc.) can be found in the Board's review of the 1982 edition (cf. *RSBR,* May 15, 1983).

Like past editions, the current one was prepared by competent authorities. Two new consultants have been added: A. Harris Stone, an expert in environmental education, and George Vuicich, professor of geography at Western Michigan University, who helped evaluate and develop improvements in the set's map program. The 1984 edition includes articles by more than 1,360 contributors, with 95 percent of articles signed.

NBK is updated by continuous revision. Events that occur as late as February of the copyright year are included. Revisions reflect curricular changes and new or expanding areas of knowledge. According to the publisher, 9,311 pages were revised between 1981 and 1984; more than 400 new articles were added; more than 2,500 articles were revised or partially rewritten; 611 full-color photographs, 60 black-and-white photographs (mostly historical), and 238 graphics were added; and (as with each annual edition) the entire Index was revised and reset.

New articles include *Acid Rain; Bangkok (Krung Thep); The Beatles; Cassatt, Mary; Copland, Aaron; Ecology; Kyoto; Von Leibnitz, Gottfried Wilhelm; Genetic Engineering; Menstruation; Milne, A. A.; National Gallery of Canada; Organization of Petroleum Exporting Countries (OPEC); Ostriches and Other Flightless Birds; Owens, Jesse; Owls; Reagan, Ronald; Robots; San Diego; Dr. Seuss; Turks and Caicos Islands; Vanuatu; Video Games;* and *Video Recording.*

Replaced, rewritten, and/or expanded articles include *Amazon River; Brontë Sisters; Castro, Fidel; Central America; Days of the Week; Elizabeth II; Eskimos (Inuit); Hypnosis; Immigration; Jesus Christ; Karate; Natural Resources; Nigeria; Peru; Photography; Sanitation; Tehran; Washington, D.C.; Water Pollution;* and *Yangtze River.* The article on Washington, D.C., has been doubled in length and given a four-color street map showing points of interest for young people visiting the city. Recent events of importance are covered in *NBK*, e.g., the 1981 eruption of Mt. St. Helens and assassination of Anwar Sadat, the 1982 Argentine invasion of the Falkland Islands, the 1983 coup in Nigeria, Jesse Jackson's mission to Syria, and the 1984 death of Andropov and election of Chernenko. *Black Americans* replaces *Negro Americans* and has been rewritten to cover the history of the black civil rights movement since the end of World War II. *Spirituals and Other Folk Hymns* is a new section added to *Hymns.* There are replacement articles on international law, Social Security, and public welfare.

Space Exploration and Travel, Rockets, Radio and Radar Astronomy, and *Satellites* have been revised totally. *Dogs* now reflects the new American Kennel Club groupings. *American Revolution* has been completely reillustrated, with historical reproductions. The picture of the Sydney, Australia, skyline has been replaced because of the construction of Centrepoint, Australia's tallest structure. Photographs in the Lebanon article were replaced because of the destruction of many buildings. A photograph of Baltimore has been replaced by one showing the new National Aquarium. Place-names have been updated; e.g., Teheran to Tehran. Information on the American Nazi party has been added to *Nazism.*

Each volume has its own Index. Among new Dictionary Index entries in 1984 are *AIDS, Agent Orange, asceptics, Eubie Blake, personal computers,* and names of various computer languages (*BASIC, LOGO,* etc.).

Accuracy remains a strong point in *NBK:* the few minor errors noted by the Board in its last overview have been corrected. The Board's 1983 description of *NBK* stands: A reliable, authoritative, accurate, and up-to-date encyclopedia for elementary school children. It is therefore recommended for homes and for school and public libraries serving elementary school students. It can also be used with junior and senior high school students with limited reading ability.

New Standard encyclopedia. 17v. Douglas W. Downey, editor in chief. Chicago, Standard Educational Corporation, 1984. illus. maps. tables. 24cm. retail $595.50; 25% off consumer price, to schools and libraries.

When the Board reviewed *New Standard Encyclopedia* on December 15, 1978, it characterized the set as a work which has maintained an efficient, continuous revision program giving priority to topics susceptible to fast obsolescence. Over the years, *NSE* has covered the basic areas of knowledge adequately, and it has sustained a high level of accuracy.

Articles are written, revised, and updated by the editorial staff; new and rewritten articles are reviewed, before publication, by authorities in pertinent fields. The editorial advisory group, headed by John I. Goodlad, professor of education at the University of California, Los Angeles, includes more than 700 contributors and consul-

Encyclopedia Summary Chart 1984 (All statistics apply to 1985.)

Encyclopedia	Approx. No. of Entries*	No. of Pages*	Approx. No. of Illus.*	Consumer Price*	School & Library Price*	RBB's Last Review
Academic American Encyclopedia	28,500	9,700	17,700	$750 plus shipping and handling	$600 plus shipping and handling	12/1/82
Collier's Encyclopedia	21,000	19,750	17,350	$1,099.50; Collier's Home Educational Program (the 1984 copyright of *Collier's Encyclopedia* along with other educational books and products): $1,299.50	$699 plus $20 shipping ($664 plus shipping per set for two or more sets)	9/1/83
Compton's Encyclopedia and Fact Index	4,276 (main text) 27,000 (capsule entries in Index)	9,606 + 700 in Fact Index +700 in Split Index	22,500	$599; less $100 for teachers	$449; $419 for two or more	5/15/83
The Encyclopedia Americana	52,000	26,700	23,700	$960 plus shipping and handling	$760 plus shipping and handling	12/1/83
Funk & Wagnalls	25,000	13,024	9,175	Available from supermarkets only at $125.81	Available from regional sales organizations only; suggested price $199.50	12/15/83
Merit Students Encyclopedia	21,000	12,300	19,200	$1,099.50; Merit Students Home Educational Program (the 1984 copyright of *Merit Students Encyclopedia* along with other educational books and products): $1,299.50	$475 plus $20 shipping ($440 plus shipping per set for two or more sets)	9/15/83
The New Book of Knowledge	13,800	10,500	23,500	$650 plus shipping and handling	$449.50 plus shipping and handling	5/15/83
New Standard Encyclopedia	17,438,	9,972	12,000	$595.50 (1985 price not yet established. Other stats will be approx. the same.)	25% off consumer price	12/15/78
The World Book Encyclopedia	18,175	14,044	29,000+	$499 blue standard binding; $549 aristocrat; $599 classical plus $29 shipping/handling	$433	2/1/84

* Information provided by publisher.

tants. Their names, their affiliations, and the titles of articles on which they worked are listed in volume 1, or, in some cases, their general fields of consultancy are cited. The authors (whether persons or corporations) appear to be well suited to the subjects assigned. For some articles, more than one consultant has been assigned. This occurs particularly where subjects are assigned to persons from business and industry.

Efforts are being made to improve the encyclopedia's cross-reference network, which serves as its only access mechanism. The number of *see* entries has been increased, and there are about the same number of cross-references within articles.

New Standard continues to focus on topics presumed to be most appropriate to family encyclopedias. Coverage of geography, of the basics in such fields as arithmetic, and of sports is more extensive than coverage for theoretical and intellectually sophisticated subjects. At the same time, there is an effort to provide comprehensive coverage. Biographical coverage continues to be somewhat less satisfactory than treatment of other topics. (Slights in coverage were noted for Elizabeth Cady Stanton, Edith Wharton, and Richard M. Nixon's recent, postpresidential activities. Abigail Adams does not appear in the *Adams Family* article in proportion to her importance historically. There are no articles on such black Americans as Sidney Poitier, Lorraine Hansberry, and Nikki Giovanni.) The editors note that over the years they have devoted more space to American than to foreign topics. These same editors state that more foreign material is now included, both in response to readers' interests and because the set is being sold abroad.

New Standard maintains a high level of accuracy. Errors noted in the Board's last review have been corrected, and new material is accurate. In treating such topics as acupuncture, sex education, homosexuality, and abortion, *New Standard* has maintained objectivity. Articles related to political topics continue, however, to project a conservative tone. And occasionally there is failure to delineate the issues and controversies that surround such topics as abortion and euthanasia.

Despite occasional awkward constructions, *New Standard* maintains acceptable standards of style. Some articles include glossaries of terms, a feature that aids readers' comprehension of subject matter and does away with need for lengthy explanations in the text.

From 1979 through 1984, the editors added between 10 and 15 new articles each year, ranging from *Country and Western Music* to *Gasohol* and *Freedom of Information Act*. Biographies added include those of Erik Erikson, John Cage, Margaret Thatcher, and Juan Carlos I. For the 1984 revision, 25 articles were added, e.g., *AIDS, Organized Crime, Toxic Shock Syndrome,* and *Pelé*. Additions thus include both general articles and articles on topics of special current interest. Bibliographies appended to major articles provide a few titles for further reference; special attention is given to identifying works intended for younger readers. Bibliographies are apparently updated when the articles they accompany are revised. Unlike the other encyclopedias analyzed in this roundup, *New Standard* is supplemented by a quarterly publication that covers major events, updates subject coverage, and provides new articles. The others have annual updates or supplementary volumes.

The number of color illustrations has increased: about 18 percent are now in color. These include maps, paintings, photographs, and reproductions of works of art. New tables and charts have also appeared. The 1984 edition includes 646 maps, all placed within the articles they illustrate. Similarly, placement of other illustrations is appropriate.

The major changes in format are the expansion of the encyclopedia through the addition of pages and the extension of the number of volumes to 17.

Based on this evidence, as well as internal evidence of continuous updating, the Board finds that the *New Standard* continues to do acceptably what it has done in the past: provide basic, up-to-date information about a variety of topics. Although it is accurate, *New Standard* is not always comprehensive in its treatment of topics, and its coverage of more difficult subjects is generally less satisfactory than that provided by the other encyclopedias analyzed in this survey.

The World Book encyclopedia. 22v. William H. Nault, publisher; A. Richard Harmet, executive editor. Chicago, World Book, Inc., 1984. illus. maps. tables. diagrs. 25cm. $599 classical;

$549 aristocrat; $499 blue standard; school and library binding $404 to schools and libraries; all prices are exclusive of $29 shipping and handling.

The Board's latest full review of *World Book Encyclopedia* (*WB*) was published February 1, 1984; its last omnibus reviews assessing *WB* as an adult and children's encyclopedia appeared December 1, 1982, and May 15, 1983. In all of these reviews, the Board commended *WB* as a superior work especially designed to meet the reference and study needs of students in grades 4–12 and to serve also as a general adult reference source. The Board's reviews commented on the caliber of *WB*'s editorial, advisory, and permanent staff and the large number (more than 3,000) of qualified contributors; *WB*'s clarity of style and judicious use of illustrations (more than 29,000; over 14,000 in color); its generally balanced, objective treatment of topics; its carefully selected Reading and Study Guides and article bibliographies; and its detailed Index of more than 150,000 entries.

In general, the 1984 *WB* continues its publisher's long tradition of excellence and timeliness, and, in general, the Board's previous conclusions on the set still apply. This newest edition includes more than 120 new articles, some 450 completely revised articles, and more than 1,700 partially revised articles. In all, according to the publisher, about 6,000 pages were revised since 1983. The following examples will illustrate the extent of revision in various fields of knowledge. Among new articles are *AIDS, Palm Springs, Virginia Beach, Congregationalist, Positivism, Pasta, Zucchini, Fire Ant, Secretarial Work, Chopsticks, Cremation, Money Market Fund, Electronic Game,* and *Amusement Park.* There are new biographical articles on such political figures as Harold Washington (Chicago mayor); Robert Hawke (prime minister of Australia); Helmut Kohl (chancellor of West Germany); Elizabeth H. Dole and Margaret M. Heckler (secretaries of Transportation and Health and Human Services in the Reagan administration); Gary Hart; Sally Ride and Guion Bluford, Jr. (the first U.S. woman and black astronauts); opera singer Placido Domingo; violinists Itzhak Perlman and Pinchas Zukerman; country-and-western musicians Roy Acuff, Eddy Arnold, Gene Autry, Jimmie Rogers, and Tex Ritter; and filmmakers Howard Hawks, George Lucas, and Steven Spielberg. The range of completely revised articles is similarly impressive, e.g., *Canada, History of; Juvenile Delinquency; President of the United States; Vietnam War; Argentina; Iran; Pickford, Mary; Poetry; Wouk, Herman; Butterfly;* and *Salt.*

Changes in partially revised articles are many and varied. They may involve revision of the text (as in *Balance of Power*), presentations of new photographs (as in *Baltimore*), or updating of statistics (as in *Corn* and *Wheat*), or a table (as in *Baseball, Basketball, Football*). Or they may update a bibliography (*Navy, United States* has a 1983 title; *Vietnam War,* a 1983 and a 1982 title; *Napoleon,* a 1981 title), provide a death date (Dame Rebecca West, British journalist, March 15, 1983; Ross Macdonald, U.S. novelist, July 11, 1983; playwright Tennessee Williams, February 25, 1983), etc. In these ways, the editors keep *WB* extremely current and internally consistent.

By and large, *WB* is quite successful in matters of revision and consistency; a random sample did, however, point up certain inconsistencies. While the sketches of Alan Cranston, John Glenn, Gary Hart, and Walter Mondale incorporate statements of their candidacy for the 1984 Democratic presidential nomination, that of Jesse Jackson does not. *Blume, Judy* cites *Wifey* (1978) but not *Superfudge* (1980), *Tiger Eyes* (1981), or *Smart Women* (1983). Twice in the *New York* (state) article, New York City is termed the seventh largest city in the world; in *New York City* it is labeled the eighth largest. The resignation in September 1983 of Israeli Prime Minister Menachem Begin and the naming of Yitzhak Shamir as his successor is mentioned in *Israel* but not in *Begin, Menachem.* (There is no sketch or index entry for Shamir.) It is not clear why in the Reading and Study Guide in *American Literature* one of the suggested headings in *Readers' Guide to Periodical Literature* (*RG*) remains "Negro literature" and not "Black literature," which *RG* has used since 1977/78. The study guide for *Communism* cites the seventh edition (not the eighth, 1980) of William Ebenstein's *Today's Isms;* the one for *China* apparently did not discover that the second edition of *Area Handbook for the People's Republic of China* (1972) has been superseded by a third edition, entitled *China, a Country Study* (1981). The guide on Drug Abuse cites the third (1974), not the fourth (1981), edition of *Mind Drugs,* edited by Margaret Hyde.

These examples notwithstanding, *WB* deserves credit for its high degree of accuracy and consistency. In short, *World Book Encyclopedia* continues to be a superior encyclopedia well suited to meet the reference and study needs of students grades 4–12 and to serve as a general reference source for adults.

SCIENCE AND TECHNOLOGY REFERENCE SOURCES FOR HIGH SCHOOL AND UNDERGRADUATE LIBRARIES

The numbers of reference sources published each year in the science and technology disciplines can present problems for limited library budgets. Many of these sources are expensive, and, in many cases, they are revised into new editions on a regular basis. The following list is intended to be a guide to some of the currently available reference sources. Titles included here represent some of the best, *relatively* inexpensive sources that might be considered as representing a rather well-balanced science reference collection. Since price was a major consideration, this list is necessarily selective and, like any such list, it may have omitted certain titles that individual libraries would consider essential. On the other hand, it attempts to identify those areas where choices are possible, e.g., two or three dictionaries in a field, all of which overlap to some extent and all of which are good sources.

This list does not include the indexing and abstracting services that are issued on a periodic basis. (Wilson publishes several, including the *Applied Science and Technology Index, General Science Index,* and the *Biological and Agricultural Index.* These indexes cover many of the general science and technology periodicals that are available in high school and undergraduate libraries.) Publications issued by the U.S. government and distributed by the Government Printing Office have also been excluded. Due to their large numbers, field guides have also been excluded here. However, two groups of these should be noted. The first is the well-known Peterson Field Guide Series, published by Houghton Mifflin. There are currently more than 25 titles in this series covering birds, tracks, mammals, reptiles, wildflowers, insects, and so forth. They are truly field guides and all are in a standard format. The other group includes the Audubon Society encyclopedias and field guides published by Alfred A. Knopf. These are well-written guides with excellent photographs. Any title in either of these series will be useful, and they are good values. Many other field guides are available and should be considered individually.

Each entry here has a one- or two-sentence descriptive annotation; complete bibliographic information is given as well as LC, ISBN, and ISSN numbers when known. The latest price is also given. Obviously, between the time of writing this article and its publication, new titles and editions have appeared; some of these may be better than what is listed. It is imperative, then, to continue to monitor review media for new publications.

Titles are listed under the following headings: General Science, Biology (including botany, zoology, and agriculture), Chemistry, Geoscience—Energy—Environment, Medical Science, Physics—Mathematics—Astronomy, and Technology (including engineering and computer science).

GENERAL SCIENCE

Asimov's biographical encyclopedia of science and technology: the lives and achievements of 1,510 great scientists from ancient times to the present chronologically arranged. By Isaac Asimov. New York, Doubleday, 1982. 984p. illus. $29.95. LC 81-47861. ISBN 0-385-17771-2.

The chronologically arranged biographies of 1,510 prominent scientists in this well-written encyclopedia provide an excellent history of science.

Biographical encyclopedia of scientists. By John Daintith and others. New York, Facts On File, 1981. 2v. bibliog. index. $80. LC 80-23529. ISBN 0-87196-396-5.

More than 1,900 scientists are listed with descriptions of their lives and contributions. A chronology of scientific discoveries and publications is included. A much more expensive and comprehensive biographical dictionary is the 15-volume *Dictionary of Scientific Biography*.

Concise encyclopedia of the sciences. Ed. by John David Yule. New York, Van Nostrand, 1982 [c1978]. 590p. illus. $17.95 pa. LC 81-70325. ISBN 0-442-29208-2.

This American edition of the British book *The Phaidon Concise Encyclopedia of Science and Technology* contains the most commonly used words in science and technology. Brief biographical sketches are included.

Handbooks and tables in science and technology. Ed. by Russell H. Powell. 2d ed. Phoenix, Ariz., Oryx, 1983. 297p. index. $55. LC 82-19842. ISBN 0-89774-039-4.

This is a partially annotated listing of handbooks and tables that covers physics, chemistry, engineering, mathematics, astronomy, biology, geology, agriculture, medicine, and dentistry. Complete bibliographical information is given for each entry.

Illustrated encyclopedia of science and technology: how it works. Donald Clarke, consulting ed. New York, London, Marshall Cavendish, 1977 [c1974–1977]. 20v. illus. $324.95.

This is a good general encyclopedia of applied science and technology that emphasizes machines or discoveries that are around us and affect our everyday lives.

Longman illustrated science dictionary: all fields of scientific language explained and illustrated. By Arthur Godman. New York, Longman, 1982 [c1981]. 255p. illus. (col.). index. $7.95. LC 82-100398. ISBN 0-582-55645-7. (Order from Caroline House, 5S.250 Frontenac Rd., Naperville, IL 60540.)

Approximately 1,500 basic scientific terms are covered in this small dictionary. It is divided into physics, chemistry, and biology. Mathematical terms are included as they pertain to these three disciplines.

McGraw-Hill dictionary of scientific and technical terms. Ed. by Sybil P. Parker. 3d ed. New York, McGraw-Hill, 1984. 1,781p. illus. $70. LC 83-11302. ISBN 0-07-045269-5.

This is a standard general science dictionary with some 115,000 definitions. Each definition includes an abbreviation that indicates the field of interest and multiple definitions are included.

McGraw-Hill encyclopedia of science and technology. 5th ed. New York, McGraw-Hill, 1982. 15v. illus. (part col.). index. $935. LC 81-20920. ISBN 0-07-079280-1.

This is the accepted encyclopedia for science and technology for school and undergraduate libraries. Articles are signed and written by authorities. Most longer articles have a bibliography. Unfortunately, pronunciation of scientific terms is not included. One-volume spin-offs covering specific disciplines are also available; see below.

Science and engineering literature: a guide to reference sources. By H. Robert Malinowsky and Jeanne Richardson. 3d ed. Littleton, Colo., Libraries Unlimited, 1980. 342p. bibliog. index. $33, $21 pa. LC 80-21290. ISBN 0-87287-230-0; 0-87287-245-9 pa.

This guide contains 2,273 annotated reference sources in science and engineering. The sources are divided by types of such references as guides, abstracts, encyclopedias, dictionaries, etc.

Scientific and technical books and serials in print. New York, Bowker, 1972– . annual. $79.50/yr. ISSN 0000-054X.

More than 80,000 books in physics, biology, agriculture, and technology are annually listed by subject and indexed by author and title. More than 16,500 scientific and technical serials from all over the world are listed with full bibliographic and subscription information.

Tables of physical and chemical constants, and some mathematical functions. By G. W. C. Kaye and T. H. Laby; rev. by E. Bailey. 14th ed. New York, Longman, 1973. 386p. $22. LC 73-85205. ISBN 0-582-46326-2.

Physics, chemistry, and mathematical functions and tables are listed in this well-known handbook.

Van Nostrand's scientific encyclopedia. Ed. by Douglas M. Considine. 6th ed. New York, Van Nostrand, 1982. 2v. illus. bibliog. $107.50/v.; $139.50/set. LC 82-4936. ISBN 0-442-25161-0/v.; 0-442-25164-5/set.

This reliable encyclopedia covers earth and space science, biology, mathematics, information science, energy, materials science, physics, and chemistry. Coverage is brief but accurate. An alternative if the *McGraw-Hill Encyclopedia* (see above) is too expensive.

BIOLOGY (INCLUDING BOTANY, ZOOLOGY, AND AGRICULTURE)

Black's veterinary dictionary. Ed. by Geoffrey P. West. 14th ed. Totowa, N.J., Barnes and Noble, 1982. 902p. illus. $28.50. LC 82-22783. ISBN 0-389-20330-0.

This standard veterinary dictionary provides reliable and up-to-date information relating to diseases and conditions of various animals.

Collegiate dictionary of zoology. By Robert William Pennak. New York, Wiley, 1974 (c1964). 566p. $32.50. LC 64-13331. ISBN 0-471-06790-3.

This is a good general dictionary of zoology that gives brief definitions.

Dictionary of biology. By Michael Abercrombie and others. 6th ed. Baltimore, Md., Penguin, 1977 (c1973). 309p. $5.95 pa. LC 73-172135. ISBN 0-14-051003-6.

This is an excellent dictionary for laypersons or beginners, covering the terminology associated with biology and its related fields.

Dictionary of botany. By John Little and C. Eugene Jones. New York, Van Nostrand, 1980. 400p. illus. bibliog. $26.50, $12.95 pa. LC 79-14968. ISBN 0-442-24169-0; 0-442-26019-9 pa.

Although this dictionary does not include the scientific or common names of plants, it is an excellent one for general botanical terminology and includes illustrations.

Dictionary of entomology. By A. W. Leftwich. New York, Crane, Russak, 1976. 360p. $27.50. LC 75-27143. ISBN 0-8448-0820-2.

More than 4,000 definitions of entomological terms and definitions of 3,000 insect species are included in this dictionary for amateur entomologists and zoological students.

Dictionary of microbiology. By Paul Singleton and Diana Sainsbury. New York, Wiley, 1978. 481p. illus. $71.95. LC 78-4532. ISBN 0-471-99658-0.

This is the most comprehensive dictionary available that covers those biological terms that pertain to microorganisms and their environments.

Dictionary of the biological sciences. By Peter Gray. Malabar, Fla., Krieger, 1982 [c1967]. 602p. $37.50. LC 81-19369. ISBN 0-89874-441-5.

Some 40,000 terms are defined in this well-known dictionary of the biological sciences.

Dictionary of theoretical concepts in biology. By Keith E. Roe and Richard G. Frederick. Metuchen, N.J., Scarecrow, 1981. 267p. $19. LC 80-19889. ISBN 0-8108-1353-X.

This is an index to the theories, laws, and ideas related to biology; it is arranged alphabetically by name. Each entry gives the biological field in which the term occurs and a number of sources that explain the topic.

Dictionary of zoology. By A. W. Leftwich. 3d ed. New York, Crane, Russak, 1973. 478p. bibliog. $27.50. LC 67-92630. ISBN 0-8448-0845-8.

This is a standard zoological dictionary that covers about 5,500 terms with brief but clear definitions.

Facts On File dictionary of biology. Ed. by Elizabeth Tootill. New York, Facts On File, 1981. 282p. illus. $14.95. LC 80-26852. ISBN 0-87196-510-0.

Twenty thousand basic biological terms are briefly defined. Only the major groups of biological organisms are included.

Grzimek's animal life encyclopedia. Ed. by Bernhard Grzimek. New York, Van Nostrand, 1972–1975. 13v. illus. (part col.). index. $500/set; $275/paperback. LC 79-183178.

This is a good, concise, descriptive encyclopedia of animal life. There are four volumes on mammals, three on birds, two on fishes and amphibians, and one each on reptiles, insects, mollusks and echinoderms, and lower animals. Evolution, description, range and habitat, feeding and mating habits, and behavioral notes are given for each group.

Guide to sources for agricultural and biological research. Ed. by J. Richard Blanchard and Lois Farrell. Berkeley, Univ. of California Pr., 1981. 735p. $47.50. LC 76-7753. ISBN 0-520-03226-8.

Arranged by nine subject chapters, this book is a guide to the resources concerned with the production of food, wildlife management, and agricultural pollution. All entries are annotated.

Henderson's dictionary of biological terms. By Sandra Holmes. 9th ed. New York, Van Nostrand, 1979. 510p. $37.50. LC 61-883. ISBN 0-442-24865-2.

This is a well-known general dictionary of biological terms that also covers related areas.

Hillier's manual of trees and shrubs. By Harold G. Hillier. 5th ed. New York, Van Nostrand, 1983 [c1981]. 575p. illus. (part col.). bibliog. $19.95. LC 82-24718. ISBN 0-442-23663-8. (out of print).

More than 8,000 plants from 700 genera are described in this manual that includes dates of introduction, flowering periods, and works of reference.

McGraw-Hill encyclopedia of food, agriculture and nutrition. Ed. by Daniel N. Lapedes. New York, McGraw-Hill, 1977. 732p. illus. index. $43.50. LC 77-12181. ISBN 0-07-045263-6.

All aspects and interrelationships of food, agriculture, and nutrition are covered in this interestingly written encyclopedia.

Mammals of the world. By Ronald M. Nowak and John L. Paradiso. 4th ed. Baltimore, Johns Hopkins Univ. Pr., 1984. 2v. illus. bibliog. index. $65. LC 74-23327. ISBN 0-8018-2525-3.

Each of the mammals of the world is described in this two-volume set arranged by taxonomic classification. The illustrations are excellent.

Oxford companion to animal behavior. Ed. by David McFarland. New York, Oxford Univ. Pr., 1982. 657p. illus. index. $35. LC 82-80431. ISBN 0-19-866120-7.

This is a well-written encyclopedia; it covers animal behavior and related topics. There is no subject index. Suggested for undergraduate libraries.

Popular encyclopedia of plants. Ed. by V. H. Heywood. New York, Cambridge Univ. Pr., 1982. 368p. illus. (col.). bibliog. index. $32.50. LC 81-21713. ISBN 0-521-24611-3.

Articles from a larger encyclopedia, *Plants and Man,* make up this work that stresses the economic importance of plants. There are close to 8,000 clearly written entries that require no scientific knowledge of botany.

Smith's guide to the literature of the life sciences. Ed. by Roger C. Smith and others. 9th ed. Minneapolis, Burgess, 1980. 223p. index. $14.95 pa. LC 79-55580. ISBN 0-8087-3576-4.

This is a library guide to the literature of life sciences. It discusses library problems, library organizations, research, and preparation of scientific papers in addition to covering the major reference sources.

World encyclopedia of food. By L. Patrick Coyle. New York, Facts On File, 1982. 790p. illus. (part col.). bibliog. index. $40. LC 80-23123. ISBN 0-87196-417-1.

Although not scholarly, this is a good source of information for about 4,000 food and beverage terms, arranged alphabetically. Each entry includes identification, description, geographic location, method of consumption, and history.

Wyman's gardening encyclopedia. By Donald Wyman. Rev. and expanded ed. New York, Macmillan, 1977. 1,221p. illus. (part col.). $29.95. LC 76-49114. ISBN 0-02-632060-6.

A good source of information on most major horticultural topics plus plant species. Contains information on pesticides, fungicides, and insecticides.

CHEMISTRY

Chemical publications. By M. G. Mellon. 5th ed. New York, McGraw-Hill, 1982. 419p. $28.50. LC 81-20947. ISBN 0-07-041514-5.

This useful guide describes the various chemical reference sources and explains how they are to be used.

Condensed chemical dictionary. Rev. by Gessner G. Hawley. 10th ed. New York, Van Nostrand, 1981. 1,135p. $46.75. LC 80-29636. ISBN 0-442-23244-6.

This is a quick reference source for technical descriptions of chemicals, raw materials, and processes; definitions of chemical entities, phenomena, and terminology; and descriptions of trademarked products used in the chemical industries.

Dangerous properties of industrial materials. By Newton Irving Sax. 6th ed. New York, Van Nostrand, 1984. 3,124p. bibliog. index. $198. LC 83-21766. ISBN 0-442-28304-0.

This is the accepted source of information on about 15,000 hazardous materials. Toxicological data for humans and laboratory animals are included.

Dictionary of named effects and laws in chemistry, physics, and mathematics. By Denis William George Ballentyne and D. R. Lovett. 4th ed. New York, Chapman and Hall in association with Methuen, 1980. 346p. illus. $19.95 pa. LC 79-41716. ISBN 0-412-22390-2.

This is an alphabetically arranged dictionary that defines the equations, laws, theorems, effects, and constants that are identified with personal names.

Facts On File dictionary of chemistry. Ed. by John Daintith. New York, Facts On File, 1981. 122p. illus. $14.95. LC 80-26857. ISBN 0-87196-513-5.

Aproximately 2,200 of the more common chemical terms are included in this dictionary. It is intended for general science students.

Glossary of chemical terms. By Clifford A. Hampel and Gessner G. Hawley. 2d ed. New York, Van Nostrand, 1981. 306p. $21.95. LC 81-11482. ISBN 0-442-23871-1.

The emphasis of the 2,000 entries in this glossary is on major chemical classification, functional terms, basic phenomena and processes, chemical elements, major compounds, and biographies.

Guide to basic information sources in chemistry. By Arthur Antony. New York, Wiley, 1979. 219p. bibliog. index. $22.95. LC 79-330. ISBN 0-470-26587-6.

The user's approach to the chemical literature is the intent of this guide. It includes information on bibliographical searching, safety manuals, style manuals, reference sources, and directories.

Handbook of chemistry and physics. 1st ed.– . Boca Raton, Fla., CRC, 1913– . annual. $64.95. LC 13-11056. ISBN 0-8493-0465-2.

This annual handbook is the accepted source of tabular data in physics, chemistry, and mathematics. Although revised annually, it is not necessary to obtain a new edition each year since much of the information never becomes dated, especially the mathematical data.

Langes handbook of chemistry. Ed. by John A. Dean. 12th ed. New York, McGraw-Hill, 1979. lv. (various paging). illus. index. $49.50. LC 78-15335. ISBN 0-07-016191-7.

This is a handy reference work that provides ready access to chemical and physics data used in the laboratory and manufacturing. There is a mathematics section.

McGraw-Hill encyclopedia of chemistry. Ed. by Sybil P. Parker. New York, McGraw-Hill, 1983. 1,200p. illus. index. $54.50. LC 82-21665. ISBN 0-07-045484-1.

Based on the *McGraw-Hill Encyclopedia of Science and Technology*, 790 articles cover analytical, inorganic, organic, and physical chemistry. It includes entries for specific compounds, processes, and techniques. Nonessential if the larger work is owned.

Use of chemical literature. Ed. by R. T. Bottle. 3d ed. Woburn, Mass., Butterworth, 1979. 306p. index. $39.95. LC 79-41061. ISBN 0-408-38452-2. (out of print).

This is a guide to the use of chemical literature including periodical literature, abstracting services, translations, handbooks, reference works, and other reference sources.

Van Nostrand Reinhold encyclopedia of chemistry. By D. Considine. 4th ed. New York, Van Nostrand, 1984. illus. index. $89.50. LC 83-23336. ISBN 0-442-22572-5.

This is one of the best, one-volume chemical encyclopedias available. It covers, in addition to all of the usual chemistry topics, environmental chemistry and the chemistry of life processes.

GEOSCIENCE—ENERGY—ENVIRONMENT

Cambridge encyclopedia of earth sciences. Ed. by David G. Smith. New York, Cambridge Univ. Pr., 1981. 496p. illus. (part col.). maps. bibliog. index. $37.50. LC 81-3313. ISBN 0-521-23900-1.

Arranged as a textbook rather than an encyclopedia, this book covers all aspects of earth science, especially the theoretical aspects.

Climates of the states: National Oceanic and Atmospheric Administration narrative summaries, tables, and maps for each state. 2d ed. Detroit, Gale, 1980. 2v. maps. $170/set. LC 80-22622. ISBN 0-8103-1036-8.

This is a reprint of 51 separate government documents issued from 1976 to 1978 giving for each state physical description, general climatic features, temperature, precipitation, floods, snowfall, winds and storms, and other climatic elements.

Dictionary of energy. Ed. by Malcolm Slesser. New York, Schocken Books, 1983. 299p. illus. $29.95. LC 82-10252. ISBN 0-8052-3816-6.

This is a very useful dictionary that defines the term and then gives more detailed terminology. It is intended to serve those in the energy profession.

Dictionary of geological terms. By American Geological Institute. 3d ed. Garden City, N.Y., Anchor Press/Doubleday, 1984. 480p. $14.95, $7.95 pa. LC 82-45315. ISBN 0-385-18100-0; 0-385-18101-9 pa.

This useful dictionary contains more than 8,500 of the most common geological terms.

Energy dictionary. By V. Daniel Hunt. New York, Van Nostrand, 1979. 518p. bibliog. $26.50, $14.95 pa. LC 78-9707. ISBN 0-442-27395-9; 0-442-23787-1 pa.

Some 4,000 terms related to the products, conservation, and environmental aspects of energy are included in this dictionary. A glossary of acronyms is appended.

Energy factbook. By Richard C. Dorf. New York, McGraw-Hill, 1981. 227p. illus. index. $22.95, $7.95 pa. LC 80-18736. ISBN 0-07-017623-X; 0-07-017629-9 pa.

This factbook examines the overall energy situation in the U.S. and the world. It discusses the various forms of energy: coal, petroleum, natural gas, electric, hydroelectric, geothermal, solar, nuclear fission and fusion, and alternative sources.

Geologic reference sources: a subject and regional bibliography to publications and maps in the geological sciences. By Dederick C. Ward and others. 2d ed. Metuchen, N.J., Scarecrow, 1981. 590p. $30. LC 81-4770. ISBN 0-8108-1428-5.

This is an up-to-date basic guide to reference sources in geology covering dictionaries, handbooks, bibliographies, serials, abstracting services, and other types of sources. Books, periodical articles, and maps are covered.

Larousse guide to minerals, rocks and fossils. By W. R. Hamilton and others. New York, Larousse, 1977. 320p. illus. (part col.). index. $15.95, $9.95 pa. LC 77-71167. ISBN 0-88332-079-7; 0-88332-078-9 pa.

Beautiful illustrations make this a good guide to 220 minerals, 90 rocks, and 300 fossils. Complete descriptions are given for each entry.

McGraw-Hill dictionary of earth sciences. Ed. by Sybil P. Parker. New York, McGraw-Hill, 1984. 837p. illus. $32.50. LC 83-20362. ISBN 0-07-045252-0.

This specialized dictionary concentrates on those terms that are used in earth sciences and related fields. Most of the material is from the third edition of *McGraw-Hill Dictionary of Scientific and Technical Terms*.

McGraw-Hill encyclopedia of environmental sciences. Ed. by Sybil P. Parker. 2d ed. New York, McGraw-Hill, 1980. 858p. illus. index. $46.50. LC 79-28098. ISBN 0-07-045264-4.

Based on the *McGraw-Hill Encyclopedia of Science and Technology*, this spin-off covers technology, conservation, waste management, climate and weather components, ecological interactions, pollution, and management. Nonessential if the parent work is available.

McGraw-Hill encyclopedia of ocean and atmospheric sciences. Ed. by Sybil P. Parker. New York, McGraw-Hill, 1980. 580p. illus. $44.50. LC 79-18644. ISBN 0-07-045267-9.

Articles on ocean and atmospheric science have been taken from the *McGraw-Hill Encyclopedia of Science and Technology* and presented in one volume. It includes articles on pollution, satellites, climate modification, and sea diving. Again, the parent work will suffice.

Mountains of North America. By Fred Becky. San Francisco, Sierra Club Books, 1982. 255p. illus. (col.). bibliog. $35. LC 82-3315. ISBN 0-87156-320-7.

The geology, biota, and history of 36 separate mountain ranges in North America are presented in this profusely illustrated book.

Ocean and marine dictionary. By David F. Tver. Centreville, Md., Cornell Maritime Pr., 1979. 358p. $18.50. LC 79-1529. ISBN 0-87033-246-5.

This dictionary provides short and concise definitions of terms associated with marine science and oceanography, including sailing nomenclature, ships, weather, currents, and related areas.

Ocean world encyclopedia. By Donald G. Groves and Lee M. Hunt. New York, McGraw-Hill, 1980. 443p. illus. maps. index. $49.95. LC 79-21093. ISBN 0-07-025010-3.

For nonspecialists, this encyclopedia covers physical, geological, chemical, and biological oceanography; instrumentation; hurricanes; organizations; and famous oceanographers.

Petroleum dictionary. By David F. Tver and Richard W. Berry. New York, Van Nostrand, 1980. 374p. illus. $24.50, $16.95 pa. LC 79-19346. ISBN 0-686-65585-0; 0-442-28529-9 pa.

This dictionary contains about 4,000 concise and easy-to-understand definitions for terms relating to all aspects of the petroleum industry.

Solar energy almanac. Ed. by Martin McPhillips. New York, Facts On File, 1983. 240p. illus. $15.95. LC 82-9362. ISBN 0-87196-727-8.

This is a compendium of topics that deal with solar energy, including history, building sites, solar cells, greenhouses, and solar homes in the U.S. A glossary is included.

Solar energy handbook. Ed. by Jan F. Krieder and Frank Kreith. New York, McGraw-Hill, 1981. lv. (various paging). illus. index. $64.50. LC 79-22570. ISBN 0-07-035474-X.

Information on solar-energy system assessment and design is brought together in this handbook. Its emphasis is on applications.

Sourcebook on the environment: a guide to the literature. By Kenneth A. Hammond and others. Chicago, Univ. of Chicago Pr., 1978. 613p. index. $25. LC 77-17407. ISBN 0-226-31522-3.

This is a fairly comprehensive discussion of three environmental areas—perspectives, case studies, and major elements of the environment. There is a bibliography following each essay. It is both a guide to the literature and an introduction for nonspecialists.

World atlas of geomorphic features. By Rodman E. Snead. New York, Van Nostrand, 1980. 301p. illus. (part col.). bibliog. index. $44.50. LC 77-28009. ISBN 0-88275-272-3.

This is an atlas of 63 landforms with accompanying text that defines the landform, describes its salient features, and enumerates reasons for its distribution and occurrence.

World energy book: an A–Z atlas and statistical sourcebook. Ed. by David Crabbe and Richard McBride. New York, Nichols Publishing Co., 1978. $32.50. LC 78-50805. ISBN 0-262-53036-8.

Approximately 1,500 terms are included in this encyclopedia. Definitions are nontechnical. Twenty-four maps in the atlas section show the available world energy resources.

MEDICAL SCIENCE

Black's medical dictionary. By William A. R. Thomson. 33d ed. Totowa, N.J., Barnes & Noble, 1981. 982p. illus. $24.50. LC 59-167. ISBN 0-389-20246-0.

Although this is a British publicaton, it is well known and adequately covers the current terminology in the various fields of medicine.

Blakiston's Gould medical dictionary: a modern comprehensive dictionary of the terms used in all branches of medicine and allied sciences. 4th ed. New York, McGraw-Hill, 1979. 1,632p. illus. $35. LC 78-21929. ISBN 0-07-005703-6.

This is one of the best American medical dictionaries that covers all branches of medicine and its allied sciences. A smaller pocket size is also available.

Dictionary of medical syndromes. By Sergio Magalini and Euclide Scrascia. 2d ed. Philadelphia, Lippincott, 1981. 944p. index. $52. LC 80-29209. ISBN 0-397-50503-5.

Some 2,700 individual syndromes or symptom complexes are defined. For each entry the synonyms, symptoms and signs, etiology, diagnostic procedures, therapy, and prognosis are given.

Dorland's illustrated medical dictionary. 26th ed. Philadelphia, Saunders, 1981. 1,485p. illus. $35.95. LC 0-6383. ISBN 0-7216-3150-9.

This is a standard, well-known dictionary of medical terms. There is also a pocket edition and a "shorter version."

Drugs in current use and new drugs. 1st ed.– . New York, Springer, 1955– . annual. $10.95/year. LC 55-1210. ISSN 0070-7392.

Drugs currently in use and new drugs are the two sections of this annual. For each entry the physical properties, proprietary names, synonyms, absorption, actions and uses, modes of administration, preparations, and specific antidotes are given.

Duncan's dictionary for nurses. By Helen Duncan. New York, Springer, 1971. 386p. illus. $6.95. LC 74-121974. ISBN 0-8261-1121-1.

Approximately 11,000 terms for nursing, medicine, and related disciplines are defined. Pronunciation, variant definitions, and synonyms are included.

Encyclopedia and dictionary of medicine, nursing and allied health. By Benjamin Frank Miller and Claire Brackman Keane. 3d ed. Philadelphia, Saunders, 1983. 1,270p. illus. $23.95. LC 82-40000. ISBN 0-7216-6363-X.

This is a comprehensive medical encyclopedia that gives brief definitions and pronunciation.

Encyclopedia of alcoholism. By Robert O'Brien and Morris Chafetz. New York, Facts On File, 1982. 378p. illus. bibliog. index. $40. LC 81-12562. ISBN 0-87196-623-9.

More than 500 entries that are directly related to alcoholism are included in this encyclopedia. It covers alcoholic beverages, alcohol abuse, institutions that work with alcoholics, laws, diseases, and slang.

Essential guide to nonprescription drugs. By David R. Zimmerman. New York, Harper, 1983. 886p. index. $26.44, $10.95 pa. LC 82-48139. ISBN 0-06-014915-9; 0-06-91023-2 pa.

This handy guide presents pertinent facts about over-the-counter drugs with the main source being the *Federal Register*. The entries are arranged under 74 conditions from acne to sore throat and mouth medicines.

The essential guide to prescription drugs. By James W. Long. 3d ed. New York, Harper, 1982. 935p. bibliog. index. $31.68. LC 76-5141. ISBN 0-06-012674-4.

The prescription drugs are listed giving dosage forms, intended action, possible side and adverse effects, and things to observe while taking the drug. Other useful information concerning drugs is included.

Gray's anatomy of the human body. Ed. by Roger Warwick and Peter L. Williams. 36th ed. Philadelphia, W. B. Saunders, 1980. 1,596p. illus. index. $79. ISBN 0-7216-9128-5.

This standard reference source on the human body is the most authoritative textbook available on anatomy. It has outstanding illustrations.

Handbook of poisoning: prevention, diagnosis and treatment. By Robert H. Dreisbach. 11th ed. Los Altos, Calif., Lange, 1983. 578p. illus. index. $11. LC 79-92918. ISBN 0-87041-075-X.

The prevention, diagnosis, evaluation, management, and legal and medical aspects of poisoning are discussed. For each material that is presented, clinical findings, prevention, treatment, and prognosis are given.

Handbook of practical pharmacology. By Bruce D. Clayton. 3d ed. St. Louis, Mosby, 1984. 698p. illus. $14.95. ISBN 0-8016-4243-4.

This useful handbook discusses the various drug types and miscellaneous medications, giving trade name, characteristics, administration and dosage, special remarks and cautions, and drug interactions.

Health sciences information sources. By Ching-chih Chen. Cambridge, Mass., MIT Pr., 1981. 767p. index. $70. LC 80-20557. ISBN 0-262-03074-8.

A comprehensive list of more than 4,000 biomedical books giving complete bibliographical information, brief evaluative annotations, and citations to published reviews is included in this guide.

Illustrated dictionary of dentistry. By Stanley Jablonski. Philadelphia, Saunders, 1982. 919p. illus. $45.95. LC 78-50053. ISBN 0-7216-5055-4.

This is a comprehensive dictionary that covers all specialties of dentistry and allied fields. It includes some terms of historical or etymological interest.

Medical books and serials in print: an index to literature in health sciences. New York, Bowker, 1972– . annual. $75. ISSN 0000-0574.

Annually, more than 52,000 in-print books are listed by subject and indexed by author and title. More than 9,000 serials from all over the world are listed with full bibliographic and subscription information.

Merck manual of diagnosis and therapy. Ed. by Robert Berkow. Rahway, N.J., Merck, 1982. 2v. illus. $19.75: v.1; $6.95: v.2. ISBN 0-911910-04-2: v.1; 0-911910-05-0: v.2.

This is a standard reference source that emphasizes medical diagnosis and treatment. Volume one covers general medicine and volume two covers obstetrics, gynecology, pediatrics, and genetics.

Nutrition and health encyclopedia. By David F. Tver and Percy Russell. New York, Van Nostrand, 1981. 569p. illus. $29.50. LC 80-19933. ISBN 0-442-24859-8.

This is a one-volume encyclopedia covering terms associated with nutrition and health. Entries are generally short.

Physicians desk reference to pharmaceutical specialties and biologicals. 1st ed.– . Ordell, N.Y., Medical Economics, 1947– . annual. ($23.95 prepaid, $25.95 billed, after Nov. 15 each will go up $2.) ISSN 0093-4461.

This technical annual, basically for physicians but useful to others, covers for each specialty or biological the dosage, contraindications, precautions, side effects, and undesirable interactions.

PHYSICS—MATHEMATICS—ASTRONOMY

A–Z of astronomy. By Patrick Moore. New York, Scribner, 1976. 192p. illus. $1.95 pa. LC 76-58876. ISBN 0-684-16913-4. (out of print).

For novice astronomers, this book covers astronomical terms, instruments, events, places, phenomena, observations, and principles. It includes brief biographical essays.

Amateur astronomer's handbook. By James Muirden. 3d ed. New York, Harper, 1983. 472p. illus. index. bibliog. $16.30. LC 81-48044. ISBN 0-06-181622-1.

This is a practical guide for the amateur astronomer covering techniques of viewing the various celestial bodies and astronomical photography.

American Institute of Physics handbook. Ed. by Dwight E. Gray. 3d ed. New York, McGraw-Hill, 1972. lv. (various paging). illus. index. $99.50. LC 71-109244. ISBN 0-07-001485-X.

This is a standard physics handbook that covers all aspects. It defines concepts and describes subfields.

Astronomy and telescopes: a beginner's handbook. By Robert J. Traister and Susan E. Harris. Blue Ridge Summit, Pa., TAB Books, 1983. 200p. illus. (part col.). index. $19.95, $14.95 pa. LC 82-19346. ISBN 0-8306-0419-7; 0-8306-1419-2 pa.

This good how-to book for amateur astronomers covers the theory, construction, and use of telescopes and auxiliary equipment.

Astronomy data book. By Hedley Robinson and James Muirden. 2d ed. New York, Halsted Pr., 1979. 272p. illus. maps. index. $29.95. LC 78-21698. ISBN 0-470-26594-9.

This useful handbook includes a wealth of information on astronomical topics as well as a chronology of important events, conversion tables, and data on radio, gamma-ray, and infrared astronomy.

Astronomy handbook. By James Muirden. New York, Arco, 1982. 189p. illus. (col.). index. $8.95. LC 82-1780. ISBN 0-668-05586-3.

Excellent illustrations make this a useful book for the amateur astronomer. It covers all aspects of astronomy in order to help the observer identify what can be seen in the sky with the naked eyes, a pair of binoculars, or a small telescope.

Atlas of the planets. By Paul Doherty. New York, McGraw-Hill, 1980. 143p. illus. (part col.). bibliog. index. $19.95. LC 80-12347. ISBN 0-07-017341-9.

For amateur observers, this handbook provides for each planet history, observing hints, descriptions of planetary features, nomenclature, and other useful information.

The Cambridge encyclopedia of astronomy. Ed. by Simon Mitton. New York, Crown, 1977. 481p. illus. (part col.). index. $22.95. LC 77-2766. ISBN 0-517-52806-1.

The excellent illustrations and well-written text make this a very useful encyclopedia for beginners and advanced amateurs. The articles are arranged by subject rather than in straight alphabetical order. A star atlas is included.

Concise dictionary of physics and related subjects. By J. Thewlis. 2d ed. rev. and enl. Elmsford, N.Y., Pergamon, 1979. 370p. $72. LC 79-40209. ISBN 0-08-023048-2.

For students and nonspecialists, this dictionary covers physics, meteorology, mathematics, photography, astronomy, crystallography, and other related fields.

Dictionary of astronomy, space and atmospheric phenomena. By David F. Tver. New York, Van Nostrand, 1979. 281p. illus. $21.95, $12.95 pa. LC 79-15372. ISBN 0-442-24045-7; 0-442-28422-5 pa.

This dictionary for laypersons covers the terminology associated with astronomy, space, atmosphere, physics, and mathematics.

Encyclopedia of physics. Ed. by Rita G. Lerner and George L. Trigg. Reading, Mass., Addison-Wesley, 1981. 1,157p. illus. index. $115. LC 80-21175. ISBN 0-201-04313-0.

Physics and astrophysics are covered in this excellent but rather expensive encyclopedia. Coverage is broad and includes survey articles on major topics such as atomic spectroscopy, hot-atom chemistry, and integrated circuits.

Facts On File dictionary of astronomy. Ed. by Valerie Illingsworth. New York, Facts On File, 1979. 378p. illus. $17.95. LC 79-17134. ISBN 0-87196-326-4.

Brief definitions are included in this dictionary. Much of the information is not found in other astronomy dictionaries.

Facts On File dictionary of physics. Ed. by John Daintith. New York, Facts On File, 1981. 217p. illus. $14.95. LC 80-26854. ISBN 0-87196-511-9.

This small dictionary contains about 2,000 entries of more common physics terms. The definitions are concise and easy to understand.

Glossary of astronomy and astrophysics. By Jeanne Hopkins. 2d ed. rev. and enl. Chicago, Univ. of Chicago Pr., 1980. 196p. $19, $10 pa. LC 80-5226. ISBN 0-226-35171-8; 0-226-35169-6 pa.

A good comprehensive dictionary of 2,350 astronomical, astrophysical, and related physics and chemistry terms. It includes definitions of specific astronomical objects, techniques, and theories.

Handbook of mathematical tables and formulas. By Richard S. Burrington. 5th ed. New York, McGraw-Hill, 1973. 500p. illus. index. $24.50. LC 78-39634. ISBN 0-07-009015-7.

All conceivable mathematical tables and formulas are included in this well-known handbook.

Illustrated encyclopedia of astronomy and space. Ed. by Ian Ridpath. Rev. ed. New York, T. Y. Crowell, 1979. 240p. illus. (part col.). index. $19.18. LC 79-7098. ISBN 0-690-01838-X.

Coverage of U.S. and Soviet space programs is included in this good encyclopedia of astronomy and astronautics.

McGraw-Hill encyclopedia of physics. Ed. by Sybil P. Parker. New York, McGraw-Hill, 1983. 1,343p. illus. $59.50. LC 82-21721. ISBN 0-07-045253-9.

This is another spin-off from the *McGraw-Hill Encyclopedia of Science and Technology*. It covers classical and modern physics including acoustics; atomic, particle, molecular and nuclear physics; mechanics, electricity, heat, and thermodynamics; and all other related areas. Again, nonessential if the parent work is owned.

Observational astronomy for amateurs. By John Benson Sidgwick. Hillside, N.J., Enslow, 1982. 348p. illus. index. bibliog. $19.95, $7.95 pa. LC 82-1499. ISBN 0-89490-067-6; 0-89490-068-4 pa.

This serious book for amateur astronomers concentrates on the various heavenly bodies and indicates how one is to observe and identify them.

Pictorial guide to the planets. By Joseph H. Jackson and John H. Baumert. 3d ed. New York, Harper, 1981. 246p. illus. (part col.). index. $22.50. LC 80-7897. ISBN 0-06-014869-1.

Each planet, including Earth, is discussed in detail in this guide. There are useful tables that give data on the planets and space exploration of them.

Use of physics literature. Ed. by Herbert Coblans. Woburn, Mass., Butterworth, 1975. 290p. index. $37.95. LC 76-353687. ISBN 0-408-70709-7. (out of print).

Libraries and the structure and control of physics literature are covered in the first part of this guide followed by the literature of specific subdisciplines of physics.

Using the mathematical literature: a practical guide. By Barbara Kirsch Schaefer. New York, Dekker, 1979. 141p. index. $19.75. LC 78-24537. ISBN 0-8247-6675-X.

This is not a comprehensive bibliography but rather a guide to the mathematical literature.

VNR concise encyclopedia of mathematics. Ed. by W. Gellert and others. New York, Van Nostrand, 1977. lv. (various paging). illus. (part col.). index. $19.95. LC 76-14575. ISBN 0-442-22646-2.

Part one of this good one-volume mathematics encyclopedia covers traditional areas of elementary mathematics, and part two covers higher mathematics. There are some basic mathematics tables and an index of prominent mathematicians.

Whitney's star finder: a field guide to the heavens. By Charles A. Whitney. 3d ed. New York, Knopf, 1981. 102p. illus. index. $8.95 pa. LC 81-47523. ISBN 0-394-74953-7.

This is an excellent guide revised for the years 1982 through 1985 and includes information on star findings, planet watching, time telling, eclipses, and other topics of astronomical interest.

TECHNOLOGY (INCLUDING ENGINEERING AND COMPUTER SCIENCE)

American electricians handbook. Ed. by Wilford I. Summers. 10th ed. New York, McGraw-Hill, 1980. lv. (various paging). illus. index. $49.50. LC 80-14757. ISBN 0-07-013931-8.

Intended for electricians, this well-known handbook covers all the essential information about circuits, equipment, motors, wiring, and lighting.

Aviation/space dictionary. Ed. by Ernest J. Gentle and Lawrence W. Reithmaier. 6th ed. Fallbrook, Calif., Aero, 1980. 272p. illus. $18.95. LC 80-67567. ISBN 0-8168-3002-9.

This is a good dictionary of more than 6,000 terms that are used in air traffic control, avionics, astronomy, computer technology, geophysics, nucleonics, civil and military aviation, meteorology, navigation, and space flight.

Building design and construction handbook. Ed. by Frederick S. Merritt. 4th ed. New York, McGraw-Hill, 1981. 1,408p. illus. index. $79.50. LC 75-6553. ISBN 0-07-041521-8.

For the building and construction trade, this is the standard reference book. It covers both building design and construction.

Computer dictionary. By Donald D. Spencer. 2d ed. Ormand Beach, Fla., Camelot Publishing, 1979. 192p. illus. $6.95 pa. LC 78-31738. ISBN 0-89218-038-2. (out of print).

This is a layperson's glossary of 2,500 words, phrases, and acronyms covering the various aspects of computers and related areas.

Computer dictionary and handbook. By Charles J. Sippl and Charles P. Sippl. 3d ed. Indianapolis, Ind., Sams, 1980. 928p. illus. $34.95. LC 79-67133. ISBN 0-672-21632-9. (Fourth ed. scheduled for publication in Jan. 1985 at $39.95.)

This is a basic reference work on computers with additional information on time-sharing and computer languages, plus a basic description of a computer.

Dictionary of computers, data processing, and telecommunications. By Jerry M. Rosenberg. New York, Wiley, 1984. 614p. $29.95. LC 83-12359. ISBN 0-471-87638-0.

This is an extensive dictionary of more than 10,000 computer, data processing, and telecommunications terms giving definitions and use. A French and Spanish glossary is appended.

Dictionary of space technology. By Joseph A. Angelo. New York, Facts On File, 1982. 380p. illus. $24.95. LC 81-3144. ISBN 0-87196-583-6.

This is a good dictionary of terms currently used in U.S. space programs. Definitions are brief and accurate.

Electronics dictionary. By John Markus. 4th ed. New York, McGraw-Hill, 1978. 745p. illus. $39.50. LC 77-13876. ISBN 0-07-04031-3.

More than 16,000 terms used in television, radio, medical electronics, industrial electronics, space electronics, military electronics, avionics, radar, nuclear science, and engineering are defined in this dictionary.

Encyclopedia of aviation. New York, Scribner, 1977. 218p. illus. index. $5.95. LC 77-7269. ISBN 0-684-16921-5. (out of print).

This general encyclopedia includes short histories of airlines, biographical data on aviation personalities, explanations of technical terms, and brief descriptions of civil and military aircraft and important air forces.

Encyclopedia of building and construction terms. By Hugh Brooks. Englewood Cliffs, N.J., Prentice-Hall, 1983. 443p. illus. index. $50. LC 82-21565. ISBN 0-13-275511-4.

This is one of the best encyclopedias covering the terminology associated with the building industry, including terms related to construction, real estate, insurance, mathematics, energy conservation, surveying, and engineering.

Encyclopedia of computer science and engineering. By Anthony Ralston and Edwin D. Reilly, Jr. 2d ed. New York, Van Nostrand, 1983. 1,664p. illus. $87.50. LC 82-2700. ISBN 0-442-24496-7.

This is a good general encyclopedia that provides 550 articles on computers for nonspecialists. A glossary of terms is included.

Engineering formulas. By Kurt Gieck. 4th ed. New York, McGraw-Hill, 1983. lv. (various paging). index. $16.95. LC 82-20337. ISBN 0-07-023219-9.

This is a comprehensive handbook of formulas used in all aspects of engineering, mathematics, physics, and chemistry.

Engineering mathematics handbook: definitions, theorems, formulas, tables. By Jan J. Tuma. 2d ed. rev. and enl. New York, McGraw-Hill, 1979. 394p. illus. bibliog. index. $34.50. LC 77-17786. ISBN 0-07-065429-8.

Intended as a desk-top reference book, this handbook covers all mathematical definitions, theorems, formulas, and tables that would be needed by engineers, scientists, students, and architects.

Facts On File dictionary of microcomputers. By Anthony Chandor. New York, Facts On File, 1981. 183p. $14.95. LC 81-4323. ISBN 0-87196-597-6.

Some 2,500 microcomputer terms are defined in layperson's language.

Facts On File dictionary of telecommunications. By John Graham. New York, Facts On File, 1983. 199p. illus. $15.95. LC 82-15675. ISBN 0-87196-120-2.

Intended for laypersons, this dictionary includes 2,000 telecommunication terms. Hardware terms and trade names are selectively covered.

IEEE standard dictionary of electrical and electronics terms. Ed. by Frank Jay. 2d ed. New York, Wiley, 1977. 882p. $37.50. LC 77-92333. ISBN 0-471-04264-1.

For electrical and electronics terms, this is a basic dictionary. In addition to the definitions, synonyms, special notes, diagrams, tables, and examples are included.

McGraw-Hill computer handbook. Ed. by Harry Helms. New York, McGraw-Hill, 1983. lv. (various paging). illus. index. $79.50. LC 83-1044. ISBN 0-07-027972-1.

This handbook covers the workings of computers, peripherals, and software. Little prior knowledge of computer science is needed to understand this handbook.

McGraw-Hill encyclopedia of engineering. Ed. by Sybil P. Parker. New York, McGraw-Hill, 1983. 1,264p. illus. index. $64.50. LC 82-18663. ISBN 0-07-045486-8.

Another spin-off from the *McGraw-Hill Encyclopedia of Science and Technology,* this work has more than 690 articles that cover civil, design, electrical, industrial, mechanical, metallurgical, mining, nuclear, petroleum, and production engineering. Again, the parent work may suffice.

McGraw-Hill's National Electrical Code handbook. Ed. by J. F. McPartland. 18th ed. Based on the current 1984 National Electrical Code. New York, McGraw-Hill, 1984. 1,205p. illus. index. $32.95. LC 81-642618. ISBN 0-07-045700-X.

This is the best handbook that covers the National Electrical Code. It discusses the code and includes many illustrations and diagrams and is intended to be a companion reference to the code itself.

Mark's standard handbook for mechanical engineering. Ed. by Theodor Baumeister. 8th ed. New York, McGraw-Hill, 1978. lv. (various paging). illus. index. $69.50. LC 16-12915. ISBN 0-07-004123-7.

This noted handbook covers properties and handling of materials, machine elements, fuels and furnaces, power generating, pumps and compressors, shop processes, instrumentation, and environmental control.

New complete encyclopedia of motor cars: 1885–present. Ed. by G. N. Georgano. 3d ed. New York, Dutton, 1982. 688p. illus. (part col.). index. $45. LC 81-71857. ISBN 0-525-93254-2.

Some 4,300 different models of cars are covered in this profusely illustrated encyclopedia. The major manufacturers are given condensed histories.

Radio amateur's handbook. By American Radio Relay League. 1st ed.– . Navington, Conn., American Radio Relay League, 1926– . annual. $17.75/year, $12/year pa. ISSN 0079-9440.

This is the bible for radio ham operators. All of the techniques, history, and know-how are included and revised on an annual basis. A Spanish edition is also available.

Radio amateur's handbook. By A. Frederick Collins. 15th rev. ed. New York, Harper, 1983. 416p. illus. index. $12.45. LC 82-48660. ISBN 0-06-181366-4.

This is a beginner's handbook that presents the fundamental theories of ham radio operations.

Standard handbook for civil engineers. Ed. by Frederick S. Merritt. 3d ed. New York, McGraw-Hill, 1983. lv. (various paging). illus. index. $79.95. LC 82-14902. ISBN 0-07-041515-3.

This is another standard handbook for civil engineers. System design, management, specifications, and applications are topics that are covered.

Standard handbook for electrical engineers. Ed. by Donald G. Fink. 11th ed. New York, McGraw-Hill, 1978. lv. (various paging). illus. index. $74.95. LC 56-6964. ISBN 0-07-020974-X.

This is a well-known handbook that is used by electrical engineers. It contains all the needed information about electricity and is oriented toward practical applications.

Welding encyclopedia. By Ted B. Jefferson. 18th ed. Lake Zurich, Ill., Monticello, 1981. 1,047p. illus. $20. ISBN 0-686-28906-4. (Anticipated publication of a complete revision due Dec. 1984.)

This well-known encyclopedia of welding terms gives good descriptions of welding subjects and includes a trade-name dictionary.—*H. Robert Malinowsky.*

REVIEWS AND NOTES

The ALA glossary of library and information science.
Heartsill Young, editor. Chicago, American Library Assn., 1983. xvi, 245p. 27cm. cloth $50 (0-8389-0371-1).
020′.3 Library science—Dictionaries | Information science—Dictionaries [CIP] 82-18512

This revised and updated version of *The ALA Glossary of Library Terms* (1943) includes definitions of terms drawn from a number of fields: librarianship and information science; educational technology; typography; computer science; administrative science; the graphic arts, etc. A broad range of entries that relate to the production, organization, storage, and dissemination of information products and to the organization, management, and delivery mechanisms of libraries and related institutions has been included. The book is designed to bring together in a single volume contemporary definitions of terms, an understanding of which is germane to the work of librarians and information scientists.

Arranged in two columns per page with approximately 4,700 entries, the editor (with the assistance of seven authorities) has chosen definitions which have been generally accepted by relevant associations and institutions. The entries vary in length but rarely exceed 75 words. Alphabetization is letter by letter; there are *see* and compare with cross-references. The Introduction states that if an acronym is clearly the most common form, an entry appears under it. Conversely, if it is a term for which the acronym is not the most common form, an entry appears under the full term. Unfortunately, there is quite a bit of inconsistency. In fact, though the Introduction specifically states that *precis* is to be found as an acronym, the entry nevertheless appears under the full term. Though *cobol* is entered as an acronym, the following terms are not: *ill, fm, com catalog, PBX,* and *ISBN*.

Any glossary which attempts to cover a variety of fields runs the risk of not covering any of the constituent areas fully. Therefore, it is not surprising that the *Glossary* has neither the extent nor depth of coverage of more specific reference works, such as Glaister's *Glossary of the Book* (Berkeley: Univ. of California Pr., 1979) or P. B. Mintz' *Dictionary of Graphic Arts Terms* (New York: Van Nostrand, 1981).

Nonetheless, *The ALA Glossary of Library and Information Science* is the only up-to-date work providing accurate, useful, and contemporary definitions for terms from a variety of disciplines that are important for librarians. An important work suitable for almost any library.

Advertising slogans of America. Compiled by Harold S. Sharp. Metuchen, N.J. & London, Scarecrow, 1984. xi, 544p. 22cm. cloth $35 (0-8108-1681-4).
659.13′Slogans | Advertising—U.S. [CIP] 83-20431

The Preface succinctly describes the evolution of advertising and the use of slogans in the U.S. The compiler gathered this collection of approximately 15,000 slogans used by some 6,000 businesses from (among other sources) television, radio, films, newspapers, letterheads, handbills, and even sandwich boards! The slogans, parent organizations, "and/or the products/ services to which (the slogans) pertain" are interfiled in one alphabetical list with slogans appearing both under the company/product name, and individually with the company/ product listed underneath.

While replete with such classics as "I can't believe I ate the whole thing" and the obscure, "Put muscle in your heat transfer applications," the veteran consumer/ad writer will find omissions, e.g., "Hey Mabel, Black Label." Also, since there is no subject access, users must remember either the company/product *or* the *exact* wording of the slogan.

This volume may help public librarians answer trivia questions, but it undoubtedly will have greater use in business/advertising collections.

African political facts since 1945. By Chris Cook and David Killingray. New York, Facts On File, 1983. 263p. 24cm. cloth $19.95 (0-87196-381-7).
960′.32 Africa—Politics and government—1945-1960—Handbooks, manuals, etc. | Africa—Politics and government—1960- —Handbooks, manuals, etc. [CIP] 81-17514

This reference book is useful in untangling the political history of Africa since 1945—a period when colonialism began to decline with the creation of many new nations. Current to the late 1970s, and, in some cases, through 1980, this book treats political events in some 60 African nations, including all of the continent. Since the evolution from colonial status to independence was not always bloodless, this handbook serves to document these changes.

One of the authors, Chris Cook, has collaborated on four other similar works dealing with Europe (1789–1973) and the British Commonwealth, which, like the present volume, present facts in combinations of tabular and summary form, as well as traditional paragraph style, in a straightforward manner, without editorial comment. The work includes the following sections typically arranged by country and then year: Major Events; Governors and Heads of State; Major Ministerial Appointments; Constitutions and Parliaments; Political Parties; Trade Unions; Conflicts, Armed Forces and Coups; Foreign Affairs and Treaties; Population and Ethnic Groups; Basic Economic Statistics; and Biographies. Perhaps the only somewhat extraneous information is that on trade unions, which have not been as great an influence as in the more industrialized countries. However, the biography section appears strong in providing information on lesser-known figures in Africa.

This handbook will, in all likelihood, contain too little information for knowledgeable scholars, but it will be of immeasurable use as a ready-reference tool for students (junior high school and up), teachers, and journalists.

Aging: a guide to resources. Edited by John B. Balkema. New York, Gaylord in association with Neal-Schuman, 1983. vi, 232p. 23cm. paper $34.95 (0-915794-48-9).
016.3052′6 Aging—Bibliography [CIP] 83-9010

Designed to draw together the reference and working tools of social gerontology, this categorized bibliography covers the usual reference tools, e.g., directories, handbooks, bibliographies, under headings that range from General Works to Ethnic Groups, Health and Housing, and Political, Legal and Sociological Aspects of Aging. Each item is numbered, followed by a complete bibliographic citation and a descriptive annotation. Subheadings within chapters and Name and Subject Indexes provide easy access. A worthwhile resource for any library whose concerns extend to aging.

Agricultural research centres: a world directory of organizations and programmes. 2v. Consultant ed., Nigel Harvey. Essex, U.K., Longman; dist in North America exclusively by Gale, 1983. 1,276p. 26cm. paper over boards $295/set (0-582-90014-X).
630′.72 Agricultural research—Directories [British CIP]

The seventh edition of *Agricultural Research Centres* (*ARC*) is the successor to *Agricultural Research Index* of 1978. *ARC* attempts to give comprehensive coverage to worldwide organizations that conduct or finance research in agriculture, veterinary medicine, horticulture, fisheries and aquaculture, food science, forestry, zoology, botany, plant production, animal production, soil science, drainage and irrigation, and land use.

Centers include official research centers, educational organizations with research programs, industrial firms, and industrial research centers.

ARC covers about 2,500 primary organizations with some 9,000 divisions, departments, and labs. The first chapter, "International Establishments," contains 117 entries. The remainder of the work is 125 alphabetical-by-country chapters. Under each country, centers are listed alphabetically according to native language. English translation is used for countries which do not use the Roman alphabet.

Entries may include titles in the orginal language, acronym, English translation of title, address, telephone number, telex, status, type of body, parent group or subsidiary, affiliation, director, sections, graduate research staff, activities, publications, and projects. Data are as thorough as the center's returned questionnaire provided or other sources provide.

The Titles of Establishments Index guides users to entries by country and entry number. The Index includes access by both non-English-language title and English translation when necessary. Acronyms are also included.

The detailed Subject Index guides users to entries according to data from the "activities" and "projects" sections of entries.

The publishers include an errata sheet for Index entries on the United Kingdom and India, but otherwise, the indexes are accurate.

ARC is a highly specialized work which provides a wealth of information in agricultural research. Because of relatively limited application, *ARC* will probably be useful in university and special libraries.

Album of science: antiquity and the Middle Ages. By John E. Murdoch. New York, Scribner, 1984. xii, 403p. 28cm. cloth $63 (0-684-15496-X).
509'.01 Scientific illustration—History | Science, Ancient | Science, Medieval [CIP]   84-1400

The third volume in the series, Album of Science, this title is an "anthology of the kinds of pictorial and diagrammatic materials to be found in the scientific literature of antiquity and the Middle Ages." However, because of the small number of illustrations that survive for these periods, this book is not intended to serve as an illustrated history of science, although the work includes more than 500 illustrations. These black-and-white photographs are of high quality and have excellent resolution. Each illustration is accompanied by explanatory text, which provides insight into the various beliefs and practices of science during these periods. Illustrations are divided into chapters covering the early production of books and text; methods of illustrating ideas by using tabulations, charts, and diagrams; the exact sciences and mathematical illustrations; and scientists' representations of scientific objects.

At the end of this volume there is a bibliography and guide to further reading. Also included are a list of sources for all illustrations and an Index with page numbers for textual material in lightface and to illustration numbers in boldface.

This volume will be a rich resource for academic and other research libraries' clients with an interest in the history of science. Previous volumes in the planned five-volume set already published include *From Leonardo to Lavoisier, 1450–1800* by I. Bernard Cohen (1980) and *The Nineteenth Century* by L. Pearce Williams (1978). Still in preparation are *The Physical Sciences in the Twentieth Century* by C. Stewart Gillmor and *The Biological Sciences in the Twentieth Century* by Garland Allen.

America the quotable. [By] Mike Edelhart and James Tinen. New York, Facts On File, 1983. xvii, 507p. hardcover $29.95 (0-87196-331-0).
973 U.S.—Quotations, maxims, etc. [CIP]   82-1592

This work reveals the nature of America through 7,000 quotes about the country and its regions, states, and cities. The authors state that the selection criteria were clarity and intrinsic interest, the degree to which a quote contributed to a full portrait of state or nation, humor or notoriety, historical importance, familiarity, and oddity of content or author.

Part I covers America through the chapters the *Nation, People, Way of Life, Politics,* and *History*, each subdivided into various categories. Part II deals with the states, cities, and regions in alphabetical order. Each state has a chapter that begins with a small map of the state and some factual material on it. Following quotes about the state (divided into sections: the "State," "Landscape," "People," "Way of Life," and "History and Politics") there are subsections of quotes on cities, towns, or regions. Chicago, Los Angeles, and New York City have separate chapters with subsections like the states. Regions (Midwest and the Great Plains, Mississippi River, New England, the South, Pacific Northwest, and Rocky Mountains) are treated similarly.

Quotes are international in origin and range from the 1800s on and are taken from books, articles, poems, songs, etc. They are arranged alphabetically by source. The accurate Index of Sources guides the reader to the proper page for each entry.

America the Quotable is an excellent supplement to general quotation collections.

American book trade directory. 30th ed. Edited and compiled by the Jaques Cattell Pr. New York, Bowker, 1984. xiii, 1,511p. 29cm. hardcover $99.50 + shipping and handling (0-8352-1890-2; 0065-759X: ISSN).
†658.809'07057 Booksellers and bookselling—U.S.—Directories | Booksellers and bookselling—Canada—Directories | Publishers and publishing—Directories | Book industries and trade—Directories   15-23627

This title (last reviewed in these pages 10/15/80) is a guide to American and Canadian booksellers and was first published in 1915. The first of four sections lists retail and antiquarian booksellers in the U.S., Guam, Puerto Rico, the Virgin Islands, and Canada and is arranged alphabetically by state or province, then by city. Each entry cites the mailing address, SAN (Standard Address Number), telephone number, names of key personnel, year established, store size, type and number of volumes stocked, subject specialities, and services offered. At the end of this section is a listing of bookstore chain and franchise headquarters in the U.S. and Canada.

The second section contains entries for wholesalers, jobbers, and distributors of trade books and magazines with equivalent directory information and the same arrangement as section I; however, import-export data, types of accounts, type of material carried, subject specialities, and special services are provided. The third section is a guide to various book industry companies and professionals. The final section is an Index to all entries.

While some of the information in the *Directory* may be found in other titles such as *Literary Market Place*, the *Directory* is a more comprehensive source on retail and wholesale booksellers.

American community, technical, and junior colleges: a guide. 9th ed. Edited by Dale Parnell and Jack W. Peltason. New York, American Council on Education & Macmillan, 1984. xvii, 956p. 28cm. cloth $85 (0-02-904210-0).
†378.154'3 Community colleges—Directories | Junior colleges—Directories | Technical education—Directories [OCLC]

This ninth edition of a standard reference work reflects, in change of title (formerly *American Junior Colleges*), the expanded academic world of two-year colleges. The entries for 1,500 schools, from large urban to rural training institutions, provide accurate information on costs, enrollment, programs, entrance requirements, facilities, and financial aid. Only schools which award associate degrees and are recognized by the Council on Postsecondary Accreditation are listed. However, unlike the eighth edition, which appeared 13 years ago, this volume includes colleges that meet degree and accreditation criteria but which offer degrees by correspondence. The descriptive exhibits (entries) were drawn from data submitted by the institutions themselves. The ERIC Clearinghouse on Junior and Community Colleges at UCLA helped to develop the data questionnaire and give reference support. Subject and Institution Indexes complete the volume.

This volume will be helpful to counselors, trainers, and students, industry and government, and in public, academic, and some special libraries.

The American counties: origins of county names, dates of creation and organization, area, population including 1980 census figures, historical data, and published sources. 4th ed. By Joseph Nathan Kane. Metuchen, N.J., Scarecrow, 1983. xi, 546p. 22cm. cloth $39.50 (0-8108-1558-3).
973 U.S.—History, Local [CIP]   82-5982

This new edition of *American Counties,* again the work of the historian Joseph N. Kane, offers few changes from the third edition published in 1972 except the addition of 1980 census figures. Considering the subject, it is not surprising that there is little new material.

Divided into nine parts, the main part is an alphabetical list of each U.S. county. Included in this, as in previous editions, is the location by state, date of creation, size, population as of 1980, county seat, nickname, source of name with descriptive matter, and a Bibliography of books about the county. Following this are sections containing most of the same information in different format, e.g., part IV is an index by year, beginning in 1634, giving dates of formation of counties. (Additional information only found here is the legislative session or act number that formed the county.) Part V is a list of counties whose names have changed. These are also found in the main part of the book. Perhaps this repetition can be justified as contributing to ready reference. The last two sections give a list of independent cities and boroughs in Alaska.

A check of dates in the bibliographies shows that 1968 is the most recent imprint; libraries owning the previous edition may not find it necessary to replace it. Nevertheless, *The American Counties* remains a standard source for information on U.S. counties.

American drama criticism: interpretations, 1890–1977. 2d. ed. Compiled by Floyd Eugene Eddleman. Hamden, Conn., Shoe String, 1979. 488p. 24cm. cloth $32.50 (0-208-01713-5).
016.792′0973 American drama—History and criticism—Bibliography | Theater—U.S.—Reviews—Bibliography [CIP]   78-31346

American drama criticism: supplement I to the second edition. Compiled by Floyd Eugene Eddleman. Hamden, Conn., Shoe String, 1984. $29.50 (0-208-01978-2).
916.812′009 American drama—History and criticism—Bibliography | Theater—U.S.—Reviews—Bibliography [CIP]   83-25410

American Drama Criticism, first published in 1967, was augmented by two supplements (1970 and 1976). The 1979 second edition includes interpretations/criticisms of American plays appearing in collected works, periodicals, and monographs published primarily between 1890 and 1977 (with a few pre-1890 items retained). The dramatists are, or were, U.S. citizens; also included are a few Canadian and Caribbean dramatists. Supplement I to the second edition, for the first time, includes general writings on some of the playwrights. Otherwise, both the second edition and its supplement retain the arrangement of the previous edition and supplements: alphabetical by playwright, with the secondary works listed alphabetically by author or (if anonymous, by title) under each play (also listed alphabetically), followed by a list of reviews in periodicals. The listings are intended to be comprehensive, so inclusion says nothing about the quality of any play, critical work, or review.

The volume concludes with a List of Books Indexed; a List of Journals Indexed; an Index of Critics; a List of Adapted Authors and Works; an Index of Titles; and an Index of Playwrights.

This volume and its supplement will help in the location of reviews and secondary literature on American plays, both classic and not so classic. And they may save students (and librarians) from exhaustive (and separate) searches of specialized bibliographies and indexes such as *MLA* and *Essay and General Literature Index,* among others. Large public and academic libraries should find *American Drama Criticism* a useful reference work.

The American electorate: a historical bibliography. Santa Barbara, Calif., ABC-Clio, 1983. xii, 388p. 23cm. cloth $28.50 (0-87436-372-1).
016.324973 Elections—U.S.—History—Bibliography | Voting—U.S.—History—Bibliography [CIP]   83-12229

Published most appropriately in a presidential election year, *The American Electorate* contains 1,425 citations and abstracts of periodical articles listed in the ABC-Clio Information Services database from 1973 through 1982. Selections for the bibliography were made by editors at ABC-Clio, and both abstracts and indexing were re-edited for this volume.

The abstracts are organized in six topical/chronological chapters: Voters and Voting Behavior, The Electoral Process, Emergence of the Electorate: Elections of 1619–1860, Civil War to World War: Elections of 1861–1919, New Era to Cold War: Elections of 1920–1959, and The Modern Years: Elections of 1960–1983. Within each chapter, citations are arranged alphabetically by authors' names, which means that one cannot access the volume by the date of an election, even in the chronological chapters. Two indexes follow the abstracts: the Subject Profile Index (ABC-SPIndex), familiar to users of *America: History and Life* and *Historical Abstracts,* and an Author Index.

As with other bibliographies in this series, libraries that subscribe to ABC-Clio's indexes or access its online database may not wish to duplicate material that is already accessible. However, students and specialists studying past elections may find the volume useful. College and university libraries, as well as specialized collections, may wish to consider it.

American family history: a historical bibliography. Santa Barbara, Calif., ABC-Clio, 1984. xii, 282p. (ABC-Clio Research Guides, no.12) 24cm. cloth $28.50 (0-87436-380-2).
016.3068′5′0973 Family—U.S.—History—Abstracts | Family—Canada—History—Abstracts | Family—Services for—U.S.—Abstracts | Family—Services for—Canada—Abstracts [CIP]   84-2955

The ABC-Clio Research Guides, of which this is a part, is a bibliography series covering high-interest history and social science topics. The publisher's database of periodical citations was the source of material. The period covered is 1973 to 1982. The four topical chapters ("The Family in Historical Perspective," "The Family and Other Social Institutions," "Familial Roles and Relationships," and "Individual Family Histories") include 1,167 article citations and abstracts from more than 2,000 history and social science journals.

Citations are arranged alphabetically by author within the chapters; Subject and Author Indexes conclude the work. Given the rather broad subject, articles range from a guide to family papers in institutions to a study of the development of shelters for battered wives from 1960 to 1981.

American Family History is an interesting and timely guide of use primarily in comprehensive history collections; it is essentially a spin-off from the publisher's *America: History and Life.* Libraries with the parent volume must weigh convenience against cost.

American Indian and Alaska native newspapers and periodicals, 1826–1924. Daniel F. Littlefield, Jr., and James W. Parins, compilers. Westport, Conn., Greenwood, 1984. xxxi, 482p. (Historical Guides to the World's Periodicals and Newspapers) 24cm. cloth $45 (0-313-23425-6).
051 Indian newspapers—U.S.—History | Indian periodicals—U.S.—History | Eskimo newspapers—Alaska—History | Eskimo periodicals—Alaska—History [CIP]   83-1483

This latest contribution to a distinguished series surveys the native American press of the area now constituting the "lower 48" and Alaska, from its known beginnings to 1924, a date significant in the history of U.S.–native American relations. An excellent Introduction provides a historical survey. It is followed by about 200 Profiles of particular serials, alphabetically arranged. These vary from a few lines to a few pages, depending on titles' duration, complexity, and importance. Accounts are followed by references to sources of further information and data on where indexed, where held, publication history, and editorship. There are numerous cross-references to variant titles (Profiles being under titles "last known"). A supplementary section profiles titles known or believed to have been issued but unavailable for examination. Then come three Appendixes which list titles chronologically (by date of first issue), by state of origin, and by "tribal affiliation or emphasis." The volume concludes with a general Subject Index citing persons, places, and topics dealt with in the Introduction and the Profiles.

The result is so satisfying—so eminently appropriate to the reference collections of libraries supporting research in American history—that one can only hope that a successor is in the offing, viz., a volume covering the native American press of the 60 years succeeding 1924.

American library directory. 2v. 37th ed. Edited by Jaques Cattell Pr., New York & London, Bowker, 1984. 2,010p. 29cm. hardcover $110 + shipping & handling (0-8352-1892-9) v.1; (0-8352-1893-7) v.2; (0-8352-1891-0) the set; (0065-910X) ISSN.
†027.097′025 Libraries—U.S.—Directories | Librarians—U.S.—Directories | Libraries—Canada—Directories | Librarians—Canada—Directories [OCLC]   23-3581

Celebrating its seventy-sixth anniversary, this indispensable source of U.S. and Canadian library statistics continues to increase; its contents (geographically arranged) are bound for the second year in two stout volumes. Since the thirty-fourth (1981) edition (cf. *RSBR,* 11/1/82), a new category has been added to the appended Library Information section—Libraries Serving the Deaf and Hearing Impaired. Since the thirty-fourth edition, a growing number of networks and consortia have emerged, while the number of library schools has dropped slightly. The number of library systems remains much the same, except for increases in some southern states. The same is true of libraries for the blind. Also listed are state and provincial public library agencies, state school library agencies, national and model interlibrary loan codes, U.S. armed forces libraries overseas, and U.S. Information Agency Centers. The Index to libraries, including branches, cites not page number but state and city—a practice satisfactory, if perhaps not ideal. Now published annually, the *American Library Directory* is updated by the bimonthly *American Library Directory Updating Service*. This long-lived directory shows no signs of diminishment. Long may it thrive!

American popular culture: a historical bibliography. Arthur Frank Wertheim, editor. Santa Barbara, Calif., ABC-Clio Information Services, 1984. vii, 246p. (Clio Bibliography series, no.14) 29cm. cloth $55 (0-87436-049-8).
016.7′00973 U.S.—Popular culture—Bibliography [CIP] 82-24285

Effective use of this tool will hang on (1) realization that its coverage is limited to periodical articles published 1973–80 and already contained in the publisher's database and (2) some understanding of its topical scope, viz., "the popular arts and entertainment, mass media and communication, religion and science, folk culture, customs, behavior, and attitudes." It is mainly an annotated list of 2,719 items grouped under seven broad headings (Popular Culture in Historical Perspective; Popular Arts; Mass Media & Communications; Folk Culture; Customs, Behavior & Attitudes; Science & Religion; and Theory, Research & the Classroom), all but the first extensively subdivided and the last (with such headings as Archives, Libraries & Research, and Bibliography & Historiography) of particular interest to librarians. The classified list is followed by Subject and Author Indexes, a list of periodicals analyzed, and lists of abstractors and abbreviations.

Considering the somewhat nebulous character of popular culture as an intellectual discipline, selection of items is difficult to quarrel with. The annotations are well written, and the Subject Index goes far toward compensating for the inherent limitations of the classified arrangement. Although libraries with the publisher's indexes or access to its online database may not need the convenience that *American Popular Culture* offers, it should be considered for the reference collections of academic and large public libraries, where its potential readership will extend far beyond self-acknowledged popular culture enthusiasts: it should be looked upon as a general resource of interest—fringe if not central—to answer a wide variety of concerns, e.g., the Boy Scouts, cemeteries, *Playboy* centerfolds, hog killing, the I AM sect, John Wayne, bartenders, and East German opinion of America—to cite but a few topics on which it presents interesting material.

American popular illustration: a reference guide. [By] James J. Best. Westport, Conn., Greenwood, 1984. x; 171p. 24cm. cloth $29.95 (0-313-23389-6).
741.64′0973 Illustration of books—U.S. | Magazine illustration—U.S. | Illustrators—U.S. | U.S.—Popular culture | Illustration of books—U.S.—Bibliography | Magazine illustration—U.S.—Bibliography | Illustrators—U.S.—Bibliography | U.S.—Popular culture—Bibliography [CIP] 83-14150

In a series of bibliographic essays, James Best examines the literature on American popular illustration, defined as artwork designed for mass consumption, e.g., images for books, magazines, posters, album covers, and ephemera, using techniques ranging from engraving to computer graphics. The bibliography begins with an overview from 1800 to the present. Subsequent chapters survey critiques, aesthetic theories, major illustrated works, prominent illustrators, the social and artistic context, techniques, and media. Complete citations for books and articles discussed in the text are found at the end of each chapter.

Best's thorough, readable, and well-organized guide is a real contribution to scholarship because popular illustration sadly exists in a gray area often ignored and rarely respected by art historians. Librarians should find it useful for both collection evaluation and selection since the bibliographies include works ranging from key nineteenth-century books to recent journal articles. Appendixes annotate relevant magazines and periodicals, describe major collections of original artwork and illustrated books, and list (by artist) outstanding examples of illustrated books. An accurate analytic Index completes the volume.

Most public and academic libraries, particularly those with emphases on art history, American studies, American popular culture, or book collecting, will want to acquire *American Popular Illustration*.

The American presidency: a guide to information sources. Compiled by Kenneth E. Davison. Detroit, Gale, 1983. xvi, 467p. (American Studies Information Guide, v.11). 23cm. cloth $48 (0-8103-1261-1).
016.973′09′92 Presidents—U.S.—Bibliography | U.S.—Politics and government—Bibliography [CIP] 73-17552

The compiler, a lifelong presidency buff and scholar, aimed "to assemble in a single reference volume the first comprehensive bibliography covering the American presidency and American presidents from 1787 to 1982." He has limited his citations to works published since 1945 and has emphasized presidential studies since 1960, unless an earlier title clearly surpasses. Titles are those likely to be found in a large public or university library. No audiovisual materials are included. Many entries are not annotated since Davison felt that the content was often self-evident, and he chose to include more entries rather than fewer, more fully annotated ones.

The first of its two parts covers such specific aspects of the presidency as presidential elections, functions and powers, and problems of the presidency. Each section contains subtopics, e.g., under "problems" are congressional relations, media, and public relations. Part 2 treats each of the presidents individually. Here entries are arranged in this order: bibliographies, source materials (private and public papers, contemporary records, autobiographies, diaries, memoirs, correspondence, and speeches), biographies, then important monographs and articles. Presidents get from 2 pages (Polk, Harrison) to 18 (Lincoln), averaging 4–8 pages. No differentiation is made between popular and scholarly works. Comprehensive and reasonably current, Gale's *American Presidency* will be of most use in academic libraries with strong American history programs.

The American presidency: a historical bibliography. Santa Barbara, Calif., ABC-Clio, 1984. viii, 376p. (Clio Bibliography series no.15) 29cm. cloth $60 (0-87436-370-5).
016.973′09′92 Presidents—U.S.—Bibliography | U.S.—Politics and government—Bibliography [CIP] 83-12245

Users of this computer-produced bibliography should keep in mind the limitations of the work, which do not appear on the title page. The work is part of the ABC-Clio database, which includes citations/abstracts of articles in some 2,000 historical periodicals, abstracted by a small army of volunteers, and appearing principally in *America: History and Life* and in *Historical Abstracts*. A second limitation is that only ten years of the database have been used, 1973–83. The work is limited, therefore, to journal articles appearing in those years.

These limitations do not necessarily diminish the value of the work to scholars. As in the basic publication, *Historical Abstracts*, the annotations run from two lines to about a dozen, and with few exceptions all are signed. They are clear and succinct, and they provide data on supplementary illustrations, tables, graphs, etc., if these exist in the article being abstracted.

The arrangement of the work is by periods, from Washington to McKinley, from Roosevelt to Roosevelt, and from Truman to Reagan. The total number of citations/abstracts (3,489) is about equally divided between these three periods.

There are Subject and Author Indexes, a list of periodicals indexed, and a list of the names of the abstractors.

Historians, political scientists, and students in these and related fields will find this work easy to use, providing much valuable information about the presidency in capsule form. Libraries with access to the publisher's indexes or its online database may not find it necessary to invest in the convenience offered by this volume.

American universities and colleges. 12th ed. Compiled and edited by the American Council on Education. New York, Walter de Gruyter, 1983. xiv, 2,156p. 29cm. cloth $99.50.
†378.73′025 Universities and colleges—U.S. | Education—U.S.—Directories [OCLC] 28-5598

This descriptive directory has grown from 401 entries in the first edition in 1938 to 1,728 in this edition, the twelfth. Along with the increase in the number of institutions, a greater number of items for inclusion have developed, thus making its compilation increasingly difficult. This is reflected in the fact that information data are for the 1980–81 academic year with a few exceptions: "degrees awarded," 1979–80; "tuition and fees," 1981–82; "financial aid," 1979–80; and "finances," fiscal year 1980. The difficulty in collecting data is understandable, but prospective students who are dependent on the most current information, for example on financial aid, will have to consult other sources.

There have been a few minor changes in introductory material, with omissions and relocation of some subjects. Some articles have been partially rewritten and made consistent with dates and data in the main section of the book, but coverage remains essentially the same.

Minor changes have been made in *Institutional Exhibits*. Instead of beginning with a brief description of the institution, exhibits now begin with *Characteristics of Institution*, which includes enrollment statistics. Other changes have been made in designation of information. For example, *Governing Board*, when given, is part of *Institutional Structure*, and *Special Academic Programs* is now *Distinctive Educational Programs*. Two years in preparation, this edition breaks down by disciplines the number of degrees conferred instead of totals by undergraduate and graduate. *Characteristics of Freshman* continues as part of the exhibits, and *Characteristics of Student Body* has been added.

Two Indexes, Institution and General, complete the volume; the latter serves as an index to introductory material with the exception of references to American Council on Education and ROTC Units, both of which are Appendixes.

The front cover of the volume is more attractive than that of earlier editions. However, the size of the book, increased by 277 pages, makes it cumbersome to handle and unlikely to withstand heavy use.

Basic changes in the content of this edition have been minor, but some efforts have been made to present information that will meet the needs of today's users. Academic and large public libraries and counselors at the postsecondary level, as well as some high school advisers, will wish to have *American Universities and Colleges*. Persons requiring the latest information on enrollment, tuition, financial aid, etc., will need to use other sources.

American working class history: a representative bibliography. [Compiled by] Maurice F. Neufeld, Daniel J. Leab, and Dorothy Swanson. New York and London, Bowker, 1983. xi, 356p. 24cm. hardcover $29.95 + shipping & handling (0-8352-1752-3).
016.331'0973 Labor and laboring classes—U.S.—History—Bibliography [CIP]   83-11845

This revised edition of Neufeld's *Representative Bibliography of American Labor History* (1964) is a thorough, current list of a wide range of useful materials. Neufeld is professor of industrial relations at the New York State School of Labor and Industrial Relations (Cornell University); Leab is professor of history at Seton Hall University and managing editor of the journal *Labor History* (which provides an annual bibliography of periodicals and dissertations on the subject); and Swanson is director of the labor library collection at New York University and a winner of the ALA John Sessions Award for library service to labor.

The compilers state that coverage (7,261 numbered entries) is not comprehensive but is representative of the variety of materials available, including dissertations, novels, plays, films, government reports, union and management publications, articles, biographies, and autobiographies. The cutoff date was January 31, 1983. Arrangement is alphabetical by author within such categories as bibliographies and guides, theories, periods of development, e.g., *American Labor before the Knights of Labor, Labor in World War II*, special aspects (*Strikes and Strike Legislation, City, Regional, and State Labor Movements and Conditions*, etc.), and sections on individual occupations, trades and industries. The last comprises one-third of the bibliography. The items represent a broad spectrum of opinion, with some antilabor materials and separate sections on women (including leaders), immigration, ethnicity and minority groups. Bibliographical information is standard; entries are not annotated; hence it is not always possible to infer the specific focus of a work—only that it is on the subject indicated by its listing under a particular heading.

An Author Index concludes the work. An Appendix lists 12 possible sources for films cited in the work. Unfortunately, the classified arrangement cannot compensate for the lack of a subject index and cross-references. Nevertheless, *American Working Class History* is an excellently produced, thorough, and current bibliography on American labor history which will be useful in a wide range of libraries.

American writers before 1800: a biographical and critical dictionary. 3v. James A. Levernier and Douglas R. Wilmes, editors. Westport, Conn., Greenwood, 1983. 1,764p. 24cm. cloth $195/set, 0-313-22229-0; v.1, 0-313-23476-0; v.2, 0-313-23477-9; v.3, 0-313-24096-5.
810'.9'001 American literature—Colonial period, ca. 1600–1775—History and criticism | American literature—Revolutionary period, 1775–1783—History and criticism | American literature—1783–1850—History and criticism | American literature—Colonial period, ca. 1600–1775—Bio-bibliography | Authors, American—18th century—Biography | Authors, American—To 1700—Biography [CIP]   82-933

The stated purpose of this set is "to provide a convenient source of information about the lives and works of a large number (786) of early American writers." Its coverage is broad: by no means limited to authors of belles lettres, it includes material on a wide range of diarists, travel writers, sermonizers, propagandists of every ilk, etc. "We have not," continues its editors, "selected writers by applying any original definition of literary quality.... Rather, we have worked inductively from the evidence of a selection of anthologies, literary and cultural histories, and bibliographies of the period." Its editors have wisely "included some very minor figures in order to provide a representative coverage of certain subgenres, such as the Puritan elegy or early nature reportage." Chronologically, coverage ranges from persons born as early as 1530 (Ralph Lane) to persons born as late as 1783 (Edward Payson). Although mainly on persons who spent their productive years in that part of British North America which eventually became the U.S., it uses *American* loosely: "The world of early America obviously had important transatlantic dimensions, and we have therefore included entries on a number of temporary residents or visitors.... In a few instances, we have included entries on writers who themselves never visited America but whose writings concern America and influenced, in some significant way, the development of an American literary heritage and cultural self-identity." Articles—all signed and written "by some 250 scholars of early American culture and literature"—are excellent. Most writers are associated with American universities, and one is glad to see that the article on Philip Freneau is (to cite but one appropriate assignment) by Lewis Leary, whose 1941 study *The Rascal Freneau* is still the last word on its subject.

Articles run from one to several pages, their length varying more or less in accordance with complexity of content and with literary and historical significance: just one page for Ichabod Wiswall, whose "efforts were foiled by Increase Mather," and for Christopher Dock, who concluded a pedagogical career by dying "quietly in his school while in a kneeling position, presumably in prayer"—but five each for Jonathan Edwards and Benjamin Franklin. Articles are arranged alphabetically. Each follows a prescribed pattern: a list of the author's works, a brief account of his/her life, a critical appraisal, and a brief list of secondary sources likely to prove useful in further study. This structural similarity facilitates ready reference as well as comparison. Cross-refereneces (*q.v.*'s) are numerous. The styles of contributors are readable, and some (as one would hope would be the case in a work of this scope) are positively attractive, with touches of grace and eloquence. Evaluations of literary merit are sympathetic but restrained. Imitators are so designated but are not therefore scorned. More original and (to modern taste) more interesting writers are so described but not overly praised: the critics avoid the temptation (one too often yielded to elsewhere) of overstating the achievements of Americans whose triumphs would, were they by British authors, seem minor.

Volume 3 includes four Appendixes (*de facto* indexes): lists of authors by year of birth, preceded by "unknowns"; place of birth (with 5 for Rhode Island, 4 for Africa, 3 for Bermuda, and 11 for Germany); principal place(s) of residence ("With only a few exceptions, no more than three ... are given for any one writer"); and "A Chronology, 1492–1800," identifies major historical events including publication of particularly significant works. These Appendixes facilitate not only access to particular articles but, by displaying categories and relationships, overviews of various sorts. The set concludes with a general Index to persons, titles, events, etc.

Nothing quite like *American Writers before 1800* appears to exist. Comparison with other generally available biographical compendia reveals surprisingly little overlap: of the 80 persons treated in its A and D sections, only 39 are treated in the *Dictionary of American Biography*—and with different emphasis. Of the same 80, only 10 are covered in H. W. Wilson's *American Writers 1600–1900*. Levernier and Wilmes are to be commended for their achievement, as are their contributors and their publisher.

American Writers Before 1800 is recommended for public and academic libraries and for historical collections; secondary school libraries will also do well to consider it—depending, of course, upon the extent to which the American colonial, revolutionary, and early federal periods are emphasized in the curricula they support.

America's corporate families and international affiliates, 1983. Parsippany, N.J., Dun's Marketing Services, 1983. xxii, 2,310p. 29cm. hardcover $295 (corporate annual subscription); $275 (libraries).

338.88 Corporations—U.S.—Directories | Holding companies—U.S.—Directories | Subsidiary corporations—U.S.—Directories | International business enterprises—Directories [OCLC] 83-3193

In early 1983 Dunn and Bradstreet brought out *America's Corporate Families: The Billion Dollar Directory*, which provides basic information about very large American corporations and their U.S. and Canadian subsidiaries. *American Corporate Families and International Affiliates* performs a similar function for U.S. multinational firms and foreign corporations with at least one U.S. subsidiary.

The main portion of the work consists of four sections. Section I is an alphabetical list of parent companies and their subsidiaries. The listing is subdivided by base country of the parent company—U.S., Canada, and all other foreign countries. Data provided for parent companies include address, telephone numbers, annual sales, number of employees, codes for up to six lines of business, stock ticker symbol and exchange on which stock is traded, corporate officers, and a list of subsidiaries. Entries for the subsidiaries include address, principal line of business, and a note regarding their subsidiary relationships; they may also list chief executive officer, annual sales, and number of employees. The remaining three sections are an alphabetical subsidiary-to-parent cross-reference list, a geographical listing of multinational businesses (U.S. and Canadian companies are further broken down by state or province), and a geographically subdivided listing by the Standard Industrial Classification scheme.

The volume will be useful as a supplement to Dun and Bradstreet's *Principal International Businesses*, which concentrates on non-U.S. firms that may or may not have operating units in this country. While many of the firms listed in *ACFAIA* can be found in both *Principal International Businesses* and the *Billion Dollar Directory*, the extensive display of information about international subsidiary relationships is unique to this volume. It is a particularly welcome addition in this field since the major directories covering this area—Juvenal Angel's *Directory of Foreign Firms Operating in the United States* (1978) and *Directory of American Firms Operating in Foreign Countries* (1979), both World Trade Academy Press, have been highly irregular in their updating and provide neither the depth of information nor the accessibility available in this volume. With the annual updating provided for *ACFAIA*, international marketers and others dealing with U.S.-foreign trade will find a ready source of current information. The volume will be particularly useful in business collections with heavy demand in the area of international business.

An annotated bibliography of the history of data processing. By James W. Cortada. Westport, Conn., Greenwood, 1983. xlii, 216p. 24cm. cloth $35 (0-313-24001-9).

001.64 Computers—History—Bibliography | Electronic data processing—History—Bibliography [CIP] 83-8539

This volume consists of about 450 journal articles, books, book chapters, encyclopedia articles, and other primary materials which trace the history of calculating machines and computers since 1100 B.C. Arranged chronologically, there are four major groupings: Reference Materials and Early History; From Punched Cards to Digital Computers, 1800–1939; Birth of the DP Industry, 1939–1955; and Computer Age, 1955–1982. Each section is topically subdivided with entry A–Z by author/main entry. An excellent Introduction covers the historical study of computers. Annotations are provided; bibliographic data are standard (except that pagination is not given for monographs).

The compiler is the author of a number of publications in data processing, and this contribution is a seminal work for historical research in the area: it is the first book-length bibliography on the subject. It is selective rather than comprehensive. For instance, the section on bibliographies lists *Readers' Guide* but does not include sources such as *ACM Guide to Computing Literature, Computer Literature Index*, and *Mathematical Reviews*. Examination of these sources, in fact, shows a number of articles which fall within the scope of this bibliography but which have not been included. Another problem is the lack of subject index.

In the Author Index, some second authors are listed while others are omitted, and there is no access via the Index to publications without personal authors. Given the size of the bibliography, these problems are not that serious; nevertheless, these are areas of improvement for future editions.

Architecture: a bibliographic guide to basic reference works, histories, and handbooks. [Compiled by] Donald L. Ehresmann. Littleton, Colo., Libraries Unlimited, 1984. xvi, 338p. 25cm. hardcover $55 (U.S.); $66 (elsewhere) (0-87287-394-3).

016.72 Architecture—Bibliography [CIP] 83-19600

This is an annotated bibliography of 1,359 sources of information on architecture, with lesser coverage of sources of information on landscape architecture and urban planning. The sources, which are limited to items published between 1875 and 1980, emphasize architecture as an art form and give little attention to engineering/technological aspects. Compiled by Donald L. Ehresmann, associate professor of the history of architecture and art, University of Illinois, Chicago, the work is intended to be a companion to his two earlier bibliographic guides, *Fine Arts* (cf. *RSBR*, March 1, 1976) and *Applied and Decorative Arts*. The first 2 of its 14 chapters list general reference works and histories, and the remaining chapters present material by period or region. Sources are limited to Western European- and Scandinavian-language books, including reprints and the most recent editions of older titles. Books for both general undergraduate readers and specialized researchers are included. Periodicals are omitted, as are exhibition catalogs, pamphlets, books on individual architects or monuments, and dissertations, although dissertations which have been rewritten and published in "widely available form" are cited.

Arrangement generally follows that used in the compiler's *Fine Arts*. Within each chapter general histories and handbooks precede all other material. Throughout the work sequentially numbered items are entered under author/compiler with full bibliographic citation, including Library of Congress card numbers. A descriptive annotation accompanies each item; a few of these include brief critical comments, e.g., "good," "well illustrated," "valuable," etc. The contents of "important" titles are analyzed. Multivolume sets are entered twice, under series title in the chapter on general works and under the subject of individual volumes in the appropriate chronological or geographical chapter. *See also* references in the annotations and at the end of sections within the chapters indicate that books are found elsewhere in the work or in the second edition of *Fine Arts*.

The compiler described his *Fine Arts* volume as a complement to Chamberlin's *Guide to Art Reference Books* (*Booklist and Subscription Books Bulletin,* June 15, 1960, p. 614–16). Although *Architecture* claims no relationship to *Chamberlin* or its successor, the well-received *Guide to the Literature of Art History* by Arntzen and Rainwater (cf. *RSBR*, October 15, 1982), the Board investigated duplication of coverage between *Architecture* and *Guide to the Literature of Art History*. Inasmuch as the Arntzen-Rainwater chapter on architecture has only 367 entries, reference librarians would reasonably expect that virtually all of the entries in *Arntzen-Rainwater* would be found in the 1,359-entry *Architecture*. This is not the case; of 61 entries on architecture in *Arntzen-Rainwater* (basic bibliographies, dictionaries and encyclopedias, histories, and handbooks), 13 are not in *Architecture*. Although *Architecture* does not include periodicals, it is regrettable that periodical indexes dealing exclusively with architecture (such as the American *Architectural Index* and the British *Architectural Index*) were not identified.

Architecture concludes with Author-Title and Subject Indexes which refer to entry number(s). The Board found a few errors in the Author-Title Index. Even though the work includes no books devoted solely to individual architects or structures, such entries can be found in the Subject Index.

Architecture: A Bibliographic Guide is recommended for public, academic, and special libraries whose readers include persons strongly interested in architecture: in such libraries, it will become a standard reference source. Librarians with smaller collections may need nothing beyond Arntzen and Rainwater's *Guide to the Literature of Art History* or even Sheehy's *Guide to Reference Books* for annotated lists of multilingual references on architecture.

Atlas of the Jewish world. By Nicholas De Lange. New York, Facts On File, 1984. 240p. illus. 31cm. cloth $35 (0-87196-043-5).

909'.04924 Jews—History | Judaism—History | Jews—Historical geography—Maps [CIP] 84-10102

A British lecturer in rabbinics has written this latest "atlas" in the publisher's series, several of which have been favorably reviewed by the Board. This one is, in a sense, the most ambitious in scope, and it is the publisher's finest yet. A combination of multicolored maps, photographs, tables, and illustrations is interwoven with a balanced text covering the historical/cultural background and the diversity of Jewish life around the world from ancient to contemporary times.

A clear Glossary, a selective but excellent Bibliography, a List of Illustrations (noting sources), accurate Gazetteer, and an Index enhance the work's value.

While the work is a coherent whole in terms of the many facets of Jewish history through the centuries, it is as an atlas that it has a special value. Produced by a British firm, the 48 maps are clearly drawn, distinctly labeled, and sufficiently detailed in localities, population movements, and ruling boundaries for ease in use by many types of readers. (There are actually more than 48 as several have detailed insets.) The maps reflect the impact on and changes in Jewish life in every time period and from all corners of the earth. Thus, the periods of greatness and persecution, life on every inhabited continent, and all of the rich cultural expression are conveyed. Some maps encompass more than a page and this will affect rebinding, but the work is sturdy.

A number of general historical and biblical atlases have similar maps but not to the extent in depth, scope, beauty, or accompanying text. Martin Gilbert's *Jewish History Atlas* (Macmillan, rev. ed., 1976) has many more specific maps but it is a smaller-size work, and the maps are all in black and white.

Atlas of the Jewish World is a distinguished reference book, and one that will be useful in home, public, school, and university libraries.

The atomic papers: a citizen's guide to selected books and articles on the bomb, the arms race, nuclear power, the peace movement, and related issues. By Grant Burns. Metuchen, N.J., Scarecrow, 1984. xiv, 309p. 23cm. cloth $22.50 (0-8108-1692-X).
016.3271'74 Atomic weapons and disarmament—Bibliography | Nuclear warfare—Bibliography | Arms race—Bibliography | Nuclear power—Bibliography | Peace—Bibliography [CIP]   84-1390

More than 1,000 annotated citations have been assembled here and arranged into 18 sections covering specific topics such as nuclear weapons proliferation, the atomic scientists, and civil defense advocates. Nearly 80 percent of the references are to books, a selection of titles published since 1945. The remaining references are to a selection of articles from the 1980s in "alternative" periodicals not covered by standard indexes and abstracts.

One section with slightly more than 100 entries is devoted to fiction, and 3 sections concentrate on aspects of the nuclear power controversy. Since an Author Index is supplied (along with a Subject Index), an opportunity was lost by arranging the book citations in alphabetical order by author rather than chronologically—an arrangement which would have highlighted trends in "nuclear publishing" in the postwar years. An occasional landmark title such as Jerome D. Frank's *Sanity and Survival* (1967, reissued 1982) and Seymour Melman's *Permanent War Economy* is overlooked. The compiler fails to cite the latest (1977) edition of the important U.S. government study *The Effects of Nuclear Weapons*, and a major UN report issued in 1980 (*Nuclear Weapons*, Autumn Press) is omitted. Nevertheless, this detailed introduction to sources dealing with the uniquely fateful set of issues facing the post-Hiroshima world will be a welcome and valuable addition to public, school, and academic library collections.

Automation in libraries: a LITA bibliography, 1978–1982. Compiled by Anne G. Adler et al. Ann Arbor, Pierian, 1983. viii, 177p. 24cm. cloth $18.95 (0-87650-157-9).
016.02504 Libraries—U.S.—Automation—Bibliography | Libraries—Automation—Bibliography [OCLC]   83-62104

This bibliography (one of the several compiled by a committee of ALA) was prepared by manually searching indexing and abstracting tools, bibliographies, and publishers announcements as well as online databases. The present volume of 2,500 citations is more than six times larger than the first volume. Its emphasis is on applications of new technologies in U.S. libraries, with sections on Canadian, British, Australian, German, and other foreign libraries. Excluded are anonymous and one-page articles, regular columns, and announcements.

Citations include complete bibliographic data. They are arranged alphabetically by main entry under 45 subject headings referring to types of libraries, library functions, networking, hardware, software, bibliographies, costs, and countries. There is no apparent significance to the arrangement of these divisions. The volume concludes with an Author Index.

The Board questions the need for such a volume, since it is now possible to search online databases, particularly *Library and Information Science Abstracts*, which allows one to retrieve materials tailored to specific needs as well as more up-to-date materials. It will, therefore, only be useful to libraries which do not have access to online searching capabilities.

BKSTS dictionary of audio-visual terms. Woburn, Mass., Butterworth, 1983. 138p. 23cm. hardcover $24.95 (0-240-51201-4).
621.38'044'0321 Audio-visual equipment—Dictionaries [British CIP]

The 2,000 brief entries in this dictionary cover the terminology of film, video, tape-slide, filmstrip, and multivision, as well as computer science. The compilers explain, "We have endeavoured to introduce and define our entries on the basis of practical operations, since this is a dictionary of the usage of terms rather than a textbook or a technical encyclopedia."

The technical terms employed in many of the definitions suggest that the work will be most useful to users who already have some expertise. For example, the concept *latensification* is defined as the "intensification of an under-exposed image by controlled fogging by a light source before development." A perusal of several entries shows the same problem, i.e., the need for further clarification. The somewhat jargonized definitions point to a related problem: the lack of illustrations to amplify complex definitions or ones more readily conveyed pictorially. There are, however, plenty of cross-references, and British spellings present no problem.

This first edition, executed through the effort of eight members of the British Kinematograph Sound and Television Society, has few competitors, at least for the decade of the 1980s. It appears to be a unique source, although some of its terms are undoubtedly covered in other wordbooks, both general and specialized. *BKSTS Dictionary of Audio-Visual Terms* will probably be most useful in comprehensive collections on the topic.

Banker's desk reference, 1983. [By] Edwin B. Cox. Boston & New York, Warren, Gorham & Lamont, 1983. xi, 339p. 26cm. paper $42 (0-8826-2920-4).
†332.1'0202 Banks and banking—Handbooks, manuals, etc. | Finance—Handbooks, manuals, etc. | Banks and banking—U.S.—Handbooks, manuals, etc. | Finance—U.S.—Handbooks, manuals, etc. [OCLC]   80-648848

This handbook offers four sections: I, the highlights of the banking year, including a chronology; II, "New Topics"; III, 38 tables on banking industry and economic statistics; and IV, a directory of professional and trade associations, federal government regulatory and special-purpose governmental agencies, and state bankers' associations. The Index refers readers to specific topics and to agencies in the directory.

The statistics and directory (part III and IV) provide the most ready-reference potential; parts I and II are meant to be studied. This title could be useful in reference and circulating collections of libraries that support business collections or curricula. The reference information is, however, available elsewhere.

Bateman New Zealand encyclopedia. Editor in chief, Gordon McLauchlan. Auckland, New Zealand, David Bateman; dist. by Sheridan House, 145 Palisade St., Dobbs Ferry, NY 10522, 1984. xv, 656p. illus. (some col.) maps. 25cm. cloth $39.95 (0-908610-21-1).
†993.1'003 New Zealand—Dictionaries and encyclopedias [OCLC]

According to its Introduction, "this encyclopedia has been designed and edited to make a popular but comprehensive and authoritative reference book available to people over a wide range of age and educational backgrounds" and to produce "a readable text unimpeded by abbreviations or esoteric language, set in highly legible type and laid out in a functional but attractive manner." For the most part, the editors have been successful.

The *Bateman New Zealand Encyclopedia* (*BNZE*) consists of hundreds of specific entries (one paragraph to two pages long) alphabetically arranged. There are numerous biographical entries for early settlers, politicians, athletes, writers, explorers, military heroes, etc. Scores of articles are devoted to cattle and sheep breeds, birds, plants, and geographical features. One finds entries on ethnic and religious groups and a strong emphasis on Maori history, culture, and traditions.

One weakness the Board found is illustrated by the fact that there are more than 60 entries for individual artists but none for art. The lack of longer essays on broad topics such as history, the economy, foreign relations, etc., makes it difficult for users to gain a real understanding of the country. Such an overview might explain the lack of entries on such social problems as unemployment, drug addiction, divorce, and crime although there are entries on *racism, censorship,* and *alcoholic liquor.* Of some help is the Subject Index which lists the specific articles under such broad subjects as *agriculture, arts, commerce and industry,* and *constitution and law.* The Board also regrets the lack of bibliographies.

More than 500 black-and-white illustrations and almost 50 pages of color photographs are well chosen and well printed. Full-color maps including a large foldout are reproduced from the *New Zealand Atlas. BNZE* provides a Chronology through 1983 and statistical tables covering population, agriculture, and trade.

High school, college, and public libraries needing more detailed information on New Zealand than that provided in a multivolume adult encyclopedia will welcome the attractive, up-to-date *Bateman New Zealand Encyclopedia.*

Benjamin Franklin, 1721–1906: a reference guide. By Melvin H. Buxbaum. Boston, G. K. Hall, 1983. xxiii, 334p. (Reference Publication in Literature series) 24cm. cloth $35 (0-8161-7985-9).
016.9733′092′4 Franklin, Benjamin, 1706-1790—Bibliography [CIP]   82-12144

The first of a projected two-volume set, this book is an indispensable tool for the study of Franklin, covering bibliographic references to him which appeared between 1721 and 1906. In his nine-page Introduction, the compiler, professor of English at the University of Colorado, Boulder, attempts to separate Franklin the man from Franklin the myth.

Arranged by year of publication, then *A–Z* by author/main entry, the work includes more than 1,600 items, both published and unpublished; only newspaper articles have been omitted. Standard bibliographic data are provided. Annotations for each entry include both descriptive and evaluative comments and range from a line or two to a half-page, the usual length being about a half-dozen lines. The Index, which lists authors and subjects by the year and then entry number, makes location of any reference a simple matter.

Compiled by the author of *Benjamin Franklin and the Zealous Presbyterians* (Pennsylvania State Univ. Pr., 1975), this bibliography will be of greatest use to scholars of early American history.

Better Homes and Gardens all about your house: your walls and ceilings, your family centers, your windows and doors, your baths, your kitchen, solar living, stretching living space. 7v. Des Moines, Meredith, 1982, 1983. illus. part col. 28cm. paper over boards $9.95 per v. (stretching: 0-696-02162-5; bath: 0-696-02165-X; windows: 0-696-02167-6; family center: 0-696-02164-1; solar living: 0-696-02166-8; kitchen: 0-696-02161-7; walls: 0-696-02163-3).

728.3′7 Interior decoration—Handbooks, manuals, etc. ∣ Room layout (Dwellings)—Handbooks, manuals, etc. ∣ Space (Architecture)—Handbooks, manuals, etc. [OCLC]		81-70035
643′.52 Bathrooms [OCLC]		81-70038
†690.1′82 Windows ∣ Doors [OCLC]		82-81723
643′.7 Dwellings—Remodeling ∣ Recreation rooms ∣ Interior decoration [OCLC]		81-70037
690′.869 Solar houses ∣ Solar energy [OCLC]		81-70039
728 Kitchens—Remodeling [OCLC]		81-70034
643′.7 Walls [OCLC]		81-70036

This series of books has been put together by more than 30 *Better Homes and Gardens* editors, designers, writers, and contributors. Each volume contains excellent color photographs, drawings, floor plans, charts, and cutaway views. These are primarily idea books that give readers a starting point on redecorating and renovating. There are some step-by-step procedures for some of the work that can be done by homeowners. Public and school libraries will find these volumes useful in their circulating rather than their reference collections. Anyone looking for home-remodeling ideas will find them extremely helpful.

The Bible book: resources for reading the New Testament. [By] Erasmus Hort. New York, Crossroad, 1983. xiv, 209p. paper $12.95 (0-8245-0557-3).
016.22 Bible. N.T.—Study—Bibliography [CIP]   83-14446

Hort has attempted to compile a bibliography of resources on the New Testament based on three basic criteria: (1) primary resources, (2) proven usefulness, and (3) the best of what is currently available. The result is a book designed for general readers that covers introductory works, the New Testament in English (including a list of major English versions), concordances, Greek New Testaments, learning Greek, dictionaries and encyclopedias, geography of the New Testament, handbooks and almanacs, and commentaries.

Following the Preface is a helpful user's Introduction to this bibliography. There are nine main chapters; these deal with the subjects mentioned above. Each chapter contains an introduction to the type of material; a listing of material in categories gives the "best" item then the "rest," and concludes with "best buys."

A Wise Buyer's Guide gives help on buying the materials listed in this work. A Quick Reference Chart (number, author, short title, publisher, binding, ISBN, date, and price) ends the text. An Author Index guides readers to book number (chapter then item number).

Hort has provided a well-rounded bibliography that is an excellent source for laypersons and beginning students interested in reading and studying the New Testament.

Bibliography of discographies. v.3: popular music. New York & London, Bowker, 1983. ix, 205p. 26cm. hardcover $45 + shipping and handling (0-8352-1683-7).
016.01697899′12 Music, Popular (Songs, etc.)—Discography—Bibliography [CIP]82-20776

Popular Music provides a descriptive compilation of phonograph-record bibliographies, of popular, rock, country, hillbilly, bluegrass, and motion-picture and stage-show music. The work is divided into two sections with the major part arranged by name and subject in a single-numbered alphabetical sequence providing cross-references to variant subjects and name forms. Subject entries are identified as musical group, label, or character. The Index cites authors', compilers', and editors' names and series titles.

Citations, selected for their usefulness, include, on a selective basis, pricing guides to out-of-print records and lists of charted popular records, with record company catalogs excluded.

Each citation is annotated by a code number that identifies non-commercial recordings or unissued recordings, personnel, matrix number, index, release dates, take numbers, differing versions of the same song, and place and date of recording information.

Although there is some intended duplication (Rhythm and Blues, Otis Clay) from volume 2 (Bowker, 1977) dealing with jazz and related music, cross-references are provided and the double classification is appropriate.

Although there are unexpected omissions, this *Bibliography of Discographies* appears to be complete. It is also unique.

A bibliography of the philosophy of science, 1945–1981. Compiled by Richard J. Blackwell. Westport, Conn., Greenwood, 1983. xviii, 585p. 24cm. cloth $75 (0-313-23124-9).
016.501 Science—Philosophy—Bibliography [CIP]   83-5671

This is a general bibliography of the contemporary (1945–81) literature on the philosophy of science. It was designed for a wide-level audience. The compiler, professor of philosophy at St. Louis University, defines the topic as "a critical reflection on the conceptual content, the methodologies, and the cultural implications of the various sciences," and not as the relationship between philosophy and science. Under this definition he excludes the "philosophy of logic, mathematics and language; philosophy of technology and of the social sciences, including history; the history and sociology of science; and value questions raised by the sciences."

The bibliography covers the monographic and serial literature consisting of original and basic research papers, but it does not include masters' theses and doctoral dissertations.

Seven typical chapters include "Bibliographies"; "Topics Related to the Disciplines: General Works"; "Aspects of Scientific Method: Philosophical Issues Concerning Science"; "Special Topics in the Philosophy of the Physical Sciences"; and "Special Topics in the Philosophy of the Biological Sciences." The last six chapters are subdivided. In each, the entries are arranged alphabetically by the author, editor, or main entry.

The 7,356 entries consist only of bibliographic citations, i.e., abstracts or commentaries. Following the bibliography are four Appendixes. Three are lists of volumes published in the following series: Boston Studies in the Philosophy of Science, Syntheses Library, and the University of Western Ontario Series in Philosophy of Science. The fourth is a list of periodicals analyzed for relevant material.

There is an Index of Personal Names, but unfortunately the only subject access to the materials is through the Table of Contents.

The classified arrangement and the lack of a topical index will limit the usefulness of this work to persons already familiar with the field. It will, however, be welcomed in libraries serving scholars of philosophy, history of science, and philosophy of science.

Bilingual-bicultural education: an annotated bibliography, 1936–1982. [Compiled by] Octavio A. Ballesteros. Jefferson, N.C., McFarland, 1983. vii, 96p. 23cm. paper $15.95 (0-89950-077-3).

016.37197 Education, Bilingual—U.S.—Bibliography | Intercultural education—U.S.—Bibliography [CIP]   83-42884

The compiler earned his doctorate in education from East Texas State University, worked in school and college bilingual education programs, and wrote a book on the subject, *Preparing Teachers for Bilingual Education* (University Press of America, 1979).

This bibliography of 556 books, articles, dissertations, and ERIC documents observes a topical arrangement in 11 chapters. Each chapter opens with several paragraphs explaining its scope. Each item is supplied with a brief descriptive annotation of a sentence or two. Many are too brief to be used as a guide to an item's value. Most items were published during the 1970s and most can be identified in standard sources.

Articles have been drawn from eclectic sources, some being journals for professional educators and others being popular mass-circulation magazines. An example of the latter is an article by Charles Kuralt published in *Family Circle* in 1976. This makes for a curious amalgam and raises questions about the bibliography's intended audience. It can be a convenience to newcomers to the field of bilingual education in identifying existing publications. It will do little, however, to assist them in evaluating the worth of these publications. Only public libraries serving a sizable bilingual population and/or academic libraries in colleges training teachers for bilingual programs need consider *Bilingual-Bicultural Education*.

Bilingual educational publications in print, 1983. New York & London, Bowker, 1983. xxix, 539p. 29cm. cloth $45 plus shipping/handling (0-8352-1605-5: ISBN; 0000-0744: ISSN).

†016.3719′7 Education, Bilingual—U.S.—Bibliography—Catalogs | Teaching—Aids and devices—Catalogs | Audio-visual materials—Catalogs [OCLC]   83-5360

To appreciate the coverage of this computer-produced bibliography, some definitions must be kept in mind. The Preface states that the work "is a listing of some 30,000 books and audio-visual materials for use in bilingual education, and English as a Second Language programs in [K-12 schools and libraries]." It then defines bilingual education as the "use of two languages, one of which is English, as mediums of instruction." It further adds that bilingual education also incorporates instruction in the history and culture of the child's native country, and thus works on, e.g., Latin American history in Spanish are listed. Also included are teachers' professional books.

The bulk of the work is arranged in a series of indexes—a Subject Index, which has entries by language (American Indian to Vietnamese); a Young People's Reading Index (subjects alphabetically, without regard to the language); an Author Index (again, one alphabet, without regard to language); a Title Index (again, all languages in one alphabet); and finally a Series Index. As might be expected, Spanish-language items outnumber all others. In the Subject Index section, Spanish books and audiovisual materials take up 190 out of 224 pages.

Items are given full bibliographic data, including price and name of publisher (abbreviated; a key appears at the end of the book). Many items have brief explanatory annotations and recommended grade level.

Bilingual Educational Publications in Print will be much in demand by teachers and school principals who are beginning or expanding their bilingual teaching and/or TESL programs. It is a much-needed source for school libraries at a bargain price.

Billy the Kid: a bio-bibliography. Compiled and edited by Jon Tuska. Westport, Conn., and London, Greenwood, 1983. 235p. 24cm. cloth $35 (0-313-23266-0).

364.1′552′0924 (B) Billy, the kid | Outlaws—Southwest, New—Biography | Southwest, New—Biography | Billy, the Kid—Bibliography [CIP]   82-5709

The life and death of the New Mexico outlaw variously known as Henry McCarty (his true name), Kid Antrim, William H. Bonney, and Billy the Kid has generated a large volume of historical and fictional books and films, and Jon Tuska has endeavored to collect them all into one volume, with chapters on Billy's life and death, and his treatment in history, fiction, and film.

The book suffers from some editorial defects. The long section of biography (110 pages) is a continuous text, unrelieved by any chapter headings (though there are 12 numbered subdivisions; none of which are explained). When they appear in the text, titles of books, journals, and films alike are printed all in capitals, sometimes a distracting device. Annotations of these books and films are more in the nature of a running commentary, but the Index does make it possible to locate any desired book or film, and bibliographies end each section.

The book will be useful primarily to persons researching the details of Bonney's life, or of the Lincoln County War, or who may wish an evaluation of some book already in print dealing with these topics—as well as those interested in American legends/popular culture. Libraries with special collections in southwestern history, outlaws, gunfighters, and so on will want to add this work, both for its biographical details and for its bibliographical evaluations.

Biographical dictionary of American labor. Editor in chief, Gary M. Fink. Westport, Conn., Greenwood, 1984. xvii, 767p. 24cm. cloth $49.95 (0-313-22865-5).

331.88′092′2 (B) Labor and laboring classes—U.S.—Biography | Trade-unions—U.S.—Officials and employees—Biography [CIP]   84-4687

This updated and expanded version of the 1974 *Biographical Dictionary of American Labor Leaders* contains, according to the Preface to the new edition, 234 new biographical sketches, bringing the total number to more than 700. Gary M. Fink, professor of history at Georgia State University, was also editor in chief of *Labor Unions* (1977), the first volume in the *Greenwood Encyclopedia of American Institutions*. He has supplied a 76-page Introduction for this edition ("The American Labor Leader in the Twentieth Century: Quantitative and Qualitative Portraits"), which is accompanied by 22 tables and a page of suggestions for further reading.

The modified title reflects the broader criteria adopted for inclusion in this edition. An effort was made to represent the diversity of the labor movement by more extensive coverage of women (who make up some 15 percent of the new entries) and by inclusion of rank-and-file trade union members. Another goal of this edition was improved coverage of labor leaders during the last quarter of the nineteenth century. Names were added in other categories such as labor intellectuals and academicians (John R. Commons, Selig Perlman) and radicals and socialists (John Reed, Kate Richards O'Hare, Michael Harrington). Labor leaders added in this edition include Douglas Fraser and Owen Bieber of the UAW, William Winpisinger of the International Association of Machinists (whose surname appears without the first n) and Leon Davis (National Union of Hospital and Health Care Employees and New York's District 1199). The bibliographies and, where appropriate, the entries for individuals included in the original edition have been updated.

The six Appendixes follow the same pattern as in the first edition listing biographies by union affiliations (national, state, and local); religious preference; place of birth (United States, other countries); formal education; political preference; major appointive and elective public offices (federal, state, local). There is a detailed Index.

Inevitably, there are omissions. Victor Gotbaum, the main focus of a recently published history of AFSCME's District Council 37 and a possible mayoral candidate in New York City, does not get an entry, and the bibliography for Norman Thomas fails to cite W. A. Swanberg's 1976 biography.

Biographical Dictionary of American Labor is recognized as a basic reference source for the study of labor history. The wider coverage and other enhancements offered in this new edition greatly extend its already considerable value.

Biographical dictionary of Latin American historians and historiography. By Jack Ray Thomas. Westport, Conn., Greenwood, 1984. xiv, 420p. 24cm. cloth $49.95 (0-313-23004-8).

980′.0072022 Historians—Latin American—Bibliography | Latin America—Historiography | Latin America—History—Bio-bibliography [CIP]   83-8558

Directories on Latin Americanists in the U.S. either by region or by discipline are sporadically available. Yet until the publication of Thomas' *Biographical Dictionary*, not even this could be said for a similar group in Latin America.

Now these historians and much of their craft are covered in this well-wrought reference book. A historian himself, Thomas knows how to evaluate his colleagues and how to assess the process of writing history. For Latin America, with its 20 republics representing Spanish, Portuguese, and French cultures and languages, this was surely no easy task.

Following a long introduction on the state of the art and its evolution are approximately 300 descriptive and evaluative biographies ranging in length from 350 to 600 words. Date and place of birth, education, and career; a brief biography of intellectual life; an assessment of contributions; and finally a bibliography of works both by and about the author are cited.

Covering everything from colonial chronicles to twentieth-century historians who died before 1983, Thomas is liberal in his interpretation of the term "historian" and includes many Latin Americans who with their renaissance backgrounds wrote in other fields besides history.

Entries are particularly clear, and even though the data are formulated as described above, Thomas manages a variety of styles remarkably well considering the mass of material incorporated.

Four Appendixes help maximize access: the first, a geographical approach, lists historians by country; the second, chronological, notes year of birth; the third, and perhaps the least useful, classifies historians by their other professions or jobs; and the fourth (and most valuable) cites historians by topics researched.

No opinions would be unanimous on who should be included within the amorphous field of Latin American history or an assessment of their contributions. Yet Thomas must be commended for producing a highly useful reference book, clearly written with multifaceted access. *Biographical Dictionary of Latin American Historians and Historiography* will be especially useful in academic libraries supporting Latin American studies.

Biographical dictionary of psychology. By Leonard Zusne. Westport, Conn., Greenwood, 1984. xxi, 563p. 24cm. $49.95 (0-313-24027-2).
150'.92'2 (B) Psychologists—Biography || Psychology—History [CIP]   83-18326

This revised edition of the 1975 *Names in the History of Psychology* contains most of that work's entries, corrections, or additions thereto, and 101 new entries. The earlier work covered deceased individuals, mainly those who expired between 1600 and 1967, and this revision includes those plus some names from antiquity, (e.g., Pythagoras) to Daniel Berlyne (d.1976). The 538 biographies are arranged alphabetically, and each entry ends with citations to biographical sources. There are three Appendixes: a chronological listing by birth date; a ranking by relative eminence; and groups of names by academic and research institutions. A 20-page Index completes this reference book. A handy reference in any psychology collection.

The biographical dictionary of scientists: astronomers, biologists, chemists, physicists. 4v. David Abbott, general editor. New York, Peter Bedrick; dist. by Harper, 1984. 204, 182, 203, 212p. illus. diagrs. 26cm. hardcover $18.95/vol. (0-911745-80-7: astronomers; 0-911745-82-3: biologists; 0-911745-81-5: chemists; 0-911745-79-3: physicists).
520'.92'4 (B) Astronomers—Biography [CIP]   84-9236
574'.092'2 (B) Biologists—Biography [CIP]   84-10972
540'.92'2 (B) Chemists—Biography [CIP]   84-9284
530'.092'2 (B) Physicists—Biography [CIP]   84-9211

The four volumes of this new biographical dictionary cover 775 scientists in the fields of chemistry, biology, astronomy, and physics. The individual volumes contain no portraits or bibliographies, but there are a few illustrations to clarify the famous principles and discoveries. Each entry briefly mentions the early life of the individual and then concentrates on the scientific discoveries and contributions. The biographies are well written in narratives that high school and undergraduate students can comprehend. Each volume begins with a brief chronological review of the important milestones in the field. The biographical entries follow in alphabetical order. Occasionally, two or more scientists who have worked together on the same scientific discoveries are included in one biography. Cross-references guide users efficiently to sources of information.

In examining the physics volume in detail, the Board found 204 biographies of which 171 subjects were deceased; 50 were born before 1800; 111 between 1801 and 1900; and 43 after 1900. Biographies ranged from a single 17-line paragraph for Petrus Peregrinus (born c.1220) to two and one-half pages for Albert Einstein (1879–1955).

Each volume includes a glossary that aids the reader in placing the terms used in the biographical entries in context with the subject and related subjects. The Subject Indexes of the individual volumes identify the entry in which a particular subject or the work of parallel researchers is covered.

Many biographical dictionaries are in-print, and many of these include more entries. However, there are few that are as readable as this series. Although the publisher gives no indication of the criteria used for selection, it is evident, from scrutinizing the physics volume in detail, that the focus is on pre-twentieth-century persons. *The Biographical Dictionary of Scientists* is therefore an excellent historical reference series that will be useful in public, high school, and college libraries. The readability and price of the books also make them attractive for general readers. Recommended.

Black access: a bibliography of Afro-American bibliographies. Richard Newman, compiler. Westport, Conn., Greenwood, 1984. xv, 249p. 24cm. cloth $35 (0-313-23282-2).
016.016973'0496073 Bibliography—Bibliography—Afro-Americans || Afro-Americans—Bibliography [CIP]   83-8537

The proliferation of bibliographies relating to some aspect of Afro-Americans in the U.S., especially since the 1950s, gave rise to a need for this book. Richard Newman is well qualified for this task. Currently a senior editor at G. K. Hall, and compiler of such bibliographies as *Black Index, Lemuel Haynes: A Bio-Bibliography, Afro-American Education: A Bibliographic Index*, and *Black Apostles*, along with numerous article-length bibliographies, Newman has provided an in-depth compilation of more than 3,000 bibliographies dealing with Afro-Americans living in the U.S. One requirement for inclusion was that the bibliography had to have an independent existence. There are a few which have "non-black origins," but these are recognized as having great significance to Afro-American history including such names as Harriet Beecher Stowe, Carl Van Vechten, and Melville Herskovits.

A strict alphabetical arrangement by author is followed throughout, with helpful and easy-to-use Subject and Chronological Indexes at the end. A seven-page Preface by the compiler suggests the thoroughness of the researchers in preparing this useful tool. The appearance of Dorothy Porter's heretofore unpublished "Fifty Years of Collecting" is a jewel in disguise.

Any library supporting research in Afro-American studies will find that *Black Access* is an indispensable aid for their patrons.

Black-Jewish relations in the United States, 1752–1984: a selected bibliography. Compiled by Lenwood G. Davis. Westport, Conn., Greenwood, 1984. xv, 130p. (Bibliographies and Indexes in Afro-American and African Studies, no.1) 24cm. cloth $29.95 (0-313-23329-2).
016.973'0496 Afro-Americans—Relations with Jews—Bibliography [CIP]   84-4685

The compiler's assessment that "oppression is the common bond that Blacks and Jews share" is perhaps one of the few perceptions on which there is general agreement. Since this is one of the few books that provides a background for research on the subject, perhaps it will serve as an incentive for others to study the matter more closely.

The work begins by listing 36 major books and pamphlets; then follow 137 general works, 21 dissertations and theses, and 1,046 journal and newspaper articles, selected from such sources as *The Nation* and *Commentary*. The first three lists are annotated. Standard bibliographic data are given. Specific subject groupings within each chapter provide further breakdowns, e.g., "Black Anti-Semitism," "Black-Jewish Relationships in the South," "Black Muslims and Jews," "W. E. B. DuBois's Opinion of Jews," "Jews as Merchants in the Black Community," "Jews and Affirmative Action," and "Jews in the American Civil War." Arrangement is alphabetical by author or title within each section; an Author Index concludes the work.

Black-Jewish Relations in the United States, 1752–1984 is an excellent introduction to a timely topic, suitable for high school, public, and academic libraries.

Book illustrators of the twentieth century. By Lucy Micklethwait and Brigid Peppin. New York, Arco, 1984. 336p. illus. 29cm. cloth $39.95 (0-668-05670-3).
741.64'092'2 (B) Illustrators—Biography || Illustration of books—20th century [CIP]   83-3745

This attractive biobibliography is misnamed. It aims at comprehensive coverage of *British* book illustrators whose work was published between 1900 and 1975.

Almost 1,000 entries ranging from a paragraph to a page are arranged alphabetically by name. A typical entry includes personal and career information and brief descriptive/evaluative summaries of the person's work. A list of books illustrated (minus publisher) and titles of periodicals in which work appeared follows. The volume is enhanced by black-and-white reproductions which accompany at least half the entries. Sources used are always cited. These include standard works such as *Bénézit* and the *Dictionary of National Biography,* specialized monographs, periodicals, and also questionnaires answered by the illustrators or their families.

Libraries with collections on children's literature, books and printing, and graphic art will want this handsome, carefully researched biobibliography.

Book marketing handbook. 1st ed. 2v. [By] Nat G. Bodian. New York & London, Bowker, 1980, 1983. 26cm. cloth $89.95/set (0-8352-1685-3: v.1; 0-8352-1686-6: v.2)
070.5'2 Book industries and trade—Handbooks, manuals, etc. | Advertising—Books—Handbooks, manuals, etc. [CIP]   80-17504

Subtitled *Tips and Techniques for the Sale and Promotion of Scientific, Technical, Professional, and Scholarly Books and Journals...,* these volumes are intended for marketing and promotional personnel in publishing. The material is based on the author's own experience with advice from others in the field. Coverage includes case histories, findings of various tests, market studies and readership surveys, analysis of successful book promotions, and critiques of promotions that failed.

The first volume has 502 entries arranged under 14 chapters, which in turn are divided into 44 parts. Topics covered include professional and scholarly book promotion by direct mail, advertising, marketing and publicity, outlets, medical-book marketing and promotion, exhibits and conventions, and international book marketing and promotion.

The arrangement of volume 2 is similar; the number of entries has been expanded to 630, but the number of parts remains the same, and there is one less chapter. While the organization is similar, the second volume has wholly new material. In addition, it adds coverage of promotion formats and cooperative mailings, headline writing and copy fitting, the school market, journal subscription studies, estimating book sales, etc. Volume 1 also has a Book Marketing Glossary, Exhibits Planning Guide, Subject Guide to Selected Card-Deck Media, and Checklists of Selected Book Review Media by Subject or Discipline. Volume 2 has an expanded glossary only.

Each volume has a Subject Index; volume 2 reprints the volume 1 Index. Bibliographic citations appear throughout the volumes in the topical parts.

Book Marketing Handbook is practical; the volumes will be valuable tools for anyone interested in book marketing and promotion.

The book publishing annual: highlights, analyses & trends. 1984 ed. New York, Bowker, 1984. viii, 236p. 29cm. hardcover $49.95 + shipping/handling (0-8352-1873-2; ISSN 0000-0787).
†070.5'05 Publishers and publishing—Yearbooks | Book industries and trade—Yearbooks [OCLC]   84-6143

Publishers Weekly Yearbook, the first issue of this annual, was published in 1983; it surveyed events in the publishing world during 1982. The title of the second issue has been changed to *The Book Publishing Annual* "to reflect a broader scope." Comparison of the contents of the two shows little difference in emphasis. Articles on scholarly publishing, religious publishing, First Amendment issues, book manufacturing, publishing economics, production statistics, award winners, best-seller lists, etc., review developments and events in 1983. Most of the authors of the 31 articles are associated with *Publishers Weekly.*

New features are the seven overviews of types of publishing (e.g., general books, scholarly, school, small press); articles on trends in hardcover and paperback publishing; and a survey of salaries in publishing. A list of all-time mass-market paperback best-sellers, headed by Benjamin Spock's *Baby and Child Care* (32,000,000 copies sold), has joined the lists of all-time best-selling hardcover books (*Better Homes & Gardens New Cook Book,* 20,331,815 copies) and trade paperbacks (*Lord of the Flies,* 7,068,345 copies). A single article entitled "The Book Industry Abroad" departs from the other articles' focus on the book industry in the U.S. A Bibliography of 1983 books and articles on publishing concludes the volume. The Index includes book titles, personal names, and subjects.

Complementing the *Bowker Annual, The Book Publishing Annual* offers interested persons a concise, authoritative summary of the industry for the year. Each library will want to judge carefully whether this should be placed in the reference or the circulating collection.

Books out of print, 1980–1983: titles which publishers have reported out-of-print or out-of-stock indefinitely in the years 1980–1983. 2v. New York & London, Bowker, 1983. 2,047p. 29cm. cloth $75 plus shipping/handling (0-8352-1604-7, set; 0-8352-1886-4, v.1; 0-8352-1887-2, v.2; ISSN: 0000-0736).
†011 Out-of-print books—Bibliography—Catalogs [OCLC]

The subtitle of this work clearly indicates its scope. Main entry is by title, and there is an Author Index, plus a Key to Publishers' and Distributors' Abbreviations.

This is a tool (scheduled for annual issue) which should be available to reference and acquisitions librarians—and to booksellers—if only via inquiry to central or regional bibliographical information centers. "Positive, negative information" often satisfies where ignorance arouses suspicion: "not guilty" is better than "guilt not proven," and "dead" than "missing." "Declared by its publisher to be unavailable" is likely to calm in situations where "I can't find it listed" will irritate. Use of this work will thus, by "closing" inquiries, save time and stabilize PR. Gertrude Jennings, whose brainchild it is said to be, is to be congratulated.

The use of titles as main entries is in line with acquisitions experience: order requests and other displays of "known data" tend, according to many authorities, to record titles correctly more often than they so record authors—especially corporate authors, foreign authors, and authors whose names have for any reason changed.

Bridge: a reference guide. By William F. Sachen. New York, Garland, 1984. ix, 171p. 23cm. cloth $18 (0-8240-9094-2).
016.79541'5 Contract bridge—Bibliography [CIP]   84-48058

The 605 books included in this guide—most published since about 1960 and selected for their instructional value—represent only a fraction of the estimated 5,000 titles in English written on contract bridge. The majority of the titles, including 23 by Goren, are favorably annotated, but weaknesses are also noted, e.g., "disorganized and some of the bidding is dated." Lists of bridge periodicals, organizations, and teaching devices are appended, plus Title and Subject Indexes. Discriminating selection and informative annotations recommend *Bridge* to public libraries and dedicated players.

British literary magazines: the Augustan Age and the Age of Johnson, 1698–1788. Alvin Sullivan, editor. Westport, Conn., Greenwood, 1983. xxxi, 427p. (Historical Guides to the World's Periodicals and Newspapers) 24cm. cloth $55 (0-313-22871-X, v.1)
820'.8 English periodicals—History | Literature—Periodicals—History | English Literature—Periodicals—History [CIP]   82-21136

British literary magazines: the romantic age, 1789–1836. Alvin Sullivan, editor. Westport, Conn., Greenwood, 1983. xxv, 491p. (Historical Guides to the World's Periodicals and Newspapers) 24cm. cloth $59.50 (0-313-22872-8, v.2)
820'.8 English periodicals—History | Literature—Periodicals—History | English literature—Periodicals—History [CIP]   82-21136

These are the first two in a projected four-volume set in the publisher's series, *Historical Guides to the World's Periodicals and Newspapers.* When completed, it will provide a reference guide to British literary periodicals from 1698 to 1982. Volume 3 will cover the Victorian and Edwardian Age (1837–1913) and volume 4, the Modern Age (1914–82). Particularly in the early years covered in these two volumes, the distinction between a "literary" and a "political" journal was rarely absolute. As a result, the editor has been generous in including titles which had some literary content. For each title listed, there is a profile of the periodical concentrating on its editor and major contributors with discussion of its general contents. The various essayists who have contributed to the work (all listed at the end of each volume) have sought to place the periodical in the context of the literary, social, and political world of its time. For each signed essay, there are three Appendixes—footnotes to the text; Information Sources (indicating bibliographical references, any existing indexes, the availability of any reprint editions, and a location guide to holdings in U.S. and British libraries); and a Publication History providing details of title changes (a very common feature in the period under review), volume and issue details, frequency, publishers/editors. Each volume has an Index, and the

British writers. 8v. Edited under the auspices of the British Council. Ian Scott-Kilvert, general editor. New York, Scribner, 1979–1984. 29cm. cloth v.I–VII, $65 each volume; v.VIII, $50; $460, 8v. set (0-684-15798-5, v.I; 0-684-16407-8, v.II; 0-684-16408-6, v.III; 0-684-16635-6, v.IV; 0-684-16636-4, v.V; 0-684-16637-2, v.VI; 0-684-16638-0, v.VII; 0-684-17417-0, v.VIII—the Index; 0-684-18253-X, set).
820'.9 English literature—History and criticism | English literature—Bio-bibliography | Authors, English—Biography [CIP]   78-23483

The 153 essays in this recently completed set will appeal to a wide audience because they provide a superior introduction to the work of writers who have made significant contributions to English literature. The series begins with the fourteenth century and follows a chronological order with the last volume's essays on writers born after 1880, e.g., Woolf, Joyce, Eliot, and Auden. Also included are seven essays concerning topics which pertain to particular periods: thus volume I contains "The English Bible" and volume VII "Poets of World War II." Each volume has its own Introduction written by the general editor and a Chronological Table which lists major international political and literary events during the period covered by the volume. Both the introductory statements and the chronological tables are an excellent historical backdrop to the essays.

The set is designed to complement the publisher's *American Writers* (New York, 1974–   ). As in that set, the essays contained here were first published as pamphlets—in this case, as part of a series initiated by the British Council in 1950 and entitled *Writers and Their Work*. Most of the original articles have been revised at least twice since their first publication. Careful editing is evident in *British Writers*, but individual contributions differ somewhat in organization. Generally, articles begin with short biographical sections and quickly develop into extended discussions of their subjects' principal works. Assessment of achievement is usually given near the ends of essays. Contributors are sympathetic toward their subjects, rarely assigning critical praise or censure. The set's Introduction states: "Since each contributor speaks with only one voice out of many, he is principally concerned with explaining his subject as fully as possible rather than with establishing an order of merit or making . . . comparisons."

Every article contains a bibliography. These are, perforce, selective and follow a specific organizational pattern: each lists its subject writings chronologically: both separate works and collections. Each bibliography concludes with a list of secondary works—books primarily, but there is an occasional journal citation. Publications of the 1960s and 1970s predominate, but standard older works are not overlooked. School and public librarians will find these bibliographies useful; librarians using larger collections and needing more extended bibliographies must turn to *The New Cambridge Bibliography of English Literature*.

Each volume contains a separate list of contributors. Most are associated with universities in the United Kingdom and are teachers of literature, poets, novelists, historians, or biographers. Some better-known contributors are Donald Coggan, Nevill Coghill, T. S. Eliot, and Peter Quennell. Eliot completed the George Herbert article two years before his death in 1965. Interestingly, his criticism of other writers' work is more frequently cited within the set than that of either Samuel Johnson or Samuel Taylor Coleridge. The editor, Ian Scott-Kilvert, was director of publications, recorded sound and literature departments, the British Council (1962–1977), a biographer of A. E. Housman, and a translator of classic texts (Plutarch's *Lives* and Polybius' *Histories*).

There is a separate index volume (v.VIII). All references include volume numbers in boldface Roman numerals and page numbers either in Arabic, to indicate the text of an essay, or in lowercase Roman to refer to a volume's Introduction. Indexing of authors and titles is complete, but indexing of more general subjects (Catholicism, expressionism, light verse, etc.) is weak. There are just under 100 subject entries, and they are not fully utilized for indexing purposes. For example, users are referred to D. H. Lawrence and Virginia Woolf for information concerning "feminism," but not to an excellent discussion of Jane Austen's female characters in Brian Southam's essay. Worse, the index entry *novel, development and structure* does not cite Jane Austen. The entry *romance* contains but one reference and *women poets* refers readers to Edith Sitwell, but not to Christina Rossetti or Elizabeth Barrett Browning.

The high level of criticism and the lucid writing styles of individual contributors make this a superior source. *The Dictionary of National Bibliography* has better biographical coverage for most of the authors discussed here and it continues to be the work to consult for genealogical information, awards, prizes, etc. *British Writers*, however, offers better coverage of writers' works. As noted above, its bibliographies are first-rate, surpassed only by individual descriptive or subject bibliographies or those in *The New Cambridge Bibliography of English Literature*.

The set is well produced. Typography, paper quality, typeface, binding are all excellent. Despite the rather weak indexing, it is highly recommended for academic, secondary school, and public libraries.

Broadway bound: a guide to shows that died aborning. By William Torbert Leonard. Metuchen, N.J. & London, Scarecrow, 1983. x, 618p. 22cm. cloth $39.50 (0-8108-1652-0).
792'.09747'1 Theater—U.S.—History—20th century—Handbooks, manuals, etc. [CIP]   83-15042

The subtitle to this handbook describes its scope; productions that opened and closed almost immediately and also those shows that were previewed but never opened on Broadway.

Each entry for the 410 productions (listed alphabetically by title) provides opening and closing dates and places; names of producers, writers, directors, and others involved in the play's production; and the cast. There follows a synopsis of the story and excerpts from critical responses. Ten indexes (chronological; actor; choreographer; composer and lyricist; costume designer; set designer; director; playwright; producer; and title) complete the volume. The Title Index is the least satisfactory to use, since the titles listed may include films, television shows, and books mentioned briefly in an entry as well as the entries themselves. And the page numbers as given do not indicate whether the reference will be of major importance.

This volume focuses on one aspect of theater history that is probably of limited interest. Thus, it would be most useful to those large public or academic libraries that support comprehensive theater collections or curricula.

Business information applications and sources. [By] Van Mayros and D. Michael Werner. Radnor, Pa., Chilton, 1983. x, 490p. 28cm. paper $27.50 (0-8019-7225-6).
658.4'038 Industrial management—Information services | Business—Information services | Industrial management—Bibliography | Business—Bibliography [CIP]   82-73545

Information sourcebook for marketers and strategic planners. [By] Van Mayros and D. Michael Werner. Radnor, Pa., Chilton, 1983. x, 326p. 28cm. paper $18.95 (0-8019-7372-4).
016.65 Industrial management—Information services | Business—Information services | Industrial management—Bibliography | Business—Bibliography | Management information systems | Information storage and retrieval systems—Business [CIP]   82-46080

Excellent subject indexing and particularly strong databases sections make these latest guides to industrial management and business information useful supplements to D. M. Brownstone's *Where to Find Business Information* (New York: Wiley, 1982) and *Encyclopedia of Business Information Sources* (Detroit: Gale, 1980).

These new sourcebooks in their first sections (Applications) divide business activity into broad categories (e.g., Marketing Planning, Sales Planning, Research and Development, etc.) and then further subdivide into specific applications. For example, a section in *Information Sourcebook* called Marketing Planning is subdivided into 16 specific applications, from competitive analysis to psychographic statistics. Under each, general reference titles, periodicals, databases, information services, and U.S. government agencies and publications are cited; full descriptions of items are then provided in the second section (Sources).

Both volumes identify those sources available in English and accessible in larger libraries or directly from the publisher/vendor. Standard directory/bibliographic data are provided along with brief descriptive material, e.g., information for each database includes acronym explanation, data source, approximate size, maintenance, profile, geographic coverage, time, online vendor(s). Each volume has a Subject Index. As is almost inevitable, some omissions were noted by the Board. On the whole, however, these are comprehensive volumes.

The Preface to each volume includes this forthright statement: "In short, most of the sources listed in this book are indeed listed in other sourcebooks." Nevertheless, academic and public libraries with strong economic and business collections will find them to be useful, complementing other guides already in their collections. Smaller libraries may find them to be particularly useful and relatively inexpensive choices in a crowded field.

Business mini-micro software directory. Compiled by Information Sources, Inc. New York, Bowker, 1984. xii, 809p. 28cm. paper $75 + shipping/handling (0-8352-1970-4; ISSN: 0000-0809).

650'.028'5425 Business—Computer programs—Catalogs | Computer software industry—U.S.—Directories [OCLC]   84-249236

This guide was compiled for the purpose of aiding potential buyers of software packages for business use in finding their way through the ever-growing maze of products. It is in two sections: an alphabetical list of software packages and a "Comprehensive Guide"—really an index. In fact, one is asked (in the brief instruction for the use of the directory) to consult the "Comprehensive Guide" first. It lists each entry under four headings: name of package, vendor, application, and compatible hardware. One must possess a fair amount of subject knowledge in order to derive full benefit from this very technical index.

The software listing which precedes the index is also alphabetically arranged and contains more than 3,500 entries. Information for each software (or software service) is comprehensive, clearly spelling out such data as who could use the product, what type of hardware to use it with, what other companies are using it, and what type of service to expect from the vendor.

As seems to be customary in this type of publication, the publisher seems disassociated from the validity of the information received from the vendors.

Libraries with business clienteles may want to add this book to their collections of computer directories and catalogs.

Business organizations and agencies directory: a guide to trade, business, and commercial organizations, government agencies, stock exchanges, labor unions, chambers of commerce, diplomatic representation, trade and convention centers, trade fairs, publishers, data banks and computerized services, educational institutions, research centers, and libraries and information centers. 2d ed. Eds. Anthony T. Kruzas, Robert C. Thomas, and Kay Gill. Detroit, Gale, 1984. 1,371p. 29cm. cloth $220. (0-8103-1199-2).

380.1'025'73 Business—Information services—U.S.—Directories | U.S.—Commerce—Directories | U.S.—Industries—Directories [CIP]   84-4179

Once again we have a directory compiled from many other directories, this one specifically geared to the requirements of people interested in business information sources of all kinds. Designed to be "a single-volume comprehensive guide to more than 16,000 organizations and agencies that are major sources of current information on American business and industry," *Business Organizations and Agencies Directory*, second edition, incorporates material from government documents, other Gale directories, and works of other publishers. The editors have been involved in editing and compiling several other Gale directories and dictionaries.

There have been a number of changes since the first edition (1980): 23 sections rather than 26; altered arrangement in several of the sections; one index rather than several; more complete information provided for some entries; more entries now numbered in one sequence; and a more pleasing appearance with the use of white paper and of serif type more varied in size and weight, which sets off entries more clearly than before.

Each section is arranged in a manner suitable to its purpose, and the amount of information included varies—some entries provide only name, address, and telephone number, others provide detailed descriptions and annotations. The arrangement of each section is explained in the Introduction, which also tells where the information was obtained and refers to one or more directories (or organizations) for the benefit of those wanting more information. The Introduction also tells if the section entries are included in the Master Index and, if so, how (by subject, name, keyword, etc.).

The first section, "Trade, Business, Commercial, and Related Organizations," is the largest. All entries come from Gale's *Encyclopedia of Associations*, but are here arranged alphabetically by name rather than by subject. Entries repeat all information given in the *E of A* except for committees and meeting schedules. Other sections cover commodity and stock exchanges, labor unions, chambers of commerce, Better Business Bureaus, etc., as well as federal, state, and regional agencies, diplomatic offices, news sources, etc. Section 7, "Federal Grants and Domestic Assistance Programs," is abstracted from the *Catalog of Federal Domestic Assistance* (Washington, D.C., Gov. Print. Off., published annually in May) and lists programs which "comprise a wide selection of business-oriented benefits and services (including research and project grants, loans, insurance, and payments) available from the federal government." Entries give name of administering agency, the program, its objectives, the types of assistance available, and eligibility requirements. *CFDA* numbers are included so one can easily check for more detailed information.

Four sections concern conventions, trade fairs, and similar matter, including lists of building facilities, visitor and convention bureaus, and trade centers throughout the world, and a list of more than 500 "worldwide expositions and trade fairs that are held on a periodic basis," e.g., the Frankfurt Book Fair. Business opportunities are listed in the section "Franchise Companies"; business travel is covered in "Hotel-Motel Systems," which includes toll-free 800 numbers to call for reservations (although all addresses are in the U.S., some entries include international coverage, e.g., Club Med, Inc., and Hilton International Co.).

Covering knowledge as a type of business information, Section 18, "Business Publishers," includes both large and small publishers which concentrate on business and related subjects; AMACOM, the Center for Urban Policy Research, and Prentice-Hall, Inc., are among the 725 entries. Only address and telephone number are given. Section 19, "Data Banks and Computerized Services," provides 320 entries for companies and organizations (producers, vendors, and services) which "process information for storage, retrieval, and dissemination to the business community." For each, name, address, telephone number, general description, and a list of computer-based products and services are given. Section 20, "Information-on-Demand," provides 81 numbered entries for library and private companies both large and small which provide research on demand. Further sections cover business schools, business libraries, and such research centers as the Brookings Institution, Predicasts, Inc., and the Rand Corporation.

With its pleasing format, sturdy binding, clearly marked running heads and index, *BOAD*, second edition, is quite easy to use if one pays attention to the Introduction, which explains the arrangement of each section and how each is indexed. Note must be taken that some sections are more selective than others. All this information can be found elsewhere, sometimes (as the Introduction is frank to state) in other Gale Research publications, sometimes in government publications, and sometimes in other directories; and inevitably compilations such as this are out-of-date compared with ongoing directory services. Yet this directory, by bringing together so many types of information of value to the business community and by providing references to sources of further information is likely to fill a real need, perhaps not as much for the libraries which have most or all of the directories drawn upon (though they will welcome the convenience of this compilation) as for smaller libraries and corporate libraries, which do not have access to all these specialized directories and yet need the information they provide. Recommended.

Business publications index and abstracts: abstracts. v.1– monthly. Detroit, Gale, 1983–   . 28cm. 12-issue subscription, paper $250 (ISSN: 0739-618X); hardbound annual cumulation $250 (0-8103-1519-X).

†016.338 Business—Bibliography | Business—Abstracts [OCLC]   83-8344

Business publications index and abstracts: subject/author citations. v.1–   . monthly. Detroit, Gale, 1983–   . 28cm. 12-issue subscription, paper $250 (0739-618X); hardbound annual cumulation $250 (0-8103-1518-1).

†016.338 Business—Bibliography | Business—Abstracts [OCLC]   83-8344

This monthly periodical service is an up-to-date hard copy version of *Management Contents* online database. It complements online access as an aid to planning a search and, of course, offers an alternative format. It enables photocopying of citations and/or abstracts without initiating an online search (and related costs). The 12 issues examined promise thorough indexing of 36,000 articles appearing in more than 700 business-oriented periodicals as well as some 3,000 books and the contents of more than 135 courses offered this year by the American Management Association. The subject/author citations and the abstracts are separate publications, each appearing monthly. The citations cumulate quarterly. The abstracts do not cumulate but are numbered sequentially and also are available in permanent hardbound annual volumes after the close of each year.

Each can be ordered separately. Academic, public, and special business libraries may wish to acquire *Business Publications Index* for their patrons who need comprehensive and current business information.

CRC handbook of chemistry and physics. 54th ed., 1984–85. Editor in chief, Robert C. Weast. Boca Raton, FL 33431, 2000 N.W. 24th St., CRC Pr., 1984. various pagings. 26cm. hardcover $64.95 (0-8493-0465-2).

†540.2′02 Chemistry—Handbooks, manuals, etc. | Chemistry—Tables, etc. | Physics—Handbooks, manuals, etc. | Physics—Tables, etc. [OCLC]   13-11056

Over the years, this title has been an invaluable source of tabular data in the areas of chemistry and physics. This edition continues the purpose, format, and subject coverage established by the first edition in 1914.

The work consists primarily of tabular data, plus the necessary information for using and interpreting the tables. Material is divided into six sections: Mathematical Tables, Elements and Inorganic Compounds, General Chemical (Constants), General Physical (Constants), and Miscellaneous. Each new edition is revised to include data from the latest discoveries, and all data have been verified. Sources are indicated and lists of references are found at the end of sections and subsections. Entries in the alphabetical Subject Index refer to section/page numbers.

CRC Handbook of Chemistry and Physics is an old standard that is still necessary for libraries serving a scientific community.

The Cambridge guide to English literature [including the literature of Great Britain, the United States, Canada, Australia, the Caribbean, and Africa]. [Edited by] Michael Stapleton. New York, Cambridge Univ. Pr., 1983. xi, 992p. 26cm. cloth $29.95 (0-521-26022-1).

820′.9(B) English literature—Dictionaries | English literature—Bio-bibliography | American literature—Dictionaries | American literature—Bio-bibliography | English literature—Commonwealth of Nations authors—Dictionaries | English literature—Commonwealth of Nations authors—Bio-bibliography [CIP]   83-1967

Covering more than a thousand years and written "to provide a guide to the literature of the English-speaking world in one volume," *The Cambridge Guide* is solely concerned with literature. Author Michael Stapleton has had a long career in publishing as editor and writer, and he writes with zest. Apparently all entries were written by him except two major ones commissioned from Barbara M. H. Strang ("The English Language") and C. H. Sisson ("The Bible in English").

More than 3,100 entries, made up of authors, titles, characters, and literary terms, are arranged in alphabetical order with numerous cross-references. The two-columned pages are interspersed with small but clear black-and-white illustrations, each in close proximity to its subject's entry. Entries contain not only factual information but also some of the author's critical opinion, thus making the book more interesting to consult without sacrificing basic material.

Entries vary in length from a few lines to several columns, depending on the importance of the subject.

Comparable to the *Oxford Companions,* but dealing strictly with literature, *The Cambridge Guide* is recommended for public and academic libraries.

Canadian almanac & directory, 1984. Editor, Susan Bracken. Toronto, Pitman; dist. in U.S. exclusively by Gale, 1984. 1,191p. 24cm. hardcover $59 (0-7730-4053-6).

†317.1 Canada—Statistics | Canada—Directories

The 137th edition of one of the two standard almanacs for Canada (the other being *Corpus Almanac of Canada*) provides directory-type information for commercial, educational, cultural, and governmental organizations; information on solar tables and holidays; statistical data about Canada; as well as a geographic directory of law firms in Canada. There is a detailed Index and a two-page Addendum of recent changes to earlier entries. The cutoff date is not given, but the Addendum includes events of November 1983.

In short, *Canadian Almanac & Directory* provides the sort of information one would expect in such a work. It is a well-established source of information about Canada, useful in all but the smallest libraries.

The challenge of aging: a bibliography. Compiled by Margaret E. Monroe and Rhea Joyce Rubin. Littleton, Colo., Libraries Unlimited, 1983. 209p. 24cm. cloth $22.50 (U.S.); $27 (elsewhere) (0-87287-387-0).

016.3052′6 Aged—Bibliography | Aging—Bibliography [CIP]   83-7942

This selective bibliography annotates approximately 500 nontechnical titles and has two purposes, as stated by the compilers: to educate laypersons in all aspects of aging and to aid librarians in selecting materials on aging.

The material is arranged according to "lifetasks" for aging as outlined in the Table of Contents. These include such topics as adjustment (e.g., retirement), major changes (widowhood), and opportunity (leisure). This arrangement is somewhat arbitrary and causes the listing of many titles in several places. Each lifetask chapter and subsection is prefaced by a brief task description followed by annotated entries. These are in no discernible order; paperback and large-print editions in addition to standard bibliographic data are given; prices are listed for items appearing in *Books in Print,* 1982. Where applicable, Library of Congress codes for nonprint format (braille, recording, talking books), available through the National Library Service for the Blind and Physically Handicapped, are listed.

Annotations are brief (one short paragraph in most cases). Clearly written, they deal honestly with the realities of aging, although a positive approach is maintained at all times. There are two Indexes: one by Author-Title, the other Subject.

Well indexed and with judicious selections of both fiction and nonfiction, *The Challenge of Aging* will be a good resource for public libraries.

Children's periodicals of the United States. R. Gordon Kelley, editor. Westport, Conn., Greenwood, 1984. xxix, 591p. (Historical Guides to the World's Periodicals and Newspapers) 24cm. cloth $49.95 (0-313-22117-0).

051′.088054 Children's periodicals, American [CIP]   83-8574

Descriptions and analyses of selected juvenile periodicals of the past and present, listing information sources for each (e.g., bibliographies, indexing availability, holdings) form the bulk of this major work. A Preface by the editor, known for his work in the field, describes and critiques the limited research on juvenile magazines. The Introduction summarizes their history, from *Children's Magazine* (1789) to *Cobblestone* (1980), followed by the articles on individual titles. A Selected Bibliography of American Children's Periodicals lists the titles alphabetically and is followed by chronological and geographical listings of the magazines.

The articles are all signed by one of the 47 contributors (listed in the back). Many are literature specialists, and some have backgrounds in library science; quite a few hold academic positions. About 100 periodicals are included, some of general interest (e.g., *Cricket, Our Young Folks*), others more specialized (e.g., *Slave's Friends, Youth's Temperance Advocate,* and church-related periodicals).

Coverage typically includes information on editorship, sponsorship, purpose, audience, format, content, authors, circulation, impact, cost, frequency, publicity, and related services and gimmicks, such as binders and T-shirts. Changes in the periodical are traced. There is some attempt to show magazines in relation to their times.

Articles are uneven as to emphasis, amount of detail, and extent of critical comment although they are usually quite informative, if modest in length. The potential audience includes readers with interests in social history, mass media/periodicals, library science, literary history, or education. *Children's Periodicals of the United States* is for children's literature, library science, or education collections.

Choices: a core collection for young reluctant readers. [v.1] Edited by Carolyn Sherwood Flemming & Donna Schatt. Evanston, IL 60204-1492, P.O. Box 1492, John Gordon Burke Publishers, 1983. 554p. 24cm. cloth $45 (0-934272-10-7; ISSN: 0735-6358).

011′.63 Slow learning children, Books for | High interest-low vocabulary books—Book reviews | High interest-low vocabulary books—Bibliography | Children's literature—Book reviews | Children's literature—Bibliography | Libraries, Children's—Book lists | Bibliography—Best books—Children's literature [OCLC]   84-644479

Compiled by librarians with a total of 20 years' experience in working with children and designed for parents and professionals who work with reluctant second through sixth grade readers, this volume identifies more than 350 currently available trade books (fiction and nonfiction) which can provide motivating and pleasant reading experiences for such children. The listing is intended to serve as an alternative to what the compilers label the "bland diet" of high interest/low reading level books.

The term "reluctant reader" covers two areas here. The emphasis is on children who read below their grade level and thus find reading a chore. The other category, designated "Group 2," covers the students who read at or even above their grade level but who find little satisfaction in reading.

An Introduction describes the method of selecting the titles included, the use and reliability of readability formulas (which were applied to the books listed), and the organization and uses of the bibliography.

The first section consists of an alphabetical listing of books by author, providing brief but sufficient bibliographic data. Each title has an annotation which often notes specific strengths and/or weaknesses in vocabulary, style, print, etc., and possible curricular use. Each listing concludes with interest level, reading level, and subject headings—which refer to the listing by subject where similar titles can be found.

The compilers think that "the most significant factor in the search for books for reluctant readers is the child's interests." Therefore, the largest section of this volume lists books by subject area. Some subjects—Baseball, Crime, Death, Courage, Family, Humorous Fiction, and Mystery and Detective Stories—have many titles listed thereunder. Others—Astronauts, Computers, Drugs, Motorcycles, Toys, and Volcanoes—have one title each. Special categories of books are also listed, e.g., Best-Sellers (guaranteed successes), Interest Levels (by grade), Reading Levels, and Reading Aloud. The bibliographic information and annotations found in the author section are repeated in the subject section—which accounts for the book's length and is a feature which is probably unnecessary. Some authors are well represented, e.g., nine titles for Judy Blume, but some others one would expect are not, e.g., only three Beverly Cleary titles.

Annotations vary in length from about 20 words to about 350 words. Ideally, the editors state, adult users should first read the book to be introduced to the child, but "because we realize that this is often impossible, we have included book descriptions so detailed and narrative that, if necessary, the adult user can rely solely upon this bibliography to introduce a book to a potential reader."

Two Appendixes contain a list of basal reading series used in compiling this bibliography and a list of publishers of high/low materials.

The Introduction states *Choices* will be revised every three years, thus allowing addition of new material and deletion of out-of-print titles.

Experienced librarians and teachers may have already compiled their own informal lists of surefire titles for reluctant readers that may include some titles not found in *Choices;* however, this detailed bibliography with its stress on materials for younger children offers valuable assistance to teachers, librarians, and parents seeking help for primary- and elementary-grade reluctant readers.

Climate normals for the U.S. (Base: 1951–80). 1st ed. Compiled by National Climatic Center. Detroit, Gale, 1983, 1984. 712p. 29cm. cloth $125 (0-8103-1025-2).
551.6973 Climatic normals—U.S. 84-126552

The National Climatic Center of the U.S. National Oceanic and Atmospheric Administration is responsible for collecting climatic data from 5,557 weather stations across the U.S. It publishes averages for a 30-year period in a series of 50 pamphlets, 1 for each state. Gale has taken the 1951–80 state reports and reprinted them in a convenient one-volume reference that will be a standard source of climate information until about 1993 (since averages are now being calculated by the government for ten-year periods). Arranged alphabetically by state and then alphabetically by station name, the following data are given for each station: temperature normals in degrees Fahrenheit—showing the average of the daily maximum, minimum, and mean—for each month; precipitation normals for each month in inches; heating degree day normals for each month (the index that has become so important in tracking fuel consumption and cold weather energy needs); and cooling degree day normals for each month (the summer weather index that helps quantify air conditioning requirements). Following the statistics are a map of the state showing the location of each weather station and a chart giving each station's latitude, longitude, and elevation.

There is no other such cumulation available in this format. Although the price seems high since the information can be purchased from the Government Printing Office on a state-by-state basis, this volume is still a bargain when one considers that it will be a standard reference work for at least ten years (a much longer life span than many reference works that cost hundreds of dollars more) and that all the data are available in one place rather than in 50 different ones. Large public, academic, and special libraries will want *Climate Normals for the U.S.*

The cold war file. By Andy East. Metuchen, N.J., Scarecrow, 1983. vii, 362p. 22cm. cloth $22.50 (0-8108-1641-5).
823'.0872'09 Spy stories, English—History and criticism | Spy stories, English—Bibliography | Spy stories, American—History and criticism | Spy stories, American—Bibliography | World politics in literature [CIP] 83-7584

Andy East's *Cold War File* is an elaborate checklist of espionage fiction published in the U.S. and U.K. during the 1960s. Seventy-seven authors are listed and discussed, including such well-known figures as Kingsley Amis, Len Deighton, Ian Fleming, and Mickey Spillane. In terms of literary quality, the spectrum is a wide one, ranging from such spy masters as John le Carré to strictly mass-marketing ventures involving a stable of writers such as the Ace Intelligence Group. Although the focus is on the 1960s (in the author's view, the peak period of cold-war fiction), some earlier works are listed, and two separate Appendixes list post-1969 fiction.

The Cold War File is notable chiefly for its arrangement, which may intrigue some spy-fiction buffs but seems sure to annoy those who prefer a more traditional format when seeking biographical or bibliographical information. A typical entry follows a "dossier" approach. For example, John le Carré's biographical background is given first, and it is noted that le Carré is the "cover identity" of David John Moore Cornwell. Following is information on cold war file agent George Smiley, a character in the novels. "Operative Data" contains brief information on Smiley's activities in the various le Carré novels, and the "Field Bibliography" lists the author's novels and refers readers to the Appendixes for post-1969 titles. The discussion of the writers and their books is not so much a literary/critical analysis as it is one which gives an overview of an author's work. *The Cold War File* should prove adequate for readers seeking general information on authors working in this enormously popular genre. It will serve well in high school, public, and popular-culture library collections.

The collector's guide to the American musical theatre. 2v. By David Hummel. Metuchen, N.J., Scarecrow, 1984. 29cm. cloth $89.50/set (0-8108-1637-7).
016.7899'12281'0973 Musical revues, comedies, etc.—Discography | Musical revue, comedy, etc. [CIP] 83-7520

Truly a labor of love by a connoisseur and record collector, this work originally began as a mimeographed list of the author's personal collection of sound recordings of American musicals. The first edition, a 60-page paperback, appeared in 1977; the second edition (1978) had 238 pages. This two-volume edition contains 893 pages, 231 of which are devoted to a faultless Index containing every composer, lyricist, author, and performer mentioned in the main listing.

The guide includes those musicals presented on stage in the U.S. and lists all the song titles whether or not these songs have been recorded. Dramas having original background music are included, as are what would sometimes be labeled "operettas." Composers, lyricists, opening dates, and number of performances are also provided. Commercial recordings on discs and tapes, as well as private cast recordings, are identified. (The author included private recordings only after verifying the contents.) Since the work is arranged alphabetically by show title, all recorded versions of a show are listed together. The various recorded versions (original cast, road company, foreign cast, film cast, revival cast, recorded selections) are indiciated by symbol notations (letters) for purposes of indexing. The guide is complex, and the front matter should be read carefully before using the work.

This is very possibly the best discography of American musicals available. It is also the best available listing of works by musical comedy composers, better than *The New Grove Dictionary* or David Ewen's *New Complete Book of the American Musical Theater* (New York: Holt, 1970).

Libraries with music collections or sound recordings will find this set to be invaluable. The author intends to include all English-language musicals in future editions.

The college money handbook: the complete guide to expenses, scholarships, loans, jobs, and special aid programs at four-year colleges. Editor, Karen C. Hegener. Princeton, Peterson's, 1983. iv, 487p. 28cm. paper $9.95 plus $1.25 for shipping/handling (0-87866-251-0).
378'.3'0973 Student aid—U.S.—Handbooks, manuals, etc. | College costs—U.S.—Directories [OCLC]   83-62921

This guide is divided into three sections: An Overview of Financial Aid Today; College Cost and Aid Profiles; and Directories (colleges grouped by specific types of scholarships/financial aids offered). It "includes all accredited institutions in the U.S. and U.S. territories that offer full four- or five-year baccalaureate degree programs." Institutions that offer primarily part-time, correspondence, or external studies and colleges that are free (for example, the U.S. service academies) are excluded. The data were collected through questionnaires sent to more than 1,700 colleges and universities as part of the spring 1983 *Peterson's Annual Survey of Undergraduate Institutions and Financial Aid Supplement.*

Like other Peterson guides, this one is current, easy to use, and, in its paperback edition, relatively inexpensive. The Profiles, arranged alphabetically by school name, make it easy to determine what employment opportunities exist and if accelerated degree programs to shorten study are possible. The reader also is introduced through detailed questions and answers to the application process. The directory enables readers to find quickly colleges offering merit, athletic, cooperative programs, ROTC, and guaranteed tuition plans. The Cost Profiles then can be used for more detailed study. *The College Money Handbook* is an excellent addition for public, academic, or school libraries.

Combat fleets of the world, 1984/85: their ships, aircraft, and armament. Edited by Jean Labayle Couhat. Annapolis, Md., Naval Institute Press, 1984. xv, 1,035p. + unnumbered pages. illus. 21cm. x 28cm. cloth $84.95 (0-87021-136-6).
623.82'5'9094 Navies | Warships [OCLC]   78-50192

Strictly for specialists, this translation is the latest in a series of "Flottes de Combat," published in France since 1897, and it is similar to *Jane's Fighting Ships*. It covers, alphabetically, all countries of the world that have even a single gunboat, from Hungary and Switzerland (one-quarter page of text each) to the superpowers, i.e., the USSR and U.S.A. (150 and 168 pages, respectively). Like *Jane's*, entries give numbers of ships or each type and class, technical data, number of personnel, etc., as well as black-and-white photographs. The work is indispensable for Department of Defense and similar governmental libraries, and it will be useful wherever there is a local interest in naval affairs.

Common Market digest: an information guide to the European Communities. [By] David Overton. New York, Facts On File, 1983. xlii, 387p. 24cm. hardcover $45 (0-87196-854-1).
341.24'22 European Economic Community | European Coal and Steel Community | Euratom [CIP]   83-14172

This handy guide to what is popularly called the Common Market aims to present succinct information on what this institution *is*, what it *does*, and *how* it operates.

Beginning with an introductory chapter on the components of the European Communities and some brief history, chapters are devoted to organizational information and broad subjects. In the chapter on industry and energy, overall purposes and policies are described, followed by descriptions of individual commitees, networks, funds, programs, etc., of the European Communities. Lists of publications are often provided in these subsections (English-language titles only).

An Index is in the front of the book together with a Table of Contents and instructions for use. Each chapter is headed by a more detailed breakdown of its content.

Any library with readers interested in international affairs or European studies will want this well-organized guide.

Communications and society: a bibliography on communications technologies and their social impact. Compiled by Benjamin F. Shearer and Marilyn Huxford. Westport, Conn., Greenwood, 1983. vii, 242p. 24cm. cloth $35 (0-313-23713-1).
016.3022'3 Mass media—Social aspects—Bibliography | Communication—Social aspects—Bibliography | Communication—Technological innovations—Bibliography [CIP]   83-12659

The purpose of this classified bibliography of 2,732 books, articles, and dissertations "is to explore the diversity of communications technologies and their impact on society from a humanistic perspective." It attempts this through nine chapters exploring mass communications theory, inventors of technology, gatekeepers, social and cultural effects, influence on public opinion, effect on political opinion, advertising, future technologies, and film and photography as art forms. This last chapter also covers "the use of computers and communications technologies in the production of fine art" as well as "the effects of technology and industrialism on literature." This variety exceeds what a single chapter of just 236 entries can adequately cover. In the other chapters, similar problems of broad scope combined with selective coverage lead to superficial treatment of the literature on important topics. The chapters' topical subdivisions sharpen internal focus and coherence. Within sections the entries are organized by author.

Articles come from both popular and scholarly periodicals. Entries for dissertations list granting university and year but do not refer to their entries in *Dissertation Abstracts International*. The Author Index works as one would expect it to. The Subject Index is not as precise as it ought to be; such topics as violence are followed by nearly 100 entry numbers without subdivision.

Comprehensive collections on mass communications need this bibliography worthy in concept but weak in execution.

Community resources directory: a guide to U.S. volunteer organizations and other resource groups, services, training events and courses, and local program models. 2d ed. Edited by Harriet Clyde Kipps. Detroit, Gale, 1984. 943p. 29cm. cloth $85 (0-8103-1794-X).
361.8'025'73 Voluntarism—U.S.—Directories | Associations, institutions, etc.—U.S.—Directories | Voluntarism—Information services—U.S.—Directories | Social service—U.S.—Directories | Community development—U.S.—Directories [CIP]   83-25349

The need for information on the services provided by the many voluntary organizations throughout the U.S. was served by the publication in 1969 of *Green Sheets*, a directory of assistance available to volunteer leaders, followed by *The Training Blue Book* and *The Pure Gold Pages* (a directory of volunteer projects), all three consolidated into *The Community Resources Tie Line* of 1980 and now superseded by this second edition under a new title. The objective of the current directory is to serve as a "basic guide to information on volunteer involvement in specific areas of human services and physical environment, and to resources and training to assist leaders of such voluntary efforts."

The editor, in her effort to make available the kind of information desired by the volunteer community, organized the contents into three major sections. Section 1 offers information on resource groups and publications. Under each category are lists of organizations followed by their relevant publications. Section 2 lists training programs alphabetically by state while the third section describes a wide range of volunteer programs.

For each resource, training program, or program in the sequentially numbered listings, the editor provides full address, telephone number, a statement on objective, and a listing of services offered. For the publications listed in section 1, users are provided with the name and address of the responsible group, name of publication, start-up date, kind of publication, type of information offered, and charge, if any. The information for each answers the question who is doing what for whom and where across the country?

Critical to accessing information stored in this directory are the contents listings (one general and one located at the start of each section) and two indexes—Organization Name Index and the Emphasis Index.

Community Resources Directory in its second edition should prove most useful in public libraries and in the hands of all public and private volunteer groups or organizations.

Companion to Russian history. By John Paxton. New York, Facts On File, 1983. xi, 503p. 23cm. cloth $21.95 (0-87196-771-5).
947'.003'21 Soviet Union—Dictionaries and encyclopedias [CIP]   82-5192

John Paxton, editor of *The Statesman's Yearbook* and author of numerous other publications on political and historical topics, now offers a one-volume reference work on Russian and Soviet history from the tenth century through the Khrushchev era. The bulk of the book consists of more than 2,500 entries, alphabetically arranged with cross-references, providing brief information on people, places, and events important in Russian history, politics, and culture. The alphabetical listing is followed by a 16-page Chronology, a 7-page Select Bibliography, and 18 maps.

Any one-volume work covering such a vast and complex subject necessarily suffers from a certain degree of superficiality, and this one is no exception. Nonetheless, there is a need for such works for the English-speaking audience. Two excellent ones are already available: *The Cambridge Encyclopedia of Russia and the Soviet Union* (1982), also in one volume but considerably heftier than Paxton's, and the multivolume *Modern Encyclopedia of Russian and Soviet History* (Academic International), begun in 1976 and still in progress. Certainly Paxton's work is no substitute for either of these, but it will still be useful, especially for small collections with very few other resources in this field. (It is regrettable that none of these works indicates the stress in Russian words and names, a feature which would have been extremely helpful for the intended audience.) Larger collections may wish to buy the *Companion* as a supplementary resource.

The complete book of U.S. presidents. By William A. DeGregorio. New York, Dembner; dist. by Norton, 1984. xi, 691p. illus. 25cm. hardcover $22.50 (0-934878-36-6).

973′09′92 (B) Presidents—U.S. [CIP]   83-23201

Over the years, publishers have issued a plethora of books about the American presidency and the 39 men who have occupied the nation's highest office. Though arguably there are dozens of men and women who have had a greater impact on American history than many of our presidents (Benjamin Franklin and John Marshall to name two), it is our presidents who seem endlessly attractive to general readers as well as scholars. The latest entry in this procession of books is *The Complete Book of U.S. Presidents*.

There are 40 chapters in DeGregorio's book—Grover Cleveland rates two separate ones as our twenty-second and twenty-fourth president. Each chapter is preceded by a full-page black-and-white reproduction of the president's portrait. The discussion of each president follows a set pattern with information on his name, physical description, personality, ancestry, father, mother, siblings, children, birth, childhood, education, religion, recreation, early romances, marriage, military service, career before the presidency, presidential nomination, opponents, campaigns and issues, election, cabinet, major events of administration, Supreme Court appointments, ranking by historians, death, quotes, and books about the president.

The volume's most attractive feature is its informal and colloquial presentation. Although organized as a reference book, it clearly is more than a source for isolated pieces of information. Each chapter gives an excellent overview of a particular president's background, achievements, and reputation. Some of the information included may seem more appropriate in a *People* magazine profile, but DeGregorio maintains his objectivity while at the same time entertaining readers.

The volume may be compared to two other currently available reference works on the presidency. Henry F. Graff's *The Presidents: A Reference History* (Scribner/see our note below) contains a biographical essay on each president, and its approach is more scholarly than DeGregorio's, and its bibliographies are superior. Joseph Kane's well-known *Facts About the Presidents* continues to be a standard in the field. In terms of the sheer mass of statistical information on each president, Kane is unsurpassed. The strength of DeGregorio is the human interest material covered. The information on physical description, personality, and early romantic interests will not be easily found in other reference works.

The Complete Book of U.S. Presidents is an informal history of the nation's presidents. Its chief virtues are a convenient arrangement and a wealth of human interest information not quickly retrievable from other reference sources. Although some of the judgments it contains on controversial matters are open to question, the factual information is generally accurate and the approach objective. DeGregorio's volume is a good source for school, public, and academic libraries.

The complete Gilbert and Sullivan opera guide. By Alan Jefferson. New York, Facts On File, 1984. 352p. 27cm. hardbound $22.95 (0-87196-857-6).

782.81′092′4 Sullivan, Arthur, Sir, 1842–1900. Operas | Operas—19th century—History and criticism [CIP]   83-20654

A delightful gift book, a perfect companion (in every sense) for G & S fans, and a "natural" for public and college library circulating collections—this charmingly illustrated "guide" probably has marginal reference potential. It is basically an album of librettos, each preceded by a creation/stage history and a synopsis, the whole preceded by perceptive front matter and followed by the briefest of disc/filmographies and a highly selective bibliography.

Builders of reference collections will want to consider the frequency and urgency of the sorts of questions put to reference staffs which this book is likely to help them answer. Do people often call to ask, "How does Josephine's song go—the one beginning, 'Refrain, audacious tar'?" *Large* reference collections (in public and academic libraries) will of course want librettos at hand—always "there," never "charged out"—of all standard operatic works—along with their complete Shakespeares, Miltons, Shelleys, Tennysons, etc. Selectors for other libraries will need to think second thoughts—their upshot being who knows what? However, there may well be smaller libraries—including secondary school libraries—that will find this book a "must"—in *both* their reference and their circulating collections: one hopes so.

The complete handbook of garden plants. [By] Michael Wright, assisted by Sue Minter and Brian Carter. New York, Facts On File, 1984. 544p. illus. (part col.) 20cm. hardcover $18.95 (0-87196-632-8).

635.9′02′02 Plants, Ornamental—Handbooks, manuals, etc. [CIP]   83-14133

The Complete Handbook of Garden Plants provides "in a pocketable (or at least easily portable) format a comprehensive guide to all the kinds of decorative outdoor garden plants . . . and the basic information needed to choose and grow such plants." Fruits, vegetables, tropical, and subtropical plants are excluded. Preface material includes a detailed map of hardiness zones, a glossary, and a list of pests and diseases with suitable treatments. Arrangement is by seven basic plant types: border and bedding perennials; bulbs, corms, and tubers; rock plants; annuals and biennials; perennial climbers; water plants; and trees and shrubs. Within each of these groupings, sections cover major botanical families, organized alphabetically. Entries for individual plants are then listed by genus, with common names in boldface. Thus, one proceeds from border and bedding perennials to Liliaceae (lily family) to the genus *Eremurus* (foxtail lilies) to five species and several hybrids and varieties. Entry information may include size (given in metric and English measurements), leaf and flower descriptions, soil and sun requirements, hardiness, season, propagation, and typical use.

This handbook has many exemplary features. A truly wide range of species are included (more than 9,000). Twenty-two artists were commissioned to do the 260 colorplates, and the illustrations for more than 2,500 plants are accurate, attractive, and nearly always face the accompanying text. A great deal of information is presented in a compact and highly organized manner. It is well designed, given the limitations of small print size and the many abbreviations necessary for a handbook format. However, there are problems in its use as an identification guide. It is not keyed to leaf and flower types; so visual identification can only be made by perusing the colorplates. One needs to know something about garden nomenclature in order to make an identification, and even then there are problems; for example, if a plant looks like a daisy, looking up the relevant family compositae in the Index will not work because only genera and common names are given, not families. If one looks up *daisy*, the pages referred to do not include the compositae under trees and shrubs; bulbs, corms, and tubers; or rock plants.

There are better books for identification and better books for encyclopedic information, but *The Complete Handbook of Garden Plants* is a well-conceived, relatively inexpensive, and sturdily bound volume which should be seriously considered by librarians and gardeners alike.

The complete social security handbook. By Bryce Webster and Robert L. Perry. New York, Dodd, Mead, 1983. 346p. 24cm. paper $12.95 (0-89696-147-8).

344.73′023 Social security—U.S.—Handbooks, manuals, etc. [CIP]   81-19443

This is an excellent guide to social security, with separate chapters on a general description of the program, benefits for the disabled, getting action from the agency, and planning for additional benefits. Five Appendixes include names and addresses for Medicare part B carriers; a list of organizations for the disabled and elderly; a feature called "The 50 Most Important Questions and Answers about Social Security"; a list of social security regional offices; and procedures, instructions, and sample forms for getting a social security card (the latter covers the Privacy Act's implication).

There are also a glossary of terms and a very good bibliography of books, magazine articles, pamphlets, federal and congressional publications and reports, and Social Security Administration publications (including the sixth edition of *Social Security Handbook*—the seventh edition of which was reviewed in *RBB,* Sept. 15, 1983). A detailed Index concludes the work.

The Complete Social Security Handbook provides information that supplements the *Social Security Handbook*; because it covers wider constituencies than the elderly and provides information in a clear, easily understood, and easily accessible way, it deserves a place in any library that deals with social security clients.

The complete word game dictionary. [By] Tom Pulliam and Gorton Carruth. New York, Facts On File, 1984. xvi, 645p. 26cm. hardcover $19.95 (0-87196-112-1).

793.73 Word games—Dictionaries | Scrabble (Games)—Glossaries, vocabularies, etc. [CIP] 84-4190

This ready reference for word-game players supplies an alphabetical list of 185,000 acceptable words drawn from standard dictionaries. Appended are four separate high-scoring word lists with a total of 45,000 words containing, respectively, the letters *J, Z, Q,* and *X.* Each group's words are subdivided by length from two to ten letters, and then each group is presented in alphabetical order, by positional order of the letter (e.g., *JUT, AJI, AJO, DJO,* etc.); and finally by scoring order of "the total Scrabble© score of all letters." The work does *not* include definitions.

The inclusiveness, recency, ease of use, and clear format of this volume give it an edge over other similar sources intended for frequent game players. Libraries, however, will probably have less use for it if they have a respectable dictionary collection. Purists should note that the book carries no "official" endorsement from any word-game producer.

Computer graphics marketplace 1983–84. John Cosentino, ed. Phoenix, Oryx, 1983. 102p. 28cm. paper $32.50 (0-89774-086-6; ISSN: 0278-2774).

†001.644'3'025 Computer graphics—Directories | Computer service industry—Directories [OCLC]

The first edition, published in 1981, contained 140 company listings; this edition lists 238 firms, plus two new indexes: a Product Index and a Geographical Index listing manufacturers by state. Company profiles include full name, address, telephone number, administrative team (chairman of the board, president, directors of marketing, sales, finance, etc.), and a product description. Founding date and number of employees are given. Sales figures or other financial data are not supplied. The Index is a listing of the names of all administrators included in the Manufacturers section.

The Product Index does not include trade names or subject analyses but is divided into three simple categories: hardware, software, and turnkey systems. Sections entitled Consultants and Services, Educational Programs, and Publications are brief. The listing of abstracts and bibliographies in the latter section provides users with little practical help. For example, the popular *Applied Science and Technology Index* (a bibliography containing thousands of references to articles on computer graphics) is not included. Neither are more specific subject indexes to the literature. A Conference and Conventions section lists meetings held in the first three quarters of 1983 and not one 1984 or 1985 meeting.

The only strength of the directory is the Manufacturers section. Librarians and people in the trade should review descriptions of other directories for computer graphic firms listed in *The Directory of Directories 1983* (Detroit: Gale, 1983) before deciding on this one.

The computer information series: the Apple index; the IBM PC index; the business computer index. Southbury, CT 06488, P.O. Box 617, Stiles Rd., B P Publications, 1983. 28cm. paper $32/6 issues (Apple): 0741-2347 ISSN; $34/6 issues (IBM PC): 0741-2355 ISSN; $38/6 issues (business computer): 0741-2363 ISSN.

†016.001'642'05 Computers—Periodicals—Indexes | Computers—Bibliography

This series provides specialized subject guides to microcomputer information by type of personal computer or on the more general topic of business microcomputers. Each bimonthly issue lists headings and subheadings alphabetically, word by word, with citations listed thereunder alphabetically. Citations include article titles, authors (where given), supplementary game material, magazine title, volume, page and date of issues, and brief annotations. The 12 to 16 magazines indexed in each guide represent current computer literature; only 3 of the titles are indexed in *Readers' Guide. See also* references are made from computer manufacturers to the names of products and also from types of hardware and software to specific names and programs. The format is easy to use and quick to skim.

With the increasing interest in computer-related materials, these indexes would be a good choice for any library serving patrons interested in personal computers or microcomputers.

Computer publishers and publications: an international directory and yearbook, 1984. 1st ed. Detroit, Gale, 1984. 379p. 29cm. hardcover $90 (0-8103-0540-2).

†016.001642 Computers—Bibliography | Publishers and publishing—Directories

This directory of English-language computer publications serves as a selection guide for booksellers and librarians and also as an informative yearbook covering new developments in the field. The book consists primarily of two alphabetically arranged chapters listing more than 600 computer periodicals and about 275 computer book publishers, mostly from the U.S., the U.K., Canada, and Australia, with a few from Ireland, Hong Kong, the Netherlands, New Zealand, and South Africa. Name, address, key personnel, representative/bestselling titles, primary audience, and other relevant data are given. For periodicals, title, publisher and address, type, brief description, circulation, price, parent company, etc., are provided. Each listing has various indexes, e.g., Index to Book Publisher by Specific Machines Covered, Index to Periodicals by Type, etc. Two other chapters are filled with recommendations for booksellers and librarians selecting publications best suited to their respective needs.

The three final chapters are indexes: Title Index: Representative and Best-selling Computer Books from Book Publishers; Who's Who in Computer Publishing; and Master Index Listing All Periodicals, Book Publishers, and Group Periodical Publishers.

A guide through this seemingly bewildering labyrinth of information is provided in the form of a very good introductory page which explains how to use the work; this is followed by an alphabetical locator Index which serves as table of contents. The directory, in this special hardbound edition for libraries, is well organized and contains a wealth of information. It will be especially useful to any librarian who, with limited funds and space, seeks to select adequate source material in this rapidly growing field. The advertising and circulation information for periodicals will surely be of use in marketing libraries.

Computers and information processing world index. Edited by Suzan Deighton, John Gurnsey, and Janet Tomlinson. Phoenix, Oryx, 1984. x, 616p. 30cm. cloth $85 (0-89774-116-1).

016.00164 Computers—Bibliography | Information science—Bibliography | Computers—Societies, etc.—Directories | Information science—Societies, etc.—Directories | Publishers and publishing—Directories [CIP] 83-6264

The goal of the *World Index* is to identify and analyze universal sources of information on computers and information processing. It is aimed at librarians, businesspersons, managers, and scholars in computer science. The work serves as both a guide to the literature and a directory of organizations and journals in computer science. It is divided into four main sections: Organizations, Reference Works, Computing Applications, and Journals.

The chapters on organizations cover 52 countries and 5 international regions. Each entry includes the name of the organization, its address and telephone number, and a brief note describing its purpose and functions. This is probably the most complete list of computer-related organizations available and one of the most valuable parts of this book.

The Journals section is also arranged by country with a list of titles alphabetically thereunder. Each entry includes title, address, frequency, price, and ISSN. An Index by journal title is included.

The sections on reference works and computing applications comprise the first guide to the literature of computer science to be published since 1974 and include abstracts of both recent and classic older materials. Entries are arranged by type of material or application and by title within each section.

In a work of this type, timeliness of the information is an important concern. This is particularly important for applications, where many of those included may already have been updated. A sample of 20 pages taken from the Computing Applications section revealed publication dates primarily between 1979 and 1981, with only two entries from 1982. As a source for information on the organizations and journals of other nations, *Computers and Information Process-*

ing World Index is excellent. It is also the only recent guide to the literature and as such is a viable purchase for large libraries dealing with computer science or international business.

A concise dictionary of law. Elizabeth A. Martin, ed. New York, Oxford Univ. Pr., 1983. 394p. 21cm. hardcover $19.95 (0-19-825399-0).

349.41′03 Law—Great Britain—Dictionaries | Law—Great Britain—Terms and phrases [CIP]   83-17323

Nine British academic and practicing lawyers have supplied clear, nontechnical definitions of about 1,500 British terms, intended "primarily for those without qualification in law." The definitions range in length from about 50 to 300 words and reflect recent British legislation. Unlike *Black's Law Dictionary*, which includes both American and English jurisprudence and gives pronunciation, *A Concise Dictionary of Law* includes only British government regulations, British agencies, e.g., *Family Division*, and British penalties for crimes, e.g., *battered child, battered wife*. American users, consulting it for comparative purposes, must be aware of British terminology (*hire purchase* for *installment buying*), because the copious cross-references do not include those from American to British usage. Well edited, it should be useful in British libraries, but less so in the U.S., except for comparative purposes or for international law collections.

The consumer protection manual. [By] Andrew Eiler. New York, Facts On File, 1984. 658p. 26cm. hardcover $29.95 (0-87196-310-8).

381′.34′0973 Consumer protection—U.S.—Handbooks, manuals, etc. [CIP]   82-1464

Drawing upon his experiences as a consumer advocate (with the Michigan Consumers Council and as consumer policy analyst for the United Auto Workers) Andrew Eiler has written a specific, helpful manual to aid buyers with problems and to help buyers avoid problems. Beginning with the purchase decision, Eiler details the procedures and safeguards that ensure consumer protection and satisfaction. He discusses laws protecting the consumer: the Federal Trade Commission Act, state deceptive sales practice laws, etc. He presents the rights and obligations of buyers and sellers and clearly details how one should proceed to ensure the action one desires, giving examples of reasonable and unreasonable expectations. He includes sample letters to use at various stages along the way and continually reiterates the importance from the very beginning of keeping documentation—keep a copy of the ad which brought you into a store, keep receipts and warranties, ask for written confirmations of verbal agreements, keep track of telephone calls and letters in trying to solve the problem, etc.

The Preface tells how to use the book; then come 75 chapters arranged in eight sections: Effective Negotiating: Combining Legal and Psychological Weapons; What You Need to Know about Consumer Protection; Fighting Deceptions and Frauds; Buying Goods: Your Rights and Obligations . . . ; Warranties: Your Rights and How to Enforce Them; Different Payment Methods: How to Protect Yourself; Consumer Credit Protections; and Suing in Small Claims Court. There are four Appendixes: State Deceptive Sales Practice Laws (state-by-state summaries giving the name of the law, what is prohibited, recoverable amounts, and special features as to notice requirements, etc.); Finding the Names of Company Officers or the Names of Businesses (one page mentioning several sources and suggesting asking your librarian); Directory of State-wide Consumer Protection Offices; and Sample Forms for Credit Transactions Prepared by the Federal Reserve Board. An Index refers one to specific subjects and includes *see* and *see also* references. The Board, however, could not find several references in the Preface to indexing. While the Preface says "check the index under 'defective products' "—there is no such entry; the closest is "*Defects: see* Magnuson-Moss Warranty Act; Uniform Commercial Code; Warranties." Under all these entries are several subheads, none specifically to defective products although the desired information will be found if one reads the textual portions cited. Also, the Preface refers to an index to specific laws; there is none—true, individual laws are mentioned by name in the Subject Index, but there is no heading which brings all of them together.

The format is pleasing; headings are in bold type and stand out well; sample letters are in italics. All is clear and easy to read. The bottom margins are extremely narrow, however, and occasionally the top margins are also. Trimming for rebinding could easily cut off a line of type.

In spite of these few problems *The Consumer Protection Manual* provides help in "understanding the basic rules that apply to consumer transactions." Its sample letters are particularly valuable; Eiler's experience allows him to zero in on what is needed and what should be avoided in all communications. If one heeds the advice given here before purchasing, one will perhaps not need all the advice on righting wrongs, but Eiler provides guidance all the way. Public libraries will want this work for their reference shelves and should also consider it for their circulating collections.

Consumer sourcebook. 2v. 4th ed. Paul Wasserman, managing editor; Gita Siegman, associate editor. Detroit, Gale, 1983. 1,427p. 29cm. cloth $148 (0-8103-0384-1).

†640.73 Commerce—U.S.—Directories | Consumer satisfaction—Bibliography | Government agencies—U.S.—Directories | Information services—U.S.—Directories | Organizations—U.S.—Directories [OCLC]   77-279

The fourth edition of *Consumer Sourcebook* has added some new materials, changed items around, and updated bibliographies, listings, addresses, etc., but remains in the Board's view a peripheral purchase, not an essential one. Many of the shortcomings noted in the Board's earlier reviews (cf. *RSBR*, Oct. 1, 1982) are still to be found: no criteria for inclusion are listed; entries are sometimes erratically classed; information is not consistently given; and while there is some subject access to organizations and agencies, it is far from complete and therefore much less helpful than it could have been. A new section, Information Centers, Clearinghouses, and Toll-Free Numbers, has been added; the other six sections remain the same. As before, the section Associations, Centers, Institutes is divided into broad subject categories (Energy Organizations, Safety Organizations, etc.); the Index to organizations (which also includes governmental listings) says there is subject access, but it is minimal; basically one must know the exact name of an organization to find it. For example, the National Rape Information Clearinghouse is in the Information Centers and Clearinghouses listings; the Rape Crisis Center is in Social Welfare and Community Service organizations under the subheading *Women;* if one looks in the Index under the word *rape*, only the Rape Crisis Center is found; neither is cited under *Women.* The Bibliography has been updated with many 1980–82 titles, but once again it is erratic in amount of information given: e.g., under *Automobiles*, of 33 titles included, 10 are annotated, 20 give prices, 2 show the number of pages, and 2 have no publication date. The continued listing of companies and trade names in one alphabet is helpful and entries have been updated, but as before, most do not include a name for consumer contacts, and there are fewer telephone numbers given than in earlier editions.

Consumer Sourcebook, 4th edition, does bring a lot of information together into one package, but because so much of it is available elsewhere, because the amount of detail is inconsistent, because the placement of entries is sometimes erratic, and because subject access is so minimal, the Board still considers it an auxiliary purchase.

Contemporary artists. 2d ed. Edited by Muriel Emanuel et al. New York, St. Martin's, 1983. 1,041p. illus. 29cm. cloth $70 (0-312-16643-5).

709′.2′2 (B) Art Modern—20th century—Bio-bibliography [CIP]   82-25048

The first edition of this authoritative biobibliography was recommended by the Board (cf. *RSBR*, Oct. 15, 1978), and this new edition continues the standard of quality set by its predecessor. The second edition covers 1,000 international painters, sculptors, and practitioners of visual performance/events selected by a distinguished advisory board. Most are living, but the editors explain that some artists deceased since World War II are included if they have "continuing influence . . . on current art activity."

A typical entry consists of brief biographical data, a mailing address, name and address of agent, and lists of all individual shows, selected group shows, collections including the artist's work, and publications by and about the artist. Many feature a statement by the artist and/or a signed analysis by an art critic as well as a black-and-white illustration of one of the artist's works.

It is unfortunate that the physical quality does not quite equal the book's contents. Paper is very thin, and print bleeds through. Gutters are so narrow that photocopying may damage the spine and rebinding will be difficult. Running heads have been omitted, an inconvenience for quick reference. Though different illustrations were chosen for this edition, they are still not of the highest quality reproduction.

The first edition with its 1,300 artists should not be discarded because the second edition was pared to 1,000 names, of which 150 are new.

Contemporary Artists will be a valuable addition to most reference collections and is nearly indispensable for libraries serving art students.

Contemporary authors: autobiography series. v.1. Dedria Bryfonski, editor. Detroit, Gale, 1984. 431p. 29cm. cloth $70 (0-8103-4500-5; ISSN 0748-0636).

†809.04 Authors—Biography [OCLC]   84-6238

Intended to complement *Contemporary Authors* by providing autobiographical information on contemporary writers of interest to current readers, the stated purpose of this new series is to "collect the autobiographical musings of contemporary authors" and to glean their statements on the "purpose of literature." Each volume will contain about 25 autobiographies of poets, novelists, dramatists, averaging from 10,000 to 15,000 words.

The publishers plan to devote a good deal of space to candid photographs supplied by authors and their families. The overall impact of these informal photographs in this first volume is rather dreary; all happy and unhappy families look alike.

This initial volume covers 23 authors, the best known being Kay Boyle, Frederik Pohl, Josef Škvorecký, and Irving Wallace. A large part of each autobiography is devoted to biographical incidents: family reminiscences, marriages, friends, first publications, and influences. Alas, far too little space is devoted to a discussion of the author's work and little attempt has been made to impose some uniformity of coverage on the authors. Paul Bowles uses his space to recount his many travels. He arrives in New York City to compose music for a Tennessee Williams play and that is all the information you get on that subject! James Purdy in his short entry frequently cites the favorable comments of others concerning his work and attacks establishment critics who have failed to recognize his genius. Erskine Caldwell gives a too long account of his life, mentioning few of his 69 publications.

Editors compiled these bibliographies and submitted them to authors for revision; U.S. and U.K. editions are noted. A bibliography of works by genre follows each entry. The reference value of the work would be increased if citations to selected book reviews of the major works and to selected criticism of an author's oeuvre were included as part of these. Attention is lavished on the Index. The editors want to show the many interrelationships between writers and thus have indexed every geographic location, significant event, personal name, and book title mentioned in the text. Thus, Bette Davis shows up by virtue of the fact that she, according to Irving Wallace's essay, wanted to play the lead in a movie that Wallace had scripted—subsequently never produced.

The impression made by the initial volume of the new set is not entirely favorable. The long, rambling entries provide little information concerning an author's work. The photographs add little value. Care must be taken in future volumes to have authors address specific topics concerning their lives, more importantly, their work. The basic idea is excellent, and the Board hopes that this series improves. However, the editors must discipline contributors so that the completed essays are more cohesive.

Conway's all the world's fighting ships 1947-1982: part I: the Western powers; part II: the Warsaw Pact and non-aligned nations. Annapolis, Marketing Dept., U.S. Naval Institute Pr., 1983. 509p. illus. 32cm. cloth $34.95 (part I); $34.95 (part II) (0-87021-923-5: set; 0-87021-418-9: pt.I; 0-87021-919-7: pt. II).

359.3'25'0904 Warships | Navies [OCLC]   82-42936

Originally published in England, this two-part volume is part of a series that will eventually cover the whole history of iron and steel warships. Volumes for 1860–1905 and 1922–46 were published in 1979 and 1980, respectively; the 1906–21 volume, which will complete the set, is in preparation. According to the Foreword, the primary aim of the 1947–82 volume is to provide a coherent overview of the post–World War II naval revolution, using newly released information (i.e., reevaluation of published information and extensive use of hitherto unavailable, unpublished sources) wherever possible. In other words, this volume improves or corrects data which may have been provided in naval annuals (e.g., Jane's Fighting Ships, 1898–) which emphasize the latest developments (often restricted in detail because of security considerations) rather than a retrospective, comprehensive picture. Part I covers the navies of the 15 NATO countries (from Belgium to West Germany) and 3 pro-Western powers (Australia, New Zealand, Japan); part II, those of the 7 Warsaw Pact and 118 nonaligned nations. The organization within each country (except for the small navies handled but briefly in part II) is presented in a standardized order: a general politico-economic, technological introduction, a statement of fleet strength in 1947, and the post-1947 classes in type and chronological sequence replete with tabular data and a design history (often with photographs and line drawings) for each class. (Canceled designs are sometimes included to throw light on a particular navy's line of development.) An Index to ships and Addenda to both parts is in part II. *Conway's* is an invaluable addition to naval reference collections of any size.

Corporate America: a historical bibliography. Santa Barbara, Calif., ABC-Clio, 1984. xii, 341p. (ABC-Clio Research Guide, no.5) 24cm. cloth $28.50 (0-87436-362-4).

016.3387'4'0973 Corporations—U.S.—History—Bibliography [CIP]   83-11232

Corporate America is a compendium of more than 1,368 abstracts of articles on American business history published from 1973 to 1982 in a wide array of economic and social science journals, selected from the database which is the basis for *America: History and Life*. Like other titles in this series, the descriptive abstracts often indicate sources used by the authors (corporation records, library collections, unpublished materials) and the presence of photographs, maps, etc. While no list of journals abstracted is given, a few titles published outside the U.S.—e.g., *Queen's Quarterly* and *Scholarly Publishing* (both Canadian), *Minerva, Economic History Review, Geography* (all from Great Britain), and some foreign-language ones—are included.

This volume is divided into ten topical chapters, each alphabetically arranged by author's name: Multinationals, Conglomerates, and Big Business; Banking, Investments, and Service Industries; Transportation; Communications; Energy; Food and Fiber; Mining; Manufacturing and Merchandising; Social Effects and Environmental Impacts; and Government Regulation and Intervention.

Excellent multiple-access Subject and Author Indexes complete the work. The likely audiences for *Corporate America* are academic, special, and larger public libraries with strong history and business/economics collections. Libraries with *America: History and Life* will need to weigh convenience/demand against cost.

The corpus administrative index. Edited by Maureen Saunders. Don Mills, Ontario, M3B 2X7, 1450 Don Mills Rd., Corpus Information Services, 1983– . various paging. 30cm. looseleaf $240 a year. (416) 445-6641 (ISSN:0703-7384).

†351'.00971'025 Canada—Politics and government—Directories

The Corpus Administrative Index is a directory of Canadian federal and provincial departments, agencies, and officers. Since 1972, it has been issued quarterly in looseleaf format; the revised pages are easily inserted in an attractive, durable plastic binder with colorful separators for the section on each province, the territories, the federal government, and intergovernmental bodies.

Each section has a list of departments with page number, an alphabetical list of officials with brief reference to their departments and telephone numbers, and then the body of information which is a directory of all departments, offices, and independent agencies including addresses as well as names, titles, and telephone numbers of officials. Regional and branch offices with addresses and telephone numbers are included for many programs and services.

Quarterly revisions appear promptly and frequently have brief addenda for changes to senior appointments announced after press deadline.

Much of the information is available elsewhere. For the federal government there is *Canadian Government Programs and Services* which is strong on descriptive information and in its currency and *Organization of the Government of Canada* (published every two years; the latest now available is 1980), and for the federal and provincial governments, the Canadian almanacs provide detailed directory-type information. However, *The Corpus Administrative Index* is possibly the most up-to-date and convenient reference tool, useful in any type of library providing information on Canada.

Crime fiction, 1749-1980: a comprehensive bibliography. [By] Allen J. Hubin. New York & London, Garland, 1984. xix, 712p. (Garland Reference Library of the Humanities, v.371) 29cm. cloth $75 (0-8240-9219-8).

016.823'0872 English fiction—Bibliography | Detective and mystery stories—Bibliography | American fiction—Bibliography | Crime and criminals—Fiction—

Bibliography | Detective and mystery plays—Bibliography | Gothic revival (Literature)—Bibliography [CIP]   82-48772

This monumental production is a revised and expanded edition of the same author's *The Bibliography of Crime Fiction, 1749-1975* (c1979; cf. *RSBR*, June 15, 1980). It lists about 60,000 titles, of which (states its Preface) nearly 6,000 are post-1975 and some 2,600 are earlier titles which the previous edition missed. Other changes include "a completely new Settings Index identifying 343 locations"; citations of discussions in standard reference works; and a selective Index to recurrent characters.

Hubin's Introduction repays careful reading: it explains not only the structure of the bibliography but its scope—what categories are included and what (regretfully) not. The bulk of the volume is an Author Index, i.e., an author/title listing, with entry under name used and with cross-references to other names used (as opposed to entry under "real" or "standard" name and cross-references from variants). Author entries include references (as noted above) to standard sources, along with miscellaneous data. Under author headings, titles are arranged alphabetically, with cross-references from variant titles. (There are thus no chronological displays of authors' outputs.) Individual title listings include reference to detectives and settings, e.g., "LA [L.A.]" for "Lew Archer, Los Angeles."

Then come four Indexes to the author/title list: Title, Settings, Series, and Series Character Chronology. The Title Index includes references from variants. The Settings Index includes, besides headings for countries, cities, etc., a few others, e.g., *Academia* and *Aircraft*: its chief curiosity is its use of the heading *England* for London, Oxford, Yorkshire, etc.—and this in sharp contrast to the specificity with which other countries are handled (cf. such headings as *Chicago, Cleveland,* and *Connecticut*). The Series Index is typified by such entries as "Avenger, The; K. Robeson" and "Poirot, Hercule; A. Christie," with, under "Sexton, Blake," references to over 100 authors, and, under "Holmes, Sherlock," references to 35. The Series Character Chronology is basically a reworking, by date of first appearance, of individuals mentioned in the Series Index, but limited to "durable" characters, defined as those "having five or more book appearances through the end of 1980." Perhaps, in another edition, Hubin will want to add an alphabetical approach to recurrent characters and an expansion of coverage to include subordinates and adversaries, e.g., Dr. Watson, Professor Moriarty, Della Street, Hamilton Burger, Captain Hastings, etc.

Crime Fiction, 1749-1980 belongs in all but the smallest public and academic libraries: it will answer a wide range of questions posed by a wide range of inquirers. Libraries aspiring to comprehensive coverage of crime fiction will find it useful in collection development. However, since it offers no descriptive or evaluative notes—and nothing to imply rankings or highlight significance—less ambitious institutions will probably find Rosenberg's *Genreflecting* (Libraries Unlimited, 1982; cf. *RBB*, Dec. 1, 1983)—or one of the many in-between tools, e.g., Reilly's *Twentieth Century Crime and Mystery Writers* (St. Martin's, 1980; cf. *RSBR*, June 1, 1981)—a more useful selection aid. This is not said in order to deprecate, in any way, Hubin's work, in so many respects a model of its kind: an achievement for all devotees of crime fiction to rejoice in, be they fans or students or both.

The critical reputation of F. Scott Fitzgerald: a bibliographical study. By Jackson R. Bryer. Hamden, Conn., Archon, 1967. xvii, 434p. 22cm. cloth $30 (0-208-00412-2).
016.813'5'2 Fitzgerald, F. Scott, 1896-1940 [OCLC]   67-24031

The critical reputation of F. Scott Fitzgerald: a bibliographical study. Supp. One through 1981. By Jackson R. Bryer. Hamden, Conn., Archon, 1983. xix, 543p. 22cm. cloth $45 (0-208-01489-6).
016.813'52 Fitzgerald, F. Scott, 1896-1940—Bibliography [OCLC]   82-25536

The 45 years since *This Side of Paradise* brought him immediate fame in 1920 saw Fitzgerald's reputation sink to near oblivion at the time of his death in 1940, followed immediately by the start of the dramatic revival of interest that in time earned him a secure position as a major writer. That period is fully documented in Bryer's 1967 study, which took its place at once as the essential Fitzgerald bibliography. The ensuing decade and a half is covered in the modestly entitled *Supplement One;* that it is a somewhat larger volume than its predecessor is itself an indication of extraordinary continuing interest in Fitzgerald.

Both books follow the same basically chronological arrangement: the first section lists reviews of Fitzgerald's books in order of their appearance; a year-by-year listing of articles about Fitzgerald comes next; lists arranged alphabetically by author follow books about (with selected reviews also cited) and graduate research on Fitzgerald. The annotations are descriptive, not evaluative, but review articles judged to be of special importance are asterisked. Each volume has a thorough, carefully constructed Index as well as a checklist of the First Appearances of Publications Containing Items by F. Scott Fitzgerald.

In view of the several films and television specials of recent years based on Fitzgerald's works, the scope of the *Supplement* was expanded to cover reviews and other material relating to stage and film adaptations both recent and early, including the silent films. The *Supplement* extends comprehensive bibliographic coverage through 1981, although a few more recent items are cited, such as the 1983 translation of André Le Vot's 1979 biography in French. It should be noted that Nancy Milford's *Zelda—A Biography* (1970) is cited in the *Supplement,* along with an ample selection of references to reviews. Also included in the *Supplement* are two new sections, a checklist of Zelda Fitzgerald's publications and a list of reviews of her *Save Me the Waltz.*

As Bryer notes in his Introduction, in the past 15 years more books by the Fitzgeralds have come into print than in their own lifetimes, and during this period Scott's books attained perennial best-seller status. Bryer's bibliographies are essential reference aids for any library supporting the serious study of our major novelists and of twentieth-century American literature and culture.

Critical survey of long fiction. 8v. Edited by Frank N. Magill. Englewood Cliffs, N.J., Salem, 1983. 3,352p., XLVIII. 24cm. cloth $350 (0-89356-359-5).
809.3 English fiction—History and criticism | American fiction—History and criticism | Novelists, English—Biography | Novelists, American—Biography [OCLC]   83-61341

The third in a projected four-part series, *Critical Survey of Long Fiction* provides brief critical essays on the long fiction (i.e., novellas and novels) of 272 "representative English-language authors, i.e., authors who regularly write in English." Thus, such writers as Nabokov appear along with American and English novelists. Other titles have covered short fiction (1981) and poetry (1982); a fourth will assess drama. In this set, as with others in the series, there are separate essays on the work of specific authors and a volume of essays on broad topics relevant to the genre.

Volumes 1 to 7 of *Long Fiction* are given over to essays on particular authors. While some authors, such as Faulkner and D. H. Lawrence, are accorded treatments of 20 pages or more, the essays on most authors average 10 pages, with most essays varying no more than 2 pages from that average. This uniformity in respect to length results in uneven treatment. For example, Jamake Highwater's three novels are covered in a 9-page essay, while Lawrence Durrell's much larger corpus of long fiction is covered in more summary fashion in the same amount of space. Each essay provides birth/death dates (and places), a list of principal long fiction, a list of works in other genres, a summary of the author's achievement, a brief biographical sketch, an analysis of the long fiction, a list of major publications other than long fiction, and a bibliography of secondary works. All essays are signed. The 170 contributors are listed in volume one. Most are from college and university literature departments; many have substantial publishing records.

In addition to the seven volumes of essays on individual authors, an eighth volume of 18 signed essays provides overviews of various aspects of the genre. The authors of these essays are listed in volume one: most are from English department faculties. Three essays cover the development of the novel from 1740, two survey the English and the American novel respectively, 14 treat special types of novels (picaresque, epistolary, etc.), and a long essay of 127 pages surveys the history and development of the novella. The volume concludes with a 13-page Glossary of literary terms and techniques and a 48-page Index to the entire set. The Index lists authors, titles, and subjects.

Unlike *Masterplots* and other such Magill publications, *CSLF* attempts a broad critical view. Essays in *CSLF* go beyond plot summaries and brief critiques of individual works and attempt to characterize the entire body of an author's fiction. Perhaps the reference works most like *CSLF* are the several parts of the Gale Literary Criticism series (*Contemporary Literary Criticism*, et al.). The Gale set, including more authors writing in many languages, attempts to give readers a flavor of the assessments by scholars through excerpts from their critical works. The Literary Criticism series provides a brief synopsis of an author's life and works but attempts no really unified assessment of his body of work. The *CSLF* series provides less critical depth in its treatment of individual authors, but its survey approach will be welcome to those desiring a source of overviews of major English-language novelists. Although it is a highly selective tool, it is a set that should see heavy use in most high school, college, and larger public libraries. Recommended.

Critical survey of poetry: foreign language series. 5v. Edited by Frank N. Magill. Englewood Cliffs, N.J., Salem, 1984. 24cm. cloth $275 (0-89356-350-1).
809.1 Poetry—History and criticism | Poetry—Bio-bibliography | Poets—Biography
[OCLC]   84-5365

Similar in format and style to other Magill critical surveys of short fiction, poetry, etc., this five-volume set covers all major poetry of the world not written in English, with emphasis on European literature.

Although each poet is discussed (in alphabetical order in the first four volumes) by a different author/specialist, a standard format and style are closely followed: place and date of birth and death; principal collections; comments on the poet's nonpoetic work; achievements; biography; analysis; major publications other than poetry (if any); and finally a bibliography. A typical entry will run to eight or more pages. The more important sections—Achievements, Biography, and Analysis—are always well done (the writer taking pains to assess the poet's achievements), while the biographical section details early influences, friendships, travels, correspondence, and other factors, which may serve to illustrate or explain the poet's life or works. The final section is made up of an essay on the poems themselves, expounding on the rhythm, or philosophy, or artistry, or whatever aspect of the poetry is significant for appreciation. All entries are signed.

Volume five consists of 27 essays on regional or national poetry, some essays being further subdivided by time periods, such as "Japanese Poetry since 1800." This last volume also contains an introductory essay on linguistics and a longer one on "The Oral Tradition." The volume concludes with a 67-page Index of Names, Titles, and Topics to all five volumes.

On the whole *Critical Survey of Poetry* is well executed, giving ample biographical and critical information concerning nearly 200 major poets of the non-English-speaking world. It will be particularly useful in public, college, and university libraries.

The Crown guide to the world's great plays: from ancient Greece to modern times. Rev., updated ed. By Joseph T. Shipley. New York, Crown, 1984. xiii, 866p. 24cm. hardcover $24.95 (0-517-55392-9).
809.2 Drama—Stories, plots, etc. | Drama—History and criticism | Theater—History
[CIP]   83-27211

The *Crown Guide to the World's Great Plays* is the second edition of a standard reference work published in 1956 as *Guide to Great Plays*. Intended for laypersons, the *Guide* offers information on approximately 750 important full-length plays, written in English or available in English translation, by Western (and three Oriental) playwrights ranging from ancient Greeks to living authors. The arrangement is alphabetical by playwright, with musical plays and a few operas rather awkwardly entered under librettist. Plays with no known authors are entered at the end of the *Guide*. For each play a synopsis and material on its significance, history, critical reaction, and prominent actors are provided. To aid readers seeking information by play title rather than playwright, the Index refers to 957 titles, including approximately 200 not treated individually in the *Guide*.

The two-page glossary of theatrical terms in the first edition has been replaced by a four-page List of Abbreviations of Organizations from the theatrical world. More importantly, a significant number of plays included in the first edition have been dropped from the current edition to make way for others. When a playwright appears in both editions, the individual plays discussed may vary, but when the same play appears in both editions, the entry is almost always unchanged.

The second edition of the *Guide*, like its predecessor, will prove useful in general reference collections where readers need concise information on a broad range of Western plays. Large reference collections may wish to retain the first edition.

Cuban literature: a research guide. By David William Foster. New York, Garland, 1985. xxxii, 522p. 23cm. cloth $72.50. (0-8240-8903-0).
016.86´09´97291 Cuban literature—History and criticism—Bibliography [CIP] 84-48099

This bibliography of Cuban literature contains approximately 7,000 unannotated items (mostly secondary sources). Books or articles in Spanish and English are arranged under 26 general reference topics and by one of the 98 authors covered. Access to the whole is via the detailed Table of Contents and the Index of Critics.

Foster's major contribution is his calling attention to many relatively unknown Cuban authors who currently are of insufficient stature to be included in standard sources. *Author* is interpreted broadly to embrace belles lettres as well as journalism and history.

In his Introduction, the compiler reveals his experience as a scholar and bibliographer and his awareness of the uniqueness of the Cuban situation and the peculiar problems it presents for bibliography, i.e., the sharp divisions since the Castro revolution. This work is the most useful, compact bibliography of Cuban literature produced to date. It is suitable for academic collections.

Cultural atlas of China. By Caroline Blunden and Mark Elvin. New York, Facts On File, 1983. 237p. illus. (part col.) 31cm. cloth $35 (0-87196-132-6).
912´.51 China—Maps | China—Historical geography [CIP]   82-675304

This beautiful book is misnamed. Much more than an atlas, it is, as the dust jacket claims, "a comprehensive survey of Chinese culture from Beijing (Peking) Man to the present" containing "75,000 words [of] text, 30,000 words [in] captions ... 58 maps specially drawn, 204 color illustrations [and] 161 black-and-white illustrations." The first part of the book covers geography and patterns of settlement. The second discusses the politics, society, and art of China from prehistory to the present day. The third part consists of thematic essays on subjects such as religion, calligraphy, and poetry.

Mark Elvin, lecturer in Chinese history at Oxford, is responsible for the text and maps, and Caroline Blunden, an authority on Chinese painting, is credited with "everything pertaining to the arts, including archeology and the selection of illustrations." The scholarly text supplemented by the voluminous captions accompanying the maps and illustrations could be read with profit by graduate students. Although coverage is strongest in history and art, the complex present is not neglected. The maps are superb and the illustrations exceptional. The well-organized and annotated Bibliography designed "for further study" could serve as a selection tool. A Gazetteer and Index complete the volume.

Because of its scholarly text, informative maps, and magnificent illustrations, the *Cultural Atlas of China* would be a suitable addition to any library serving young adults and adults interested in China.

DataMap: index of published tables of statistical data, 1984. 2d ed. Compiled by Jarol B. Manheim and Allison Ondrasik. New York & London, Longman, 1984. xvi, 1,069p. 26cm. hardcover $200 (0-582-28509-7; ISSN 0264-7745).
†310.16 Statistics—Indexes

The second edition of this computer-generated index to all tables in 29 published statistical sources is organized in three sections. Section I bibliographically identifies the 29 sources, 17 of which are U.S. government publications (e.g., *Agricultural Statistics, County and City Data Book, Sourcebook of Criminal Justice Statistics, Digest of Educational Statistics, Statistical Abstract of the United States*); 6 are United Nations' documents (*Compendium of Social Statistics, UN Statistical Yearbook, UNESCO Statistical Yearbook,* etc.); and 6 are the work of other organizations (e.g., *Commodity Yearbook, Information Please Almanac, World Almanac, Municipal Year Book*). More than 13,000 tables are indexed. By contrast, the 1983 edition indexed 28 sources containing more than 10,000 tables. Twenty-seven sources are common to both editions, but in the second edition, *Annual Survey of Manufactures* has been replaced with *Index to International Public Opinion* (adding 1,580 tables) and *State and Metropolitan Area Data Book* (142 tables). In the 1984 edition, 19 sources have been updated, usually by a year. Eight sources use the same edition—e.g., the 1979 edition of *Business Statistics* and *Handbook of Labor Statistics* and the 1977 edition of *County and City Data Book*. (Presumably the 1982 edition of *Business Statistics,* the 1983 editions of *County and City Data Book* and *Handbook of Labor Statistics*—three well-known, heavily used government documents—will be indexed in a subsequent edition of *DataMap*.) According to the Introduction, the sources selected are those thought to be most widely held and used by social scientists and reference librarians in various types of libraries.

Section II lists titles and pages of every table in each of the indexed sources. Each table is coded (AS0001 is the first table in *Agricultural Statistics*, WA0461 is the 461st—or last—table in *World Almanac*, etc.) for citation in Section III, the Subject Index. Here, as the Introduction explains, direct access is only to primary terms. To illustrate: in a table reporting fire deaths by number, percentage, age, and sex, the term "Fires—Deaths" would be assigned primary importance as the term most likely to be used to access a table; "Number," "Percentage," "By Age," and "By Sex" would be secondary terms used to summarize or describe the table but *not* used as index entries (cf. p.547).

All in all, *DataMap* is a clean, efficient index to a wide variety of social, political, economic, and other statistical data found in a variety of sources frequently held in most libraries. It is an appropriate selection for libraries with some or all of the sources indexed, although each library must determine whether the demand for statistical information justifies the convenience of this somewhat expensive reference.

Datapro/McGraw-Hill guide to CP/M software; IBM PC software; Apple software. 3v. New York, McGraw-Hill, 1983, 1984. 28cm. paper $19.95 each (0-07-015404-X: CP/M; 0-07-015424-4: IBM; 0-07-015403-1: Apple).

001.64′25 CP/M (Computer operating system) | Computer programs—Purchasing [CIP]   83-19607
001.64′25 IBM Personal Computer—Programming—Handbooks, manuals, etc. | Computer programs—Handbooks, manuals, etc. [CIP]   83-24888
001.64′2 Apple Computer—Programming | Computer programs—Purchasing [CIP]   83-23848

These guides to nongame software are designed for owners and users of microcomputers in homes or businesses. In each, software packages are arranged by application (e.g., accounting, education, graphics, word processing, text editing, etc.). Entries include vendor, machine(s) supported, operating environment, language, pricing, maintenance support, training and installation services, documentation, media format, and a full description of the program.

The guides recommend that users also consult the vendor profiles to help estimate the viability of the companies. Data provided here include number of employees, sales revenues, and the extent of their product line.

Each guide includes a Vendor Index which lists products by name under vendor, a Product Index, and a Glossary.

These guides to software should be very popular in libraries serving microcomputer owners.

Day by day: the sixties. 2v. By Thomas Parker and Douglas Nelson. New York, Facts On File, 1983. 1,115p. 34cm. cloth $90 (set) (0-87196-648-4: set; 0-87196-384-1: v.1; 0-87196-460-X: v.2).

909.82′02′02 History, Modern—1945— —Chronology [CIP]   80-22432

The *Day by Day* series aims to give quick chronological reference to specific events, as well as a broad overview of the years following 1940. These two volumes cover the 1960s, and to provide a sense of that era, entries use terminology of that time (e.g., "Negro" not "black," "Russia" not "Soviet Union"). Sources are the publisher's yearbooks, major newspapers, and other reference works.

The "Yearly Summaries" section establishes the format for the entire work. Material is given in chart form on two-page spreads with columns 1–5 (World Affairs; Europe; Africa and the Middle East; the Americas; and Asia and the Pacific) dealing with international affairs. Columns 6–10 (U.S. Politics and Social Issues; U.S. Foreign Policy & Defense; U.S. Economy and Environment; Science, Technology, and Nature; and Culture, Leisure, and Life Style) cover national affairs. The row labels are the dates. The bottom row provides content information on each column heading.

The section for each year begins with two pages of black-and-white photographs and a monthly summary in the format as described above. Following this is the day-by-day listing of events in the same format, with six days covered on each two-page spread. Entries are given in each category for each day when possible, but some days have as few as one entry.

Volume I covers 1960–64, volume II 1965–69. A 136-page Index concludes the second volume. General headings refer to U.S. events. Subject entries for foreign countries are listed under the name of the country.

Day by Day: The Sixties is a valuable tool for those interested in that turbulent decade. It will probably be of greatest use in school and public libraries.

The Democratic and Republican parties in America: a historical bibliography. Santa Barbara, Calif., ABC-Clio, 1984. xii; 290p. (ABC-Clio Research Guide) 24cm. cloth $25.50 (0-87436-364-0).

016.324273 Democratic Party (U.S.)—History—Bibliography | Republican Party (U.S.)—History—Bibliography [CIP]   83-12230

This volume of more than 1,000 abstracts—drawn from the publisher's database of citations to articles from over 2,000 journals in 42 languages—is limited to the periodical literature of 1973 to 1982 on the topic and is alphabetically arranged by the first-named author's surname. The first chapter includes a range of topics (including third parties) not necessarily falling into one of the time periods covered in chapters 2 through 5: The Emerging Two-Party System (1789–1860); The Republican Ascendancy (1860–1932); The Democratic Resurgence (1932–1960); Redefinitions and Realignments (1960–1982). Abstracts, while descriptive, frequently pinpoint the types of sources (newspapers, private papers, government documents, etc.) utilized by the author(s). Random sampling suggests that a very wide range of historical/social science journals is represented: at least six British journals, at least one each from India, Australia, Italy, USSR, and Switzerland, and many U.S. historical and political science titles.

Excellent Subject and Author Indexes direct readers to entry numbers of the abstracts. *The Democratic and Republican Parties in America* will be most useful in academic, public, and special libraries with access to an extensive variety of scholarly historical, political science, and general social science periodicals. Those libraries with the publisher's *America: History and Life* will have the coverage already and will need to weigh convenience against the cost.

Demography of racial and ethnic minorities in the United States: an annotated bibliography with a review essay. [By] Jamshid A. Momeni. Westport, Conn., Greenwood, 1983. xv, 292p. 24cm. (Bibliographies and Indexes in Sociology, no.2) cloth $35 (0-313-23975-4).

016.3058′00973 Minorities—U.S.—Statistics—Bibliography | Minorities—U.S.—Economic conditions—Bibliography | Minorities—U.S.—Social conditions—Bibliography | U.S.—Population—Bibliography | U.S.—Foreign population—Bibliography [CIP] 84-6724

Momeni's *Demography of the Black Population in the United States* (1983) was reviewed in these pages in August 1984. The present work similarly approaches the literature of other minority populations and updates its predecessor's coverage of publications dealing with blacks. Its emphasis is upon Asians, Hispanics, Jews, and native Americans. Topics covered include group status and fertility patterns, health and mortality, migration, urbanization, and population growth, to cite but a few. Entries (688 in all) are accompanied by long and authoritative annotations. The whole is preceded by a bibliographical essay and followed by Author and Minority Subject Indexes (the latter citing population group as well as topics).

History and sociology students and persons interested in the status of particular minorities will welcome this bibliography. The character of its introductory essay and of its annotations will make it useful even where there is not ready access to the literature cited. One hopes that Momeni will continue his investigations and perhaps, in another volume, not only update his existing surveys but do more with the literature of groups—chiefly from northern and eastern Europe—on which judging from the scarcity of citations thereto in its Subject Index, comparatively little is reported in the present volume.

Dictionaries: the art and craft of lexicography. By Sidney I. Landau. New York, Scribner, 1984. xiii, 370p. 24cm. hardcover $30 (0-684-18096-0).

413′.028 Lexicography [CIP]   83-27112

Landau's book is described on its dust jacket as "the first comprehensive practical guide to what dictionaries are—or should be—how they are produced, and how to evaluate, choose, and use them best." Written from an insider's viewpoint (as a lexicographer of eminence, Landau scarcely needs introducing), it should be read—and read carefully—by all would-be and practicing reference librarians, English teachers, writers, editors, and reviewers. One is likely to have one's own favorite chapter (one's "first among equals"): the Brief History, perhaps, or one of the discussions of Key Elements, Definition, Computer Use, Dictionary Making, Usage, etc., the last-named includes a particularly perceptive survey of recent usage manuals. Landau's last chapter, A Miscellany, includes a thought-provoking treatment of criticism of dictionaries, which pinpoints deficiencies in dictionary reviewing and suggests how it can be improved. For some readers, nothing will be more delightful than his Preface, in which he tells, all too briefly, of his own experience as a lexicographer. Who can fail to appreciate what Landau writes of Albert H. Marckwardt—"He was incapable of dismissing any idea without rational consideration. If it was worthless, he would get to the heart of its worthlessness swiftly, but with such clear vision that one was compelled to see its emptiness too. His criticism was deft but never hurt, because he so patently meant no hurt."

Whether *Dictionaries* belongs in their reference collections, their circulating collections, or both is something that public and academic librarians must individually decide. Basically a treatise, to be read consecutively, it is well indexed and is, to a degree, appropriately consulted at random. In addition, it has "reference features": a 21-page Critical Bibliography of Selected Monolingual Dictionaries and a 4-page Selective Bibliography of Nondictionary Sources. The former lists and describes more than 50 titles, most of them basic to public and academic library reference collections and ranging from the general to the specialized; its scope is of course less comprehensive than that of Kister's *Dictionary Buying Guide* (1977), but is broader than that of *RBB*'s recent "Desk Dictionaries: A Consumer's Guide" (cf. our issue of Dec. 1, 1983). Landau's list of "Nondictionary" sources covers secondary works, i.e., books and articles *about* dictionaries; among items listed is his own extraordinary article which appeared in these pages November 15, 1980.

The style of *Dictionaries* is, by the way, so superior to that of most professional writing as to suggest that a great many productive scholars in library and information science would do well to study and imitate Landau's rhetoric.

A dictionary of American composers. [By] Neil Butterworth. New York, Garland, 1984. xi, 523p. (Garland Reference Library of the Humanities, v.296) 24cm. cloth $75 (0-8240-9311-9).
780'.92'2 (B) Music—U.S.—Bio-bibliography [CIP]   81-43331

More than 1,000 composers of serious music are covered here, about 30 of them active mostly in the eighteenth century, 50 in the nineteenth, and the rest in the twentieth. The selection is an orthodox one that reflects solid homework; there are very few omissions or inclusions to dispute. The sketches range from a few hundred words to several thousand for Copland, Ives, and Thomson. The descriptive information is honestly stated, the opinions minimal, and the facts usually accurate. Only in a few instances is updating needed. No bibliographical references are included; nor are the compiler's sources cited, his counsel acknowledged, or his research practices and policies for presentation described in detail. Although an admirable accomplishment, one is forced to ask, "Is this book really needed?" Butterworth's compilation seems an unnecessary duplication of Charles Eugene Claghorn's *Biographical Dictionary of American Music* (West Nyack, N.Y.: Parker, 1973) or Rugh Anderson's *Contemporary American Composers* (2d ed., Boston: G. K. Hall, 1982)—both admittedly somewhat briefer in their entries. Compared to general sources more conspicuous in their authority, like the *New Grove Dictionary* (New York, London: Macmillan, 1980, for which an American version is now being prepared), or *Baker's Biographical Dictionary of Musicians* (6th ed., New York: G. Schirmer, 1978, for which a new edition has just been announced), *A Dictionary of American Composers* seems pale indeed. Only for the most comprehensive collections.

Dictionary of American medical biography. 2v. Martin Kaufman, Stuart Galishoff, Todd Savitt, editors; Joseph Carvalho III, associate editor. Westport, Conn., Greenwood, 1984. 1,027p. 24cm. cloth $95 (0-313-21378-X/set; 0-313-24333-6, v.1; 0-313-24334-4, v.2).
610'.92'2 (B) Medicine—U.S.—Biography | Public health personnel—U.S.—Biography | Healers—U.S.—Biography [CIP]   82-21110

A biographical dictionary of nearly 1,200 prominent American physicians, surgeons, and other medical personnel who lived between 1613 and 1976, the *Dictionary of American Medical Biography* is designed to extend the coverage of the classic *Dictionary of American Medical Biographies*, a 1928 publication edited by Howard A. Kelly and Walter L. Burrage. However, the scope of the present work is broader; it includes not only physicians and surgeons but also chemists, biochemists, nurses, engineers, medical manufacturers, and unorthodox medical practitioners who made significant contributions to American medicine. It also strives to include the two classes of medical people who were often ignored: blacks and women. Thus, it not only cites members of the Mayo family but also Ernest Krebs of laetrile fame; Sylvester Graham after whom the graham cracker is named; Mary A. (Baker) Eddy, the founder of Christian Science; Daniel Coit Gilman, the first president of Johns Hopkins University; George Edwin Waring, a sanitary engineer; and Relliford Stillmon Smith, a pioneer black physician in Georgia. Entries are informative and well written. Unlike the entries in Kelly and Burrage, the entries in the present work are much more standardized and the information presented therein is terse, emphasizing factual data.

An entry typically cites the place and date of birth and death, occupation and area of specialization, educational background, career highlights, contributions to medicine, and a list of writings and other references (including other biographical dictionaries) where additional information can be located. Six Appendixes present special lists (by date of birth, place of birth, state where prominent, specialty or occupation, medical college or graduate-level college, and females). There is an excellent Name-Subject Index. The *Dictionary* concludes with brief sketches of the more than 100 contributors to the work. Many are medical historians, and some are medical librarians.

The *Dictionary of American Medical Biography* is an excellent addition to medical or history of science collections.

Dictionary of American military biography. 3v. Roger J. Spiller, editor; Joseph G. Dawson III, associate editor. Westport, Conn., Greenwood, 1984. 24cm. cloth $145/set (0-313-21433-6).
355'.0092'2 (B) U.S.—Armed forces—Biography | U.S.—Biography [CIP]   83-12674

Arranged in alphabetical order by surname, this collection of biographical essays on more than 350 persons covers major events in American military history. Biographies were selected by nearly 50 American military historians who interpreted this area of our history in the widest possible sense. Thus, the volumes include native Americans, civilians, inventors, writers, educators, physicians, etc., as well as the expected generals, admirals, etc.

The essays are signed, and most are 1,500 words in length. More than 225 scholars, including historians, military and naval officers, and a few graduate students contributed essays. Each entry includes brief biographical data (place and date of birth, death, if appropriate, and career) followed by a narrative of the subject's career. The final part contains the author's own evaluation of the importance of the subject in U.S. military history. Short selective bibliographies are given for each subject; numerous cross-references are included.

Volume 3 includes six Appendixes: Chronology of American Military Developments (through 1975), American Military Ranks, Military Units, Persons by Birthplace, Entries by Conflict, and Entries by Service. There is also an Index and an alphabetical list of contributors and brief credentials.

The editors (Roger Joseph Spiller, an American military historian, and Joseph Green Dawson III, a specialist in American history) have compiled a collection of essays that will serve those who require only brief information and evaluation of persons who have played important roles in our military history. Those desiring in-depth information will need to consult other resources, but the bibliographies included in these volumes can serve as a guide. For large public and academic libraries which have requests for this type of information.

Dictionary of animals. Consultant editor, Michael Chinery. New York, Arco, 1984. 379p. illus. (col.) 27cm. cloth $17.95 (0-668-06155-3).
591'.03'21 Animals—Dictionaries [CIP]   84-716

Insects, birds, amphibians, mammals, and earthworms are all included in this concise, colorful, and well-written encyclopedic dictionary. Beginning with *aardvark* and ending with *zorille*, users can find brief information on more than 2,000 species. Many of the entries have full-color illustrations; both drawings and photographs are used. Entries are brief and informative; they are written in language easily comprehended by laypersons. The technical names for the order, the family, and the species are given at the end. There are also some special features—set off by colored background and boxes—under such general terms as *apes, camouflage, hibernation, parasite,* and *scavengers*. The tight binding prevents the book from lying flat; this may eventually cause the spine to break even though the binding appears to be very durable. *Dictionary of Animals* is one of the better animal dictionaries available for family use; it will also be an excellent reference for high school and public libraries. The editor has been writing about nature for nearly 20 years; *The Family Naturalist* (Macdonald), *The Natural History of the Garden* (Collins), and *Nature All Around* (Purnell) are among his many works.

Dictionary of business and economics. Revised and expanded edition. [By] Christine Ammer and Dean S. Ammer. New York, Free Press, 1984. x, 507p. 24cm. cloth $29.95 (0-02-900790-9).

330′.03′21 Economics—Dictionaries | Business—Dictionaries [CIP]   83-48175

The original edition of this subject dictionary received favorable comment in these pages (*RSBR*, Apr. 15, 1979), and this new edition continues to provide clear, jargon-free definitions suitable for use by general users, business administration students, and economists. It is the only recent dictionary that defines both economic and business terms.

Easily understood and well-produced charts and graphs provide the needed illustrated dimension for many explanations. Brief biographies of important economists emphasize their theories. Many entries include cross-references. Included in the longer discussions are references to books, although bibliographical data are incomplete. However, complete bibliographic information is provided in the Selected Bibliography that ends the work.

This work contains more definitions (over 3,000) than *The McGraw-Hill Dictionary of Modern Economics* (New York: 1973) and should be more useful to users having a general interest in the subject. However, the two complement one another, and large public and academic libraries should have both.

Dictionary of business biography: a biographical dictionary of business leaders active in Britain in the period, 1860–1980, A–C. Stoneham, Mass., Butterworths, 1984. xxxi, 878p. 25cm. cloth $185, $925/set (0-406-27340-5/set: 0-406-27341-3/v.1).

650 Businessmen—Great Britain—Biography—Dictionaries [OCLC]

Produced by the London School of Economics, this projected five-volume set will be a biographical dictionary of business leaders active in Britain for the period noted. The volumes will be issued about once every six months and will include some 1,000 biographies. The first volume contains about 250 entries. Contributors include academicians, business leaders, editors of business-related publications, and archivists.

The biographies are signed and arranged in alphabetical order and range from two pages to more than six. All articles include lists of both published and unpublished sources of information, and some include black-and-white portraits of biographees and lists of their publications.

In selecting subjects for this set, the compilers have provided a wide coverage of the whole spectrum of business in the United Kingdom. Based on the evidence of the first volume, coverage and quality of the entries will make *Dictionary of Business Biography* an excellent source for individuals beginning research in British business history. The cost and specialized nature of the set, however, will make it attractive primarily to large business research collections that emphasize business history.

Dictionary of computing. Oxford, Oxford Univ. Pr., 1983. x, 393p. 24cm. cloth $34.95 (0-19-853905-3).

001.64′03′21 Computers—Dictionaries | Electronic data processing—Dictionaries [British CIP]

This title is similar in coverage and format to *Dictionary of Computing* by Galland (cf. *RBB*, November 1, 1983). Both volumes have been compiled by computer practitioners in the U.S. and U.K. While *Galland* seems written for the serious data-communications and computer student, the *Oxford* product suggests a broader coverage than just computers. Its more than 3,750 *A–Z* terms include such related fields as communications, law, electronics, mathematics, and logic. The definitions for the same terms in each book may vary in length; and although several entries appear in both texts, some computer/communications words (e.g., *teleconferencing*) are to be found only in the *Oxford*. Galland concludes with conversion tables that underscore its practical approach. The *Oxford* could be studied by the beginner who has just pruchased a computer, although serious students or practitioners will find it useful as well.

There is some duplication between the two titles, but both can complement each other in a reference or circulating collection. If a library can afford to purchase only one title, *Galland* is probably better for more specialized collections; *Oxford*, with its somewhat broader coverage, may be more suitable for general reference.

Dictionary of computing and new information technology. 2d ed. by A. J. Meadows et al. New York, NY 10024, P.O. Box 96, Nichols for Kogan Page (London), 1984. 229p. 21cm. cloth $24.50 (0-89397-197-9).

001.5′03′21 Electronic data processing—Dictionaries | Telecommunications—Dictionaries | Office practice—Automation—Dictionaries [CIP]   84-4874

Dictionary of Computing and New Information Technology lists more than 3,000 terms in the areas of computers, telecommunications, information storage and retrieval, expert systems, and online databases. It is oriented toward nonspecialists who, nevertheless, have either interest or expertise in some aspect of information technologies. Entries are arranged letter by letter, and the definitions for the terms are concise, well written, and generally informative. Many entries go beyond providing brief definitions by including relatively extensive information on the topic. Cross-references both explicit and implicit are ample. For instance, italicized words within definitions indicate that those terms are entries themselves.

This dictionary differs from other computer dictionaries in its emphasis on information science. For instance, it has as entries such terms as *journal*, *Ringdoc*, *TOXLINE*, and *World Patents Index*, *TAXADVISOR*, *MYCIN*, and *Dendral*. It also lists various information centers and vendors, e.g., *INIS* (International Nuclear Information Service), *INSPEC* (Information Services: Physics, Electrical and Electronics, and Computers and Control), *Lockheed*, and *BCPA* (British Copyright Protection Association).

There are, of course, areas where the dictionary could be improved. For instance, *OCLC* ceased to be Ohio College Library Center in 1977, and it currently means Online Computer Library Center, Incorporated. *Libris* is defined as a "teleordering" system—which is true in Britain (where the dictionary was first published)—but the American counterpart is an online acquisitions system. Some terms could have more definitions—e.g., *CAS* stands for, among others, Chemical Abstracts Service, and some terms have been omitted, e.g., *full-text searching*, *menu-driven systems*, *communication processor*, and *multi-tasking*. There are some stylistic inconsistencies. For example, *BATAB* and *LIBRIS* are centered as if they were not acronyms.

Despite these criticisms, the dictionary has much to contribute to information technology.

A dictionary of drug abuse terms and terminology. By Ernest L. Abel. Westport, Conn., Greenwood, 1984. 187p. 24cm. cloth $29.95 (0-313-24095-7).

362.2′93′0321 Drug abuse—Dictionaries [CIP]   83-22865

Ernest Abel, research scientist at the Research Institute in Buffalo, New York, and author of three previous drug-related books, offers this source on the premise that "language carries cultures." Dealing with words that have resulted from the subcultures that naturally form in the world of drug users and abusers, this comprehensive dictionary defines more than 3,700 slang and formal terms "pertaining to drugs, drug use, drug vendors, drug effects, legal enforcement of drug laws, and other related aspects of drug manufacturing, selling and use." Entries, arranged alphabetically in boldface, apply to the use of illicit drugs as well as the misuse of medically approved drugs. Terms unique to sex, race, or area of the country are included, but they are not labeled. A short (often just one or two words) precise definition is provided for each entry; formal terms requiring more explanation have an adequate paragraph. Cross-references are used throughout.

As etymology is almost impossible to determine with most slang terms, only a few entries have any reference to origin. Abel states that the vast number of alcohol- and tobacco-related terms have been omitted unless extremely common.

A Glossary, presenting more than 125 terms, most of which are located in the text, and a short Bibliography are included for further reference. This compact dictionary will become a valuable source for public and school libraries and anyone whose work requires knowledge of drug-related terms.

A dictionary of eponyms. 2d ed. [Compiled by] Cyril Leslie Beeching. London, England, Clive Bingley; dist. by Shoe String, 1983. 214p. 22cm. cloth $17.50 (0-85157-329-0).

920′.02 Biography | Eponyms | English language—Eponyms—Glossaries, vocabularies, etc. [British CIP]

Claiming to list "well over a hundred eponyms" not covered in its first (1979) edition and to have amended a few 1979 articles, the second edition of *A Dictionary of Eponyms* explains, in 400 numbered entries, words derived from the names of real persons, e.g., *peach melba, salmonella,* and *teddy bear.* The 400 articles explain more than just 400 eponyms, as there are several "clusters," e.g., *Hansen's bacillus* and *Hansen's disease* are both covered in number 164. Discussions are literate, and some are mildly amusing; they are also informative, with connections between persons and eponyms spelled out in considerable detail. The result is a book ideal for individual purchase and for circulating collections of school, public, and academic libraries—and of possible value in their reference collections, the problem, from a reference service point of view, being its extreme selectivity (the rationale for which is, though stated, not very clear and is in any case not likely to be recalled by one who consults only occasionally); it is difficult to predict what awaits discovery and what does not. For this reason, many reference librarians will prefer to rely on Ruffner's *Eponyms Dictionaries Index* (Gale, 1979), which covers some 33,000 eponyms and, though it says very little about each, cites sources of further information. A check of Beeching's *A, B,* and *C* sections against the 1981 *Webster's Third New International Dictionary* suggests that 80 percent of Beeching's eponyms are explained, albeit less fully, in the latter tool. (No count was made of eponyms listed in Webster but *not* in Beeching.) Perhaps Beeching will want to consider, in a third edition (sure to be demanded), a considerable expansion—at *least* a doubling—in coverage.

The dictionary of historic nicknames: a treasury of more than 7,500 famous and infamous nicknames from world history. [By] Carl Sifakis. New York, Facts On File, 1984. xvii, 566p. 26cm. hardcover $29.95 (0-87196-561-5).

920'.02 Nicknames | Biography [CIP]   82-15430

"Nicknames can be pithy word portraits of a man, his era and indeed ourselves, depending on how we use them." So declares the former crime reporter and author of *The Encyclopedia of American Crime,* whose collection of nicknames of historic figures from the pharaohs to Hank Aaron is more selective than Jennifer Mossman's *Pseudonyms and Nicknames Dictionary* or Harold S. Sharp's four-volume *Handbook of Pseudonyms and Personal Nicknames.* It differs from these recent sources by adding brief identifications for each name which vary in length from a few lines for James Couzens (1872-1935, *The Croesus of the Senate, The Poor Man's Friend*) to 26 lines for Jeremy Bentham (*The Father of Utilitarianism*). No sources are cited so there is no authority for the comment on Sarah Bernhardt (*The Divine Sarah*): "She is credited with having had more than 1,000 lovers." There are many other colorful figures— Texas Guinan (*Queen of the Speakeasies*) and *The Flying Monk,* as well as the staider Sarah Josepha Hale (*The Mother of Thanksgiving*). An Index to categories or vocations lists a large number of literary, religious, and political figures; there are many from the world of crime, with fewer businessmen and industrialists, astronauts and aviators. Rulers, nobility, and musicians are well represented. Unless the nickname is better known (e.g., *Tex Guinan*), all are listed by real name, with *see* references from nicknames; all are in pleasantly large type which sets the entries apart from the text.

Just as the compiler makes no claims to completeness, he notes in his informative introduction on the nature of nicknames, that some origins or meanings of certain sobriquets will be disputed. But the wide selection and lively text recommend this stoutly bound, well-printed volume for use in academic and public libraries.

Dictionary of historical terms: a guide to names and events of over 1,000 years of world history. [By] Chris Cook. New York, Peter Bedrick; dist. by Harper, 1983. 304p. 23cm. hardcover $15.95 (0-911745-16-5).

903'.21 History—Dictionaries [CIP]   83-13377

The author's stated goal is to include the most frequently used historical terms, worldwide, in one volume. For foreign terms, the language of origin is indicated as well as the translation of the term. The length of the definitions ranges from very brief to extensive. The background of the term and its use in a historical context is discussed.

Arrangement is alphabetical with cross-references included. Researchers and history students will find *Dictionary of Historical Terms* a valuable personal reference book, and it will also be a good addition to library reference collections serving such a clientele.

Dictionary of library and educational technology. 2d ed. rev. and expanded. By Kenyon C. Rosenberg with the assistance of Paul T. Feinstein. Littleton, Colo., Libraries Unlimited, 1983. vii, 185p. 24cm. cloth $24.50 (U.S.); $29.50 (elsewhere) (0-87287-396-X).

621.38'044 Audio-visual equipment—Catalogs | Audio-visual equipment—Dictionaries [CIP]   83-19641

A revised and updated version of *Media Equipment: A Guide and Dictionary* (1976), this volume is designed for users of all kinds of library and educational technology. This revision has been expanded to include coverage of micrographic and reprographic equipment as well as computer hardware and software and software equipment. The authors reflect this broad spectrum of technology with their backgrounds in electronics, engineering information, teaching, and instructional technology. Both are affiliated with the National Technical Information Service.

The major portion of the book consists of an alphabetically arranged dictionary of nearly 800 terms including definitions of equipment, specifications, processes, and the like. Definitions range from several sentences to one-half page in length. Terms used in definitions which are also separate entries are highlighted in darker type; *see* references are also provided.

The volume also includes a 30-page narrative on criteria for selection, arranged by type of equipment. A selective Bibliography covering general topics, audiovisuals, computers, microforms, photography, television, and word processing concludes the volume.

Because of the increasingly heavy use of technology by almost all kinds of libraries, *Dictionary of Library and Educational Technology* should be useful in almost any reference collection.

Dictionary of medieval civilization. [By] Joseph Dahmus. New York, Macmillan, 1984. viii, 700p. 24cm. cloth $60 (0-02-907870-9).

909.07'03'21 Civilization, Medieval—Dictionaries [CIP]   83-25583

A fairly bare-bones dictionary of persons, places, and things medieval, covering 12 centuries (A.D. 300–1500), this is a useful volume which, according to its Preface, contains "no original analyses" and in which the definitions will "strike the informed reader as conventional."

Coverage of topics is good, based on a judicious balance between "what would suffice for the majority of readers" and the limitations of space in a book of only 700 pages.

Entries range in length from two or three lines to a full, double-column page or more, for topics such as *Church and State; Papacy, History of,* and the like. But the majority of entries consist of 10 to 20 lines, sufficient to identify the person, place, or thing, to ascribe dates, and (usually) to relate the topic to other persons or events. The greatest number of entries (about 70 percent) are for persons; places, such as the *Cinque Ports, Llandaff, Salonica,* make up about 15 percent; and the remainder refer to such medieval ideas or objects as *Misericord, Pipe Rolls,* or *Sicilian Vespers* that students might run across in their reading and need to identify briefly or clarify.

There are no pronunciations, and very few etymologies are given. The latter are likely to be sorely missed by scholars and others interested in word derivation.

On the whole, *Dictionary of Medieval Civilization* is well done and will find ready acceptance in academic and public libraries, especially those with a readership oriented toward history.

The dictionary of modern economics. Rev. ed. General editor, David W. Pearce. Cambridge, Mass., MIT Pr., 1983. 481p. 24cm. paper $12.50 (0-262-66051-2).

†330'.03 Economics—Dictionaries [OCLC]   83-42516

This revised and updated edition was originally published in Britain by Macmillan. The general editor and most of the contributors are from the University of Aberdeen or other Scottish universities. Designed to lead the "average undergraduate" beyond the "conventional first year economics course," to provide "coverage of the words and phrases, concepts and institutions that a first year student might want, and more," the 2,500 entries include single words (e.g., *collusion*), phrases (*life-cycle hypothesis*), institutions (*International Development Association*), laws (*Gresham's Law, Clayton Act*), and biographies of both living and deceased economists. Definitions range from brief one-sentence identifications to longer discussions of over three columns. All are generally clear and understandable, sometimes including formulas and diagrams, and frequently citing important publications. There are *see* references for synonymous terms, and, at the end of many entries, to related terms. Terms used in a definition which are themselves entries are printed in italics. Alphabetization is letter by letter, a change from the word by word of the 1981 edition. Spelling is generally British: e.g., American Federation of Labo*u*r, program*me* budgeting. No pronunciations are given. While one can always think of terms not found, the combination of words and biographies presents students with comprehensive coverage of the field from classic to modern. This will be most useful in academic libraries, but any public or special libraries whose clientele is working in economics will also find this helpful.

A dictionary of mottoes. [By] L. G. Pine. London, Routledge & Kegan Paul, 1983. xiii, 303p. 24cm. cloth $12.95 (0-7100-9339-X).
080 Mottoes—Dictionaries [CIP]   82-21463

This work deals with the first three definitions of *motto* in the *Concise Oxford Dictionary*: a "sentence inscribed on some object and expressing appropriate sentiment; a word or sentence accompanying a coat of arms or crest; [or a] maxim adopted as rule of conduct...." The vast majority here have been taken from the second category. The author, a genealogist, lists the motto, gives translations as necessary (Latin was much favored for mottoes), and occasionally adds explanatory notes, and then gives the name of the family, military unit, or other institutional body which has adopted the motto. There is an Index of Names of those associated with the mottoes. *Dictionary of Mottoes* is probably of interest only to comprehensive collections in British history and genealogy.

A dictionary of pictorial subjects from classical literature: a guide to their identification in works of art. [By] Percy Preston. New York, Scribner, 1983. xxii, 311p. illus. 24cm. cloth $39.95 (0-684-17913-X).
704.9'47'0938 Mythology, Classical, in art | Mythology, Classical—Dictionaries [CIP]   83-4470

The subtitle of this work is probably more indicative of its potential usage in a reference collection than the title. Following generally along the line of earlier works on Christian iconography, such as Bles' *How to Distinguish the Saints in Art*... (1925), this work covers classical mythology in a similar way. Given certain objects or symbols in a painting, such as a book, a hearth, a horse, a river, a snake, etc., one can, by use of this dictionary, identify the person(s) depicted, or the myth exemplified, in the painting or mosaic. Each symbol listed is briefly explained, and the classical writer (Aristophanes, Seneca, Vergil, etc.) whose story best narrates the event is cited, with chapter and verse as appropriate.

A single brief example wil suffice to show the operation of the alphabetical listings: "Hearth (see also Fire; Stick) Attribute of Hestia; Vesta. Penelope sits at the hearth with a beggar whom she does not recognize as her husband Odysseus (Od. 19.53f)."

Literary citations are abbreviated (*Met.*; *Ars Amat.*, etc.), but there is a "List of Works Cited" explaining them. There is no index, but a brief bibliography is provided.

Classical scholars, art librarians, museum directors, and others who have to deal with or explain classical or Renaissance paintings, tapestries, mosaics, and the like, will find that *A Dictionary of Pictorial Subjects from Classical Literature* fills a long-felt need.

A dictionary of symptoms: a medical dictionary to help sufferers, by easier self-diagnosis, to eliminate groundless fears and to know when to consult their doctor. By Joan Gomez. New York, Stein and Day, 1983. viii, 312p. 24cm. hardcover $16.95 (0-8128-2887-9).
616.07'2 Medicine, Popular | Symptomatology—Dictionaries [CIP]   82-42525

Librarians wary of medical reference tools which emphasize "self-help" at the expense of "doctor knows best" will be reassured by Gomez: explicit as to what to look for and what it might mean, she is, nevertheless, quick to say that one must consult one's physician or dentist. Her approach is interesting: a brief Table of Contents refers one not to the "real" text but to a second finding aid (called part I—Table of Symptoms) which, for the most part, anticipates the organization of part II—Analysis of Symptoms (where the full data display is provided). A Glossary and an Index conclude the book. Part II—its heart—is strong, as one would hope it would be, in symptoms and what they may mean; and it features a plain—and occasionally witty—style. Many sentences are, however, of telegraphic terseness, and some suggest lack of proper editing, e.g., "Even in childhood, males predominate among adults." Layout could also be better: hanging indentation would have clarified many pages. Despite obvious efforts to update, e.g., use of small type to squeeze in the latest on venereal complaints, revision is not extensive; and there are still lags in respect to descriptions of treatments, e.g., under arteriosclerosis no reference to bypass surgery or to angioplasty.

Despite shortcomings, Gomez' book is one which public libraries—and some academic and special libraries—should consider. S. S. Miller's *Symptoms: The Complete Home Medical Encyclopedia* (Crowell, c1976) may, however, prove more useful, despite its age, in most reference situations: its prose is more "eased out," hence more readable; its explanations are fuller, its page layout better, and its use of illustrations more effective. An alternative (and up-to-date) source which should be considered is Lendon Smith's *Feed Yourself Right* (McGraw-Hill, c1983), which is stronger than *Gomez* or *Miller* on nutritional aspects of health and disease and which features many entries under symptom, e.g., "Cold Hands and Feet"—though it is not so consistently symptom-oriented, nor is it so nearly comprehensive in coverage.

Directory of federal technology resources 1984: expertise, services, and facilities available to engineers, scientists, and technology oriented businesses. Prepared by the Center for the Utilization of Federal Technology. U.S. Dept. of Commerce, National Technical Information Service, 1984. PB84–100015/TCY. 137p. plus indexes 28cm. paper $25 (ISSN: 0747-7880).
†620.0025 Laboratories—U.S.—Directories | Engineering—Research—U.S.—Directories | Federal government—U.S.—Directories [OCLC]   84-644400

Compiled to promote the sharing of technological advances between the federal government and private industry, the approximately 800 federal laboratories and engineering centers selected for description in this directory "offer a variety of know-how and services." Introductory statements point out that although there may be restrictions on use of technology developed by some agencies, the research centers included have shown a desire to share their knowledge and expertise. Notification of studies completed by or for many of the research centers included is usually distributed through the National Technical Information Service and is indexed and described in the *Government Reports Announcements and Index*.

This directory helps locate addresses, telephone numbers, directors, and information officers. The major section, Resource Summaries, is divided into 23 categories from aeronautics and aerodynamics to transportation. Facilities are listed alphabetically thereunder and their research activities and services are described. A Subject Index provides more specific access, and a Geographic Index lists research centers by state. An alphabetical list of all entries concludes the work.

In order to keep this directory current, the editors plan revisions every two years and suggest the possibility of providing online access. The *Directory of Federal Technology Resources 1984* should be popular in research or business libraries. It supplements locational information found in the publisher's *Government Reports Announcements and Index* and the *Research Centers Directory* (Gale, 1960–).

Directory of financial aids for minorities, 1984–1985. By Gail Ann Schlachter. Santa Barbara, ABC-Clio, 1984. xiv, 305p. 29cm. hardcover $35 (0-87436-371-3).
378'.3'02573 Minorities—Scholarships, fellowships, etc. [CIP]   83-21226

Because available scholarship directories "rarely cover more than a few programs designed primarily or exclusively for minority groups," this directory was brought into being; it is scheduled to appear biennially. Programs are listed under six categories: Scholarships, Fellowships, Loans, Grants, Awards, and Internships. Under each are the same subdivisions: Minorities in General, Asian Americans, Black Americans, Hispanic Americans, and Native Americans. More than 800 programs/organizations are listed alphabetically in each subdivision with addresses, telephone numbers, and short paragraphs describing the purpose, eligibility requirements, duration, and limitations, etc., of each program.

"State Sources of Information on Educational Benefits" identifies state agencies providing financial aid and the organizations in each state administering the Guaranteed Student Loan Program. Each section is alphabetical by state. The "Annotated Bibliography of General Financial Aids Directories" includes sources on internships/work-experience programs, as well as the standard grant directories. It also, rather inexplicably, includes the guides to entering contests by Alan Gadney—scarcely of interest to the presumed audience of this work, i.e., college and graduate-school-bound minority students. Program Title, Sponsoring Organization, Geographical, Subject, and Calendar Indexes complete the work; the latter are keyed to the arrangement of the body of the work identifying the months in which applications are due for specific programs.

The *Directory of Financial Aids for Minorities, 1984–1985* will be beneficial in any high school, public, or college library serving minorities.

Directory of food and nutrition information services and resources. Edited by Robyn C. Frank. Phoenix, Ariz., Oryx, 1984. vi, 287p. 28cm. paper $74.50 (0-89774-078-5).

641'.072073 Food—Information services—U.S.—Directories | Nutrition—Information services—U.S.—Directories [CIP] 83-42505

This directory covers a variety of information sources: 627 organizations; 61 databases; 102 microcomputer software programs; more than 180 journals and newsletters; 19 abstracts, indexes, and current awareness services; more than 400 producers of books, audiovisuals, and microcomputer software; more than 140 key reference books on food, human nutrition, and food service management; and regional, state, and area agencies and organizations. The latter are listed first by government agency (general, agricultural, and health and human services) and then by private organizations. Tables of nutrient values and three Indexes (Subject, Organization, and Geographic) conclude the work.

Organizations are numbered and arranged alphabetically. Address, contact person, purpose, geographic area served, eligible clientele, audience, area of interest, service, and (when appropriate) educational program and degree(s) offered are included. The section on databases discusses six major services and then lists databases with producers, addresses, telephone numbers, contacts, and distributors, followed by information subject areas, food and human nutrition subjects, database size, source documents indexed, thesaurus/search aids, corresponding print products, and systems/vendors. Microcomputer software is grouped under nine subjects, and each entry includes producer/distributor, with address, telephone number, and contact; host system; source language(s); sales condition(s); audience; documentation; and description.

Directory of Food and Nutrition Information Services and Resources is an excellent resource for food/nutrition or related subject collections in libraries.

Directory of online databases. Santa Monica, Calif., Cuadra, 1979– . v. 28cm. paper $75 annual subscription (ISSN:0293-6840).

†001.644'04'025 On-line bibliographic searching | Information storage and retrieval systems [OCLC] 79-54776

For years Cuadra Associates has been advocating broader perspectives on the use of online databases than just the bibliographic ones which have been heavily used by many libraries. One of their more effective means of broadening awareness of these "nonbibliographic" databases (as librarians sometimes call them—Cuadra prefers to not use that term) has been the publication since 1979 of *Directory of Online Databases*.

The Introduction to the directory defines *online databases* as "computer-readable collections of data" that are "available for interactive access by users from remote computer terminals." In 1,546 entries (in the Fall 1983 edition), the directory covers 1,878 databases and files within database families. It groups them into two principal types, reference and source. Reference databases are further divided into bibliographic and numeric, and source databases into three categories: numeric, textual-numeric, and full text. Each database description in the directory includes (in addition to type) subject, producer, online service which makes the database available (i.e., vendor), conditions or requirements for gaining access to the database, the language or languages used in the database, geographic coverage, time span covered, and the frequency with which new information is added. Descriptions of contents are mostly quite full, one or more paragraphs in length. The scope of the directory is worldwide.

Following the main portion of the directory, there is a directory of database producers and online services. Several indexes conclude the work: a Subject Index which lists databases under broad rather than narrow headings (e.g., *coffeeline* under "Agriculture" but not under "Coffee"); an Index which lists, for producers, the databases they compile; one which lists, for online services, the databases they provide; one which lists the telecommunications systems which provide access to the online process; and a Master Index to databases, database producers, and online services. An annual subscription to the *Directory of Online Databases* not only includes the semiannual directory issues (published in spring and fall), each of which replaces all previous issues, but also two interim update issues which cover new and revised information. A pocket is provided at the back of each main directory for its update issue. Considering the excellent layout, the frequency of updating, and the importance of the subject, this directory represents perhaps the best investment for libraries which are active users of online databases or that may have business, professional, or home users involved in online information retrieval.

In comparison, *Online Bibliographic Databases* (3d ed.; Aslib, 1983), by James L. Hall and Marjorie J. Brown, covers only 179 databases and gives briefer information about each, while Martha Williams' *Computer-Readable Databases: A Directory and Data Sourcebook* (Knowledge Industry Publications, 1982), which covers 773 databases, primarily bibliographic ones, has an unappealing, awkward format.

The directory of software publishers: how and where to sell your program. Edited by Eric Balkan. New York, Van Nostrand, 1983. ix, 310p. 29cm. hardcover $25.50 (0-442-21429-4).

338.7'610016425'02573 Computer service industry—U.S.—Directories [CIP] 83-6730

The introductory chapters concern marketing techniques for selling software packages to publishers and stress the importance of an easily understood manual. Legal protection and copyright are addressed, and, for those unable to locate a publisher or not wishing to use one, there is advice on selling directly to users.

The heart of the directory is information gleaned from questionnaires sent to software producers and returned to the author between January 1981 and January 1983. Publishers responded to 17 questions designed to reveal their business profiles and program requirements; the resulting data from 150 companies is arranged alphabetically by company name, along with address, telephone, and a contact person/department. A "Quick Reference Section" matches specializations ("North Star," "Oasis") hardware with companies seeking software programs for them. Additional Company Listings provides name, address, and telephone number for several software publishers, with an identification of the hardware for which the company markets software.

The editor, a consultant working in the industry and former editor of the *Computer Consultant Newsletter*, inserts an important disclaimer concerning the questionnaire: "The questions varied from time to time, so not all companies have answered all questions." There is also no complete index.

The Directory of Software Publishers is a useful guide for freelance programmers. It surely will be of interest particularly to public libraries in this age of personal computers.

Directory of United States traditional and alternative colleges and universities. By Jean-Maximillien de La Croix de Lafayette. Washington, DC 20016, 3843 Massachusetts Ave., NW, NASACU/ACUPAE, 1984. xviii, 476p. 28cm. paper $30 + shipping/handling.

†378.73'025 Universities and colleges—U.S.—Directories | Non-formal education—U.S.—Directories 83-73182

This directory identifies schools that offer legitimate degrees but do not necessarily have accredited, traditional programs. Schools are listed alphabetically according to a "National Survey and Reliable Sources." Thus, under North Carolina appears a list of Public Institutions, Religious Institutions, and one of Colleges and Universities Legally Empowered to Grant Academic Degrees. Since many states do not approve/license schools, the authority for listing institutions "legally empowered" is unclear.

There are 23 chapters. These discuss variously such topics as accreditation, alternative education, education in the military, and honorary degrees. Schools listed are rated on traditional and nontraditional programs, with no explanation of the assessment procedure. Later editions are to list schools with optional attendance and those without campuses.

The scope of this directory is extremely broad; the result is inadequate depth. It is often difficult to distinguish quoted material, of which there is a great deal, from original. The style of the latter is often subjective.

Listings are not complete; definitions of categories are imprecise; and information on institutions is often limited. A particular school can only be found in the Index under such a heading as *nontraditional programs*. Although this book offers information not readily available elsewhere, it is such a mélange of data with such poor access mechanisms that one is apt to miss the wealth of facts therein. Better focused, less idiosyncratic future editions, based on an authoritative and fully described information-gathering process, could make *Directory of United States Traditional and Alternative Colleges and Universities* a valuable complement to standard directories of colleges and universities.

Discipline in our schools: an annotated bibliography. Compiled by Elizabeth Lueder Karnes, Donald D. Black, and John Downs. Westport, Conn., Greenwood, 1983. ix, 700p. 24cm. cloth $49.95 (0-313-23521-X).
016.3715 School discipline—U.S.—Bibliography [CIP]   83-12847

Designed "to provide educators with the most comprehensive source of information available regarding social behavior problems and discipline in American schools," this bibliography is indeed timely.

The work is divided into four categories (Books, Dissertations and Papers, Journal Articles, and School District Publications and Nonprint Materials) and provides 1,642 annotated citations. Most of the items date from the 1970s and appear alphabetically by author, except in the last section where they appear by name of the particular school board or district. Standard bibliographic information is provided. Author and Subject Indexes cite item numbers; the latter has fairly broad terms as entries, resulting in, e.g., over 200 members listed under *Elementary School Students*. Thus, it is frequently less than useful.

In view of what appears to be coverage limited to works of the 1970s, the claim of comprehensiveness seems excessive. The Preface provides no discussion of parameters for inclusion/exclusion, and the inadequate subject indexing makes *Discipline in Our Schools* difficult to use. Nevertheless, there is a wealth of material here. The book will be most suitable for academic libraries.

Do-it-yourself medical testing. [By] Cathey Pinckney and Edward R. Pinckney. New York, Facts On File [1983, 1984]. xxii, 290p. illus. 24cm. hardcover $16.95 (0-87196-705-7); paper $7.95 (0-87196-972-6).
616.07′5 Diagnosis | Self-examination, Medical [CIP]   82-12069

Librarians will want to know that this work was published in 1983 with 266 pages and that the slightly larger revised edition came out in October 1984. Both works have 1983 copyrights and their dust jackets are similar. The earlier book described 160 tests; the "revised, updated and expanded" 1984 version analyzes 165 tests. *Do-It-Yourself Medical Testing* aims to help consumers make a better assessment of what their symptoms are so that they may discuss them more accurately with their physicians. For each group of tests, four main sections are included: What is Usual, What You Need, What to Watch Out For, and What the Test Results Can Mean. The tests cover urine, breath and lung, heart and circulation, eye and vision, ear and hearing, brain and the nervous system, the gastrointestinal and genitourinary systems, and several miscellaneous. There are three Appendixes: a list of routine tests, a disease-related Index, and a citation to sources of equipment and supplies. The text and instructions are well written and should be easily understood. *Do-It-Yourself Medical Testing* will be useful in homes and school and public libraries.

Drug use and abuse: a guide to research findings. v.1—adults, v.2—adolescents. By Gregory A. Austin and Michael L. Pendergast. Santa Barbara, Calif., ABC-Clio, 1984. 955p. 29cm. $110/set (0-87436-414-0: set).
616.86′3 Drug abuse—Abstracts | Psychotropic drugs—Abstracts | Drug abuse—Periodicals—Indexes | Psychotropic drugs—Periodicals—Indexes [CIP]   84-3015

This comprehensive guide summarizes and indexes the findings of federally funded research conducted between 1970 and 1980 (including both published and unpublished reports) on the psychosocial aspects of drug use and abuse. Volume 1, dealing with the adult population, divides the 125 citations (most dealing with opiate usage) into six categories, among them: characteristics of opiate use and adult users; treatment of drug dependence; and relationship between drugs and crime. Volume 2, devoted to the adolescent and college-age population, divides its 113 citations (primarily covering marijuana and hallucinogens) into four subjects: drug use among high school students and adolescents; drug use among college students and young adults; ethnic minorities and drugs; and studies on marijuana and hallucinogens. Citations are numbered sequentially throughout both volumes and are arranged alphabetically by author within major categories. Each entry consists of the citation, summary table (ten fields in chart form that specify various characteristics of the research), purpose of the study, definition, a list of findings, and conclusions.

Each discrete research finding is referred to as a separately numbered and indexed "kernel." The Author Index and nine Subject Indexes (in both volumes) provide reference to these "kernels" within an abstract. With the exception of the Age Index (which is chronological) and the Drug and Topic Indexes (arranged by category), the Indexes are alphabetical. The Indexes appearing in the first volume refer only to that volume, while volume 2 has cumulative Indexes to both volumes.

"Not intended to replace the original documents," the abstracts provide an orderly and detailed presentation of the procedures, findings, and conclusions of a study, and it is this, and the ability to access each finding by subject area, that make *Drug Use and Abuse* unique. It is a useful resource for professionals in the field and for academic and medical libraries.

Drugs and sex: a bibliography. Compiled, with an introduction, by Ernest L. Abel. Westport, Conn., Greenwood, 1983. xviii, 129p. 25cm. cloth $29.95 (0-313-23941-X).
016.615′78 Generative organs—Effect of drugs on—Bibliography | Psychotropic drugs—Physiological effects—Bibliography | Drugs and sex—Bibliography [CIP]   83-5656

Drugs and Sex is a sequentially numbered 1,432-item bibliography on the effect of psychoactive substances on human and animal sexuality. The bibliography is arranged under 16 headings. Fifteen of these sections are either specific drugs or classes of drugs such as alcohol, amphetamines, barbiturates, caffeine, LSD, marijuana, and tobacco. Under each heading, the items are arranged alphabetically by author. The last section lists general material. The bibliography is preceded by a 12-page Introduction which defines commonly occurring terms in the literature (e.g., *impotence*) and summarizes the sexual effects of each of the 15 classes of drugs. The Subject Index that follows the bibliography refers to entry numbers. It allows access to the items in the bibliography by specific sexual effect, e.g., feminization. Where there are a large number of citations, they are classified. For example, items under the subject "sexual arousal ... produced by" are first arranged by drug (e.g., alcohol), and then by the categories animals, men, and women.

Abel is prolific; he has compiled numerous other bibliographies and published a number of books on such subjects as fetal alcohol syndrome, marijuana, alcohol and reproduction, and smoking and reproduction. He is a senior research scientist at the Research Institute on Alcoholism of the New York State Department of Dental Hygiene. The readable, informative, and brief Introduction shows his grasp of the subject matter.

Citations were mostly obtained from such professional journals as *Endocrinology, Neuroendocrinology*, and *American Journal of Psychiatry* and include some foreign-language titles. Standard bibliographic data are provided and most items date from the late 1960s through the 1980s. The work is limited by lack of access to authors who are not first authors.

Drugs and Sex is suitable for medical libraries which need a convenient tool on the subject. Most of the items can undoubtedly be located in other sources, and the nature of the topic suggests that *Drugs and Sex* will need future updates to retain its usefulness.

EPA index: a key to U.S. Environmental Protection Agency reports and Superintendent of Documents and NTIS numbers. Edited by Cynthia E. Bower and Mary L. Rhoads. Phoenix, Oryx, 1983. vi, 385p. 29cm. cloth $35 (0-89774-032-7).
016.6285′05 U.S. Environmental Protection Agency—Bibliography [CIP]   82-73733

This index, designed for libraries that have collections of EPA reports, and those that frequently use these reports or which are involved in environmental research, will assist in identifying and locating the approximately 8,000 EPA reports published prior to 1982 that were distributed to federal depository libraries or cited in the *Monthly Catalog*.

Entries are listed in two sequences: alphanumeric by the report number (EPA report number or NTIS accession number—the latter are *see* references) and alphabetically by title. Titles beginning with numbers are listed separately at the beginning of the title sequence. The 21,000 entries provide at least two complete bibliographic citations, taken directly from the publication, for each report.

Entries, listed in three columns per page, with approximately 16 entries per column, are clearly delineated. Running heads in both sequences aid in rapid location of the number or title of report. Citations in either sequence include the full title, date, EPA-assigned and other report numbers, depository library distribution/format symbols, SuDocs (Superintendent of Documents) classification number, and NTIS accession number. Alternate-title entries and cross-references for report and NTIS accession numbers are also given. The Introduction presents an enlarged sample entry from each sequence, clearly identifying each element. Filing rules and an explanation of symbols are also covered.

The three Appendixes provide identification of the SuDocs numbers that were given to eight series of EPA technical reports, a listing of federal regional depository libraries, and a reproducible order form for use when ordering from NTIS.

Individuals or libraries dealing with EPA documents will find this index extremely useful.

Earth and astronomical sciences research centres: a world directory of organizations and programmes. Consultant editor, Jennifer M. Fitch. Harlow, Essex, Longman; dist. exclusively in the U.S., its possessions and Canada by Gale, 1984. 742p. (Longman Reference on Research) 25cm. hardcover $200 (0-582-90020-4).

550′.72 Earth sciences—Research—Directories | Astronomy—Research—Directories [British CIP]

This volume covers 3,500 research centers in 131 countries that conduct research in geology, cartography, surveying, ocean studies, meteorology, climatology, planetary and galactic observations, geochemistry, mineralogy, petrology, mining, and earthquake control. Most of the information is up to date as of 1983. Each entry provides the full title of an organization with acronym (if used), followed by address, telephone and telex numbers, type of organization, products, affiliation, name of director, sections, number of graduate research staff, annual expenditure, activities, publications, and liaisons with other groups. The directory is arranged alphabetically by country and organization name and has a detailed Subject Index and a Titles of Establishments Index, i.e., an alphabetical list of all research centers. Non-English titles have been translated, and the translation is included in the Index.

Earth and Astronomical Sciences Research Centres will be useful primarily in university and research libraries specializing in the geosciences and astronomy.

Education-for-health: the selective guide: health promotion, family life and mental health, audiovisuals, and publications. Edited by the Mental Health Materials Center for the National Center for Health Education. Detroit, Gale (exclusive distributor to libraries worldwide), 1983. 927p. 29cm. hardcover $90 (0-914617-00-1).

016.613′07′8 Health education—Audio-visual aids—Catalogs | Health education—Book reviews | Mental health education—Audio-visual aids—Catalogs | Mental health education—Book Reviews | Family life education—Audio-visual aids—Catalogs | Family life education—Book reviews [CIP] 83-22106

The almost 2,200 items in this catalog include films, videos, slides, and cassettes in part one; and books and pamphlets (including many from voluntary agencies and from the government) in part two, with about 1,200 audiovisuals and 900 publications. The whole work is concerned with health education, broadly defined. All titles cited met criteria established by the two cooperating organizations and are therefore "recommended" by health professionals. For each title, complete bibliographic information is given, including (for audiovisuals) producer and running item. Vendor addresses, prices, and a paragraph describing recommended audience use are provided for each item.

Arrangement is by topical chapters for broad categories (Awareness for Health, Emergencies and Crisis Intervention, etc.). A separate page for each chapter lists subheadings, arranged alphabetically. There are separate title and subject headings to each part in an Appendix.

Education-for-Health is a good compendium for those needing clear, well-written evaluations chosen by professionals for materials suitable for preschool and primary grades, the general public, patients, and health professionals—this last category including social workers, clergy, counselors, general physicians, psychiatrists, and psychologists, among others. School, public, academic, and medical libraries will find it an invaluable reference source as well as an excellent acquisitions tool. An update called *Center*, also produced by the National Center for Health Education five times a year, keeps *Education-for-Health* current by providing a regular feature of reviews of new material.

The elementary school library collection: a guide to books and other media. 14th ed. Lois Winkel, editor. Williamsport, Pa., Brodart, 1984. xv, 1,055p. 29cm. cloth $79.95 (0-87272-090-X).

011′.62 Children's literature—Bibliography | School libraries—Book lists | Audio-visual materials—Catalogs [CIP] 83-14383

As stated in the Introduction, *The Elementary School Library Collection* "is primarily designed to serve as a resource to assist in the continuous maintenance and development of existing collections or for the establishment of new library media centers. It also functions as a reading, listening, viewing guidance tool and as a cataloging aid."

The scope of the collection is governed by the guidelines noted in the American Association on School Librarians' *Media Programs: District and School*—"a minimum collection of quality print and audiovisual materials recommended as essential for a school library media center serving 250 or more students." A total of 13,314 titles has been included, representing 8,906 books, 160 periodicals, and 4,248 audiovisual materials, and all were readily available for purchase as the fourteenth edition went to press. Titles were mostly selected by school librarians.

Following a discussion of selection criteria, the work first lists reference and nonfiction works by Dewey class. Fiction titles are listed by author as are the "easy" titles. Periodicals are listed by title, and the final listing of professional books is organized by Dewey class.

Elements given for each entry are Dewey number, full bibliographic information (including price), ISBN, phase of acquisition (Ph-1 for all libraries, Ph-2 continuing development, Ph-3 specialized significance), readability estimate (for books), interest level, annotation, and subject headings (LC headings for children's literature).

The annotations are mainly descriptive; however, they occasionally "note particular critical points and indicate particular audiences and/or uses of the recommended title." The Author, Title, and Subject Indexes are accurate.

This well-balanced, carefully prepared list achieves its goal as a resource for the continuous maintenance and development of existing collections or for establishing new collections in library media centers serving preschool through sixth grade children in the U.S. and Canada. It can also function as a cataloging aid.

Encyclopaedia Iranica. v.1 (3 fascicles). Edited by Ehsan Yarshater. London, Boston, Routledge & Kegan Paul, 1983. 336p. illus. 28cm. paper, fas.1, $20; fas.2, $37.50; fas.3, $37.50 (0-7100-9090-0).

955.003 Iran—Dictionaries and encyclopedias [OCLC]

Seven years in preparation, this first-ever comprehensive reference tool on the 2,500-year-old Persian and Iranian civilization will be used primarily by scholars and students in Iranian studies. The Board examined only the first three unbound fascicles (parts of volume 1, 112 pages each). The alphabetical entries have proceeded only as far as "Ab." The publisher has not stated how many total volumes the final work will encompass or the projected date of completion, but it appears that the work will be produced in fascicles of 112 pages each.

The editor is affiliated with the Center for Iranian Studies, Columbia University, and each article is signed, with the affiliations of the contributors from all over the world listed at the end of each fascicle. The scope of *Encyclopaedia Iranica* is broad, extending from prehistory to the present. Reciprocal influences between Iran and its neighbors are shown. Particularly stressed are Near Eastern, Indian, and Greco-Roman relations; Indo-Muslim culture; Caucasian and central Asian civilizations; Shiite studies; Iranian ethnography and folklore; history of science; and art and music. Biographies of living persons are excluded. Transliteration is explained. (Entries appear under the New Persian form—not English words—except for Latinized forms in current English, e.g., Xerxes); Iranian calendar dates are given in the Introduction in fascicle 1 only. Primary-source materials are cited within articles, with secondary sources listed at their ends. Following the Introduction are a General List of Abbreviations, Short References and Abbreviations of Books and Periodicals, and a Glossary of Persian and Arabic Terms. With only a small portion of the total work to examine, the Board cannot, by policy, provide a definitive evaluation. However, based on what has been examined, this appears, thus far, to be an authoritative work which maintains a high level of scholarship. Articles examined were thorough and well written and included illustrations where appropriate. Cross-references and bibliographies direct one to other articles and sources. Subject matter covered includes discussions of water in ancient and modern Iran, a Zoroastrian hymn, a caliphate of the eighth to tenth centuries, silk production and textiles through the centuries, and biographies of a twelfth-century scholar, a seventeenth-century poet, and a fifteenth-century leader.

Libraries experiencing extensive demand for materials on Iran through the centuries will want to consider the *Encyclopaedia Iranica* even though it is incomplete. Other reference sources (e.g., the incomplete sets of *Encyclopedia of Islam* and *The Cambridge History of Iran*) cover some of the material, but none is as comprehensive as *Encyclopaedia Iranica.*

Encyclopaedia of drawing: materials, technique and style. [By] Clive Ashwin. Cincinnati, OH 45242, 9933 Alliance Rd., North Light, 1983. 264p. illus. 26cm. paper over boards $22.50 (0-713401-33-8).
741.2 Drawing [OCLC]

Ashwin, a noted arts educator and contributor to many art periodicals, has created an encyclopedia intended to be of use to "anyone who draws or uses drawings for whatever purpose." The inclusion of topics is catholic, ranging from computer graphics, frottage, and photography to watercolor and printmaking. The latter sections are so well written that they alone justify the price of the book, moderate in any case. As well as being comprehensive, the book is up-to-date to judge from the inclusion of such topics as graffiti and conservation.

A Table of Contents briefly lists all entries. There is an Index to Artists who are discussed in the Text; entries in italics under the artist's name indicate that an illustration of his/her work is included. Unfortunately, the work lacks a bibliography, although the author has provided a brief bibliographic essay in his Preface. Within individual entries, the author competently explores various topics. A particularly useful feature is the reference structure. Words printed in boldface refer readers to related entries. For example, under chalks, one is referred to *pastels* and *aux deux crayons*. Sometimes, related terms are cited at the end of a section in the form of *see also* references, and *see* references are also sprinkled throughout.

One of the work's outstanding features is its illustrations. While the expected works by master draftspersons such as Raphael, Durer, and Piranesi are here, so too are many unusual illustrations, running the gamut from works by aboriginal artists to outstanding contemporary designers. Most are printed in black and white; a depiction of contemporary air-brush illustration is an excellent choice for one of the few in color. All are clearly printed, conveying the difference in texture between an aquatint, lithograph, or a conté sketch. To be sure, there are a few omissions. In the excellent section on printmaking, a drypoint is illustrated, but the author has not related this particular technique to engraving. More diagrams might have been included to illustrate perspective. But this is quibbling. To those who love drawing and want to learn more about it, *Encyclopaedia of Drawing* is a delightful book to consult. It is appropriate for public, school, and special/art libraries.

An encyclopaedia of Napoleon's Europe. By Alan Palmer. New York, St. Martin's, 1984. xxiv, 300p. illus. maps. 24cm. cloth $22.50 (0-312-24905-5).
940.2′7′0321 France—History—1789-1815—Dictionaries | Europe—History—1789-1815—Dictionaries | Napoleon I, Emperor of the French, 1769-1821—Dictionaries, indexers, etc. [OCLC]

As its dust jacket states and as its title suggests, this book is "intended for people who are interested in the years 1797 to 1815 as a whole." Particularly fascinating are numerous articles on the Bonaparte family and "circle." But in addition to articles on matters of obvious political, military, and dynastic import, there are articles on cities, regions, and population groups—and even on musicians, painters, poets, and novelists. Emphasis, in treatment of peripheral developments, is on how they absorbed and reflected the energy generated by him of whom the prince de Ligne is quoted as saying, "One could forgive the fiend for becoming a torrent, but to become an earthquake was really too much."

Articles (alphabetically arranged and very well written) run from a few lines to nearly a page—just over a page for Napoleon I *ipse*. There are numerous cross-references and a classified display of article titles; both facilitate study of the "universe" in question, as opposed to retrieval of specific bits of information. Other features include a clutch of maps, a Select Chronology, and a superb Bibliographical Note. There are numerous illustrations, to be enjoyed as evocations of atmosphere rather than valued as sources of data.

Palmer is a distinguished historian whose numerous books include several on the Napoleonic period. Students of history will find his latest contribution helpful, and its emphasis on ramifications may broaden their perspectives. Students of literature, art, and music will gain from its useful insights into the social and political context of romanticism. Public and academic libraries will want to acquire it—as will some high school libraries and some individuals.

Encyclopedia of American forest and conservation history. 2v. Richard C. Davis, editor. New York, Macmillan, 1983. 871p. 29cm. cloth $150 (0-02-907530-2: set; 0-02-907750-8: v.1; 0-02-907770-2: v.2).
333.75′0973 Forests and forestry—U.S.—History—Dictionaries | Forest conservation—U.S.—History—Dictionaries [CIP] 83-311

The editor's purpose is "to produce the standard, authoritative guide and reference to the history of forestry, conservation, forest industries, and other forest-related subjects in the United States." The 203 contributors, including scholars and practitioners, have written 413 articles that range from several hundred to several thousand words. The alphabetically arranged articles are signed, and they include cross-references in the text and references for further reading. Written for both specialists and laypersons, the articles present factual as well as interpretive commentary on significant facts covering everything from the national parks, important personalities, associations, and controversial issues to industry and recreation. The articles include numerous black-and-white photographs, many from the Forest History Society Media Archives. Five Appendixes cover the national forests of the U.S., giving names, dates established, history, legislation that established them, acreage when established and acreage as of September 1981; National Parks of the U.S. with similar data; Chronology of Federal Legislation Cited, which established the national forests and national parks; Chronology of Administrations giving presidents of the U.S. and their secretary of interior, general land office commissioner, national park service director, secretary of agriculture, and forest service chief, with the terms of each; and an atlas.

Print appears to be somewhat larger than is usual in works of this type and is extremely legible. Paper is opaque and the binding strong. *Encyclopedia of American Forest and Conservation History* is an excellent set which belongs in any library serving those interested in American forestry, conservation, and ecology. Recommended.

Encyclopedia of American political history: studies of the principal movements and ideas. 3v. Jack P. Greene, editor. New York, Scribner, 1984. 1,420p. (American Civilization Series) 28cm. cloth $180 (0-684-17003-5).
320.973′03′21 U.S.—Politics and government—Dictionaries | Political science—U.S.—History—Dictionaries [CIP] 84-1355

Its format modeled on Scribner's *Encyclopedia of American Economic History* and *Encyclopedia of American Foreign Policy*, this three-volume collection of 90 articles on American political history claims to represent "a broad range of ideological positions and historical points of view." The essays, ranging in length from 5 to 20 pages, have been written especially for this reference source by historians with imposing credentials.

The topics covered cut a wide swath through the thickets of American political history. Although its emphasis is on political movements and ideas, coverage also includes important political events and documents which embody crucial themes, constitutional issues, government policies, political parties and elections, and federal, state, and local government. Each chapter ends with a short bibliographical essay and cross-references to related articles in the encyclopedia. A detailed Subject Index for the whole set appears at the end of the third volume.

The writing is consistently authoritative and clear, and the breadth and depth of coverage are impressive. But what truly distinguishes this encyclopedia from others is the unique way it treats American political history. Simply put, this is a topically arranged intellectual history of American politics. The very first article—an overview of American political historiography—sets the tone for succeeding chapters. Its thrust is to survey different approaches to U.S. political history and to compare, contrast, and interrelate the ideas behind historical theses. The essays on political movements—egalitarianism, pacifism, nativism, radicalism, conservatism, liberalism, federalism, and feminism, to name only a few—follow the same pattern, concentrating on delineating the philosophical roots of each movement, tracing its intellectual evolution, and portraying its impact on American political history. For example, the article on the New Freedom of Woodrow Wilson is almost entirely a study of contrasts with Theodore Roosevelt's New Nationalism; the Civil War is treated as a case study of American historiography rather than as a series of events, linearly recounted; and the Bill of Rights, though discussed in a chronological context, is analyzed thoroughly as a composite of different philosophies of colonial government.

What is particularly interesting about this work is what it omits. There is, for example, no full descriptive or evaluative account of all the presidents' terms of office (although there is an article on the presidency). Nor are foreign policy and American participation in major wars such as the War of 1812, the Spanish-American War, both world wars, the Korean War, and the Vietnam War considered. However, the *Encyclopedia of American Foreign Policy* covers this area of U.S. political history (cf. the *RSBR* April 1, 1979 evaluation). Election campaigns are covered selectively.

In a reference source of such arrangement and treatment cutting horizontally across political events, the Index assumes great importance. The Index here is adequate, but access to the work would be greatly improved by the addition of more cross-references.

A sturdy binding and excellent page layout commend the set physically.

Because of the exclusively horizontal treatment of political history and its emphasis on movements and ideas, *Encyclopedia of American Political History* is not a ready reference source crammed with dates, events, short biographies and the like—nor does it pretend to be. It is, however, an impressive achievement which provides for students of U.S. political history a rare overview of the stuff of politics which many studies have ignored, viz., ideas. It not only informs but also whets one's appetite for further study in a rich field. As a unique topical encyclopedia that lends itself well to extended reference work and a starting point for in-depth study, it is indispensable for academic and medium- and large-size public libraries. Community college libraries should also consider it. Recommended.

Encyclopedia of associations. 4v. 18th ed., 1984. Denise S. Akey, editor. Detroit, Gale, 1983. V.1: National Organizations of the U.S.; v.2: Geographic and Executive Indexes; v.3: New Associations and Projects; v.4: International Organizations. 27cm. cloth (v.1 in 2 pts., $180/set: 0-8103-1687-0; v.2, $160: 0-8103-1688-9; v.3. $175 (2-issue subscription): 0-8103-0130-X; v.4, $130 (3-issue subscription): 0-8103-0143-1).
†061.025 Associations, institutions, etc.—U.S.—Directories [OCLC]   76-46129

Originally conceived as a source of information about nonprofit membership organizations in the United States, the *Encyclopedia of Associations* has expanded its scope to include organizations of other types; among them, nonmembership groups which "conduct research, collect data, or act as clearinghouses" (e.g., the National Referral Center at the Library of Congress) and which have potential value as information sources; overseas organizations of interest to Americans, particularly those which have no counterparts in the U.S.; and for-profit organizations whose names and activities may suggest that they are nonprofit entities (e.g., Research Institute of America) for which "informational entries" are provided to alert the user to their for-profit status.

The 1984 edition of volume 1 has been expanded by 1,470 entries, bringing the number of organizations covered to approximately 17,750. Revisions were made to an estimated 90 percent of the entries included in the previous edition. Unrevised entries are identified with an asterisk. The Alphabetical and Keyword Indexes provide access to the entries, which are arranged in the body of the work under broad subject categories, by specific fields, and by organization name (including each significant work in the title). Inactive and defunct organizations are also indexed, as are "missing organizations" (those whose entries have been dropped since they have not responded to requests for information for the last three editions).

The Geographic Index in volume 2 arranges the organizations by country, state, and city and lists them alphabetically by name within cities. Volume 2 also includes an Executive Index which lists the chief official of each organization alphabetically by surname and includes address and telephone number. Listings in both these Indexes include the entry numbers in volume 1.

Volume 3 is issued "periodically" (actual frequency is not stated) between editions of the *Encyclopedia* (now annual) to provide information on new and recently formed organizations. These initial listings are sometimes less detailed than those provided in volume 1, and some of the items of information usually included may not be available for new organizations. In such cases, fuller entries are anticipated in the next edition of the *Encyclopedia*.

Volume 4 is new to this edition and "focuses on organizations that are nonprofit, international in scope and membership, and headquartered outside the United States" (Introduction). Entries do not duplicate those for overseas organizations included in volume 1, but concentrate "on those international groups that are considered to be the major coordinating bodies for their respective professions or areas of interest and that are represented by members in many countries." The editors point out that the emphasis of this volume differs from that of the *Yearbook of International Organizations*, which is also distributed by Gale.

This volume is issued in three installments; the first of which includes 500 of the projected 2,000 entries. Organizations are arranged under the same broad subject categories used in volume 1, with the omission of those not applicable to international organizations. Entries follow the format of those in volume 1, but include, in addition, information on the official and/or working languages of the organization and its telex number when available.

The *Encyclopedia of Associations* is useful not only for its data about individual organizations but also as a guide to locating information on many subjects through the information resources of these organizations. Since the individual volumes are sold separately, libraries can select those best suited to their needs. Volume 1, the basic encyclopedia, can stand alone as a work of reference. The need for the interedition supplements which constitute volume 3 may be somewhat diminished now that the encyclopedia is being issued annually, especially since these supplements cost virtually as much as the basic encyclopedia itself. The new volume 4, with its international coverage, may be a better investment for libraries desirous of supplementing the basic encyclopedia. Most libraries can probably get along without volume 2 as few patrons are likely to ask how many of the listed organizations are located in a particular city or region or whether "a particular individual is associated as a chief executive with more than one organization" (among the limited uses cited for this volume in the Introduction).

Encyclopedia of banking and finance. 8th ed. [By] Glenn G. Munn; revised and expanded by F. L. Garcia. Boston, Bankers Publishing Co., 1983. 1,024p. 29cm. cloth $89 (0-87267-042-2).
332'.03'21 Banks and banking—Dictionaries | Finance—Dictionaries | Banks and banking—U.S.—Dictionaries [CIP]   83-8845

Since the first edition of this special encyclopedia in 1924, it has become a standard reference source in libraries with business collections. The seventh edition, published in 1973, had 3,050 entries; the current edition with 4,000 entries (many revised and extended) promises to be indispensable for some years to come. The work defines thousands of banking, business, and financial terms in short entries and also features essay-length discussions of relevant subjects: *Debt Limit, Federal Farm Loan System, International Balance of Payments*, etc. Absent is extensive information on loans made by U.S. banks to foreign countries or a discussion of the possible consequences if countries, such as Mexico or Argentina, were to default on these loans. However, the discussions of default and coverage of the International Monetary Fund are excellent.

Statistical tables showing historical trends are numerous, and there are also examples of standard banking forms. Suggested readings follow most entries and, though brief and with incomplete bibliographic data, are an important feature. The more recent printed materials are dated in the early 1980s.

A "Quick Index" lists all entries alphabetically; although it is complete and serves the stated purpose of the author (to help users review topics covered without having to scan the large volume), it is no substitute for a detailed subject index. However, cross-references within the body of the work are plentiful. *Encyclopedia of Banking and Finance* is a standard for almost any business collection.

Encyclopedia of community planning and environmental management. By Marilyn Schultz and Vivian Kasen; illus. by Diane Caro. New York, Facts On File, 1984. x, 475p. photos. 28cm. hardcover $45 (0-87196-447-3).
307'.12'0321 Land use—Planning—Dictionaries | Environmental protection—Dictionaries | Municipal engineering—Dictionaries | Regional planning—Dictionaries [CIP]   82-7366

This work proposes to incorporate the diverse aspects of the field of planning, e.g., land use, economic development, and flood control, into one easy-to-use volume. It contains 2,000 articles in an alphabetical arrangement, with entries ranging in length from a brief descriptive paragraph to a full page, with the typical entry a few paragraphs. Entries cover organizations (purpose, activities, publications), federal agencies (including recent program changes and amendments through 1983), legal decisions (early landmark cases through recent ones), general topics, (e.g., *Demand-Responsive Transportation, Group Home, Sprawl, Thermal Window*), and British activities in community planning. Original illustrations and photographs (with credit noted) enhance the text.

The 36-page Index is accurate; it lists article titles and is arranged alphabetically under major topics. Many cross-references at the end of each entry and in the Index make the work's contents very accessible.

The *Illustrated Book of Development Definitions* (Rutgers, 1984) contains fewer definitions, and they are usually confined to one sentence. *The Dictionary of Development Terminology* (McGraw-Hill, 1975) has similar one- to two-sentence definitions. *The McGraw-Hill Encyclopedia of Environmental Sciences* (1980, 2d ed.) was reviewed by *RBB* (April 15, 1981) and found useful, although it has more specific focus than the work under review.

The *Encyclopedia of Community Planning and Environmental Management* is well done, comprehensive, and easy to use. Many large public, academic, and special libraries will find it valuable.

Encyclopedia of crime and justice. 4v. Sanford H. Kadish, editor in chief. New York, Free Press (a div. of Macmillan), 1983. 1,790p. 29cm. cloth $300/set (0-02-918110-0).

364'.03'21 Crime and criminals—Dictionaries ǁ Criminal justice, Administration of—Dictionaries [CIP]   83-7156

Designed for a wide audience, this four-volume set offers 286 original articles covering topics related to crimes, criminal behavior, criminal law, and the criminal justice system.

The alphabetically arranged, signed articles, ranging from one page to more than ten pages in length, were written for this work by noted specialists in the field. These include primarily law professors, but well-known psychologists, judges, sociologists, and consultants in criminal justice have also contributed.

In general, articles explain basic concepts and theories and provide historical background, interpretations of research findings, court cases, and decisions. To assist the reader, articles contain bibliographies as well as *see also* references. For those readers unfamiliar with technical terminology related to criminal justice, a 24-page Glossary is provided in volume four. An Introduction and a Guide to Legal Citations are also included in volume one for the same purpose.

The volumes are sturdily bound; both print and paper are of high quality, and the format is arranged to facilitate ease of reading and use. There are two indexes in volume four; the first, Legal Index, is divided into a Table of Cases (covering all court decisions cited) and a Topical Index containing all other legal documents cited. The second General Index includes references to authors, titles, and subjects in detail.

The interdisciplinary scope of this work enhances its usefulness to informed general readers, students, and teachers in criminal justice, law, law enforcement, and sociology, as well as to criminal justice and court personnel. Given the importance of the subject area in today's society, the work is recommended for all but the smallest academic and public libraries.

The encyclopedia of drug abuse. By Robert O'Brien and Sidney Cohen. New York, Facts On File, 1984. xxvii, 454p. 26cm. cloth $40 (0-87196-690-5).

362.2'9 Drug abuse—Dictionaries ǁ Drugs—Dictionaries [CIP]   82-5034

O'Brien, a reference book author and editor, and Cohen, former director of the Division of Narcotic Addiction and Drug Abuse for the NIMH, have produced a comprehensive work which includes not only articles on drugs themselves but also "on medical and biological aspects, ethnic groups, geographical areas, organizations, laws and other topics." Intended for both laypersons and professionals, it is a companion volume to *The Encyclopedia of Alcoholism* (cf. *Reference Books Bulletin*, Oct. 15, 1983) and includes a number of references to alcohol and its abuse. This work, however, concentrates on other drugs: the medical and physical effects, psychological factors, political and legal factors, and drug use in more than 25 countries. After a highly readable chapter entitled "History of Drugs and Man," more than half the book is devoted to definitions and explanatory entries, arranged alphabetically and varying in length from four lines (*California Poppy*) to five pages (*Controlled Substances Act*). Included are many trade-name drugs and a number of tangential entries, e.g., one on AIDS because of the link between intravenous drug abusers and that disease, another on advertising which questions the public interest versus alcohol and drug advertising, as well as the problematic area of pharmaceutical advertising. There are tabulated histories of amphetamines, barbiturates, cocaine, heroin, LSD, marijuana, morphine, and opium and entries on topics ranging from the American military to organized crime. Several 1982 studies and reports are noted. Appendixes include a glossary of street language and drug synonyms, an extensive Bibliography, and more than 50 tables on drug laws and violations, treatment units, users in treatment, patterns of usage, trafficking in and growth of cocaine abuse, and public attitudes toward alcohol and drugs. Invaluable to researchers is a list of sources of drug information in the U.S., Canada, and foreign countries, as well as international agencies and major English-language periodicals concerned with drug and alcohol abuse. A complete Index ends the work.

Because of its scope, currency, and clear writing style, *The Encyclopedia of Drug Abuse* should be essential for guidance counselors, school administrators, public-health workers, school health personnel, and in almost any library serving students from the middle school through graduate school.

Encyclopedia of frontier and western fiction. John Tuska and Vicki Piekarski, editors in chief. New York, McGraw-Hill, 1983. xviii, 365p. cloth $29.95 (0-07-065587-1).

813'.0874'9 American fiction—West (U.S.)—Bio-bibliography ǁ American fiction—West (U.S.)—History and criticism—Dictionaries ǁ Western stories—History and criticism—Dictionaries ǁ West (U.S.) in literature—Dictionaries ǁ Frontier and pioneer life in literature—Dictionaries ǁ Authors, American—West (U.S.)—Biography [CIP]   82-14831

The Preface to this collection of biographies and bibliographies of writers of western fiction uses as its definition "fiction of all kinds if set on the North American continent." It is therefore not limited to the conventional "cowboys and Indians" or "pioneer life" types of popular fiction.

Approximately 300 writers are included, each entry giving some biographical data and a list of writings, including works published in series and, where appropriate, a list of films made from novels. Entries vary from about a quarter-page to about ten pages for the prolific Zane Grey. Among the earliest names are Cooper, Irving, and O.Henry; later famous names include Jackson Gregory, James Oliver Curwood, Conrad Richter, and Louis L'Amour. Though the majority of the writers are late-nineteenth- and early-twentieth-century figures, many are listed as still living.

In addition to the 300-odd sketches, there are five subject essays, arranged (and in effect buried) alphabetically through the book, along with the authors' sketches. There are Historical Personalities (such as Kit Carson, Frémont, Custer); House Names (publishing houses specializing in such fiction, particularly if serial in form); Native Americans (Indians as topics of fiction); Pulp and Slick Western Stories (largely a history of the "dime novel" and of a few slicks such as the *Saturday Evening Post*); and finally, Women on the Frontier (an essay on women as topics of western fiction). Since there are no running heads in the book, these valuable essays are hard to find and easily overlooked.

A few other editorial peculiarities were noted—the listing of titles is presented in paragraph rather than in columnar form, and there are some typos. Despite these minor infelicities, *Encyclopedia of Frontier and Western Fiction* covers in adequate detail the biobibliography of almost every writer of importance who has fictionalized the West. It will find ready acceptance in almost all types of libraries.

Encyclopedia of historic places. 2v. by Courtlandt Canby. New York, Facts On File, 1984. 1,052p. 29cm. cloth $120 (0-87196-126-1: set; 0-87196-397-3: v.1; 0-87196-125-3: v.2).

903'.21 History—Dictionaries ǁ Gazetteers [British CIP]   80-25121

The *Encyclopedia of Historic Places* is a two-volume gazetteer of locations having historical interest. Entries for political entities, regions, geographical features (lakes, rivers, and mountains), sites of battles and forts, shrines, and archaeological digs are arranged in one alphabetical sequence. Coverage is global and ranges from the "remains of human beginnings" to the present. Although similar to *Webster's New Geographical Dictionary* and the *Columbia-Lippincott Gazetteer of the World*, the *Encyclopedia* is more limited in scope. Places and sites without historical interest are omitted. For each of the places included, a brief description of the historical significance is given. Entries are identified by regional location in the current country and then by distance/direction from a nearby large city (e.g., "approx. 73 mi E of Houston"). Alternate names are entered with a reference to the form preferred (Brugge, *see* Bruges; Aix-la-Chapelle, *see* Aachen; St. Petersburg, *see* Leningrad) and are repeated in the principal entry.

Within entries, names spelled in capital letters indicate places which have separate entries. Chinese names are spelled according to the Wade-Giles system of transliteration rather than the newer Pinyin system because the names "are more familiar" to readers in the older spellings. The *Encyclopedia* is readily usable in its straightforward two-columns-per-page format. There is a one-page Preface and a list of illustration credits, but no index, bibliography, or other supporting material. Some entries are illustrated with black-and-white photographs of adequate clarity.

For libraries which can afford its price, the *Encyclopedia of Historic Places* will be a helpful supplement to the more comprehensive gazetteers found in general reference collections, but it is not a necessary purchase except in larger history collections.

The encyclopedia of mammals. Edited by David Macdonald. New York, Facts On File; c.Equinox (Oxford) Ltd., 1984. xv, 895, xlviiip. 29cm. cloth $45 (0-87196-871-1).

599 Mammals [CIP]   84-1631

See *RBB* news item Nov. 1, 1984, p.349. Breadth of coverage, authority of contributors, readable text, and number and good quality of well-captioned photographs distinguish this encyclopedia, whose editor, an authority in mammalian biology and natural history, is a fellow in animal behavior at Oxford. The articles, signed by 180 qualified professors and personnel of research institutes over the world (chiefly Britain and U.S.), cover all existing mammals in essays ranging from 2 pages for *Coyote* to 16 pages for *Squirrels*. Intended for students and natural history enthusiasts, the clear, often dramatic accounts of playing, hunting, and breeding habits will appeal to general readers, especially if they are partial to television nature programs. Fact boxes provide distribution maps and other data. The essays often reflect recent research and field experiences, as in the explanation of the gray squirrel's destructive habit of bark stripping. Also recent are the titles, chiefly published since 1970, in the bibliography of works consulted, far fewer than the thousands of titles in Walker's *Mammals of the World* (3d ed., 2v., 1975). But more handsome than Walker's are the color photographs, 1,150 plus 72 commissioned color illustrations, which appear on almost every page. Appended are a list of species, a glossary of about 350 briefly defined terms, and a good Index. This *Encyclopedia of Mammals* is an excellent source for school and public libraries as well as for homes.

The encyclopedia of North American wildlife. By Stanley Klein. New York, Facts On File, 1983. [315p.] illus. (part col.) 29cm. cloth $35 (0-87196-758-8).

596.097 Zoology—North America—Dictionaries [CIP]   82-5183

This one-volume encyclopedia, covering major species of wildlife in the continental U.S., Canada, and northern Mexico, is divided into five major sections: mammals, birds, reptiles, amphibians, and fish. Subsections are used with reptiles (snakes, crocodilians, lizards, and turtles) and amphibians (frogs and toads and salamanders). Entries, which describe the domain, physical characteristics, living habits, and when appropriate, the importance and usefulness to humans, are arranged alphabetically within sections or subsections with titles in boldface followed by the species' Latin name. Alternate terminology is listed as an entry with cross-referencing. There are 325 entries with more than 600 cross-references and 350 full-color photographs. Included among the Appendixes are National Organizations for the Conservation and Protection of Wildlife; a Bibliography; Endangered Species of North America; and an Index of Latin Names, arranged as the entries are. The text and photographs make *The Encyclopedia of North American Wildlife* a desirable addition to any library, but the lack of a general index is a major drawback.

Encyclopedia of occultism & parapsychology: a compendium of information on the occult sciences, magic, demonology, superstitions, spiritism, mysticism, metaphysics, psychical science, and parapsychology, with biographical and bibliographical notes and comprehensive indexes. 2d ed. v.1, A–G. Edited by Leslie Shepard. Detroit, Gale, 1984. xi, 570p. 29cm. cloth $200 (3v. set) (0-8103-0196-2).

133′.03′21 Occult sciences—Dictionaries | Psychical research—Dictionaries [CIP]
84-3990

The first edition of the *Encyclopedia of Occultism and Parapsychology* was published in 1978 and given a rather unfavorable review by the Board in *RSBR,* Jan. 15, 1979. A number of the objections raised then have been addressed and corrected in this edition. (The Board examined only one volume of what will be a three-volume set.)

Based on two earlier encyclopedias, Lewis Spence's *Encyclopedia of Occultism* (1920) and Nandor Fodor's *Encyclopaedia of Psychic Science* (1934), the first edition reproduced their entries photographically as originally published, interfiling them and adding some new entries. This caused confusion, however, for an article might start out "This contemporary" but mean 1920, not 1978, although there was no indication of this in the article. Some (but by no means all entries) were identified as being from one or the other original, and if users did not read the introductory material, they could easily be misled. Also, there was no acknowledgment of authorship for new entries. At the time of the Board's review, one supplement had been published; in 1982 a cumulative volume incorporating four supplements and providing a comprehensive Index to the entire set was published. The editor then felt it was time to undertake a major revision, and this second edition is the result.

All entries were reviewed and revised as necessary; facts and sources were checked; errors corrected; entries updated and expanded, and new articles added. The original Spence and Fodor articles with their "different viewpoints" were "integrated into an overall text after careful evaluation," and responsibility for this "presentation and opinion" is accepted by Leslie Shepard, the editor. All original subjects have been retained, and, says Shepard, "although tempted to reduce some of the longer, more discursive, material (particularly from Spence)," he "felt it was on balance better to retain the material in the new edition rather than eliminate facts and opinions already published. Moreover, such detailed treatment (often quotations form source works) was felt to have value for researchers."

Entries therefore may be short, one-sentence identifications or be many pages long; they include persons both living and dead, places, publications, terms, phenomena, mythical beings, etc. A sampling of entries showed that about 25 percent are unchanged from the original or supplements, but also identified many minor changes and corrections, some extensive expansions, and some totally new articles. Bibliographies have been added or expanded and citations made more complete. All have been reset in a larger uniform typeface for a more pleasing appearance which is also easier to read. Running heads have been added to facilitate finding articles. There are many cross-references; boldface in an entry indicates a term or name which has its own article, and there are also specific *see* or *see also* references.

If a library has the first edition and the cumulative supplement, it may need to weigh carefully whether the relatively few major changes, but greater ease of use and better understanding, are worth the price. (Minor changes clarify greatly at times, however—from "About 20 years ago" to "About 1900" makes considerable difference in understanding.) If a library did not buy the first edition and has a constituency interested in the supernatural and psychic phenomena, this new edition may prove to be a useful source.

Encyclopedia of occupational health and safety. v.1 & 2. 3d rev. ed. Technical editor, Luigi Parmeggiani. Washington, DC, 20006, 1750 New York Ave., NW, International Labor Organization, 1983. 31cm. cloth $155 (92-2-103290-6; v.1: 92-2-103291-4).

†613.62′03 Medicine, Industrial | Industrial safety [OCLC]

After 12 years of research, the third edition of *Encyclopedia of Occupational Health and Safety* presents a comprehensive overview of all aspects of health and safety for workers. Ranging from *Abattoirs* to *Zoonoses,* from *Ergonomics* to *Whaling,* it contains more than 1,150 articles prepared by 900 specialists from 60 countries. Each article is signed, and the Appendix contains each author's affiliation. According to the publisher, more than 70 percent of the entries have been revised from the second edition, and approximately 200 new articles have been added.

The book is intended to be a "source of practical information . . . even for those with no specialized medical or technical knowledge." It provides information about accidents or illnesses caused by industrial processes and/or materials, describes occupational terminology and specific types of work, and then recommends procedures for prevention of accidents or illnesses. Each article includes a bibliography, and there are many cross-references throughout as well as hundreds of black-and-white illustrations.

The Encyclopedia of Occupational Health and Safety is an excellent standard source on the topics; libraries with older editions will want this more up-to-date one.

Encyclopedia of psychology. 4v. Raymond J. Corsini, editor; Bonnie D. Ozaki, assistant editor. New York, Wiley, 1984. illus. 29cm. cloth $199.95 (0-471-86595-X).
150′.3′21 Psychology–Dictionaries ‖ Psychology–Indexes [CIP]   83-16814

This new work is edited by Raymond J. Corsini; consulting editors are also former presidents of the American Psychological Association; associate and foreign editors are leaders and specialists in their fields, and many other contributors are well known. Its Preface states that the set is intended for "psychologists, psychiatrists, social workers, counselors, sociologists, anthropologists, and other professionals"; and it is also meant to be useful to laypersons interested in the subject. Three volumes are devoted to text, and the last contains Indexes and Bibliography. This ambitious work claims to contain some 2,150 separate entries—1,500 on subjects and about 650 on persons. It offers timely coverage of such traditional subjects as Freud, Jung, and schizophrenia and on such current concerns as sports psychology, psychodrama, and crisis intervention. The work is primarily textual—most of the articles are about a page in length—but there are some line drawings, graphs, and charts. Articles are signed except for those on living persons who sent basic information to Wiley where the material was edited and rewritten. Alphabetizing is letter by letter, but articles, conjunctions, prepositions, etc., are ignored. Thus, *Psychology and the Arts* falls between *Psychology in Africa* and *Psychology in Australia*. The Board finds this practice confusing—especially since it is not explained in the prefatory matter.

The articles, although varying in comprehensiveness and depth, are mostly of high quality and authoritative. There is an especially useful series of articles on psychology as it developed, exists, and is taught in various countries. Although this set is a welcome addition to reference literature in psychology, there are some problems with access and arrangement. Some subjects are so scattered that neither the Subject Index nor the cross-references at the ends of some articles can be relied upon to bring them together. For example, there are articles entitled *Cultural Bias in Tests*; *Race Bias in Testing*; *Culture Fair Tests*; *Psychological Testing: Its Survival Problems*; but not all of these have cross-references (and in two cases *Cultural Bias in Tests* is cited incorrectly as "Cultural Bias in Testing" and "Cultural Biases in Testing"). *Racial Differences* also has a discussion of testing and refers to A. R. Jensen (who is the author of *Cultural Bias in Tests* and himself a rather controversial figure), but there is no cross-reference to the Jensen article. In the Index under testing, only one of the five references—test bias—leads directly to one relevant article. Readers must look under *Cultural Bias in Testing* or *Race Bias in Testing* to locate the other articles, or they must rely on the cross-references—which are not consistent. The same problem crops up in other areas, e.g., articles on psychology and law. The impression is that some articles were indexed in detail but not indexed in relation to the work as a whole.

The Subject Index is alphabetized in letter-by-letter sequence, which again is not explained. Also, the Index citations are rather perverse: *trait psychology, trait theories,* and *traits* mostly all refer to two articles. The Board wonders why there are three separate Index entries. Articles do not necessarily conclude with bibliographies; some include bibliographic references within the text (in which case an author and year are given). Entries which are followed by bibliographies cite author and title only. In either case, for full details the reader must go to the Bibliography in volume 4: it contains 15,000 references, listed alphabetically by author not by subject. Since some subjects are treated in several articles, readers will have difficulty building a bibliography on a subject. Still, the references are, for the most part, well chosen.

The physical aspects of the set are good: type is attractive and easy to read, but article headings are almost the same size as the boldface subheadings and cross-references. The binding is satisfactory.

Encyclopedia of Psychology is more up-to-date and comprehensive than Eysenck's three-volume *Encyclopedia of Psychology* (Herder & Herder, 1972) and has a narrower focus than Wolman's twelve-volume *International Encyclopedia of Psychiatry, Psychology, Psychoanalysis and Neurology* (Aesculapius, 1983). Briefer dictionary-type information can be found in the new *Longman Dictionary of Psychology and Psychiatry* (Longman, 1984) and the *Harvard Guide to Modern Psychiatry* (Harvard Univ. Pr., 1976).

The *Encyclopedia of Psychology* will be useful for students (college and up), professionals, and the general public. However, users must be cautioned to search under a variety of entry points for any one topic, mindful of the alphabetization practices. Recommended for large public, academic, and special libraries, although those with *Wolman* may find *Encyclopedia of Psychology* duplicative in some respects.

Encyclopedia of religion in the South. Edited by Samuel S. Hill. Macon, Georgia, Mercer Univ. Pr., 1984. vii, 878p. 27cm. hardcover $60 (0-86554-117-5).
277.5′003′21 Christianity–Southern States–Dictionaries ‖ Southern States–Religion–Dictionaries ‖ Christian biography–Southern States–Dictionaries [CIP]   84-8957

Samuel Hill, a professor at the University of Florida, with the help of "more than 200" scholars associated with colleges, seminaries, universities, and religious institutions, has compiled an impressive overview of religion in the southern U.S. from the colonial period to the present. The religion of the native Americans of the region has been omitted. Geographical coverage includes the former Confederate states plus Kentucky, Maryland, Missouri, Oklahoma, and West Virginia. "More than 500 articles," ranging in length from less than a half column (e.g., *Deputies*) to more than 17 pages (e.g., *Virginia*), cover the history of religion in each state (the longest articles); denominations (both large and small); doctrines and theological movements of special significance to the South; prominent families and individuals; places, institutions, and organizations; events; ecclesiastical offices; titles and jurisdictions; social movements; religious practices; and a wide variety of miscellaneous topics.

Articles are arranged alphabetically under subject headings, with numerous cross-references within the main alphabetical sequence. Unfortunately, running heads are not used, hampering searches for particular articles. An alphabetical Subject Index provides access to topics treated within articles. Articles conclude with name and institution of the authors. Some articles provide references to related articles, and the longer articles tend to have bibliographies appended. Bibliographic citations for books are limited to author and title.

The lack of subdivision under main heading in the Subject Index makes many entries difficult to use. Under "Baptist(s)," for example, are listed nearly 200 undifferentiated column references. This and many other general headings would have been much more useful if subheadings had indicated the aspect treated in particular articles, e.g., with respect to Baptists: abolitionism, in Alabama, American Baptist Association, etc.

Nevertheless, the editor and his contributors have succeeded in providing a useful summary of facts and scholarly interpretation relating to this broad and important subject. Libraries serving students and scholars in religious studies will want to consider this work for their collections.

The encyclopedia of second careers. [By] Gene R. Hawes. New York, Facts On File, 1984. xi, 444p. 29cm. hardcover $49.95 (0-87196-692-1).
650.1′4 Career changes [CIP]   82-5195

This source is designed to help persons planning a career change, and as such it presents data on a wide range of jobs/professions. An introductory section suggests developing a career-locator profile consisting of personal interests, abilities, education one has or would get, ease of entry into the occupation, and present and future income sought. This analysis leads users to several lists of careers, first accessed according to interests and then by abilities; skeletal information is given for each career. Other tables list highest income careers, those with easiest entry, education needed (from on-the-job to doctorate), and helpful prior experience.

Almost two-thirds of *The Encyclopedia of Second Careers* consists of more detailed descriptions of the jobs listed, organized topically. For each of some 200 occupations, the text notes the character of the field; required prior experience; personal qualities; training and education; employment opportunities; getting the first job; growth anticipated in the field; income that can be expected; career path and work settings; and source(s) of additional information. Other sections of the work deal with starting a business, growth regions (Sunbelt, Rocky Mountains), and locating and landing a job. Schools where additional training may be obtained are listed: two-year colleges, colleges and universities with continuing education programs, and accredited trade and correspondence schools. Employment services are also briefly mentioned.

This sourcebook has unusual breadth; the career descriptions are

The encyclopedic discography of Victor recordings: pre-matrix series, the Consolidated Talking Machine Company, Eldridge R. Johnson, and the Victor Talking Machine Company, 12 January 1900 to 23 April 1903.... Compiled by Ted Fagan and William R. Moran. Westport, Conn., Greenwood, 1983. xxxii, 393p. 24cm. cloth $49.95 (0-313-23003-X).

016.7899'12 Victor Talking Machine Company—Catalogs | Sound recordings—Catalogs | Music—Discography—Catalogs [CIP] 82-9343

Begun in 1963, an incredible amount of research and work has gone into the compilation of a complete catalog of Victor recordings for the companies and time span indicated in the subtitle. More volumes are forthcoming to bring the period of coverage up to the present day and the present company, RCA Records of New York.

Working from archives (which have "suffered the ravages of time") and other published and unpublished sources, the authors, both connected with the Stanford Archive of Recorded Sound, have unscrambled numbering systems and put together an ordered catalog of pre-matrix recordings. It has been published while some problems yet remain in the hope of eliciting additional information from collectors and historians.

The introductory material is an essential part of the work, containing not only the vital Users Guide but also details of the company, development of the labels. Librarians may want to note for their files the inclusion of a complete reprint of *The Victor Talking Machine Company* by B. L. Aldridge, of which only one copy is known.

Pages 1–219 contain the discography, arranged by pre-matrix number. A complex system of indicators permits the inclusion of a variety of information about the recording to be shown in very little space. It is followed by a Chronological Listing of Recording Sessions, 12 Jan. 1900 to 1 Nov. 1903; and Artist and Title Indexes. All are keyed to the pre-matrix number of the discography.

Meticulously prepared and presented, *The Encyclopedic Discography* is more than just a catalog of one company's publishing. It is a history of the very beginning of the recording industry and an insight into "the way we were." It will be a boon to archivists, musicologists, collectors, and social historians and should be available in most academic and public libraries.

Energy research guide: journals, indexes, and abstracts. Cambridge, Mass., Ballinger, 1983. xi, 284p. 24cm. hardcover $42 (0-88410-097-9).

016.33379'05 Power resources—Periodicals—Bibliography [CIP] 81-1640

More than 500 periodicals, indexes, and abstracts covering energy or related fields are included in this guide. Alphabetically arranged by title, each entry includes full title, short annotation, price, address, and telephone number. All titles are included first in a master list that indicates which are indexes and/or abstracts and then in seven subject lists: Energy Use and Conservation, Renewable and Alternative Energy Sources, Oil and Gas, Coal, Electric Power including Nuclear, Environment, and World Energy. Only English-language publications are included, and emphasis is on print sources with no mention of online databases. Although the publication date is 1983, users should be aware that many titles may have ceased, and the listed subscription prices may have changed. The publishers should be encouraged to produce new editions on a regular basis. This would be useful to almost any library.

Entomology: a guide to information sources. [Comp. by] Pamela Gilbert and Chris J. Hamilton. London and Bronx, N.Y., Mansell, 1983. viii, 237p. 24cm. paper over board $29 (0-7201-1680-5).

595.7 Entomology—Information services | Entomology—Bibliography [British CIP]

The foundation of the First Aurelian Society in London in 1745 is evidence of Britain's early and continued interest in entomology. Thus it is fitting that two British librarians, long involved in the literature, should compile this guide. The briefly annotated lists of books, journals, newsletters, libraries, and museums and their collections, and the clear description of computerized information retrieval services, will aid both novices and specialists in the study of insects. The compilers regret that bees were omitted for lack of space. The 1,305 numbered items, indexed by number except as noted, are grouped under eight chapters, each further subdivided. Among them is one on entomologists and their organizations, including directories, learned societies, and sources of obituaries. Another on miscellaneous services gives an annotated list of translation services and guides. Both foreign and English-language titles are included; the British titles are more up-to-date, e.g., Winchell's *Guide to Reference Books* (1951) is described as not as strong in entomology as Walford's *Guide* (1980), with no mention of *Sheehy*. Nor is the latest edition of Blanchard and Ostvold's *Literature of Agricultural Research* cited.

This well-organized and -indexed volume is broad in coverage; it will serve academic and special libraries well.

The essential jazz records: ragtime to swing, v.1. By Max Harrison, et al. Westport, Conn., Greenwood, 1984. xii, 595p. (Discographies, no.12) 22cm. hardcover $39.95 (0-313-24674-2).

016.7899'12542 Jazz music—Discography [CIP] 84-7926

The first volume of a two-volume set, this book describes the 250 best jazz records from the origins of jazz through the twenties and thirties. Entries are arranged in roughly chronological order to facilitate viewing of jazz styles and artists in their historical context. All of the recordings selected are considered by the three editors to be either the most representative or the most progressive of the time. Although the vast majority of recordings are of American music, there are two chapters on European jazz music and the influence of jazz on classical composers.

For each entry as much information as possible is given about the recording, including titles, dates, personnel, and instrumentation of each song in the collection. Both American and European catalog numbers are provided. All of the entries are indexed by album title, song title, and musician.

Reviews average two pages in length and provide critical evaluations of all of the songs on each record. These reviews provide valuable insight into the evolution of jazz by comparing various recordings and artists. Although the editors do not always agree on the value of an individual song or performer, all listings had some impact on the history of jazz. *The Essential Jazz Records* is a valuable starting point in studying the history of jazz music and in building a jazz collection. It will be extremely useful for anyone interested in the subject.

Ethnic genealogy: a research guide. Edited by Jessie Carney Smith. Westport, Conn., Greenwood, 1983. xxxix, 440p. 24cm. cloth $37.50 (0-313-22593-1).

929'.1'072073 U.S.—Genealogy—Handbooks, manuals, etc. | U.S.—Genealogy—Library resources | Afro-Americans—Genealogy—Handbooks, manuals, etc. | Asian Americans—Genealogy—Handbooks, manuals, etc. | Hispanic Americans—Genealogy—Handbooks, manuals, etc. | Indians of North America—Genealogy—Handbooks, manuals, etc. [CIP] 82-12145

The genesis of this work was an Institute on Ethnic Genealogy for Librarians held at Fisk University in 1979. It will be useful to librarians, to genealogists, and to persons searching American Indian, Asian-American, black American, and Hispanic-American ancestries.

The extensive Introduction by the editor, university librarian at Fisk, summarizes the various chapters. Each is written by a specialist, e.g., the president of the Afro-American Historical and Genealogical Society, a specialist in East Asian genealogy at Brigham Young University's Honolulu campus, a specialist in family associations and periodicals, a researcher in Spanish-language sources, an author of a computer instructional package for Afro-American history, and a researcher in American Indian records. Several of the contributors have worked with the extensive genealogy records of the Mormon Genealogical Society in Salt Lake City.

There are detailed chapters on genealogical sources, basic genealogical techniques, researching family history, the resources of the National Archives and Records Service, the huge library of the Mormon Genealogical Society, and sources available on the four specific ethnic groups covered. Detailed explanations of the National Archives, the Genealogical Society, and census records, as they pertain to the ethnic groups, are provided. Each chapter has thorough documentation, annotated bibliographies, and, in some cases, lists of periodicals, directories of societies and repositories, etc. Throughout, the style is one of helpfulness for both novices and advanced searchers. Gaining a sense of the whole history that surrounds a family is stressed. A general Index concludes the work.

Although other works such as *Black Genealogy* (1977) and *Black Genesis* (1978) (cf. *RSBR*, July 15, 1978), have similar information, *Ethnic Genealogy* is the first inclusive work that covers several ethnic minorities and provides more general information as well. Family researchers or librarians will find this comprehensive, user-friendly work invaluable.

Ethnic information sources of the United States. 2d ed. 2v. Paul Wasserman, managing ed.; Alice E. Kennington, assoc. ed. Detroit, Gale, 1983. xix, 1,380p. 29cm. cloth $135 (0-8103-0367-1).
301.45′1′071073 Minorities—U.S.—Societies, etc.—Directories | Minorities—U.S.—Information services | Ethnic groups—U.S.—Directories | Minority groups—Directories | Societies—U.S.—Directories [OCLC]   76-4642

A sturdy reference source reviewed by the Board in its 1976 edition (cf. *RSBR*, April 1, 1977) has now been updated. The purpose of the work is to bring together in one location information about nearly 90 ethnic groups in the U.S. It does not cover black Americans, American Indians, or Eskimo, as they are covered in other sources. The work provides for each group lists of fraternal and professional organizations, foundations, museums, newspapers, radio and television programs, festivals, etc. Standard directory/bibliographic data are provided; some items with brief descriptions. Although no count of organizations is provided, an estimate from the Organization Index is 1,800. A new feature is a general chapter on groups, especially study centers, which focus on ethnicity as a phenomenon itself, rather than on any particular ethnic group. New ethnic categories added are Asians, Indochinese, and Byelorussians.

The arrangement is alphabetical by ethnic group and under each type, source of information appears with cross-references. The Organization Index lists the group by its full name but without cross-references. Organizations are located across the U.S. but especially on the East Coast. Their interests run the gamut from support for activities in the homeland to the perpetuation of ethnic heritage in the U.S. to opposition to the current government in the mother country. A sample of books, pamphlets, and audiovisual materials on one ethnic group revealed that half of the items date from 1976 to the present, including one from 1980.

As noted in the Board's review of the first edition, librarians will need to weigh carefully the work's value in terms of other sources that might be available. Information about most of the organizations in a small sample was also located in the current *Encyclopedia of Associations*. *The Encyclopedic Directory of Ethnic Organizations in the U.S.* (1975), reviewed by the Board (cf. *RSBR*, July 15, 1976), lists organizations, and the *Guide to Ethnic Museums, Libraries, and Archives in the U.S.* (1978) describes 830 institutions. Still, the wide-ranging nature of *Ethnic Information Sources of the U.S.* makes it a convenient tool, especially in public libraries.

The Eugene O'Neill companion. By Margaret Loftus Ranald. Westport, Conn., Greenwood, 1984. 827p. 24cm. cloth $65 (0-313-22551-6).
812′.52 O'Neill, Eugene, 1888-1953—Handbooks, manuals, etc. | O'Neill, Eugene, 1888-1953—Dictionaries, indexes, etc. [CIP]   83-22671

This huge work, intended for general readers, provides synopses of the plays, identifies characters, and supplies biographical data for many O'Neill associates and family members. Information in the many Appendixes includes a chronology of plays; film and musical adaptations; information on manuscripts; and selected lists of critical studies and dissertations on O'Neill written after 1960. There is also a brief but not very helpful section on the future of O'Neill scholarship.

Arrangement is alphabetical; cross-referencing is good. Where necessary, bibliographic sources are noted both in the text and at the end of entries. There are several bibliographies. The main bibliography contains full reference information for all sources cited in the body of the work. Another bibliography concerning O'Neill criticism gives complete bibliographic information, but coverage is selective and limited to work written since 1953.

Scene-by-scene plot summaries of the major plays are detailed, perhaps too detailed. The plot summary for *A Moon for the Misbegotten* is more than 6,000 words; *Long Day's Journey into Night* is just under 8,000 words. The critical comments of the author following many summaries are helpful to beginning students. An essay entitled "O'Neill's Theory and Practice of the Theatre: An Assessment" is not fully developed and provides little insight into the expressionistic and naturalistic elements in his work. However, O'Neill's important contribution to American theater and his work as an experimenter are fully documented in this book.

The Europa biographical dictionary of British women: over 1,000 notable women from Britain's past. Edited by Anne Crawford et al. London, Europa; Detroit, Gale (exclusive distributors in U.S. and possessions), 1983. ix, 436p. 25cm. hardcover $55 (0-8013-1789-3).
920.72′0941 Women—Great Britain—Biography [British CIP]

This biographical dictionary lists more than 1,000 deceased British women who have made their mark in history. Entries range from early times through the twentieth century. Included are women "whose place in history is recognized"; women involved in public affairs; women who participated "in a movement which allowed women greater scope than was usual at the time"; women who were philanthropists and/or those close to government ("wives, mistresses, ladies-in-waiting, and society hostesses"); and those in the arts.

The entries, alphabetically arranged, are each initialed by one of the 78 contributors (both men and women); many of the writers have academic affiliations. Entries provide the woman's full name, birth and death dates, a biographical essay (which lists creative works and their dates of publication as appropriate), and usually end with references to other sources, mostly monographs (with incomplete bibliographic data). Most are a column or less in length; there are no illustrations.

The text includes limited cross-references—generally from pseudonym or commonly known name to proper name. Within entries, names in caps indicate separate entries in the work.

This is a balanced work in terms of historical periods and coverage of the areas outlined in the Introduction. Most of the women included were born in the British Isles, but others were from areas which are or were part of the British Empire.

Because of its specific nature, *The Europa Biographical Dictionary of British Women* will probably be most appropriate for collections specializing in British history or the history of women.

European writers: the Age of Reason and the Enlightenment. v.3 & 4. George Stade, editor in chief. New York, Scribner, 1984. 718p. 28cm. cloth $130/set (0-684-16594-5: v.1 & 2); (0-684-17914-8: v.3 & 4).
809′894 European literature—History and criticism—Addresses, essays, lectures [CIP]   83-16333

These two volumes continue the series on European writers, of which v.1 and 2 were reviewed earlier (cf. *RBB*, Sept. 15, 1984). They contain 27 chronologically arranged essays on 29 writers, chiefly French, with a few German and Italian, from Descartes to André Chénier. As in the first two volumes, they are written for a general audience by qualified scholars and are distinguished for their clarity and balanced treatment of the lives and works of such great figures as Corneille, Molière, Pascal, Racine, Voltaire, and Lessing. Current critical opinion is reflected as in Gita May's essay on Diderot, whose "originality as a bold, imaginative scientific thinker . . . would be uncovered only quite recently, thanks to the work of dedicated scholars on both sides of the Atlantic." Recent titles also appear in the appended bibliographies for each essay which include a selection of standard editions, translations, and biographical and critical studies. As the Board observed for the first two volumes, "The judicious selection of writers and genres and their interesting treatment recommend this well-designed and stoutly bound set to academic and public libraries, and to preparatory schools where the classics are taught."

European writers: the Middle Ages and the Renaissance. 2v. William T. H. Jackson, editor; George Stade, editor in chief. New York, Scribner, 1983. 956p. 29cm. cloth $130 (less 20 percent discount for standing orders) (0-684-16594-5).
809′.894 European literature—History and criticism—Addresses, essays, lectures [CIP]   83-16333

These two volumes, the first of 11 in a series on European writers, contain 36 articles, 25 on individual writers from Prudentius (348–   ) to Calderón de la Barca. The rest cover a movement or genre, such as Renaissance pastoral poetry or Renaissance short fiction. This series augments and updates the coverage of *Ancient Writers: Greece and Rome* (Scribner, 1982) and, with the latter, serves as a companion to the publisher's multivolumed *American Writers* and *British Writers*.

Aimed at a general audience, the articles (each about 15,000 words) are distinguished by a lucid and interesting selection of facts on the writers and good interpretations of their work. Articles on medieval writers emphasize their works, since little is known of their lives, with lives of Renaissance writers more fully treated.

The chronologically arranged articles were written by 29 "young scholars and professors emeriti; by critics, translators, poets, and novelists; by experts in an era or movement or figure," chiefly from large American and British universities. Unfortunately, the editor, William T. H. Jackson (Columbia University), died shortly after completing the Introduction, which gives an excellent overview of the periods covered. Also supplied in volume 1 is a Chronology of Medieval and Renaissance Europe. An index will, it is hoped, appear in volume 11.

Evaluating Chicago sociology: a guide to the literature, with an annotated bibliography. By Lester R. Kurtz. Chicago & London, Univ. of Chicago Pr., 1984. x, 303p. (Heritage of Sociology series) 21cm. cloth $22 (0-226-46476-8).

016.301 Sociology—U.S.—Bibliography | Chicago school of sociology—Bibliography [CIP]   84-53

This contribution to the Heritage of Sociology series is by an assistant professor of sociology at the University of Texas at Austin. Kurtz' stated purpose is a twofold one. First, there is a critical analysis of the Chicago School of Sociology—a coterie of sociologists (e.g., Albion Small, William I. Thomas, and Robert E. Park) and nonsociologists (e.g., John Dewey, George Herbert Mead, and Thorstein Veblen) at the University of Chicago whose outstanding contributions and those of their disciples gave Chicago intellectual domination of sociology for about 60 years, from 1892 (when the world's first university sociology department was founded at Chicago) to 1950 (by which date Chicago's dominance had waned). This is followed by a selected, annotated bibliography. The breadth of the critical analysis (the "guide to the literature" of the subtitle) is evident in the range of topics addressed in seven lucid chapters on persons behind the movement, substantive areas, and methods of research, etc.

The excellent annotated bibliography of some 1,000 primary and secondary references includes material published through 1983: books, articles, and dissertations. As expected, most of the references are to sociological items (including a few in French, Italian, Swedish, German, etc.); in addition, a few journal sources as varied as *American Heritage, Atlantic Monthly, Technology and Culture, Phylon,* and *Teachers College Record* are also included. So too are a few works by anthropologists, economists, historians, philosophers, etc.—that is to say, persons associated with Chicago sociology, such as the previously mentioned Dewey, Mead, and Veblen.

The comprehensive Index includes author and subject references to both sections of the work. Scholars and students interested in the history of sociology will find this work invaluable. Sociology collections, particularly those in academic libraries, will certainly need it.

The Facts On File dictionary of archaeology. Ruth D. Whitehouse, editor. New York, Facts On File, 1983. 597p. 25cm. cloth $24.95 (0-87196-048-6).

930.1'03'21 Archaeology—Dictionaries [OCLC]   83-16396

The intended audience for this comprehensive, brief-entry dictionary is wide ranging, from professionals and student archaeologists to the general public. Some 3,500 entries cover sites from all over the world, cultures, archaeological techniques and terminology, and a few biographees. The time span is "some four million years, from the emergence of man or his immediate ancestors to recent centuries." All contributors are professional archaeologists, most of whom are identified with academic/research institutions in the U.S., Canada, England, or Australia.

Ruth D. Whitehouse is lecturer in prehistoric archaeology at the University of Lancaster. She is coauthor (with David Whitehouse) of *Archaeological Atlas of the World* (San Francisco: Freeman, 1975). (See *RSBR*, June 1, 1976.) Whitehouse has clearly succeeded in blending extensive use of nontechnical language and well-defined technical terms with numerous cross-references and well-placed black-and-white illustrations and pertinent chronological tables.

The dictionary concludes with a Subject Index (rearranging the entries in some 30 categories) and Further Reading (similarly subdivided), providing references as current as 1983. Those familiar with another British archaeological dictionary, Sara Champion's *Dictionary and Terms of Archaeology* (New York: Facts On File, 1980) may recall that, unlike Whitehouse's, Champion's is not a comprehensive title; for it defines only about 300 terms and deliberately omits cultures and artifacts. (Cf. *RSBR*, June 1, 1981.)

Clearly, *The Facts On File Dictionary of Archaeology* will be a useful addition to archaeology, anthropology, and general reference collections in high school, public, and academic libraries.

The Facts On File dictionary of botany. Elizabeth Tootill, general editor; Stephen Blackmore, consultant editor. New York, Facts On File, 1984. 390p. diagrs. 23cm. hardcover $21.95 (0-87196-861-4).

580'.3'21 Botany—Dictionaries [CIP]   83-25309

Like those in any good dictionary in a special field, the 3,000 entries in this botanical dictionary include fuller definitions and a number of terms not found in general dictionaries. Embracing the major fields of pure and applied plant science, with selected items from such related fields as agricultural botany, horticulture, and microbiology, and some laboratory equipment and techniques, it omits named species or genera but includes higher ranks of plant groups and some larger families, e.g., *Rosaceae*. In this respect it resembles George Usher's *Dictionary of Botany, Including Terms Used in Biochemistry, Soil Science and Statistics* (1966), whose brief definitions for high school and college students omit genera and species. The clear definitions, some augmented by line drawings and charts, were prepared by ten British contributors, seven with bachelors of science, three with higher degrees. Pronunciation is not given.

Published simultaneously in the United Kingdom as *The Penguin Dictionary of Botany*, it should be useful to its target audience: undergraduate students in botany and biology.

The Facts On File dictionary of design and designers. By Simon Jervis. New York, Facts On File, 1984. 533p. 22cm. cloth $24.95 (0-87196-891-6).

745.4'03'21 Design—Dictionaries | Designers—Biography [CIP]   83-25350

Europe and North America are emphasized in this historical dictionary covering the period from 1450 to the present and including not only designers but "some patrons, impresarios, pundits, and historians" as well as exhibitions. Although some styles, concepts, and motifs are covered, a detailed glossary of design and ornament is not attempted, readers being referred to dictionaries of architecture and decorative arts. However, the compiler, on the staff of the Victoria and Albert Museum, has drawn from Thieme and Becker's *Künstlerlexikon* and other art and architecture sources. Jervis modestly describes his introductory essay as the "sketchiest outline of the designer in history," but it gives a good idea of the difficulties of defining the subject. Biographical entries, 50 to 1,000 words in length, emphasize the biographee's work in design, e.g., as in Aalto's contribution as a designer rather than as an architect or urban planner. Entries for design journals are evaluated as to their usefulness as sources. Movements (Art Nouveau) and societies (Art-Workers' Guild) include many cross-references in their texts. There are no appended bibliographies.

In a field "where modern literature is both sketchy and patchy," *Dictionary of Design and Designers* is a convenient source of identification of major and minor figures, as well as organizations and journals. It will be welcomed in comprehensive collections.

The Facts On File dictionary of religions. John R. Hinnells, editor. New York, Facts On File, 1984. 550p. 22cm. cloth $24.95 (0-87196-862-2).

291'.03'21 Religions [CIP]   83-20834

Though produced by an international team of 29 scholars, this dictionary is a predominately British enterprise. It has four sections: the Dictionary (the largest), Maps, Bibliography, and General and Synoptic Indexes. It intends to promote understanding of the specialized vocabulary used by those who write about and practice religion. The bulk of the work has been allocated to "living" religions, but the work includes new religious movements, astrology, magic, and the occult, as well as "secular alternatives to religion" such as Marxism and humanism. The clarity of the definitions varies, and no pronunciation is given. There are ample cross-references within entries but no main-entry cross-references. The valuable, scholarly bibliographies, arranged under broad subject headings, are keyed by Roman numerals and numbers to the entries. Because use of the General Index is frequently essential, this is often a two-step dictionary, for example, there is no entry under *Muslims*, but the General Index refers readers to *Islām*. For American Indians, the Index refers to *Amerindians*. Charismatic, Malcolm X, Gandhi, and

Krishnamurti are not separate entries, but the Index points to references in the text.

The Synoptic Index groups related entries under broad categories. There are some omissions—Reinhold Niebuhr, Pierre Teilhard de Chardin, and Martin Buber, for example. The work's strength is in its coverage of Eastern religions and concepts. In fact, the entries for *Zoroastrianism, Hinduism,* and *Neo-Confucianism* are longer than those for *Judaism, Protestantism,* and *Roman Catholicism.*

For general collections, this will not be as useful as Brandon's *Dictionary of Comparative Religions* (Weidenfeld & Nicholson, 1970) or the *Abingdon Dictionary of Living Religions* (Abingdon, 1981). *The Facts On File Dictionary of Religions* will be useful primarily in larger academic collections or libraries specializing in the subject.

Fantasy for children. 2d ed. [Compiled by] Ruth Nadelman Lynn. New York and London, Bowker, 1983. xiv, 444p. 24cm. cloth $24.95 plus shipping & handling (0-8352-1732-9).
016.80883'876 Children's stories—Bibliography | Fantastic fiction—Bibliography | Bibliography—Best books—Children's stories | Bibliography—Best books—Fantastic fiction [CIP]   83-11868

The first edition of *Fantasy for Children* (c1979) was a bibliographic guide for parents, teachers, and librarians to more than 1,650 recommended fantasies for children, grades three through eight. This second edition includes more than 2,000 recommended fantasy novels and short story collections for the same age users and audience. Science fiction is excluded. All were published in English in the U.S. (including translations into English) between 1900–1982. Such earlier classics as *Alice in Wonderland, Gulliver's Travels,* and *Princess and the Goblin* have been included if they are historically significant and were published in recommended editions after 1900.

Unlike the first edition, the out-of-print titles have been interfiled with the in-print ones here.

The books listed in the "Annotated Checklist of Fantasy Literature for Children" are arranged in 11 topical chapters. Some chapter titles have been slightly changed since the previous edition. The chapters include "Animal Fantasy," "Imaginary Beings and Creatures," "Time Travel Fantasy," "Witchcraft and Wizardry Fantasy," etc.

Within each chapter the titles are alphabetical by author; full bibliographic information is given, along with grade level, a brief descriptive note, a listing of reviews and, where applicable, a notation of awards won and a listing of sequels and related works by the author. Cross-references have been liberally supplied.

Entries for in-print titles include specific recommendation: an asterisk indicating outstanding quality; *R,* recommended; and *A,* acceptable. However, the basis for inclusion is that each work must have been recommended by at least *two* review sources from a select list of 17 book review journals and literature texts. Therefore, the 185 titles labeled "marginal" in the 1979 edition have been dropped.

New to this edition are an Introduction that provides an overview of the critical literature published on children's fantasy and a bibliography of 1,725 critical and biographical books, articles, and Ph.D. dissertations on children's fantasy, divided into three parts—Reference Works, History and Criticism, and Author Studies.

The volume concludes with a Directory of Publishers, Author and Illustrator, and Title Indexes.

Fantasy for Children is a valuable reference tool for librarians, teachers, and students of children's literature. It can be a guide to build collections, to locate specific titles or kinds of fantasy, and to stimulating research.

Festivals sourcebook: a reference guide to fairs, festivals, and celebration... 2d ed. Paul Wasserman, managing ed., Edmond L. Applebaum, associate ed. Detroit, Gale, 1984. xi, 721p. 23cm. cloth $110 (0-8103-0323-X).
394.2'6973 Festivals—U.S. | Festivals—Canada [OCLC]   76-48852

The Board recommended the first edition of *Festivals Sourcebook* (cf. *RSBR,* March 1, 1979), but gently chided it for minor flaws, mostly specific omissions. Such problems are unavoidable given the nature of the book, and users must tolerate and easily forgive them. The purpose—to list annual or otherwise regularly scheduled festivals, fairs, folk celebrations, theater and drama fests, and other community events of more than local interest held in the U.S. and Canada—and the format—a listing by broad type and by state or province within types—remains the same. The number of events has increased from 3,813 to 4,247. The major categories under which they are listed remains 18 in number, although the number of headings in the more specific Subject Index has been increased from approximately 180 to 226.

Entries list name of event, location, usual date(s), address and telephone number (the latter a new feature), a description, and year the event was first held. In addition to the Subject Index, there are Chronological, Event Name, and Geographic Indexes. Canadian events account for only 370 entries.

The editors acknowledge that there are omissions which should be remedied and deletions which should be made in the next edition and ask for users' input in both areas. Herewith, the *Reference Books Bulletin* Editorial Board offers its suggestions of events which fit the book's scope (i.e., there are no local celebrations of a national holiday, sports events, horse shows, county fairs, holy days, rodeos, or beauty pageants which are not a part of a larger festival). Events omitted include the annual Labor Day walk from north to south across the Mackinac Bridge; the annual Air Fair in Dayton, Ohio, North America's largest air show; the annual Kraut Festival in Franksville, Wisconsin; and the Old Town Art Fair in Chicago. An event to delete is Chicagofest, a music festival described as being held at Chicago's Navy Pier. Chicago's political wars moved it to Soldier Field in 1983; it lost money and subsequently was discontinued. This serves as a caution that users should confirm not only dates of events, but their continued existence.

Festivals Sourcebook is as complete as one can reasonably expect it to be. If users take the editors' invitation to submit additions and corrections, the next edition will be an even more useful planning tool to travelers with special interests and to public relations professionals looking for opportunities to put their clients in the public eye.

Fiction 1876–1983: A bibliography of United States editions. 2v. New York and London, Bowker, 1983. 2,328p., 1,050p. 29 cm. hardbound $99.50 + shipping/handling (0-8352-1726-4: set; 0-8352-1880-5: v.1; 0-8352-1881-3: v.2).
016.80883 Fiction—Bibliography | U.S.—Imprints [CIP]   83-21376

Like other recent Bowker bibliographies (e.g., *Biographical Books,* see *RSBR,* 9/15/81), these volumes were compiled from the Bowker database utilized for *Books in Print* and *American Book Publishing Record.* Among its 170,000 titles, chiefly by twentieth-century American authors, are novels, novellas, short story collections, and anthologies, both adult and juvenile. The two main alphabets, volume 1, Author Index, and volume 2, Title Index, contain similar bibliographic data for each entry and at the most include: author, coauthor, editor, translator, title, original title, edition, whether a reprint, LC number, whether illustrated, pagination, date of publication and/or copyright, publisher and distributor (if different), type of binding (if other than cloth over boards), price, ISBN, and imprint. In many cases, of course, far fewer data are provided. Titles were selected on the basis of all editions for which Library of Congress cataloging was available, supplemented by Bowker's database. Out-of-print mass-market paperbacks were generally omitted.

A 41-page Classified Author Index groups approximately 80 percent of the authors by nationality and century, e.g., *Authors, African, 20th Century,* according to LC practice of linking authors with nationalities. Birth and death dates, not given in either the Author or Title Index, are sometimes supplied in the Classified Author Index. Volume 2 contains an appended Key to Publishers' and Distributors' Abbreviations/Directory of Publishers and Distributors, which serves to establish full name and address for 15,000 publishers currently in business, but not for others cited in abbreviated form in the Author and Title Indexes.

No inconsistencies in alphabetizing were found in the two volumes, but as noted above, full bibliographic data are often lacking. For example, pagination is seldom given, nor is date of publication in some cases, although the LC number often gives a clue to the approximate date. Price is found more often than not, but there are some omissions. Also, various editions of the same title appear in no discernible order.

The editor states that "virtually every fiction title that appeared in the U.S. in the period covered will be found in these volumes." Such a sweeping statement invites reviewers to dig for omissions, and in fact, the Board's random checking of other bibliographies revealed titles published in the U.S. within the period which do not appear in *Fiction 1876-1983.* (Since a mere six columns are devoted to Henry James, one could intuitively suspect the comprehensiveness of this set.) Thus, if a complete list of an author's fiction is needed, further checking will be necessary.

Nevertheless, in spite of these weaknesses, *Fiction 1876-1983*, in bringing together nearly 100 years of American imprints of America's most popular literary form, will prove a useful time saver in large public and academic libraries and is a useful addition to American enumerative bibliography. Recommended.

The fifty billion dollar directory: marketing guide to 10,750 mail order companies. 1984 ed. [Edited by] Anitra Earle. Publishers Services, 6318 Vesper Ave., Van Nuys, CA 91411-2378, 1984. ix, 630p. 29cm. hardbound $65 (0-916145-00-X; ISSN: 0741-8892).

381'.14'02573 Mail-order business—U.S.—Directories [OCLC]   84-644925

This marketing guide consists primarily of two major lists amounting to 478 double-column pages. One is of those mail-order companies advertising specific products; the other is of mail-order book dealers. Both are arranged in zip-code order. There is no separate alphabetical listing provided to help locate a known firm by name or to group firms by product interest. The work also includes more than 100 pages of discussions on the direct-marketing business in general and advice for those contemplating it.

Basically this is a work designed for the mail-order sales market and for firms or individuals wishing to establish contact with those firms. Libraries needing directories of mail-order firms are better served by two titles having good subject arrangements and useful indexes: *The New Wholesale-by-Mail Catalog* (The Print Project, New York: St. Martin's Press, 1982) and Richard Gottlieb's *Directory of Mail Order Catalogs* (New York: Grey House, 1981).

Film directors: a complete guide. 2d annual international, 1984 ed.. Beverly Hills, Calif., Lone Eagle, 1984. viii, 384p. 28cm. hardcover $32.95 (0-943728-05-3; ISSN: 0740-282).

†791.43'0233'092 Moving-picture producers and directors [OCLC]   83-4926

This updated, revised, and expanded international edition includes full-length feature and telefeature credits for more than 1,200 filmmakers (American and foreign). The title has been changed in this edition (from *Directors: A Complete Guide*), and a new section has been added, "From the Director's Chair," containing interviews and photographs of six prominent directors. A third edition is planned for publication in December 1984.

The compiler, a motion picture researcher and production associate who lives and works in Los Angeles, has included self-nominated individuals who meet the general criteria of being fairly active directors whose works have been distributed in the U.S. In addition to these nominees and others that he receives or selects himself, he has added some retired film "greats," and a few independent filmmakers.

Each entry gives the date and place of birth and contacts (agents and/or home address) wherever possible, a list of films with their dates of release if known, names of the production company, and whether a U.S. or foreign release. Notation indicates whether a director is a member of the Director's Guild and whether a film was an Academy Award or Emmy winner or nominee.

The Index of Directors opens with an "In Memoriam" tribute, listing 12 directors or actor/directors who died in 1983 and is followed by an Index of Film Titles. The guide concludes with a directory of agents/managers.

Much of this information can be found in such other resources as Halliwell's *Film Companion* or Sternberg's *Film Facts*, but *Film Directors* provides easy access for students, fans, or aspiring directors. It will be especially useful in larger film collections. Practitioners in the industry might also use it.

The films of the seventies: a filmography of American, British and Canadian films, 1970–1979. By Marc Sigoloff. Jefferson, N.C., McFarland, 1984. viii, 424p. 24cm. cloth $29.95 (0-89950-095-1).

791.43'75 Moving-pictures—Dictionaries [CIP]   83-42887

An alphabetical listing of 942 mainstream films, by a compiler who believes that the seventies were the most productive period to date for Anglo-American cinema, this work lists for each film the year, a quality rating (one to five stars), company, length, production and directorial staff, complete cast (and the names of the characters played), audience rating (G, PG, R, or X), and U.S./Canadian box-office rental (gross minus theater's expenses and share). Films from Canada and Britain are so labeled. Fifty- to 100-word annotations summarize and critique each film, note genre, and often relate the film to others.

A Name Index (actors, producers, cinematographers, etc.) refers users to the entry number, not page. While the focus of *The Films of the Seventies* is popular rather than scholarly, a great deal of information is given for each film. Critiques are decidedly idiosyncratic, but interesting. Because of the focus, the inherent appeal of the subject coupled with a format that makes for easy browsing, and the comprehensive nature of the coverage, this is a good source for both popular libraries and research film collections. However, it should be noted that *Films of the Seventies* undoubtedly overlaps to a certain extent with many other film reference sources, but it is probably the most detailed for the period covered.

The financing of American higher education: a bibliographic handbook. By Richard H. Quay and Peter P. Olevnik. Phoenix, Oryx, 1984. xvi, 142p. 29cm. cloth $27.50 (0-89774-047-5).

016.3791'214'0973 Universities and colleges—U.S.—Finance—Bibliography [CIP]   83-13192

This bibliography focuses on perhaps the most important and persistent problem in higher education today—finance. Reflecting the development of an academic specialization over two decades, it brings together the major records of published scholarship in the field from 1960 to 1981, although it emphasizes works published between 1971 and 1981, with a few 1982 titles.

Following an extensive literature search, the authors selected those items which generally met one of eight criteria: authorship by a prominent scholar; addressing of theoretical constructs, their application, or criticism; focus on highly specialized subjects; "where lack of volume precluded greater selectivity"; authorship by a corporate body important to higher education; and frequent citation as determined by a citation analysis. More comprehensive coverage was afforded to the four-year college and university setting, with more selective coverage of community colleges and little of other postsecondary institutions. Also, works not readily available in print or through ERIC were usually rejected.

The work is organized by a descriptive classification scheme developed by the authors that reflects their view of the dominant themes of higher education finance over the last two decades. The four major sections (covering the Political Economy of Higher Education; Institutions, Programs and Coalitions; Human Resources; and Research, Planning, and Policy Development) are further subdivided into 19 subject areas. The alphabetically arranged (by author) citations in each section include standard bibliographic information and a one-paragraph annotation.

Supplementary information includes appendixes listing and annotating related bibliographic sources on financing American higher education and higher education financial data sources. Author and Subject Indexes are also appended.

Students and instructors of higher education as well as college and university administrators, government officials, and individuals with policymaking responsibility in all areas of higher education, whether public or private, will find this resource highly useful. Academic libraries and those libraries serving government bodies will want to buy it.

Find that tune: an index to rock, folk-rock, disco & soul in collections. Edited by William Gargan and Sue Sharma. New York, Neal-Schuman, 1984. vii, 303p. 29cm. hardcover $39.95 (0-918212-70-7).

784.5'4'0016 Rock music—Indexes | Disco music—Indexes | Soul music—Indexes [CIP]   82-22346

This guide to more than 4,000 songs from 203 sheet-music collections has five indexes/lists: the collections themselves and then indexes by song titles, first lines, composer/lyricist, and performer. The Title Index forms the main body of the work with publisher name, copyright date, and the names of performers, composers, and lyricists. The collections indexed represent the broadest spectrum of music. *Phonolog Reporter, Rock On,* and *Popular Music* were used to verify or correct information; cross-references are generous. *Find That Tune* is a good source for music collections and sheet-music dealers.

Finding answers in science and technology. By Alice Lefler Primack. New York, Van Nostrand, 1984. xv, 364p. 24cm. hardcover $22.50 (0-442-28227-3).

507 Science—Library resources—Handbooks, manuals, etc. | Technology—Library resources—Handbooks, manuals, etc. | Libraries—U.S.—Handbooks, manuals, etc. [CIP]   82-20082

A guide to science reference sources for high school, junior college, and undergraduate students, and for "hobby" scientists, this volume includes only those sources which are suitable for both nonstudents and students. Emphasis is on U.S. materials which are current, in print, and easily accessible. How-to-do-it books and books expressing particular points of view have been excluded.

The author is a science/technology librarian. Previously she wrote *How to Find Out in Pharmacy*. The first two chapters discuss the types of scientific and technical information and how to find answers by using library resources and computer searching. These are followed by chapters on specific subjects arranged in order of Library of Congress classification from general science to engineering. Subsections in three chapters reflect current concerns and interests. The mathematics chapter has a section on computer science; natural history has sections on nature conservation and ecology; and engineering has a section on energy. Each subject chapter is divided as follows: introductory materials, suggested subject headings and classification numbers for locating materials, bibliographic materials, secondary literature, current awareness materials, and quick reference tools. Lists of the major journals in the subject area are included under secondary literature. In a number of chapters, sample pages from reference tools are reprinted.

The Appendix includes a list of U.S. libraries having major collections in science and technology, U.S. government depository libraries, NASA information centers, and U.S. patent depository libraries. These are not exhaustive lists, but they would be helpful for interlibrary loan purposes.

The Index is an alphabetic list of titles and authors mentioned in the text.

Finding Answers in Science is not in the usual bibliographic or guide-to-the-literature format but is written as essays. When reference sources are cited, the title is followed by place of publication, publisher, edition, date, and a brief description. In the few cases where a source was listed under more than one subject, this information was repeated. *Finding Answers in Science* is an important tool for public, high school, and college libraries which will aid students in locating information and in using libraries.

Fine and applied arts terms index: an alphabetical guide to sources of information on more than 45,000 terms used by museums, art galleries, and auction galleries in the English-speaking world, and by artists, artisans, designers, and professionals in associated fields, including words and phrases that describe objets d'art, objets de vertu, bibelots, antique furnishings.... 1st ed. Laurence Urdang, editor in chief. Detroit, Gale, 1983. 773p. 24cm. cloth $85 (0-8103-1544-0).
701'.4 Art—Terminology—Indexes | Decorative arts—Terminology—Indexes [CIP] 83-16532

Fine and Applied Arts Terms Index is an index to definitions of terms from the visual arts found in 23 standard reference sources, 123 auction catalogs from Christie's and Sotheby's, and three volumes of *Kovels on Antiques and Collectibles*. The *Index* provides more than 45,000 references to the titles covered. Terms and personal names from the decorative arts are emphasized, although painting and sculpture are covered; architecture and urban planning are omitted. The primary user will be the student or collector of decorative objects.

The various sources and auction catalogs are cited after each of the alphabetically arranged entries by alphanumeric symbols which are identified in the Bibliography. The existence of an illustration for that term in a particular work is indicated. A two-page, How-to-Use-This-Book section explains the construction of the symbols.

Compiled by experienced editor Laurence Urdang, the *Index* lists terms as they were found in the various sources. As a result, multiple entries for the same term or person abound: *Huet, J–B* and *Huet, Jean-Baptiste; cries of London* and *cris de Londres; Mudjur carpet* and *Mudjur rug; Pergolesi, M. A., Pergolesi, Michael Angelo, Pergolesi, Michelangelo,* and *Pergolesi, Michele Angelo*. The Board observed duplicate entries on virtually every page.

Despite the duplication of similar entries, *Fine and Applied Arts Terms Index* will have value in art and general reference collections serving patrons interested in the decorative arts.

First editions: a guide to identification. Edited by Edward N. Zempel and Linda A. Verkler. Peoria, IL 61614, P.O. Box 3635, Spoon River Pr., 1984. vi, 231p. 23cm. hardcover $20 (0-930358-07-4).
002.075 Book collecting | Bibliography—First editions [OCLC] 83-51139

This guide is composed of two books known to reference librarians: Henry Sherman Boutell's *First Editions of Today and How to Tell Them* (Berkeley: Univ. of California Pr., 1949) and *A First Edition?* (Peoria: Spoon River Pr., 1977), which was compiled and edited by the editors of the title being reviewed. The Introduction begins with the statement, "This book has a complex history." This turns out to be an understatement. The work contains statements from the first, second, and third editions of Boutell's book. There is no explanation as to why the fourth edition (updated by Wanda Underhill and published by Peacock, 1965) is not included. The editors further state that the 1977 edition of *A First Edition?* is used here. No mention is made of the second edition, 1983, listed in the most recent *Books in Print*. Bibliographic references indicate that the title may be a paperback edition of the 1977 imprint. Is there a second edition? If so, does it have recent information not included here? Librarians should check further before ordering this assembled listing.

Publishers have supplied most of the information used in this guide. An introductory statement defines "first edition," "first impression," and "first printing." Publishers are listed alphabetically and their statements are dated. There are cross-references to indicate name changes and, with individual entries, *see* references call attention to additional information: "*See* 1937 Statement." Publishers listed are located in the U.S., the U.K., British Commonwealth, and Ireland. Many relatively new commercial publishers are included (surprised not to find David R. Godine), and there is good coverage of important small presses.

For librarians, scholars, and book collectors, this is a useful listing of first edition statements. Beginning book collectors are advised to read works on bibliography and study descriptive bibliographies on writers of interest to them. Only then will they properly interpret this 1936 printed statement in the entry for Random House, Inc.: "As far as Random House first editions are concerned, with the exception of limited editions where all the necessary information is contained in the colophon, all books are plainly marked 'first edition' on the copyright page."

Foundations. Edited by Harold M. Keele and Joseph C. Kiger. Westport, Conn., Greenwood, 1984. 516p. (Greenwood Encyclopedia of American Institutions) 24cm. cloth $49.95 (0-313-22556-7).
361.7'632'09 Charities—U.S.—Societies, etc.—History | Social service—U.S.—Societies, etc.—History | Corporations—Charitable contributions—U.S.—History | Endowments—U.S.—History [CIP] 83-10750

Designed as concise histories of voluntary and nonprofit organizations in American society, the volumes of the *Greenwood Encyclopedia of American Institutions* cover labor unions, social service organizations, research institutions, learned societies, and the like. This volume surveys the 234 largest American foundations.

The editors were aided in their work by a panel of 56 foundation officers/personnel staff and 21 academics who have contributed signed pieces; unsigned entries are presumably the work of the editors.

The front matter contains a detailed Table of Contents with cross-references, a list of contributors, and a lengthy Preface which provides an overview of the history and character of charitable foundations. The body of the volume presents the historical sketches of the foundations, their purposes, and usually a few sources for further information. Entries vary widely in length, from 250 words for the Adolph Coors Foundation to well over 3,000 words for organizations such as the Carnegie Corporation of New York. Entries average 750 to 1000 words. Arrangement is letter by letter by the official name of the foundation. Both the Table of Contents and the Index facilitate locating entries. Five Appendixes follow the text: foundations listed by asset size, family connected foundations, foundations listed by state, a chronology, and a "genealogy" of foundations listing the interrelationships among various foundations.

Much of the general information about the origin, areas of interest, assets, etc., can be found in other works such as the Foundation Center's *Source Book Profiles* or the *Taft Foundation Reporter*. These tools provide more detail regarding both current assets and recent grants, plus other information of particular interest to the reader contemplating an application to one of these organizations; the number of organizations they cover is also substantially larger than is provided here. However, *Foundations* will prove useful when the need is for fuller information on the history and development of a foundation. It will be a wise acquisition for larger reference collections in American studies and for the reference shelves of those doing fund-raising. It will be an excellent addition to a distinguished series.

Foundations of moral education: an annotated bibliography. James S. Leming, comp. Westport, Conn., Greenwood, 1983. xv, 339p. 24cm. cloth $35 (0-303-24165-1).

016.17'07 Ethics—Study and teaching—Bibliography ‖ Moral development—Bibliography [CIP]   83-12834

The writings on moral education (often referred to as values education) published from the 1960s through 1981 are the subject of this 1,532-entry annotated bibliography. The text is divided into three parts: "Reflections on the Domain of Moral Education" (philosophical material); "Moralization: The Learning of Morality" (behavioral sciences); and "Additional Topics" (sociological, historical, cross-cultural, political, etc., material). Within these sections, material is arranged topically and then alphabetically by author. Entries include articles, dissertations, and monographs in English and provide standard bibliographic data. Collections of readings have their own section at the end of the text. Unpublished material is not included since accessibility was a priority in selection. Items listed in *Dissertations Abstracts International (DAI)* have volume/page references to *DAI*, and items available as ERIC microfiche provide the ERIC access number.

The text concludes with accurate Author and Subject Indexes to entry number. *Foundations of Moral Education* is suitable for academic and special libraries with an interest in education and/or moral philosophy. However, libraries should be aware that since much of the material can be located through *DAI, Current Index to Journals in Education, Education Index*, etc., this is a convenience tool.

The Frankenstein catalog: being a comprehensive listing of novels, translations, adaptations, stories, critical works, popular articles, series, fumetti, verse, stage plays, films, cartoons, puppetry, radio & television programs, comics, satire & humor, spoken & musical recordings, tapes, and sheet music featuring Frankenstein's monster and/or descended from Mary Shelley's novel. [Comp. by] Donald F. Glut. Jefferson, N.C., and London, McFarland, 1984. x, 525p. 24cm. cloth $29.95 (0-89950-029-3).

016.823'7 Shelley, Mary Wollstonecraft, 1797-1851. Frankenstein—Bibliography ‖ Shelley, Mary Wollstonecraft, 1797-1851. Adaptations—Bibliography ‖ Frankenstein films—Catalogs ‖ Monsters in literature—Bibliography ‖ Monsters in mass media—Catalogs [CIP]   81-6026

Its subtitle says it all—or just about. High school, public, and academic libraries will, in support of a wide range of recreational and scholarly pursuits, want to acquire this beautifully annotated bibliography. There are 2,666 entries, grouped as suggested in the subtitle, and there are Name and Title Indexes.

"Fumetti" differ, by the way, from ordinary captioned photographs by being, according to Glut, "stories made up from still photos and/or motion-picture frame enlargements, arranged to tell the story of the film, and to which have been added comic strip style dialogue balloons and/or captions."

Glut's previous publications include *The Frankenstein Legend* (Scarecrow, 1973), in a sense a rehearsal for the far more nearly comprehensive *Frankenstein Catalog*.

Freedom in the world: political rights and civil liberties, 1983-1984. By Raymond D. Gastil. Westport, Conn., Greenwood, 1984. x, 474p. 24cm. cloth $35 (0-313-23179-6).

†323.4 Civil rights—Addresses, essays, lectures [OCLC]

This is the sixth yearbook since 1978 (and the eleventh year of work) by the nongovernmental Freedom House, which surveys the status of freedom in the world. Survey ratings, tables, and individual country summaries enable users to look at a variety of facts and informed interpretations, written by the director of the Comparative Survey of Freedom. Less useful for reference purposes is a 200-page section that includes presentations and discussions at a 1983 conference on freedom in China (mainland and Taiwan) sponsored by Freedom House. This concise gathering of data on the subject should be of use to public and academic libraries.

From museums, galleries, and studios: a guide to artists on film and tape. Compiled by Susan P. Besemer and Christopher Crosman. Westport, Conn., Greenwood, 1984. xvi, 199p. (Art Reference Collection, no.6) 24cm. cloth $35 (0-313-23881-1; ISSN: 0193-6867).

016.7'092'2 Artists—U.S.—Interviews—Film catalogs ‖ Artists—U.S.—Interviews—Phonotape catalogs [CIP]   83-22710

A "mediography" of 600 films, videocassettes, and audiocassettes in which artists describe their own work, the selection is confined to contemporary visual artists (painters, sculptors, photographers, architects, film and video makers, and craft and folk artists). As well as the expected modern, experimental, and performance artists, primarily of American origin, the work also includes such subjects as gold- and silversmith Tor Scwanck, illustrator Maurice Sendak, and saddlemaker Austin Green.

The main section is arranged by artist, with an additional section, arranged by titles, for the films/videos treating multiple artists.

Citations provide title, format, producer, distributor, date, running time, sound/color details, and order or rental information as well as a descriptive annotation on the contents. The directory which follows is an alphabetic list of producers, distributors, collections, and organizations to which requests for rental or purchase may be addressed. The Index includes persons, places, museums, works, and types of art which provides easy access to and selection of films, videos, and tapes on particular topics.

From Museums, Galleries, and Studios is a useful, unique source which will be of great interest to libraries serving public and academic audiences interested in contemporary art.

The frontier experience: a reader's guide to the life and literature of the American West. Edited by Jon Tuska and Vicki Piekarski, with Paul J. Blanding. Jefferson, N.C., McFarland, 1984. xiv, 434p. 23cm. cloth $29.95 (0-89950-118-4).

016.978 West (U.S.)—History—Bibliography ‖ West (U.S.)—History—Fiction—Bibliography ‖ West (U.S.)—History—Film catalogs ‖ Frontier and pioneer life—West (U.S.)—Bibliography ‖ Frontier and pioneer life—West (U.S.)—Fiction—Bibliography ‖ Frontier and pioneer life—West (U.S.)—Film catalogs [CIP]   84-42611

In the General Introduction to this bibliography, Tuska and Piekarski (coeditors of the *Encyclopedia of Frontier and Western Fiction*, McGraw-Hill, 1983), state that their intention is to "assist and guide the general reader through the vicissitudes of studying the American frontier and the Westward expansion." The book does this quite successfully, providing the general reader (but perhaps not the specialist) with 400 pages of fascinating reading, in the form of a score of introductory essays, and long annotations of several hundred recent monographs on some 20 different aspects of the American frontier.

The various sections of the book cover a wide variety of topics—western history in general, pioneer women, native Americans, Mexican Americans, missionaries, fur traders, the military, outlaws, cowboys, miners, the overland trail, stage-coaching, railroads, literature, and painting; even such diverse topics as poetry on the frontier and buffalo have separate and sometimes lengthy sections to themselves. Nor is the coverage limited to books; at the end of each section is a list of "Suggested Fiction" and "Suggested Films."

Both the essays and the annotations are written in a smooth, unpretentious style, not without an occasional touch of humor. For example, in the essay on western women, the author speaks of several female stereotypes to be found in the traditional western movie, such as the prostitute with the heart of gold, as well as the "hot-blooded Mexican, who has many problems adjusting to the Anglo-Saxon world, but whose main problem is keeping her peasant-style blouse from slipping off one of her shoulders."

The *Frontier Experience* will be especially valuable in public libraries, but it will also be useful in any library that endeavors to keep abreast of this century's output of literature dealing with the frontier and the West.

Gary Null's nutrition sourcebook for the '80s. [By] Gary Null. New York, Macmillan, 1983. 328p. 22cm. cloth $15.95 (0-02-590900-2).

641.1'0212 Food—Composition—Tables ‖ Nutrition—Tables [CIP]   83-713

This sourcebook gives the nutrient value (presumed average serving size is 100 grams) of readily available food in the form in which it is usually eaten, i.e., cooked or raw. Foods selected for inclusion are arranged according to eight categories; protein, carbohydrates, fat, cholesterol, fiber, sodium, vitamins (seven), and minerals (four). Foods are listed according to nutrient value, in descending order. At the bottom of the lists are those foods with the least amount of the quality measured: protein, fat, etc. To find the food value of the various foods included, users must check the Index and much page turning results. For the sweet potato there are 26 page references to 7 different listings (lists average 39 food items to a page). Also the Index lists foods only, containing no references to such subjects as fiber and polyunsaturates which are treated in the text. There are, however, separate entries for bread, whole wheat bread, and white bread. The lists are easily understood, listing food, calorie count, and nutritional value. The text is general and the source(s) for the nutritive information is not given.

The author has written dozens of books and articles on health subjects. *Gary Null's Nutrition Sourcebook* is not as comprehensive as Jean A. T. Pennington's *Food Values of Portions Commonly Used* (Harper and Row, 1980).

Gevers international consultants: world-wide professional directory. 3v. 3d ed. Lausanne, Seminar Services; dist. in the U.S. and Canada by Gale (Detroit) 1983. 31cm. cloth $185 (price includes midyear supplement).
†658.46′025 Consultants—Directories

The purpose of this annual directory is to provide worldwide information about international consultants, such as accountants and auditors, intellectual property consultants, lawyers-members of the local bar or law society, lawyers who are not members of the bar, and management and tax consultants. Each issue is updated by a midyear supplement published in August. The Introduction does not indicate the methods used for identifying and collecting the information provided. It does state that "firms listed in the directory have been checked as having the highest professional standards." Consulting firms from 119 countries (Algeria to Zimbabwe) have been identified in this issue.

Arrangement is alphabetical, first by name of the country, then by name of city (in the case of larger countries), then by type of consulting service, and finally by name. The maximum information provided for each firm is the address; brief description of the firm's practice; name and full address of associated firms in other cities or countries; language capabilities of the personnel; such other data as countries covered by the firm, references, and typical clients; data concerning each individual member of the firm: year and place of birth, degrees, professional experience, etc. The minimum amount of information under a firm is its exact name, address, and international telephone and telex numbers. Name and Professional (subject) Indexes are included for each country but not for the whole set.

Gevers International Consultants will be a useful work for libraries which serve businesses, particularly those involved in international trade.

The good book guide for business: an indispensable guide to more than 600 essential business books for today's managers. From the publishers of *The Good Book Guide* and *The Economist*. New York, Harper, 1984. 318p. illus. 22cm. cloth $20 (0-06-181877-1).
016.65 Management—Bibliography | Business—Bibliography | Economic history—1945- | Bibliography [CIP]   84-47601

The editors of the British publications *The Economist* and *The Good Book Guide* have prepared an annotated list of more than 600 books deemed most useful for practicing managers. Arranged topically in five chapters, the books included cover the world business environment, the management of organizations, the individual in business, and business history, as well as reference works. Two- to three-paragraph (unsigned) reviews are provided for each book. An Author-Title Index and Subject Index are also included.

It is difficult to determine exactly what criteria were used for the selection of books for this volume. While the editors clearly state that all books were written in English and are currently available (as of July 1984), the major selection criterion of "books that have something to say and stand out as being 'best of their type' " leaves many questions unanswered. In addition, the lack of publication dates for the books listed and the lack of any particular organization within each chapter make the guide difficult to use.

Keeping the above disadvantages in mind, librarians building business collections in small or medium-size libraries might wish to use this volume in conjunction with *The Basic Business Library*, reviewed in these pages August 1984.

Government programs and projects directory. 1st ed. Compiled and edited by Anthony T. Kruzas and Kay Gill. Detroit, Gale, 1983- . v. 28cm. paper $85 (3 parts) (0-8103-0422-8; ISSN 0737-5255).
353.07′8′025 Administrative agencies—U.S.—Directories | U.S.—Executive departments—Directories [OCLC]   83-645478

This new directory is being issued in three paperbound parts scheduled to appear at four- to six-month intervals; the Name and Month Keyword Index in each will be cumulated in the later issues. Entries are listed in two sections: cabinet departments and independent agencies (alphabetically by agency name) and program/project name. Each issue is expected to contain about 400 hundred entries. Programs of all types are covered: social services, research, law enforcement, defense, conservation, etc. Again, the rationale for directories in parts (like other titles from Gale) as opposed to single volumes is not apparent.

Included in each entry are the address of the sponsoring agency; U.S. statutory authorization (when available); a program description; funding data (when available); and sources from which the information was obtained. The 1982 *Catalog of Federal Domestic Assistance* and agency annual reports of earlier years are frequently cited as sources; more current data will therefore already be available in any library with the 1983 *Catalog of Federal Domestic Assistance* and the latest agency reports. Other libraries could, however, find this compilation useful, and since a number of entries note that no funds were provided for fiscal 1983, this directory will also serve as a convenient guide to the recent rapid contraction of federal government civilian functions. Other than that, libraries with the basic government information sources will probably not need this title.

Grants in the humanities: a scholar's guide to funding sources. 2d ed. By William Emmet Coleman. New York, Neal-Schuman, 1984. 168p. 23cm. hardbound $24.95 (0-918212-80-4).
100.4′4 Humanities—Research grants—U.S.—Directories | Research grants—U.S.—Directories | Humanities—Research grants—U.S. | Research grants—U.S. [CIP]   83-27069

This manual, like the first (1980) edition (cf. *RSBR*, November 15, 1980), is intended for scholars seeking grants in postdoctoral humanities research. It follows closely the arrangement of the earlier edition: brief chapters on the art of grantsmanship and proposal writing, a sample proposal and sample budget, and five appendixes. Appendix A (Granting Agencies)—about half of the book—has been revised and rewritten and has grown to include 197 grant programs (only 136 in the previous edition). Several of the new listings are for "facilities" appointments—"appointments or affiliations with universities and research centers which do not involve a money grant, but which instead give a scholar an office, some secretarial help, the use of a research library, or the like." More foreign study centers for scholars doing research abroad have also been included. The remaining appendixes list deadlines for submitting proposals, federal information centers, the Foundation Center and its cooperating libraries, and state humanities committees. The Index to Places and Study in the first edition has been dropped; the Index to Subjects in the Humanities has been revised. Coleman notes that since the first edition of this title, Neal-Schuman has inaugurated a series on grants, fellowships, and fund-raising under his editorship. The 1984 edition is a part of that series. By reason of the extent of revision and expansion of grant programs included and the continuing needs of scholars for information on funding sources, *Grants in the Humanities* will be useful in academic libraries.

The great song thesaurus. By Roger Lax and Frederick Smith. New York, Oxford Univ. Pr., 1984. 665p. 24cm. cloth $75 (0-19-503222-5).
784.5′0016 Music, Popular (Songs, etc.)—Indexes [CIP]   83-24927

The Great Song Thesaurus (*GST*) identifies popular songs from the sixteenth century to the present, including some 10,000 of the best-known songs in the English-speaking world. The book is divided into nine categories or chapters: "The Greatest Songs"; "The Award Winners"; "Themes, Trademarks, and Signatures"; "Elegant Plagiarisms"; "Song Titles"; "British Song Titles"; "Lyricists and Composers"; "American and British Theatre, Film, Radio, and Television"; and "Thesaurus of Song Titles by Subject, Key Word, and Category." Taken together, the various chapters provide basic data on an amazing number of popular songs and jingles composed in the last 400 years. The longest section, "Song Titles," provides in an alphabetical sequence by title, information on the song's date of composition, composer/lyricist, famous performers, and musicals/movies, etc., from where it comes. The lyricists and composers section lists them alphabetically along with their song titles.

The Great Song Thesaurus will be an invaluable source for any library with a popular music collection and for those libraries without access to such reference tools as *Popular Music Periodicals Index*. It will also be extremely useful in general reference collections.

The great symphonies. Edited by Clive Unger-Hamilton. New York, Facts On File, 1983. 235p. 29cm. hardcover $29.95 (0-87196-549-6).
785.1′1′09 Symphonies—History and criticism ‖ Symphony [CIP]   83-1493

This is a guide to the symphonic form from the eighteenth century to the present. Intended for nonspecialists, it provides biographical information for 58 composers, discusses the symphonic production of each composer and analyzes selected masterworks, profiles major conductors and orchestras, and offers a discography of recommended performances. The text is abundantly illustrated with photographs, some of which are in color.

The main body of the book is divided into nine chapters, which are in chronological order. Within each chapter, however, page layouts are confusing. For example, the main text for the Mahler chapter briefly surveys his symphonies and concludes with a detailed analysis of the fourth, but most pages also include one or two marginal columns that give biographical information about Mahler as well as Roussel, Schönberg, Nielsen, and Elgar (the critical discussion of Schönberg, though, is in the next chapter, "The Twentieth Century").

The next part of the book provides short profiles of 41 modern conductors. The double-text format is especially distracting here because of the brevity of these entries and because there is no distinction between analysis and biography. Happily, the following chapter briefly describing 24 major orchestras abandons this arrangement. The critically annotated discography will be useful as a buying guide. A Glossary and Index increase the book's value, but there is no bibliography.

All of this information is available in fuller treatment from other sources, but for concertgoers and record collectors, *The Great Symphonies* will be appreciated both as a quick-reference guide and as a readable history of symphonic development and orchestral performance. It is probably more suitable for circulating collections, although its reference value is not insignificant.

Growing up with science: the illustrated encyclopedia of invention. 25v. Westport, Conn., Stuttman (to homes only); to schools and libraries, from Marshall Cavendish, 1984. illus. 26cm. hardcover $199 to schools or libraries (0-87475-830-0).
503′.21 Science—Dictionaries, Juvenile ‖ Technology—Dictionaries, Juvenile ‖ Inventions—Dictionaries, Juvenile [OCLC]   82-63047

Described as "an alphabetic encyclopedia that answers for younger readers the 'Hows,' 'Whats,' and 'Whys' of the scientific world in which they live," this set offers an attractive and accurate introduction to the physical, biological, and practical sciences. Its subtitle seems a misnomer, however, since the set covers more than just inventions—a wide range of natural phenomena are also described.

The first 22 volumes provide an easy-to-understand, interestingly written series of extremely well-illustrated, alphabetically arranged articles on machines, devices, manufacturing processes, biological sciences, and scientific discoveries and techniques, ranging from early developments such as the wheel and the telescope to modern developments such as computers and nuclear power. From a detailed examination of these volumes, it appears that much of the information is based on the British set *How It Works: The Illustrated Encyclopedia of Science and Technology*, also published by Marshall Cavendish, 1978 (cf. *RBB* Nov. 15, 1978, evaluation). Unlike the 1978 title, the material in *Growing Up with Science* is definitely written for children.

Information is accurate and up-to-date; thus, reference is made to the space telescope that is scheduled for launching in 1986; to the invention in 1984 of a scalpel which cuts around corners; and to COMSAT, a satellite operator scheduled to begin direct satellite-to-home television transmission in 1985.

Occasionally there are boxed items of unusual or special interest, such as the part sulfuric acid played in a murder case, the distance at which a male moth can detect the pheromones of a female moth, etc.

The numerous full-color photographs, detailed drawings, and diagrams, many of them large, are quite informative and appealing. Many illustrations are those used in *How It Works*, with the captions somewhat simplified and with British terms replaced by American ones (e.g., *gritblasting* becomes *sand-blasting*). Labeling of parts on detailed drawings is in clearer type than that used in *How It Works*.

Volume 23 contains articles concerning discoveries and inventions, arranged in approximate chronological order, from prehistoric tools to the microchip. This volume corresponds to volume 21 in *How It Works*, with the writing directed to a younger audience, and with about 77 percent of the illustrations repeated. Some subject headings are changed for juvenile users, e.g., *Semiconductor* to *Transistor, Generation of Electricity* to *Electricity,* and *Volto's Pile* to *Pile Battery.* In addition, some subjects are covered in *Growing Up with Science* which are not covered in *How It Works;* cf. *Anesthetics, Jet Engine, Computers, Laser,* and *Microchip.*

Volume 24 presents brief biographies of about 100 scientists, arranged alphabetically, ranging from such early ones as Hero (first century A.D.), Gutenberg, and Isameel al-Jazari to such modern ones as Vladimir Zworykin. (In *How It Works* biographies are scattered throughout the set.)

Volume 25 begins with 40 science projects. Among these are directions for making a telescope, a fire alarm, a photogram, and a crystal radio, and an introduction to optical illusions, a demonstration of yeast in action, and a game of chance. Safety precautions are emphasized.

Following the projects is a Glossary (no pronunciation guides) and then an Index to the entire set. No blind entries were found in the latter.

The design and format of the set are attractive, with the text in two columns. Paper is of good quality and the type is clear. Pages lie flat when the volumes are opened.

Growing Up with Science is an up-to-date, inviting set of scientific and technological information for elementary and junior high school children, with a strong emphasis on good graphics. Much of the material can also serve as a basic introduction to science subjects for older students and adults. Useful for both reference and browsing, *Growing Up with Science* is recommended for school, public, and home libraries.

A guide to critical reviews: part I: American drama, 1909–1982. 3d ed. By James M. Salem. Metuchen, N.J. & London, Scarecrow, 1984. x, 657p. 22cm. cloth $42.50 (0-8108-1690-3).
016.8092 Theater—New York (New York)—Reviews—Indexes ‖ Moving-pictures—U.S.—Reviews—Indexes [CIP]   84-1370

The Guide to Critical Reviews series provides citations to reviews of plays, musicals, films, and literature. This volume claims coverage of almost 2,500 plays, by some 350 American dramatists, produced in New York on Broadway, Off-Broadway, and Off-Off-Broadway and published in *The New York Times* and other periodicals.

Arranged alphabetically by playwright, plays are then listed in alphabetical order by title, with citations to reviews following each play. Some entries include opening dates and number of performances.

Five tabular listings provide further information on playwrights, awards, and performance totals. Accurate and thorough Coauthor, Adapter, and Original Author and Title Indexes conclude the work.

Although most of the information in this guide is available via general periodical indexes, this work is worthwhile because it consolidates material by genre and author for easier access. It is a good source for in-depth theater collections.

A guide to fairs and festivals in the United States. [By] Frances Shemanski. Westport, Conn., Greenwood, 1984. viii, 339p. 24cm. cloth $35 (0-313-21437-9).
394′.6′025 Festivals—Directories ‖ Fairs—Directories [CIP]   82-21080

Describing some 250 fairs and festivals in the 50 states plus American Samoa, Puerto Rico, and the Virgin Islands, this directory provides selective coverage; the author based her decisions on such criteria as age of the festival, number of people attending, how the event influenced its area, etc. The author collected data by sending questionnaires to festival organizers and also by drawing upon her own experience as a free-lance travel writer. In addition, follow-up interviews were conducted as needed.

The work is arranged alphabetically by state and then city or town. Entries include information about the time of the event, its origin, history, purpose, special features, achievements, and future plans. A Calendar of Fairs and Festivals (arranged alphabetically by state listing events chronologically by month) and an Index add to the value of the work. The alphabetical Index lists fairs and festivals by name and subject. Thus, persons interested in a particular subject need only turn to the Index for a list of appropriate events.

This guide differs from Paul Wasserman and Edmond L. Applebaum's *Festivals Sourcebook* (2d ed., Gale, 1984) in several respects, the most obvious being that the *Sourcebook* claims to cover over 4,200 fairs, festivals, and celebrations in North America—far more than Shemanski. Also Shemanski does not list contact persons, offices, addresses, or telephone numbers. Although not as comprehensive as the *Sourcebook* (and less expensive), *Shemanski* in part provides a more detailed discussion of each event. It will be particularly useful to travelers, festival organizers, and individuals interested in tracing the history of the individual events. *Shemanski* is probably most suitable for larger and more specialized reference collections. *Festivals Sourcebook* is a more obvious choice for most libraries.

Guide to industry special issues. 1st ed. Cambridge, Mass., Ballinger (a subsidiary of Harper & Row), 1984. 733p. 26cm. hardcover $65 (0-88410-944-5; ISSN: 0740-9907).

†011.34 Periodicals—Bibliography

The data displayed in this guide are, according to its Preface, "derived from the *Harfax Industry Data Sources* database, which is available through Bibliographic Retrieval Services, Data-Star, Dialog Information Service, and Mead Data Central's NEXIS system." It claims to cite "some 6,900"—actually, 6,907—"articles in 1,800 journals." The "articles" include not only "regularly appearing [special] issues" but recurring "features," i.e., not necessarily whole issues. Coverage of the U.S. and Canada is thorough; that of other countries, admittedly less so.

The bulk of the *Guide* is an annotated list of "Journals and Their Special Issues," arranged alphabetically first by journal title, then by issue or feature. Then come six indexes: first, by industry, citing title of journal and citation number of issue or feature; then by a Geographical/Industry Index, which recapitulates the Industry Index but regroups its components under place-names; then a Publisher Index, citing journal titles; then a Product Index, in two parts: (1) a Classified Index, by Standard Industrial Classification Code, and (2) an alphabetical Subject Index; then an Index to Recurring Statistical and Directory Issues and Features; and last, an Index to Titles of Issues and Features.

With its good coverage, perceptive annotations, and thorough indexing, *Guide to Industry Special Issues* promises to be a useful tool in large public libraries, in academic libraries supporting the study of business, economics, and engineering—and of course, in many special libraries.

Guide to Islam. By David Ede et al. Boston, G. K. Hall, 1983. xxiv, 261p. 29cm. cloth $55 (0-8161-7905-0).

016.297 Islam—Bibliography || Civilization, Islamic—Bibliography [CIP]   83-6134

The *Guide to Islam* is one of a series of annotated bibliographies prepared by the Project on Asian Philosophies and Religions, a cooperative undertaking of scholars and teachers supported by the National Endowment for the Humanities. "The project's basic objective . . . has been to provide an authoritative guide to the literature, both texts in translation and commentary and analysis, for teachers and advanced undergraduate and beginning graduate students who are not specialized scholars with access to primary texts in their original languages" (series Preface).

In keeping with this objective, the *Guide to Islam*, which was prepared under the direction of David Ede of Western Michigan University, seeks to "introduce the English-language reader to significant publications on Islam as a religion and a civilization." Each section of the volume (e.g., Historical Development, Religious Thought, Religious Practices, Sacred Places, Institutions, Art and Architecture, and Research Aids) was prepared by a specialist in that particular aspect of the subject. Other scholars in the field critically reviewed the preliminary draft of the guide.

The 2,962 items included consist mostly of books and journal articles in English published prior to 1977. Because events since 1976 have generated a significant body of recent material on Islam, a supplement to the guide is in preparation.

Succinct descriptive and critical annotations enable users to match the contents of works to their interests and identify works of recognized authority (e.g., the new edition of the *Encyclopedia of Islam* is characterized as "absolutely indispensable for students and scholars alike"). A Subject Index provides access to the entries by specific topic. The Author Index includes title entries for works frequently referred to by title. Better use of indentation and the employment of boldface would have made the Table of Contents easier to use. But this is a minor defect in an otherwise admirable work.

In view of the importance of Islam both as a religion and a civilization and the recent enlargement of its role in world affairs, this guide should be a valuable resource in academic and many public libraries. Many of the listed items, which are out-of-print or not otherwise readily available, can be obtained in microform from the Institute for Advanced Studies of World Religions.

Guide to microforms in print incorporating international microforms in print, 1983: authors/titles/subject. Editor, Ardis Voegelin-Carleton. 4v. Supplement. Westport, Conn., Meckler, 1983. 29cm. harcover $102.50; supplement: paper $50. Authors/titles, v.1 (0-930466-72-1); v.2 (0-930466-76-4); set (0-930466-78-0); ISSN (0164-0747) subject, v.1 (0-930466-73-X); v.2 (0-930466-77-2); set (0-930466-79-9); ISSN (0163-8386) supplement (0-930466-74-8); ISSN (0164-0739).

686.4'3'025 Microforms—Catalogs | Microcards—Catalogs [OCLC]	78-64852
016.099 Microforms—Catalogs [OCLC]	78-649060
011'.36 Microforms—Catalogs [OCLC]	83-643092

This annual guide consists of a two-volume author/title listing of books, journals, newspapers, government publications, archival material, collections, and other items in microform currently available from micropublishing organizations throughout the world. The same titles are listed under appropriate subject classifications in the two-volume companion, *Subject Guide to Microforms in Print*. The 135 subject groupings are derived from the Library of Congress classification system and are, therefore, extremely broad, e.g., social sciences. The paper *Supplement* identifies items published in between the annual editions. The entries include appropriate purchasing information and identify the relevant microform type. Theses and dissertations are excluded.

The Introductions in both parts appear in English, French, German, and Spanish; each part has a directory of publishers listed alphabetically and by code or acronym.

Like other "in print" guides, this set will be useful as an acquisitions tool and also can be used for verification of interlibrary loan requests, although it undoubtedly has omissions. Large public, academic, and special libraries needing access to and/or acquiring microforms will want to obtain this work.

Guide to musical America. By Lynne Gusikoff. New York, Facts On File, 1984. xii, 347p. illus. maps. 24cm. hardcover $17.95 (0-87196-701-4).

781.773 Music–U.S.—History and criticism [CIP]   82-7377

As stated in the Introduction, the purpose of this book is twofold: "to present historic highlights of different styles of music as they developed in particular regions of the U.S. at various times; and to specify certain geographic locations where one may hear different styles of music today."

Regions covered are the Northeast, the South, the Midwest, the West, and the West Coast. Brief introductory essays discuss the development/growth of idioms (jazz, swing, classical, country and western as well as dance) in the regions as relevant. For example, there is an essay on the Northeast which begins with the Pilgrims and the influence of the Psalms and progresses to disco and rock in the 1970s. At the end of each regional section, a general map of the region and maps of its larger cities are annotated to show music halls, clubs, performing arts centers, etc. Each section also lists festivals by state. These directory features are perhaps the most notable reference use feature of the volume; the music history material is rather brief for reference purposes.

Guide to Musical America is a good source for public libraries.

Guide to nonsexist teaching activities (K–12). Developed by Northwest Regional Educational Laboratory Center for Sex Equity. Phoenix, Oryx, 1983. xii, 99p. 28cm. paper $22.50 (0-89774-100-5).

016.37019'345 Sex discrimination in education—U.S.—Bibliography | Sexism—U.S.—Bibliography | Sex role—U.S.—Bibliography | Education—U.S.—Curricula—Bibliography | Teaching—Aids and devices—Bibliography [CIP]   83-42515

Developed to provide teachers, librarians, and others involved in education with information on innovative, nonsexist resources, this bibliography will be helpful in adapting or supplementing biased instructional materials, appropriate for K–12 students. The compilers suggest that this work be used in conjunction with *Bibliography of Nonsexist Supplementary Books*, also published by Oryx Press. Organized into eight categories, e.g., General Awareness and Counseling, and Career Guidance, each grouping has further topical subcategories subdivided into types of material, e.g., lesson plans, course outlines, bibliographies, supplementary texts, photographs, periodicals, multimedia programs, and audiovisual materials. Items are arranged alphabetically by title. A sample lesson plan or course outline is provided for each major category.

Each item includes bibliographical data, ordering information, annotation, recommended grade level, and, as appropriate, availability in microfiche or hard copy from the ERIC Document Reproduction Service. Various Appendixes provide additional information including Guidelines for Developing Nonbiased Instruction. A Title Index concludes the work. *Guide to Nonsexist Teaching Activities* will be valuable in K–12 libraries or those serving education students.

A guide to reference and bibliography for theatre research.
2d ed. By Claudia Jean Bailey. Columbus, Ohio, The Ohio State University Libraries, 1983. xi, 149p. 28cm. paper $18.95 (0-88215-049-9).
†016.792 Drama—Bibliography | Theater—Bibliography | Reference books—Drama—Bibliography | Reference books—Theater—Bibliography | Reference books—Bibliography [OCLC] 83-61581

Bailey, a librarian and associate professor at the Community College of Rhode Island, has compiled an annotated bibliographic guide to research in theater arts and drama that should prove very useful to students in those areas.

The first part of the volume introduces users to basic library sources of information, e.g., national and trade bibliographies, biographical sources, and government publications.

The final 400-plus entries focus on theater and drama sources by type (bibliographies, theses, directories) and subject (theory and criticism, costumes, theater architecture). Excluded are material on Shakespeare, techniques of acting and directing, and books published after fall 1979.

All Items are consecutively numbered and include adequate bibliographic data. A detailed Table of Contents and an Author/Title Index are provided. This guide is for libraries serving theater or English majors.

A guide to reference books for small and medium-sized libraries, 1970–1982. By G. Kim Dority. Littleton, Col., Libraries Unlimited, 1984. xx, 410p. 24cm. cloth $28.50 (U.S.); $34 (elsewhere) (0-87287-403-6).
011′ 02 Reference books—Bibliography [CIP] 84-7849

This compilation "is designed to maximize each library's return on the limited acquisitions dollars, shelf space, and staff time available to invest in the reference collection." Similar in format to the same publisher's *American Reference Books Annual*, it lists 1,179 titles of "the most appropriate and highly recommended reference books in English" published between 1970 and 1982. Some important reference works predating 1970 and some 1983 imprints are included. Government publications, references for children, and media-related titles are included on a highly selective basis. An initial chapter covering general works is followed by 43 subject-oriented chapters divided by topic or format. Author/Title and Subject Indexes refer to entry numbers.

ARBA (which began publication in 1970) is the source for many of the titles. However, *ARBA* reviews have been condensed and updated so that an annotation may include references to similar works published later than the work reviewed. Titles have also been selected from other Libraries Unlimited publications including such standard sources as Sheehy's *Guide to Reference Books*. All entries are annotated, some with several lengthy paragraphs. Full bibliographic information is provided, and most annotations conclude with a list of citations to reviews in *ARBA* and 19 other journals.

Comparison with the fourth edition of *Reference Sources for Small and Medium-Sized Libraries* (ALA, 1984) is inevitable. The arrangement of the two works is markedly similar; *Reference Sources* provides much the same subject coverage within 22 classifications that are in approximate Dewey order. *Reference Sources* has 609 more entries than Dority's *Guide*, but smaller print and a two-column format make it 158 pages shorter. The length and quality of annotations are comparable, although the *Guide*'s annotations provide many references to other titles and citations in review journals—two valuable features. Since *Reference Sources* includes some works appropriate for young adult and juvenile collections, online databases, and nonprint media, and coverage is not limited by date of publication, its coverage is broader. Both books include important out-of-print titles. *Reference Sources* has no subject index; the *Guide* does not index titles appearing in annotations.

Both of these works are admirable compilations and are excellent selection tools for all but the largest public and academic libraries.

A guide to the architecture of London. [By] Edward Jones & Christopher Woodward; photos by William Harrison. New York, Van Nostrand, 1983. 416p. illus. maps. 29cm. cloth $24.95 (0-442-24355-3).
914.21′04858 Architecture—England—London—Guide-books | London (England)—Buildings—Guide-books | London (England)—Description—Guide-books [CIP] 82-4930

The authors, practicing architects, have produced both a guide to and a critical appraisal of London's architecture from Roman Walls to the Tate Gallery additions (1979).

The nearly 900 entries include the expected public buildings, churches, palaces, and museums as well as bridges, cemeteries, department stores, housing developments, memorials, and parks. Arrangement is chronological within sections devoted to each area of London. A brief essay on the social and architectural history of the area and a map on facing pages showing site locations precede each section. A photograph or drawing and full information (address, architect and/or engineer, closest mass transit stop, and map locators) accompany the descriptions which are both scholarly and a delight to read. Some examples follow. On *Gospel Oak Comprehensive redevelopment*, "This entry is included as representative of many well-intentioned architectural crimes committed in London since the war by the Welfare State." On *Keate House*, "It is unlikely that this two-storey stuccoed house would have gained entry to this guide without its literary associations: it is not particularly distinguished, and was rescued from destruction in the 1920s only by courtesy of money from the USA." The *Hampstead Garden Suburb* gives "the impression of being a benign sanatorium." On the public library in Hampstead, "It did not occur to the architects of the Welfare State, as it certainly had to the Victorians, that public buildings might be as good as private ones and perhaps even better." Finally, on *Golders Green Crematorium* and its group of chapels, "Good red-brick Romanesque make it a handsome place from which to depart."

Architecture buffs, anglophiles, travelers, and reference desks will welcome this compact, well-organized, comprehensively indexed, erudite, and reasonably priced *Guide to the Architecture of London*.

Handbook of Latin American art: manual de arte Latinoamericano: a bibliographic compilation. v.I, pts., 1 & 2. Joyce Waddell Bailey, general editor. Santa Barbara, Calif., ABC-Clio, 1984. 1,195p. 24cm. cloth $75 each part (0-87436-384-5: pt.1; 0-87436-385-3: pt. 2; 0-87436-386-1: set).
016.7′098 Art, Latin American [CIP] 83-26656

This reference, the first of a projected three-volume bibliography on Latin American art, divides its more than 11,000 unannotated items (in English, French, Spanish, and Portuguese) into two parts: (1) North America, with the Caribbean and Central America and (2) South America. Two companion volumes, the *Colonial Period* and the *Ancient Period*, will soon follow, making this the most complete bibliography to date on the neglected field of Latin American art.

Entries provide complete bibliographical information and, when appropriate, entries may be cited from the *Handbook of Latin American Studies*: a major reference for all fields and the model for the present work. A very detailed introductory section and three Indexes (Author, Institutional Authors, and Artists from Monographic Studies) provide access to this mammoth work. With the mass of items involved, additional scholarly apparatus such as annotations, introductory essays, and a subject index would probably have extended the work to unpublishable lengths. However, more concentration might have been spent on reference tools, since these, more than anything else, will expand the user's field of information.

Yet in all, Bailey and her team of scholars, funded by the National Endowment for the Humanities, are to be commended for the realization of the formidable task of bringing bibliographical control to Latin American art.

Handbook on the aged in the United States. By Erdman B. Palmore. Westport, Conn., Greenwood, 1984. 458p. 24cm. cloth $49.95 (0-313-23721-2).
305.2′6′0973 Aged—U.S.—Handbooks, manuals, etc. 84-4463

This handbook provides a state-of-the-art report on what is known about aging and aged persons in the U.S. The contents are divided into four parts, one each for demographic, religious, and ethnic groups and one for groups representing special concerns. Within each part are chapters on subgroups: e.g., demographic groups include centenarians, veterans, and the widowed, while the section on special groups has material on criminals, the disabled, homosexuals, and the institutionalized. Each chapter is written by an expert, most of whom are faculty members at U.S. universities.

Chapters generally include discussions of current demographic and socioeconomic data about subgroups of the elderly. Also covered are the subgroup's history, special problems and advantages, psychological characteristics, research issues, organizations and services, and lists of sources for additional information. Some chapters also summarize current research findings.

Palmore's introduction provides a review of basic facts and misconceptions about older Americans in general, which is supplemented by statistical tables in appendix B. Other features of the book are a list of academic research centers on aging, a bibliography of texts and handbooks, a list of contributors, and an Index (neither appendix B nor the Index was included in the proof copy reviewed by the Board).

Handbook on the Aged is a fascinating and useful compilation of data. As a current source, it will be useful on reference shelves; however, those who want an overview of a topic may wish to read entire chapters. As a systematic effort to present details on segments of the elderly population, it effectively refutes the view that all old people are much the same.

The Harlem renaissance: an historical dictionary for the era. By Bruce Kellner. Westport, Conn., Greenwood, 1984. 476p. illus. 24cm. hardcover $45 (0-313-23232-6).

700′.899607307471 Afro-American arts—New York (N.Y.)—Dictionaries | Harlem Renaissance—Dictionaries [OCLC]   83-22687

Like the *Oxford Companion to American Literature*, this historical dictionary includes, in an A–Z arrangement, brief biographies of literary figures, theater personalities, and musicians; book synopses; descriptions of newspapers, periodicals, and musical comedies; citations to groups and other topics, e.g., riots, pertinent to the Harlem Renaissance (1917–35). Unlike the *Oxford Companion*, its entries are signed, two-thirds of them by Kellner, the rest by one of seven contributors, chiefly American university professors. All entries have appended references and citations to sources in the text when pertinent. Also, Kellner has written a rather full prefatory overview of a period when three powerful figures were predominant: W. E. B. DuBois, James Weldon Johnson, and Marcus Garvey, all treated more fully in the text. Appropriately, all biographees are treated from the standpoint of the Harlem Renaissance. Thus white poet Vachel Lindsay's support of young black writers is given more prominence than his literary works. Also, Mary McLeod Bethune, who was "far removed from Harlem" is included because "she exerted a powerful influence over the movement of the Renaissance." Only O'Neill's plays using black material are discussed in his brief entry. More fully covered are magazines like *Opportunity*, groups such as Pan-African Congresses, and labor leader A. Philip Randolph.

Biographies of entertainers abound—Eubie Blake, Bessie Smith, and many lesser knowns. Of the five Appendixes, three give chronologies: events; books by or about blacks; and plays by, about, or featuring Afro-Americans. The other two list appropriate serial publications and a glossary of Harlem slang. An appended bibliography includes quite a number of publications of the 1970s.

References to related articles in the text are indicated by asterisks. There are 28 illustrations, mostly photographs, caricatures, and drawings, and a good analytical Index provides access to the contents. Both add to the reference value of this alphabetical approach to a very significant period in Afro-American history. *The Harlem Renaissance* is an excellent addition to American history collections in academic and public libraries.

Harrod's librarian's glossary of terms used in librarianship, documentation and the book crafts and reference book. 5th ed. Rev. and updated by Ray Prytherch. Brookfield, VT 05036, Old Post Road, Gower, 1984. xi, 861p. 23cm. hardcover $69.95 (0-566-03460-3).

020′.3 Library science—Dictionaries | Information science—Dictionaries | Bibliography—Dictionaries | Book industries and trade—Dictionaries [CIP]   83-17174

The editor, a faculty member at Leeds Polytechnic School of Librarianship, states that this is a transitional edition of a well-respected reference. Although Harrod has now become advisory editor and the publisher has changed, the work is still based solidly on *The Librarians' Glossary*, 4th ed., rev. (London: Andre Deutsch, 1978). The brief Preface by the editor details the work's publishing history and cites revision of 700 entries and the addition of 300 new terms, primarily in the fields of automation, telecommunications, and information technology. Because the glossary goes far beyond explanations of professional terminology and includes historical descriptions of institutions and programs, it serves as a valuable handbook as well. It is particularly strong on developments in Great Britain, the U.S., Canada, and Australia. Using words sparingly, the editor has nevertheless steered a straight course between too brief, meaningless definitions and encyclopedic entries. While coverage of acronyms and modern concepts is a major emphasis, the editor wisely concedes that "to many in the profession, knowledge of books remains a principal concern, and with the fading of historical bibliography from librarianship courses the Glossary's coverage of printing and analytical terms assumes a new importance." With nearly three times as many entries as the *ALA Glossary* (Chicago, American Library Assn., 1983), *Harrod's* entries are longer, and its scope and coverage are broader. Despite its price, *Harrod's* is a worthwhile addition to any professional collection worthy of the name.

Herbs: an indexed bibliography, 1971–1980: the scientific literature on selected herbs, and aromatic and medicinal plants of the temperate zone. [Compiled by] James E. Simon, Alena R. Chadwick, and Lyle E. Craker. Hampden, Conn., Archon Books, 1984. xviii, 770p. 26cm. cloth $69.50 (0-208-01990-1).

016.582′063 Herbs—Indexes | Aromatic plants—Indexes | Medicinal plants—Indexes | Herbs | Aromatic plants | Medicinal plants [CIP]   82-24493

Both an information book and a bibliography, *Herbs* should be considered for large public libraries, for academic libraries, and some special libraries—and this despite weaknesses (on which more below). Part I describes more than 60 plants (even more, if one counts subdivisions, e.g., the several mints), with references to Parts II and III, which together constitute a classified bibliography of nearly 7,900 items. The volume concludes with Subject and Author Indexes.

The descriptions in Part I include, besides botanical data, information on agricultural, ornamental, culinary, cosmetic, and medicinal applications: a "Warning" on the copyright page very sensibly disclaims responsibility for misuse of such information. The bibliography itself is comprehensive and is, on the whole, well set up, despite some overlapping, e.g., between section 6.1 Colorants, Condiments and Flavorings and section 6.4 Applications in Food and Flavor Industry, and despite lack of cross-references linking related sections and/or entries: as the Introduction is frank to state, "Considerable overlap of the subject areas occurs in some articles, and since each article is listed only once the reader should always review related subject areas." This approach, besides laying the whole burden upon readers, ignores the likelihood that authors may perceive and report fresh connections, i.e., ones which inquirers can scarcely be expected to anticipate.

The Author Index is comprehensive (it cites authors besides those first named), and it cites particular items in the bibliography; but the Subject Index cites sections only, *not* particular items. Thus "phenols 1.1, 1.2, 1.8, 7.2, 7.5, 7.6, 8.2" directs one to sections which list 999 items altogether: apparently one is to page through all seven sections, trusting that here and there among the 999 will be items whose titles refer to or allude to phenols. No justification is offered for this extraordinary lack of specificity.

Perhaps in a second edition (sure, before long, to be needed), the editors of *Herbs* can improve it: where it falls, it falls hard; but where it rises, it rises grandly.

The historic preservation yearbook: a documentary record of significant policy developments and issues. 1st ed., 1984–85. Edited by Russell V. Keune. Bethesda, Md., Adler & Adler, 1984. xiv, 590p. 29cm. cloth $78 plus $3.50 shipping and handling (0-917561-00-7; ISSN: 0748-8823).

†363.69 Historic buildings—Conservation and restoration   84-7297

This is the first of a projected series in the field of historic preservation in its legal, tactical, and economic aspects. Documentation of events of the past few years (not just 1984–85) is included.

There are 29 chapters, covering such things as techniques for local preservation; outstanding examples of successful (and some unsuccessful) building or roadway preservation; tax incentives for preservation; the problem with marking churches as "historic landmarks"; and other specific problems or procedures. Covered in detail are the National Register of Historic Places and some typical state registers, notably those of Massachusetts and Connecticut; the National Park Service; and several typical state actions, such as the Louisiana Act of Demolition of State-owned Buildings, as well as some in California and Montana. One of the California actions was particularly interesting, as it involved the world-famous La Brea Tar Pits, whose archaeological and paleontological value was threatened by a proposed rail subway. Another interesting chapter deals with shipwrecks ("Who controls shipwrecks, the salvors or the states?").

The volume has valuable appendixes and a good topical Index. It is specifically aimed at "preservationists, architects, developers, government officials, lawyers, and city planners." To these might be added state and local historical societies, especially those with historical buildings for which they are responsible. And in an academic situation, students of law, civil government, architecture, economics, and local history would also profit from the work. The Preface promises that issues will be appearing annually.

Historical dictionary of Egypt. By Joan Wucher King. Metuchen, N.J., & London, Scarecrow, 1984. xiii, 719p. (African Historical Dictionaries, no.36) 22cm. $47.50 (0-8108-1670-9).
962'.003'21 Egypt—History—Dictionaries [CIP]   83-20247

The title of this work is misleading, as it does not cover ancient Egypt at all. There is, at the beginning of the book, a brief chronology of Egyptian history that begins in 30 B.C. (death of Cleopatra) and covers the period up to A.D. 639 (first Muslim entry into Egypt) in two pages. But from the year 640, when Muslim domination of Egypt begins, the chronology and the entries in the dictionary itself are far more detailed. A more accurate title would have been *A Historical Dictionary of Islamic Egypt*.

Because of the dictionary format, biographies are interspersed with topics, such as *Agriculture, Education, Geneva Conference*, and the like. The biographies are informative accounts of all major sultans, pashas, viziers, presidents, and other rulers, as well as of important lawyers, teachers, generals, politicians, and others.

The entries are concise, informative, and (on the basis of some random checking with other authorities) accurate. Entries vary in length from about one-third of a page to four or five pages for such entries as *Ottoman Egypt* or *Nasser, Gamal Abdal*. Recency of events is as late as 1982, in the article on President Mubarak.

A lengthy bibliography, arranged chronologically, with separate listings for Arabic and non-Arabic books, completes the work. There is no index.

For academic and public libraries with a history-minded clientele.

Historical dictionary of Napoleonic France, 1799–1815. Owen Connelly, editor. Westport, Conn., Greenwood, 1985. xiii, 586p. 24cm. cloth $65. (0-313-21321-6).
944.04'5 France—History—Consulate and Empire, 1799–1815—Dictionaries | Europe—History—1799–1815—Dictionaries [CIP]   83-22754

This dictionary attempts to present a panoramic view of the age of Napoleon, and the result is very satisfying. Owen Connelly, a historian who has written other works on the subject, is not only the book's editor but the author of many of its articles. There are, in fact, roughly 500 entries, most of them signed, and written by others in the field; unsigned material is written by Connelly.

As explained in the Preface, the material is not limited to Napoleon in his native France. It encompasses the entire Napoleonic era in a worldwide setting, its cultural atmosphere, and the people who helped to shape this time and whose lives were touched by this giant figure of history. Connelly justifies the relative short shrift he gives to Napoleon's campaigns by noting the availability of Chandler's *Dictionary of Napoleonic Warfare*, which he recommends as an excellent source of military information. Connelly's treatment of campaigns is, however, more adequate for history buffs; serious students may do well to turn to other sources. Articles are arranged alphabetically, vary in length, are clearly written, and are followed by ample cross-references.

It is not completely clear why 1799 was chosen as the starting point; some earlier events, such as the "Terror" of 1793–94 are also listed. The year of Napoleon's first consulship, 1800, might have been a better choice. The book would have been improved by more articles on individual artists such as Delacroix, who immortalized Napoleon and his family through his paintings.

These, however, are minor flaws in a work containing much information on a colorful period in history. It will be welcomed in academic and public libraries.

Historical maps on file. New York, Facts On File, 1984. various pagings. maps. 29cm. looseleaf hardcover $145 (0-87196-708-1).
911 Geography, Ancient—Maps | Outline maps | Atlases [CIP]   82-675379

The third in a series of looseleaf collections of black-and-white graphics on heavy stock, this "atlas" is designed for easy photocopying, like its predecessors *Maps On File* (cf. *RSBR*, August 1982) and *The Human Body On File* (cf. *RBB*, April 15, 1984). The approximately 300 maps are grouped into nine sections; following the first (Ancient Civilizations), the arrangement is by continent: Europe (to 1500, 1500–1815, 1815 to the present); the United States; Western Hemisphere (Canada and Latin America); Africa and the Middle East; Asia; and Australia. The tenth and concluding section is an Index containing some 5,000 entries.

The sequence within each section is generally chronological. A map of Greece at the time of the Peloponnesian War, however, carries no indication of dates and is misleadingly numbered to file after a map of Alexander the Great's empire, ca. 323 B.C. Coverage of U.S. history is ample (89 maps); two noteworthy sets within the U.S. group are seven maps showing the distribution of immigrants from various European countries in 1910, and 21 maps indicating the electoral vote in select presidential elections, including the last nine. The latest map of Latin America, on the other hand, is of the pre-1850 period. The Hundred Years' War gets no map, and while the American Revolution and the European revolutions of 1820–1831 and 1848 are covered, the French and Russian revolutions are not.

To insure that clear reproductions can be obtained on standard copiers, not only is the use of color ruled out, but text is restricted to the absolute minimum—the barest captions, legends, and only essential names. No interpretative commentary is supplied either on the maps or elsewhere. Where several varieties of shading are employed on a map, it can be difficult to distinguish bodies of water from land.

This set of maps does not pretend to be a substitute for a standard historical atlas, but in school libraries and in other situations where legally reproducible maps are needed, and where the loss of individual map pages can be guarded against, this set could prove useful.

The hockey encyclopedia: the complete record of professional ice hockey. [By] Stan Fischler and Shirley Walton Fischler. New York, Macmillan, 1984. 720p. 24cm. hardcover $24.95 (0-02-538400-7).
796.96'2'0922 Hockey—Records | Hockey—Dictionaries [CIP]   83-16224

This comprehensive record of facts and figures associated with ice hockey provides data on players, coaches, and teams of the National Hockey League (NHL) and the World Hockey Association (WHA). Following an Introduction on the history of the game, the sections, Awards and Achievements and All-Time Leaders, provide brief information and lists of trophy winners, record holders, etc. The Player Register is the largest section giving, in alphabetical order, more than 3,000 players who have played major league hockey and listing year-by-year statistics, birth date, place of birth, and height and weight. Similar data follow in the section on goaltenders and coaches. Data on teams, the NHL, the WHA, the Stanley Cup playoffs, etc., conclude the work.

Any hockey enthusiast will want this encyclopedia, and any library with a sports reference collection will find it very handy.

The home how-to sourcebook. [By] Mike McClintock. New York, Scribner, 1984. xii, 384p. hardcover $24.95; paper $14.95 (0-684-18015-4: hardcover; 0-684-18045-6: paper).
643 House construction—Amateurs' manuals | Dwellings—Remodeling—Amateurs' manuals [CIP]   83-20219

The jacket accurately describes the contents of this useful handbook: "More than 1,500 sources for top-quality tools, materials, products, and services for designing, constructing, remodeling, restoring and repairing the home." McClintock (author of six books and about 250 articles in the home-consumer field) states that he has included here only those that he has had success with or who responded to his inquiries. "I did not go looking for bad apples." His selections are arranged under ten sections: Planning and Design; Building Materials; Tools and Equipment; Homebuilding; Restoration and Remodeling; Repairs and Maintenance; Furnishings and Fixtures; Appliances; Heating and Cooling; Plumbing and Electrical. Each is further divided by directories of private firms, professional societies, government agencies, sources for consumer education (including Better Business Bureaus), and informally annotated lists of books for reading and reference. Of a book on A-frames he says, "It's the kind of book I've almost donated to the library a few times, but I haven't because it's still useful." Titles range from books on photovoltaic systems to compost toilets.

The Subject Index, listing individual firms and organizations only under appropriate subjects, includes a number of references to hand tools, shop equipment, and restoration and remodeling. This refreshingly informal as well as informed source (by virtue of McClintock's ten years as a house builder) is both a directory and a bibliography. It should be considered by public and trade school libraries.

Human food uses: a cross-cultural, comprehensive annotated bibliography. Supp. Compiled by Robert L. Freedman. Westport, Conn., Greenwood, 1983. xxxiii, 387p. 29cm. cloth $65 (0-313-23434-5).
016.3941 Food habits—Bibliography | Diet—Bibliography [CIP]   82-25163

The first volume of this annotated bibliography of more than 9,000 print and nonprint citations was "developed for scholars and scientists requiring data on various aspects of food in human culture" (cf. *RSBR*, June 15, 1982). This supplement includes about 4,000 additional entries consisting of "many recent publications as well as some classics . . . held aside in order to provide adequate annotation." Like the first volume it is international in scope including basic bibliographic information and some with annotations a half-page long. A Keyword Index provides subject access to the alphabetical author arrangement of the bibliography. Added cross-references greatly improve the Index from that of the first volume, but there are still weaknesses, the most serious being the inclusion of subject entries with long lists of citation numbers without any further subject subdivision, e.g., *Germany* includes 35 citations with no other subject refinement, and *Uganda* includes 73 entries; however, the 67 entries under *France* are subdivided. Users must also note that the Index is not cumulative.

Libraries with the parent volume will want to add this supplement. Others will have to consider their need for such a comprehensive bibliography on a rather specialized topic, the cost of the two volumes ($130), and the Index problems—especially in the first volume.

Human sexuality: a bibliography and critical evaluation of recent texts. By Mervyn L. Mason. Westport, Conn., Greenwood, 1983. viii, 207p. 24cm. cloth $35 (0-313-23932-0).
016.612'6 Sex—Bibliography [CIP]   83-12688

This book critically examines 180 books dealing with various aspects of human sexuality. The author uses nine topical groupings for arrangement: Female Sexuality, History and Sex, Male Sexuality, Philosophy and Sex, Physiology and Sex, Sex Education, Sex Research, Sex Therapy and Counseling, and Sexual Minorities. Each entry has a brief summary and a critique of strengths and/or deficiencies. The author examined each book and selection was made according to "availability, excellence in a specified category, popular usage by professionals in the field, widespread knowledge of a particular book by professionals, and the scientific-sexological approach of a particular book to its subject." *Human Sexuality* will be useful in all academic and research libraries covering human sexuality as well as in libraries serving counselors, lawyers, judges, clergy, physicians, and various paramedical practitioners.

I stand corrected: more on language from William Safire. New York, Times Books, 1984. ix, 468p. 24cm. cloth $19.95 (0-8129-1097-4).
428'.00973 English language—Usage—Addresses, essays, lectures [CIP]   83-40090

Like his *On Language* (1980) and *What's the Good Word* (1982), Safire's *I Stand Corrected* is excerpted from his *New York Times Magazine* column. It consists of pithy remarks on many linguistic topics, with responses from readers—agreeing, disagreeing, amplifying, inquiring further, etc. The result is witty, stimulating, opinionated, occasionally tedious, and on the whole very much worth reading. Public and academic libraries will want to acquire copies for their circulating collections.

As a reference tool it is not very satisfactory. Although alphabetically arranged, it does not employ captions likely to be thought of by inquirers. Thus Safire has excellent things to say about restaurant jargon; but who would think to look under *carte before the horse?* Some captions are simply mysterious, e.g., *twenty hundred* for verbal rendering of numbers and *word order* for misplaced modifiers. Worse, the Subject Index—for indeed there is one—does not use terms on the order of *restaurant, numbers,* and *modifiers* to help one locate this material. (In all fairness, there are Index entries for *euphemisms* and *hyphenation,* to cite but two informative topical headings, and for specific words, e.g., *geezer* and *image.*) There is, then, much good material, but much of it is difficult to access randomly and efficiently. Safire would do well to see that the Index to his next compilation routinely employs the standard vocabulary of usage handbooks and dictionaries: to do so would enhance reference value without detracting one iota from overall charm.

An Ibsen companion: a dictionary-guide to the life, works, and critical reception of Henrik Ibsen. By George B. Bryan. Westport, Conn., Greenwood, 1984. 437p. 24cm. cloth $49.95 (0-313-23506-6).
839.8'226 Ibsen, Henrik, 1828–1906—Dictionaries, indexes, etc. | Ibsen, Henrik, 1828–1906—Handbooks, manuals, etc. [CIP]   83-18551

This book will be useful to students of Ibsen and therefore belongs in the reference collections of all but the smallest public and academic libraries. It consists mainly of articles (alphabetically arranged) on plays, on characters, and on persons and organizations associated with Ibsen's life and career and with the subsequent history of Ibsen production, criticism, etc.—but no topical articles as such, i.e., none on themes, character types, aesthetic concepts, and the like. Many articles include bibliographic references. Articles on particular plays will be useful to readers at a variety of levels; they include detailed synopses, brief structural analyses, and stage histories (the last in the form of chronologies). The body of the work is preceded by an illuminating essay on Ibsen the dramatist and by a general chronology and is followed by a good Selected Bibliography (generally not citing items referred to in articles), by an Appendix listing early translators of Ibsen, and by an Index.

In all respects admirable, *An Ibsen Companion* is especially notable for its coverage of stage history; cf. the many entries for actors who have interpreted Ibsen characters. For this reason it will be particularly helpful to readers to whom Ibsen's plays have existed mainly as works to be read rather than as works to be produced, performed, and witnessed.

Idioms and phrases index. 3v. 1st ed. Laurence Urdang, editor in chief. Detroit, Gale, 1983. 1,691p. 29cm. cloth $150 (0-8103-1547-5).
423'.1 English language—Terms and phrases | English language—Idioms—Dictionaries [CIP]   83-17192

This index provides access to 32 reference works that define English-language idioms and phrases. Standard works such as *Brewer's Dictionary of Phrase and Fable* (Harper and Row, 1981), *The Random House Dictionary of the English Language* (Random House, 1966), and the final edition (10th) of *The Oxford Companion to Music* (London: Oxford Univ. Pr., 1972) are included. Eight of the sources indexed are presently out-of-print, and four titles included have subsequently come out in new or revised editions. An annotated bibliography of sources describes each work indexed, but the editors do not explain why these and not other sources were selected. For example, subject dictionaries for music, advertising, medicine, computers, architecture, publishing, etc., are included but none for fine arts, business and economics, and many other fields.

The format is attractive and contributes to the reference value of the set. Typeface is clear and the phrases, printed three columns to a page, are easy to read. A most useful feature is the inclusion of a user's guide and the annotated bibliography of sources in all volumes.

Each idiom or phrase is listed alphabetically by its first significant word and by every other significant word that is part of the expression. Spot-checking revealed no errors. A symbol appears before the first word of the expression under which it can be located in the cited source. Source designations (alphanumeric) are readily understood and, for quick reference, printed on the inside front and back covers of each volume.

Like the publisher's *Biography and Genealogy Master Index,* this new tool is a timesaver, indexing more than 140,000 different phrases and idioms. The inclusion of out-of-print works, superseded editions, and a rather narrow selection of indexed sources poses problems. Nevertheless *Idioms and Phrases Index* is an outstanding new reference source and will be highly useful in any academic or public library. A revised and expanded edition should be encouraged.

Illustrated dictionary of art terms: a handbook for the artist and art lover. [By] Kimberley Reynolds with Richard Sedon. London, Ebury; dist. by Harper, c1981, 1984. 190p. 24cm. hardcover $15.95; paper $8.95 (0-911745-31-9; hardcover: 0-911745-31-7: paper).
703'.21 Art—Dictionaries [CIP]   83-15739

This work succeeds in its stated aim of providing "a simple guide to terms frequently encountered in books, magazine articles, catalogues, and even television programmes on making and looking at works of art." It offers clear and thoughtful definitions of approximately 1,000 terms which, with the captions to some 150 accompanying drawings and photographs, provide a minicourse in art history and methods. The fine arts, as opposed to the purely decorative or applied arts, are stressed, although relevant terms from the latter fields are included. The inclusion of abbreviations is a helpful feature. Cross-references abound. A bibliography of suggested readings concludes the work.

Both authors are British and write extensively on art; Sedon is a recognized painter as well. Their *Dictionary of Art Terms* will be valuable to high school and public libraries in particular; academic libraries will find it useful but may prefer something more technical.

Index to America, v.3: life and customs—nineteenth century. By Norma Olin Ireland. Metuchen, N.J. & London, Scarecrow, 1984. xxiv, 350p. 23cm. cloth $25 (0-8108-1661-X).
016.973 U.S.—History—Indexes [CIP]   76-7196

This third volume in the author's *Index to America* series appears after a six-year hiatus. Intended for use by public, school, and academic libraries, it is an index to 161 popular and, for the most part, recent books about the life and customs of the period. The books selected for indexing are titles likely to be found, according to the author, "in major libraries."

Indexed titles include general historical works such as Daniel Boorstin's *Americans*, biographies, texts, and popular sets such as the *American Heritage New Illustrated History of the U.S.* There also are books especially suited for younger readers, which are marked with an asterisk in the list of titles indexed.

Arranged in alphabetical order by subject, the volume includes topics that range from *ague* and *air-conditioning* to *midwives, Tammany Hall, urbanization*, and *water closets*. Many biographical references are included, and there also are entries for some historical events. However, the purpose of the book is primarily to refer readers to general information on nineteenth-century culture, and the entries on events, government, and politics are not intended to be exhaustive. Numerous cross-references are provided, and a separate list of the women's names included in the index is provided as an Appendix. *Index to America* is a particularly good source for public and high school libraries.

Index to international public opinion, 1982-1983. Elizabeth Hann Hastings and Philip K. Hastings, eds. Westport, Conn., Greenwood, 1984. xix, 651p. 29cm. cloth $95 (0-313-24050-7).
016.3033'8 Public opinion polls—Indexes—Periodicals [CIP]   80-643917

This is the fifth volume of an annual begun in 1978-79 by Survey Research Consultants International. The work brings together highlights of important opinion surveys conducted by the world's leading opinion research organizations. This volume presents "polls conducted and/or referenced" in more than 125 countries and regions. The surveys cover not only attitudes on present-day interests (e.g., the Middle East) but also problems of continuing concern shared by people throughout the world (e.g., family size). The volume covers surveys completed mainly between the springs of 1982 and 1983, conducted by 99 survey organizations (selected because of their professional standards), and listed by country in the preliminary pages. (It is unclear if all of these surveys were actually conducted in this time period as the abbreviations used for them in the body of the work indicate that less than half took polls which are reported in the volume.)

Arrangement of the survey results is by major topic and then by more specific subcategory, e.g., "Business and Industry—Attitude Toward." Results of polls on these topics are arranged alphabetically by the countries in which such surveys were conducted and then by month/year if more than one was taken. Each entry includes the abbreviation of the interviewing organization, sample size, question(s) asked (in English), and the responses/percentages. The bulk of the volume covers surveys conducted in one country; data on multinational surveys are organized by region. Results of world surveys are also included. A Bibliography lists the published sources for these surveys. The three Indexes (by topical categories, by countries and regions in which the surveys were conducted, and by countries and geographic areas referenced in surveys) were examined and found accurate. Because there is no table of contents, the Indexes are vital.

Index to International Public Opinion will be a very helpful reference in large public, academic, and special libraries concerned with public attitudes throughout the world. It is a useful companion to the *American Public Opinion Index*.

Index to legal essays: English-language legal essays in Festschriften, memorial volumes, conference papers and other collections, 1975–1979. Compiled for the British and Irish Association of Law Librarians under the editorship of Barbara Tearle. London, Mansell; dist. in the U.S. and Canada by H. W. Wilson, 1983. xii, 430p. 26cm. cloth $40 (0-7201-1653-8).
016.34 Law—Addresses, essays, lectures—Bibliography [British CIP]

The *Index*—the first of several projected volumes—provides comprehensive bibliographical coverage of more than 5,000 legal essays in English published between 1975 and 1979. The 342 collections indexed reflect truly international coverage, for titles included were published in more than 30 different countries. Inasmuch as existing legal bibliographical sources do not adequately cover essays in collective works, the *Index* fills a lacuna. Divided into four sections, the volume facilitates finding essays on a specific subject, on a particular geographical area or jurisdiction, or by a given author. In the first section, List of Collections, full bibliographical information on each collection indexed is provided as is the code used to identify the collection in the second section—the Subject Index, the heart of the volume. The *Index* is alphabetical by topic, subdivided by country/state and form headings (bibliographies, history, statistics, etc.), and by author within a subject; it concludes with the previously mentioned code. Geographical Index (the third section) lists all jurisdictions and geographical areas used as subdivisions in the Subject Index, with topical headings where works covering that area may be found. The concluding section, Author Index, lists authors in the Subject Index and refers to the subject headings under which they will be found. Both the Subject and Geographical Indexes include numerous cross-references.

Index to Legal Essays, by providing thorough coverage of an important segment of the legal literature, will be a valuable reference for law librarians and other legal researchers.

An index to microform collections. Edited by Ann Niles. Westport, Conn., Meckler, 1984. xviii, 891p. 29cm. cloth $95 (0-930466-75-6).
011.36 Microforms—Indexes | Books on microfilm—Indexes [CIP]   84-4452

An Index to Microform Collections (IMC) analyzes 26 monographic collections containing more than 9,000 titles selected from Suzanne Dodson's *Microform Research Collections* (2d ed.). Excluded are four collections that already have published indexes—American Culture Series, Black Culture Series, Landmarks of Science, and Library of American Civilization.

IMC is organized in three parts: an alphabetical list by title of contents of each of the 26 collections; Author Index; and Title Index. Users should read the Introduction, particularly the latter part that deals with some idiosyncrasies of the computerized Index. For example, Mc or Mac are filed letter by letter rather than interfiled as in most library catalogs.

An Index to Microform Collections is a valuable access tool. It is obviously designed for academic libraries and those large public libraries serving serious researchers. Easy to use, its only major drawback is its cumbersome size.

Index to poetry for children and young people, 1976-1981: a title, subject, author, and first line index to poetry in collections for children and young poeple. Compiled by John E. Brewton, et al. New York, H. W. Wilson, 1984. xxxii, 320p. 28cm. cloth $35 (0-8242-0681-9).
016.821'008'09282 Children's poetry—Indexes [CIP]   83-10459

Sixth in a series of poetry indexes which began in 1942 with *Index to Children's Poetry*, this volume follows two supplements and three five-year cumulations. The present volume indexes more than 7,000 poems in 110 collections suitable for the very young child through twelfth graders. Collections were chosen by 14 consulting librarians and teachers; most were published between 1976-81, although some older works have been included.

Analysis of Books of Poetry Indexed provides complete bibliographic information, suggested grade (K–12), and content notes. Poems are then indexed by title, author, first line, and subject. More than 2,000 subject headings are used with ample cross-references. Subject headings have been consistent from volume to volume in the series. The book concludes with a directory of distributors and publishers.

Index to Poetry for Children and Young People, 1976–1981 is a worthwhile reference book for its designated time period and audience, suitable for children's or young adults' collections.

Index to poetry in popular periodicals, 1955–1959. Compiled by Jefferson D. Caskey. Westport, Conn., Greenwood, 1984. [xv] 269p. 29cm. cloth $29.95 (0-313-22227-4).
016.811'008 American poetry—20th century—Periodicals—Indexes | American periodicals—Indexes [CIP]   83-22584

Poems found in 45 periodicals, mostly magazines indexed in *Readers' Guide to Periodical Literature* during the late fifties, are listed here in separate Title, First-Line, Author, and Subject Indexes. Entries in the latter three are keyed numerically to listings in the Title Index, where an abbreviated citation notes poet's name, periodical title, volume, date, and page; more than 7,400 poems are included in this easy-to-use source. Among periodicals analyzed are *Poetry, Horn Book, ALA Bulletin, Commonweal, New Yorker, Redbook,* and *Ladies' Home Journal*—suggesting an unevenness among the worth/quality of the poems indexed.

Probably useful only in those libraries with strong poetry needs and interests and periodical backlists from 1955 to 1959.

Indexed journals: a guide to Latin American serials. [Compiled by] Paula Hattox Covington. Madison, WI 53706, Secretariat Seminar on the Acquisition of Latin American Library Materials, Memorial Library, Univ. of Wisconsin–Madison, 1983. iv, 458p. (Seminar on the Acquistion of Latin American Library Materials, Bibliography series, 8) 28cm. paper $20 + $2 shipping and handling.
016.98 Latin America—Periodicals—Indexes | Latin American periodicals—Indexes [OCLC]   83-176434

"This guide consists of (1) a description and evaluation, by discipline, of the principal indexes and abstracts which cover journals published in or relating to Latin America, and (2) a list of these journals with an indication of those indexes in which each is covered."

The inclusion of 1,500 periodicals, noted in more than 100 abstracting and indexing services, provides the following information: index in which journal appears; a guide to indexing and abstracting services; journals available through indexes; and an identification of journals on Latin America by discipline and by country. The four-part division further defines this reference's range and purpose. Under the subject guide to indexes are listed 25 fields from both the social sciences and the humanities (pure and technical sciences excluded) with a descriptive annotation of each indexing tool and a final paragraph that summarizes the entire field. The second part consists of an alphabetical listing of periodicals with initials indicating where they are indexed. In part 3, the periodicals are arranged under 23 various disciplines that incorporate Latin America. And finally, a geographical index arranges the periodicals by country.

Covington's guide, for its scope, its accessing of materials difficult for retrieval, and its organization (allowing for entry through subject or geographical area) is a boon to Latin Americanists. *Indexed Journals* will take its place next to the *Handbook of Latin American Studies* and the *Hispanic American Periodicals Index* as one of the major sources of information on a large area of the world.

Indexing and abstracting 1977–1981: an international bibliography. Compiled by Hans H. Wellisch. Santa Barbara, Calif., ABC-Clio, 1984. xix, 276p. 29cm. cloth $45 (0-87436-398-5).
016.0253 Indexing—Bibliography | Abstracting—Bibliography [CIP]   84-3064

With this volume, Hans Wellisch, professor of library and information science at the University of Maryland, recognized authority on indexing and abstracting, and currently president of the American Society of Indexers, has brought his comprehensive coverage of the literature of indexing and abstracting up through 1981. The first volume of this bibliography (ABC-Clio, 1980), covering the early literature through 1976, was well received and has proved to be a most valuable contribution to the bibliographic control of this literature. The Board called it "an extremely well-designed bibliography . . . worthy of emulation by all subject bibliographers."

This continuation lists more than 1,600 items arranged according to the author's own classification of the field. Nonprint items, such as tape-slide presentations and video recordings, have been added to the wide variety of printed documents covered. The subject focus continues to be on verbal indexing, with classification as a form of indexing largely excluded. Emphasis on international coverage continues, with 26 languages represented. Separate Author Indexes are provided for each script, followed by a Title Index for works not entered under personal author and a detailed Subject Index. At least one incorrect referent was found in the Author Index.

Changes in the classification of the literature covered reflect recent changes in the field. Among the new categories added are classificatory principles of indexing languages; subject heading lists and thesauri; probabilistic indexing; the indexing process; indexing of numerical data, fiction and poetry, patents, personal files, films, video recordings, and videotex; expertise indexes; concordances; and professional indexing and abstracting societies. In the section on abstracting, sections have been added for production of abstracting and indexing services and print versus online.

As in the previous volume, each entry includes a full bibliographic citation, and most are followed by an annotation or abstract written or edited by the compiler. The practice of using only forenames in the Author Index, which the Board had criticized in its review of the first volume, continues.

This work, like its predecessor, is a valuable contribution to the bibliography of indexing and abstracting. It, too, will be welcomed by students and scholars—for these, access to the literature has been greatly enhanced by Wellisch's painstaking labor.

Indians of North America: methods and sources for library research. [By Marilyn L. Haas]. Hamden, Conn., Shoe String, 1983. xii, 163p 23cm. cloth $21.50 (0-208-01980-4).
016.970004'97 Indians of North America—Bibliography | Indians of North America—Library resources—U.S. | Reference books—Indians of North America | Indians of North America—Research—Methology [CIP]   83-14007

Marilyn L. Haas, a reference librarian, has written a guide to library research on North American Indians which is "meant to help college students writing papers, Indians studying their tribal history, anthropologists and archaeologists, historians and hobbyists, teachers of Indian children, lawyers seeking background information—and the librarians who help them all—to find written information on North American Indians." Haas has succeeded in producing the basic tool for research in this area, giving guidance through the maze of subject headings and access words to the various formats in which information is stored. The classics are listed as well as the up-to-date sources which have resulted from the renewed interest in North American Indians in the last ten years. The three sections cover library methodology and an annotated list of reference works, including online databases; standard monographs—extensively annotated—with pertinent subject headings for further searches; and a bibliography of books on individual tribes.

Indians of North America is a sound, clearly written, and concise guide for independent research on this topic.

Information America: sources of print and nonprint materials available from organizations, industry, government agencies and specialized publishers. 3 issues per yr. Editor, Tracy Davis. New York, Neal-Schuman, 1983. 28cm. paper $80 (ISSN: 0738-1522).
027'.0025'73 Information services—U.S.—Directories | Associations, institutions, etc.—U.S.—Directories | Government publicity—U.S.—Directories | Publishers and publishing—U.S.—Directories | Library materials—Catalogs [OCLC]   83-647144

This set, formerly titled *Sources: A Guide to Print and Non-Print Materials Available From Organizations*, has been redesigned in response to a subscriber survey. Now organized by broad subject areas, it is easy to use. Each entry offers a complete address and telephone number of the organization when available, a purpose statement, and a description of information services. Since a majority of these are not publishers in the commercial sense, their offerings are usually listed under formats (e.g., Books and Pamphlets, Film, Periodical).

The Board examined volume 6, numbers 1 and 2. These open with a user guide; a minidirectory feature (number 1 on money management; number 2 on Vietnam veterans' organizations); selected U.S. government publications; and then the Directory of Sources grouped into such categories as Arts and Leisure, Education, Health, History, Religion, etc. Four indexes—to free and inexpensive materials, periodicals, subjects, and sources—complete the issue. They are cumulative.

The compilers describe this periodical as a beginning access tool and as a resource to publications published by nontraditional as well as mainstream organizations; it could be an important reference work although much of the information it contains is available elsewhere. Libraries that wish to supplement more traditional guides to companies, associations, and publications, and who need or wish to maintain an awareness of the changing materials that are being produced (and the people or groups producing them) may want to add this to their reference collections. The paper binding will not withstand heavy use.

Insular art: an annotated bibliography. By Martin Werner. Boston, G. K. Hall, 1984. xxxiv, 395p. (Reference Publications in Art History) 24cm. cloth $68 (0-8161-8327-9).
016.7'0941 Art, Anglo-Saxon—Bibliography | Art, Celtic—Bibliography [CIP]   84-10914

Martin Werner of the art history department at Temple University has compiled a guide to Insular art, defined here as "the art produced in England from the coming of the Saxons in the early fifth century to the beginning of the Age of Alfred in 871 and in Ireland between the fifth century and 1017." Insular art is characterized by intricate designs and abstract ornaments and survives primarily in manuscripts, metalwork, and sculpture. Generally, the study of Continental influences and works made on the Continent by Insular peoples has been excluded.

The book includes more than 2,000 entries for monographs, festschriften, and scholarly journals published before the end of 1979. A short Appendix lists some 1982 imprints. Annotations are descriptive and range in length from several sentences to a full page; reviews are cited frequently. Bibliographic information for each source includes the number of plates and figures. There is an Author Index; the absence of a subject index and adequate cross-referencing is compensated for somewhat by a lengthy Table of Contents. The book begins with chapters covering such ancillary subjects as language, literature, and ecclesiastical history and then proceeds to discuss genres (e.g., "Metalwork, Textiles, Beads"). Subsections are chiefly geographical (e.g., "Ireland: Brooches"). An introductory essay traces the historical development of scholarship in Hibero-Saxon art.

This fine, selective bibliography conveys the vitality of research in Insular art; it will be sufficiently comprehensive for all but the most scholarly collections of art history.

Interlibrary loan policies directory. 2d ed. By Leslie R. Morris and Patsy Fowler Brautigam. Chicago, American Library Assn., 1984. iv, 448p. 21cm. x 26cm. paper $27.50 (0-8389-0393-2).
025.6'2 Inter-library loans—U.S. | Libraries—U.S.—Directories [CIP]   83-11897

Here are presented pertinent data on types of material loaned, charges, copying services, and loan periods, based on returned questionnaires from 832 public, academic, and special American libraries. These are primarily libraries with high interlibrary loan volume as lenders and/or with large book budgets. Updating Thomson's 1975 edition, the work is alphabetical by state, then library; an Index by keywords in the libraries' names completes the volume. The latter uses such keywords as *city, medical,* etc.—a rather dubious practice. It is a far cry from Winchell's book on interlibrary loan, published in 1930. This directory should facilitate efficient interlibrary loan borrowing. However, many libraries listed here are members of OCLC, which has (or will eventually have) *ILL* profiles available online to readers. Thus, the *Interlibrary Loan Policies Directory* may be more useful in small and/or non-OCLC libraries.

International bibliography of special directories. 7th ed. [Edited by] Helga Lengenfelder. New York, Saur; dist. by Gale, [1983]. xix, 474p. 24cm. cloth $85.
†016.06 Directories—Bibliography [OCLC]

English-language readers should realize that this is the new edition of what was formerly called the *International Bibliography of Directories* (last revised in 1978 by the same publisher); the parallel German title, *Internationale Bibliographie der Fachdressbücher,* remains the same. The work lists and briefly describes some 5,630 "address books and membership lists published regularly or irregularly in some 50 countries worldwide." Although containing almost 1,200 fewer entries than the previous edition and lacking current information on new editions of some serial directories, the present edition includes more complete and appropriate information, such as publishers' addresses. The front matter appears in English and German, the headings and annotations in English except that French and German works are described in those languages.

The classified arrangement of the work consists of seven major sections and the addenda as follows: General; Cultural Affairs, Arts, Sciences and Technology; State and Society; Commerce and Industry; Individuals; Classified List of Trades and Industries (the largest section has 35 subdivisions); and Public Transportation and Transport Communication. Larger subdivisions are further divided by country wherever possible. Although there is no index to the numbered entries, the detailed outline of contents enables searchers to locate information without too much difficulty. For libraries needing more extensive coverage than that provided in, e.g., *The Directory of Directories*.

International Center of Photography encyclopedia of photography. New York, Crown, 1984. 607p. illus. 29cm. cloth $50 (0-517-55271-X).
770'.3'21 Photography—Dictionaries [CIP]   84-1856

The ICP has provided a much-needed, convenient, one-volume reference source for general information on photography from the "aesthetic and historical to the technical and practical aspects." Previously published encyclopedias are either outdated or present information in inconvenient multivolumes. The stated objective here, "to give the general reader a comprehensive view of the medium in a single volume," is certainly met, although additional sources will be needed for more detailed information. The more than 1,650 entries, arranged alphabetically, three columns to a page, document the scope of photography since its invention; demonstrate "in words and images its power and range of artistic expression"; and provide information on pioneers of the medium who have by invention or creation provided something unique. Of these entries, more than 1,300 are concerned with the current state of the "aesthetic, communicative, scientific, technical, and commerical applications" of photography; 250 of the 350 biographical entries deal with photographers whose work "shaped and defined the expressive and communicative uses of the medium," and another 100 deal with the scientists, inventors, and others who have influenced or are responsible for the growth and development of the medium in ways other than through photographs. The photographers whose biographies and works are included were chosen by an international board of advisors and limited to those born before 1940. A supplement to these biographical entries is provided by an Appendix (on which subject, see more below). There are 64 pages of beautifully reproduced color photographs, numerous scientific illustrations, and more than 250 black-and-white pictures, all excellent examples of the versatility and power of the camera. The text of unsigned articles was written by 43 contributors—all listed but not identified.

There are some errors, e.g., the Gernsheims sold rather than donated their collection to the Universtiy of Texas at Austin; Edwin Land, Polaroid inventor, did not graduate from Harvard; and Carl Mydans was not one of the first four photographers for *Life* magazine. There are other discrepancies, involving spellings, dates, etc. The Ur-Leica is referred to as both a 1913 and 1914 prototype; Paul Strand's film is spelled variously *Manhatta, Mannahatta,* and *Manahatta;* the National Archive should be Archives; Alfred Stieglitz' name is spelled two different ways in one paragraph and misspelled twice again; Daguerre's process was presented in Paris in 1839, not 1939; and there are frequent errors in German words and titles as well as the absence of proper accent marks. The diagram of the camera on page 92 is numbered, but there is no key to identify these numbers.

There are two Appendixes: the Biographical Supplement of Photographers is an alphabetical list of more than 2,000 prominent photographers, which cites their nationality, dates of birth and death, and type of photography. Photographic Societies and Associations lists organizations concerned with various aspects of photography and its uses and applications with addresses and purpose.

Even with its errors, this *Encyclopedia of Photography* is an extremely complete source that would be valuable in any library; it is, by far, the best of its kind.

The international directory of little magazines and small presses. 19th ed., 1983–84. Len Fulton and Ellen Ferber, Editors. Paradise, CA 95969, P.O. Box 100, Dustbooks, 1983. 581p. 23cm. cloth $25.95; paper $17.95 (0-913218-64-2).
051.025 Little magazines—Directories | Little presses—Directories [OCLC]

This annual directory presents in this issue 3,535 entries for periodicals and presses. Data on periodicals (in addition to the kind found in the *Standard Periodical Directory*) are length of reporting time on manuscripts, payment rates, and copyright arrangements. Comments by editors on audience, recent contributors, and material sought will also interest writers.

Information on presses that will concern writers are average press run, type of manuscripts sought, reporting time, payment or royalty arrangements, and number of titles printed in 1983 and 1984.

Subject and regional indexes to the entries are included along with a list of some 200 book distributors, book jobbers, and magazine agents.

A Key to Directory Listings is provided, but no mention is made of intended audience except for the cover notation "over 4,000 markets for writers." Neither criteria for inclusion nor a definition for "little" are found. Among the "little magazines" are long established ones, e.g., *American Literature, Daedalus,* and *Drama Review* and the 100,000 circulation *Creative Computing*.

The magnitude of independent publishing can be gauged by the fact that despite the hundreds listed, some are missing, e.g., Hazlett Publishing, Inc., Hemlock's Publications printed by Economy Self Publishing, and Golden-Lee Books.

Reference and acquisitions librarians in public and academic libraries as well as writer patrons will find *The International Directory of Little Magazines and Small Presses* an invaluable supplement to the *Directory of Publishing Opportunities in Journals and Periodicals* and *Literary Marketplace*.

International discography of women composers. Compiled by Aaron I. Cohen. Westport, Conn., Greenwood, 1984. xxii, 254p. 24cm. cloth $35 (0-313-24272-0).
016.7899'12'088042 Women composers—Discography [CIP]　　83-26445

This work complements the author's *International Encyclopedia of Women Composers* (Bowker, 1981), which provided needed coverage for thousands of women composers throughout history. The discography volume lists the recorded performances of 468 women from 40 countries, many of whom are still living. Americans account for 168 of the total. Because predominantly they have been issued by small companies, most of these recordings are not listed in standard catalogs. However, nearly all are commercially available, and a valuable Appendix to the book is a directory of the 286 recording companies cited in the text.

The main listing is arranged alphabetically by composer, and entry information includes birth and death dates, nationality, and compositions. Only concert or art music and music issued in phonorecording format have been included. For each composition, major performers are given, if known, and the releasing label and disc number. Indexes are Composers by Country, Composer by Instrument and Music Form, and Titles.

International Discography of Women Composers is an up-to-date, comprehensive discography. While international in scope, the work still includes 77 more American composers than the Institute for Studies in American Music's *American Music Recordings*. Thought should be given to incorporating the discography into future editions of the *International Encyclopedia of Women Composers*.

International encyclopedia of psychiatry, psychology, psychoanalysis, and neurology: progress volume I. Benjamin B. Wolman, editor. New York, Aesculapius Publishers, 1983. xxxiv, 509p. 29cm. hardcover $89 (0-918228-28-X).
616.89'003'21 Psychiatry—Dictionaries | Psychology—Dictionaries | Psychoanalysis—Dictionaries | Neurology—Dictionaries [CIP]　　83-2505

Continuing the fine tradition of the 12-volume set of 1977 which received a very favorable review from the Board (cf. *RSBR*, Oct 1, 1978), and which was the recipient of ALA's Dartmouth Medal in 1978, is this first supplement—*Progress Volume*. Editor Benjamin B. Wolman says in his Preface, "The twelve volumes of the Encyclopedia are as up-to-date as they were five years ago, and only certain limited areas required a new approach and a fresh appraisal." The 136 signed articles by 125 authors (more than half of whom also contributed to the original volumes) are as authoritative and clear as before. New topics include, for example, *Pairbonding and Limerence* by John Money, *Senile Dementia* by Robert D. Terry, and *DSM III* by Henry Pinsker. All except for the 22 biographical entries contain bibliographies. Although most of the biographies are of persons who have died since the publication of the *Encyclopedia,* one is of a living person, and five died well before it went to press. As before, emphasis in biographical articles is on concepts and contributions, not on dates, degrees, etc.

Entries range from one-half column (for most biographies) to seven or eight pages, with the majority being three or four pages long. Once again there is a list of "Major Cross-References"; these lead to entries in the *Progress Volume* which, if they also relate to entries in the main set, contain the phrase: "For a complete list of articles see Volume_____, page_____." Name and Subject Indexes complete the volume.

The Board characterized the *Encyclopedia* as a basic reference work by and for scholars, scientists, and professionals which also would have value for students and members of the general public interested in these fields. The *Progress Volume* is an integral—and worthy—continuation of the set. All who purchased the original *Encyclopedia* will want to add this supplement.

The international foundation directory. 3d ed. Consultant editor, H. V. Hodson. London, Europa; dist. in the U.S. by Gale, 1983. xxviii, 401p. 24cm. hardcover $78 (0-8103-2032-0).
361.7'632'025 Endowments—Directories [OCLC]　　73-90303

Philanthropic foundations are now an established feature of modern-day life. This new edition shows a 10 percent increase in listings over the previous edition of 1979 with just more than 700 foundations, trusts, and similar nonprofit institutions included. The criterion for inclusion is that an organization should operate on an international basis (interpreted somewhat generously); there are listings from 46 countries although the majority are located in North America and Europe: the lists for the U.S. and the U.K. total 125 pages. Arrangement is alphabetical by country and then alphabetical by name. Name, address, foundation date, history, activities, financial details, officers, and any publications are given for each entry. There are two indexes—one by title and one under broad subject groupings.

For large collections *The International Foundation Directory* provides a useful complement to the *Foundation Directory*, but most libraries will probably find it too limited in scope and/or too specialized to be of much practical use.

International index to recorded poetry. Compiled by Herbert H. Hoffman and Rita Ludwig Hoffman. New York, Wilson, 1983. xlvi, 529p. 27cm. cloth $70 (U.S. &. Canada); $80 (other) (0-8241-0682-7).
011'.38 Poetry—Indexes | Poetry—Discography [CIP]　　83-16659

This index analyzes more than 1,700 recordings of poetry issued through 1981 in the U.S. While most of the entries are for phonodiscs, there are some for tapes, filmstrips, and cassettes and most selections are English-language; yet more than 33 languages, from Anglo-Saxon to Xhosa and Yiddish are also represented. The book is divided into six sections. The first is the list, with publisher/code number of each recording analyzed. The second and largest section is the Poet Index, arranged alphabetically by name. Each of these entries includes the poet's birthdate (if known) and language of composition. Following this is a list of poems, by title, including the first line and relevant record code. The First Line and Title Indexes refer users to the author's name. A Reader Index and a Register of Poets by Language of Composition complete the work. While this work answers the frequent need to find recordings of poems as read aloud by the poet, the access provided for this particular need is somewhat cumbersome, e.g., although the Author Index indicates that there are, for example, five recordings of *Sweeney Among the Nightingales*, one must then check the Reader Index to find if Eliot recorded his own poetry, and that listing does not indicate individual poems but recordings by code number. One must then flip back and forth between the two Indexes to match poet with poet-as-reader. This is an irritant but not a major flaw (it can easily be corrected in subsequent editions). The volume will be most welcome in both public and academic libraries.

International organizations: a dictionary and directory. [By] Giuseppe Schiavone. London, Macmillan Pr.; Chicago, St. James Pr., 1983. 321p. 22cm. cloth $39.50 (0-912289-03-1).
†060.25 International agencies—Directories [OCLC]

Schiavone lists and describes in this directory more than 350 organizations in which national states "are associated in a common purpose" for economic or political reasons. There is, of course, an ongoing need to represent these bodies in a reference format with essential information, clarity of style, and rapid accessibility. The author has achieved this purpose. The entries are characterized by the following information: full-name entry, acronym, purpose, activities, legal basis for formation, history, procedural rules, function of subdivisions, location of secretariat, relationship to other international organizations, recent history, problems dealt with, rules for membership, and more specific data (director, address and publications). The term "dictionary" in the title is at times an understatement since some of the articles, with a maximum length of almost 3,000 words, seem proportioned for an encyclopedia. Another quality feature is the objectivity of the writings. Ease of access to these entries is expedited by an Index of acronyms and full names; those in italics note bodies no longer in existence, reorganized, or renamed.

Other features include a long Introduction wherein the author indicates his grasp of the subject in an encompassing essay where contextual themes are broached: assessment of international organizations in their goal for world government, the inadequacy of bilateral diplomacy, the League of Nations, the formation of the UN, economic cooperation, and post-1965 history. Perhaps here the author might have noted his criteria for selections, his intended treatment for each organization under study, and his relegating of certain bodies to a separate listing with minimal data at the end of the book. Yet this is caviling in considering what he has accomplished.

Two other sections complete this volume: a chart listing all of the countries of the world and their membership in the UN, its separate agencies, the International Atomic Energy Agency, and the General Agreement on Tariffs and Trades (GATT), and a chronological Index of Foundation Dates from 1815 to 1982.

Schiavone, for his interpretative introduction and his concise entries, has done an excellent job, and this encyclopedic reference belongs in most academic and public libraries.

Jailhouse rock: the bootleg records of Elvis Presley, 1970–1983. By Lee Cotten and Howard A. DeWitt. Ann Arbor, Mich., Pierian, 1983. xxxix, 367p. (Rock and Roll Reference Series 8) 24cm. cloth $17.95 to individuals; $22.95 to institutions (0-87650-158-7).
789.9′136454′00924 Presley, Elvis, 1935–1977—Discography | Copyright—Unauthorized reproductions of sound recordings—Discography [OCLC]   83-61755

This guide offers serious collectors of Elvis Presley records a discography/buying guide to original issues, reissues, and counterfeits of illegal, unauthorized releases of his material. The volume includes an introductory essay on the bootleg-record industry, including a glossary of terms and a list of bootlegged performances. The main discography includes a Song Title Index to albums, LPs, and singles. There also are chapters on recorded interviews and press conferences (talking albums) with topical index; overseas pirated releases; and novelty albums with a Song Title Index. The special lists or indexes include a Label Index; Personal Name Index; and lists of bootlegged cassette tapes, super eight millimeter films, and videotapes.

The authors bring a strong interest in Elvis as well as experience in teaching rock-and-roll music history and as biographers to their role as compilers. Their numbered entries include record producer, date of production, packaging, highlights of each album side, and evaluative summary for the prospective collector. The illustrations are black and white and include album covers and labels.

Jailhouse Rock will be extremely useful to collectors of Presley records and related media or to those rock-and-roll fans and historians interested in the bootleg phenomenon. Larger public libraries may want to add this to their reference collections with a second copy for circulation.

Jane's 1983–84 aviation review. Edited by Michael J. H. Taylor. New York, Jane's, 1983. 176p. 28cm. hardcover $14.95 (0-7106-0285-5).
†629.13′05 Aeronautics—Yearbooks | Airplanes—Yearbooks | Astronautics—Yearbooks [OCLC]   83-12286

Even though the designation "1983–84" is misleading (How can a 1983 publication review what happened in 1984?), the third annual edition by a publishing house known internationally for its excellent reference works on everything from military and commercial vehicles to containers to ships continues to inform, to be well written, and to contain excellent photographs. Actually, this edition reviews 1982–83 as shown by a new feature—"Chronology: June 3, 1982–June 3, 1983." Two other special features have been added to this volume: "New Aircraft of the Year," which covers the more important and interesting types that were released during 1982–83 with complete descriptions and in some cases specifications; and "Jarrett's Jubilees," being a historical essay on some interesting airplanes. The annual follows the same outline as the previous two volumes with individually written, encyclopedic articles on various aircraft that have had noteworthy achievements during the period. The 18 articles cover commercial and military aircraft, the U.S. space shuttle flights, balloons, and the "Paris Salon of 1983" air show. Each article is well written for a general readership and includes numerous excellent photographs. An index would have been useful, especially for the names of all the aircraft that are mentioned in the articles.

Any library that has found the Jane's reference works useful will probably want to obtain this annual as well.

Jane's spaceflight directory: a comprehensive guide to the past, present and future activities of the world's space powers. Edited by Reginald Turnill. New York, Jane's, 1984. 311p. illus. 32cm. cloth $50 (0-7106-0208-1).
†629.41′025 Astronautics [OCLC]

Jane's adds to its collection of the world's most complete reference sources on aircraft, ships, and weapons systems with this sourcebook on international space programs, spacecraft, and astronauts. It is up-to-date, comprehensive, and authoritative.

The section on individual space programs includes data for each of the 19 nations involved in space exploration and utilization and for 27 international space projects. Entries range from a single paragraph on Argentina to more than 100 pages on the U.S. For both the USSR and the U.S., each series of missions is described, from *Sputnik* to *Salyut* and from *Explorer* to the space shuttle. Every launch within each series is covered, with information on the dates, purpose, and success. Other major sections of the book cover the military's use of space, launch vehicles, and astronauts. The military section contains brief information on communications and spy satellites; the launch vehicle chapter lists data on all of the rockets known to have been developed throughout the world, and the biographical section contains brief information about every person to have flown in space.

All of the information in this book is accurate and complete. It is well illustrated and is especially valuable for information on the Soviet and other foreign space programs. This directory is recommended for any library with a serious interest in spaceflight and should become the standard reference for aerospace information.

Keats's major odes: an annotated bibliography of the criticism. By Jack Wright Rhodes. Westport, Conn., Greenwood, 1984. 224p. 24cm. cloth $35 (0-313-23809-X).
016.821′7 Keats, John, 1795-1821—Bibliography | Odes—History and criticism—Bibliography [CIP]   83-16634

A chronological arrangement of more than 700 critical essays or articles that deal with any one or all of Keats' five major odes (*Ode on a Grecian Urn, Ode to a Nightingale, Ode on Melancholy, Ode to Psyche,* and *To Autumn*), this bibliography has entries from 1820 to 1980. All are annotated (from two to about eight lines). There is an Author Index, as well as a Subject Index, the latter including topics both within the text of Keats' odes as well as in the annotations.

There is a 34-page Introduction, which is essentially a history of the impact of Keats on English literature and especially on literary criticism. It is well documented, containing no less than 91 citations to books, theses, and literary articles.

The bibliography demonstrates that while in the nineteenth century the commentators were mostly well-known poets or critics, such as Shelley, Swinburne, Wilde, Ruskin, Meredith, Palgrave, Hopkins, and so on, the twentieth century has not been lacking in critical appreciation, with names such as Saintsbury, William Henry Hudson, Conrad Aiken, and André Gide appearing amid hundreds of less well known names. *Keats's Major Odes* will be invaluable to students of Romantic English poetry, and probably no academic library supporting a curriculum in English literature should be without it.

Kister's atlas buying guide: general English-language world atlases available in North America. Phoenix, Oryx, 1984. xii, 236p. 24cm. cloth $37.50 (0-912700-62-9).
912 Atlases—Bibliography [CIP]   82-42920

Kenneth F. Kister, author of *Encyclopedia Buying Guide* (Bowker, 1981) and *Dictionary Buying Guide* (Bowker, 1977), has now assembled profiles of 105 world atlases ranging from the comprehensive *Times Atlas of the World* to small, inexpensive paperbacks. A 25-page introductory essay offers detailed advice on selecting an atlas, focusing on such elements as extent and balance of coverage, scale and projection, accuracy and currency, and legibility. The importance of accessibility of atlas content is stressed; a thorough, six-point checklist is furnished as an aid to evaluating indexes in atlases.

The individual atlas profiles supply such items of information as publisher and distributor; edition and publication date; number of total pages and map pages; number of index entries; ISBN; size; and price. Each profile includes an evaluative review by the *Guide*'s author, which is supplemented by citations to other reviews in major atlas evaluation sources. The closing date for inclusion in the *Guide* was September 1, 1983. (The atlas evaluations in the Board's "World Atlas Survey," which appeared in the September 1, 1983, premier issue of *RBB*, are among the reviews cited.)

There are several useful Appendixes. A set of five charts facilitates comparison of atlases by type (adult-large, medium, small; children's; paperback) with respect to number of map pages; number of index entries; total pages; publication date; and price. A 17-page annotated bibliography in two parts ("evaluating" and "making and using" maps and atlases) cites selected books, articles, and nonprint materials. Two directories (of selected dealers in out-of-print maps and atlases and of atlas publishers and distributors) complete the section of Appendixes, which is followed by a Title-Subject Index to the *Guide*.

The author's evaluations of individual atlases are well informed and to the point, although there will inevitably be differences over particular judgments. (Some might take issue, for instance, with his rather harsh assessment of the *Great Geographical Atlas*.)

A good general world atlas is an essential component of home, school, and library reference collections, and the baffling variety of available titles makes choice difficult. This reliable, up-to-date *Buying Guide* meets a real need.

Knock on wood: an encyclopedia of talismans, charms, superstitions & symbols. New York/Toronto, Beaufort Books, 1983. viii, 263p. 23cm. paper $10.95 (0-8253-0144-0).
001.9′6′0321 Superstition—Dictionaries [CIP] 82-24440

Informal tone and lightness of touch—which make it ideal for circulating collections in school, public, and college libraries—should not lead one to overlook *Knock on Wood*'s reference value. It even features a good (if brief) bibliography packed with data. And in concentrating on superstition, it touches on other phenomena, including some that are quite borderline, e.g., *Smoky the Bear*. One may be surprised to learn that "in Panama, the man in the moon was sent there as punishment for incest" and that "anyone walking under a rainbow will be transformed into the opposite sex"—but relieved to know, if one is left-handed, that one is no longer likely to be burnt at the stake therefor.

Knowledge encyclopedia. Edited by John Paton. New York, Arco, c1981, [1984]. 415p. illus. (part col.) 28cm. hardcover $16.95 (0-668-06137-5).
032 Encyclopedias and dictionaries [OCLC] 83-73345

At first glance—but see below, on its age and orientation—this one-volume encyclopedia would appear to be a work suitable both for older children and for adults, with coverage reasonably comprehensive and, though superficial in many areas and weak in recent political history, fairly strong in science and technology. Its generous use of illustrations would also seem to recommend it, its best graphic effects being, as one might expect, in science and technology (e.g., the illustrations for *Electromagnetic Waves* and *Sea Urchin*). The result is something one would expect to prove useful in homes lacking more substantial encyclopedias but not very useful in libraries, as the latter would surely have verbal and graphic sources of equal or superior quality. Articles are very short, cross-references are numerous, and there is an adequate Index. Page format is curious: each page (except for those few given over to graphics) is in three columns, with those next to gutters (separated by a gray bar) providing text supplementing the texts of some articles (in the other two columns): double coverage is not linked, nor is there any sure way to predict what data will go in inner columns and what will not.

So far, so-so. Unfortunately, there are basic difficulties: age and orientation. According to its copyright page, this work, although "Published 1984," is "Copyright 1979, 1981 by Grisewood & Dempsey Ltd." Although the American edition is silent on this point, this "1984" publication *appears* to be a republication of a 1979 British publication, itself (one infers) scarcely a model of currentness. Statistics, where dated, are from the 1970s; and there are even lingering pre-1979 lapses, e.g., Robert Lowell (1917-77) is listed as yet living, and the independent existence of Bangladesh (1971-) is, though recorded under *Bangladesh*, not recognized on the map of Asia. Orientation is strongly British (and Commonwealth), with articles on Toronto, Alice Springs, and Newcastle but none on Baltimore, Denver, or Detroit, with an article on English literature but none on American, with a list of English sovereigns but none of U.S. presidents, and with such entries as *Tumour* and *Tyre* (the latter a form unlikely to occur to many Americans at the presumed level of readership).

Knowledge Encyclopedia is, then, a work unlikely to prove very useful in American homes and libraries except as, in the most extreme and charitable senses of the term, a "supplementary" source.

The labor almanac. [By] Adrian A. Paradis [and] Grace D. Paradis. Littleton, Colo., Libraries Unlimited, 1983. 205p. 24cm. cloth $25 (U.S.); $30 (elsewhere) (0-87287-386-2).
331′.0973 Labor and laboring classes—U.S.—Handbooks, manuals, etc. | Trade-unions—U.S.—Handbooks, manuals, etc. | Labor policy—U.S.—Handbooks, manuals, etc. [CIP] 83-915

The authors of this volume note that as a result of their experience in researching and writing two previous titles, *Labor in Action* (1963) and *Labor Reference Book* (1972), they became convinced that there was a need for a labor almanac—hence the present volume.

It is in eight sections: Labor History Highlights presents, in 25 pages, a year-by-year chronology of historical facts and data about labor; National Labor Organizations lists almost 300 unions (with addresses, principal officers, and total number of union members) plus other labor-related organizations; Prominent Labor Leaders lists major union leaders in an alphabetical arrangement; chapter IV summarizes major labor laws and lists executive orders affecting labor; chapter V enumerates federal agencies concerned with labor laws, lists the commissioners and secretaries of labor (with periods of service), and summarizes the areas of responsibility of the major organizational units; chapter VI lists the major state agencies concerned with labor matters; and the last two sections (chapters VII and VIII) provide statistical data and a glossary of labor terms. It is not clear whether this work is intended to be a serial; certainly, parts of the work will be out-of-date relatively soon.

Information for the almanac was obtained from questionnaires sent to unions, from government publications, and from a variety of reference sources. A 31-page Index listing, in a single alphabetical sequence, organizations, persons, laws, terms, and publications facilitates access to the material. The information in *The Labor Almanac* is available in other reference sources, but the almanac constitutes a handy and useful compilation. Reference departments in public, academic, and appropriate special libraries will want to consider it.

Lambert's world of trade, finance & economic development: an international directory of government contracts. 2v. 1030 Fifteenth St., NW, Washington, DC 20005, Lambert, 1984. (Lambert Network of International Publications) 28cm. paper $250, U.S. & Canada; $270, elsewhere (0-939304-08-2).
†380.1′025 Commerce—Directories | Development banks—Directories | Government financial institutions—Directories [OCLC] 84-44384

Other publications in this series include *Lambert's Worldwide Government Directory*, *Lambert's Worldwide Defense Authorities*, and *Lambert's World of Energy*. This business directory lists 60,000 key government officials concerned with national and international trade and economic activities in more than 170 countries. Information for each country includes names of key personnel in relevant government agencies, state-owned trading and manufacturing corporations, banks, stock exchanges, chambers of commerce, and diplomatic missions, as well as selected general economic data (labor force, inflation rate, exports, and imports). No sources are cited for these figures. The directory is replete with street and cable addresses, telephone and telex numbers. A uniform organizational scheme is used for each country—basically, hierarchical: head of state, then ministries, major banks, stock exchanges, transportation and tourism, chambers of commerce/trade groups, and public enterprises. Commercial representatives of foreign diplomatic missions accredited to the country are then listed, followed by the economic data. Volume I includes Africa and the Americas (including the U.S.); Volume II, Asia and Europe. Each volume has an Index, listing under individual nations all state organizations listed in the body of the work. Subsequent annual editions will be in one volume covering all countries.

Much of this information is available in other sources, including *The Statesman's Year-Book, International Marketing Handbook,* and *The Rand McNally International Bankers Directory*. However, *Lambert's* includes more locational information for many more governmental officials, and this and other related directories from the publisher are produced annually to provide up-to-date information to "a network of contacts in governments worldwide." On the other hand, no information is given in the front matter concerning methods used to keep information current. (Much of the statistical data are three to four years old.) The question is, Is the statistical and locational information the very latest available in official government or UN sources? References to specific official yearbooks, annuals, directories, etc., used in gleaning the information presented here would inspire more confidence. *Lambert's World of Trade* is probably of most interest to special business libraries, particularly those in international corporations or exporting companies.

Lands and peoples. 6v. Danbury, Conn., Grolier, 1983. illus. maps. 28cm. hardcover $245 + $15 (shipping/handling) to homes; $149.50 + $4 (shipping/handling) to schools and libraries (0-7172-8009-8).
909 Geography [CIP]   83-1649

Lands and Peoples was last reviewed in these pages February 1, 1973, and it has remained a work of quality through the succeeding ten years mainly because of continuous updating and revision. It provides up-to-date information, and material is presented so that the set's purpose, "to promote understanding among people of the world," is fulfilled by selecting content "that develops those concepts and attitudes basic to a good understanding of the interaction between man and his social, his cultural and his physical environment."

The 1973 version consisted of seven volumes: the first six dealt with North and South America, Asia, Africa, Australia, and Europe respectively, and the seventh with Arctica, Antarctica, a miscellany called Facts & Figures, a reading list, and the Index. The new version's six-volume format was suggested by consultants. Thus, *Arctica*, formerly in v.7 is now in v.5 (North America); *Antarctica*, Facts & Figures, and the Index were transferred to v.6 (Central and South America). Within the volumes, the arrangement was changed from alphabetical by country to geographical, i.e., articles follow a north to south arrangement. Each volume, however, has an alphabetical list which makes it easier for those unfamiliar with geography to find what they seek. In 1973, Facts & Figures primarily consisted of lists of various data (e.g., largest islands of the world, governmental leaders, and historical events) and thematic world maps. Much of this material is now integrated throughout the set—a distinct improvement.

The Index helps provide access to the set's contents. It and Facts & Figures are available to libraries in a paperbound separate.

The level of authority of the authors and consultants continues to be impressive (some articles were reviewed by the U.S. embassy staff of the various countries); the illustrations are excellent, and the treatment is objective. Although in its present edition, *Lands and Peoples*' new, logical arrangement reveals the interrelationship of the world's people, the set cannot be used as a starting point for further study because of the lack of reading lists. However, the publisher will add a 16-page reading list in the 1985 edition, which will be published this spring. This comprehensive list of readings will include identifiable titles for both younger and older readers.

Over the years *Lands and Peoples*' contents and format have been revised extensively. This combination of improvements has resulted in a 1983 edition which is recommended as a social studies reference for those who read at the fifth-grade level and above. *Lands and Peoples* will be a handsome addition to school and public library collections.

Large type books in print, 1984. [6th ed.] New York, Bowker, 1983. xiv, 1,273p. 29cm. cloth $45.50 + shipping/handling (0-8352-1618-7).
†011.63 Large type books—Bibliography [OCLC]   74-102773

This title provides much of the same information as *Books in Print* and other compendia from Bowker, except that *Large Type BIP* is itself printed in large (18 point) type. Besides the usual Key to Abbreviations, Author and Title Indexes, and Publishers' Directory at the end, the body of the work consists of two main listings—General Reading and Textbooks.

Both sections are subdivided—Fiction, Literature, Reference, Religion, etc., for the first section (including a subdivision on children's books) while textbooks are listed by subject category, e.g., business, health and hygiene, mathematics, science, and so on. There are some 5,000 titles from about 90 publishers in this edition.

Entries provide bibliographic data, including price, and also give size of type (usually 16 to 18 point).

Improvements since the fifth edition (1982) include the updating of over 1,000 prices, and expansion of the children's books section, adding up to a revision of about 40 percent since the fifth edition.

Large Type Books In Print is primarily intended for librarians and booksellers, but the visually handicapped may also use it to select books for themselves. With this idea in mind, the publishers might consider providing running heads in future editions which would make browsing far easier.

This book is for any library serving the visually impaired at any age.

Larousse encyclopedia of archaeology. 2d ed. New York, Larousse, 1983. 432p. illus. 29cm. paper $24.95 (0-88332-316-8).
930.1 Archaeology [OCLC]   83-80485

The first edition (1972) (cf. *RSBR*, Oct. 15, 1974), published by Larousse and Hamlyn, was distributed in this country by Putnam. This edition has the Larousse imprint and, except for a few necessary changes on the verso of the title page, is an exact reprint of the 1972 edition. There is not one book added to the "Further Reading List" (consisting primarily of works published in the 1950s and 1960s), and the Index has no added items. The text is the same, and no new illustrations have been added.

Emphasis is on classical archaeology and the major discoveries of the nineteenth and twentieth centuries. The illustrations and their captions are the book's strongest feature. Citing many of these illustrations in the Index contributes to the ready-reference value of the work, helping users locate photographs of famous archaeological sites.

Libraries needing introductory works are probably now better served by Robert J. Sharer and Wendy Ashmore's *Fundamentals of Archaeology* (Benjamin-Cummings, 1979). Libraries without the highly important *The Princeton Encyclopedia of Classical Sites* (Princeton Univ. Pr., 1976) should save their money for it. Needless to say, libraries with the 1972 edition of *Larousse* should not bother with this edition.

Late Georgian and Regency England, 1760–1837. [By] Robert A. Smith. London, New York, Cambridge Univ. Pr., 1983. ix, 114p. 22cm. cloth $29.95 (0-521-25538-4).
016.94107'3 Great Britain—History—1714–1837—Bibliography [British CIP]

Few periods have been as eventful and decisive for modern England (and indeed, all of Europe) as the time covered by this bibliography. In just over three-quarters of a century, the French and American revolutions, the defeat of Napoleon, the Industrial Revolution, the Reform Bill, and the accession of Victoria influenced the rise of Great Britain to a nineteenth-century world power and set its course for the twentieth. A wealth of scholarship and good reading about the history and historiography of Georgian and Regency England awaits casual readers and inquiring researchers.

This listing, produced for the Conference on British Studies, is one of a series of bibliographical handbooks on English history. It is comprehensive in scope, excluding only literary history and criticism, and provides listings of items published before January 1981. Limited to 2,500 entries, it is intended to be a selective rather than exhaustive tool for students and nonspecialists. The emphasis is upon recent literature rather than on older interpretations in general works.

The book's 14 topical chapters include general bibliographies, guides, and surveys, and the staples of social, political, and economic history. Subjects frequently given less coverage—the fine arts, science, religion, and intellectual history—also receive attention here. The editor provides brief annotations for many entries, and an Index of Authors, Editors, and Translators concludes the work.

This excellent guide provides a careful selection of books, articles, and printed primary sources. It should satisfy the needs of all except more advanced scholars. For academic and large public libraries.

Latin America, 1979–1983: a social science bibliography. By Robert L. Delorme. Santa Barbara, Calif., ABC-Clio, 1984. 225p. 29cm. cloth $45 (0-87436-394-2).

016.98 Latin America—Economic conditions—1945- —Bibliography | Latin America—Social conditions—1945- —Bibliography | Latin America—Politics and government—1948- —Bibliography [CIP]   84-11133

Complementing the author's earlier work, *Latin America: Social Science Information, 1967–1979*, the 3,728 unannotated entries are arranged geographically by 32 countries and then according to format, i.e., book, chapter, or article. English-language items far overwhelm those in Spanish and Portuguese. Retrieval is facilitated by Author and Subject Indexes.

Unfortunately, this does not fulfill the potential need for a good bibliography of social sciences in Latin America. There are omissions; only easy-to-find titles are cited. Many basic monographs and Spanish-language journals are neglected for the various countries. Compounding this neglect is the failure to incorporate standard reference works that treat entire geographical areas country by country, and U.S. government documents experience the same fate. Without annotations, an introductory essay highlighting both resources and lacunae for each country is a necessity. Or perhaps an occasional title might be highlighted as essential for research in a given area. Neither type of directional signal is given. Finally, the methodology for compilation does not indicate the author's comprehensiveness or his resources. The vague audience identifier, "social scientists," focuses on no specific clientele. Are these student researchers, laypersons, or Ph.D.'s in one of the social science areas? Standards like the *Handbook of Latin American Studies* and the *Hispanic American Periodicals Index* will serve all sorts of searchers better than *Latin America, 1979–1983*.

Latin American politics: a historical bibliography. Santa Barbara, Calif., ABC-Clio, 1984. viii, 290p. (Clio Bibliography series, no.16) 29cm. cloth $60.50 (0-87436-377-2).
016.98 Latin America—Politics and government—1948- —Periodicals—Indexes [CIP]   83-27156

As with others of the Clio Bibliography series, readers must remember that this work covers abstracts of journal articles only, published between 1973 and 1982; monographs are not cited. All materials are abstracted from the publisher's large historical database used to produce more comprehensive products ("more than 2,000 periodicals," according to the Preface). Approximately 500 journals are covered; these and a list of authors and of abstractors and a detailed Subject Index are cited at the end.

There are 3,005 entries; each includes name of author, article title (with translation if not originally in English), name of journal, volume, number, and pagination. Then follows the abstract. The average abstract is about 8 lines, but some are as short as 4 lines, and others as long as 20 lines. Unless the summary was staff prepared, the abstractors' names are appended.

Arrangement is by country (after an introductory section, "Latin American Politics in Historical Perspective"), with some grouping of related countries, such as the West Indies and the Andean nations.

Although browsing through coverage of specific areas or countries is profitable, best access to the material is via the Subject Index. *Latin American Politics* is suitable for libraries with Latin American studies collections, but libraries with the parent *America: History and Life* should weigh convenience against cost.

Libraries in American periodicals before 1876. Compiled by Larry J. Barr et al.; edited by Haynes McMullen. Jefferson, N.C., McFarland, 1983. xx, 426p. 24cm. cloth $65 (0-89950-066-8).
016.02 Library science—Bibliography | Library science—Abstracts | Libraries—Bibliography | Libraries—Abstracts [CIP]   83-780

H. G. T. Cannons' *Bibliography of Library Economy from 1876 to 1920* (1927) was a classified index to English-language articles on librarianship and related fields appearing in periodicals from 1876–1920. This present work extends *Cannons* back from 1876 insofar as U.S. periodical articles are concerned. Included are 1,473 articles on libraries which appeared in 153 periodicals. Brief items are reprinted in their entirety while longer ones are abstracted. Locations symbols from the *Union List of Serials* are provided for each entry.

The major portion of the work is devoted to articles on U.S. libraries; listed first are articles on types of libraries in the U.S. and then following, articles on libraries in U.S. states and cities. Smaller sections are devoted to articles on libraries in Europe and other countries. In each section, articles are chronologically arranged by date of publication. A detailed Index provides access by names of persons and libraries, as well as by subject. This is a most useful tool for library historians; it is suitable for large library service collections.

Lite English: popular words that are OK to use no matter what William Safire, John Simon, Edwin Newman and the other purists say! By Rudolf Flesch. New York, Crown, 1983. x, 207p. 21cm. hardcover $10.95 (0-517-55139-X).
427 English language—Usage—Dictionaries | English language—Slang—Dictionaries [CIP]   83-7793

In many ways *Lite English* is an informative and potentially helpful book, suitable for public and academic libraries and worth considering for school libraries. Some readers will be annoyed or puzzled by Flesch's constant harping on the sins of "purists" and by his frequent attacks upon the *New York Times*; and not all will be persuaded that if you use, e.g., *literally* in the sense of *figuratively*, *prof* for *professor*, and *hanky* for *handkerchief*, you will thereby improve your prose. Still, we must remember that many writers shun plain words—consistently preferring *assist, engage, render, ascend, ascertain, instruct, engagement,* and *hypothesis* to their plain but sturdy cousins *help, hire, give, climb, find out, teach, date,* and *hunch*. Sometimes Flesch is right for the wrong reasons; cf. *hopefully*. Such slips are, thankfully, few. In short, his advice adds up to an understandable reaction against stuffiness, but it must not be swallowed whole.

For the record, there are, according to the dust jacket, 250 entries; but there is probably material on more words than that figure suggests: *lunch* is, for example, covered under *ad*, but with no cross-reference from *lunch*. And note that not all words Flesch lists are ones he approves: he warns—and quite sensibly too—against, e.g., *cute* and *heck*.

Literature criticism from 1400 to 1800: excerpts from criticism of the works of fifteenth, sixteenth, seventeenth, and eighteenth-century novelists, poets, playwrights, philosophers, and other creative writers, from the first published critical appraisals to current evaluations. v.1. Dennis Poupard, editor; Mark W. Scott, associate editor. Detroit, Gale, 1984. 618p. illus. 29cm. cloth $68 (0-8103-6100-0; 0740-2880 ISSN).
809'.03 Criticism [OCLC]   83-20504

This is another in the fine Gale Literary Criticism series. While earlier Gale sets cover nineteenth- and twentieth-century writers, this title encompasses authors who died between 1400 and 1800. Significant passages from published criticism of 16 authors (mainly British, a few French, and 1 Chinese) form the core of the work, and 300 more authors are listed for future volumes. Defoe, Fielding, Richardson, and Swift are the major authors covered in the initial volume. The length of each entry represents the author's critical reception in English or foreign criticism in translation, ranging from 8 to 112 pages (the latter for Swift). Each entry includes a historical overview of the critical, social, and historical forces of the writer's time. Because entries are intended to be definitive overviews, 15–20 authors will be included in each volume, as compared with some 60 authors in other volumes of the series.

Variations or other names under which the author wrote are indicated, as well as birth/death dates and biographical and other background information. There is also a chronological list of each writer's principal works. To provide perspective on changes over the years, the extensive excerpted critical passages are also arranged chronologically. Explanatory notes precede and clarify each criticism. Annotated bibliographies at the end of each entry direct readers to further sources, and illustrations add to the book's attractiveness (e.g., a title page of a first edition). An Index to Titles is accurate, and a Cumulative Index to Authors in all the Gale Literary Criticism series is also included. Public and academic libraries will find this volume a useful sourcebook for the Renaissance/early modern periods of English literature.

The literature of chess. By John Graham. Jefferson, N.C., McFarland, 1984. vi, 250p. 23cm. cloth $18.95 + $1.50 shipping/handling (0-89950-099-4).
794.1 Chess—Abstracts [CIP]   83-26759

The extensive literature of chess has been reviewed by the editor of the chess magazine *En Passant*, and the result is this selection of 132 titles, old and new. Each is fully discussed and arranged under one of nine categories, such as Openings, Middle Game, Biographies, and Chess Lore. Extended head notes and Graham's informed commentary are enlivened by illustrations of piece positions in games and anecdotes. As a noted chess expert writes in his Foreword, "John

Graham has selected, tasted, digested, and enjoyed practically all of the modern chess literature worthy of study." Thus, libraries with game collections will find it a necessary purchase.

The London stage, 1920–1929: a calendar of plays and players. 3v. By J. P. Wearing. Metuchen, N.J., Scarecrow, 1984. 1,788p. 23cm. cloth $89.50 (0-8108-1715-2).
792'.09421 Theater—England—London—Calendars | Theater—England—London—History—20th century—Sources [CIP]   84-10665

Continuing the author's earlier surveys listing plays presented on the London stage since 1890, this volume lists close to 4,000 productions at 51 theaters. As with the earlier volumes, plays are arranged chronologically by first date of production and include the following details in a code format: title; genre of play and number of acts/scenes; author; theater; date; length of run and number of performances; cast; production staff; and a bibliography of first-night reviews. The Introduction gives details for interpreting the codes. A Title Index and a General Index facilitate use.

The London Stage, 1920–1929 provides a wealth of detail from original sources such as playbills. It should be purchased for in-depth theater or English literature collections.

MASA: medical acronyms, symbols, & abbreviations. Edited by Betty Hamilton and Barbara Guidos. New York, Neal-Schuman, 1984. 186p. 29cm. hardcover $39.95 (0-918212-72-3).
610'.148 Medicine—Acronyms | Medicine—Notation | Medicine—Abbreviations [CIP]   83-4191

Arranged in an alphabetical letter-by-letter array with beginning or internal numbers disregarded in interfiling, this collection of abbreviations and acronyms is extensive and contains about 25,000 terms. It is important to read the Introduction which explains that other abbreviations for the same term(s) are indicated by "also." For terms no longer used, the phrase "See . . . " is used to show correct current use. For closely related terms, "see also" directs users. When an abbreviation does not match the term (as in Latin terms), the source is given in parentheses, e.g., "PP after meals (postprandial). Nonalphanumeric symbols are not included.

While the book works from the abbreviation to the term, it is not intended that one can find the proper abbreviation, although many rarely found terms are easily located.

MASA will be a useful acquisition for medical and public libraries with patient/health-care collections.

MBA's dictionary. Edited by Daniel Oran [and] Jay M. Shafritz. Reston, Va., Reston, 1983. vii, 448p. cm. casebound $26.95 (0-8359-4146-9); paper $15.95 (0-8359-4145-0).
650'.03'21 Industrial management—U.S.—Dictionaries | Business—Dictionaries | Law—U.S.—Dictionaries [CIP]   83-4524

Using as its core the subject matter one encounters in courses required for the BBA and MBA degrees, *The MBA's Dictionary* provides broad coverage of business, finance, accounting, management, and related disciplines. The terms covered in the volume range from common business concepts, such as *leverage* and *research and development*, to aspects of business research, such as *Likert scale* and *Chi-square*. Terms selected for coverage reflect current usage, e.g., *Reaganomics* and *Pac-man strategy*. The persons highlighted in the dictionary include economists (e.g., Friedman), psychologists (e.g., Maslow), and a wide range of other business researchers such as Frederick W. Taylor and Frank Gilbreth. Other topics represented here include institutions (e.g., Brookings), specific laws and cases (e.g., Hatch Act), and events in business history (e.g., Haymarket riot). The volume also gives good coverage both of common abbreviations and of many current slang terms, the latter being covered with surprising frankness (cf. *CYA* and *Brownie Points*). The text is supplemented by nearly four-dozen well-placed charts, graphs, formulas, and other graphic illustrations. It has more than 4,300 main entries which, because of the book's grouping of related terms under broader headings, represents closer to 6,000 separate terms. While entries for broad headings such as *investment* or *reserve* may run to 500 words or more, most entries are between 50 to 100 words long.

The method used to refer readers to other entries is to set the referent word in boldface. Unfortunately the typeface selected makes it sometimes difficult to distinguish the boldface from the very black type of the regular text. This is, however, a minor annoyance in an otherwise beautifully executed work.

There are a number of recent, comparable business dictionaries; *Kohler's Dictionary for Accountants* (cf. *RBB*, Dec. 1, 1983) is specific to a narrow business specialty. Jerry Rosenberg's *Dictionary of Business and Management* (Wiley: 1983) is perhaps the best general business dictionary with which to compare this work. The number of terms is roughly similar as is the level of detail provided in the definitions. There is, however, surprisingly little overlap between the works, probably less than 50 percent. Where there is overlap, Oran and Shafritz are usually more concrete in their definitions and tend to give more specific examples than does Rosenberg. The works clearly complement each other.

The MBA's Dictionary is a volume that should find steady use in collections of most academic and many public libraries.

The MEED Middle East financial directory, 1983. London, Middle East Economic Digest; dist. by Bradford Mountain Book Enterprises, 125 E. 23d St., Suite 300, New York, NY 10010, 1983. xii, 430p. 29cm. hardcover $75 plus $2.50 shipping/handling (0-946-51001-6; ISSN 0264-2727).
†332.1'0956'025 Banks and banking—Near East—Directories | Financial institutions—Near East—Directories [OCLC]   83-8462

Now in its seventh edition, and with 200 new entries, this directory supplies information on activities, finances, management personnel, subsidiaries, etc., for financial institutions and worldwide affiliated banks and institutions of all 24 Arab nations. A brief profile for each country gives facts of interest to businesspersons (heads of state, languages spoken, business hours, visas, hotels). Indexes to persons, institutions, and shareholders (new to this edition) add to ease of use by citing columns as well as pages. Large business reference services will find it useful if their clients do business with Arab countries.

McGraw-Hill concise encyclopedia of science & technology. Sybil P. Parker, editor in chief. New York, McGraw-Hill, 1984. lxxiv, 2,065p. illus. diagrs. 28cm. hardcover $89.50 (0-07-045482-5).
503'.21 Science—Dictionaries | Technology—Dictionaries [CIP]   83-26794

Most of the information in this concise encyclopedia has been extracted from the fifth edition (1982) of the 15-volume *McGraw-Hill Encyclopedia of Science & Technology*. In addition, material has been extracted from the *McGraw-Hill Encyclopedia of Electronics and Computers* (1984), the *McGraw-Hill Dictionary of Scientific and Technical Terms* (1984), the *McGraw-Hill Encyclopedia of Astronomy* (1983), the *Synopsis and Classification of Living Organisms* (1982), and the 1978 *McGraw-Hill Encyclopedia of the Geological Sciences*. For libraries that cannot afford the parent work and its spin-offs, the one-volume version will be a welcome addition. The *McGraw-Hill Encyclopedia of Science & Technology* was very favorably reviewed in detail in these pages in August 1983. Since the abridged version contains extracts from the full set, the content of the articles will not be reevaluated here. It should be noted that the publishers have attempted to retain the same ratio between length of article and importance. There are 7,300 alphabetically arranged articles, individually signed and including numerous cross-references. The illustrations are excellent, and the two-column format (with adequate margins) is easy to read. At the end of the main part is a bibliography which lists (alphabetically by author) citations to key works, arranged by subject areas; some 1983 imprints were noted. The listing also contains key journal titles for each subject area. Eighty-one databases are also listed, with full name and brief annotation of coverage. A 40-page Appendix precedes the Index and includes such useful information as chemical elements, animal and plant taxonomy, and units of measurement. The Index provides instant access to virtually all of the specific information in the text.

The only other comprehensive one-volume science encyclopedia, almost 1,000 pages longer, is *Van Nostrand's Scientific Encyclopedia* (6th ed., 1982). The main difference between the two is that *Van Nostrand* is more advanced, has longer articles, and substitutes cross-references within the volume for a detailed index. It also does not contain the many appendixes that *McGraw-Hill* has. In spot-checking subject coverage, the Board found comparable articles in both works about one-third of the time. Half of the remaining articles were unique to *McGraw-Hill* and half to *Van Nostrand*. *Van Nostrand* may have a few more articles, but this is probably due to the lack of an analytical index and the need to have more entries to cover all topics. For libraries that own *Van Nostrand*, *McGraw-Hill Concise Encyclopedia* is complementary—not duplicative. There will be overlap in coverage, but each has its unique articles, and between the two, one should find information about almost any scien-

McGraw-Hill dictionary of chemistry. Sybil P. Parker, editor in chief. New York, McGraw-Hill, 1984. 665p. 24cm. hardcover $32.50 (0-07-045420-5).
540′.3′21 Chemistry—Dictionaries [CIP]   84-12205

McGraw-Hill dictionary of engineering. Sybil P. Parker, editor in chief. New York, McGraw-Hill, 1984. 659p. 24cm. hardcover $32.50 (0-07-045412-4).
620′.003′21 Engineering—Dictionaries [CIP]   84-12206

These two dictionaries, spin-offs from the *McGraw-Hill Dictionary of Scientific and Technical Terms* (3d ed., 1984), are to be added to the long list of other specialized McGraw-Hill dictionaries. The chemistry volume contains more than 9,000 terms representing the fields of analytical chemistry, biochemistry, chemical engineering, crystallography, geochemistry, inorganic chemistry, organic chemistry, physical chemistry, and spectroscopy, as well as related terms in the field of physics. The engineering volume is somewhat larger, with more than 16,000 terms representing the engineering disciplines of aerospace, civil, design, industrial, materials science, mechanical, metallurgical, mining, petroleum, and systems. It excludes, however, chemical, electrical, and food engineering. In addition, the engineering volume identifies each term with the field with which the term is associated.

One may well ask how the *McGraw-Hill Dictionary of Engineering*, with six pages less than the chemistry dictionary, can have 7,000 more terms. The engineering volume is printed in smaller type, two columns per page; the chemistry volume has larger type, one column per page. Both are easily read. Since the chemistry volume has many formulas, the one-column-per-page format makes reading much easier. Both have keywords in bold print, with the engineering volume having both first and last terms printed as running heads; the chemistry volume gives only the first term. Definitions are brief and easy to follow. The chemistry volume focuses on the vocabulary of theoretical and applied chemistry rather than on that of chemicals and materials.

The engineering volume presents those terms that are fundamental to the basic understanding of engineering principles. The terms in each dictionary are alphabetized on a letter-by-letter basis with word spacing, hyphen, comma, and prime in a term ignored in the sequencing. Cross-references are made from synonyms, variant spellings, acronyms, abbreviations, and symbols. Both dictionaries include the statement: "Synonyms, acronyms, and abbreviations are given with the definitions and are also listed in the alphabetical sequence as cross-references to the defining term." Chemistry definitions may include either an empirical formula or a line formula, whichever is appropriate. Within definitions are such statements as "Also known as," "Also spelled," "Abbreviated," "Symbolized," or "Derived from."

For those who cannot afford the *McGraw-Hill Dictionary of Scientific and Technical Terms*, these two volumes are to be recommended. Their only serious flaws are that they do not lie flat when in use because of very tight bindings. They are useful reference books for professionals, students, educators, librarians, and writers. High school, college, university, and special libraries will find these dictionaries good additions to their reference collections.

McGraw-Hill dictionary of earth sciences. Sybil P. Parker, editor in chief. New York, McGraw-Hill, 1984. 837p. 24cm. hardcover $32.50 (0-07-045252-0).
550′.3′21 Earth sciences—Dictionaries [CIP]   83-20362

This is a bare-bones scientific dictionary—no pronunciations, etymologies, or derivations are provided. Definitions are brief, seldom more than four lines, and usually three or less. However, more than 15,000 terms (pertaining to 18 different earth sciences) are defined. Chemical formulas are given for compounds and/or geological ores.

It is difficult to fault any part of what this dictionary offers, but its omissions are sometimes disappointing. The pronunciation of such terms as *breccia, foehn, gneiss, paar,* and *sikussak* would have been welcomed. And the origin of certain words would have been both interesting and enlightening. Thus, the connection between sodium and natron is ignored; a definition of *halcyon days* is given ("a period of fine weather"), but there is no attempt to relate it to the fascinating legend of the nest of the kingfisher bird, which gave rise to the expression "halcyon days."

In defense of some of these minor defects, it may be argued that the inclusion of such omitted data would have enlarged the work considerably without adding significantly to the merit of the definitions. Nevertheless, the definitions sometimes border on the cryptic.

For patrons desiring short, clear, and succinct definitions of terms in the literature of the earth sciences, *McGraw-Hill Dictionary of Earth Sciences* is very practical, and it will find ready acceptance for this purpose in all types of libraries.

McGraw-Hill dictionary of science and engineering. Sybil P. Parker, editor in chief. New York, McGraw-Hill, 1984. xviii, 942p. 24cm. cloth $32.50 (0-07-045483-3).
503′.21 Science—Dictionaries | Technology—Dictionaries [CIP]   83-26768

Containing approximately 35,000 terms, which the editors felt constitute the essential vocabulary of approximately 100 scientific and technical disciplines, all terms and definitions in this dictionary were selected from the third edition of the *McGraw-Hill Dictionary of Scientific and Technical Terms* (cf. *RBB*, August 1984).

Entries are exactly as they appear in the parent volume. Each includes the term in boldface, an abbreviation of the subject field in brackets, the definition in lightface, and, if appropriate, a cross-reference. Cross-references direct users to appropriate entries for synonyms, variant spellings, acronyms, abbreviations, and symbols. Preceding the entries are a listing of subject field abbreviations and a section of notes describing the scope of each of these fields. Entries in the dictionary are alphabetized on a letter-by-letter basis. This abridgment also lacks the illustrations and Appendix of the parent work. This version of the larger *McGraw-Hill Dictionary* is primarily for personal use; libraries may want to pass it up in favor of the more comprehensive parent work.

McGraw-Hill encyclopedia of electronics and computers. Sybil P. Parker, editor in chief. New York, McGraw-Hill, 1984. 964p. illus. 29cm. cloth $59.50 (0-07-045487-6).
621.381′03′21 Electronics—Dictionaries | Computers—Dictonaries [CIP]   83-9897

The McGraw-Hill Encyclopedia of Electronics and Computers (*MEEC*), a by-product of the fifth, 1982 edition of the *McGraw-Hill Encyclopedia of Science and Technology* (*MEST*), contains 477 articles dealing with scientific principles of electronics, electronic devices and their applications, and engineering. The articles, many of which are extensive, are written by 272 eminent scientists and engineers. A list of contributors, with their addresses and titles of their contributions, is included at the end of the encyclopedia. The articles are arranged alphabetically word by word and are followed by an Index by subject. The articles are very readable although, as the Board pointed out in its review of the fourth edition of *MEST* (cf. *RSBR*, Jan. 1, 1978), a technically trained person with appropriate mathematical background would benefit most. The length of the articles varies from a paragraph to 15 to 16 pages. The entries are, usually, accompanied by illustrations, photographs, and tables. Each article is signed by one or more persons, has an ample number of *see also* references and generally an up-to-date Bibliography.

MEEC is more or less a spin-off of *MEST*. A comparison of the two shows that a vast majority of pertinent *MEST* articles appear verbatim in *MEEC* with minor cosmetic changes such as the elimination of some cross-references and, in a few instances, updating of bibliographies. Some substantial changes have been made. For example, the articles *Electronic Publishing, Programming Languages,* and *Digital Optical Disk Recorders* were written for *MEEC*. The *MEST* article on microcomputers appears in *MEEC* as two articles: *Microcomputer* and *Microcomputer Development Systems*, although, in the transition, two figures relevant for the second article were dropped. The *MEST* article *Transmission Lines* has been truncated by dropping the section on power transmission lines and by correspondingly adjusting the Bibliography. Two sections, software portability and software piracy, were added to the *Software Engineering* article. *MEST* used color in its illustrations and colorplates; *MEEC*, on the other hand, contains only black-and-white illustrations.

Although the Preface claims that *MEEC* places "particular emphasis on computer science and engineering," it is obvious that its coverage of computer science is limited. For instance, it does not cover topics such as time-sharing, terminals, text-editing systems, and computer tomography.

Libraries with a great demand for information on electronics should consider *MEEC* although those owning *MEST* must weigh

Macmillan biographical encyclopedia of photographic artists and innovators. [Compiled by] Turner Browne and Elaine Partnow. New York, Macmillan, 1983. xiii, 722p. photos. 25cm. cloth $45 (0-02-517500-9).

770'.92'2 (B) Photographers—Biography [CIP]   82-4664

Including more than 2,000 entries alphabetically arranged, the *Macmillan Biographical Encyclopedia of Photographic Artists and Innovators* presents a history of photography in biography from the early 1800s to the present. The earliest birth date noted was 1787 for Louis-Jacques-Mandé Daguerre, identified as physicist-painter and known as the developer of the "first widespread, practical photographic process." Persons included are (or were) photographers (e.g., Berenice Abbott, William Henry Jackson, Edward Steichen), scientists (Dennis Gabor, Robert Koslowsky), inventors (Edwin Herbert Land, Carl Zeiss), teachers (Robert D'Alessandro, Clyde H. Dilley), photojournalists (Eve Arnold, Ut Cong Huynh), photohistorians (Fritz Kempe, Hans Christian Adam), critics (Max Kozloff, Pier Paolo Preti), and curators (Brian Walter Coe, David Travis). The primary criterion for inclusion was dedication to photography; it had to be a "major passion if not the major pursuit" in the biographee's life; second came visibility in the profession "attained through appearances in important photographic journals, books, permanent collections in museums, or through grants and awards." Coverage is worldwide; entries range in length from about one-fourth of a column to nearly three columns.

Each biographee is identified by field(s) of work, then a prose narrative gives facts on birth (and death, if applicable), education, mentors and major influences, area and type of work, etc. Living persons were sent questionnaires and frequently their work is characterized in their own words. Lists of publications, portfolios, collections holding their works, dealers, agents, archives, and addresses follow as applicable. An added bonus is a section of 133 black-and-white plates and 11 colorplates illustrating the work of 144 of the biographees. Abbreviations are used for some major organizations, etc.; these are explained in "How to Use This Book"; locations of collections of major journals also are included here. Lists of museums and galleries worldwide which hold photographic collections/exhibitions complete the volume.

A fascinating and useful volume, *Macmillan Biographical Encyclopedia of Photographic Artists and Innovators* brings together in one place for the first time biographical data on the artists and scientists of photography, some of it previously very hard or impossible to find. Libraries or persons interested in photography will discover a wealth of facts and inspiration here.

Macmillan dictionary for students. Judith S. Levey, executive editor. New York, Macmillan, 1984. 1,190p. illus. 27cm. hardcover $16.95 (0-02-761560-X).

423 English language—Dictionaries, Juvenile [CIP]   84-3880

This dictionary has had earlier incarnations, the most recent as the *Macmillan Contemporary Dictionary* (1979) and as the *Macmillan Dictionary* (1981). Ninety thousand entries present approximately 120,000 definitions of words selected from everyday language and from "the language of literature, history, and science" studied in schools. Etymologies are supplied for 19,000 of the terms; usage notes have been included more selectively. In both usage notes and labels, the dictionary adopts a descriptive approach to language.

Entries indicate each word's syllabication, pronunciation, meaning, and part of speech. They also illustrate meaning through sentences. As appropriate, entries also include inflected forms, identify subject areas, and describe shades of difference between and among synonyms. The simple pronunciation key appears at the bottom of each page. Entries are alphabetized letter by letter. Geographical and biographical entries are integrated into the single vocabulary. The front matter clearly and thoroughly explains all these practices.

The Reference Section, actually a series of Appendixes, includes a brief handbook of style, a list of U.S. presidents, a selective chronology of U.S. history, an introduction to computers, and a glossary of computer terms. The last was borrowed from *The Apple IIe User's Guide* (Pumpkin Press, 1983).

Comparison of *Macmillan* and the slightly larger *Webster's New World Dictionary of the American Language* (students ed., Simon & Schuster, 1981) reveals *Macmillan*'s strengths. Both are aimed at the junior high/high school student. *Macmillan* generally offers more concise definitions, sometimes at the expense of nuance, but not of clarity. *Webster's* holds an advantage in coverage of scientific vocabulary, probably a consequence of its having a 108,000-term word stock. It is difficult to compare illustrations since few are common to both. *Webster's* more detailed illustrations outnumber *Macmillan*'s, most of which are in two colors. Either dictionary can capably serve the needs of the full range of its intended audience. However, *Macmillan* is a better choice for use with students who lack extensive experience in using dictionaries since it offers them remedial assistance through its clear, step-by-step introductory explanation of how to use the dictionary and interpret its entries.

The Macmillan guide to correspondence study. Compiled and edited by Modoc Press, Inc. New York, Macmillan, 1983. xii, 497p. 29cm. cloth $65 (0-02-921550-1).

374'.473 Correspondence schools and courses—U.S.—Directories | Correspondence schools and courses—U.S.—Handbooks, manuals, etc. [CIP]   83-9854

This guide gives admission requirements and procedures, tuition fees, and course descriptions for correspondence study programs offered by 174 schools accredited by the National Home Study Council or other accrediting agencies recognized by the U.S. Department of Education. Information was supplied by the schools, and only names and addresses are given for the few schools that did not reply to the questionnaire.

The schools are alphabetically arranged under two sections: (1) Colleges and Universities (chiefly state universities) and (2) Proprietary Schools, which range from Hadley School for the Blind to the Truck Marketing Institute. As is to be expected, the former offers mostly academic courses, the latter vocational.

For each institution, a general description of its correspondence programs is followed by names of chief administrative officers, academic level of courses, details of admission, accreditations, fees, etc., and course descriptions resembling those found in college catalogs. The variety is impressive. For example, the University of California offers an extension course "In Search of the American Dream," while the University of Alaska gives five semester credits for Elementary Inupiaq (the language of the Unalakleet). Among the proprietary schools, the Farmland Training Center not only offers courses in animal science but also offers a course in agribusiness writing. The Subject Index lists 11 schools offering correspondence courses in library science, 26 in journalism, 37 in philosophy, 56 in mathematics, and 8 in truck driving, not to mention courses in sail and doll making. The compilers of this well-edited directory urge users to write for catalogs since these may note changes in fees, etc. But the information they have collected and conveniently arranged will be quite helpful to prospective correspondence students and will serve to steer them away from nonaccredited programs. Libraries will find it a valuable adjunct to their other education guides to colleges.

Macmillan illustrated animal encyclopedia. Edited by Philip Whitfield. New York, Macmillan, 1984. 600p. 29cm. cloth $35 (0-02-627680-1).

591'.03'21 Zoology [OCLC]   84-3956

This well-written and beautifully illustrated animal encyclopedia is a welcome supplement to the numerous comprehensive animal encyclopedias that are now available. It is a carefully selected representation of the individual animals of the world. Arranged first by class (mammals, birds, reptiles, amphibians, and fishes) and then by family, a brief introduction to each class gives readers an indication of the number of species, diversity of the animals included in that class, and a brief historical evolution statement. Each family is then represented by a number of species—usually ones that are commonly known. The narrative faces the page that has color illustrations of the species under description. Both common and scientific names are given along with geographical range, natural habitat, size, physiology, conservation status, food consumption, and reproduction, including gestation and litter size. The illustrations are beautifully done in full color. A helpful addition would have been a size indication next to each illustrated animal so that a comparison could be made quickly.

Definitely a book that will appeal to families with children and to any library that cannot afford the more expensive comprehensive volumes, it is a selection of Book-of-the-Month Club, Outdoor Life Book Club, Library of Science Book Club, and Natural Science Book Club.

The Macquarie dictionary. St. Leonards, Australia; dist. exclusively by Facts On File, c1981, 1983. 2,049p. illus. 35cm. hardcover $45 (0-949757-00-4).
423 English language—Dictionaries | English language in Australia [National Library of Australia CIP]

Australians have a predilection for abbreviating words and phrases—so the first major dictionary of the Australian English has already become known simply as "The Macquarie." A series of useful Prefaces by different authors examine the need for this compilation and surveys the historical development of Australian-English and Australian pronunciation. It includes not only the meanings of everyday words but also provides a very generous coverage of Australian idioms and slang expressions. The entries themselves give pronunciation, definitions, and, where known, derivation. There is a generous use of small, black-and-white illustrations throughout, although not all are helpful in clarifying the term to which they refer. Current technical terms are included; Australian flora and fauna are covered extremely well. As might be expected, the dictionary is exhaustive on both current and historical slang terms. The resources of Macquarie University, aided by the Australian National University, have been drawn upon for the ten years this work has been in preparation. Spin-off versions—*The Budget Macquarie, The Pocket Macquarie, The Concise Macquarie, The Handy Macquarie,* and *The Little Macquarie*—have followed, and The Macquarie Dictionary Society was established to enable any purchaser of the Macquarie to participate in the work of keeping the dictionary both current and correct. *The Macquarie Dictionary* will be a very useful addition to any comprehensive English dictionary collection or in any library requiring works on varieties of English.

Made in America. Edited by Jerome M. Rosow. New York, Facts On File, 1984. xviii, 266p. 24cm. hardcover $14.95 (0-87196-294-2); paper $7.95 (0-87196-884-3).
381'45'00029473 Consumer education | Brand name products [CIP]   84-20679

Rosow, the president of Work in America Institute, has compiled an unusual directory which, according to its subtitle, is "a consumer's guide to more than 12,000 products made in America, for Americans, and 100 percent by Americans"—although the front matter states that a product is listed if it is "manufactured 100 percent within the United States" as claimed by the manufacturer. This is not a kind of "look-for-the-union-label" list. Omissions (and there are many—only two computer companies are listed) are accounted for by the failure of companies to reply on time or not reply to a series of three questionnaires. Firms which supplied information are simply listed by broad categories of products (apparel, appliances, food, etc.) under two sections: Consumer Products and Industrial Products. There are appended Indexes to company names and product categories, but not to brand names of individual products, since "space limitations prevented us from doing so." Information on individual companies, such as that given in the multivolumed, fully indexed *Thomas' Register of American Manufacturers*, is not found. For example, all we find on *Comet, Joy,* and *Mr. Clean* is that they are manufactured by Proctor & Gamble in the United States, though this is unverified by Rosow. Thus, this consumer's guide is a guide only for those who want to buy American, since no information on quality of a product is supplied. Because of omissions, scant information on individual products, and lack of a brand name index, *Made in America* has very limited library reference use.

The Marshall Cavendish illustrated encyclopedia of World War I. 12v. Editor in chief, Peter Young. New York, Marshall Cavendish, 1984. 3,628p. illus. 31cm. hardcover $460. (0-83307-181-3).
940.3 World War, 1914-1918—Chronology [CIP]   83-20879

This lavishly illustrated, well-written, and comprehensive history of the events of 1914-18 is presented as a monument to a war which, in the words of the Introduction, "has very probably had a more profound effect . . . than any other single event of modern times." Its stated objective is threefold: to offer a complete, comprehensive, and objective reference source on the war; to provide the student of that war with a research facility of depth, authority, and integrity; and to help the general reader to understand these momentous years by use of a lively text and stimulating illustrative material.

The set achieves these objectives beautifully. Edited by Brigadier General Peter Young, with the aid of a 13-member editorial board, all of whose members either served in the British army or are historians at British universities, it presents the history of the war in approximately 550 short, concisely written chapters, with contributions by as many as 200 different authorities including American and British historians and former officers of the American, British, and German armed forces. Each chapter is illustrated; many pictures or maps occupy a full page, and a surprising number are in color. The ratio of text to illustration is about 50/50. The chapters follow a general chronological sequence, from the 1914 assassination at Sarajevo to the signing of the armistice in November 1918. However, they are episodic in the sense that one chapter does not necessarily follow from the preceding one. In this way all the varied aspects of the war—political, social, economic, military, literary, and so on—are covered. Each chapter ends with a brief biography of the contributor and a "Further Reading" list of some five to ten appropriate books for that section.

There are separate chapters on air warfare, zeppelins, dreadnoughts, submarines, the trenches, propaganda, tanks, hospitals, prisoners, and the like, as well as on specific battles and precise areas, such as the Somme or the Dardanelles, and even chapters on such subjects as "The Code Breakers" and, in a chapter entitled "The Rendezvous with Death," war poetry. There is almost no aspect of warfare, if it occurred during World War I, that is not covered in detail in these volumes. Each contributor seems to have been chosen for his or her expertise on a precise topic. The style of each chapter varies slightly, but it is evident that tight editorial control was maintained throughout.

The final volume contains "The War in Perspective" and a year-by-year chronology. This is followed by an extensive bibliography of some 1,000 book titles arranged by broad subject. "Air Warfare," for example, has 50 entries; "Belgium" has 22; and "United States" has more than 150. These bibliographical citations are not annotated; they give surnames, first and middle name initials and do not give pagination. However, they identify authors and titles adequately. Following the bibliography is a General Index, then several topical ones for commanders, statesmen, ships, and illustrations. Finally, there is a list of Major Battles, a Glossary, and a List of Contributors.

It is difficult to find fault with any aspect of this set, with the exception of the Index, which might have been easier to use if the pagination in lines after the first were indented. The triple-columned pages of the text in the main volumes are a bit formidable at first glance, but the books' overall design is excellent, and the frequent use of captioned illustrations in the text helps make the historical account very much alive. Despite the fact that most of the authors are British and the Central Powers are often termed "the enemy," there is a serious attempt to portray each belligerent country as it saw itself, fighting a grim battle for survival in a world at arms.

Many books have been written on World War I, but few if any have covered the subject in as much depth or breadth, or with as many contributing experts and authorities as *The Marshall Cavendish Encyclopedia of World War I*. With its excellent illustrations, its variety of writing styles, and its clear maps and diagrams, this major historical encyclopedia on an important phase of European history is recommended for libraries of all types, as well as for homes where persons are interested in the history of Europe and the world.

Materials for occupational education: an annotated source guide. 2d ed. Edited by Patricia Glass Schuman with Sue A. Rodriguez and Denise M. Jacobs. New York, Neal-Schuman, 1983. vii, 384p. 24cm. cloth $35 (0-918212-17-0).
016.3317'02 Vocational guidance—Information services | Vocational guidance—Bibliography [CIP]   83-8195

This source guide provides annotated lists of professional and trade associations, government agencies, specialized publishers, and private businesses that provide materials of all kinds for occupational education. This is the second edition of a work first published in 1971 with 500 entries: this edition has been expanded to more than 800 entries. Although emphasizing material relevant to two-year college instructional programs, the guide also provides career information and materials appropriate for various occupational levels, including vocational high schools and four-year colleges.

Under 30 occupational areas, e.g., agriculture, business, fashion trades, paralegal, mortuary science, etc., source organizations are arranged alphabetically. Each organization has one main annotated entry listed under the most pertinent subject category with cross-references in other relevant categories. Annotations include address, telephone number, description of purpose, and a selection of sample titles and prices. Subheadings are provided in the chapters on business, engineering technology, and health occupations.

Two sections—General Sources, a listing of agencies and publishers that offer materials for a wide range of occupations, and Occupational Education, a listing of agencies that provide background materials on vocational training in general and curriculum guides for specific purposes—precede the subject chapters. For quick reference, the alphabetical List of Sources provides the name and address and identifies subject areas of each organization, and the Index of Occupational Categories lists occupations used as subject headings and alternate terms as cross-references.

Educators and librarians dealing with occupational education programs will find *Materials for Occupational Education* a valuable reference source.

Medical research centres: a world directory of organizations and programmers. 2v. 6th ed. Consultant editors: Leslie T. Morton and Jean F. Hall. Essex, Longman; dist. in the U.S., its possessions, and Canada by Gale, 1983. 1,087p. 26cm. hardcover $320 (set) (0-582-90017-4).
610'.72 Medical research—Directories [British CIP]

The sixth edition of *Medical Research Centers*, previously entitled *Medical Research Index* (5th ed., 1979), is a "world directory of establishments conducting research in the medical and biochemical fields." Included are more than 11,000 organizations and laboratories in some 100 countries. Covered are universities, industrial research laboratories, medical schools, pharmaceutical houses, professional societies, and organizations that provide funding for medical research.

Entries are arranged by country and then alphabetically by parent organization and include the organization's name and acronym in the original language and English, address, telephone number, affiliation and parent body, and the director of research. Where available, some entries include more detailed information such as the number of individuals involved in full-time research, annual expenditures for research and development, and scope of activities and publications. There are two indexes, by titles of establishments and subject.

Organizations that are international in scope appear in a separate section preceding the country listings. The editors note that entries are limited for the USSR and China due to linguistic and other difficulties.

Since this is a high-priced item, even large academic libraries should consider if they need the international coverage of this directory. Those libraries just requiring information on U.S. and Canadian medical research centers will be adequately served by *Research Programs in the Medical Sciences* (New York: Bowker, 1980; $79.95).

Medical science and the law. Rev. ed. Edited by Paula Goulden and Benjamin Naitove. New York, Facts On File, 1984. vii, 197p. 24cm. cloth $19.95 (0-87196-818-5).
†340.04 Medical laws and legislation—U.S. | Medical ethics | Ethics, Medical | Jurisprudence—U.S. [OCLC]

Based largely on Facts On File's weekly reports on world affairs, with added cases and public reports, this summary is arranged under nine controversial issues intended "to serve as a record of 'life and death' topics." Among them is Abortion, giving background federal and state legislation, actions of concerned groups, and party platforms to August 1982. Another, Insanity Defense, is devoted primarily to the Hinckley case. Some are more briefly treated than others, e.g., Birth Issues (covered to late 1982) and Experimenting on Human Subjects. Contraception, Death and Dying, and Science and Technology (e.g., genetic research, test-tube babies) are covered to early 1983; Drugs to 1980. An interesting section, Ethical Issues and Health Care, deals with unnecessary surgery and health costs.

The widespread interest in these subjects and their unbiased treatment in *Medical Science and the Law* make this compilation a valuable source, particularly for public and high school libraries.

Melville dissertations, 1924–1980: an annotated bibliography and subject index [Compiled by] John Bryant, with the sponsorship of the Melville Society. Westport, Conn., Greenwood 1983. xxi, 166p. 24cm. cloth $35 (0-313-23811-1).
016.813'3 Melville, Herman, 1819–1891—Bibliography | Dissertations, academic—Bibliography [CIP]   83-5683

Herman Melville is one of the most researched and written-about figures in American literature. Few other American writers have been the subject of as many doctoral dissertations. Indeed, since 1924 the number of such dissertations has about doubled every ten years. While such exponential growth must end sooner or later, the recent sensational discovery of a major archive of Melville papers suggests that it may well be later. Bryant lists 531 dissertations from universities in North and South America, Europe, and Asia, arranged by year and then alphabetically by author. Where applicable, the *Dissertation-Abstracts*, or *English-and-American-Studies-in-German* references are given. Complete bibliographic information is also given for published books or articles which have resulted from the dissertations. Annotations are descriptive, not critical, and are based on the compiler's examination of the originals in the Melville dissertation archives at the Newbery Library. The list is followed by Author and University Indexes, and lastly by a Subject Index. Here, more than a thousand names of people, books places, things, events, and ideas, which are mentioned in the dissertation titles or in the annotations, are listed.

Melville Dissertations 1924–1980 is a valuable handbook which consolidates and updates previous bibliographies of Melville dissertations. It should be in the reference section of any graduate-level collection supporting research on Melville.

The Metropolitan Opera on record: a discography of the commercial recordings. Compiled by Frederick P. Fellers. Westport, Conn., Greenwood, 1984. xix, 101p. (Discographies, no.9) 24cm. cloth $25 (0-313-23952-5).
016.7899'1221 Metropolitan Opera (New York, N.Y.)—Discography | Operas—Discography [CIP]   83-22587

Some 477 commercial recordings by the Orchestra or Chorus of the Metropolitan Opera in New York are listed in this catalog. Whether they involve any official sanction of the company or not, they do document the traditions of our country's best-known opera company. Both excerpts and complete operas are cited here. They begin as early as 1906 with single acoustical discs; extend through the successive periods of special contracts with Victor, Columbia, or the Book-of-the-Month Club; and end in 1972 when the company ceased lending its official auspices to particular recordings. The works and names as cited here may be briefer than our cataloging codes call for, but no user will be bothered in the least. More important, the compiler has gone to great and valuable pains to search out dates of the recordings, matrixes and take numbers, and other crucial discographic data. The result should prove to be definitive for a long time to come. *The Metropolitan Opera on Record* will be a valuable reference in all libraries that serve opera fans, whether browsers or specialist researchers. Coincidentally (or perhaps intentionally), this is an excellently timed work celebrating the Met's centennial season in 1983–84.

Modern English-Canadian prose: a guide to information sources. [Compiled by] Helen Hoy. Detroit, Gale, 1983. xxiii, 605p. (American Literature, English Literature, and World Literature in English v.38) 23cm. cloth $48 (0-8103-1245-X).
016.818'508 Canadian fiction—20th century—Bibliography | Canadian prose literature—20th century—Bibliography [CIP]   73-16996

This title follows the familiar format of other Gale information guides; an introductory section on basic reference sources for Canadian literature is followed by entries for individual authors. Compiled by an associate professor of English at the University of Lethbridge (Alberta) whose interest is Canadian fiction, this volume surveys 68 established English-language fiction writers followed by 10 English-language prose writers of the twentieth century. For each author, a brief biographical sketch is followed by a list of the author's works arranged by genre (monographs, short stories, articles, etc.) and then critical works, also arranged by genre (bibliographies, book reviews, etc.). Author, Title, and Subject Indexes complete the volume. This is a very useful compilation for academic libraries and others interested in Canadian studies.

Modern Latin American art: a bibliography. James A. Findlay, compiler. Westport, Conn., Greenwood, 1983. vi, 301p. 24cm. cloth $35 (0-313-23757-3).
016.7'098 Art, Latin American—Bibliography | Art, Modern—20th century—Latin America—Bibliography [CIP]   83-10743

This welcome bibliography reflects, for the most part, the collection of the Library of the Museum of Modern Art in New York City. Some 2,400 entries are organized by broad geographic area (Latin America) and by country, and subarranged by subject and type of material (Architecture; Costumes and Native Dress; Graphic Arts—

Periodicals; Painting—Dictionaries, etc.). Findlay includes monographs, exhibition catalogs, journals, bibliographies, handbooks, and histories. He excludes monographs on individual artists and references to periodical articles. Full bibliographic information and brief but helpful descriptive notes are provided. Spanish-language material predominates. The thorough Index includes references to museums, galleries, and individuals. Findlay's bibliography of *Modern Latin American Art* fills a gap in the documentation of this field and will facilitate research in art history and Latin American culture. An essential purchase for art reference collections.

The money encyclopedia. Edited by Harvey Rachlin. New York, Harper, 1984. 672p. 24cm. hardcover $26.50 (0-06-181711-2).
332.4'03'21 Finance—U.S.—Dictionaries | Financial institutions—U.S.—Dictionaries | Money—U.S.—Dictionaries [CIP] 83-48801

A large number of qualified persons connected with government agencies, stock exchanges, trade and professional associations, corporations, and universities have contributed a wide range of topics to this up-to-date, adequately cross-referenced encyclopedia. The signed articles, some brief, but mostly three or more pages, are nontechnical in style and range from expected subjects such as estate planning, Dow Jones averages, savings and loan associations, Medicare, and Social Security to advice on buying an automobile, renting an apartment, collecting autographs, and all kinds of insurance. Tables accompany many of the articles, e.g., savings bonds, stock market indexes, and minting of coins, while the long article on credit includes a glossary. There are no appended bibliographies, but sources are sometimes cited. Also, publications of a corporation (such as Standard & Poor's) are described.

Broader in scope and more up-to-date than Munn's *Encyclopedia of Banking and Finance* (6th ed., 1962), but lacking Munn's bibliographies and with fewer tables than Thorndike's *Encyclopedia of Banking and Financial Tables* (1973), *The Money Encyclopedia* reflects the changes in banking practices and the increasing complexity of the financial services industry. Both public and academic libraries will find it a ready source of practical information on all aspects of money.

Money management information source book. [By] Alan M. Rees and Jodith Janes. New York, Bowker, 1983. xii, 299p. (Consumer Information Series). 24cm. hardcover $35 + shipping and handling (0-8352-1738-8).
016.332024 Finance, Personal—Bibliography [CIP] 83-9258

Focusing on popular publications rather than on professional/technical literature, Reese and Janes provide an evaluative guide to information resources on money management and personal finance. Rees, a professor in the library school at Case Western, specializes in information sources for consumers. Janes is also on the staff of Case Western. Following a brief introductory chapter describing the rapid changes in the condition of the financial world over the past decade or so, the authors devote the next six chapters to bibliographies of over 600 recent (1978 or later) publications on topics such as consumer money management, real estate, taxes, and financial planning. Another four chapters survey more than 100 magazines, newspapers, and newsletters; some 600 pamphlets; and a sampling of professional reference sources in the field. The volume concludes with a Glossary; a directory of organizations providing pamphlets; and Subject, Author, and Title Indexes.

With the exception of the pamphlets, all other entries contain annotations of from 12 to more than 200 words, most in the range of 75 to 100 words long. The books listed here range from the guides by financial mainstays such as Sylvia Porter, Venita Van Caspel, and Howard Ruff to less staid titles such as *Turn Your House into a Money Factory*.

Rees and Janes not only describe each work and highlight its unique strengths, they also offer definite judgments. In addition to the high recommendations and comments such as "sane and challenging" for the works they feel to be worthwhile, they have also cited a number of items currently on the market of which their evaluation is less sanguine. Geoffry Abert's *After the Crash*, for example, receives the stinging notes, "Alarmist nonsense mingled with economic piffle."

The organization of this sourcebook is clear, indexing is thorough, and the information it imparts useful. *Money Management Information Source Book* should prove to be a valuable acquisition both for reference and for collection development purposes, especially in public libraries.

More notes from a different drummer: a guide to juvenile fiction portraying the disabled. By Barbara H. Baskin and Karen H. Harris. New York, Bowker, 1984. xv, 496p. 23cm. hardcover $27.50 + shipping/handling (0-8352-1871-6).
808.06'8 Children's stories—Bibliography | Handicapped in literature—Bibliography | Physically handicapped in literature—Bibliography | Mentally handicapped in literature—Bibliography | Emotions in literature—Bibliography [CIP] 84-12283

Believing that literature is a way to promote positive attitudes toward impaired people, the authors here describe and critique 450 children's books concerned with disability. A continuation of *Notes from a Different Drummer*, which examined juvenile fiction published between 1940 and 1975, *More Notes* focuses on books from 1976 to 1981. Titles for preschool through young adult audiences are included; formula romances, folklore, stories "written for academic purposes," works for sectarian presses that espouse a specific belief, and adaptations from other formats (e.g., film) have been omitted. In addition to books emphasizing the disabled, stories with characters exhibiting mild or unlabeled but obvious impairment are within the work's purview; books in which characters' behavior is incongruent with their stated disabilities are not.

The authors, one in library education and the other in special education, sought to identify and review all possible relevant books. Titles are arranged alphabetically by author; citations include number of pages, reading level (young child, mature child, young adolescent, mature adolescent), and disability. Extent of plot summaries is commensurate with the book's complexity (e.g., five paragraphs for *Westmark*, one for *Peter Gets a Hearing Aid*). An analysis, usually one paragraph long, comments on literary merit and on how the disability is handled. Title and Subject Indexes help access contents. The reviews are prefaced by surveys of the disabled in society and in literature.

More Notes is useful for pinpointing books on disability, many of which would not otherwise be easily identified. The authors' determination that books must stand up both as literature and as having accurate portrayals of disability results in tough, knowledgeable critiques (e.g., "melodramatic and patently absurd," "pleasant, although simple view of remediation procedures," "unique, demanding, tightly constructed"). Comments are sometimes didactic. The extensive summaries, if sometimes a little too detailed for clarity, are still helpful.

More Notes from a Different Drummer is a high-quality reference suitable for any children's literature collection and for libraries serving professional needs of teachers, librarians, therapists, social workers, and the like.

A multimedia approach to children's literature: a selective list of films (and videocassettes), filmstrips, and recordings based on children's books. 3d ed. Edited by Mary Alice Hunt. Chicago, American Library Association, 1983. xxix, 182p. 23cm. paper $15 (0-8389-3289-4).
011'.37 Children's literature—Bibliography—Catalogs | Children's literature—Study and teaching—Audio-visual aids—Catalogs | Teaching—Aids and devices—Catalogs | Libraries, Children's—Activity programs—Audio-visual aids—Catalogs [CIP] 83-15517

A recommended list of books and stories available in nonprint format for preschool to sixth grade children, this bibliography identifies 568 books plus one or more audiovisual productions of each (153 films/videocassettes, 365 filmstrips—mostly sound, and 348 disk and cassette recordings). Prefatory material includes programming ideas, information on the selection of entries, and a bibliography of resources on choosing and using audiovisual materials. This edition was compiled by a committee of the Association for Library Service to Children which reviewed contents of the second edition, deleting some items and adding materials which appeared between 1977 and January 1983.

Entries are arranged alphabetically by book title, with the audiovisual versions then following each title. Entries contain purchase information, suggested audience level (preschool, primary, intermediate), annotations, and for audiovisual entries, at least narrator, composer. Sometimes other credits are listed. A final section lists nonprint presentations on such popular children's authors as Beverly Cleary, Dr. Seuss, Virginia Hamilton, etc. Separate Indexes of authors, film titles, filmstrip titles, record titles, broad subjects (e.g., Newbery Medal Books, Picture Books—Mood, U.S.—Family Life), and a Directory of Distributors complete the listing.

This edition, like the earlier ones, is selective and only those audiovisual materials true to the spirit of the original book have been included. Librarians, teachers, and parents will find *Multimedia Ap-*

proach useful both for identifying and for selecting material for children's programming and individual use.

Music psychology index, v.3: the international interdisciplinary index of the influence of music on behavior, references to the literature from the natural and behaviorial sciences, and the fine and therapeutic arts for the years 1978–1980. Edited by Charles T. Eagle, Jr., and John J. Miniter. Phoenix, Ariz., Oryx, 1984. xvii, 269p. 28cm. paper $65 (0-89774-144-7; ISSN 0195-5802).

†016.78115 Music—Psychology—Bibliography | Music—Physiological aspects—Bibliography

This "index of literature pertaining to the psychological and physiological influence of music" is described as "an outcome of the Computer-Assisted Information Retrieval Service System (CAIRSS) for Music Project." Its coverage of 400-plus serial titles (including *Dissertation Abstracts*) results in less overlap with *Music Index* and *Psychological Abstracts* than one might expect or fear. Subject coverage is in fact broad (cf. the illuminating prefatory note "Philosophical Foundation of the Index"), and sources from outside music and psychology (as those disciplines are usually perceived) are freely tapped. Access is via author and subject. Author entries are made for all cited authors, not just those listed first. Subject access is via keywords in titles, with some standardization, e.g., titles using *language art, language delayed,* and *laryngeal* are listed under *language arts, language delay,* and *larynx* respectively. There are also some *see also* references which further refine the natural language approach. Although such indexing can result in missed opportunities and unintended victims (if titles lack essential terms or use terms loosely or figuratively), in practice it seems to work, i.e., the hit rate is high. True, some headings, e.g., *analysis* and *application,* are of questionable value, in that their significance depends on associated terms; analysis of what? A more serious difficulty is the very large number of entries under certain terms, e.g., nearly 300 under *music* (fortunately, such phrases as *music ability, music aptitude, music notation,* and *music therapy* are also used as entry points: they yield more manageable returns). Presumably all such awkwardnesses would vanish in online retrieval employing Boolean logic.

Music Psychology Index is something all musicologists, psychologists, and health professionals—and librarians serving these groups—should be aware of; and it should be considered for large research libraries and for special libraries supporting musical-therapy programs, broadly defined.

The musical woman: an international perspective 1983. Judith Lang Zaimont, editor in chief; Catherine Overhauser and Jane Gottlieb, assoc. eds. Westport, Conn., Greenwood, 1984. xvi, 406p. 24cm. cloth $49.95 (0-313-23587-2; ISSN 0737-0032).

780'.88042 Women musicians [OCLC]   83-1637

Except for solo concert performers, theatrical singers, and singer/songwriters, most women music professionals remain largely unrecognized in spite of their significant contributions to the music world. *The Musical Woman* seeks to remedy this lack by providing information on the achievements of women music professionals in the twentieth century in all areas except solo performance. Volumes will be published at regular intervals and will consist of two sections: a "gazette" which provides data on women's musical activities and a series of signed essays treating eight areas of musical activity (e.g., Featured Musicians, Music Education, Music Scholarship, etc.). Although each topic will be covered in every volume, the emphasis will vary in each.

The gazette section in the 1983 volume covers "Performances," "Festivals," "Prizes and Awards," "Publication," and "Discography," and includes data for 1980 with a forecast for the first part of 1983.

All but one of the 15 articles in the essay section of the 1983 volume were commissioned especially for this volume. Included are essays on women music critics and opera conductors in the U.S., surveys of women composers in Britain and the U.S., and treatments of three individual composers and four entrepreneurial pioneers.

Since much of the information in *The Musical Woman* is not easily available elsewhere, this series will be a worthwhile acquisition for many music and/or women's studies collections.

Mystery, detective, and espionage magazines. [By] Michael L. Cook. Westport, Conn., Greenwood, 1983. xxiv, 795p. (Historical Guides to the World's Periodicals and Newspapers) cloth $65 (0-313-23310-1).

809.3'872 Detective and mystery stories—Periodicals—History | Spy stories—Periodicals—History [OCLC]   82-20977

"The intent of this work," states its Preface, "has been to gather together as much information as possible and to make it available in one source. It is hoped," Cook continues, "that this encyclopedia of mystery, detective, and espionage magazines will be of interest and assistance to both the layman, who reads for pleasure, and the serious scholar, in doing further research, as well as for collectors of this type of popular fiction, and that the nostalgic value will be of benefit to all." His hope concerning "nostalgic value" may or may not be realized; but his other hope probably will be. Public and academic libraries will want to consider *Mystery, Detective, and Espionage Magazines,* particularly if their users include mystery buffs and/or students of popular literature. Cook's accounts of periodicals are consistently informative, clear, and penetrating: his sensitivity to trends, to possibilities, to the ups and downs of genre writing is, like much of what he discusses, at times positively uncanny.

The bulk of the volume is given over to "The Magazines in Profile": accounts of more than 400 publications, ranging from the short-lived (one issue) to the seemingly everlasting. Each profile consists of an essay (from a few lines to several pages), a brief list of Information Sources (e.g., indexes and location tools), and a Publication History. Numerous cross-references reflect incessant title changes. Then come two essays—Overviews of Foreign Magazines and Book Clubs in Profile—plus seven Appendixes (including Sherlock Holmes Scion Society Periodicals and a valuable Chronology), a Selected Bibliography, and an Index to persons, publishers, titles, and some fictional characters—but not to motifs and to character types (matters which might be, in another edition, the foci of additional Appendixes or of an expanded introductory essay, should Cook prefer not to catch them in his index).

National continuing care directory: comprehensive information on retirement facilities and communities offering prepaid contracts for long-term care. Edited by Ann Trueblood Raper for the American Association of Homes for the Aging. Glenview, Ill., Scott, Foresman, 1984. 618p. 24cm. paper $13.95 (0-673-24813-5).

362.6'1'02573 Life care communities—U.S.—Directories | Retirement communities—U.S.—Directories | Aged—U.S.—Care and hygiene—Directories [CIP]   84-417

The extended life expectancy of most persons has led to rapid growth of the retirement industry. This directory is a guide to what is known as Life Care Retirement Communities: facilities which provide medical services contractually guaranteed, combined with independent living arrangements and other services usually rendered in retirement communities. These facilities generally require payments of a substantial entrance fee as well as monthly sums.

The work begins with excellent consumer advice on what to look for and which questions to ask prior to signing an agreement. Included in the directory proper are 277 retirement communities which either were in service or under actual construction in December 1983. It updates information in a similar directory of 1982 and is the result of collaboration between the American Association for Retired Persons and the American Association of Homes for the Aging. A two-page spread is devoted to each facility; cited here are name, address, sponsor/owner; manager; year opened/stage of development; location; current number of residents; fees, etc. For each, general and medical services (e.g., cleaning, laundry, utilities, parking, dental care, occupational therapy, routine physical examinations, etc.) are described as being either included in fees, available with charge, or not available.

Two indexes at the end give further help in locating material. The Metropolitan Area Index identifies communities by the nearest metropolitan area, and a Special Features Index actually is a chart showing the existence of certain amenities (e.g., athletic and library facilities, beauty salon, cable television, etc.) in each facility. A short bibliography follows.

The *National Continuing Care Directory* is of great value for those who need to choose a retirement location. It is an excellent source for public or social service libraries.

The national job bank: a comprehensive guide to major employers in the nation's key job markets. Senior ed., Robert Lang Adams; managing ed., J. Michael Fiedler. Brighton, MA 02135, 2045 Commonwealth Ave., Bob Adams, Inc., 1983. 1,432p. (Job Bank series) 23cm. cloth $79.95 (0-937860-07-7).

331.12'8 Vocational guidance—U.S. | Professions—U.S. | U.S.—Occupations | U.S.—Industries—Directories [OCLC]

The National Job Bank aims to show "specifically where to find professional employment in the nation's ten key job markets . . . selected because of the size of their professional workforces and their relatively strong employment outlooks." The ten markets are—in order of presentation—the metropolitan areas of Atlanta (including "major employers throughout Georgia"), Boston (i.e., Massachusetts), and Chicago; metropolitan New York (including northern New Jersey, Long Island, Westchester County, and southwestern Connecticut); northern California; Pennsylvania; southern California; the Southwest (including Colorado, New Mexico, Utah, and Arizona); Texas; and metropolitan Washington, D.C. (including the Baltimore and northern Virginia areas). Documentation for declaring these areas "key markets" is not given; nor is "major employers" in the subtitle explained. The methodology or criteria for collecting the data on each employer: firm name, address, telephone number, contact person, brief description of firm's business, headquarters location, listing on New York or American stock exchange (if applicable), and approximate area work force (from "small employer" for under 200 employees to "very large employer" for more than 5,000 employees) are also omitted. For some listings the employer's tentative professional employment outlook, ranging from Stable (i.e., "little or no hiring expected") through Moderate, Average, and Good is also included.

About 10,000 employers are reportedly included in this volume (surely a rather small number given the regions covered); material is based upon ten separate titles from the same publisher, each covering one of the areas listed above (all published 1981 or later). In no case is the date of the information supplied—a most important consideration in light of the rapidity with which personnel resources and requirements change in today's job market. The fullness of entries varies widely from perhaps one-third of a page to five lines or less; for example, more than 200 of some 600 Boston entries have no more than five lines. It must also be pointed out that the regional volumes—but not the national one—include chapters on job-search techniques with sample résumés, interview questions, cover letters, lists of employment agencies and services, etc.—essential information for today's job hunters. Considering that much of a typical entry is directory information, users might have profited by a reminder of the usefulness of telephone directories (including the yellow and blue pages) and such business tools as Dun & Bradstreet's *Million Dollar Directory* and *Reference Book of Corporate Managements, Moody's Manuals, Standard Corporation Descriptions* (including a *Daily News Section*), and *Standard & Poor's Register of Corporations, Directors, and Executives*—examples of titles found in many public, academic, and special libraries, providing much the same information (albeit not in the same format) and increasingly supplemented by computerized databases. And, of course, for up-to-date information on job opportunities, the importance of local and national newspapers, professional journals, and job lines cannot be overstated.

The regional volumes also include not-for-profit prospective employers (hospitals, colleges and universities, governments, etc.) as well as private businesses. The title under review treats primarily the for-profit sector, although a few nonprofit agencies are included. All volumes include cross-indexes by industry wherein the names of firms/organizations are listed in one or more of 31 broad categories from Accounting/Auditing to Utilities. In the *National Job Bank*, the Industrial/Geographical Cross-Index concludes the volume. Under each of the alphabetically listed categories, the subarrangement is alphabetical by name of region and thereunder alphabetical by company/organization name.

The National Job Bank: A Comprehensive Guide to Major Employers in the Nation's Key Job Markets falls short of being the comprehensive guide claimed. It does not clearly define the concepts of the "ten key markets" and "major employers" and the data collection methodology; it omits chapters on job-hunting techniques (which appear in the regional job market volumes on which it is based); and its coverage is not comprehensive. This work is essentially a limited directory, with no stated frequency of publication or a time frame for the information given. Not recommended.

Native American folklore, 1879–1979: an annotated bibliography. Compiled by William M. Clements and Frances M. Malpezzi. Athens, Ohio, Swallow, 1984. xxiii, 247p. 29cm. cloth $34.95 (0-8040-0831-0).
016.398′08997073 Indians of North America—Folklore—Bibliography | Folklore—North America—Bibliography [CIP]   83-6672

Defining folklore in rather broad terms, as explained in the Introduction, the editors of this bibliography have produced a briefly annotated list of 5,450 publications, both serial and monographic, from the founding of what came to be known as the Bureau of American Ethnology in 1879 to 1979.

Arrangement is geographical, with subdivision by American Indian tribes. Within each subdivision, items are listed by author (occasionally by title), with an annotation seldom longer than two lines. *See also* references follow each subdivision. Subject and Author Indexes conclude the work. The Subject Index includes both broad and narrow topics. Unfortunately, the larger topics (e.g., Death, Games, Linguistics, etc.) are not subdivided, so that there are sometimes from 100 to 200 undifferentiated references under one Index entry.

Since the bulk of this literature appears in minor, hard-to-locate serial publications, this extensive bibliography will be welcomed by all scholars in the field of native American ethnology and folklore.

Native American periodicals and newspapers, 1828–1982: bibliography, publishing record, and holdings. Edited by James P. Danky; compiled by Maureen E. Hady. Westport, Conn., Greenwood, 1984. 532p. 24cm. cloth $49.95 (0-313-23773-5).
016.973′0497′005 Indians of North America—Periodicals—Bibliography—Union lists | Indian periodicals—Bibliography—Union lists | Indian newspapers—Bibliography—Union lists | Catalogs, Union—U.S. [CIP]   83-22579

This union list bibliography is the fourth produced by the News and Periodical Unit of the State Historical Society of Wisconsin Library. Preceding works include *Undergrounds* (1974), *Asian American Periodicals and Newspapers* (1979), and *Women's Periodicals and Newspapers* (1982). The work under review is a "guide to the holdings and locations of 1,164 periodical and newspaper titles by and about Native Americans." Included are literary, political, and historical journals as well as general newspapers and magazines. The book's purpose is not to be comprehensive but to provide "a description of those titles still in existence."

The 468 pages of main text are an alphabetical listing of titles. Entries can include up to 23 items, and full bibliographic information is provided. Notation is given also if the title is in English. The work concludes with six accurate and thorough Indexes: Subject, Editors, Index of Publishers, Geographic, Catchword and Subtitle, and Chronological. Reference is to entry number.

Native American Periodicals and Newspapers is a quality publication which the Board commends to libraries with in-depth collections in this field.

The new book of American rankings. By FYI Information Services. New York, Facts On File, 1984. 320p. 26cm. hardcover $29.95 (0-87196-254-3).
317.3 U.S.—Statistics [CIP]   84-4115

This edition, similar to the first, contains numerous tables which compare such topics as climate, cost of living, health, crime rate, etc., in the 50 states. There are 33 broad categories with approximately 332 key topic subsections and tables. The broad topics cover geography, population, family unemployment, income, taxes, energy, pollution, sports, and politics. Within each major topic is detailed comparative information on such subjects as divorce/marriage ratio, average farm acreage, pupil/teacher ratio, average residential gas bills, and the number of registered automobiles, etc.

An introduction to each major topic provides an overview. Then follow specific data presented with an interpretive, well-written narrative. The narratives also provide references to other relevant tables and compare data found in other sections. In each key topic subsection, tables are clearly labeled with the date and source of the data.

Appended to the main body of this volume are short summaries on each state. Profiles are listed alphabetically along with their rankings in several different areas. A Bibliography and an alphabetical Subject Index conclude the work.

On the whole, *The New Book of American Rankings* provides an excellent portrait of each state's standing in many various categories. The comparative data will be useful to general audiences in public, school, special, and academic libraries.

The new book of popular science. Danbury, Conn., Grolier, 1984. 6v. 28cm. hardcover $245 + $15 (shipping/handling) to home; $149.50 + $4 (shipping/handling) to schools and libraries (0-7172-1213-0/set).
500 Science—Popular works—Collected works | Technology—Popular works—Collected works [CIP]   83-26595

The New Book of Popular Science (hereinafter *NBPS*) is an outgrowth of *The Book of Popular Science*, first issued more than a half-century ago and extensively revised—and retitled *New*—in 1978. Since 1978 it has been revised five times; material received from its publisher states that in the 1984 edition, approximately a third of its chapters have been updated, that five have been added on new topics (alternate energy sources, acid rain, biofeedback, office automation, and personal computers), that five chapters have been replaced, and that illustrations have been revised and updated in proportion. *NBPS*'s authority rests mainly on its publisher's reputation for high-quality material, upon the expertise of its editorial staff (headed by writer and editor Lynn G. Blum), and upon the qualifications of its contributors (mainly persons associated with institutions of higher learning and with research laboratories, along with experienced writers in the area of science education).

NBPS is in six volumes: (1) *Astronomy & Space Science; Computers & Mathematics*; (2) *Earth Sciences; Energy; Environmental Sciences*; (3) *Physical Sciences; General Biology*; (4)*Plant Life; Animal Life*; (5) *Mammals; Human Sciences* (including anatomy, physiology, psychology, and medicine); and (6) *Technology*; Appendix; Index. This distribution of editorial space would appear to reflect current educational emphases and the perceived interests of young adults and of adult laypersons. History and philosophy of science are to some extent covered, but only incidentally, i.e., within large subject divisions and within chapters: thus the excellent chapter "How To Do an Experiment" is under *General Biology*, between viruses and embryology. Future editions might consider adding separate sections on such topics, possibly in volume 1 (to form an Introduction) or possibly in an Appendix.

Except for the Appendix and the Index, each half or third of a volume consists of chapters (most of them signed) on specific topics, e.g., under *Energy* there are eleven chapters, including "The Energy Picture," "Petroleum," "Coal," "Natural Gas," "Solar Power," and six others. Each group of chapters is effectively arranged, moving from familiar and/or easy and/or basic matters to matters more esoteric and/or complex, thus facilitating continuous reading—*Plant Life* is a readable botany "text"—although it is often possible to read later chapters with understanding despite not having read earlier ones. Chapters feature language and pace which will make them readily understood—and enjoyed—by upper elementary students, junior and senior high school students as well as adults. Among especially fresh and readable presentations are the chapters on "Minerals" and on "Collecting Minerals and Rocks," by F. H. Pough; on "Stars," by Cecilia Payne-Gaposchkin; on "Heat Transmission," by John Albright; and on "Mosses and Ferns," by T. G. Lawrence. Throughout, effective use is made of subheadings; and there are running titles, curiously and atypically set below, not above, the text. Cross-references are few, i.e., little is done to encourage one to trace lines of thought or inquiry different from what the chapter sequence implies. The material on viruses in the general chapter "What is Life?" is thus not linked to what is said in the separate chapter "Viruses" in the same volume; nor are the several references, in the *Earth Sciences* section, to tidal waves linked; and early in the chapter on "Printing," half-tone work is mentioned without explanation—and with no hint that the subject will be discussed a few pages later. While chapters do not include bibliographies, each volume includes a section of up-to-date and well-chosen Selected Readings, arranged more or less in chapter sequence and consisting mainly of titles likely to be considered for school and public libraries; however, the text does not routinely refer to the Selected Readings.

Illustrations are numerous, running from one to several per double-page spread, including sidebars and charts. On the whole they are interesting and effective; many of the line drawings are of very high quality. But some could be better placed. Thus, a chart on inflorescence appears three pages from relevant text, with reference neither to nor from; an excellent graphic on how airplanes land appears two pages from a verbal account, despite the fact that on the text page there is an illustration which belongs where the graphic on landing is; and the caption for an illustration of climates of the past refers to a "little Ice Age" implied in the illustration but not mentioned in the chapter's text (and this despite the fact that the Ice Age in question played an important part in the history of northern Europe).

The Appendix consists of the Selected Readings for volume 6 (which should have preceded the Appendix) and useful material on Nobel Prize winners, Mathematical Symbols, Important Constants for the Physical Sciences, etc. The Index (also in volume 6) is to both text and illustrations, cites persons, places, and topics, and is analytic. The Appendix and Index are available as a paperbound separate—a boon to libraries.

NBPS is clearly printed on quality stock; its page layout is attractive; and its binding is both colorful and sturdy, with pages lying flat when volumes are opened. Individual volumes are small enough to be easily handled at student work stations.

As a set for continuous reading, *NBPS* is excellent, being above the comprehension level of the *Raintree Illustrated Science Encyclopedia* (cf. *RBB*, August 1984) and thus facilitating transition from juvenile to adult reading. As a reference set, it will depend for its usefulness upon the availability and effective use of its Index. In short, *NBPS* is a good, solid multivolume survey of the pure and applied sciences; it is sufficiently up-to-date; and it has particular potential as collateral or "free" reading and as a tool of self-education. Its possibilities in reference service are considerable. More effective use of running titles, better coordination of text with illustrations, and bibliographies would facilitate its use even further. *New Book of Popular Science* is recommended for school libraries (upper elementary, junior and senior high schools) and for public libraries, and it should be considered for academic libraries. It is also recommended for home purchase, as it can be used, for both pleasure and profit, at a variety of levels.

The new book of world rankings. By George Thomas Kurian. New York, Facts On File, 1984. xxiv, 490p. 26cm. hardcover $29.95 (0-87196-743-X).
310 Statistics | Social indicators | Economic indicators | Quality of life—Statistics
[CIP] 82-7380

Kurian has held here to the patterns of his 1979 *Book of World Rankings (RSBR,* Sept. 1, 1980), but has added a number of new subjects (liquor consumption, slum population) and dropped 32 old ones. Chiefly 1980 statistics for more than 190 nations and for 349 discrete subjects were derived for the most part from UN, World Bank, International Monetary Fund, and the U.S. Agency for International Development statistics. These are arranged under 23 broad topics—important segments of national activities—Politics, Military Power, Crime, Education, Economy, Geographical Climate, etc., selected by the same criteria: availability, comparability, usability, reliability, and rankability. The same brief profiles of each country, based on ranking shown in the statistical tables, and a Subject Index are appended. This source on a wide variety of data reflects Kurian's experience as a compiler of reference books, notably among them the *Encyclopedia of the Third World,* and will be an excellent ready-reference tool in almost any library where a question like "Who has the most . . . ?" is an everyday occurrence.

The new compleat astrologer: the practical encyclopaedia of astrological science. Incorporating: astrology ancient and modern; how to cast, interpret and make predictions from your own birth chart; aspects; progressions; planetary positions and tables; and an atlas of astrology in full colour explaining the secrets of celestial mechanics. 21st-century edition, completely revised, updated and extended. By Derek and Julia Parker. New York, Harmony (a div. of Crown), 1984. 288p. illus. 30cm. cloth $20 (0-517-55503-4)
133.5 Astrology [CIP] 84-3764

About 900 astrology books from 140 publishers worldwide were in print in 1981, evidence of continuing interest in the subject. Now a British journalist/playwright and his wife, a former president of the Faculty of Astrological Studies (London) and author of many books on astrology and health, have updated their guide to astrology to include astrological tables valid for all birthdays through the year 2001. First published in 1971, with new editions in 1975 and 1981, this latest revision is filled with illustrations, most of them in color, which accompany a lively text. A historical section precedes another on zodiac signs, giving traits, character, mind, career, and emotional and parent/child relationships. A section headed "Interpretations: The Birth Chart Revealed" treats briefly (two pages) 18 subjects, including synastry, astrology and sex, and planetary myths. Also brief are the biographies of astrologers from Rameses II to the present. Brief astrological profiles illustrate various signs of the zodiac, e.g., Marilyn Monroe and Edgar Degas under Neptune.

While the publisher's claim that "*The New Compleat Astrologer* is simply the lushest, most definitive, most painstakingly produced and designed work ever published on this subject" may be a bit exaggerated, it will certainly interest people who read their horoscopes in the daily press. Public libraries will want to consider it.

The new Grove dictionary of musical instruments. 3v. Edited by Stanley Sadie. London, Macmillan Press Ltd; New York, Grove's Dictionaries of Music Inc., 1984. illus. 26cm. cloth $350. (0-333-37878-4, British ed.; 0-943818-05-2, U.S. ed.).
781.91'03'21 Musical instruments—Dictionaries [CIP]   84-9062

The New Grove Dictionary of Musical Instruments expands and updates the coverage provided in its parent work, *The New Grove Dictionary of Music and Musicians* (reviewed in these pages May 15, 1982). Expansion of substantial proportions has been affected in the areas of non-Western and folk instruments and of modern instruments and their makers. While the parent work has separate entries for only 300 of the most important non-Western and folk instruments, the *Dictionary of Musical Instruments* provides 10,000 entries: "all significant instruments from every culture."

The new dictionary also includes more than 200 articles on electronic instruments in addition to the 33-page general article on the subject. The corresponding article in the *Dictionary of Music and Musicians* occupies only three-fourths of a page and refers to only eight additional articles on individual instruments. One of these, the article on the synthesizer, has been expanded from two and one-half to four and one-half pages in the *Dictionary of Musical Instruments*. Significant expansion has also occurred in coverage of inventors, makers, and manufacturers of instruments.

Although the articles on the instruments of classical Western music are based on those in the *Dictionary of Music and Musicians*, few have been reprinted without alteration. Some have been extensively rewritten or revised, and others have been updated to incorporate significant new information. *Harpsichord* has been expanded by five and one-half pages, and 50 additional items have been added to its bibliography, 27 of which have been published since the original bibliography was compiled. Fewer changes have been required in the articles on performing practice, "though all have been reconsidered by their authors or others and in some areas... advances in research have necessitated a fresh treatment." Stanley Sadie, who was music critic of the London *Times* for 18 years, edited *New Grove* dictionaries. He also is editor of *Musical Times* and the forthcoming *New Grove Dictionary of Music in the United States*.

Aproximately 400 contributors were involved in the preparation of the entries. About two thirds are from the U.K. and the U.S. The remainder reside in 30 other countries in various parts of the world. Although contributors are identified only by their last known place of work or residence, the editor notes that the entries pertaining to non-Western and folk instruments "were supplied or editorially prepared by scholars with specialist knowledge based on fieldwork in the regions concerned."

The text is enhanced by more than 1,600 black-and-white photographs and drawings ranging from historical illustrations to technical diagrams. There are numerous photographs of performers playing non-Western and folk instruments. The articles on performance practice include many musical examples.

Bibliographies, many of which have been expanded and updated since they first appeared in the *Dictionary of Music and Musicians*, are appended to all except the briefest entries. While a few of the longest bibliographies are arranged by category, most merely list the cited sources chronologically by first date of publication. In a bibliography with almost 200 entries, such as the one provided for *Organ*, this lack of categorization is a drawback.

Neither the parent work nor the *Dictionary of Musical Instruments* has a general index. Although the *Dictionary of Music and Musicians* provides an Index of Terms Used in Articles on Non-Western Music, Folk Music and Kindred Topics, this finding device was not included in the *Dictionary of Musical Instruments*, where many additional terms of this nature are to be found. Pronunciations are not indicated even for those specialized terms not likely to be found in other dictionaries.

While cross-references compensate in part for the lack of an index, they do not fulfill this function adequately. The 77-page *Organ* article (the longest) is supplemented by a number of separate articles (e.g., *Chamber Organ, Cinema Organ, Electronic Organ, Reed Organ, Theatre Organ, Organ Stop, Registration*), only a few of which are cross-referenced from the main article. *Reed Organ* includes at least a dozen terms and names for which separate entries are provided but for which no cross-references are given. These entries often provide fuller information than does the article itself.

Physically, the *Dictionary of Musical Instruments* resembles its parent. Although the small type is adequate when the dictionary is merely being consulted, it seems likely that extended reading may cause eye fatigue, especially since the clarity of the print is sometimes obscured by insufficiently opaque paper. The type used for the bibliographies and lists is even smaller than that used for the text.

The *New Grove Dictionary of Musical Instruments* achieves its aim of providing "the most comprehensive treatment... of the musical instruments of the entire world." Music libraries and libraries that place special emphasis on music materials will find it essential. Other libraries owning the parent set will want to assess their need for the expanded and updated information which this more specialized tool provides. Recommended.

New Iberian world: a documentary history of the discovery and settlement of Latin America to the early 17th century. 5v. Edited, with commentaries, by John H. Parry and Robert G. Keith, with the assistance of Michael Jimenez. New York, Times Books, 1984. 28cm. cloth $500 (0-8129-1070-2—set; 0-8129-1071-0—v.1; 0-8129-1072-9—v.2; 0-8129-1073-7—v.3; 0-8129-1074-5—v.4; 0-8129-1075-3—v.5).
980'.01 Latin America—History—To 1600—Sources | America—Discovery and Exploration—Sources [CIP]   82-19664

For English-language readers, the *New Iberian World* is the first comprehensive collection of source materials available on the conquest of Latin America. "In these volumes, an attempt has been made to include samples... of all the principal types of documents that occur in the colonial archives (primarily in Spain or Latin America) and within each type to select documents for their significance, for their interest as illustrations of particular situations, and ... for their value as entertainment."

Each volume runs chronologically from about 1500 to 1600, and an approach based mainly on geography organizes the five volumes: I, *The Conquerors and the Conquered*; II, *The Caribbean*; III, *Central America and Mexico*; IV, The Andes; and V, *Coastlines, Rivers, and Forests*. Only the titles of the first and last volumes do not seem self-explanatory.

Accessibility is facilitated through a master table of contents in the first volume plus individual tables of contents in the others. Access to materials on specific topics is through the 65-page Index (in v.V), mainly by place-name and surname but also by some subjects. Whereas introductions to each volume focus on the contents thereof, more specific aid comes from the editors' introductory paragraphs to each document. Given the difficulty of translating certain Spanish and indigenous terms into English, a five-page Glossary is provided in each volume.

That this work exists can be attributed to the persistence of the Harvard-based editors, who not only collected and edited the documents but, more importantly, recognized the need for such a scholarly accumulation. Earlier collections have been briefer, sporadic, and without the chronological or thematic intensity of the work under review.

Another attribute is that Spain and Portugal, normally serving as backdrops to the more important action on the American continent, are here integrated into the total imperialistic venture. The second and third parts of the first volume focus on Iberian precedents including the Muslims, exploration into West Africa, and the structure of empire. In this same volume are presented the American native societies both preceding and coincidental to conquest.

As historians the editors have been remiss in their selection, for unnoted are *Popol Vuh* of the Mayas, *El Ollantay* of the Incas, and the poetry of the Aztecs. Although in oral form, they were recorded in Spanish and as original literature contribute an indigenous perspective on pre-Columbian life. Their inclusion here would be in keeping with the collection's multiplicity of perspective.

The attractive print, adequate margins, and sturdy binding make the set very handsome. However, the 110 black-and-white rather lackluster illustrations with explanations on separate pages neither encourage nor invite use. In short, they are highly dispensable.

New Iberian World is a contribution to the understanding of Latin America in the English-language world. For scope, uniqueness, and variety, this collection of documents should be acquired by all university libraries interested in Latin America and by all large public libraries.

New rock record. [By] Terry Hounsome. New York, Facts On File, 1983. 719p. 25cm. cloth $17.95 (0-87196-774-X); paper $9.95 (0-87196-770-7).
016.7899'12454 Rock music—Discography [CIP]   81-12489

The persevering rock-music aficionado with good eyesight will find a wealth of valuable information in this discography, an update of *Rock Record* (1981), reviewed in detail in *RSBR*, Sept. 15, 1982. The format of the latter, which the Board previously found difficult to use, has not been changed. Pages are crowded; presentation is columnar with little or no white space between columns; columns are not headed; and print is all capitals with no spacing to set off a new entry from its predecessor. Reader assistance may be found preceding the text: key to column content, Introduction, and list of abbreviations.

Entry, each given an alphanumeric designation, is by group or artist's surname. The entry lists musicians who played or sang for each record listed, their instruments, record title, date of issue, record label, country of origin, and catalog number. Code symbols link musicians and LPs within the entry. A Name Index, also visually difficult to use (five columns to a page), enables one to locate every listed LP on which an artist has performed.

New Rock Record contains approximately 6,000 main entries listing some 35,000 musicians and 40,000 LPs. It is 200 pages longer than, and adds some 1,500 entries and 10,000 musicians to, the 1981 version. Despite the format, both public and academic libraries should have it available; rock-music buffs and researchers will willingly dig for its treasures.

The New York Times encyclopedia of film, 1896–1979. 13v. Gene Brown, editor. New York, Times Books, 1984. illus. 31cm. cloth $2,000 a set (0-8129-1059-1).
791.43 Moving-pictures—Collected works [OCLC]   81-3607

This is not an encyclopedia but rather a collection of facsimiles of articles on film in the *New York Times* from April 23, 1896, through December 31, 1979. It is similar in format to *The New York Times Film Reviews, 1913–1968* (reviewed by the Board Dec. 1, 1973), a six-volume set that reprinted more than 16,000 reviews. However, the *Encyclopedia* complements the reviews by presenting "every New York Times film article ever printed, including over 5,500 news items, profiles, and interviews, complete with thousands of photographs, illustrations, and advertisements." Intended users are film historians and other scholars, as well as cinema buffs.

The scope of the articles is wide; many concern the activities of individual movie stars, but others take up subjects as diverse as corporate finance, censorship, inventions and technology, sociological impacts, and moral issues.

The first 12 volumes contain the articles arranged chronologically, and the thirteenth volume is an Index. The volumes are not numbered, so users must consult the spines, covers, or title pages. The first volume begins with a short introduction by Harry M. Geduld, the set's advisory editor and a prolific writer on film. Articles are presented in three or four columns to a page.

Volume 1's first entry is a short announcement in the amusement listings: "Koster & Bial's Music Hall, 34th St., To-night, First Time, Edison's Marvel, The Vitascope, Chevalier and all the Foreign Stars." The next day's report is entitled "Edison's Vitascope Cheered," and the reporter notes that "When the hall was darkened last night a buzzing and roaring were heard in the turret, and an unusually bright light fell upon the screen."

The first volume (1896–1928) sets the tone: there was an almost immediate recognition of the impact of motion pictures on American life. The other volumes cover time spans that range from two to eight years. Every article is dated, but original page numbers and columns are not given. Other inclusions are photographs and illustrations that accompanied original articles and a selected number of newspaper advertisements for films at New York City theaters. All these enhance the page layout.

The 338-page index volume cites the "most significant people, places, things, and themes." Each entry gives the month, day, and year of the published article (pages in the set are unnumbered, but month and year are given at the top of every right-hand page). There are two kinds of listings under index terms. A subtopic or short phrase preceding the article's date is an "indication of the most important of the articles on the subject." For example, the entry for Charlie Chaplin first lists 360 dates from 1915 through 1979. Then come citations of 110 articles under 77 alphabetized headings such as "appeal of," "denial of communism," and "marriage to O'Neill." Presumably these latter news articles are the more substantial ones, although the chronological list will be useful for researchers wanting a year-by-year approach. Very few cross-references are used, and it is admittedly difficult to derive exact identification of persons from the context of some articles. Overall, the Index is fairly comprehensive and workable, but is not as useful for reference as the Index for the earlier set.

The New York Times Encyclopedia of Film, 1896–1979 is printed on acid-free paper and is bound in a sturdy buckram. The chief physical drawback is the obscurity of some reproductions. Because of the unavailability of actual pages from the newspaper, 35mm microfilm was used as source material. Variances in the original filming of the newspaper caused occasional portions which are too light, too dark, or too out of focus to be easily legible.

This set will be warmly received by film researchers who spend long hours with *The New York Times Index* and microfilm readers. It is the most extensive and important collection of facsimile articles on film to appear in book format. This is readily accessible source material from America's foremost newspaper; the encyclopedia will be a boon to researchers, and it will provide needed balance to the recent flood of published movie histories, biographies, and memoirs. Most libraries may want to purchase the earlier set first, but even so *The New York Times Encyclopedia of Film, 1896–1979* is recommended for special collections of film history and popular culture.

Novel verdicts: a guide to courtroom fiction. By Jon L. Breen. Metuchen, N.J. & London, Scarecrow, 1984. xii, 266p. 23cm. cloth $18.50 (0-8108-1741-1).
016.823'008'0355 English fiction—Bibliography | Courts in literature—Bibliography | American fiction—Bibliography | English fiction—Stories, plots, etc. | American fiction—Stories, plots, etc. | Law in literature—Bibliography | Lawyers in literature—Bibliography | Judges in literature—Bibliography [CIP]   84-14110

Courtroom fiction has been defined by Breen as those books either entirely devoted to describing a trial or including a courtroom scene or scenes of significant length. Most of the 420 annotated titles and the supplementary list of about 500 titles are mystery/detective novels, with a few from such serious writers as Dickens, Dreiser, Galsworthy, and Cozzens. In fact, Breen includes *An American Tragedy* among his "Golden Dozen," the best of the novels with a British or American setting.

Full annotations include not only plot and type of courtroom action, but usually an assessment of the book as a work of fiction. Breen can be quite blunt as in his description of *The Missing Witness*: "There are numerous unlikely happenings, unbearably corny dialogue in the man-woman scenes, and a general soap-opera aura to the whole enterprise."

In his selection, he has used *Crime Fiction, 1749–1980* by A. J. Hubin (Garland, 1984) and other pertinent sources. Three indexes are appended: (1) Author-Title, including names of real persons or real cases mentioned in annotations; (2) place of trial, with England, California, and New York leading; and (3) cause of action, with divorce, libel, robbery, and larceny most frequent.

Discriminating selection and excellent annotations distinguish this useful source for such information as the first English and American editions of Erle Stanley Gardner's *Case of the Careless Kitten* or the name of the detective in *Lawful Pursuit*. Suitable for public and academic libraries with popular culture collections.

Nuclear weapons databook, v.I: U.S. nuclear forces and capabilities. By Thomas B. Cochran et al. Cambridge, Mass., Ballinger, 1984. xix, 340p. 28cm. cloth $38 (0-88410-172-X); paper $19.95 (0-88410-173-8).
355.8'25119 Atomic weapons [CIP]   82-24376

This work, the first of eight volumes scheduled to appear in the *Nuclear Weapons Databook* series, is based on research sponsored by the National Resources Defense Council. Next to appear will be *Soviet Nuclear Weapons*. Subsequent volumes will include one more on U.S. weapons and others on foreign nuclear weapons, on the environment, on command and control of nuclear weapons and strategy, on arms control in general, and finally a history of nuclear weapons. Dates for these have not been announced.

In the present work, after an introductory overview, eight chapters give details of army, navy, and air force nuclear weapons in the U.S. Details include black-and-white photographs, function, modifications, safeguards, history of manufacture, deployment, and location (names of countries only). There are some 150 photographs and 75 tables of statistical or other data. One map shows the location of 722 military units "certified" for nuclear warfare in the U.S.

The Foreword states that the work "is for those who want to understand the nuclear arms race." Since libraries, especially public libraries, exist partly for the purpose of ensuring "an informed citizenry," this book and its subsequent volumes will be valuable additions in all public and academic libraries. The series will certainly "inform" citizens about a very important subject.

O'Dwyer's directory of public relations firms, 1983. Publisher and editor, Jack O'Dwyer; associate editor, Maureen Ward. New York, NY 10016, 271 Madison Ave., J. R. O'Dwyer Co., Inc., 1984. 315p. illus. 28cm. paper $70 (0-941424-03-0; ISSN 0078-3374).

338.7'61'659202573 Public relations—Directories [OCLC]   70-86913

The 1984 edition of *O'Dwyer's Directory of Public Relations Firms* lists 1,400 public relations firms and PR departments of advertising agencies. The directory is in 11 sections including a list of the 50 largest U.S. public relations firms, independent and ad agency owned; a list of the largest independent U.S. public relations firms excluding ad agency owned ones; and a list of the largest public relations firms associated with advertising agencies. Finally there is a cross-index to client companies of all public relations firms listed in the directory. The entry for the directory section includes the full name of the firm, address, telephone number, type of public relations handled, number of employees, officials of the company, date founded, and a list of major clients. Spiral-bound, the work will not withstand heavy usage.

As a reference tool, *O'Dwyer's* will serve any number of valuable functions. As a job-finding tool, it will enhance several other business/marketing directories. Undoubtedly business libraries in particular will find it useful.

Office automation and word processing buying guide. By Tony Webster et al. New York, McGraw-Hill, 1984. 328p. 28cm. paper $19.95 (0-07-068962-8).

652 Office practice—Automation | Word processors—Purchasing | Office equipment and supplies—Purchasing [CIP]   83-18694

Office automation, as used in this book, "refers to a total office perspective where word, data, image and voice processing" are all parts of the office. This guide is intended for buyers and users of such systems. It is divided into two parts: Part I—Theory; and Part II—Detailed Product Summaries.

Part I includes chapters on office automation concepts, applications and systems, technology, word processing, private branch exchanges (PABXs), local area networks (LANs), and office automation planning. Part II includes chapters that are product summaries of such equipment as electronic typewriters, word processing, PABXs, LANs, and microcomputer word processing. A Glossary is included as well as a list of other publications, presented in the form of advertisements.

Office Automation and Word Processing Buying Guide is fairly comprehensive and up-to-date. The text is easy to follow, and specifications for products are given. The book will be a helpful addition to library business and automation collections and a wise purchase for office automation planning.

1000 most important words. [By] Norman W. Schur. New York, Facts On File, 1982. 193p. 24cm. hardcover $15.95 (0-87196-869-X).

428.1 Vocabulary [CIP]   83-25371

1000 most practical words. [By] Norman W. Schur. New York, Facts On File, 1983. 255p. 24cm. hardcover $15.95 (0-87196-868-1).

428.1 Vocabulary [CIP]   83-25372

These books list words, mainly of Latin origin and far from picturesque, which are in the vocabularies of educated speakers and writers and with which every young person needs to become familiar: *arduous, cache, exculpate, gullible, ineluctable, noisome, peccadillo, sartorial, unique,* etc. Entries are, as it were, "eased-out" dictionary entries, i.e., short articles on meanings, origins, figurative uses, etc., with a greater than usual number of real and manufactured quotations. Each book is described on its dust jacket as a "vocabulary builder and dictionary." As vocabulary builders, they will interest and instruct adults and young adults and should therefore be seriously considered for school, public, and academic libraries. As dictionaries, i.e., as reference tools, they are of limited value—the difficulty being that they are so very selective that the likelihood of finding in them material on particular words is not, in the end, very great.

Their titles are unfortunate: they promise more than they deliver. If one browses at length, one discerns a slight difference in emphasis between *important* and *practical*, but not enough to indicate in which volume a particular word might be discussed. And there is Schur's use of *most*—not just important and practical but *most* important, *most* practical. Arguments will no doubt arise concerning his choices (one misses, among words said to be most important, *authority, democracy, freedom, love, patriotism,* and *race*): arguments endless and, in the long run, unprofitable.

Online database search services directory. 1st ed. John Schmittroth, Jr., and Doris Morris Maxfield, editors; Amy F. Lucas, associate editor. Detroit, Gale, 1984. 1,186p. 28cm. paper $120 (0-8103-1698-6; ISSN 0741-0077).

†001.644'04 On-line bibliographic searching—Directories | On-line data processing—Directories | Data base management—Directories | Computer service industry—Directories [OCLC]

This directory seeks to identify users and organizations which provide search services from a variety of databases. The listing of public, academic, and special libraries, private information firms, and other organizations in the U.S. and Canada is concise. The alphabetically arranged entries may furnish up to 17 categories of information: full name, address, and telephone number; year service was established; key contact; number of staff conducting searches; online system accesses; subject areas; service availability; fee policy; names of search personnel; and related remarks. Six Indexes list the organizations by name and acronyms; by online systems' access; by databases searched; by subject areas searched; by search personnel; and by state or province. (It should be emphasized that the work describes the *organizations* providing online database searches, not the databases themselves.)

Information has been gathered through questionnaires returned by organizations originally identified through library and online user group directories and related guides. A copy of the questionnaire is provided for those who wish to have their organization considered for inclusion in future issues.

Public and academic libraries and some information centers which are engaged in online searching or whose patrons need to find searching agencies may wish to add this helpful resource to online reference work.

Opposing viewpoints sources: criminal justice; nuclear arms; 1984 supplements to criminal justice and nuclear arms; foreign policy; death/dying; American/Soviet relations; and human sexuality. Bruno Leone, executive editor. Greenhaven Pr., 577 Shoreview Park Rd., St. Paul, MN 55112, 1983, 1984, 1985. 29cm. looseleaf $79.95 each major volume; $16 each supp.; $.80 each replacement viewpoint (0-89908-500-8, criminal justice; 0-89908-501-6, nuclear arms; 0-89908-504-0, foreign policy; 0-89908-503-2, death/dying).

†080 Social sciences—Addresses, essays, lectures

Each sourcebook presents 100 topical articles matched pro and con; they are arranged by subtopic, e.g., in *Nuclear Arms,* the 13 sections include The Soviet-American Debate, Economics of the Arms Race, Missiles in Western Europe, and The Morality of Nuclear Weapons. Articles range from Caspar Weinberger's statement before the Senate Armed Services Committee to an excerpt from a British book *The Case for Nuclear Disarmament. Criminal Justice* includes harder-to-find topics under such sections as Reforming the U.S. Judicial System, Rights of Crime Victims, and The Insanity Defense, as well as The Death Penalty, Juvenile Crime, and The Prison System.

Each Table of Contents surveys the coverage and viewpoint of each article in one or two sentences. A Glossary of acronyms and terms and a descriptive list of organizations connected with the topic are also provided, and each volume has the sources used and a Subject/Personal Name Index. Excerpts range from two to eight pages, short enough to be useful for students of varying ability; the paper is heavy and opaque. Social studies teachers with foreign policy, sociology, or contemporary issues courses as well as librarians serving secondary school or community college populations or the general public will find the content and the pro/con arrangement invaluable. Space is allowed for two additional annual supplements. Librarians will be pleased to note that "The viewpoints may be photocopied by library users for personal and/or non-commercial use."

The Overlook martial arts dictionary. By Emil Farkas and John Corcoran. New York, Overlook, 1983. xiii, 305p. illus. hardbound $16.95 (0-87951-133-8).

796.8'15'03 Martial arts—Dictionaries [CIP]   81-47415

This selective, specialized dictionary presents the more popular terms of martial arts, listed alphabetically letter by letter with pronunciation and language of origin. Good photographs accompany some definitions. Japanese entries are more numerous than Chinese or Korean, mainly due to the reluctance of many Chinese kung-fu masters to reveal information that they may regard as a betrayal of closely guarded secrets. This will be a useful book for school, public,

The Oxford companion to American literature. James D. Hart, compiler. 5th ed. New York, Oxford Univ. Pr., 1983. 896p. 24cm. cloth $49.95 (0-19-503074-5).
810'.9 American literature—Dictionaries | American literature—Bio-bibliography
[CIP] 81-22469

Students of American literature and librarians will rejoice in this fifth edition of a standard tool. Its format—always acceptable—has been improved; and it claims to include articles on "more than 240 authors" and "over 115" not separately discussed, if at all, in the fourth edition and "over 115" new summaries and "over 590" articles extensively revised. An overview of its pages and a detailed examination of several sections supports this claim: of about 325 articles in the first 47 pages, 26 are new and 39 revised, with 11 from the fourth edition dropped—that last figure cited suggesting that libraries with the fourth edition should retain it. Canadian material has been dropped, it now being the subject of a separate *Oxford Companion*. The Chronology, paralleling literary and general history, has been updated through 1982.

Coverage continues to be broad, with a high percentage of articles on topics other than authors or titles of belles lettres and other strictly literary matters. Particularly praiseworthy is continuing coverage of authors less talked about now than in their heydays. An interesting inclusion is articles on foreign authors, e.g., Dickens, in so far as they commented on America. Many ostensibly nonliterary articles include literary information, e.g., the one on Abraham Lincoln considers his portrayal in fiction, drama, etc., and articles on cities, universities, etc., refer to their literary associations. But some articles do not mention literature, e.g., those on Lyndon Johnson and on the Chautauqua movement: the rationale for their inclusion is implied in the term *companion,* viz., like dictionaries which include "encyclopedic" material, this book appears to be intended primarily as a *vade mecum,* as a resource for individuals lacking instant access to tools on aspects of American civilization other than literature. In any case, the *OCAL*'s continuing emphasis upon literature as an expression of general culture and upon books which, regardless of their present popularity or lack thereof, were in the past highly esteemed or were influential, may prove, for students of American literature, something of an antidote to approaches which limit attention to works valued today for their literary excellence and/or their relevance to problems now perceived to be urgent.

As an information storage and retrieval system, *OCAL* offers some not-so-pleasant surprises. Even those who sympathize with its overall emphasis may question the presence of more than 40 articles on works by Poe, 12 on books by Howells, 2 on works by Mary Austin, 7 on poems by Freneau, 9 on poems by Bryant—but only one on a work by Katherine Anne Porter (and that one by no means her best) and none at all on works by Eudora Welty. Nor is its cross-reference network perfect: thus, the article on Whitman cites articles on several of his poems but fails to cite the articles on "Song of Myself," "Out of the Cradle," and "Chanting the Square Deific."

But such deficiencies should not lead one to conclude (as did Paull F. Baum, some years since, concerning Tennyson's "Ulysses") that the *OCAL* represents the "triumph of rich color over bad drawing." Overall, it "works." Moreover, it is an absolute gold mine of useful information, carefully selected and thoughtfully interpreted. It is a tool which can, without exaggeration, be called "essential" to public and academic libraries as well as to personal collections. For more than 40 years, it has been virtually a one-person production: if ever a compiler of a reference tool deserved a lifetime-achievement award, it is James D. Hart.

The Oxford companion to American theatre. Compiled by Gerald Bordman. New York, Oxford Univ. Pr., 1984. vi, 734p. 24cm. cloth $49.95 (0-19-503443-0).
792'.0973 Theater—U.S.—Handbooks, manuals, etc. | Drama—Handbooks, manuals, etc.
[CIP] 83-26812

The Oxford Companion to the Theatre (1983) now has a companion, *The Oxford Companion to American Theatre,* compiled by Gerald Bordman, also author of two works on American musicals. Arranged in dictionary style with brief articles, this new work includes articles on personalities, acting schools and companies, theater-related subjects, and several hundred plays. According to its Preface the book intends to give a broad picture of the popular American stage. In fact, there are articles on all nonmusical American plays which have achieved New York runs of a prescribed number of performances (number varies according to chronological period) and for all musicals which usually had longer runs. Plays and musicals with less than the prescribed number of performances but of special interest are also included. There are articles on a number of foreign plays which had long runs or a special impact on the American stage. Articles vary in length depending upon the subject, e.g., plays usually have one-fourth of a page and important playwrights a full page. Related articles are cross-referenced. The work is quite comprehensive, and there is much on the history of American theater. There are brief articles on general topics, e.g., "Blacks in American Theatre and Drama," "Censorship in American Theatre," "Minstrel Shows," and "Dog Dramas."

The Preface admits to two areas of omission—some off-Broadway or more venturesome regional theater favorites and a number of rising young talents—believing that these do not belong to the theatrical mainstream. It also acknowledges that material is often difficult to unearth for figures who were important away from New York. Dates given apply to New York City unless otherwise stated. Thus *Children of a Lesser God,* which was first mounted in Los Angeles at the Mark Taper Forum, is described in terms of its New York premiere at the Longacre Theater without mention of the original production. Because of these stated policies, the work emphasizes traditional mainstream theater with a New York emphasis. The Board suggests that the next edition consider enlarging its scope to represent more accurately "American" rather than "New York" theater—which, of course, does predominate. As it is, this *Companion*'s stress on New York City and the mainstream is evident.

There are, however, some unexplained omissions: *The Desperate Hours,* which won a Tony in 1955, and its star Karl Malden, who also appeared in the original production of *A Streetcar Named Desire*; Brendan Behan and his *Borstal Boy,* also an award winner; David Mamet is included but not Jean-Claude van Itallie; and Kim Stanley, but not Kim Hunter.

Articles frequently quote critics, and some offer criticism on their own, e.g., the article on Tennessee Williams concludes: "His preoccupation with social degeneracy and homosexuality, which had heretofore been contained by his sense of theatre and poetic dialogue, overcame these saving restraints and lost him a public for the newer works." And the conclusion of the Liza Minnelli entry: "During the run of this last show it was said that she was not actually singing one song on stage but mouthing the words to a recording. She is popular in films."

Symbols identify winners of Pulitzer Prizes and New York Drama Critics Circle Awards, but winners of Tony Awards are not indicated except sometimes in the text.

Close in intention to this new *Oxford Companion* is Bronner's *Encyclopedia of the American Theatre, 1900–1975* (Barnes, 1980), which has Appendixes on awards and Broadway statistics. However, *The Oxford Companion to the American Theatre* is broader in scope, and it continues the honored tradition of the *Oxford Companions.* The Board recommends it for school, public, and academic libraries and hopes that future editions will be more catholic and less parochial in scope.

The Oxford companion to Canadian literature. General editor, William Toye. New York, Oxford Univ. Pr., 1983. xviii, 843p. 24cm. cloth $49.95 (0-19-540283-9).
810'.3'21 Canadian literature—Dictionaries | Canadian literature—Bio-bibliography
[Canadian CIP]

A welcome addition to the Oxford companions, this work updates and expands Norah Story's *Oxford Companion to Canadian History and Literature* and its *Supplement* (1967, 1973). William Toye, the general editor for the new companion, was also general editor for the *Supplement* and is editorial director of Oxford University Press in Canada.

Almost 200 contributors (including academics, translators, and librarians) have written 750 signed articles that cover Canadian literature (which, of course, includes works in both English and French). Arranged alphabetically, articles cover specific authors, titles (single works and periodicals), and genres, as well as general surveys. Happily, one finds such articles as *Collective Creations* (improvised theater), *Translations* (French to English and English to French), *Governor General's Literary Awards* (with a list through 1982), and six entries on regional literatures, in addition to a broad range of articles on fiction, poetry, drama, biography, folklore, science fiction, etc. Coverage is strong for the period since World War II. Some of the longer articles have separate bibliographic essays; all have bibliographic references cited within the article, and there are occasional critical references at the end of articles. There are numerous cross-references, including pseudonyms, and authors not treated individually but within other articles. Within articles, capitals are used to signal those terms treated elsewhere as individual entries.

The Oxford Companion to Canadian Literature is an extremely useful reference work for public and academic libraries.

The Oxford companion to the theatre. 4th ed. Edited by Phyllis Hartnoll. New York, Oxford Univ. Pr., 1983. 934p. 24cm. illus. cloth $49.95 (0-19-211546-4).
792'.03'21 Theater—Dictionaries [British CIP]

This new edition reflects changes in world theater since the publication of the third edition in 1967. Thus, it describes acoustics and sound, lighting, and fringe theater as well as more traditional subjects—actors, playwrights, country surveys, theaters, etc. The editors have added new material on American theater and its history and on some contemporary actors, writers, directors, and companies. It continues the survey of world theater that began with the first edition. For the first time, illustrations (more than 200 in black and white) have been added. Extensive bibliographies conclude the volume.

Each article has been checked for accuracy, and most have been rewritten. Entries generally are two paragraphs in length, although a few may be one or two pages. Other changes include resetting of the text for better readability.

Considering the 1983 imprint, some entries seem less than up to date, presenting events only through 1980 or 1981, if that. Names familiar to theatergoers are not found as entries, e.g., Tom Conti, Michael Bennett, Bob Fosse, and David Mamet. Some topics are not covered (e.g., the concept of national theater), or, if they are, the lack of a subject index makes finding the information well nigh impossible, despite the numerous cross-references. Nevertheless, this volume offers a great deal of information in a readable format. It belongs in reference collections of public, academic, and special libraries serving theater enthusiasts or students.

Paris Opéra: an encyclopedia of operas, ballets, composers, and performers: genesis and glory, 1671–1915. By Spire Pitou. Westport, Conn., Greenwood, 1983. xii, 364p. 24cm. cloth $45 (0-313-21420-4).
782.1'0944'361 Opera de Paris—History [CIP]   82-21140

This first of a planned four-volume set includes three features: a narrative story of the Paris Opéra from 1671 to 1982, heavily factual but engagingly written; an encyclopedic section for 1671–1715, with alphabetical entries ranging from roughly a hundred to a thousand words for the major productions, forms, composers, librettists, and performers of the opera and including bibliographies; and an Appendix that lists the repertory chronologically. Four more Appendixes list alphabetically about a thousand of the major singers and dancers from 1671 to the present. The plan is for three subsequent volumes to carry the encyclopedic section through the eighteenth, nineteenth, and twentieth centuries. The scholarship is occasionally rather ingenuous—for instance, the encyclopedic section includes an entry for J. S. Bach on the strength of Opéra performances of the twentieth century which used his music. The sources, while well documented, include neither *Loewenberg* nor the latest edition of *Grove*. While it seems likely that considerable archival source work was involved, there is no direct evidence of this; nor are any notable discoveries or new perspectives conspicuously announced. The book would seem appropriate mostly for comprehensive music and/or dance collections and primarily as a supplement to standard reference works and scholarly studies.

Peoples and places of the past: the National Geographic illustrated cultural atlas of the ancient world. Joan Tapper, editor. Washington, D.C., National Geographic Society, 1983. 242p. illus. maps. tables. 47cm x 33cm. cloth $69.95 (0-87044-462-X).
909.07 Civilization, Ancient | Civilization, Medieval [CIP]   83-2208

This lavishly illustrated, coffee-table-size book hardly classes as a reference work. Its plan is to illustrate, rather than explain, cultural and social achievements from the dawn of civilization to about the year 1500 of our era. All of the well-known monuments of history are pictured—the Palace of Knossos, the Roman Forum, the Alhambra, Mont-Saint-Michel, Stonehenge, Luxor, the Taj Mahal, the Great Wall, the Pyramids, and all the rest—in hundreds of magnificent photographs covering much that is best in human beings' achievements.

The text accompanying these fine pictures, though concise and omitting many details, is adequate to convey the sense of beauty, grandeur, or intricate artwork involved in the buildings, paintings, carvings, or other works illustrated.

Nor is the coverage confined to the world of art; social development, including such things as husbandry, hunting, the democratic process, economic and community life, sports, and religion—as well as the less desirable aspects of life such as war, conquest, and the destruction of fortresses—also accounts for a large portion of the book's content.

Many of the illustrations are imaginative drawings or paintings, done in the manner made familiar to readers of the *National Geographic*, illustrating such things as a family of primitive cave dwellers, or a group of Greek laborers building the Agora, or a Roman family living in their country house in Campania.

The reference value of this work is dependent largely on its ten-page, six-columned Index and on its excellent maps. With its very large (over 18-inch) full-page illustrations, this work will be highly valued as collateral reading for high school students or adults interested in archaeology, early history, anthropology, comparative civilizations, or the history of art. A classified Bibliography (following the topical organization of the book) cites many standard works on specific topics.

Reference librarians in public and school libraries should know about this fine work, even if they decide to shelve it elsewhere than with "reference books."

Perspectives of new music: an index, 1962–1982. By Ann P. Basart. Berkeley, CA 94709, P.O. Box 10034, Fallen Leaf Press, 1984. 127p. 21cm. paper $13.95 (0-914943-00-X).
780'.5 Perspectives of new music—Indexes | Music—20th century—History and criticism—Periodicals—Indexes [CIP]   83-82609

Although *Perspectives of New Music* (*PNM*) has been analyzed in *Music Index* since the journal began, Basart's compilation will be welcomed by those working in the field of contemporary music. The body of the work is an Author Index; 685 consecutively numbered entries in the Author Index are keyed to entries in the Index to Artistic Works and Subject Index. Prefatory material includes sample entries and cross-references (which are used freely throughout the Index) from each section with a detailed explanation of their content, as well as a statement of alphabetizing practice and an abbreviations list. While *PNM* regularly publishes two issues per volume, it is somewhat inconsistent in numbering so that the listing of volume and issue numbers with date of issue (p.vi) is helpful.

PNM publishes scores, poems, drawings, interviews, text compositions, book reviews, and evaluative articles. All are entered in the Author Index, with compositions (e.g., drawings, scores) also in the Index to Artistic Works. The Subject Index is detailed, including persons, institutions, and topics; headings are not necessarily those used by *Music Index*.

Major music libraries, particularly those supporting research in twentieth-century music, will want this inexpensive volume for its convenience and detail. Other academic and public libraries probably will find the indexing in *Music Index* to be adequate.

Peterson's annual guides/undergraduate study: four-year colleges, 1984. 14th ed. Princeton, N.J., Peterson's Guides, 1983. xx, 2,005p. 28cm. paper $11.95 (0-87866-215-4; ISSN: 0737-3163).
†378.7'025 Universities and colleges—U.S.—Directories | Universities and colleges—Canada—Directories | Education—Directories | Schools—Directories | Universities—Directories [OCLC]

This weighty (six pounds) edition covers accredited colleges in the U.S., Canada, and overseas in more than 2,000 densely printed pages. The alphabetically arranged College Profiles and Special Announcements section provides brief data on the student body, admissions, expenses, financial aid, academic programs, housing, and campus life for each of the institutions. From here users are occasionally referred to Messages from the Colleges, a two-page description provided by 647 of the institutions. These provide somewhat more information in essay form.

This material is supplemented by the Majors Directory (lists the colleges alphabetically under 435 subject majors), the Entrance Difficulty Directory (most difficult to noncompetitive) and Cost Ranges Directory (less than $2,000 to $10,000 and over).

To all of this add a tabular "Geographical Listing of Basic College Data and Test Score Ranges," advice on choosing a college, information on financial aid and standardized tests, and indexes to the Majors Directory and to the colleges.

Although other college directories are available, most high school and college libraries will want this reasonably priced directory to supplement the easier to use *Comparative Guide to American Colleges* and the briefer *Lovejoys.*

A pictorial history of Blackamericans. 5th rev. ed. By Langston Hughes, Milton Meltzer, and C. Eric Lincoln. New York, Crown, 1983. 380p. illus. 29cm. hardcover $19.95 (0-517-55072-5).

973'.0496 Afro-Americans—History [CIP]   83-7742

Since the first edition of this book in 1956, revisions have appeared periodically; all designed to keep up with changing attitudes and conditions of Afro-Americans.

The first edition was hailed by one reviewer as "popular history at its most popular with emphasis on little known facts." Another wrote that it was an "unforgettable record." Packing more than three centuries of Afro-American history into 316 pages *was* quite a feat, although the current edition has increased to 380 pages. The rather large number of black-and-white illustrations helps tell the story succinctly and picturesquely.

This edition demonstrates for our time how changing tactics and revisionist practices brought about such drastic changes in just a short while. There is very little change in the earlier portions of the book, but as one gets nearer to the last 20 years, great changes become apparent. New sections help to update the information to 1983. Excellent black-and-white pictures help to tell the story of the last two or three decades.

Some may resent the omission of many important and history-making names, but considering the authors' desire to provide a simplistic but authentic story, this can be understood. The few factual errors in the book appear minor, so the book remains an excellent teaching tool for novices.

An elaborate Index leads users to names, events, and organizations, some mentioned only casually. With the dearth of other available references, even elementary school users will have additional sources to which they can turn for further information.

A Pictorial History of Blackamericans remains a very good beginning book on Afro-Americans and should have a place in public, school, and college libraries.

Political dissent: an international guide to dissident, extra-parliamentary, guerilla and illegal political movements. Compiled and written by Henry W. Degenhardt. Detroit, Gale, 1983. xiii, 592p. (Keesing's Reference Publications) 26cm. cloth $90 (0-8103-2050-9).

322.4'2'025 Government, Resistance to—Societies, etc.—Handbooks, manuals, etc. [CIP]   83-14096

Based on information collected in Keesing's *Contemporary Archives,* this publication complements Keesing's *Political Parties of the World.* "Political dissent," as defined in this guide, "embrace(s) various kinds of political opposition outside the legal structure of the state concerned, i.e., forces which constitute an actual or potential threat to the stability of the state." The coverage, however, excludes one-issue groups (like antinuclear weapons movements) which "have not, so far, presented a challenge to the legal structure of the states in which they operate."

The book divides the world into nine regions under which individual countries are treated; the section Palestinian [Arab] Movements appears under *P* in the section on the Middle East. Included are governments in exile as well as dissenting indigenous political movements—whether to the right or left of the political spectrum. For each country entry, its political structure and organization and a brief political history are provided followed by the history, activities, and leadership of the dissenting groups and movements. Entries range from very brief (e.g., *Denmark*) to several pages (e.g., *Poland*). The volume concludes with a Select Bibliography and Subject/Name Indexes.

The author attempts to apply the "standards of accuracy, detachment, and impartiality" in discussing the controversial movements covered here. By and large, he is very successful, but there are instances where the concern for impartiality leads to understatement or qualification which blurs the truth. For example, in the section on Kampuchea (Cambodia), it is stated that Pol Pot and the Red Khmers "carried out the most radical communist policy program ever implemented anywhere, involving the forcible removal of the country's urban population to rural areas and mass executions of alleged reactionaries." True enough, but who would know that "most radical" means that an estimated 3 million civilians were annihilated? Similar meticulous care with words leads to similar misleading information in the articles on the IRA and the PLO. Also, the terms *left-wing* and *right-wing* are misleadingly applied in the sections on El Salvador, France, and Lebanon.

Overall, however, this is a comprehensive and very valuable survey of dissenting political movements not often covered in other reference sources. Appropriate for academic, large, and medium-sized public library reference collections covering politics and political science.

Politics in America: members of Congress in Washington and at home. Washington, D.C., Congressional Quarterly Pr., 1984. xix, 1,734p. 24cm. cloth $29.95 (0-87187-259-5).

328.73'073'025 U.S. Congress—Biography | U.S. Congress—Committees | Election districts—U.S.—Handbooks, manuals, etc. [CIP]   83-7640

Another valuable reference source on the U.S. Congress is this second biographical directory of members of the 98th Congress in action, the first, on the 97th Congress, having appeared in 1981. Although the work includes the same names as the *Congressional Directory* and its bare facts, the resemblance ends there; for the editors and many contributors have here provided assessments of "members (of Congress) as nearly as possible on their own terms," based on "watching senators and representatives in action, examining the public record of their work, and interviewing them about each other" (but not about themselves). CQ's fine reputation adds credence to the editors' claims that value judgments are avoided.

The lively and generally bias-free text is arranged by state, each prefaced with a statistical profile based on the 1980 census, a short biography of the present governor, and a map of congressional districts; then follows the profiles of the senators (seniors then juniors) and the representatives (by district number). Assessment of various activities of each member is augmented by lists of committee appointments, election returns, campaign finances, voting studies, key votes, and interest group ratings, e.g., AFL/CIO, as well as political and personal data on the member. A description of the relevant congressional district accompanies each profile. A list of memberships on all senate, house, and joint committees and an Index (to personal and geographic names) complete this informed record of who does what in Congress. The wealth of information, so conveniently arranged and indexed, recommends this volume to all types of libraries where current information on the states and on Congress is needed.

Pop culture mania: collecting 20th-century Americana for fun and profit. By Stephen Hughes. New York, McGraw-Hill, 1984. xii, 330p. 24cm. hardcover $17.95 (0-07-031114-5).

745'.075'0973 Collectibles | Antiques [CIP]   83-14941

Although collecting antiques, fine art, rare books, and furniture is a centuries-old passion, the avid pursuit of what has come to be known as "collectibles" is a much more recent phenomenon. In *Pop Culture Mania,* Stephen Hughes, a collector, dealer, and consultant on collectibles, traces the history of this particular form of collecting and relates it directly to a combination of nostalgia and hardheaded business sense. In the 1960s increasing numbers of new collectors saw the collectibles of earlier eras as somehow superior in design and craftsmanship to current products, and at the same time they recognized in them a hedge against galloping inflation. Hughes' book is a lively and informative discussion of this phenomenon, with practical advice on more than 50 areas of interest to collectors.

The book is divided into two sections. In part I the author provides historical perspective on the subject and gives detailed advice on buying and selling strategies. The various collectible forums, flea markets, garage sales, auctions, etc., are discussed, and the opportunities and possible pitfalls of dealing with each are indicated. This section also includes suggestions on opening a business, founding a collector's club, as well as displaying, storing, and insuring collections.

In part II, specific areas of collecting interest are discussed, including advertising items, board games, comic books, dolls, Hummels, maps, mechanical banks, photographs, teddy bears, toys, trade cards, World's Fair collectibles, etc. Each category is introduced with a very brief summary listing the value range of that particular collectible, the most popular items in the area, and sources of supply. Following this is a brief history of the collectible (generally two to five pages), a section on factors to consider in collecting, and then a listing of books, periodicals, and clubs that deal with the collectible. Following part II are several Appendixes listing general publications relating to collecting and bibliographical information on some collecting interests (buttons, clocks, jewelry, keys, etc.) not covered in the text of the work. A useful though far from complete Index concludes the volume.

At present there is a plethora of books on collecting and collectibles, with so-called price guides on everything from toothpick holders to cookie cutters. The Hughes volume stands out from these and may be considered the best overview of present-day collecting trends. Most price guides become quickly outdated, but Hughes avoids this danger by generally listing ranges rather than spot prices.

The book is also superior to most in the historical background that it provides. The volume's faults, the absence of illustrations and an occasional superficiality, presumably necessitated by space limitations, are greatly outweighed by its merits: conciseness of treatment, sound practical advice on all aspects of collecting, and good bibliographical references for those who wish to pursue a particular collecting interest. *Pop Culture Mania* is an excellent choice for public libraries.

Popular music: an annotated guide to recordings. By Dean Tudor. Littleton, Colo., Libraries Unlimited, 1983. xxii, 647p. 24cm. hardcover $65.(U.S.); $78 (elsewhere) (0-87287-395-1).

016.7899′13 Music, Popular (Songs, etc.)—U.S.—Discography [CIP]   83-18749

Popular Music provides an annotated survey of 6,200 significant, long-playing, and currently available recordings spanning the history of recorded popular music. This is an updated, revised, and combined edition of four separate volumes published in 1979 by Libraries Unlimited; two of the major divisions of the new book, Black Music and Jazz Music, correspond to the original volumes on those genres. The contents of the other two earlier volumes, *Grassroots Music* and *Contemporary Popular Music,* are covered in this volume under Folk Music, Mainstream Music, Popular Religious Music, and Rock Music.

According to the compiler, approximately 35 percent of the listings are for new recordings or for new reissues. About 20 percent of older recordings previously listed have been replaced by better reissues, while information has been updated for nearly 50 percent of the recordings carried over from the original volumes.

Selection has been based primarily on the significance of the recordings in terms of their influence, impact, and importance, rather than on the significance of the artist, although innovators are singled out for special attention. Entries include discographic information (name of artist or group, title, label, serial number, and country of origin if other than U.S.), and dates of the recordings are frequently, but not always, given. Consistent inclusion of dates would have enhanced the historical and reference values of the work. Similar albums are grouped together within subdivisions of the six major groupings.

Annotations averaging 300 words describe the recordings and explain their particular significance. Disks recommended for first purchase are identified with an asterisk.

The brief "Introduction to Popular Music" and introductions covering the origins, development, and characteristics of each major category and the principal subgenres make the volume usable as a reference source on popular music. Supplementary features include a 15-page Bibliography of key books arranged by broad subject categories and a list of 42 periodicals devoted to popular music with subscription information. A Performing Artists Index is also provided as well as a brief list of specialty stores/mail-order services.

Popular Music should prove useful to libraries and individuals both as an information source and as a buying guide for developing collections of recorded popular music.

Popular music: an annotated index of American popular songs, 1970–74 and 1975–1979. v.7 & 8. Edited by Bruce Pollock. Detroit, Gale, 1984. 24cm. cloth $55 each (0-8103-0845-2, v.7; 0-8103-0846-0, v.8).

784.5′00973 Music, Popular (Songs, etc.)—U.S.—Bibliography [CIP]   64-23761

This series, of which these volumes are a part, is intended to be a "selective, annotated list of significant popular songs of our times." Earlier volumes covered the years 1920 to 1970 in five- or ten-year segments. After an 11-year hiatus, the series is being continued by a new publisher (Adrian Press published v.6); the basic format remains unchanged. Song listings are based on LC data or sheet music and are arranged alphabetically by title within year of original copyright. For each title, names of composer(s) and lyricist(s) are given, as well as current publisher(s), the production in which each song was introduced, and by whom, if inaugurated on television, in the theater, or in films. Any other performers important to the song are also noted. Also noted are initial or best-selling recordings, with performer, recording company, and any other relevant data. Songs are cross-referenced from other years, as needed, e.g., for a song copyrighted 1977 but a best-seller in 1979, there is a reference from 1979 to 1977. A Supplement lists songs copyrighted earlier but of some significance in the period covered by the volume. Annotations are often only one line and indicate the reason(s) for inclusion, e.g., best-selling record, award nominee or winner, significant performer and/or place of introduction. Access is facilitated by Title and Lyricists & Composers Indexes; a list of publishers, with addresses, completes the book.

Each volume starts with directions for use, followed by a survey of popular songs of the period. *Popular Music* is intended to be practical, and surely popular usage of a list of songs so long after the fact is likely to be limited. And it is selective; so even the scholar is thwarted. *Popular Music* can be used to verify titles, track down published music, and trace creators and performers, and it will, therefore, be useful as a verification source in comprehensive collections.

Population information in nineteenth century census volumes. By Suzanne Schulze. Phoenix, Oryx, c1983 [1984]. ix, 446p. 29cm. cloth $65 (0-89774-122-6).

304.6′0973 U.S.—Census—Indexes | U.S.—Population—History—19th century—Sources—Indexes [CIP]   83-17380

For those unacquainted with the scope and variety of U.S. census publications, locating information therein can pose considerable problems. Complete sets of the census publications are uncommon, and the standard list, Henry J. Dubester's *Catalog of Census Publications, 1790–1940,* (1950) provides primarily bibliographic assistance. Suzanne Schulze's listing arranges the censuses for 1790 through 1890 in chronological order, and within each decennial census, the publications are arrayed by numbers assigned by Dubester. In addition to bibliographic information for each publication (including reprint information), Superintendent of Documents, Library of Congress, and Dewey classification numbers are provided, along with LC card numbers. The existence of microform copies also is indicated, and contents notes provide the detail required to locate specific statistics.

In place of an index, the endpapers contain a "Guide to Volumes—By Dubester Number." This consists of a subject listing of information by broad categories; for example, under "Social and Economic Characteristics," subjects range from citizenship and crime to slavery and transportation. Each subject included in a given census and volume is indicated according to Dubester number; users can then turn to the entries for individual publications to determine which tables are pertinent.

Several additional features enhance the book's value: a glossary of terms provides notes on data definitions and changes through the years; there is a list of states and territories with information on their changes of status in successive censuses; and also a list of Congressional Serial Set Volumes containing census information. A list of state censuses also is included, and the volume ends with blank forms for developing a union list of library holdings of census volumes.

Librarians considering acquiring this volume should be aware that it does not provide assistance with the manuscript censuses (or even indicate that as a result of a tragic fire the detailed schedules of 1890 are for the most part lost to posterity). The book does, however, promise to help those who want to find aggregate statistics in a complicated series.

Prefixes and other word-initial elements of English: a compilation of nearly 3,000 common and technical free forms, bound forms and roots that frequently occur at the beginnings of words, accompanied by a detailed description of each, showing its origin, meanings, history, functions, uses and applications, variant forms, and related forms, together with illustrative examples, the whole arranged in alphabetical order with entries numbered for easy reference, supplemented by a detailed index containing all sample words, variants, and etymological source words and roots described in the text. Laurence Urdang, editorial

director. Alexander Humez, editor. Detroit, Gale, 1984. 533p. 24cm. cloth $58.50 (0-8103-1548-3).
425 English language—Suffixes and prefixes | English language—Word formation [CIP] 83-20662

If all books had such expressive subtitles—and if all library catalogs recorded them in their entirety—how much more informative would the catalogs be! This dictionary of prefixes (in the broadest sense) may prove to be the last word on the subject, telling one all one wants to know and possibly more. Numbered entries—2,860 in all—tell, in more detail than do general dictionaries, how prefixes and other "initial" linguistic building blocks originated and how they function. An extraordinary Index cites not only all words and word elements discussed but also meanings (de facto translations)—"abnormally long," "dark blue color," "flexible rod-shaped organ," and "martyrdom of Christ," to cite but four instances.

Prefixes belongs in large public and academic library reference collections—which is not to imply that smaller libraries should not consider it: they should, as should builders of personal collections if they love to contemplate language.

The Prentice-Hall standard glossary of computer terminology. By Robert A. Edmunds. Englewood Cliffs, N.J., Prentice-Hall, 1985. xv, 489p. 28cm. cloth $34.95 (0-13-698234-4); paper $26.95 (0-13-698226-3).
001.64'03'21 Electronic data processing—Dictionaries | Computers—Dictionaries [CIP] 84-4765

This work contains more than 4,700 words. Its author has succeeded in being comprehensive, although he has excluded terms specific to a particular computer language. "All terms are described in a way that will make them as comprehensible as possible to the nontechnical reader without, at the same time, rendering the explanations useless to the information processing professional."

This work has large, easy-to-read print and makes good use of white space, allowing readers to scan with ease. Boldface print is used for guide words and defined terms. Key terms are highlighted with an asterisk. Entries may be acronyms, abbreviations, cross-references, or words followed by a parenthetical word "placing" its meaning, e.g., indicating its hierarchical position as: Access Time (*Processing) indicates that access time is used in connection with retrieval of data. A few biographies are given for persons influential in computer development.

An excellent resource for those working with computers and those attempting to read or converse intelligently about them, *The Prentice-Hall Standard Glossary of Computer Terminology* is suitable for almost any library.

The Prentice-Hall university atlas. Englewood Cliffs, N.J., Prentice-Hall, 1984. Various paging. maps. 32cm. cloth $27.50 (0-13-698259-X).
912 Atlases [CIP] 84-675201

This new edition of a standard atlas that has gone through 21 editions in Britain is now being made available in the U.S. The physical-political maps that make up the bulk of the 176-page map section are mostly reduced (8 by 9 ¾ inches on the page) and updated versions of those appearing in Prentice-Hall's *Great International Atlas* (1981), and these were prepared by the reputable British firm of George Philip. Nearly a third of the total are double page.

Relief is depicted on the attractive maps by means of layer tints enhanced by shading and selective use of contour lines; spot elevations are given in metric numbers. The type of projection, scale (both as a fraction and by a kilometer bar), and a color bar explaining the scheme of relief tints are provided in the margin. Railroads are shown as black lines, roads as red lines.

Good comparability of scale is maintained. Characteristic scales employed for particular continents run as follows: Europe, 1:2.5M; Asia and North America, 1:6M; Latin America and Africa, 1:8M. As one might expect, the British Isles get very detailed treatment, and while North America gets adequate coverage, it is by no means emphasized. A political map and a few thematic maps (geology, climate, population) normally precede the section of more detailed maps for a given continent, and a similar set of world maps occupies the first several pages of the map section.

The Index contains some 60,000 names and locates places on the maps by coordinates of latitude and longitude. A one-page list following the Index gives for principal places in China the Pinyin equivalent for the Wade-Giles form of name shown on the maps. Other supplementary features include a two-page guide to foreign geographical terms and a one-page list of recent place-name changes in Angola, Iran, Madagascar, Mozambique, Vietnam, and Zimbabwe. Special maps display in contrasting solid colors the French departments and, for the U.K., both the old counties and the new administrative divisions.

The thoroughly professional cartography, the detailed Index, and the reasonable price make *The Prentice-Hall University Atlas* a welcome addition to the group of world atlases currently available in the U.S. It is especially suitable for school, public, and home libraries.

The presidential-congressional political dictionary. Compiled by Jeffrey M. Elliot and Sheikh R. Ali. Santa Barbara, Calif., ABC-Clio, 1984. xiv. 365p. (Clio Dictionaries in Political Science, no.9) 24cm. hardcover $28 (0-87436-357-8).
320.473'03'21 Presidents—U.S.—Dictionaries | U.S. Congress—Dictionaries | U.S.—Politics and government—Dictionaries [CIP] 84-6316

This work provides readable explanations of more than 300 entities and terms that pertain to the offices of the president and the Congress. They are grouped in 12 broadly titled chapters—equally divided between the branches of government. Each entry, which averages about one page in length, begins with a paragraph or two on the historical "significance" of the term. For example, one can learn about such concepts as *apportionment, executive agreement, privileged legislation,* and *seniority system*. Chapter 3, "The Presidents," consists of brief sketches and assessments of their administrations. Chapter 5, "The Presidential Establishment," explains executive departments and major bodies such as the Council of Economic Advisors and the Office of Management and Budget.

In addition to cross-references following entries, an Index leads users to appropriate entries, as well as to names and terms found in the contents of various entries. Ten figures in the Appendix provide graphic depictions of official relationships and tabulations of data.

This expanded subject-arranged dictionary will be particularly useful to students. *The Presidential-Congressional Political Dictionary* will be appropriate for high school, college, and almost any general or political science reference collection.

The presidents: a reference history. Henry F. Graff, editor. New York, Scribner, 1984. xi, 700p. 29cm. cloth $65 (0-684-17607-6).
973'.09'92 (B) Presidents—U.S.—History | Presidents—U.S.—Biography | U.S.—Politics and government [CIP] 83-20225

The Presidents consists of 35 essays, each by a historian or a political scientist who is a specialist on the presidency of which he writes. The list of contributors includes such notables as Arthur S. Link on Woodrow Wilson, David Burner on Herbert Hoover, and Robert H. Ferrell on Harry S. Truman, and even these choices must have been difficult since more than one author is well qualified to write on several of the subjects. The volume ends with Jimmy Carter. In three cases (Harrison/Tyler, Taylor/Fillmore, and Garfield/Arthur) the subjects are combined in a single essay.

The essays range from 10 to 30 pages in length, roughly in proportion to the usually ascribed importance of the presidencies (for example, Franklin Pierce's administraton is treated briefly while Woodrow Wilson's receives the most extensive coverage). Each essay is a careful appraisal of the accomplishments and impact of the administrations, followed by a bibliography of the most important primary and secondary sources.

These essays represent a distillation of many years of scholarly experience and study and should be useful to both students and scholars. Written in a readable style, without the burden of scholarly documentation, they are suitable both for reference and general reading.

Prime-time television: a pictorial history from Milton Berle to "Falcon Crest." Compiled by Fred Goldstein and Stan Goldstein. New York, Crown, 1983. 384p. illus. 29cm. hardcover $24 (0-517-55071-7).
791.45'75'0973 Television braodcasting—U.S.—Pictorial works [CIP] 83-7804

Primarily a pictorial review presenting what was on television year by year from 1948 through 1982, *Prime-Time Television* covers the best as well as the worst, "the shows that made you laugh and those that made you cry, the series that made you wish TV was never invented and those that you wished would never go off the air." This nostalgic journey covers shows that appeared for as few as three weeks to record-breaking telecasts including such memorables as, "Arthur Godfrey's Talent Scouts", "Mr. Ed", "Peter Gunn," "77

Sunset Strip," and "Bonanza." Regular weekly series and specials, spectaculars, miniseries, made-for-television movies, and programs that made a major contribution to television history, even though not aired during prime time (e.g., "Howdy Doody" and "Saturday Night Live"), are also included. Each chapter covers one television broadcast season (September–August), with shows presented under the year first aired regardless of the length of their run. The brief text for each chapter generally refers to the most successful shows of the season or ones still being televised. Other shows for that season are covered by the over 2,000 black-and-white photographs that are used throughout.

Photographs are captioned with the show's name, first and last telecast dates of the original run, broadcast network, and the names of the performers and any guests appearing in the photograph. *Prime-Time Television* is an enjoyable browsing source, the Title/Performer Index makes it a good reference tool for hard-to-answer trivia questions. At the same time the book portrays the growth and evolution of American television over the past 35 years. Since complete credits for each show are not provided, the work is most suitable for public or school rather than academic libraries.

Print index: a guide to reproductions. Compiled by Pamela Jeffcott Parry and Kathe Chipman. Westport, Conn., Greenwood, 1983. xx, 310p. 24cm. cloth $35 (0-313-22063-8).
769'.016 Prints—Indexes | Prints—18th century—Indexes | Prints—19th century—Indexes | Prints—20th century—Indexes | Printmakers—Indexes [CIP]   83-12824

Print Index locates reproductions of fine art prints produced from the early eighteenth century through the mid-1970s by more than 2,000 graphic artists (primarily European and American). Sources indexed are limited to 100 monographs, exhibition catalogs, and collection catalogs "available at most museum, college, or large public libraries with art book holdings."

The body of the work (after a brief section of anonymous works) is arranged by artist. Information provided includes nationality and dates of artist when known, title of print, date, print technique employed, and the code for the "List of Books Indexed."

The Subject and Title Index provides such genre entries as *portraits, self-portraits, still lifes, nudes,* and theme entries, e.g., *love, mother and child,* and *seascapes* as well as access to those items with distinctive titles. The material is printed two columns to a page in rather small type which appears to be from a dot matrix printer and ranges from gray to heavy black.

There are incongruities of coverage due to the sources indexed, so one finds only a few prints listed for some prominent printmakers and 20 plus for lesser-known artists.

Despite limitations of format and sources indexed, *Print Index* should be a useful resource for librarians serving the general public as well as art students and art historians.

The private lives of English words. 1st ed. By Louis G. Heller, et al. Detroit, Gale, 1984. xxxi, 334p. 24cm. cloth $44 (0-8103-1012-0).
422'.03 English language—Etymology—Dictionaries [CIP]   84-8095

Articles half a page to a full page in length explain the histories and etymologies of some 400 English words. The articles eschew most of the technical vocabulary of linguistics in favor of a popular approach, treating words much as if they were people whose biographies were being written. Learned without being ponderous, the articles summarize philological controversies in an intelligible manner. The few technical terms included tend to be those describing processes of change which words can undergo. These processes are explained in the Foreword.

Except for some words discussed in a cluster with related terms, articles are arranged alphabetically. An Index (called List of Headwords) precedes the articles. In addition to this, an Index at the back of the book contains all headwords, cited variant forms, cited meanings, and types of linguistic changes. An Appendix lists the 400 words alphabetically and tells which processes of change each one illustrates. A second Appendix reverses this, listing the processes and the words illustrating them.

Because of its selectivity and its popular approach, *The Private Lives of English Words* cannot in justice be compared to the standard English etymological dictionaries by Eric Partridge, W. W. Skeat, and C. T. Onions. Rather its purpose is to entertain and stimulate the intellect as much as to inform. It succeeds in these roles. Anyone interested in words will find it impossible to resist extended browsing among these private lives made public. *The Private Lives of English Words* is ideal for high school and public libraries.

Psychocriticism: an annotated bibliography. Compiled by Joseph Natoli and Frederick L. Rusch. Westport, Conn., Greenwood, 1984. xxiii, 267p. (Bibliographies and Indexes in World Literature, no.1) 25cm. cloth $35 (0-313-23641-0).
016.801'92 Psychology and literature—Bibliography [CIP]   84-4689

As its Preface notes, coverage of *Psychocriticism* is "restricted . . . to articles and books" published 1969–82 "in which a fairly recognizable school or method of psychology is applied to literature." Works on characterization, mood, etc., which make "no reference to any formal psychology" are excluded. With its scope in mind, reference librarians in many public and academic libraries will find *Psychocriticism* an exceedingly useful finding aid. For further light on its orientation and scope, one should read its superb introductory essay, "A Survey of Psychocriticism."

The bibliography of 1,435 entries opens with generalia and is thereafter organized by period, then by literary author, then by author of secondary work. Annotations are excellent and are worth reading apart from particular literary investigations, i.e., as revelations of the many ways in which psychology and art illumine each other. Besides cross-references, there are efficient Subject and Author Indexes: the former focuses on topics, e.g., *sex roles,* as well as literary figures whose works are treated; the latter cites authors of secondary works.

Psychware: a reference guide to computer-based products for behavioral assessment in psychology, education, and business. Compiled and edited by Samuel E. Krug. Kansas City, Mo., Test Corp. of America; dist. exclusively to libraries in North America by Gale, 1984. xiv, 801p. 24cm. cloth $65 (0-9611286-5-8).
155.2'8 Behavioral assessment—Data processing—Catalogs | Psychodiagnostics—Data processing—Catalogs | Educational tests and measurements—Data processing—Catalogs | Vocational guidance—Data processing—Catalogs | Personnel management—Data processing—Catalogs [CIP]   84-16461

Psychware is a unique guide to nearly 200 computer-based tests utilized for assessing personality and behavior in the areas of psychology, education, and business. Most of the products listed, however, go beyond simple test scoring and may be described as "computer-based interpretation." By eliminating the possibility of clinician bias, these computer-based interpretations better ensure the statistical reliability of the tests.

The product list, which forms the body of the directory, is presented in alphabetical order by product name. For each item the following categorized information is supplied: name; supplier; product category, of which there are seven (Career/Vocational, Cognitive/Ability, Interest/Attitudes, Motivation/Needs, Personality, Structured Interview, and Utility); primary applications totaling seven (Behavioral Medicine, Clinical Assessment/Diagnosis, Educational Evaluation/Planning, Personal/Marriage/Family Counseling, Personnel Selection/Evaluation, Training/Development, and Vocational Guidance/Counseling); sale restrictions; and service type and cost. Then comes a description of the product and an actual sample of the product in reduced format. (The latter are sometimes so reduced that reading is difficult.)

Facilitating use of *Psychware* are five indexes: Product Title, Product Category, Product Application, Service, and Supplier.

Although *Psychware* is somewhat overwhelming at first glance, it is easy to deal with if one reads the Introduction, which is complete with definitions. Growing use of computers makes *Psychware* a very timely reference tool, and this should encourage use of the material listed. The realization that computer-based psychological testing provides greater reliability in test results and reduces computing time is bound to increase its use by educators and test administrators. For in-depth behavioral science collections.

Publishers directory, 1984–85. 2v. 5th ed. Linda S. Hubbard, editor; Monica M. O'Donnell, associate editor. Detroit, Gale, 1984. 1,729p. 29cm. hardcover $200 (0-8103-0412-0; ISSN 0742-0501).
†070.5'025 Publishers and publishing—U.S.—Directories | Publishers and publishing—Canada—Directories

Formerly entitled *Book Publishers Directory,* this new edition includes information on about 9,350 publishers in the U.S. and Canada, excluding only vanity presses and publishers listed in Bowker's *Literary Market Place.* The directory is descriptively subtitled "A Guide to More than 9,000 New and Established, Commercial and Nonprofit, Private and Alternative, Corporate and Association,

Government and Institution Publishing Programs and Their Distributors [Including] Producers of Books, Classroom Materials, Reports, and Databases." Utilizing information gathered from questionnaires, the numbered entries include some or all of the following information: name, address, telephone number, Standard Address Number, ISBN, CIP participation, principal officials, annual output for three years, total titles in print, brief description (including marketing activities and book sales volume), subject specialties, mergers, discount schedule, sales breakdown to various marketing segments, returns policy and address, imprints (divisions and subdivisions), and selected titles. Defunct and other publishers that did not answer queries are so designated. About 120 distributors also appear with relevant information in an added section.

The three Indexes are an invaluable part of the work. The first provides in one alphabetically arranged sequence the names of all publishing/distributing organizations and imprints covered by both the *Directory* and those listed in the 1983 issue of *Literary Market Place*. This provides effective access to the approximately 14,500 publishers in Anglo-America. The second and third Indexes provide a broad subject approach (*abortion* to *yoga*) and state/province by city listing (with addresses).

A unique work, *Publishers Directory* incorporates the features and quality that the Board has come to expect from the publisher. It will be exceedingly useful when libraries need to go beyond the more familiar, traditional publishing houses and organizations. It will suggest possibly overlooked sources on a wide array of topics. It should be especially useful in public and academic libraries.

Quantities and units of measurement: a dictionary and handbook. By J. V. Drazil. London, Mansell; Weisbaden, Brandstetter; dist. in the U.S. and Canada by H. W. Wilson, 1983. 313p. 22cm. paper over boards $25 (3-87097-117-7 Brandstetter; 0-7201-1665-1).
†530.8′03 Units—Dictionaries | Physical measurements—Dictionaries | Weights and measures—Dictionaries | Physics—Tables [OCLC]

This second edition of a combined dictionary/handbook of physical measurements is intended for use by scientific and technical students and professionals. The text is divided into three parts: a dictionary of units of measurements, their symbols, and abbreviations; a dictionary of quantities and selected constants; and symbols for denoting quantities and constants. In the chapters appearing before the main text, there is information on the arrangement of entries and the types of data found under the entries in each section. There is also a short chapter on the symbols and abbreviations used in the text and another on systems, units, expressions used in names of units, and prefixes and their symbols. Additional information is found in four appendixes: definitions of SI units (International System of Units), table of units used in the U.S. and the U.K., recommended values for fundamental constants, and a bibliography of international and national standards relating to units and quantities.

Cross-references are found throughout the text referring from French or German terms to their English equivalents, from abbreviations to the full term, and to terms with the same meaning. *See also* references are used for related terms. There are two indexes, one French, the other German. Each lists in alphabetical order the French or German equivalent of names of all quantities and constants in the text. Libraries which serve physical scientists and engineers should acquire *Quantities and Units of Measurements*.

The quotable woman: from Eve to 1799. By Elaine Partnow. New York, Facts On File, 1984. 24cm. hardcover $24.95 (0-87196-307-8).
082′.088042 Women—Quotations | Quotations, English [CIP] 82-15511

Elaine Partnow, self-styled "inveterate quote plucker" has extended the time range of *The Quotable Woman: 1800–1981*, to include 724 women from Eve to Mrs. Trollope in this new companion volume. Sources are cited for each quotation, and explanatory notes are added. All quotations are in English, often in translation. The chronological arrangement by birth date allows users to contrast the seventeenth-century Brilliana Harley, who urged her son "Do exercise, for health can no more be had without it," with Violante do Céu, who spoke dolefully of "the end which ends with no way out." Typically, Anne Bradstreet observed that "man at his best is vanity." Many women are represented by a number of quotations, including Aphra Behn who said pithily, "She's a chick of the old cock." Women of the Renaissance are well represented by more than 1,000 quotes.

A Biographical Index briefly identifies the quotable women while a Subject Index reveals a diversity of subjects in its copious cross-referenced entries. This companion is a unique addition to myriad quotation books and will be welcomed in public and college libraries.

Rand McNally atlas of the United States: its people, land, and economy. Chicago, Rand McNally, 1983. 192p. illus. maps. 39cm. hardcover $40 (0-528-83099-6).
912 U.S.—Maps [OCLC] 83-61911

Rand McNally contemporary world atlas. Chicago, Rand McNally, 1984. 224p. illus. maps. 28cm. paper $8.95 (0-528-83146-1).
912 Atlases [OCLC] 84-60927

Reader's Digest wide world atlas. Pleasantville, N.Y., Reader's Digest; dist. by Rand McNally, 1984. 240p. illus. maps. 39cm. cloth $29.95 (0-528-83148-8).
912 Atlases [CIP] 78-65321

The maps of the states that form the core of the first atlas in this group come from the "Cosmo" series used in a standard line of Rand McNally world atlases. Their legibility and visual appeal have been much enhanced here by the introduction of a fresh color scheme and a more effective rendering of relief by means of light shading. Facing each state map is a page containing descriptive text and a set of basic data, a bar graph in color depicting the economy in terms of the number of people employed and the dollar value of major sectors, and a color photograph of a picturesque scene. Two inset-size maps portray land use and some distinctive feature of the particular state, e.g., for Washington, volcanic forces; other types of color illustration, such as graphs, are sometimes substituted for the second inset map. A set of five double-page essays along similar lines on the major regions of the country precede the main state section. An Index with more than 40,000 entries completes the atlas. School, public, and academic libraries will find this a useful atlas.

The 1984 edition of the *Family World Atlas* (one of the "Cosmo" group) is now available in paperback—a fact which the title of the paper version (*Contemporary World Atlas*) fails to point out. For comments on *Family*, cf. *RBB*, Sept. 1, 1983. Individuals and libraries with the *Family World Atlas* may ignore the paperbound version.

The *Wide World Atlas* is now available in an updated edition. The 52 double-page physical/political maps are a selection from the superb series developed for the *International Atlas* and are supplemented by sets of maps that have appeared in various other Rand McNally atlases: physical maps of the continents; maps of metropolitan areas at 1:300,000; environmental maps of the continents; a set of thematic maps; and ocean floor maps. An Index containing some 35,000 entries completes the atlas; this relatively sparse Index limits the usefulness of the atlas as far as library reference purposes are concerned, but in other respects this is a fine atlas. One particularly noteworthy feature is the use of a very limited number of carefully matched scales (mostly 1:3M, 1:6M, and 1:12M) for the main map set, making for unusually good comparability among maps. Also included in this atlas are six pages of tabular data. School, public, and academic libraries should consider purchase.

Rand McNally family world atlas. Chicago, Rand McNally, 1984. 32A, 224p. maps. 29cm. hardcover $12.95 (0-528-83145-3).
†912 Atlases [OCLC] 84-60927

The core features of this new edition of one of the standard atlases in the Rand McNally line follow the arrangement and format found in the 1981 "Census edition" (cf. *RBB*, Sept. 1, 1983): an 89-page set of political maps; a 59-page section of data tables for the world and the U.S.; and an Index containing some 30,000 entries. Map coverage emphasizes North America, with most states and Canadian provinces getting full-page treatment.

The maps do not show relief, and scale is indicated only by mile and kilometer bars in the lower margins. Railroads are shown but not highways. A page preceding the map section explains the symbols used and the alphanumeric grid-reference system employed in the Index.

The statistics section is in two parts: world data and comparisons (including population figures for all urban centers of 50,000 or more), and U.S. data (including population figures for some 20,000 places, arranged by state). Unlike the 1981 tables, these U.S. tables provide the final 1980 Census totals.

The major change with this edition occurs in the separately paged preliminary material, which is new to the *Family World Atlas* and also represents a sizable reduction from the 1981 edition's 96 pages. The front matter now consists of a set of thematic maps (half- or quarter-page) for each of the continents, depicting such matters as annual rainfall, vegetation, population, economic resources, energy, landforms, and natural hazards. (These thematic maps first appeared in the 1982 edition of *Rand McNally Goode's World Atlas*.) Preceding the group of thematic maps for each particular continent is a two-page spread which combines a short descriptive text with a "global view" of the as-seen-from-space variety and an inset-size map showing just the individual countries in contrasting solid colors. Along with the substitution of this new and much less extensive preliminary section comes a reduction in price: this edition costs four dollars less than the 1981 Census edition. Libraries with the 1981 edition may want this newer one for the final Census figures; otherwise, the older edition will probably be just as useful as before.

The Random House thesaurus. College edition. Edited by Jess Stein and Stuart Berg Flexner. New York, Random House, 1984. 812p. thumb index. 25cm. hardcover $14.95 (0-394-52949-9).
423'.1 English language—Synonyms and antonyms [OCLC]   84-4914

This collection of synonyms and antonyms is a de facto revision of *Reader's Digest Family Word Finder*, published in 1975 and reviewed in these pages July 15, 1976. The revision appears to expand the original by more than 10 percent more entry terms (to a claim of about 11,000) and by as many as 10 percent more synonyms and antonyms for entry terms carried over. However, it drops the numerous notes on word origins, pronunciation, spelling, etc., which are an attractive feature of the original—which is still in print.

The revision, like the original, is alphabetically arranged, provides well-devised illustrative sentences, separates shades of meaning, provides some labels (e.g., *slang*), and arranges alternatives (within meaning) by presumed frequency. Neither the original nor the revision discusses, i.e., discriminates among, alternatives in the sense in which *Webster's New Dictionary of Synonyms* so brilliantly does.

The Random House Thesaurus should certainly be considered for school, public, and academic libraries and for individual purchase. In choosing between it and its predecessor, one should consider the extent to which one's collection already covers etymology, usage, and the like; for this reason all but the smallest libraries will probably prefer *The Random House Thesaurus*, whereas individual purchasers may prefer *Reader's Digest Family Word Finder*—which offers somewhat less in the way of synonyms and antonyms but more on other linguistic phenomena.

Rare books, 1983–84: trends, collections, sources. Edited by Alice D. Schreyer. New York and London, Bowker, 1984. x, 581p. 24cm. cloth $39.95 + shipping and handling (0-8352-1756-6).
†011.44 Rare books | Rare books—Bibliography | Book collecting [OCLC]

This is the first volume in a series that will provide year-in-review essays and directory information on rare books and manuscripts. Similar in format to *The Bowker Annual*, it is intended for the specialized community of collectors, dealers, and rare book librarians. There are five sections: "Reports from the Rare Book and Manuscript Field," "Review of Bibliographical Scholarship and Publishing," "Issues and Programs in the News," "Educational Opportunities," and "Directory of Collections and Sources." The first three parts are essays; the last two are directories. The 19 original essays are written by a diverse and well-qualified group of subject experts. Their short reports cover the 1983 calendar year and are consistently articulate and informative. The introductory essay gives an overview of the antiquarian book trade and is followed by survey chapters for autographs and manuscripts, the auction year, private collecting, and institutional collections in the U.S., Canada, and Great Britain. Part II is a review of bibliographical scholarship and publishing, with articles by G. Thomas Tanselle, Daniel Traister, and Peter M. VanWingen. The work concludes with chapters on automation, trends in preservation, the Oberlin conference on theft, tax incentives, and programs such as those at Columbia University, the American Antiquarian Society, and the Center for the Book. There is a general Index for the essays.

Much of *Rare Books, 1983–84* consists of directory information. The auctioneers and appraisers sections are taken from *American Book Trade Directory*. A selected list of rare books and manuscripts libraries is arranged by state and province and includes information on staff, holdings, subjects, published guides, and access policy.

Other chapters list relevant library school courses, important fellowships and lectures, and professional associations.

Approximately one-half of this volume is devoted to a directory (culled from *American Book Trade Directory*) of nearly 2,000 dealers in rare books and manuscripts. It is the best single quick-reference source of names of antiquarian dealers in the U.S. and Canada. Arrangement and format are identical to the parent volume with the important addition of an Index of specialties.

This new series will be widely acquired by those involved with the antiquarian book trade, but nearly all libraries will find the directory of booksellers useful for acquisitions work and reference desk referrals.

Reader's Digest consumer adviser: an action guide to your rights. Pleasantville, N.Y., The Reader's Digest Assn., 1984. 416p. 24cm. hardcover $21.50 (0-89577-180-2).
640.73 Consumer education [CIP]   84-2044

Designed to offer guidance for almost every consumer good or service, from the supermarket purchase to real estate and from selecting a lawyer to utilizing credit, this *Adviser* intends to make the reader an "informed, prudent buyer of goods and services." It also tells readers how to find the direct route to the relevant federal, state, or local government agency.

The editors of *Reader's Digest* and the Maxwell Associates acknowledge source material from such agencies as the American Arbitration Association, the Automotive Information Council, the National Better Business Bureau, and several consumer-advocate agencies. Even though the text is up-to-date, the editors caution readers to check laws and regulations listed before using them, and they provide the appropriate addresses.

The work begins with a chapter of general information on consumer rights, followed by others on wise buying habits, "frauds, scams and rip-offs," homes, automobiles, door-to-door solicitation, service businesses, banks and credit, insurance and investments, leisure-time activities, professional services, complaint routes, and going to court, etc. The brief Index is adequate; cross-references are few.

The highly readable format uses color to highlight areas of special information including "Buyer Beware" and "Consumer Alert" hints. Addresses of the many agencies of particular help to consumers are listed in appropriate chapters. Many other titles cover essentially the same information, e.g., Richard George's *New Consumer Survival Kit* (1978); John Strossel's *Shopping Smart . . .* (1980); and the Better Business Bureau's *Guide to Wise Buying* (1980). This one has the advantage of being more current and is easy to use. It is a good buy for families and for public and school libraries, especially in schools which offer consumer education classes.

Reader's Digest 101 do-it-yourself projects. Pleasantville, N.Y., Reader's Digest [c1983, 1984]. 384p. illus. 29cm. hardcover $25.50 (0-89577-163-2).
684 Handicraft | Do-it-yourself work [CIP]   82-61581

Many do-it-yourself project books contain a collection of weird, useless, and out-of-date projects that most individuals would ignore. It is refreshing, therefore, to find a book such as this that includes useful and decorative projects. Projects range from making all kinds of furniture, cabinets, and objects and building picket fences or brick barbecues to laying out brick walks or rock gardens. Degrees of complexity in doing the projects are indicated by listings in the front of the book under one of three headings—apprentice, journeyman, and craftsman. For each project, a picture of the final item is included with a narrative instruction followed by schematics, lists of the tools, parts, and materials needed; and complete step-by-step narrative and illustrative instructions. All 101 finished projects are presented in color pictures. *Reader's Digest 101 Do-It-Yourself Projects* is a necessity for do-it-yourselfers, and it will be a useful circulating book for school and public libraries. Schools that have 4–H, Future Farmer, and Future Homemaker groups will certainly find this to be a useful source of ideas.

A reference companion to the history of abnormal psychology. 2v. By John G. Howells and M. Livia Osborn. Westport, Conn., Greenwood, 1983. 1,056p. illus. 24cm. cloth $95/set (0-313-22183-9).
616.89 Psychology, Pathological—Miscellanea | Psychology, Pathological—Early works to 1900—Miscellanea [CIP]   80-27163

John G. Howells, chair of the Section in the History of Psychiatry of the World Psychiatric Association, and M. Livia Osborn have compiled this delightful *Reference Companion to the History of Abnormal Psychology* for writers, researchers, and students. Alphabetically arranged letter by letter, giving many cross-references and providing bibliographical citations for further reading, the *Reference Companion* presents a fascinating history of the field in short articles. The more than 4,200 entries include concepts; diseases; persons; mythological, literary, and biblical characters; publications; hospitals; operas; associations; drugs; etc.—anyone or anything thought at one time to be connected in any way with abnormality, "the unusual as well as the frankly pathological." Definitions vary from one sentence to almost a page in length; the majority fall in between. Most entries have *q.v.*'s, *see*, or *see also* references to other terms to give further information and to broaden the range of the definition. In addition to these, an Appendix lists entries by 43 subject categories: e.g., Clinical States, Concepts and Theories, Instruments and Contraptions, Suicide; and an Index lists each term and refers to other entries in which that term is mentioned. With these multiple aids one should be able to find all entries relating to one's special interest. There are 16 clearly reproduced black-and-white illustrations depicting historical conceptions of madness or apparatus to treat it.

Almost every entry has a bibliographic citation; book citations give only author or editor, date, and title; journal citations are fuller. Some citations are to seminal works and classics; others are to more general compendia and anthologies. The entries are written in an engaging style ("We have deliberately paused on any unusual, intriguing, or humorous note; flesh has been added to bare bones, without deviating from the truth"). *A Reference Companion to the History of Abnormal Psychology* is fun for browsing; it also provides information about abnormal psychology under a broad and detailed range of topics and in a different manner than one finds in other dictionaries or encyclopedias of psychology and psychiatry. General readers and trivia buffs will have a field day, but students and researchers will also find this two-volume set full of useful facts and information.

A reference guide to modern fantasy for children. [By] Pat Pflieger; Helen M. Gill, advisory editor. Westport, Conn., Greenwood, 1984. xvii, 690p. 24cm. cloth $65 (0-313-22886-8).
823'.0876'099282 Fantastic fiction, English—Dictionaries | Fantastic fiction, American—Dictionaries | Children's stories, English—Dictionaries | Children's stories, American—Dictionaries [CIP]   83-10692

This is an interesting and complete guide to the 36 authors and approximately 100 books selected for inclusion. It employs brief-entry dictionary format to describe authors, book titles, major and minor characters, places, and magical objects. Plot synopses and descriptions of characters are good, and the author entries are also a strong feature, providing biographical information, themes, a well-prepared bibliography of primary works, and a selection of the best available literature covering these works. Unfortunately, illustrators are not included, although an Appendix contains a listing of illustrators of the first editions of titles discussed.

In an interesting Preface the author explains the purpose of the work and why certain authors (Charles Dodgson, L. Frank Baum, A. A. Milne) and a primary fantasy genre—science fiction—are not included. The author has selected fantasies concerning place, time, conflict between good and evil, incredible beings, and animals. Works selected "represent a century crucial in the development of fantasy as an art form."

This good, one-volume survey of some of the major writers of fantasy for children complements Ruth N. Lynn's bibliography, *Fantasy for Children* (New York: Bowker, 1983) and secondary sources such as Zena Sutherland's *Children and Books* (Glenview, Ill.: Scott, Foresman, 1981).

Reference sources for small and medium-sized libraries. 4th ed. Compiled by the Ad Hoc Committee for the Fourth Edition of Reference Sources for Small and Medium-sized Libraries, Reference and Adult Services Division, The American Library Association. Jovian P. Lang and Deborah E. Masters, coeditors. Chicago, American Library Association, 1984. xvi, 252p. 26cm. paper $20 (0-8389-3293-2).
011'.02 Reference books—Bibliography [CIP]   84-6513

This latest edition of a respected work will be welcomed in school, college, and public libraries—especially, perhaps, in the last. It lists and describes 1,788 titles—considerably more than the third edition's 1,046—with, according to the ALA press release, more than half of them being new titles or new editions. Its Preface reports: "The scope of the book was expanded to include reference materials for children and young adults as well as adults; sources in other formats such as microforms and databases were added, and out-of-print sources considered to be basic reference sources were included." The resulting compilation stands somewhere between Sheehy's *Guide to Reference Books* and Cheney and Williams' *Fundamental Reference Sources*, being far more selective than the former and covering a wider range of specialized tools than the latter: so far as general libraries serving primarily adult clienteles are concerned, all three deserve the labels "essential" and "indispensable," whether looked upon as selection tools or as finding aids and switching centers.

The arrangement is, as in earlier editions, classified along lines suggestive of Dewey, e.g., Language separated from Literature by Science and Technology, Art, Music, etc., Major sections carry bylines, e.g., *Philosophy, Religion*, and *Ethics* by Janet Sheets and *Political Science and Law* by Wiley J. Williams. Sections and subsections include succinct and useful introductions. Entries include standard bibliographical and order data, and each is annotated—annotations being brief and mainly descriptive, with those features cited which are most relevant to reference work; such evaluative commentary as is provided is perceptive. Items particularly suited to use by children and/or adolescents are labeled *J* and/or *Y*. There are occasional cross-references, e.g., in Mythology and Folklore, a reference to *Index to Fairy Tales...*, listed and described in Indexes to Collections, under Literature. The volume opens with a Table of Contents and concludes with an Index to authors and titles (including ones mentioned in annotations but not separately listed). The Table of Contents is sufficiently detailed to compensate, at least in part, for the lack, in the Index, of topical headings; still, addition of such headings is surely something to consider for the next edition.

Inevitably, selectivity leads to exclusions open to question, e.g., Glaister's *Glossary of the Book* and the *Random House College Dictionary*; but selection is generally superior. Similarly, classification can lead to controversy. A subclass on linguistics *per se* would have made room for *Encyclopedic Dictionary of the Sciences of Language*, now awkwardly ensconced among such titles as *Longman Dictionary of English Idioms*. The Literature class mingles indexes to criticism broad in scope, e.g., *Articles on American Literature*, with ones as specific as Bevington's *Shakespeare*. And there are apparent misplacements, e.g., Rosenberg's *Genreflecting* among dictionaries of literature (not guides to literary types) and Field's *Special Collections in Children's Literature* among such analytic indexes as *Short Story Index*. Basically, however, the classification works—and one suspects that this is a tool more likely to be used by staff or with the help of staff (familiar with its structure) than by one-time inquirers proceeding without assistance.

The ALA Reference and Adult Services Division is to be commended for its continuing sponsorship of an important bibliographical enterprise.

Reference sources in library and information services: a guide to the literature. [Compiled by] Gary R. Purcell with Gail Ann Schlachter. Santa Barbara, Calif., ABC-Clio, 1984. xxvi, 359p. 24cm. cloth $45 (0-87436-355-1).
011'.02 Reference books—Library science | Reference books—Information science | Library science—Bibliography | Information science—Bibliography [CIP]   83-19700

Purcell and Schlachter, two reference literature authorities, have prepared an annotated guide to reference publications covering the field of library and information services. Although there are numerous sources which provide limited coverage of this subject (e.g., *American Reference Books Annual, Guide to Reference Material,* and *Guide to Reference Books*), there has been no single comprehensive reference source on the topic until now.

The criteria for inclusion are carefully developed and clearly defined in the Introduction. Only works which are primarily concerned with library and information services are listed, and the principal types of reference publications are included. With few exceptions, the titles are in English and the time period covered is the twentieth century.

The volume is divided into two major parts. Part I is arranged by type of publication (bibliography; terminology; encyclopedias, yearbooks, handbooks, and manuals; biographical and membership directories; directories of libraries and archives; and sources of library statistics). Part II covers more than 100 special services and operations (e.g., acquisitions, buildings, map libraries). Within each part the sections are further subdivided according to format or geographic coverage.

Reference Sources in Library and Information Services contains more than 1,000 descriptive/evaluative annotated entries. They vary in length from two or three lines for some state library directories to nearly an entire page for major reference works. Entries contain extensive cross-references; separate Author, Title, and Geographic Indexes are provided as well as a detailed Contents.

Reference Sources in Library and Information Services is an accurate, current, and reasonably comprehensive guide to the subject. It is well organized and should prove valuable to practicing librarians as well as to library school educators and students.

Research guide to philosophy. Compiled by Terrence N. Tice and Thomas P. Slavens. Chicago, American Library Association, 1983. xii, 608p. (Sources of Information in the Humanities, no.3) 24cm. cloth $40 (0-8389-0333-9).
107 Philosophy—Study and teaching—History | Philosophy—Historiography [CIP] 83-11834

Tice and Slavens, professors of philosophy and library science respectively, at the University of Michigan, have created a tool which belongs in all academic libraries, in some public libraries, and in the personal collections of philosophy students. Reference and collection development librarians will find it helpful as an updating mechanism and as a buying guide.

Basically, it consists of bibliographical essays (by Tice) surveying problems and suggested solutions, i.e., philosophy and commentary relating thereto, with 30 such essays grouped under two headings, *The History of Philosophy* and *Areas of Philosophy*. The *History* section consists of 13 bibliographical chapters, starting with general works and proceeding from "Ancient Philosophy" to the present, with 7 of the 13 on twentieth-century developments. The *Areas* section has 17 such chapters, some (like "Logic," "Epistemology," and "Ethics") on "pure" fields, others (like "Philosophy of Science," "Philosophy of History," and "Philosophy of Education") on applications to various areas of human endeavor. Throughout, Tice's style is readable, with complex ideas plainly set forth. His coverage is balanced; his tone, dispassionate.

The essays are followed by *Reference Works,* a 13-page, beautifully annotated list (by Slavens) of 25 bibliographies, 13 encyclopedias and dictionaries, three digests and handbooks, three directories, one index to philosophical dissertations, and, surprisingly, eight series (e.g., Boston Studies in the Philosophy of Science). Selection is good; it supplements (as it is supplemented by) that of Rogers' *Humanities* (ALA, 1979). Slavens' annotations should prove, on the whole, more helpful than those in Sheehy's *Guide to Reference Books* (1976) or Walford's *Guide to Reference Materials* (1981). Last come two indexes (Tice's work): an Author-Title Index, remarkably thorough and covering both primary and secondary sources; and a Subject Index, comprehensive in coverage and rich in subdivision and in provision of cross-references. Both indexes will facilitate access to the contents of Tice's bibliographical essays.

Research guide to the arid land of the world. By Stephen T. Hopkins and Douglas E. Jones, with the technical assistance of John A. Rogers. Phoenix, Oryx, 1983. vi, 391p. 29cm. cloth $74.50 (0-89774-066-1).
016.33373 Arid regions—Bibliography | Arid regions—Research—Bibliography [CIP] 83-42500

The purpose of this annotated bibliography is to gather and evaluate "bibliographies, directories, abstracting journals, statistical sources, online databases, atlases and gazetteers deemed most useful to researchers in the physical and human geography of the world's drylands."

Covering 120 countries and their various political subdivisions and encompassing 28 fields of study, this research guide is intended as an "interdisciplinary tool of greatest value to researchers outside their professional specialties."

It is organized by geographic region/country and includes a black-and-white political outline map for each region; a geographic summary; an aridity measurement chart; and a classified, briefly annotated Bibliography of research sources with appropriate cross-references for each country. Each entry is numbered consecutively, and annotations are largely descriptive rather than evaluative (database sources list vendors). Two Appendixes and two Indexes follow the main text. The Appendixes define technical terms used in the charts and list sources used to prepare the work. One Index lists authors of sources cited in the Bibliography; the other is a subject index, listing the types of reference tools and fields under which appear the geographic regions and countries.

Researchers from many disciplines (botany, climatology, anthropology, and women's studies—to name a few) will find this to be an effectively organized and comprehensive bibliography and an excellent starting point in work dealing with the vast drylands of the world.

Research on adolescence for youth services: an annotated bibliography on adolescent development, educational needs, and media, 1978–1980. Edited by Gerald G. Hodges and Frances Bryant Bradburn. Chicago, American Library Assn., 1984. 148p. 23cm. paper $15 (0-8389-3297-5).
016.3052'35 Youth—U.S.—Bibliography | Youth—Canada—Bibliography | Mass media and youth—Bibliography | Youth—Books and reading—Bibliography | Education, Secondary—Bibliography | Adolescent psychology—Bibliography [CIP] 83-25785

Compiled by the Media and Young Adult Subcommittee of the Research Committee of the ALA's Young Adult Services Division, this is the third volume of an ongoing bibliographic project. The two previous, *Media and the Young Adult: A Selected Bibliography, 1950–1972* (ALA, 1977) and *1973–1977* (ALA, 1981), when combined with this volume, provide summaries of research from 1950 to 1980 related to adolescence—defined as those in grades 7–12 or ages 12–18.

Articles selected from 27 "core journals and abstracts" were considered for inclusion if the research was applicable to professionals concerned with: "the factors that influence adolescents' needs for information; the methods adolescents use to seek and process information; and the improvement of the quality of services and information accessible to youth." The first 219 entries are divided into five broad categories: Psychological Development; Adolescent Sociology; Education; Reading; and Media (Media Characteristics; Media Influence and Preferences; and Media in Instruction); in each, items are alphabetical by author. Each category, with the exception of Media Influence and Preferences, contains both reviews of research and research studies, each providing a complete citation and thorough annotation. More than 100 dissertations and theses, grouped into the same general categories, are listed but not annotated. Subject and Author Indexes conclude the work.

This selective guide is useful from a historical/academic perspective, but like all too many sources published for use in education, the value of the information is by now dated. In our rapidly changing society, to rely on research four to six years old (such as a 1978 report on influences on career decisions; a 1979 report on adolescent sexual behavior; or a 1980 report on racial attitudes and perceptions of black television characters) to (as stated by the editors) "design meaningful programs for adolescents" would be a mistake. A useful tool for academicians, this selective compilation will be of limited value to teachers and librarians serving today's adolescents.

Revistas: an annotated bibliography of Spanish language periodicals for public libraries. Compiled by Bibliotecas Para La Gente Periodical Committee. Berkeley, University of California, 1983. 31p. (Chicano Studies Library Publications Series, no.9) 27cm. paper $5 (0-918520-07-X).
†016.0561 Spanish language—Periodicals—Bibiography [OCLC]

Fifty-nine Spanish-language periodicals are evaluated in this guide. Provided for each are date, edition, frequency, place of publication and publisher, U.S. distributor, price, recommendation code, annotation, and major subject heading. Four categories of ratings (highly recommended, recommended, additional, and marginal) suggest to librarians the importance of each periodical. Annotations consider such topics as current contents, past articles, illustrations, and languages.

The information, gathered from northern California, is from urban, suburban, and rural public libraries. Included because of their popularity with patrons, the magazines are assured to satisfy varied interests: art, books, cars, child care and family, children, cooking, fashion, mechanics, men, politics, sports, women, etc.

In addition to an alphabetical arrangement, the periodicals are also accessed through Appendixes ranking them according to the evaluation criteria mentioned above and also by subject. The directory of publishers and distributors will also be useful. This reference should be in any public library serving a Spanish-speaking clientele.

Rolling rivers: an encyclopedia of America's rivers. Richard A. Bartlett, editor. New York, McGraw-Hill, 1984. vii, 399p. illus. 24cm. hardcover $29.95 (0-07-003910-0).
333.78'45'0973 Rivers—U.S. 83-18745

Rolling Rivers is a collection of essays dealing primarily with the history of more than 100 of America's most important rivers and streams. Each essay begins with a small box of basic facts about the river under discussion describing the river's source, length, tributaries, mouth, and agriculture and industry. Essays are about three to six pages in length and are signed; most of the more than 90 contributors are historians. Most essays include suggestions for further reading, and some have accompanying illustrations or photographs. Besides tracing the history of each river, essays include discussions of inhabitants and their settlements as well as Indian tribes, battles, trade patterns, construction and industry, and such current perspectives as recreation, flora and fauna, environmental problems, damming, flooding, and legislation. Some essays also include legends, poems, and songs about the rivers discussed.

This encyclopedia is divided into six geographical sections: the East Coast, the Northeast Mississippi Valley, the Northwest Mississippi Valley, the Southeast and Texas, the Great Basin and Arizona, and the Pacific Coast and Alaska. An Index cites geographic place-names, bodies of water, personal names, and subjects. Although some of the factual information here can be found elsewhere, *Rolling Rivers* is an attractive resource for high school and public libraries, especially for its historical information.

The schoolroom poets: a bibliography of Bryant, Holmes, Longfellow, Lowell, and Whittier with selective annotation. By Jeanetta Boswell. Metuchen, N.J., & London, Scarecrow, 1983. vii, 303p. 22cm. cloth $18.50 (0-8108-1659-8).

016.811'3 American poetry—19th century—Bibliography [CIP]   83-19276

The title of this compilation—eminently suited to the reference collections of public and academic libraries—clearly indicates its scope and charmingly evokes the status of the writers concerned. As Boswell remarks, "We seem to have outlived the fashion of decrying every line they wrote, as witness so many critics who say there is a portion of their works which should not be allowed to slip into utter oblivion." Surely the creators of "Thanatopsis," "The Last Leaf," "Nature," "Auspex," and "The Brewing of Soma" (to cite but five semiprecious but exquisitely polished gemstones) are among our national treasures—not that *any* efforts, even Boswell's, seem likely to brighten their reputations to the point that they equal the accomplishments of some of their contemporaries.

The bibliography has 2,462 entries, including books, chapters, articles, dissertations, and relevant passages within discourses on larger topics. (Most of this material can be derived from other sources, but not so expeditiously.) Entries are grouped under poet, and arranged thereunder alphabetically by author. Many are crisply annotated. There is generous repetition, e.g., an essay by E. S. Ward on three of the poets is listed under all three, with different annotations. The volume concludes with five indexes (again, one per poet), each in two parts: Coauthors, Editors, and Translators, i.e., of the items listed; and Subjects, including individual works—use of the subject indexes thus facilitating access to material on particular poems. *The Schoolroom Poets*, in short, is an excellent source for the study of American literature.

Perhaps Boswell will want to consider a companion volume on other "premodern" American writers of fading and/or never very glowing poetic reputation, e.g., Very, Tuckerman, Chivers, Thoreau, Melville, Timrod, Hayne, Lanier, Boker, Tabb, Stedman, Aldrich, Reese, Hovey, and Moody—perhaps using, as her point of departure, Jay B. Hubbell's old (1936) but still unsurpassed survey, *American Life in Literature*.

Science fiction, horror and fantasy film and television credits. 2v. Compiled by Harris M. Lentz, III. Jefferson, N.C., McFarland, 1983. 1,374p. 24cm. cloth $69.95 (0-89950-071-4).

791.43'09'0915 Science fiction films—Dictionaries | Horror films—Dictionaries | Fantastic films—Dictionaries | Science fiction television programs—Dictionaries | Horror television programs—Dictionaries | Fantastic television programs—Dictionaries [CIP]
82-23956

The subtitle tells much: "Over 10,000 Actors, Actresses, Directors, Producers, Screenwriters, Cinematographers, Art Directors, and Make-up, Special Effects, Costume and Other People; Plus Full Cross-References from All Films and T.V. Shows." This is a vast collection of detail compiled "in an attempt to give credit to the many men and women who have helped create science fiction, horror and fantasy films and television." The compiler, an editor for *Famous Monsters* magazine, has included U.S. and foreign features, serials, shorts, and individual television episodes through the fall of 1982.

The first volume contains an alphabetical list of actors and actresses usually giving their birth and, if appropriate, death dates; film and television credits including title, date, and character played; and country of production if not American, British, or Canadian. A similar section follows for directors, producers, etc.

Volume 2 contains lists by film title and by television show or series, citing director, actors and actresses and characters played, production dates, and country of production if not North American or British. Film titles range from *Miracle on 34th Street* to *Shoes of the Fisherman* to *Jack and the Beanstalk* to *Cat People*. Television shows range from "Batman" to "Hallmark Hall of Fame" to "Shirley Temple Theater."

Useful for specialized film and television collections.

The science universe series: an illustrated encyclopedia. 8v. New York, Arco, 1984. 29cm. paper over boards. $79.60/set; $9.95 per volume (v.1, Exploring space and atoms, 0-668-06175-8; v.2, Language and communications, 0-668-06176-6; v.3, Sight, light and color, 0-668-06177-4; v.4, Energy, forces and resources, 0-668-06178-2; v.5, Machines, power & transportation, 0-668-06179-8; v.6, Measuring and computing, 0-668-06180-4; v.7, Earth, sea and sky, 0-668-06181-2; v.8, Patterns of life on earth, 0-668-06182-0).

500 Astronomy—Juvenile literature | Atoms—Juvenile literature | Outer space—Exploration—Juvenile literature | Chemistry—Juvenile literature [CIP]   83-26623
001.51 Communication—Juvenile literature [CIP]   83-26651
535 Light—Juvenile literature | Vision—Juvenile literature | Color—Juvenile literature [CIP]   83-26645
621.042 Power resources—Juvenile literature | Force and energy—Juvenile literature | Power (Mechanics)—Juvenile literature [CIP]   83-26619
620'.9 Machinery—Juvenile literature | Power (Mechanics)—Juvenile literature | Transportation—Juvenile literature [CIP]   84-6449
530.8 Mensuration—Juvenile literature | Physical measurements—Juvenile literature | Computers—Juvenile literature [CIP]   84-6307
551 Geophysics—Juvenile literature [CIP]   84-6312
574 Biology—Juvenile literature | Life (Biology)—Juvenile literature [CIP]   84-6318

These eight, beautifully illustrated books provide brief information on scientific topics. Although the volumes are labeled encyclopedias, they are not arranged alphabetically. Instead, each volume covers a broad topic (as indicated by its title) and presents subtopics in each volume, arranged in roughly chronological order, with two pages devoted to each topic. A brief Introduction prepares the reader for what is included in the volume, and a closing summary reviews what was covered. Thus, volume 5, *Machines, Power & Transportation*, is in chapters—"The First Machines," "The Lever and the Wheel," "The Early Civilizations," through "Factory Automation," "The First Generation of Robots," and "Robots with Artificial Intelligence." The latter topics indicate that the set is up-to-date. There is a Glossary; within the text certain words are printed in boldface. Each volume has an index; there is no overall index to the eight volumes. There are also no photographic credits or bibliographies.

Articles are brief, well written, and accurate and are accompanied by exceptionally good color photographs and line drawings. The editors have presented as up-to-date information as possible, as seen by pictures of Sally Ride on the space shuttle mission in the article "Living and Working in Space" in volume 1.

The formats of the volumes are identical: 64 pages, Introduction, 27 articles, Summary, Glossary, and Index. The bindings are attractive and durable using a different highlighting color on each spine, continued on the cover and the endpapers. The covers have full-color illustrations that suggest the contents of particular volumes.

While *The Science Universe Series* is not set up for ready reference, it is a good source of information often sought by students. It would be, therefore, an excellent addition to any school or public library and would be a good choice for home libraries.

Scientific and technical books and serials in print, 1984. 3v. New York, Bowker, 1983. 3,698p. 29cm. cloth $110 + shipping/handling (0-8352-1649-7: set; 0-8352-1809-0: v.1; 0-8352-1810-4: v.2; 0-8352-1888-0: v.3; ISSN 0000-054X).

016.5 Science—Indexes | Engineering—Indexes | Technology—Indexes [OCLC]78-640940

This annual bibliography was first published in 1974. Originally limited to books, its coverage was expanded in 1978 to include serials. Prior to this edition, it was published as a single volume.

The contents of the Index are derived from the databases of the publisher, particularly its *Books in Print* and its other "in print" listings. The bibliography not only lists scientific and technical book and serial titles of interest to professionals in the field but also those of interest to laypersons, young adults, and children. While this edition has been expanded to include additional types of publications and subject areas, no major changes have been made in its subject scope. Included among the works on all aspects of physical and biological sciences and their applications and engineering are relevant biographies, philosophical works, and histories of science and technology. Excluded are titles pertaining to business, economics, marketing, or management aspects of science and technology; architecture as design or as a social phenomenon; hobbies; and medicine. The book section is limited to titles which are published or distributed exclusively in the U.S.

The serials section lists titles published by the United Nations, the European communities, and in 22 major countries. Only the translations of Soviet serials are listed.

Volume 1 lists books by subject; volume 2, books by author; and volume 3, books by title, serials by subject, and serials by title, and it ends with the Key to Publishers' and Distributors' Abbreviations including directory information. As with other Bowker listings, subject headings are alphabetical by LC rules—surely confusing to laypersons. Entries in each of these indexes (ca. 103,000 books and ca. 17,000 serials) contain all available bibliographic and ordering information except that entries in the serials by title section refer to the subject listing for complete information.

This continues to be a useful tool for use in both reference and acquisitions in scientific and technical libraries.

Scribner desk dictionary of American history. New York, Scribner, 1984. vii, 631p. 24cm. cloth $24.95 (0-684-18154-1).
973'.03'21 U.S.—History—Dictionaries [CIP]   84-14019

This is the second abridgment of Scribner's eight-volume *Dictionary of American History*, the second edition of which was favorably reviewed by the Board July 15, 1977. In 1983 Scribner published a one-volume 1,140-page condensation of the set, and this book, entitled *Concise Dictionary of American History*, also was favorably evaluated by the Board (cf. *RBB*, May 15, 1984).

Now comes a yet briefer (631p.) condensation, based largely on the 1983 volume. In many instances the wording is identical, some space being saved by use of abbreviations—*R* for river, *NW*, etc., for directions, and the like. More frequently, articles in the *Concise Dictionary* have been shortened still further for the *Desk Dictionary*; e.g., *Georgiana* (a proposed Mississippi River colony, 1763) has been shortened from 12 lines to 6, with some loss of historical detail.

The lack of adequate cross-references, mentioned in prior reviews, has to some small extent been remedied in this new version by the occasional use of smaller-type capitals within the text. The slight advantage is more than offset by the fact that in some instances, the information in the *Desk Dictionary* is so brief as to be of little value. *Hollywood*, e.g., is reduced to two and one-half lines, or 16 words. The article *Jackson Hole* is likewise only two and one-half lines.

The book does not, as stated on its dust jacket, "answer all questions pertaining to American history." Even so, *Scribner Desk Dictionary of American History* will be welcomed by school librarians as a handy source for quick identification of most places, events, and movements in U.S. history. In libraries catering to more mature readers, a wiser purchase will be Scribner's *Concise Dictionary of American History*.

Secretarial word finder. Compiled by Linnea Leedham Ochs and Susan van der Reyden. Englewood Cliffs, N.J., Prentice-Hall, 1983. 540p. 22cm. hardcover $19.95 (0-13-798157-0).
428.1 English language—Syllabication | English language—Orthography and spelling | Secretaries—Handbooks, manuals, etc. [CIP]   83-8640

Claiming to list "close to 40,000 English words," *Secretarial Word Finder* indicates primary and secondary stresses and divides words into syllables, with slashes indicating permissible end-line breaks. Following the word list (the bulk of the book) is "Secretarial Reference Data"—17 brief presentations of such diverse topics as Word Division, Greek Alphabet, Proofreaders' Marks, and Common Fractions Reduced to Decimals. Sharp's *Follett Vest-Pocket 50,000 Words* does the same thing with words and costs less, but is less legible and lacks the "reference data." Neither book, sad to say, lies open flat—which books consulted by typists ought surely to do.

Secretaries, copy editors, etc., should find this book helpful; libraries, unless they need *very* quick access to the sort of information it provides (notably, what it tells in regard to line-end breaks), will probably find that their collegiate-level dictionaries do most of what *Word Finder* does in regard to words—and of course much more.

Selected film criticism: foreign films, 1930–1950. Edited by Anthony Slide. Metuchen, N.J., and London, Scarecrow, 1984. xi, 207p. 22cm. cloth $17.50 (0-8108-1673-3).
791.43'75 Moving-pictures—Reviews [CIP]   81-23344

This sixth volume of *Selected Film Criticism* "provides contemporary reviews, printed in their entirety, of more than 160 foreign-produced feature films released in the U.S. between 1930 and 1950." The majority were released in the 1930s and 1940s when almost all British films were screened in the U.S.

The reviews, written by 36 well-known film critics, were selected from 19 periodicals including popular magazines, film trade papers, and "serious" film periodicals. As with the earlier volumes, attempts were made to include only those reviews that had not been reprinted elsewhere.

Arranged alphabetically by the title under which the film was released in the U.S., cross-references are provided from the original title. Included in each entry is the U.S. title, original language title, original production company, original U.S. leasing company, and date of the film release in its country of origin. The U.S. release date coincides with the year of the review's appearance.

The two Indexes provide access by country and director. Fourteen countries (the U.S. followed by France and Germany are the leading countries of origin) and 95 directors are represented. A useful tool providing sources unavailable elsewhere, the most unique feature, however, is that the original reviews are reprinted *in toto*, maintaining the style of the critic and the flavor of the times. Given the films covered and the time span, *Selected Film Criticism* will probably be most useful in comprehensive film collections.

Self-help: 1400 best books on personal growth. By Bill Katz and Linda Sternberg Katz. New York, Bowker, 1985. xvii, 379p. 24cm. hardcover $29.95 + shipping & handling (0-8352-1939-9).
011'.7 Self-help techniques—Bibliography | Life skills—Bibliography | Bibliography—Best books—Self-help techniques | Bibliography—Best books—Life skills | Public libraries—Book lists | Libraries, University and college—Book lists [CIP]   84-24163

How does one choose a book from the array available on retirement or personal grooming? What are authoritative nontechnical sources of information on stress or investments? Readers, librarians, and booksellers are the intended audience for this selective, annotated bibliography of the "best" books on personal growth—those that "help an individual improve, modify, or otherwise understand his or her physical or personal characteristics." Used with its companion volume, *How-To: 1400 Best Books on Doing Almost Everything* (Bowker, 1985, $29.95, 0-8352-1927-5), the Katzs offer "complete coverage of the literature of improvement," from fixing your image to fixing your roof.

A bewildering variety of books is published on self-help. The current *Books in Print* lists 284 titles under the heading "stress"; almost 100 of these are popular works. *Self-help* narrows the field to 18 titles, covering several aspects of the subject, including job stress, anger, burnout, and stress in children. Most titles are very current, being published 1980–84. Arrangement is by subject under 165 topics; each entry has standard bibliographic information, price at publication, and Dewey Decimal Classification number. The informally written annotations are both evaluative and descriptive, giving clear ideas of books' content, quality, and format. There are detailed Table of Contents and combined Author, Title, and Subject Indexes for this title and its companion volume. The combined indexes are useful since, while the scope of each work is fairly clear, there are gray areas. Thus, home buying and jogging are treated in *Self-Help*, home renovation and tennis in *How-to*.

Although choices can always be second-guessed and updates will be needed, *How-To* and *Self-Help* will be very useful to anyone facing the sea of possibilities in the areas of self-help books and how-to manuals.

Send me a memo: a handbook of model memos. By Dianna Booher. New York, Facts On File, 1984. vi, 201p. 24cm. hardcover $16.95 (0-87196-906-8).
651.7'55 Memorandums [CIP]   83-14058

The same consultant's *Would You Put That in Writing?* (Facts On File, 1983) was reviewed on Feb. 1, 1984, in these pages, where it was described as "a how-to book" suitable for circulating collections but not, despite the high quality of its content, organized for ready reference. The Introduction to *Send Me a Memo* echoes the advice set forth in Booher's earlier book; its remaining five-sixths is given over to models, alphabetically arranged by topic—from Accomplishments, To Document, through Dismissals, Farewells, "No" Replies, and Promotions/Raises (To Announce, To Request, To Grant, To Decline), to Resignations, Sympathy, and Welcomes. Model memos are followed by explicit and perceptive analyses of weaknesses and strengths. Sample memos are generally (as the subtitle claims) "models"—although now and then Booher overdoes informality: should a dismissal of Shirley X *really* commence: "Shirley,"—an opening at one time reserved for truly "friendly" communications? Running heads (the lack of which in *Would You Put That in Writing?* the Board complained of) are omnipresent—and facilitate searching.

Secretaries, administrative assistants, and managers—anyone who needs to achieve clear and effective business communication—will find this work a helpful and easily accessed compendium. It supplements and, for many users, will probably be even more helpful than R. W. Poe's *McGraw-Hill Handbook of Business Letters* (1983; cf. *RBB*, Jan. 1, 1984). In short, here is a good acquisition for offices (including those of library administrators, regardless of level) and for public, academic, and special libraries.

Shakespearean criticism: excerpts from the criticism of William Shakespeare's plays and poetry, from the first published appraisals to current evaluations. v.1. Laurie Lanzen Harris, editor; Mark W. Scott, associate editor. Detroit, Gale, 1984. 683p. 29cm. cloth $70 (0-8103-6125-6).
822.3′3 Shakespeare, William, 1564–1616—Criticism and interpretation—History | Shakespeare, William, 1564–1616—Criticism and interpretation—Addresses, essays, and lectures [CIP]   84-4010

Shakespearean Criticism, an important new addition to the Gale Literary Criticism Series, is directed to students "in late high school and early college who are beginning their study of Shakespeare." The first five volumes will contain excerpts from published criticism on six or seven plays, each having "an equal balance of genres and an equal balance of plays based on their critical importance." The first volume covers *Hamlet, Timon of Athens, Twelfth Night, The Comedy of Errors,* and *Henry IV*, parts I and II. Future volumes will contain essays on such topics as Shakespeare's poetry, the authorship controversy, and costume and set design.

The initial volume is well edited. Major critics have been selected for inclusion, and entries include introductory material on dates, text, and sources. There are brief statements about scholars whose work is included and about the significance of their criticism. The bibliographies at the end of each section are selective and serve to guide students to additional sources. Complete bibliographic information is supplied for the latter and for the sources of the excerpts.

Critical excerpts on each play are organized chronologically, and the editors have maintained a balanced collection of criticism for each. Most of the criticism presented is taken from 201 books (prefaces to various editions of the plays, chapters from composite books, etc.). Ninety-one of the books are pre-1930 publications; 91 were written between 1930 and 1970, and 19 were written in the 1970s. Of the 98 periodical articles selected for inclusion, 18 were written in the 1970s, 52 between 1930 and 1970, and 28 before 1920. Unfortunately, most if not all the excerpts are abridged. This becomes obvious as one reads these essays: thoughts do not always flow logically from one paragraph to the next. Page numbers at certain points in the text indicate original pagination, but no other indication is given of what is omitted from the original source.

Students beginning to study the plays would probably appreciate essays grouped according to subject rather than chronologically as is done here. A careful reading of these essays is necessary before users can locate specific comments on such topics as character development, the meaning of important soliloquies, the dramatic structure of a particular play, etc. However some of the later volumes may in fact provide this kind of coverage. Libraries having limited book and periodical collections will find this and subsequent volumes useful. Users of larger libraries will probably use *Shakespearean Criticism* more as a guide to the literature than as a critical guide to the plays.

Given the enormous amount of secondary material on Shakespeare, this volume provides a convenient introduction for beginning students and as such is recommended for high school, public, and college libraries.

Simon and Schuster's guide to garden flowers. By Guido Moggi and Luciano Giugnolini; U.S. editor, Stanley Schuler. New York, Simon and Schuster, 1983. 511p. illus. 20cm. cloth $19.95 (0-671-46674-7); paper $9.95 (0-671-46678-X).
635.9 Flowers | Flowering woody plants | Flower gardening [CIP]   82-19678

Translated from Italian, this book has 369 illustrated entries, each coded in full color as to type of plant (e.g., annual, water plant, perennial, etc.) and suitability (for cut flowers, for borders, rock gardens, etc.). A small map shows distribution and whether indigenous, cultivated, or hybrid.

Each half-page entry is accompanied by a half-page color photograph facing it. Colors are vivid and true. Entries are arranged by scientific term and include common name, family, description, height of plant in inches and centimeters, size of flower, place of origin, flowering time, cultivation, propagation, and qualities. There are a few exceptions to the half-page: one page has three entries with one large and two small photographs facing; *Rosa* expectedly runs longer—to 12 pages and 17 illustrations; 14 other entries run longer than the standard.

There is an 11-page Glossary of 350 to 400 terms, an Index by common name, and a brief Bibliography. There is also a fine 80-page Introduction which covers the history of gardens and flower cultivation, mentions some of the major botanists, and describes the characteristics of various types of gardens, and some of the outstanding gardens of the world.

While it is regrettable for reference purposes that the book has such narrow inner margins, it is true that, as the publisher states, "This is one of the most stunning and informative books a gardener can own." Its coverage, arrangement, and indexes make it excellent for libraries or home collections.

Social reform and reaction in America: an annotated bibliography. Santa Barbara, ABC-Clio, 1984. viii, 375p. (Clio Bibliography series, no.13) 29cm. cloth $55 (0-87436-048-X).
016.306′0973 U.S.—Social conditions—Bibliography | Canada—Social conditions—Bibliography | U.S.—Economic conditions—Bibliography | Canada—Economic conditions—Bibliography [CIP]   82-24294

This bibliography series began in the 1970s; *RBB* has reviewed some of the earlier titles (e.g., *American and Canadian West*, Sept. 15, 1980, and *European Immigration and Ethnicity in the United States and Canada*, Feb. 1, 1984) and found them valuable as selective sources covering diverse topics in American history. This volume's 2,993 abstracted journal articles and chapters in books were originally published between 1973 and 1982 and were extracted from the publisher's database (used to produce *America: History and Life*, etc.).

Ninety countries and 42 languages are covered. The book is arranged in six chapters organized by chronological periods, covering both U.S. and Canadian experience. Each is then subdivided by specific topics. Standard bibliographic data are given. Within chapters and subdivisions, arrangement is alphabetical by author in double columns; generally, abstractors are noted. Each abstract cites the existence of a bibliography, type of research sources, and whether the work includes illustrations. A list of journals cited appears at the end—after detailed Subject and Author Indexes. The whole is clearly written using comprehensible language.

The 1974 revision of *Harvard Guide to American History* lists many books on social reforms, but *Social Reform and Reaction in America*'s dual-nation bibliography of articles, drawn from a rich database of modern scholarship, makes it extremely valuable. Within the limitations noted, and alerted to the fact that the entries are also to be found in *America: History and Life*, this volume can be useful in academic and large public libraries.

Social welfare in America: an annotated bibliography. Walter I. Trattner and W. Andrew Achenbaum, editors. Westport, Conn., Greenwood, 1983. 324p. 24cm. cloth $35 (0-313-23002-1).
016.361′973 Public welfare—U.S.—Bibliography | Charities—U.S.—Bibliography | U.S.—Social conditions—Bibliography [CIP]   83-10855

The history and philosophy of public welfare in the U.S. are covered in this annotated bibliography of 1,410 monographs, articles, dissertations, and documentaries. It is arranged in a "cradle-to-grave" framework with sections on general welfare, infant and child, youth, adulthood (domestic and economic), and the aged.

The Introduction provides a brief state-of-the-art essay and clearly delineates the scope of the work; specific notes on the selection, compilation, and organization of the bibliography follows. An epilogue suggests topics for future search. Accurate Author and Subject Indexes conclude the work.

The six chapters are all subdivided into four sections, *Syntheses and Overviews, Period Pieces, Salient Variations,* and *Age-Specific and Life-Cycle Studies*. Within these, entries are further subdivided by specific topic or genre (e.g., Classic Case Studies) then arranged alphabetically by author. Entries contain full bibliographic information; annotations are evaluative.

Social Welfare in America is comprehensive; it will be particularly useful in public and academic libraries supporting social service and American history programs.

The solar energy directory. Sandra Oddo, senior editor; Martin McPhillips, associate editor; Richard Gottlieb, general editor. New York, H. W. Wilson edition of a Grey House Publishing Directory, 1983. viii, 312p. 29cm. cloth $50 (U.S. and Canada); $60 (other) (0-939300-06-0).

6212.47'025'73 Solar energy—U.S.—Directories [CIP]   83-5498

"Solar energy," states the Introduction to this work, "is one of the newest and fastest-growing of the technical and business fields in the United States." *The Solar Energy Directory* will therefore meet a real need in public libraries, some special libraries, some academic libraries, and some offices. Its stated scope is the "direct use of solar energy," i.e., "Solar heating and cooling / Solar thermal energy / Photovoltaics"—with "such indirect uses as wind, biomass, or hydropower" excluded. Data, chiefly but not exclusively derived from responses to questionnaires, are arranged under ten headings: Professional, Industry, and Trade Organizations; Private Organizations and Advocacy Groups; Government; Utilities; Regional, State and Local Organizations; Manufacturers; Education and Training; Research Institutions and Foundations; Solar Professionals; and Sources of Information. Appendixes include Manufacturers Listed by Product; Manufacturers Listed by State; Solar Product Catalogs; and Groups Offering Workshops and Seminars. Coverage is good; information on particular institutions, etc., is ample and relevant; and presentation is clear (as are instructions for use). There is an Index to names of institutions, firms, and publications (but not names of persons).

One suggestion: this is a work which will need frequent updating, so rapidly is the solar industry growing and changing; perhaps the publisher will want to look into ways to revise the work at regular intervals.

Spanish literature, 1500–1700: a bibliography of Golden Age studies in Spanish and English, 1925–1980. Compiled by William W. Mosely et al. Westport, Conn., Greenwood, 1984. lxiii, 765p. (Bibliographies and Indexes in World Literature, no.3) 24cm. cloth $75 (0-313-21491-3; ISSN 0742-6801).

016.86'09'003 Spanish literature—Classical period, 1500–1700—History and criticism—Bibliography [CIP]   84-8965

This bibliography, intended as ready reference for generalists and for advanced students of Golden Age literature, lists 11,181 unannotated items of secondary literature in English and Spanish. Citing books, dissertations, and articles, entries are arranged under the following headings: *Festschriften*, General, General Bibliography, Drama, Picaresque, Poetry, Prose, *Romancero*, and Individual Authors and Anonymous Works. (Students of lesser-known figures of the period will be particularly pleased with this last and largest section.)

In spite of the overwhelming importance of the Golden Age in Spanish literary history, surprisingly few general bibliographies of it exist. Most concentrate on single authors and genres. Hence, the compilers have indeed done a service to the field with their special focus on the needs of students and nonexperts. Yet, as in every bibliography, not everyone will agree on inclusions and methodology.

The beginning year (1925) for entries is presented without having been placed in context, i.e., is there a basic pre-1925 bibliography covering the earlier years? Is the year a benchmark in Golden Age studies? The 55-year coverage of this bibliography coincides with the introduction of nonprint media. This factor should be duly recorded.

In spite of these shortcomings, *Spanish Literature* is a contribution to a very broad field. As the most recent and comprehensive bibliography, it should be in all large public and university libraries serving Spanish programs.

Standard directory of advertisers, 1983 classified: guide to 17,000 corporations. Skokie, IL 60077, 5201 Old Orchard Rd., National Register Pub. Co., a Macmillan Co., 1983. various pagings. 28cm. paper $235; $347/set (0-87217-000-4).

659.1 Advertising—Directories || Advertising—U.S.—Directories [OCLC]   5-21147

Standard directory of advertising agencies June–September, 1983. Skokie, Ill., National Register, 1983. 949p. 28cm. paper $219, $347/set (0-87217-056-14).

†659.1'025 Advertising—Directories [OCLC]   66-6149

The "Advertisers Red Book," as the *Standard Directory of Advertisers* is commonly known, is the most comprehensive and authoritative source on advertisers and their agencies doing regional or national advertising. The classified edition, which lists companies by 51 product classifications, is published in April, and the geographical edition is published in May. An updating service is also available which consists of biweekly bulletins and five cumulative monthly supplements.

Each company listing includes address, telephone number, type of business, key personnel, number of employees, dollar volume of sales, ad agency, account executive, appropriation for advertising, and type of media used. In addition to the main directory, an alphabetical Index of Companies and a Trade Name Index of approximately 30,000 names are included.

In order to be included, a company must have spent at least $50,000 on national or regional advertising in the prior year. Information for the directory is provided by the companies listed. The 1984 edition includes approximately 300 new listings.

A companion volume, the *Standard Directory of Advertising Agencies*, commonly known as the "Agency Red Book," is issued three times a year—February, June, and October. It lists approximately 3,650 advertising agencies in the U.S. and abroad. For each agency the address, telephone number, year founded, number of employees, key personnel, annual billings, major clients, and percentage of billings by media type are included. Special features include a Geographical Index and a Market Index, which lists agencies by specialty.

Both works are standard reference items for any business, academic, and public library serving business students or patrons.

Statistical information on the financial services industry. 2d ed. Washington, DC 20036, 1120 Connecticut Ave., NW, American Bankers Assn., 1983. ix, 208p. 29cm. paper, to members $50; to nonmembers, $66.

332.1'0973 Finance—U.S.—Statistics || Financial institutions—U.S.—Statistics || Banks and banking—U.S.—Statistics [OCLC]   83-134480

Designed to "help bankers plan for the future," this sourcebook contains ten chapters of statistical data for the years 1971–81. Information presented in the prior edition (1981) has been updated and supplemented in many areas to reflect important developments in the industry during a decade of significant changes.

Chapters deal with banks and their relationship to the credit markets and financial services industry, depository institutions, and international banking. Other topics include demographic and asset growth data, trends of nonfinancial sectors, payments system, and consumers. Information is presented in a variety of formats, including tables, illustrative maps, and graphs. Most material has been drawn from outside sources such as government documents, journals, and reports. In most cases, the information has been clearly labeled and is understandable for the knowledgeable reader. In a few cases, however, inclusions lack explanation as to their origin or relevance to the topic at hand.

The high price and specialized nature of this volume will make it attractive primarily to research or business libraries. Bound in paper, the book will not withstand heavy use.

Statistics sources: a subject guide to data on industrial, business, social, educational, financial, and other topics for the United States and internationally. 8th ed. 2v. Paul Wasserman, managing ed. Jaequeline O'Brien, assoc. ed.: Daphne A. Grace and Kenneth Clansky, asst. eds. Detroit, Gale, 1983. xxx, 1,875p. 29cm. cloth $185 (0-8103-0391-4).

†016.31 Statistics—Bibliography || Statistical services   81-13451

This new eighth edition of *Statistics Sources* occupies 1,875 pages in two volumes in contrast to its predecessor, which occupied 1,388 pages in one volume. It indexes in depth a wide variety of U.S. and foreign statistical publications. Examples of these publications are yearbooks and statistical compilations issued by organizations such as the U.S. Bureau of the Census, United Nations, and Organization for Economic Cooperation and Development. The main section lists 30,000 citations under 20,000 fairly specific subject headings. While the entries for the U.S. are dispersed alphabetically under subjects from Abortions to Zoology—Degrees Conferred, those of foreign countries are brought together under each country's name.

Statistics Sources uses cross-references sparingly. In general, a complete bibliographic citation is repeated under each relevant heading, which, of course, saves users time but increases the bulk of the work. Sometimes this practice leads to rather strange sequences as found starting at Fiji—Health—Number of Dentists to Fiji—Health and Medical Services, where the same source is cited over and over again. Also, a very high percentage of entries results from in-depth indexing of a few sources. For instance, almost half of more than 220 entries under *Fiji* result from one source—the *United Nation's Statistical Yearbook*. In fact, of the 25 sources which are indexed under *Fiji* and its subdivisions, 5 account for more than 75 percent of the entries. The same pattern recurs under other countries. The Board must question whether such extensive indexing of relatively few titles is really worthwhile inasmuch as we hope that most librarians would use sources like the *United Nations Statistical Yearbook* as a matter of routine when asked for statistics on foreign countries.

The eighth edition represents a substantial updating of its predecessor with both new subject headings and new sources.

In its review of this work's sixth edition (cf. *RSBR*, March 1, 1982), the Board had some reservations about the in-depth indexing of relatively few titles. The sixth edition (1980) sold for $85; the eighth edition is $185. Librarians will be well advised to think carefully about the need for this rather limited tool particularly if they already subscribe to the more comprehensive *American Statistics Index* and *Statistical Reference Index*.

Style manuals of the English-speaking world: a guide. By John Bruce Howell. Phoenix, Oryx, 1983. xiii, 138p. 24cm. cloth $22.50 (0-89774-089-0).
016.808′02 Authorship—Style manuals—Bibliography [CIP]   82-42916

Although writers of academic papers and manuscripts for publication will, in most instances, have to conform to the dictates of prescribed style manuals, it is good to have this bibliography of 231 such tools—ranging from the very general (e.g., *The Chicago Manual of Style*) to the highly specialized (e.g., *Writing the Biomedical Research Paper*), and from the lengthy to the very brief (five pages being the minimum allowed). As its Introduction notes, usage manuals (in the Fowler tradition) are excluded, as are technical writing guides and manuals addressed specifically to students at particular institutions. (The Introduction also includes a brief history of style manuals—pages which reference librarians would do well to read.)

Selection seems good. The basic arrangement is classified, with the last four items comprising Appendixes on Disabled People (i.e., how to refer to them) and on Nonsexist Language. Annotations are perceptive, and cross-references numerous and helpful. *Style Manuals* should be considered for academic, special, and large public libraries—where it should prove useful both in advisory service and in collection development.

A subject bibliography of the history of American higher education. Compiled by Mark Beach. Westport, Conn., Greenwood, 1984. vii, 165p. 24cm. cloth $29.95 (0-313-23276-8).
016.37873 Education, Higher—U.S.—History—Bibliography [CIP]   83-22565

An earlier work by Beach, *A Bibliographic Guide to American Colleges and Universities* (Greenwood, 1975), carried an all-encompassing title but was actually a very useful compilation on one subject: published histories of specific colleges and universities. This new book lists 1,325 citations pertaining generally to the history of American higher education. Sources include books, articles, dissertations, and government documents. A classified arrangement cites entries under topics from Academic Freedom to Zoology. There are no annotations, but there are some internal cross-references and referrals to Beach's earlier work.

While the 1975 work was a comprehensive treatment of a narrow topic, this book is a very selective listing covering a broad field. Unfortunately, there is no discussion on what constitutes "historical writing." The chief drawback is the book's limited number of citations, e.g., there are all of 7 citations under Accrediting, 15 under Administration, and 7 under Physical Education. The Board hopes that the classification Libraries is not typical of the quality of coverage—the 12 citations consist of five books, three dissertations, one U.S. document dated 1880, and three journal articles. Needless to say, this hardly seems a good showing unless Beach's definition of *historical writing* is extremely narrow indeed.

There is an Author Index keyed to entry numbers, but the Subject Index is merely a table of contents containing the list of classifications and cross-references along with the range of entry numbers for each term.

A Subject Bibliography of the History of American Higher Education is probably of most use only in comprehensive education collections.

Surveys, polls, censuses, and forecasts directory: a guide to sources of statistical studies in the areas of business, social science, education, science, and technology. 1st ed. Detroit, Gale, 1983– . 28cm. paper $175/3 issues per year (0-8103-1692-7; ISSN: 0737-545X).
016.0014′33′0973 U.S.—Statistics—Bibliography—Periodicals | Social surveys—U.S.—Directories | Public opinion polls—Directories [OCLC]   84-640501

Surveys, Polls, Censuses, and Forecasts Directory includes such diverse organizations as Louis Harris and Associates, the U.S. Department of Commerce, and the National Fire Protection Association; it deals with topics such as economic and industrial forecasts and opinion polls on public policy issues. The first three issues of the *Directory* contain 1,159 entries organized alphabetically by the name of the poll or survey. The entries are based on responses to questionnaires completed by sponsoring organizations. A full entry contains the address and telephone number of the sponsoring or conducting organization, contact, year started, description, frequency, time coverage, geographic coverage, format and availability, and sources for further information. The entries are followed by Subject Indexes which cumulate in each issue.

There are, of course, omissions, e.g., the U.S. Advisory Commission on Inter-Governmental Relations' annual survey on taxation is not listed. One Dun & Bradstreet publication is listed while there is nothing from Standard & Poor's. The work also lists what appears to be one time surveys/polls, the results of which are published, e.g., as journal articles. Some of this material is undoubtedly covered in other reference sources.

As with other directories issued in parts from Gale, it is difficult to know if subsequent editions will increase coverage or whether the next edition of three issues will cumulate the contents of the first. While this appears to be a timely if not unique source, librarians may wish to examine subsequent issues before acquisition.

Telephone services directory: a guide to counseling information; referral services; private social agencies; federal, state, and city agency hotlines; volunteer groups; medical and legal organizations; businesses; and other related subjects. 1st edition. Detroit, Gale, 1983. 117p. 28cm. paper $85/3 pt. set (0-8103-1542-4; ISSN: 0737-5360).
†384.64 Information services—U.S.—Directories | Hotlines (Counseling) [OCLC]

The premise underlying the publication of this directory is that telephone communication is becoming increasingly important in seeking services and providing information. This first edition will be published in three parts and will list 1,300 telephone services in the U.S. (The Board examined the first two, which contained 850 entries.) The directory is arranged by broad subjects and then subarranged by geographic area. The entries include name of service/organization, hot-line number, description of services offered, region served, address of service, and name of a contact person, service hours and staffing, sponsor, and founding date.

Some of the listings are for toll-free 800 or 900 numbers, while others are for local numbers. Many of the entries are for crisis-intervention assistance services, though other topics (e.g., job hunting) are also included. Each entry is numbered, and each issue has cumulative indexes by subject and by names. Again, as with other Gale titles, the rationale for a three-part as opposed to a one-volume work is not clear.

Telephone Services Directory is expensive considering the coverage provided, and some of the information is available in standard reference tools. Although *Telephone Services Directory* may be useful for public library reference desks or for referral agencies, librarians might be wise to wait for all three issues before purchasing or wait for later editions.

Television comedy series: an episode guide to 153 TV sitcoms in syndication. By Joel Eisner and David Krinsky. Jefferson, N.C., McFarland, 1984. xvi, 866p. illus. 24cm. cloth $49.95 + $1.50 (shipping and handling) (0-89950-088-9).
791.45′09′0917 Comedy programs—U.S.—Plots, themes, etc. [CIP]   83-42901

This hefty volume provides episode coverage for "every prime time situation comedy series, live or animated, broadcast from 1949 to 1980 and still available for syndication." For 153 sitcoms, every episode has been listed in order of production—more than 11,000 shows. Entry information for each series consists of dates when first aired, days and times of broadcast, network, number of episodes, filming format, producer, production company, syndication company, cast, and a descriptive paragraph with a statement on how the series has fared in syndication. Information for individual episodes includes a title, director and writer (when known), guest stars, and a one- or two-sentence plot summary.

Eisner and Krinsky have carefully set the boundaries for their book within the subtitle. Although certainly browsable—and comprehensive in what it attempts—this is not a general guide to television comedy. Only prime-time situation comedies are listed, and then with these important exclusions: live shows that were never filmed or taped, those series not in syndication (when a show is offered to several stations instead of just a single network), banned shows, and shows that originated after 1980. Thus, there are no entries for many shows that one might expect to find here: e.g., "Mr. Peepers," "Facts of Life," and "Private Benjamin."

What distinguishes *Television Comedy Series* from books such as *The Complete Directory to Prime Time Network TV Shows* is the episode information. The "M*A*S*H" entries, for example, run to 15 pages. The Personal Name Index is particuarly useful, as it includes all people mentioned in the text (cast, writers, directors, guest stars, etc.). The 58 black-and-white photographs of series stars illustrate a well-formatted and sturdy reference book.

A prodigious amount of research has been devoted to the compilation of this guide, and it should answer many questions from sitcom fans. *Television Comedy Series* is suitable for public libraries and specialized collections on television.

Tennyson: a bibliography, 1827–1982. By Kirk H. Beetz. Metuchen, N.J., Scarecrow, 1984. vi, 528p. (Scarecrow Author Bibliographies, no.68) 23cm. cloth $35 (0-8108-1687-3).
016.821'8 Tennyson, Alfred Tennyson, Baron, 1809–1892—Bibliography [CIP] 84-1274

Striving for comprehensiveness, this bibliography lists 5,147 books, articles, reviews, and dissertations on Tennyson published between 1827 and 1982. In the chronological arrangement, each year's output is organized by type. Descriptive annotations accompany some of the items, but no pattern of selection for annotation can be discerned. The Author-Editor Index is straightforward and performs its function. The Subject Index is of paramount importance, given the bibliography's chronological arrangement. It lists persons, poems, and topics and subdivides these adequately, underlining entry numbers of book-length studies.

A topical approach would have been more responsive to user needs than is the chronological approach. For this reason, although it is nearly 20 years old and is very selective, Charles Tennyson and Christine Fall's *Alfred Tennyson: An Annotated Bibliography* (Athens: Univ. of Georgia Pr., 1967) remains useful. Its annotations are more thorough than Beetz'. This new bibliography will, of course, be useful to serious students of Tennyson who want to retrieve as many secondary works as they possibly can. However, the arrangement will test their determination to get it all.

Terminals and printers buyer's guide. [By] Tony Webster. New York, McGraw-Hill, 1984. x, 345p. 28cm. paper $19.95 (0-07-068968-7).
621.3819'533'0294 Computer terminals—Catalogs | Video display terminals—Catalogs | Printers (Data processing systems)—Catalogs [OCLC] 84-883

This is a four-part buying guide to visual display and graphics terminals, as well as printers and printing terminals. Part 1 forms the introduction and technical overview of printers and terminals. Parts 2–4 consider 270 models of video display terminals from 55 manufacturers; the IBM 3270 Information Display System and 22 other vendors' terminal products compatible with the IBM 3270; and 400 models of printers and printing terminals from 75 different manufacturers.

Each entry in parts 2–4 provides a one- to two-page product report and includes a list of models available; specifications; prices; and the address of the manufacturer's main office. Often there is an accompanying photograph of the equipment. Products are listed under the company name. In addition, part 3 offers a 12-page essay on communication protocols.

The volume concludes with a glossary, i.e., listings by manufacturers of models of each type of equipment and cross-reference tables.

The compiler, manager of the Computer Reference Guide Division, McGraw-Hill, has computer experience in the U.S., England, and Australia. While the idiom of this text is predominantly British, it is understandable, and the products described are from the U.S. Public, academic, and special libraries will find *Terminals and Printers Buyer's Guide* useful for both reference and circulating collections serving data processing personnel.

Tests: a comprehensive reference for assessments in psychology, education and business. Richard C. Sweetland and Daniel J. Keyser. Kansas City, MS 64112, 330 W. 47th St., Suite 205, Test Corporation of America, 1983. VII, 890p., LXXII. 25cm. cloth $39.95 (regular ed.); $69.95 20 percent library discount plus $2.90 (shipping/handling) (0-9611286-0-7: reg. ed., 0-9611286-1-5: lib. bdg.).
150'.28'7 Psychological tests | Educational tests and measurements | Business—Examinations [CIP] 83-5074

Designed as a quick reference for finding the most appropriate, currently available test to be used for assessments in psychology, education, and business, *Tests* presents brief descriptions of some 2,300 English-language tests and tells how to obtain them. The book is arranged in three sections, each of which is then further divided and subdivided for a total of 60 subsections, e.g., *reading* in the education section is subdivided into elemetary, high school and above, multilevel, and library skills. Under each heading, entry is alphabetical by name. If a test can be used in various capacities, *see* references are provided as appropriate. Each entry is well set off; the format makes it easy to assess quickly which test in any category may be the best one to use. Under each title, symbols show whether the test requires an examiner or whether the test is self-administered. An age level (child, teen, adult) and a grade level (if appropriate) is indicated. A clear, concise statement of purpose comes next, followed by a description, cost, and availability information. No data on validity are given; nor are there any references or evaluations as in Buros' *Mental Measurements Yearbook* (8th ed., Highland Park, N.J., Gryphone Pr., 1978) or *Tests in Print* (III, Lincoln, Nebr., Buros Institute of Mental Measurements, 1983). Some of the same tests are included in *Tests* as in the *Buros'* volumes; each also has unique listings. *Tests* has indexes by publisher with address, test titles, author, and scoring service. Tests which can be used for the visually impaired are also indexed.

Designed by psychologists for psychologists, educators, and human resource personnel, this will be a useful volume for anyone seeking information on tests. It does not provide the in-depth treatment which is available in Buros' works, but it is easier to scan and presents at a glance what a test is about, its purpose, description, and availability. *Tests* should be most helpful to persons and libraries involved with testing in these fields.

Tests in print III. James V. Mitchell, editor. Lincoln, Nebraska, dist. by the Univ. of Nebraska Pr., 1983. xxxi, 714p. 26cm. cloth $85 (0-910674-52-3).
†016.3712'6 Educational tests and measurements—Bibliography | Examinations—Bibliography 83-18866

Tests in Print III (*TIP III*) like its two predecessors is an index to tests, test reviews, and the literature on specific tests. *TIP III* is in the tradition of Oscar Buros who for 40 years was editor of the *Mental Measurement Yearbooks* (*MMY*), *Tests in Print,* and other test-related monographs.

As with its predecessors, the main purpose of the work is to "stimulate increased awareness of the necessity for improvement in the construction, validation, and use of tests."

The 2,672 tests listed in this new volume are set in alphabetical order by title (which appears in boldface). Information provided with each listed test includes age group or type of person for which test is intended, date of publication, author, publisher, references to all original test reviews that have appeared for this test in all the *Mental Measurements Yearbooks* to date, and references to professional journal articles in which the test has a role of some importance. Theses and dissertations have been excluded in this edition; citations have been analyzed chronologically. References are also given for tests which are no longer in print.

To facilitate use of this monumental reference tool, four major indexes are provided: (1) an Index of Titles also includes out-of-print or status-unknown tests listed in *Tests in Print II* or *The Eighth Mental*

Measurements Yearbook; (2) a Classified Subject Index (here all tests in *TIP III* are grouped under 17 major subject headings running the gamut from Achievement Batteries to Vocations); (3) a Publishers Directory and Index: this is a listing of publishers, their addresses, and entry numbers for tests attributable to each publisher; and (4) an Index of Names: this is a list of authors of tests, reviews, or references dealing with a specific test.

TIP III should prove invaluable to all who are involved in the field of testing and is a must for educators, psychologists, social workers, researchers, and academic libraries supporting behavioral sciences programs.

Thinkers of the twentieth century: a biographical, bibliographical and critical dictionary. Editors, Elizabeth Devine et al. Detroit, Gale, [1984]. 643p. 25cm. cloth $75 (0-8103-1516-5).

920.00904 Biography—20th century—Dictionaries | Philosophy, Modern—20th century—Bio-bibliography | Philosophy, Modern—20th century—History and criticism [OCLC]

The term *thinkers* in the title is the key to this fine selection of biographies of approximately 430 men and women of the present century who have had an important influence on the intellectual, cultural, or religious life of the Western world. Most of these people were also writers, in the sense that it was primarily through their writings that they exerted their influence, but very few of them were "literary" figures in the usual sense of that word.

Aside from a number of outstanding thinkers from continental Europe, such as Benedetto Croce, Sigmund Freud, Étienne Gilson, Jacques Maritain, and Paul Valéry, the majority of the entrants are British or American, with such well-known names as C. S. Lewis, Robert Hutchins, J. Robert Oppenheimer, and several hundred others. There is a sprinkling of names from non-Western or non-European countries, notably Nicolas Berdyaev, Mahatma Gandhi, D. T. Suzuki, and Che Guevara.

Each entry is divided into three parts: a brief who's-who style biographical summary; then an extensive list of publications by the biographee frequently followed by a list of biographies, critical appraisals, and bibliographies; and finally the signed essay of about 2,000 words, summarizing the life and influence of the person in question. These have been written by contributors knowledgeable in the various fields, and they constitute the major strength of the work. They are generally sympathetic yet critical and written in a style that is scholarly but not too erudite.

Thinkers of the Twentieth Century will find a useful niche in reference collections of academic and public libraries.

The Times atlas of the oceans. Edited by Alastair Couper. New York, Van Nostrand, 1983. 272p. illus. maps. 38cm. cloth $90.50 (0-442-21661-0).

912'.155146 Oceanography—Maps [CIP]   82-675461

The Times Atlas of the Oceans is a comprehensive thematic atlas-cum-encyclopedia on the oceans of the world and their relationship to humans and their environment and survival. Edited by Alastair Couper, noted educator and consultant to United Nations agencies on shipping, the atlas was designed for use by a wide range of "specialists and non-specialists." The atlas presents data in essay, tabular, and map formats on "the physical and biological interactions, the trans-national character of living resources, the reasons behind the flow of merchant ships and deployment of naval vessels, management concepts, and the legal regime of the oceans." Covering every aspect of the ocean environment in thorough, concise, and easily understood articles, a broad overview of the world's oceans is presented.

Information is organized into four main divisions: The Ocean Environment (e.g., geography, ocean basins, ocean/atmosphere); Resources of the Ocean (e.g., fisheries, aquaculture, offshore oil, seafloor minerals); Ocean Trade (e.g., ports, patterns of trade, navigational aids, collisions); and The World Ocean (e.g., health, pollution, naval operations, undersea archaeology, territorial claims). Each division is subdivided into four or five subject areas containing from 4 to 12 articles. The Table of Contents clearly presents the relationship of the articles, subject areas, and divisions by its arrangement. Arranged for easy access, the articles, with few exceptions, are complete on two facing pages with maps and paragraphs adjacent to the text.

More than 142 full-color photographs, 320 multicolor charts, graphs, diagrams, or lifelike drawings, and 284 maps are used throughout to highlight or further explain the articles. All are beautifully produced and well labeled. The end section contains 11 Appendixes (mostly lists and statistics, e.g., shipping routes and distances between ports), a 7-page Glossary, a list of sources, a Bibliography, and a 15-page Index. The latter uses roman type for the subject entries and italic type for gazetteer entries of sea features, accompanied by grid references.

A wealth of information beautifully presented in an intriguing and interesting manner, *The Times Atlas of the Oceans* should be a valuable source for almost any reference collection in both libraries and homes.

The Times atlas of world history. Rev. ed. Edited by Geoffrey Barraclough. Maplewood, N.J., Hammond, 1984. 360p. maps. charts. diagrs. 38cm. cloth $75 (0-8437-1129-9).

911 Geography, Historical—Maps [CIP]   84-675088

This revision continues the high quality established by the outstanding first edition (1978) of what has become a standard reference source. This interpretive atlas, edited by Oxford historian Geoffrey Barraclough, departs from the "Eurocentricity" of other historical atlases, which tend to concentrate on the history of Europe, particularly Western Europe. The aim here has been "to present a view of history which is world-wide in conception and presentation and which does justice, without prejudice or favour, to the achievements of all peoples in all ages in all quarters of the globe."

Concise text accompanies more than 600 maps produced by the latest techniques of cartography and printing. According to Hammond, many maps were produced by computer-based graphics.

The work begins with a 12-page chronology of major events in world history to 1984 and "The Geographical Background to World History," a two-page physical map of the world. This is followed by the seven major sections of the work: The World of Early Man, The First Civilisations, The Classical Civilisations of Eurasia, The World of Divided Regions, The World of the Emerging West, The Age of European Dominance, and The Age of Global Civilisation. Then follow a Glossary of supplementary information on individuals, peoples, events, and treaties and an Index. The latter almost exclusively cites place-names. The work, therefore, lacks subject access except through the six-page Table of Contents in the forematter.

In this new edition, corrections have been made, and new material has been added. Particular attention has been paid to plates dealing with the period since 1945 which, according to the publisher, "have been updated and in some cases radically altered." The revision also reports on new historical discoveries as well as recent events. Thus, fossil finds in Kenya, South Africa, Israel, and Europe are cited. Maps illustrating early African history and those depicting the classical and medieval periods were revised. New and updated information on the Middle East is presented. Maps of Israeli settlements on the West Bank and of the Lebanese civil war have been added.

In an age of visual communication, this graphically striking presentation of history is a bargain at $75, and it will be useful in any general reference collection.

Tools in the learning trade: a guide to eight indispensable tools for college students. By Barbara Currier Bell. Metuchen, N.J., and London, Scarecrow, 1984. xi, 179p. 22cm. cloth $15 (0-8108-1655-5).

011'.02 Reference books | College students—Books and reading | Study, Method of [CIP]   83-15105

Contending that college students, like carpenters, must have the right tools to do their job, the author discusses eight types of tools and makes recommendations within each category: dictionaries, synonym books, writing guides, one-volume encyclopedias, research guides, style manuals, calculators and computers (written by Winifred Asprey), and handbooks for creative thinking. Each chapter sets up relevant criteria such as scope, timeliness, readability, and format. The chapters on dictionaries and synonym books are enhanced by reprinting pages of five leading collegiate-level dictionaries and two synonym books. Sample questions requiring the use of the type of reference tool are included at the end of each chapter. (The Board doubts that these will ever be used.) Somewhat amateurish drawings scattered through the book add little. In each chapter, books are critically annotated—either individually or as a group—and in several they are also rated as recommended, good, fair, or not recommended. The short chapter on calculators and computers concentrates on giving criteria for purchasing these tools. One Appendix guides students to works about reference tools, and another reprints a chapter from *Sheehy*; these seem more geared to library school students than to average college students.

Since *Tools in the Learning Trade* brings together useful titles in a variety of learning areas, it could be helpful for personal reference at high school, college, or public library reference desks. Most librarians will learn nothing new.

Twentieth-century author biographies master index: a consolidated index to more than 170,000 biographical sketches concerning modern day authors as they appear in a selection of the principal biographical dictionaries devoted to authors, poets, journalists, and other literary figures. 1st ed. Edited by Barbara McNeil. Detroit, Gale, 1984. xix, 519p. (Gale Biographical Index series, no.8) 29cm. hardcover $60 (0-8103-2095-9); paper $25 (0-8103-2096-7); ISSN 0747-7279.

809'.04 Authors—20th century—Biography—Indexes [CIP] 84-10349

Users familiar with the publisher's *Author Biographies Master Index* (the second edition, 1983, provides citations to some 413,000 persons cited in 140 biographical dictionaries and directories) will appreciate the value of this latest addition to the Gale Biographical Index series. Derived in part from the master work, this index includes approximately 171,000 citations to an estimated 90,000 persons contained in 55 biographical dictionaries (210 volumes)—many of which emanate from the publisher as well. This complements similar efforts dealing with journalists, the performing arts, and writers for children and young adults.

Following a Bibliographic Key to Publication Codes for Use in Identifying Sources, which describes the source works, author entries appear alphabetically by surname in three columns to a page along with years of birth/death and the appropriate citation(s). The scope includes authors, broadly defined, who were born or who died in the twentieth century. To support statements of currentness, the publisher claims to have included 30,000 new citations gathered since the parent work's appearance in fall 1983.

For public and academic libraries serving persons needing access to sketches of modern authors in a wide array of biographical sources, this index will be most useful.

Twentieth-century culture: a biographical companion. Edited by Alan Bullock and R. B. Woodings. New York, Harper & Row, 1983. xxx, 865p. 24cm. cloth $35 (0-06-015248-6).

†920.009'04 Biography—20th century | Scientists—Biography Artists—Biography | Scholars—Biography [OCLC] 83-48331

This companion to the *Fontana Dictionary of Modern Thought* contains 1,945 brief biographies signed by some 300 contributors, chiefly from British university faculties. It includes, with few exceptions, those who died after 1900 or are still living whose work has had an impact on modern thought in any field. The editors say these embrace "not only thinkers and writers but also the most important of those whose activities created the problems with which many of the former have been preoccupied." European and American figures predominate, with a few from other countries, e.g., Nigerian novelist and critic, Chinua Achebe.

Intended for those who know the important names in their own field, but not those outside it, the informative sketches range widely, from surrealist filmmaker Luis Buñel to Pierre Mendès-France and Beatrix Potter. A Classified Index by broad categories (further subdivided) reveals a high percentage of physicists and creative writers, especially British, American, and French, with a few from the world of technology, business, and politics. While biographical material on most of these men and women will be found in a well-stocked library reference collection, its well-written sketches, with appended bibliographies, are a convenient source of twentieth-century biography, and it is also suitable for home purchase.

Twentieth-century short story explication: supplement II to third edition: with checklists of books and journals used. [Compiled by] Warren S. Walker. Hamden, Conn., Shoe String Press, 1984. 348p. 24cm. hardcover $35 (0-208-02005-5).

016.8093'1 Short stories—Indexes 80-16175

The first edition of this highly important bibliography was published in 1961, followed by the second edition in 1965 and the third, carrying coverage through 1975, in 1977. This second supplement to the third edition includes primarily those critical studies of short stories published during 1979 to 1981. Included also are items previously "overlooked or unavailable, as well as recent reprintings of earlier works." Transparent organization facilitates use: two sections, "A Checklist of Books Used" (arranged alphabetically by author) and "A Checklist of Journals Used" (listed alphabetically by title), may be easily annotated with holdings information. There is a separate Index of the short story writers included in the supplement. Bibliographic citations throughout the work follow accepted practice; the publisher has not stinted on punctuation and use of italicized typeface to help make references more easily understood by users. Working with prepublication copy, the Board found no mistakes in the citations to criticism or omitted author or title references in the two important checklists.

So far, 1,298 short story writers are cited in the third edition and its two supplements. Coverage is international, but emphasis is on English writers, and entries refer predominantly to studies written in English. However, there are 76 foreign-language titles included in the periodicals listing of approximately 300 journal titles. Many of these foreign-language journals include articles written in English.

This worthy bibliography provides accurate and easy access to short story explication located in books and periodicals and will be useful in any library serving students of English literature.

Ulrich's international periodicals directory: a classified guide to current periodicals, foreign and domestic. 22d ed., 1984. 2v. New York, Bowker, 1983. 1,969p. 28cm. cloth $110 plus shipping/handling (set) (v.1, 0-8352-1620-9; v.2, 0-8352-1621-7; set, 0-8352-1619-5).

†011.34 Periodicals—Bibliography | Periodicals—Directories 32-16320

The current edition of this standard bibliographic annual, providing information on the world's periodicals, continues the high quality of past annual issues. According to the publisher, the present work contains information on some 64,800 periodicals of which more than 40,000 have been updated from the last edition; 6,800 titles have been added. The format, now familiar, continues unchanged; since the Board's last evaluation (cf. *RSBR*, Sept. 15, 1981), the work has been split into two volumes for easier handling.

The Classified List of Periodicals is the primary listing in which titles, fully described, appear under some 556 subject headings, with liberal use of cross-references. Here one finds vital facts on publication, price, circulation, indexing, classification, and ISSN. This edition, for the first time, includes telephone numbers of U.S. and Canadian publishers.

Volume 2 includes a Cessations list (citing in alphabetical order, and with as much detail as possible, periodicals that have ceased since the previous edition); Index to Publications of International Organizations (listing serials in the main listing and in the publisher's *Irregular Serials and Annuals* under their respective publishers); and Title Index.

The set begins with a helpful User's Guide and a number of special aids. In all, this work continues to be a valuable work for reference, acquisition, and processing.

U.S. government directories, 1970–1981: a selected, annotated bibliography. Compiled by Constance Staten Gray. Littleton, Colo., Libraries Unlimited, 1984. xi, 260p. 24cm. cloth $35 (U.S.); $42 (elsewhere) (0-87287-414-1).

016.35304'025 Administrative agencies—U.S.—Directories—Bibliography | U.S.—Executive departments—Directories—Bibliography [CIP] 83-26801

This is the second directory of federal government directories from the 1970s to appear; for Donna Rae Larson's *Guide to U.S. Government Directories, 1970–1980* (Oryx, 1981), see *RSBR*, September 1, 1982. This list extends coverage one year further into the eighties but is limited to titles made available to federal depository libraries and includes fewer directories (575) than *Larson*. The entries are grouped into 12 broad subject areas (e.g., Areas and Places; Businesses and Industries; Individuals); arrangement within each chapter is by Superintendent of Documents classification. A descriptive annotation indicating the purpose, scope, and arrangement of each directory is supplied. Other elements of information furnished include first year of publication, if known; last year, if ceased; and frequency. Prices, being subject to change, are not noted; an Appendix contains a description of the microfiche *GPO Sales Publications Reference File* reprinted from the Government Printing Office's *PRF User's Manual*. Three other Appendixes list regional depository libraries, GPO bookstores, and U.S. government departments and agencies. Title and Subject Indexes complete the bibliography.

While the *PRF* remains the primary source for current information on directories for sale by the Government Printing Office, more comprehensive collections, especially those without Larson's *Guide*, will want to consider acquiring this bibliography.

U.S. industrial outlook 1985: prospects for over 350 manufacturing and service industries. 26th ed. Washington, D.C., U.S. Dept. of Commerce, 1985. various pagings. 28cm. paper $15. S/N:003-008-00195-5.

338.0973 U.S.—Industries—Periodicals [OCLC]   84-645436

The annual volumes of the *U.S. Industrial Outlook* provide data for "improving the information base needed for decision making" in business. Standard Industrial Classification (SIC), used by all federal statistical agencies, most state agencies, and many nongovernmental bodies is followed. (The Motor Vehicles group, for example, includes as component industries Passenger Cars, Trucks and Buses, Motor Vehicle Parts and Stamping, Truck and Bus Bodies, and Truck Trailers.)

Each chapter begins with an analysis of the industry group based on its performance over the past several years and its long-term prospects. The industries included in each group are then treated individually in terms of their current situation (as of late 1984 when the data were compiled), outlook for 1985, and long-term prospects. Tables of Historical Trends accompany the narrative description for most industries. Additional tables, graphs, and black-and-white photographs are included for many industries.

Most of the basic data in the volume were obtained from the Bureau of the Census, and the price indexes were compiled by the Bureau of Labor Statistics. The use of a uniform database permits meaningful comparisons among industries. "Additional References" are provided at the conclusion of many chapters or industry sections. Users should study the section entitled, "How to Get the Most Out of This Book," which explains the method used in developing the forecasts and other concepts relevant to interpreting the data (e.g., the distinction between industry and product data).

The analyses and data provided in *U.S. Industrial Outlook* will be valuable to students and persons involved in business and industry. The book is indispensable for general business collections.

U. S. nonprofit organizations in development assistance abroad: TAICH Directory, 1983. 8th ed. Managing ed., Wynta Boynes; editors, Florence M. Lowenstein and Roger B. McClanahan. New York, Technical Assistance Information Clearing House; UNIPUB, 1983. xiv, 584p. 23cm. paper $24.50 (0-932140-02-5).

309.2′233′73 Technical assistance, American—Societies, etc.—Directories | Economic assistance, American—Societies, etc.—Directories [OCLC]   78-27776

Persons thinking about doing development work abroad and others needing information on overseas assistance will find in this directory detailed information about 497 American organizations concerned with development-assistance programs.

Besides each organization's name and address and the names and titles of its officers, one learns the objectives and programs of the organization, the countries in which it operates, its financial resources, the number of salaried and volunteer persons serving it in the U.S. and abroad, and its publications. The organizations are of varying sizes with diverse goals and programs. Most, but not all, are affiliated with churches. Giants like the Ford Foundation, which spent $35 million in 1982, appear with smaller operations like the Missionaries of Our Lady of La Salette, which spent $300,000. Others spent much smaller amounts.

The alphabetical arrangement is supplemented by four indexes. The Category Index serves as a very general subject index listing the organizations under 14 such broad categories as communications, nutrition, and population and family services; some organizations appear under several headings. The Country Index shows where the organizations are active, and the State Index shows where in the U.S. the organizations are incorporated and have their home offices. The Organization Index lists, in addition to the official names, secondary or popular names, former names, and sometimes acronyms.

The Technical Assistance Information Clearing House (TAICH) receives some support from the U.S. Agency for International Development; organizations registered with the agency are indicated by an asterisk. Information was gathered by questionnaires or compiled from reports or promotional information and then checked by each organization. The last previous directory was completed in 1978.

This directory would be even more useful if the Category Index showed fields of interest in greater detail and/or if an index ranked the organizations by their approximate annual expenditures. Despite these minor shortcomings, *U.S. Nonprofit Organizations in Development Assistance Abroad* is a primary source of information on overseas development-assistance programs in the nonprofit sector. It will be useful in academic and public libraries where this kind of information is called for.

U.S. television network news: a guide to sources in English. Compiled by Myron J. Smith, Jr. Jefferson, N.C., McFarland, 1984. xx, 233p. 24cm. cloth $29.95 (0-89950-080-3).

016.0701′9 Television broadcasting of news—U.S.—Bibliography | Documentary television programs—U.S.—Bibliography [CIP]   82-42885

Described as a "working guide" to more than 3,200 English-language sources (predominately from the U.S.) on network television news from the late 1940s through 1982 (the Addendum extends coverage through the fall of 1983), this bibliography is organized into nine chapters, from reference, general works, and histories to network television and reporting, programming, controversy, domestic affairs, U.S. presidents, presidential elections, and foreign affairs. The last chapter covers biographies. Books, scholarly papers, periodical articles, government documents, dissertations, and masters' theses are included. The Table of Contents forms a topical guide; each chapter begins with a brief introduction to the topic(s) covered. Brief annotations for books and some articles are provided. Author and Subject Indexes refer readers to entry numbers. A lack of white space and no boldface type for headings make the work unattractive and hard on the eyes.

This tool should be useful to casual students of television networks or to more serious researchers. Journalism collections will want *U.S. Television Network News*.

Urban development in the Third World. Pradip K. Ghosh, editor. Westport, Conn., Greenwood, 1984. xvii, 546p. (International Development Resource Books, v.2) illus. tables. figures. 24cm. cloth $45 (0-313-24138-4).

307′.12′091724 City planning—Developing countries | Urbanization—Developing countries | City planning—Developing countries—Bibliography | Urbanization—Developing countries—Directories | Cities and towns—Developing countries—Statistics [CIP]   83-22859

This is the second in a 1984 series of what will eventually be 20 International Development Resource Books. They are being prepared under the auspices of the Center for International Development (University of Maryland) and the World Academy of Development and Cooperation, based in Washington, D.C. The editor is a visiting fellow at the Center and president of the World Academy. The series intends to span the range of issues confronting international development in the Third World. Each title will be similar in format, with current readings (reprints of articles, etc.) comprising more than one-half of each book, then an annotated Bibliography and a directory of information sources.

The title under review is particularly pertinent because most of the world's projected population increase by the year 2000 will live (usually poorly) in cities of developing nations. The book documents and analyzes current trends and future needs in effective urban development of the Third World. It evaluates progress made during the past decade in attaining sustained economic growth and improvement in the quality of living in the developing countries and their crowded cities.

This first section of reprinted articles, mostly from UNESCO publications, includes items by Lester R. Brown and other experts and covers broad topics ("Can Third World Cities Cope?") and specific case studies, such as Jamaica and Kenya. The statistical tables and figures in the second section are drawn mainly from World Bank and UN publications and include such comparative statistics as those on adult literacy and population density. The resource bibliography covers 621 English-language books, periodicals, and specialized publications since 1970, with the most recent dated 1982. A Subject Index to it facilitates use. The last section, a directory of information sources, includes relevant research institutions in Third World countries. The book's Index is accurate and includes references to footnotes in the first section's readings.

Urban Development in the Third World is a useful, accessible work on a vital topic; it will be valuable in academic and public libraries concerned with international development.

The Board's evaluation of volumes 1 and 3–20 in the series of International Development Resource Books will be published in a future issue of *Reference Books Bulletin*.

Victorian science and religion: a bibliography with emphasis on evolution, belief, and unbelief, comprised of works published from c. 1900–1975. By Sydney Eisen and Bernard V. Lightman. Hamden, Conn., Archon, 1984. 696p. hardcover $49.50 (0-208-02010-1).

016.575 Biology—England—History—Bibliography | Evolution—History—Bibliography | Evolution and religion—History—Bibliography | Religion and science—History—Bibliography | Geology—England—History—Evolution [CIP]   82-24497

An exhaustive bibliography on a rather specialized but important topic, this work has 6,267 bibliographic citations, for the most part, unannotated and drawn primarily from English-language books and journals published in Western Europe between 1900 and 1975. The work is divided into sections covering natural theology, geology, evolution and ethics, the Church of England, nonconformity, Christian socialism, atheism, positivism, etc. Included also are 24 subdivisions, each covering such specific writers as Coleridge, Huxley, Kingsley, Mill, Newman, and Tennyson.

There are Subject and Author Indexes. Broad topics, especially writers, are subdivided: thus, Matthew Arnold's monographic works are listed separately, and even his better-known poems, such as "Dover Beach," have separate citations. So with Newman: "Lead, Kindly Light" has 4 citations, and *The Idea of a University* has 11.

Victorian Science and Religion is a much needed bibliographical guide to a major issue in Victorian intellectual life, and it will be useful in almost any academic or large public library with a clientele interested in nineteenth-century studies.

The vocational-technical core collection, v.2: films and video. [By] Jack Hall and Victoria Cheponis Lessard. New York, Neal-Schuman, 1984. V, 250p. 29cm. hardcover $22.95 (0-918212-47-2).

025.2'1877 Libraries, University and college—Book lists | Technical education—Bibliography | Vocational education—Bibliography [CIP]   81-11048

Volume 2 of *The Vocational-Technical Core Collection* is an annotated bibliography of films and videotapes for vocational-technical instruction. (Volume 1, covering books, was reviewed in *RSBR*, Dec. 15, 1982.) The 347 entries have been selected and reviewed for one or more of the following reasons: "1. They were previously noted in an established review source such as *Voc Ed., School Shop,* or *Industrial Education;* 2. They were recommended in bibliographies published by technical or trade associations; 3. They were recommended by vocational educators or technical trades practitioners; and 4. They supplied information generally unavailable in a given subject area." Entries are arranged alphabetically by title under one of 26 subject headings in the areas of business, communications, construction, graphics, personal services, manufacturing, transportation, and vocational health. Each entry includes title, format, price, producer/distributor, date of production, subject, series, and annotation. The latter are descriptive, very well written, and include safety/storage precautions, hygiene practices, indicate study guides, teacher's guides, bibliographies, and tests accompanying the program, and state whether or not sex-role stereotypes are depicted. Title and Subject Indexes and a distributor's directory are included.

The authors are to be commended for compiling this excellent companion to the earlier volume on books. Even though the book is intended to be used in vocational-technical high schools, it would be useful to library media specialists, teachers and curriculum developers in technical and community colleges, as well as to film and video selectors and catalogers in public libraries. Professionals engaged in adult training programs will find it serviceable too.

Ward's directory of 51,000 largest U.S. corporations. Petaluma, Calif., Baldwin H. Ward Publications, 1984. various pagings. 24cm x 28cm. hardcover $195 (0-913482-00-5).

†338.74'025 Corporations—U.S.—Directories | Manufacturers—U.S.—Directories [OCLC]

This is the latest in a series in which the titles and numbers of companies change with each issue. This one includes data for more than 8,000 public and 43,000 private corporations in the United States. Information is divided into four sections: alphabetical, geographical, and two SIC industry sections (one ranking all corporations by sales size under their SIC industry fields and the other ranking the public companies by sales size under SIC fields, also including 30 financial items from their annual and 10-K reports).

Information incorporated into the various listings includes corporation name, address, name of major officer(s), telephone number, sales volume, number of employees, number of plants, etc. Financial information for publicly held companies is extensive—assets, long- and short-term debt, P/E ratio, number of shareholders, etc.

Special features include lists of the top 1,000 corporations (by number of employees, highest four-year growth rate, highest current ratios, lowest debt to equity ratios, largest capital expenditures, etc.).

Ward's Directory is an extremely useful item for business libraries.

The wars in Vietnam, Cambodia and Laos, 1945–1982: a bibliographic guide. By Richard Dean Burns and Milton Leitenberg. Santa Barbara, Calif., ABC-Clio, 1984. xxxii, 290p. (The War/Peace Bibliography series, no.18). 29cm. cloth $58.50 (0-87436-310-1).

016.9595704'3 Vietnamese Conflict, 1961–1975—Bibliography | Indochina—History—1945- —Bibliography | Indochina—History, Military—Bibliography [CIP]   80-13246

Published for the Center for the Study of Armament and Disarmament, California State University, Los Angeles, this exhaustive bibliography of books, articles, theses, and documents relating to the three countries from the end of World War II to 1982 emphasizes the period of active American involvement (1965–75) in the region. It is based in part on the same publisher's *Vietnam Conflict: Its Geographical Dimensions, Political Traumas, and Military Developments* (1973).

After a chapter on general reference aids, the work indexes 6,202 citations, arranged in topical chapters covering an overview of Southeast Asia; Vietnam; U.S. intervention; congressional opinions/policies, international reactions, etc.; strategy; combat operations; human costs of the war; and U.S. domestic reaction (which includes more than 100 citations to novels, plays, etc., in the section on artists and the war). Each chapter is subdivided, either by type of material, subtopic, or chronologically as appropriate. Full bibliographic data are given but generally without annotation.

The work is further enhanced by a nine-page Introduction—essentially a brief summary of the various Indo-Chinese wars from 1946 to 1979. In addition, each of the nine main chapters is preceded by a one- or two-page introduction. There are three maps, and 15 statistical tables, including data on Vietnam veterans. Also included are a Chronology and a Glossary; an Author (or Agency) Index concludes the work. The classified arrangement, even with a good Table of Contents, cannot fully compensate for the lack of a subject index. Nevertheless, this excellent bibliography on this controversial topic will be welcomed in all large public and academic libraries.

Watergate: an annotated bibliography of sources in English, 1972–1982. By Myron J. Smith. Metuchen, N.J., Scarecrow, 1983. xiii, 329p. 22cm. cloth $27.50 (0-8108-1623-7).

016.3641'32'0973 Watergate Affair, 1972- —Bibliography [CIP]   83-4408

The bulk of this work consists of 2,565 annotated citations to material on this famous American political crisis. An additional 17 audiovisual items round out the materials. Reference sources are separately listed.

Entries cover the wide scope of topics that came from the original incidents. Annotations are usually one sentence but longer as necessary, e.g., a book on conservatism in the Nixon and Ford administrations. Especially useful is a listing of all the court cases and congressional proceedings, including supporting documentation, decisions, and findings.

Prefacing the main section is a daily chronology of events for 1972 to 1975. A section on personalities briefly identifies participants in one alphabetical list. The House Committee impeachment investigation report is reprinted. An accurate Subject Index concludes the work.

Watergate is certainly one of the most comprehensive bibliographies on the subject. The volume will be useful in American political science/history collections.

Webster's new twentieth century dictionary of the English language unabridged. 2d ed. Based upon the broad foundations laid down by Noah Webster, extensively revised by the publisher's editorial staff under the general supervision of Jean L. McKechnie. New York, Simon & Schuster, 1983. xiv, 2,129, 160p. illus. maps. 29cm. hardbound $69.96 (0-671-41819-X).

423 English language—Dictionaries [OCLC]   83-42537

Jean McKechnie, assisted by a permanent lexicographical staff, has served as editor of this dictionary since its predecessor, *Webster's New World Dictionary of the English Language,* was extensively revised. No editorial board or contributing editors are listed. Though some additions to the vocabulary have been made, there has been no extensive revision since then.

The active vocabulary of American English is emphasized, but "a considerable number of obsolete, archaic, and rare words that are likely to be encountered in the earlier standard literature" are included. Its entries (the publisher says there are 320,000), arranged letter-by-letter, are supplemented by separately paged Appendixes for place- and personal names, etc.; see below. The actual number of words is considerably less, about 156,000 based on the Board's sample. Newer terms are less fully covered than in some other dictionaries, especially scientific/technical terminology. Widely used terms such as *acid rain, anorexia, laetrile,* and *pacemaker* are found, but few of the newer scientific words in *The Second Barnhart Dictionary of New English* (1980) appear. In other fields, the sense of *anchor* as anchoring a television program is noted, as well as *ballpark figure,* but not *bag lady.* Contemporary slang, however, is fairly well covered. At any rate, the editors' claim that the work "includes virtually all those words that a prolific reader in English will ever be likely to investigate" is at best extravagant and at worst misleading.

Conservative American spelling practice appears to be followed, but no authority or guidelines are given. Variant spellings and pronunciations are shown without, however, indicating common American practice. Thus, *honor, honour* and *theater, theatre* are provided without an indication that the second spellings are British—a peculiar practice in view of the claim to identify current American practice. A typical entry gives: hyphenated word, showing pronunciation by diacritical marks; part of speech; brief etymology; definitions/senses in no particular order; and for some entries, a brief illustrative quotation. Brief pronunciation keys on each page are augmented by a fuller prefatory key. Many of the etymologies are briefer than those in *American Heritage Dictionary,* deliberately simplified for lay users. Rare, obsolete, and slang words are so labeled, but fields less often. Labeling is inconsistent. *Nigger* is accurately described as "a vulgar, offensive term of hostility and contempt, as used by Negrophobes" but *queer,* in the sense of homosexual, is merely identified as slang. *Broad,* in the sense of any female, is described only as a "vulgar term" and is identified as slang. Its pejorative sense is omitted. On the whole, racial, religious, and ethnic pejoratives tend to be better described as such than terms of possible contempt relating to gender or sexual preference. Many other dictionaries suffer from the same problem, but this one may be especially criticized in view of its claim to emphasize contemporary usage.

Definitions are brief and usually clear, with derivatives treated as main entries, e.g., *capacious* and *capaciously,* the latter defined as "in a capacious manner or degree"—an unnecessary and dubious practice inasmuch as it can be viewed as mere padding. The definitions sometimes follow historical order, sometimes not, since the editors believe it is impossible to give the prevailing current meaning first. Such a position is at best moot. Quotations from English classical writers, cited by author, and brief phrases supplied by the editors are less frequent than in some *abridged* dictionaries, e.g., *World Book Dictionary.* Synonyms are sometimes given but not analyzed as in some other dictionaries, both abridged and unabridged. Antonyms are not provided.

The "several thousand" small, black-and-white, well-chosen illustrations are supplemented by 32 colorplates of a miscellany—cats, reptiles, ocean depths, eggs, state flags—inserted in two places. Since these are not related to entries by references in definitions, these more or less exist in a void and are of dubious value. There are also Hammond maps (12 pages in color) at the end. These constitute the color in the deluxe color edition.

Proper names appear in separate Appendixes: about 6,000 briefly identified persons, giving pronunciation; about 1,600 place-names, with location and population; about 2,000 fictional names; some 2,500 foreign words and phrases; about 2,400 biblical names; and about 1,500 abbreviations. These and other miscellaneously appended material will be of less use in libraries than in the home.

Format is satisfactory: the stout binding and opaque paper are adequate for continued use. The small type is usually clear and while not overwhelmingly attractive, the page layouts are clear, with adequate white space for clarity.

Since *Webster's New World Dictionary (WNWD),* second college edition, is also a Simon & Schuster publication, and since, in many cases, its definitions strongly resemble those in *Webster's New Twentieth Century Dictionary (WNTCD),* it is pertinent to note some differences. Under the experienced editorship of David Guralnik, with the assistance of some distinguished contributing editors, the *WNWD* appears to have undergone more continuous revision than the *WNTCD.* The former contains terms, chiefly scientific, not in *WNTCD,* e.g., *half-cell, hadron, halocline, heat sink,* and *hemodialysis.* Newer meanings are given for some terms, such as *halfway house, happening,* and *headhunter.* Some of *WNWD*'s definitions are clearer, e.g., *half gainer.* Unlike *WNTCD,* synonyms are discriminated in *WNWD.* Thus the latter is, in some ways, much more attractive as a working tool than *WNTCD.*

Although *Webster's New Twentieth Century Dictionary* is a source of clear, simple definitions of American English, the random arrangement of the definitions, the failure to add newer scientific terms, to supply adequate illustrations of use, and to discriminate synonyms are major flaws. In fact, the Board is somewhat puzzled at the appellation of "unabridged" for this work, since, in some cases, better definitions, fuller etymologies, and more new words appear in some abridged dictionaries. Libraries needing an unabridged dictionary would do better to select *Webster's Third New International Dictionary* or the *Oxford English Dictionary* and its supplements, further supported by smaller dictionaries of new words. Home dictionary buyers will probably get better value by purchasing a good college-level desk dictionary (see *Reference Books Bulletin,* Dec. 1, 1983). Not recommended.

Webster's II new Riverside university dictionary. Boston, Houghton Mifflin, 1984. 1,536p. illus. 25cm. cloth $14.95 (0-395-33957-X).
423 English language—Dictionaries [CIP]   83-3799

Although, as the *University* in its title implies, *Webster's II* (as it will surely come to be called) is clearly aimed at the collegiate level—with technical usages, etymologies, etc.—it may be thought of as being in some respects not only an updated but a slightly condensed version of the same publisher's *American Heritage Dictionary, 2d College Edition* (cf. *RBB,* Dec. 1, 1983). Coverage is satisfactory—and timely—with, however, somewhat less coverage of slang and disapproved terms and usages than one might wish for. Its vocabulary is presented in four alphabets, i.e., with separate lists of Biographical Names, Geographic Names, and Foreign Words and Phrases. Definitions are clear and concise, with conciseness occasionally achieved at some cost to instant communication of meaning, e.g., *Fabry's disease* is said to involve "impaired renal functioning," whereas *American Heritage* says it involves "impaired functioning of the kidneys." Usage labeling is adequate and clear, although some users will regret the lack of labels indicating that particular terms and usages are regarded as offensive, e.g., *broad* in the sense of "a woman or girl." Etymologies precede definitions (in *American Heritage* they follow). Synonyms are cited, with interesting explications of "core meanings" and, in many instances, discussions of differences. Special strengths include numerous word histories, which go far beyond the usual etymological summary; good (and fresh) use of examples; and excellent usage notes (see the discussion of *fulsome*). Pictures, while not numerous, are well chosen and are clearly presented, hence informative. Page layout is fairly tight, but the overall effect is uncrowded, as such things go; typography is clear, e.g., hyphenation is readily distinguished from syllabication.

Front matter includes, among other features, clear and helpful "Explanatory Notes" and "A Concise Guide to Style, Usage, and Diction"—the latter well done but probably of more interest to individual than to institutional purchasers; its highlights are its lists of clichés and of redundant expressions.

All in all, *Webster's II* is a worthy addition to one's roster of acceptable college-level dictionaries; it should be considered for high school, college, and public libraries and for homes and offices.

The Westminster dictionary of Christian theology. Edited by Alan Richardson and John Bowden. Philadelphia, Westminster, 1983. xvi, 614p. 24cm. hardcover (0-664-21398-7).
250'.03 Theology—Dictionaries [CIP]   83-14521

One of a series of religion-oriented dictionaries (really more like encyclopedias), the emphasis in this work is on theology, with good articles on *Christology, God, Holy Spirit,* and *Scripture,* and shorter but satisfactory articles on *Chrism, Epiphany, Montanism, Paraclete,* etc. Topics in the fields of liturgy, church discipline, veneration of individual saints, and the like, are not included, but may be found in other Westminster dictionaries.

All articles are signed, with academic or other affiliation given. A large number of contributors appear to be British, although many U.S. universities are also represented, and there are many identifiable Catholic contributors.

The work is admirably free of bias—neither Catholic/Protestant bias, nor old-line vs. recent-foundation. On the other hand, churches outside the mainstream of Orthodoxy, Catholicism, or Protestantism may feel that their doctrines have been slighted. For example, there are no specific articles on Mormons or Mennonites; on the other hand, there are articles on Anglo-Catholics, Baptists, Congregationalists, Lutherans, Orthodox, Quakers, Roman Catholics, etc. Most of these are general in nature, dealing with theological, not doctrinal or disciplinary, distinctions.

The Westminster Dictionary of Christian Theology is excellently done and deserves a place in any library where there is an interest in theological matters.

Wheeled armoured fighting vehicles in service. [By] B. T. White; illus. by Peter Sarson and Tony Bryan. Poole, Dorset, Blandford Pr.; dist. by Sterling, 1983. 128p. illus. (part col.) 26cm. hardcover $16.95 (U.S.); $21.95 (Canada) (0-7137-1022-5).

623.74′75 Armored vehicles, Military [British CIP]

Though similar in size and format to the more general work, *Military Vehicles of World War 2* (cf. *RBB*, Dec. 1, 1983), this work is limited to vehicles as cited in the title, describing and illustrating in black-and-white and color the 50-odd types currently in use by about 20 countries. The illustrations are clear, and the text sufficiently detailed to give a good idea of the capabilities of each vehicle, both on land and water, since many of them are amphibious.

The wheeled vehicles described may be grouped into three types, depending on intended usage—reconnaissance, light attack (including occasionally, armor-piercing projectiles), or troop carrier. The work shows how most basic models can be or have been converted from one use to another.

Like other Blandford publications of this type, the work will appeal primarily to military buffs and historians; its general reference value is somewhat limited.

Where to find what: a handbook to reference service. Rev. and updated by James M. Hillard. Metuchen, N.J. and London, Scarecrow, 1984. xviii, 357p. 22cm. cloth $22.50 (0-8108-1645-8).

011′.02 Reference books—Bibliography | Reference services (Libraries)—Handbooks, manuals, etc. | Research—Handbooks, manuals, etc. [CIP] 83-14272

Many of the problems identified by the Board (cf. *RSBR*, Mar. 15, 1975) in the first edition of this work remain. Like that edition, the updated version is "intended as a working assistance to the reference librarian or to the general public seeking specific information." It does this by organizing reference books under 595 subject headings, the intention being that the inexperienced reference librarian or a veteran confronted with a question outside his or her expertise will turn to this work for guidance to appropriate resources.

Some of the subject heading selections are perplexing. For example, "demons" is used, but "witchcraft" is not, nor is there a *see* reference from the latter to the former. A fault of the first edition, the lack of a *see* reference from "crafts" to "handicrafts" persists. The disproportionate number of headings for sports and military subjects may reflect the compiler's personal interests more than demand in most libraries.

Many subject sections open with a brief introductory note referring to other sections of the book or briefly explaining the nature of most questions asked on that subject. Some of these notes add nothing to their sections, especially in the case of "disasters," consisting only of citations of general purpose almanacs.

Annotations describe and briefly evaluate most of the works. The most thorough annotations tend to be in the military and sports sections.

Since many of the introductory notes imply that the book is intended for smaller libraries, some of the works selected are surprising. For example, rather than the *Concise Dictionary of Scientific Biography*, it recommends the full *DSB*, a set too expensive for most small libraries. The compiler allows that "certain essential reference books are included, however, which are too expensive for any but large libraries but are necessary for adequate coverage in their field." Yet under "Jewish People" he does not list the *Encyclopedia Judaica*.

While it is well intentioned, the volume's unevenness is a notable weakness; librarians and patrons are better served by such tools as Sheehy's *Guide to Reference Books* or Cheney and Williams' *Fundamental Reference Sources*.

Who lived where: a biographical guide to homes and museums. By John Eastman. New York, Facts On File, 1983. xxii, 513p. illus. 29cm. cloth $29.95 (0-87196-562-3).

973 Dwellings—U.S.—Directories | Historic buildings—U.S.—Directories | Historical museums—U.S.—Directories | U.S.—Directories [CIP] 82-7376

The author, a free-lance writer, has reviewed hundreds of state guides, local and regional gazetteers, and individual biographies to produce this interesting reference work. For inclusion, the author selected 600 persons (all deceased) whose careers affected U.S. cultural and political history—broadly defined, since the persons range from Abraham Lincoln to Gypsy Rose Lee. Biographical information is, perforce, brief.

Arrangement is by region and individual states within each region. There is a separate chapter for New York City, placed between the New England and Middle Atlantic Region chapters. For each region and state there is a brief introduction, usually too general to be of much value. Unfortunately there are too few illustrations.

A Name Index and Gazetteer is the primary index. Arranged by name, it enables users to locate all homes for an individual. Symbols and abbreviations are used to indicate illustrations in the book, status (landmark, park, historic site), and/or extant dwelling privately owned.

Who Lived Where is a charming book, useful for travel/biography collections especially for locating nonlandmark sites.

Who was who on screen. 3d ed. [By] Evelyn Mack Truitt. New York & London, Bowker, 1983. ix, 788p. 29cm. cloth $65 plus shipping and handling (0-8352-1578-4).

†791.43′028′0922 Moving-picture actors and actresses—Biography | Entertainers—Biography

Who was who on screen. Illus. 3d ed. [By] Evelyn Mack Truitt. New York & London, Bowker, 1984. ix, 437p. 29cm. paper $23.95 (0-8352-1867-8).

†791.43′028′0922 Moving-picture actors and actresses—Biography | Entertainers—Biography

This A–Z biographical dictionary claims to cover all film stars who had at least one film credit and who died between 1905 and 1982. Some 13,000 entries, representing American, British, French, and German film personalities, are included. Typically, entries include minimal personal information—birth and death dates, vocation, sometimes marriage information, and a chronological list of film credits with year and name of film. In many entries only the name of the individual, dates of birth and/or death, and occupation are given.

There are cross-references from the real names to professional names. There are a few inconsistencies in referencing names. Data were gathered by the compiler from her years of collecting memorabilia about film stars. She includes a select bibliography. Entries range from 1926 to 1982, with most of them being recent.

The basic work contains more biographical information than does the two-volume *Forty Years of Screen Credits, 1929–1969* (Metuchen, N.J.: Scarecrow, 1970). However, *Who Was Who* does not list Oscar-winning films. The work under review complements *The Film Buff's Checklist of Motion Pictures, 1912–1979* (1st ed., Hollywood Film Archive, 1979). As with many film reference sources, there is both overlap among these titles and information unique to each.

The illustrated compilation is a condensed version covering 3,100 persons most of whom were from the U.S., Great Britain, France, and Germany. Sixteen pages of portraits serve as illustrations. The concise edition is arranged like the parent work.

As a source for those interested in film stars and general Hollywood information, *Who Was Who on Screen* may be used profitably by persons involved in popular culture either seriously or as a hobby. It will be useful in college, university, or public libraries.

Who's who in American music: classical. 1st. ed. Edited by Jaques Cattell Pr. New York, Bowker, 1983. xiii, 582p. 29cm. hardcover $125 (0-8352-1725-6); ISSN (0737-9137).

†780.973′092′025 Musicians—U.S.—Bio-bibliography | Musicians—U.S.—Directories [OCLC]

Dealing with classical music only, this new work is well described by its title except that *Who's Who in Music in America* might be more accurate. A mélange of brief biographies, with emphasis on professional preparation and achievements, the work provides "data on 6,800 members of the music community who are currently active and influential contributors to the creation, preservation, performance, or promotion of serious music in America." Selection of persons to be included was entrusted to the editors and an advisory committee, as were the content and format of the entries. Information was gathered by questionnaire, and the entrants limited as to the amount of information to be supplied—e.g., no more than five memberships, three honors/awards, seven roles, etc. Entries were compiled by the editors for persons of importance who did not reply. A sample entry shows 15 possible elements: classification (e.g., singer, librarian), birth date, study/training, works (original), recorded performances, roles, positions (career outline), teaching, honors/awards, bibliography (about), memberships, research interest, publications, representative/agent, and mailing address.

No indication is given of the sources used in compiling the list of prospective entrants, and coverage is inconsistent. For example, the principal cellist, percussionist, and violist of the Detroit Symphony Orchestra are included, but the concertmaster is not. The principal conductor of the Lyric Opera of Chicago appears, but not its general manager. A Geographic Index, arranged by state and then by city, with separate entries for Canada and "Other Countires" (few) is followed by a Professional Classification Index reaching from the expected composer, vocalist, etc., to administrator, artist manager, patron, and librarian, among others.

Ranging from the very important to the lesser figures in the broadly defined classical musical world of the United States, *WWAM* is a unique work, planned to be biennial. Inconsistent though it may be, with surprising inclusions as well as omissions, it should find a place on the reference shelves of any academic or public library, budget permitting. The editors should attempt to cover some of the more noticeable omissions in future editions.

Who's who in aviation and aerospace. U.S. ed., 1983. Compiled by the National Aeronautical Institute, with the assistance of Jane's, New York, Grey House, 1983. vii, 1,415p. 29cm. cloth $95 (0-88262-875-5).

629.1'0922 Aeronautics—U.S.—Biography | Aerospace industries—U.S.—Biography [OCLC] 83-641838

Covering a subject of primary importance in today's technology, the National Aeronautical Institute has put together an impressive biographical directory of leading professional men and women in U.S. aviation and aerospace. Biographees submitted the basic information which was then edited for the directory. Data were rechecked by the biographees before publication; some entries (those indicated with an asterisk) have data supplied from other sources.

The most complete entries include "current position, firm, business address, and telephone; primary aviation/aerospace activity; relevant previous employment; education; professional affiliations and honors; pilot certificates held (when applicable), flight hours, aircraft owned and flown; and military service. Useful personal information such as date of birth, nonprofessional affiliations and honors, and home address also is provided in most cases." Two very useful Indexes provide additional access: a Geographic Index and a Primary Professional Activity Index are alphabetically arranged by state and then by city within each state, followed by the individual names listed under one or more of the 20 professional activity categories, ranging from aerospace engineer to test pilot. The second Index is arranged alphabetically by firm or affiliation with individual names following. The directory is legible, well designed, and easy to use.

Who's Who in Aviation and Aerospace is a well-done "who's who"-type source, and if future revisions appear at intervals (no clues were in the front matter), it should become a standard reference in science/technology collections in public and academic libraries.

Who's who in science in Europe: a biographical guide in science, technology, agriculture, and medicine. 3v. 4th ed. Harlow, Essex, Longman; dist. exclusively in the U.S. and Canada by Gale, 1984. 2,556p. 25cm. hardcover $500 (0-582-90109-X).

509'.2'2 Scientists—Europe—Biography [British CIP]

Previous editions of this important biographical directory appeared in 1967, 1972, and 1978. It covers western and central Europe including Turkey but excluding the USSR. European Communist bloc countries are included. There are 25,000 entries, and coverage includes 30 countries and the natural and physical sciences, engineering, agriculture, and medicine. Entries are alphabetically arranged and include for each, as available, full name, year of birth, higher education and degrees obtained with name of granting institution(s) and subject(s) studied, present job (including employer and year appointed), previous professional experience, directorships held, appointments to national committees, memberships in societies (with year of appointment and highest position held with years of service), major publications (including titles of books written or edited and journals on which the individual has served in an editorial capacity),

main professional and research interests, telephone number, and full postal address. A Country/Subject Index lists each person under one or more of eight subject areas—agriculture and food science, chemical and materials science, earth and astronomical sciences, electronics and avionic sciences, energy sciences, engineering science, medical and biochemical sciences, and physics and nuclear science—within country of residence. This publication complements *European Research Centres: A Directory of Organizations in Science, Technology, Agriculture, and Medicine,* published by Longman in 1982. Although there are biographical dictionaries of particular countries, there is no other comprehensive directory of European scientists. It will be useful in academic and research libraries with strong science programs.

Who's who in special libraries, 1983–1984. New York, Special Libraries Association, 1983. 380p. 28cm. paper $16 (ISSN: 0278-842X).

026'.00025'7 Special Libraries Association—Directories | Special librarians—U.S.—Directories | Special librarians—Canada—Directories | Librarians—U.S.—Directories | Librarians—Canada—Directories [OCLC] 82-644142

Who's Who in Special Libraries is the membership directory of the Special Libraries Association (SLA). Members are listed alphabetically, by SLA chapters, and by names of their employers. Page references in these three lists lead to a fourth listing, by SLA divisions and sections, in which members' addresses are provided. No biographical data are included.

Parts I and II of the directory are devoted to general information about SLA. Part I contains the SLA bylaws, membership information, and statistical and historical data. Part II includes lists of officers, directors, chapters, and committees and has its own Name Index.

Published annually, this directory may be wanted by SLA members and by special libraries, library science collections, and some general collections.

Who's who in television and cable. Steven H. Scheuer, editor. New York, Facts On File, 1983. 579p. illus. 26cm. hardcover $49.95 (0-87196-749-2).

791.45'092'2 (B) Television personalities—U.S.—Biography [CIP] 82-12045

Public libraries—and academic and special libraries supporting curricular and/or other activity in journalism and/or radio and television—will want to consider this collection of "well over 2,000" biographical sketches of persons associated with television as performers, producers, agents, etc. Coverage seems, on the whole, satisfactory, although there are puzzling omissions, e.g., Harvey Korman, Louise Lasser, Mary Tyler Moore, Carl Reiner, and Lauren Tewes. Factual data were derived from biographees' responses to queries: at this late date in history, a surprising number of people were reticent as to year of birth. Articles follow a rigid format: name, occupational category or title, business address, date and place of birth, education, career highlights, achievements and awards, and personal (the last very often on the order of "Resides in Ventura, CA, with husband, Cal, and daughters, Muffy and Ginny"). Many sketches are accompanied by black-and-white photographs. The volume concludes with a Corporation Index, grouping entries under ABC, CBS, etc., and an index by Job Title or Position, with such headings as Producers, Actors and Actresses, Anchors, and Reporters. There is no provision of access via program title—something the compilers may want to consider in subsequent editions.

William Morris in private press and limited editions: a descriptive bibliography of books by and about William Morris, 1891–1981. By John J. Walsdorf. Phoenix, Oryx, 1983. xxvi, 602p. 26cm. hardcover (in slip case) $74.50 (0-89774-041-6).

016.821'8 Morris, William, 1834–1896—Bibliography | Printing—Bio-bibliography | Printers—England 82-42923

The title and subtitle given above tell enough of the content of this labor of love. The work is divided into two parts: a descriptive listing of the 53 books printed by Morris (many of them also written by him) at the Kelmscott Press from 1891 to 1898; and a similar descriptive listing of books by or about William Morris on private presses in England and America from 1891 to 1981. Each book is given one or two pages of detailed description, and many have reproduced title pages. The balance of the book (approximately 170 pages) is made up of Kelmscott Press auction and sales catalogs, photostatically reproduced. There is also a bibliography, a list of recent dealers' catalog prices, and three indexes—names, titles, and presses.

William Morris will have strong appeal in universities with special collections in English literature, especially the Pre-Raphaelites, and in any library with an interest in fine printing.

Women and folklore: a bibliographic survey. Compiled by Francis A. de Caro. Westport, Conn., Greenwood, 1983. xiv, 170p. 24cm. cloth $27.50 (0-313-23821-9).
016.398'088042 Women—Folklore—Bibliography | Folklore—Bibliography [CIP] 83-12837

Containing more than 1,600 entries, this bibliography is an attempt to bring "together knowledge about what has been published on women's folklore, and folklore about women, and related topics." It is not intended to be exhaustive.

Divided into two parts, the Essay Guide functions as a sort of classified index, referring to appropriate works in its sections on Women's Speech, Quilt Making, Witchcraft, Healers, Sex Roles, etc. Dates of bibliographic citations range from the 1820s to as late as 1982, with most of them falling within the last 50 years.

A Subject Index cites entry numbers from the Bibliography—which results in long lists after some index terms, e.g, more than 150 after *folksong and music* and more than 100 after *sex roles*. Such a scheme is of dubious help in searching out the wealth of material provided here. However, the Essay Guide is some compensation.

Nevertheless, this volume, compiled by an English professor whose previous writings are in related subject areas, will be useful in large public libraries and academic libraries supporting courses in women's studies and/or folklore.

Women and sexuality in America: a bibliography. Compiled by Nancy Shali. Boston, G. K. Hall, 1984. xv, 404p. (G. K. Hall Women's Studies Publications) 24cm. cloth $49.95 (0-8161-8099-7).
016.3067'088042 Women—U.S.—Sexual behavior—Bibliography | Women—U.S.—Sexual behavior—History—Bibliography [CIP] 84-10751

This 1,684-item bibliography was created to "document change over time" in the area of American women's sexuality. In comprehensiveness the text has been restricted in several ways: only English-language nineteenth- and twentieth-century printed material, mostly published in the U.S.; narrow definition of "sexuality" (no items on child care or birthing practices); and professional (but not highly technical) literature only. The remainder is what the author hopes to be a "balanced presentation in terms of topics and time periods" which maintains "a humanist perspective." Following the Preface and Introduction, the text is divided into 15 topical chapters covering such diverse subjects as contributions of psychoanalysis, children and adolescents, lesbians, and sexual dysfunction and related problems. The brief introduction to each chapter is followed by annotated lists (primarily of books) and then checklists (primarily of periodical articles). Citation is to the edition of the work which was examined (generally the earliest) except for the works of Freud and Ellis, for which standard editions are cited. Accurate Author/Title and Subject Indexes conclude the volume.

Within its self-imposed limitations, Shali's bibliography is worthwhile. The goals of balanced coverage and creating a work for "most humanities researchers" have been achieved. *Women and Sexuality in America* will be of special interest in libraries with psychology and women's studies collections.

Women composers, conductors, and musicians of the twentieth century: selected biographies. 2v. By Jane Weiner LePage. Metuchen, N.J. & London, Scarecrow, 1980, 1983. vii, 293p. 23cm. cloth $18.50 (0-8108-1298-3, v.1); x, 373p. 23cm. cloth $21.50 (0-8108-1597-4, v.2).
780'.92'2 (B) Women musicians—Biography [CIP] 80-12162

This reference work has been compiled "to make readily available [information concerning] the contributions and accomplishments of some of the gifted women musicians of the twentieth century." Its scope is limited to 34 prominent persons, among whom Margaret Hillis, Wanda Landowska, and Sarah Caldwell are perhaps best known.

The composers, conductors, and performing musicians were, with a few exceptions, interviewed by the author. Excerpts from reviews and descriptions from other secondary sources are also included in the biographies. Each sketch concludes with (for composers) a partial list of compositions chosen by the subjects themselves, and many also have discographies that include distributors' addresses. Each volume also contains a detailed index.

Libraries with extensive collections in twentieth-century music and those needing biographical material on major female musicians may find this set a useful reference tool.

Women in China: a selected and annotated bibliography. [Compiled by Karen T. Wei.] Westport, Conn., Greenwood, 1984. xvii, 250p. (Bibliographies and Indexes in Women's Studies, no.1) 24cm. cloth $35 (0-313-24234-8).
016.3054'0951 Women—China—Bibliography | Women—Taiwan—Bibliography [CIP] 84-10863

This selective bibliography on the role of women in Chinese society from antiquity to the present emphasizes the nineteenth and twentieth centuries (in accordance with the increasing importance of women during those time periods). Most of the 1,102 publications included were published between the end of the nineteenth century and 1982. The vast majority are English-language materials, but there are also some Dutch, French, German, and Russian publications. The book is obviously aimed at Western users, since no Chinese-language sources are included. There is no geographic limitation to the entries—both Taiwan and the mainland are covered.

The major subject emphases of the work are the economic condition, status, and liberation of Chinese women. The book is organized into 14 broad subject chapters such as "Bibliography"; "Biography, Autobiography, and Memoirs"; "Economics and Employment"; "Education"; and "Family Planning, Fertility and Health." Within each chapter, entries are arranged alphabetically by author or title. Most (85 percent) of the entries have both descriptive and analytical annotations. Books, journals, conference papers, theses and dissertations, chapters or parts of books, microforms, and nonprint media have all been included. Author and Title Indexes conclude the work.

Women in China takes the first step toward documenting the role of women in non-Western cultures. It will be useful to any serious students of women in Chinese history and culture. For women's or Asian studies collections.

Women in Western European history: a select chronological, geographical, and topical bibliography: the nineteenth and twentieth centuries. Compiled and edited by Linda Frey, Marsha Frey, and Joanne Schneider. Westport, Conn., Greenwood, 1984. liv, 1,024p. 24cm. cloth $55 (0-313-22859-0).
016.3054 Women—Europe—History—Bibliography [CIP] 81-20300

Continuing the excellence of their bibliography, which provided sources of information on women from antiquity to the French Revolution, the compilers (all professors of history) in this second volume bring the study of the historical development of women's place in society in Western Europe from 1789 to 1982. Although the compilers point out that "European history for the past two hundred years does not lend itself to neat chronological divisions," they have arbitrarily used specific dates in chapter divisions. The first chapter incorporates nineteenth-century developments, 1789–1914; the twentieth century is divided into two chapters, 1914–45 and 1945–82. Coverage is international within the chapters, entries appear under geographical/political divisions and within these, under broad as well as narrow topics such as Literature, Science, Art, etc., some of which are further subdivided. In any given section, entries are listed alphabetically by author. Standard bibliographic data are provided; there are no annotations. Cross-references appear at the ends of sections.

Although a few cross-references are provided in the Subject Index, either more specific indexing or the use of titles (only entry numbers are used) would increase ease in using the work. For example, under such entries as *Family* or *Feminism* are hundreds of references.

Name and Author Indexes are also included. *Women in Western European History* is a most valuable resource for college and university libraries supporting courses in women's history and for public libraries having patrons interested in the changing role of women in society in Western Europe.

Women novelists, 1891–1920: an index to biographical and autobiographical sources. By Doris Robinson. New York, Garland, 1984. li, 458p. 25cm. cloth $38 (0-8240-8977-4).
016.823'912'09 (B) Women novelists—19th century—Biography—Indexes | Women novelists—20th century—Biography—Indexes [CIP] 83-49334

Public and academic libraries—especially the latter—will want to consider adding Robinson's bibliography/index to their reference collections—less, perhaps, for major authors (already well covered in standard tools) than for minor ones (on whom material may prove difficult to identify). Coverage includes about 1,500 authors and is international, with emphasis upon English-language authors and sources—an emphasis suggestive not of bias but of realistic assessment of demand. Still, one surprising omission is Sigrid Undset.

The volume consists of a list of the nearly 300 biographical compilations and other reference tools analyzed; the body of the work—listing under literary figure, autobiographies, biographies (including but not limited to material in the compilations analyzed), obituaries, and (in some cases) published bibliographies; and an Index by country of origin, notable for its preliminary list of black authors and for its distinction between English, Scottish, and Welsh authors (a useful distinction, and one not always made).

It is to be hoped that Robinson will extend this work backward, forward, and (as it were) sideways—possible sequels including similar coverage of women novelists 1921–1950 and women poets 1891–1920.

Women of the future: the female main character in science fiction. By Betty King. Metuchen, N.J., Scarecrow, 1984. xxi, 273p. 23cm. cloth $18.50 (0-8108-1664-4).

813'.0876'09352042 Science fiction, American—History and criticism—Addresses, essays, lectures | Science fiction, English—History and criticism—Addresses, essays, lectures | Science fiction, American—Bibliography | Science fiction, English—Bibliography | Women—Fiction—Bibliography [CIP] 83-20130

Arranged by decades from the 1930s to the 1980s, this work identifies female characters in science fiction novels and sections of anthologies, giving for each: (1) main character; (2) physical characteristics, e.g., "Seldom climaxes in sex until her marriage to Bran Tregure, and then has quite normal sexual desires; has dark hair, cropped close to her head . . ."; (3) mental/emotional characteristics, e.g., "Is an 'interplanetary explorer' and a 'woman of considerable intellectual power,' but is afraid of the stars and of unfamiliar wild animals . . ."; and (4) story particulars, given in about 400 words. Each of these is separately indexed, with an added Title/Author Index. A historical overview giving some plots covers 1818–1929. Three short Appendixes list collections and anthologies of stories about women characters; women in erotic science fiction, e.g., John Norman's *Gor* series, labeled "soft-core sadomasochistic pornography housed in SF trappings"; and Amazon women. The author points out that "not even nearly half" of the women are feminist characters, but is convinced that "sf remains one of the best, if not the best, type of literature for feminist fiction." Sf readers and feminists will be interested in this unique bibliography.

Words of love: a complete guide to romance fiction. By Eileen Fallon. New York and London, Garland, 1984. XXII, 386p. (Garland Reference Library of the Humanities, v.382) 23cm. cloth $19.95 (0-8240-9204-X).

809.3'85 Love stories—History and criticism—Addresses, essays, lectures | Love stories—Bibliography [CIP] 82-49132

The love story has come out of the closet. In this guide, 66 no longer living and more than 150 current romance writers (chiefly British and American women) are described, either in interesting biographical sketches or by the writers themselves. The latter are living authors who tell how they came to be published, name their favorite authors, and give their thoughts on writing. Principal works are listed chronologically after each entry.

Compiled by a literary agent and former editor who has worked closely with such romance novelists as Barbara Cartland, she was assisted by Kay Mussell whose Foreword helps to explain the current romance book and who supplies a list of critical works. Other contributors have written an informative historical overview (from the fourth century A.D.) and essays on the Regency romance and the romance boom. Subgenres (e.g., Edwardian, family saga) are treated somewhat sketchily under ten categories, which are used to classify the writers in an appended list. Aspiring writers will find the descriptions of associations, publications, and conferences of interest. (For example, the Romance Writers of America was not founded until 1980 and had its first national conference in 1981.)

Many of the writers use pseudonyms and a list of these is appended, but there is no index.

Since one out of four books sold in the U.S. is a romance, this biobibliography should be popular with inveterate readers of such prolific writers as Roberta Gellis as well as with would-be writers of this popular form. Social historians will also find it of interest.

Words of Wall Street: 2,000 investment terms defined. [By] Allan H. Pessin [and] Joseph A. Ross. Homewood, Ill., Dow Jones-Irwin, 1983. xi, 297p. 23cm. cloth $22.50; paper $9.95 (0-87094-382-0).

332.6'03'21 Investments—Dictionaries | Securities—Dictonaries | Finance—Dictionaries [OCLC] 82-73632

Pessin and Ross, drawing upon their extensive experience in teaching and writing about the securities industry, have compiled this work defining 2,000 terms in lay language. Items chosen include abbreviations/acronyms (e.g., *PV, PX, FOCUS Report, QT, STANY, WHOOPS*), slang (*White Knight, daisy chain, whipsaw,* etc.), SEC rules (10b-13, 13E, 433), various securities regulations acts (*Securities Act of 1933, Securities Exchange Act of 1934; Regulations A, G, Q, T, U, and W of the Federal Reserve Board, Glass Steagall Act*), and basic investment terms and phrases (*Fortune 500, Forbes 500, cumulative voting, holder of record, quick asset radio, Moody's investment grade, Standard & Poor's Index,* etc.). Entries are often not merely defined but are amplified with examples, alternative designations, or cross-references. Entries are alphabetized letter by letter. One word of caution noted in the Preface is the "Table of Cross References" (nearly 150 such references) preceding the A–Z glossary proper, which must be checked if one does not find a term. The Preface does not explain the rationale for this artificial separation of related items. In format and style, *Words of Wall Street* is similar to and will update Peter Wyckoff's *Dictionary of Stock Market Terms* (Englewood Cliffs, N.J.: Prentice-Hall, 1963; published by Hopkinson & Blake in 1963 as *The Language of Wall Street*), a well-known popular-language investment dictionary which has served well in public and academic libraries. *Words of Wall Street* is also appropriate for libraries and for individual purchase.

The wordtree: the handbook of physical and social engineering. Authored, compiled, & edited by Henry G. Burger. 1st ed. 7306 Britanny, Merriam, KS 66203-4699, The Wordtree, 1984. 381p. 28cm. cloth $149 (0-936312-00-9).

423'.1 Vocabulary | English language—Synonyms and antonyms [CIP] 84-13007

Surprises are in store for materials selectors who examine Henry C. Burger's *The Wordtree*: it is truly a dictionary with a difference. Its two main parts are a "Hierarchy" (a classified display which faintly recalls Roget's) and an alphabetical index thereto. Its subtitle rivals Kant in use of unfamiliar words and inflections: *A Transitive Cladistic for Solving Physical & Social Problems; The Dictionary That Analyzes a Quarter-Million Word-Listings by Their Processes, Branches Them Binarily To Pinpoint the Concepts, Thus Sequentially Tracing Causes to Their Effects, To Produce a Handbook of Physical and Social Engineering.* The "transitives" appear to be 24,600 verbs taking direct objects; "cladistic" seems to refer to "branching"—up, down, sidewise, allowing one to move intellectually in many directions, not just one, and recording all sorts of metaphysical relationships. The result is juxtaposition of notions along startling lines—with levels of diction, degrees of specificity, etc., displayed in truly mind-boggling and mind-expanding fashion. Promotional material is encouraging: "Pinpoint any idea, then skip-branch (don't plod) to its causes and effects!" But as anyone who has tried to reduce multidimensional reality to one-item-after-another verbal strings could predict, the result is not wholly successful. That Burger's reach exceeds his grasp will come, then, as no surprise; but it is refreshing to behold someone reaching for the stars when so many content themselves with reinforcing their holds upon the nearby. The front matter (54 jammed-with-type pages) is worth reading, especially the "Decoder" (p.0–1) and the "Synopsis" (p.12–15).

Linguists, social psychologists, information scientists, and others will find *The Wordtree* thought provoking—and conceivably of use in practical situations. But regardless of its status as an innovative approach to word finding—its emphasis being on just that, not on presenting data about "given" words—it leaves much to be desired as a working tool in typical public and academic library situations. Its "system" is complex; its typography is not only small but gray; its page layout is so crowded and lacking in emphasis as to make it virtually illegible to all but the most assiduous readers; and in general it labors to bring forth modest hillocks in a way suitable to the parturition of Everest—a comment which may prove unfair, but surely the best achievements of communication are best described contrariwise. Burger's prose is sometimes vivid and in all senses "telling"; but much of it reads like literal translation from some unknown tongue. Surely if there is in this book as much good as its compiler claims—and one suspects there is nearly as much—it can be presented in such a way as to be almost as readily accessible to casual users as to initiates and devotees. Such, at any rate, is one's faith in the possibilities of standard English and familiar and simple display techniques.

World directory of energy information: the Americas including the Caribbean. v.3. Compiled by Cambridge Information and Research Services Ltd. New York, Facts On File, 1984. x, 316p. 30cm. cloth $95 (0-87196-483-X).

333.79 Power resources—Information services—Directories [CIP]   81-754

The third and final volume of the *World Directory of Energy Information* follows the design of volumes 1 (Western Europe, *RBB*, June 15, 1982) and 2 (Middle East, Africa, Asia/Pacific). It provides for the U.S., Canada, Central and South America, and the Caribbean a survey of key energy production and consumption, information on energy industries, and statistics of energy trade. Data are current through 1981. State and provincial data are provided for the U.S. and Canada. Part 3 lists public and private sector organizations engaged in the energy field, and part 4 is a bibliography, by country, of energy publications.

Statistics provided here can be found in numerous other sources such as the UN's *Yearbook of World Energy Sources*, but this volume's advantage is its useful guide to publications and organizations in the Western Hemisphere which are responsible for energy development and management. It will be useful in large public and academic libraries although revisions of the set will be necessary to keep it up-to-date.

World directory of modern military vehicles. By Bart Vanderveen. New York, Arco, 1984. 256p. illus. 25cm. hardcover $19.95 (0-668-06022-0).

623.74 Vehicles, Military [CIP]   83-17177

With some slight changes of title, from *Observer's Military Vehicles Directory* to the present one, and some changes in format, this is essentially the fourth volume of an ongoing series dealing with unarmored vehicles; this one covers the decade from 1970 to about 1981. Like its predecessors, each entry has one black-and-white photograph (occasionally two or three, to show variations) and six to ten lines of technical data, including country of origin (coded by international registration letters—*E* for Spain, *ROK* for South Korea, etc.). Vehicles are grouped by type and appear in no readily discernible order. The reference value, aside from the obvious use to ascertain technical data about a given or known model, is minimal. The Index is solely by name of manufacturer, and the entries merely refer to page numbers. Thus, the entry *GMC* is followed by 15 page numbers. There is no index by country, either of origin or of usage, though the text indicates that many vehicles are sold abroad; for example, the Toyota "jeep" is pictured as modified for use in Australia, Jordan, and the Netherlands.

The work will have some value for military vehicle specialists and perhaps in libraries catering to movie and TV studios, where accuracy of detail is a factor. General libraries that have purchased earlier volumes will doubtless want this update to the series but probably only for their circulating collections.

World guide to abbreviations of organizations. 7th ed. [Compiled by] F. A. Buttress. Detroit, Grand River, 1984. 731p. 25cm. cloth $115 (0-8103-2049-5).

060'.148 Associations, institutions, etc.—Abbreviations [British CIP]

This is a new seventh edition of a standard guide which appeared first in 1954. It is 50 percent larger than the sixth edition of 1981 (cf. *RSBR*, June 1, 1982), and it contains some 42,500 entries. Arranged alphabetically, the entries consist of the abbreviation, initialism, or acronym, followed only by the complete name of the organization. Occasionally the country or parent organization (e.g., UN) is cited, but no address or other information is given. The work identifies companies, institutions, international agencies, and government departments in Europe, Africa, Asia, Australia, and the Americas and includes a selected bibliography for Russian and Near Eastern acronyms. There is also a general bibliography which includes such sources as the *World of Learning*, the *Encyclopedia of Associations*, and Gale's *Acronyms, Initialisms and Abbreviations*.

Since this is the age of acronyms, *World Guide to Abbreviations of Organizations* is very useful, especially for large academic and research libraries.

World guide to special libraries: Internationales Handbuch der Spezialbibliotheken, v.17. 1st ed. Munchen, Saur; dist. by Gale, 1983. XXX, 990p. 30cm. cloth $120 (3-598-20528-7; ISSN: 0724-8717).

†026.00025 Libraries, Special—Directories [OCLC]

Designed to supplement the *World Guide to Libraries* (volume 8 in the same series), this compilation includes 32,099 entries of special libraries in 159 countries. Above all other types of libraries, the "special" library is the one most difficult to define. The compilers have included here not only independent libraries but also departmental libraries in educational institutions "provided they are accessible as separate collections and are catalogued separately as such" together with governmental and legal libraries. A minimum book collection of 3,000 volumes was set for inclusion, although this criterion is not always met. Entries are grouped under five broad headings: Generalities—1 percent of the entries; Humanities and Theology—27.5 percent; Social Sciences—23.5 percent; Health Sciences and Life Sciences—13.5 percent; and Sciences and Technology—34.5 percent. Under these headings the entries are by country in alphabetical order and then alphabetical by name. A Subject Index analyzes entries under 271 terms. The main editor admits that this broad grouping under five terms supplemented by the subject headings is "still not entirely satisfactory, and may not meet every need." It may be possible to refine this approach in future editions. The publisher also plans to issue national directories of special libraries with extensive subject indexes. At the most, entries contain name, address, telephone, telex, telegram address, year of foundation, name of director, important holdings, special collections, statistical information on holdings, participation in data networks, interlibrary loan programs, and library associations. Many entries, of course, have briefer descriptions.

While this is an impressive first attempt at what is an immense undertaking, the call for this information may be limited in many libraries. Most libraries may find Gale's *Directory of Special Libraries* sufficient for their needs.

World view, 1984: a comprehensive look at the news behind the news. New York, Pantheon, 1983. 470p. illus. 22cm. hardcover $22.50 (0-394-53363-1); paper $11.95 (0-394-72154-3).

†320.9'048 World politics—1975–1985—Yearbook

World View, an encyclopedic yearbook on international affairs, was initiated and first published in France as *L'Etat du Monde.* For the English-language version (published also in Great Britain by Pluto Press, London), some material was retained and translated, but additional articles were commissioned.

Like encyclopedia yearbooks, *WV* begins with a chronology of events covering June 1982 through May 1983. But unlike them, reading lists of articles from *The Times,* the *New York Times, New Statesman,* and the *Nation* are placed after many entries.

The rest of the volume is devoted to articles on issues, countries, and areas of the world. The one-to-eight-page signed essays on issues cover such varied topics as "Strategic Questions" and "Debating Points."

More than half the yearbook is made up of articles in the section on the major countries and regions of the world in which the principal political and economic developments of 1982 and early 1983 are analyzed. The signed articles on 34 countries focus on a significant trend (e.g., Mexico: The Curse of Oil), include a political fact box (head of state, nature of regime, parties), and a chart of demographic, military, and economic statistics for 1965, 1975, and 1982. The essays (unsigned) and statistical charts on 35 major regions of the world are similar in content to those in the countries section except that maps are provided. In the last section of *WV,* culture and ideology topics as diverse as Pac-Man, feminist fiction, and video games are discussed.

The editors make no claim to evenhandedness or objectivity; their objective was to produce an "authoritative, scholarly and reliable yearbook that also provides an alternative, critical view of the world." The essays, often subjective, are lively, very readable, and they are enhanced by political cartoons.

Contributors sign their articles but are not otherwise identified. The dust jacket tells us that the "European contributors . . . are all experts in their fields . . . [are] published regularly in . . . well-known newspaper and journals" and that the American contributors include political columnists for the *Village Voice* and a military analyst for Washington's Institute for Policy Studies.

The reference value of *World View* is strengthened by clearly explained and well-documented statistics and numerous bibliographies. The latter (which include books, journal articles, and organi-

Worldmark encyclopedia of the nations. 6th ed. 5v. (v.1 United Nations, v.2 Africa, v.3 Americas, v.4 Asia & Oceania, v.5 Europe) Moshe Y. Sachs, editor and publisher. New York, Worldmark Press: J. Wiley, exclusive world distributor, 1984. illus. maps. tables. 29cm. $199.95 (0-471-88622-X: Wiley)
910′.3′21 Geography—Dictionaries | History—Dictionaries | Economics—Dictionaries | United Nations | Political Science—Dictionaries [CIP]   83-26013

The sixth edition of this standard reference is much the same as the earlier editions in terms of purpose and scope; the major change is the full incorporation of updated information which has been contributed by professors, authors, subject experts, and government officials. Moshe Y. Sachs continues as editor and publisher.

The Preface explains the encyclopedia's purpose: "to offer the reader a portrait of the world—the individual nations and their main meeting ground, the United Nations system." Volume 1 focuses on the United Nations, and volumes 2 through 5 concentrate on individual countries of the world. The first part of the UN volume contains a survey of the UN and its main organs and concludes with a bibliography (most are dated in the 1980s). The second part of volume 1 discusses the agencies related to the UN; the first volume also includes world tables, glossaries, an abbreviations list, conversion tables, an Index to Countries, an Index to the UN and Related Agencies, and data on polar regions.

Within each of the next four volumes countries are arranged alphabetically. The sixth edition contains 172 country articles compared to 162 in the fifth edition. Discussion on every country covers 50 different topics. (This familiar scheme permits comparison of topics between countries.) In this edition, two topics are new: environment and science and technology. The topics banking and securities and communications and the press have been combined in this edition. Included for each country are capital city, flag, anthem, monetary unit, system of weights and measures, holidays, and a black-and-white map of the area.

Worldmark Encyclopedia of Nations continues to provide readable, up-to-date information; it is an extremely useful reference for school, academic, and public libraries.

Ye gods: a dictionary of the gods. 1st ed. By Anne S. Baumgartner. Secausus, N.J., Lyle Stuart, 1984. 201p. 24cm. hardcover, $14.95 (0-8184-0349-7).
291.2′11′0321 Gods—Dictionaries | Mythology—Dictionaries [CIP]   83-18146

Approximately 188 gods and goddesses from both the East and West (Greece, Arabia, Persia, Prussia, Mexico, India, Egypt, China, etc.) are succinctly and humorously defined in this aptly titled reference book. Arranged alphabetically and intended for a popular audience, the book has no introduction, no criteria for selection, and no bibliography to credit the information given. Also the term "god," judging by the entries, is very loosely defined. Yet the frivolous attitude of the author and her breezy style make a potentially dull subject highly readable. *Ye Gods* is most suitable for public and school libraries.

Year by year in the rock era: events and conditions shaping the rock generations that reshaped America. By Herb Hendler. Westport, Conn., Greenwood, 1983. xxv, 350p. 24cm. cloth $29.95 (0-313-23456-6).
784.5′4′00973 Rock music—Miscellanea | Music and society | Music, Influence of | U.S.—Social life and customs [CIP]   82-11722

After an Introduction and Preface in which Hendler briefly describes the rock era and indicates the arrangement of this book, he steps back and allows the events of 1954 through 1981 to present their own story. For each year, Hendler lists the artists performing; juke box hits; rock industry news as well as other news of the era; statistics and other information descriptive of the period; fashion, fads, jargon of the period; and trivia of the year. Each year of the 1954–81 period is covered in this fashion.

The next section includes statistical information of the rock era: cost of living; product price data; tuition fees; relevant facts and "firsts" that took place; important contests; major films made; and other facts that will be of interest to rock buffs.

A Bibliography which cites sources used in compiling this work completes the book.

This chronological account of the rock era and its evolution will appeal to many researchers interested in the period. This book will also appeal to trivia buffs with its inordinate amount of little-known information.

Young people with problems: a guide to bibliotherapy. By Jean A. Pardeck and John T. Pardeck. Westport, Conn., Greenwood, 1984. 176p. cloth $29.95 (0-313-23836-7).
616.89′166′088055 Bibliotherapy | Child psychotherapy | Adolescent psychotherapy | Child psychopathology—Juvenile literature—Bibliography | Adolescent psychopathology—Juvenile literature—Bibliography [CIP]   83-18601

"The primary purpose of this book is to provide counselors, psychologists, psychiatrists, social workers and other helping professionals with readily available information about bibliotherapy, including annotations of recommended books for working with young people with problems." An introduction citing specific research on bibliotherapy explains how to use books in therapy and discusses situations in which such therapy is effective. Chapters deal with alcohol and drugs, divorce and separation, emotional and behavioral problems, moving to a new home, physical handicaps, pregnancy and abortion, serious illness and death, sexual awareness, sibling relationships, and stepparents. Facts about each topic are introduced, and several related books are cited. Most titles are post-1970 publications; interest and grade levels K–12 are given. Annotations are typically four to six sentences long and indicate if the book is available in paperback, large-type, braille, or as a talking book, but not its print status. Although school psychologists may find the text preceding the annotations more helpful in actual therapy, the annotations are sufficiently comprehensive that other professionals could use the lists to recommend titles. (Psychologists advise the Board that youngsters prefer talking to reading.) Librarians helping students prepare health or social problems papers may find *Young People with Problems* a useful roundup of familiar and lesser-known titles.

DATABASES

Marquis who's who. Marquis Who's Who, Inc. Vendor: DIALOG file 234. $95/hour standard rate, prices vary for online and offline records. Coverage as of May 1984: *Who's Who in America*, 42d edition, 1982–83, to date (75,000 records) and *Who's Who in Frontier Science and Technology* (15,000 records). Updated quarterly.

The exciting possibilities of being able to search *Who's Who in America* online via the *Marquis Who's Who* database became apparent to the Editorial Board after it studied the DIALOG Bluesheet for file 234, several additional brochures about the file, and the full DIALOG chapter on the database. The last, which was sent to the Board in its final draft stage, amounts to more than 50 pages of explanatory text and illustrations of every aspect of the database. Though an experienced DIALOG searcher could often search the file successfully based on the brief information on the four-page bluesheet, the Board believes that most users will benefit from reading the full chapter carefully.

Since this database has 43 searchable indexes and six searchable suffix fields of the basic index, space limitations preclude full description and commentary on all of them. In general, the 43 indexes are grouped into seven different categories of information: vital statistics, such as name, birth city, birth state, and year of birth; career information, such as company name, company location, occupation name, and position held; education information; achievements, such as awards, honors, etc.; affiliations and memberships, such as clubs, civic or political activities, professional memberships, and religious affiliations; family information; and address information. The basic index searches virtually every word in the database, and the six suffix fields of the basic index function as, in effect, logical groupings of the 43 additional indexes.

Placement of information in each entry appears to be determined, in part, by the choice of the biographee. For instance, one person included in *WWA* might list an Olympics medal as an award (searchable online by *AW=olympic?*), and another person would list it as a special achievement (searchable as *SA=olympic?*). The Board hopes that such discrepancies can soon be cleaned up in the editing process. In the meantime, instead of trying to outguess the system, a searcher could simply search *olympic?/id* to cover the identifier suffix subfield of the basic index, which includes awards, special achievements, and a number of other categories.

The power of the online *Marquis Who's Who* database to turn out intriguing results is only as limited as the imaginations of the people using the file. For example, how many prominent Americans work in Altoona versus Johnstown, Pennsylvania (rival cities), or live in Des Moines, Iowa, or were born in Santa Barbara, California? How many Cuban-born American lawyers have made it into *Who's Who in America*? Compare several major state universities, such as the Universities of North Carolina, Texas, Minnesota, Wisconsin, Illinois, Michigan, and California at Berkeley. How many graduates—or employees—prominent enough to be in *WWA* have won Guggenheim fellowships or Rhodes scholarships? For that matter, what librarians have received one either? All of these searches are possible. Fund-raising efforts could be aided by an online search. For example, a list of company chief executive officers in a particular city, region (by truncated zip code), or state who have included a particular activity, such as arts organizations, in their civic activities lists can be compiled. Trying as many of these possibilities as time allowed, the Editorial Board was favorably impressed with the potential uses of the file. (However, one error should be pointed out here: the Board selected company location (CO)=Los Angeles or Los(w)Angeles and got only two responses. Either there is a massive conspiracy against that part of the world, or, more likely, the database has a tagging error of some sort.)

Marquis promises quarterly unpdating of the database, but the Board found it difficult to determine fairly how effectively this updating is being done. For example, Elliott Carter's winning the Edward MacDowell Medal (1983) is not reported in Carter's online biographical sketch (which, as of May 1984, had been updated in June 1982). The publisher does not indicate whether he intends to update individual biographical sketches more frequently online than their traditional once every two years in print, hence it is not clear how useful the online file will be for very current information, such as address and job changes.

One problem the Board had in using the online file was with abbreviations, an issue that Marquis had addressed in publications which accompany the database. A separate list of abbreviations, which will be incorporated into the DIALOG file 234 chapter, is essential to consult when searching online since the same abbreviations, which are essential in order to crowd 75,000 biographical sketches into two thick volumes, are used in the online file (e.g., *Bapt* for Baptist, *Mpls* for Minneapolis, or *obs* for observatory). Thus, *MIT* and *UCLA* are authorized abbreviations of those universities, but to find Penn State one has to combine the abbreviations to come up with *Pa State U*.

The *Marquis Who's Who* database includes more than just the online version of the 1982, 42d edition, of *Who's Who in America*. Newer editions will be added to the database every two years, and "future updates . . . will include other titles in the *Who's Who* series," according to the bluesheet. In May 1984 the publisher added nearly 15,000 additional biographical sketches to the database corresponding to a new work, *Who's Who in Frontier Science and Technology*. It was relatively easy for the Board to limit individual search requests to just the WWA subfile by selecting *SF=WA42* (i.e., subfile equals WWA 42 edition) and combining that set with any other search results; however, the Board suggests that DIALOG and Marquis consider establishing these subfiles with the limiting capability as well. In that way, a searcher could do a *limitall* to the WA42 subfile and not be bothered by the other subfiles for the rest of the search session (this would be comparable to DIALOG's present capability in ERIC of limiting a search to the *CIJE* subfile at the beginning of the search).

Marquis plans to continue its process of improving its online database, including controlled terms, numeric coding schemes, and more spelled-out words and corporate names. The Editorial Board is impressed with the extent of Marquis' achievements, recognizes the difficulty of developing an online database out of a print product, and encourages the publisher to continue improving the file to solve such problems as the inconsistent use of abbreviations and the lack of standard placement of information. As indicated above, the possibilities for locating information on prominent Americans are very great, depending only on the creativity of the user. The only major reservation the Board has with this new database is its price—$95 per connect hour, plus charges for online printing of records ranging from $.20 to $2.50, depending on the print format chosen. Although it is the publisher's prerogative to make its own market analysis and determine its most profitable pricing structure, the relatively high charges will discourage many libraries from experimenting with the database in order to gain a good feeling for its many potential uses and will restrict the uses which libraries and their nonbusiness patrons can make of a potentially exciting reference tool.

MICROFORMS

Any-Book: [microform]. Microfiche negative 10 x 15cm. Authors, titles $39; words $24; subjects $11; areas $12.

Any-Book promises "astonishing access to almost every book published in the English language during the past eight years, plus earlier titles still in print." Indeed, the claim is that a book "can be identified from any word or words located anywhere in the title." After examination, the Board was more stunned than astonished.

Published in microfiche in February, June, and October, each issue supersedes the last. The set the Board examined consisted of 233 negative fiche in a box with labeled dividers (the same size as the fiche!), four user guide cards (Introduction; Note to New Subscribers; Helpful Hints; Symbols), and a copy (full size, folded) of the *LC Classification Outline*, 4th ed.

Any-Book is in seven sections: Titles; Words; Authors; Subjects; Areas; ISBNs; and Publishers. The "Titles" fiche have 39 columns each with material arranged vertically. According to the guide cards, this section is supposed to have complete information on each title. Some of the entries on the first fiche are as follows: *An A.B.C. of Literary magazines/by; The ABC of the Foreign Exchanges/George Clar; The A, B, C's (and 912's) of Porsche Engines, or; The A.D.C. being personal reminiscences of the; Abortion, an annotated indexed bibliography/by; Abortion/Brautigam*; and *Abortion and the Roman Catholic Church/by Susa.* Needless to say, when some of these titles were checked in *Books In Print (BIP)*, full bibliographic and ordering information was found.

The Board hurried on to the "Words" fiche because here was to be the librarian's dream—a keyword in context index using title words. These fiche are also printed with 39 narrow columns to a fiche. A typical entry looks like this: *agency income,* ⊠ *Sources of voluntary* with the ⊠ indicating the start of a title. The problem with this arrangement is that only one line is used for each entry, and consequently, so many titles are truncated, sometimes to near-meaningless phrases, e.g., *accomplishments of the* ⊠ *Recent.* Sometimes other information appears (e.g., ISBNs), and it is conceivable that a patron who has a sketchy idea of a title *might* recognize the correct one and could then go to the "Titles" section (or more likely, to another tool) for complete information.

The "Authors" fiche were rife with missing information and misinformation. When we discovered 35 books under Austin (no first name) ranging from *Agroindustrial projects analys* to *Vampires, Spies, and Alien beings* and checked *BIP* for the full name of this versatile author, the Board found that he/she was, of course, really many different people.

The "Subjects" fiche is actually an Index by LC subject headings to the "Areas" fiche which list titles in LC class order. Typical entries in the latter are *PM5039 Deductions suggested by the geographical* and *PM7871 Issues in English creoles: papers from t.* The Introduction states that only about two-thirds of the titles appear in the "Areas" fiche. "ISBNs" fiche list publishers and addresses numerically by the ISBN five-digit identifiers, and the "Publishers" fiche provide the same data but arranged by the publisher abbreviations.

The publishers explain that most of the data are taken from publisher-supplied computer tapes. "Clerical proofing of data would delay publication with resultant decay in current value. Data are presented as received. Timely data of current value are preferred to clean, out-of-date information." While the Board concedes the point, the question still arises as to just how valuable *Any-Book* can be given the great number of truncated entries, incomplete names, and entries with little data other than title. The Board also doubts that the constant changing of fiche necessary to use this source is any more efficient than flipping through pages of *BIP.* The latter, despite its peculiarities, is at least less prone to provide what amounts to useless information.

The Board suggests that libraries await improvements in *Any-Book* before purchasing it.

News bank. [negative microfiche with hard-copy index]. New Canaan, Conn., News Bank, 1983. 11 x 15cm. $1,675 for initial annual subscription. (ISSN 0737-3813)

News Bank is a current issues and events reference service which consists of articles from U.S. newspapers on microfiche with a hard-copy Subject Index. Complete articles on a wide range of topics—socioeconomic, political, international, and scientific subjects—are selected from 114 newspapers in the 50 states. The articles (minus illustrations) are grouped into 14 subject categories and distributed monthly with a hard-copy Index which is cumulated quarterly and then annually.

The Board examined fiche that covered three months and a quarterly cumulation. Instructions for using the Index and fiche are a model of clarity. In the Index, broad subjects (e.g., *religious sects and movements; fads, hobbies and leisure; Mexico*) with many subdivisions are used. Scope notes and cross-references are generously provided. There are also entries for figures in the news subdivided appropriately, e.g., *Jackson, Jesse—Attitudes and Opinions; Presidential Primary Candidacy; Profiles; Speeches.* The names of states are often used as subdivisions, which facilitate research, e.g., under *Women in the Work Force—Salaries—Comparable Worth,* you find *Alaska EMP-54:E14, EMP-60:F8-9; Minnesota EMP-54:F1-2;* and *Vermont EMP-60:F10-11.* The bottom of the page informs users that *EMP* stands for employment (green headers on the microfiche); each of the 14 subject categories has color-coded fiche, and the numbers refer to fiche number (prominently displayed on the upper right-hand corner of each fiche and grid coordinate, respectively). The fiches are easy to access and file, with color codes and large-print dates and numbers. The articles are clearly reproduced; one document per frame, 98 frames per fiche, and the frames run horizontally (comic-book mode). Because it is negative fiche, copies look like the original, black print on white. Articles on a specific subject, e.g., *Toxic Shock Syndrome* are usually on one fiche, a convenience for readers. City, name of newspaper, and date are printed at the beginning of each article. The quality of information retrieved, its depth, completeness, accuracy, and objectivity depend on the source newspaper. Newspapers of record, e.g., the *New York Times,* the *Washington Post,* and the *Wall Street Journal,* are not included in the service.

News Bank also publishes *Review of the Arts* ($490), which includes reviews and articles about film, television, fine arts, architecture, literature, and the performing arts, and *Names in the News* ($230), a current biographical reference service. These services were not examined.

High school and academic libraries, whose budgets permit, may want to consider this service which provides local and regional views of current issues as a supplement to the *New York Times Index* and microfilm and *Facts On File.* It might be useful to have the separate list of newspapers arranged by state printed in the Index volume.

NEWS AND COMMENTS

ABC's of nature
A delightful 1977 imprint was *Joy of Nature: How to Observe and Appreciate the Great Outdoors* (Reader's Digest Assn.). Now from the same publisher (and retailing for $21.50) comes *ABC's of Nature: A Family Answer Book*. There is some duplication of content with the earlier work but not enough to justify distress. Many of the same people are involved, e.g., art editor G. L. Nielsen, associate art editor D. R. Schmidt, and consultant D. R. Allen. The *ABC's* in its title may suggest "dictionary" or "encyclopedia"; but this book is neither. It is rather a collection of questions and answers "logically" arranged, i.e., its arrangement is classified in four sections: The World Itself, The World of Plants, The Animal World, and Many Worlds of Life. It concludes, however, with an Index which may make it something to consider for school and public library reference collections—but buy a copy for circulation and *then* consider for reference. The intended readership is the "family," i.e., everyone from older children to adults—and conceivably younger children, too, where guidance of the "let's-look-it-up-together" variety is both offered and welcomed. Like its predecessor, it features solid content, clear and attractive prose, and superb graphics.—*Robert M. Pierson.*

Abstracts and indexes in science and technology
This guide consists of extensive bibliographic descriptions of 223 scientific and technical indexing/abstracting services. These are arranged under eleven broad categories, e.g., astronomy, biological sciences, health sciences, etc. For each index or abstract, title, publisher, bibliographic history, arrangement, coverage, scope, manner of locating information in the source, description, related bibliographic sources, existence of lists of periodicals scanned, and related databases are identified. This new edition has been expanded to cover more titles; the identification of related databases is a new feature. Although not intended to be "definitive," it will be very useful in almost any science collection, building reference and bibliographic instruction (Scarecrow, 0-8108-1712-8; $17.50).—*Rao Aluri.*

Address book
It is not true that Chita Rivera, Julie Harris, Paul Williams, Sammy Davis, Jr., and Valerie Harper are living together at 151 El Camino Drive in Beverly Hills. But it might seem that way to readers of the second edition of Michael Levine's *Address Book: How to Reach Anyone Who's Anyone* (Facts On File, 1984, $15.95), because he lists that address under *many* celebrities' names without noting that their talent agency (William Morris) is at that address! This list of celebrities, executives, associations, and VIPs superficially covers so much ground that it is difficult to know when to use it. One could look for the addresses of *Time* magazine, the Nudist Information Center, Delta Airlines, the Tonka Toy Corporation, and Murray Goralnick, president of the Beverly Hills Computer Store, but why would you? Some entries are obvious (write to Jane Pauley c/o NBC New York), and some are astonishing (Dr. De Sade, editor of *Fetish Times*). The Introduction in a Q-and-A format informs readers of the dos and don'ts of writing to "notables" and offers "professional tricks" which might improve the chances of a letter being read and answered by the likes of Cary Grant and Bo Derek.—*Mona McCormick.*

Adult video index '84
Chastely and appropriately bound in plain brown covers, Keith L. Justice's *Adult Video Index '84* (McFarland, 1984, $20) is a filmography of adult videocassettes (for "adult," you may read "erotic," "pornographic," or just plain "dirty" as you wish—"hardcore" perhaps says it best). Arranged alphabetically by title, running times, formats, casts, distributors, synopses, prices, etc., are provided, although in some cases, data are sketchy. A distributors directory, a list of titles by distributors, and indexes by name and by genre (e.g., "Gay Male," "Large Bosom," etc.) are also provided. The black-and-white illustrations appear to be reproduced from package covers, all of which are at least suggestive if not downright obvious.

Needless to say, most if not all school libraries will pass on this title. Academic libraries with strong popular culture or perhaps behavioral sciences collections should probably consider this listing; law libraries with an emphasis on civil liberties might also find it useful. Public librarians wishing to kill off the "Marian the Librarian" image for good may find that the acquisition of this title will do the trick, although, depending upon local circumstances, it might also do in the librarians themselves as well. Whether or not a public library has a responsibility to help a patron find a vendor for such films as *Liquid Lips* or *Seven in a Barn* is a question that cannot be answered here.

On a final note, the Library of Congress has assigned two subject headings to this work: "Video recordings—Catalogs" and "Sex in moving-pictures," the latter being so suggestive of a more innocent past that it almost disguises the not-so-innocent contents.—*Stuart W. Miller.*

African books in print
The third edition of the two-volume *African Books in Print* (Mansell, $169), complete through 1982, is considerably larger than the two previous editions, with an increase of subject headings and cross-references to 1,320. The coverage of 102 languages is impressive, but the editors remain dissatisfied with the absence from these pages of many publishers, particularly from the Maghreb and Francophone countries. Another major omission includes books in Portuguese. The objective continues to be the provision of a "systematic, reliable and functional reference tool and buying guide to African published material currently in print." The appearance of introductory information in both French and English (Scope of Arrangement and Progress in Black Africa, 1978–1982), along with a table of currency information, enhances the usefulness of this title as an ordering and a reference tool.—*A. P. Marshall.*

American and British poetry
Harriet S. Alexander has compiled a well-organized bibliography but has misleadingly entitled it *American and British Poetry: A Guide to the Criticism, 1925–1978* (Athens, Ohio, Ohio Univ. Pr., 1984, 486p., $42). It indexes criticism of American and British poets from Caedmon to the contemporary published in more than 400 books and 160 journals. Despite the title, most of the books were published since 1960, the time at which indexing of many of the journals commenced. This quirk is not explained. Once one understands its limits, the bibliography is a joy to use. Organized by poet and then by individual poem, journal citations employ full titles, and book citations include author, title, and page numbers. Full citations for the books are given at the end of the volume. The bibliography makes it easy to locate fairly recent criticism of more than 600 poets; many of the items would be difficult to find through other bibliographies since few of them analyze so many books so thoroughly.—*James Rettig.*

American eccentrics

Recently received in the *RBB* office are proofs of Carl Sifakis' *American Eccentrics* (Facts On File, November 1984, $17.95). It consists of articles on (to quote promotional material) 150 "imposters, misers, gamblers, lovers, fools, benefactors." Not all readers will find the subjects of all articles quite so remarkable as Sifakis seems to; still, his coverage of the amusing and the sensational may refresh adolescents and others who have had it, as they may say, "up to here" with lives of great persons tediously reminding them that they too, etc., etc. Sifakis' style is what is sometimes called breezy—at its worst, brash ("Clearly the weird doctor had gone round the bend"), even gauche ("Police fine-combing New Orleans . . ."). School, public, and academic libraries not wholly committed to thrift and/or solemnity will want to consider *American Eccentrics* for their reference and circulating collections, where it will supplement more sober and straitlaced items.—*Robert M. Pierson.*

American education 1622–1860

Did the process systematically impart knowledge? This is the question used by Cornelia S. King, compiler of *American Education 1622–1860* (Garland, 1984, $64.50, 0-8240-8966-9), to determine whether items from the collections of the American Philosophical Society, The Historical Society of Pennsylvania, and The Library Company of Philadelphia should be included in this cloth-bound educational bibliography. The 4,865 items listed include treatises on pedagogy, official publications of educational organizations and institutions, systems of school education, addresses delivered by individuals to these organizations, and guides for the conduct of life—all published prior to 1861. *American Education* will be a valuable sourcebook for historians and researchers concerned with the development of the American school system. It is the third of what is to be a four-volume set.—*Vira C. Hinds.*

American Indian novelists

Citing novels, other primary literary works (poems, short stories, etc.), and associated critical secondary sources, *American Indian Novelists* (Garland, $28, 0-8240-9199-X) is an annotated bibliography with citations to the work of 21 American Indian novelists, living and dead. (Annotations are generally descriptive rather than critical, and they are only provided for novels and secondary sources related to the novels.) The work includes novelists "who share in common the quality of both considering themselves and being considered by their communities as American Indian by heritage." The compilers, Tom Colonnese and Louis Owens, have excluded American Indian writers such as John Rollins Ridge, whose works are not fiction, and have included novelists like Jamake Highwater, whose Indian heritage is being challenged, and novelists whose stories treat Indian characters only marginally. A paragraph of biographical information prefaces each section, and unannotated reviews of the cited novels and sources of biographical information are also cited. An alphabetical Index of writers and cited works (including works mentioned in the annotations) ends the volume. Since American Indian novelists are not covered adequately in literature indexes, *American Indian Novelists* is a valuable contribution to American literature bibliography.—*Jack Forman.*

American landmark legislation

The first volume (the only one seen of a five-volume set, Oceana, $375/set; $100/volume) is a photoreproduction of source material on the Railway Labor Act of 1926. It consists of the text of the law, plus selected pages from the *Congressional Record* of 1926, two congressional hearings, two congressional reports, one book excerpt, one law review article, and one Supreme Court case. All sources are reprinted without editorial comment, even though the title page says "compiled and edited by Irving J. Sloan."—*Wiley J. Williams.*

America's meeting places

If you have conference or meeting planners among your library's clientele, you may want this new directory compiled by Redtree Associates (Facts On File, 0-87196-995-5, $35). It provides information on more than 400 inns, hotels, conference centers, and nonprofit and historic sites in the U.S. with meeting facilities for ten to several hundred persons. Arranged by state, data are presented in tabular form and include site description; number, price, and type of rooms; equipment available; transportation; and contact person. Black-and-white photographs accompany some entries. Indexes organize sites by capacity, location (e.g., in the mountains, by water), and features (e.g., golf, tennis, historic interest). Although not a substitute for more comprehensive directories, this directory includes many sites of unusual interest.—*Josephine McSweeney.*

Anglo-Saxon and Anglo-Scandinavian art

This 1984 annotated bibliography of more than 600 books and articles is compiled by Robert Deshman and is part of G. K. Hall's Reference Publications in Art History series. Deshman has gathered literature pertaining to works of art influenced by the Vikings and created in England from the last part of the ninth century to the early twelfth century. Arrangement is by medium with subdivisions as needed; standard bibliographic data are provided. A majority of the references (some in foreign languages) are on illuminated manuscripts and stone sculpture; coins and architecture were excluded. Indexes include one for authors and editors and a detailed one on subjects and places. This work is clearly for comprehensive, academic art collections (0-8161-8344-9, $45).—*Frances Corcoran.*

Animal rights and the law

What are the rights of animals according to the law? is a question that has been asked many times over the past years. Daniel S. Moretti has tried to help answer it by alerting interested persons to the statutes in his book, *Animal Rights and the Law* ($7.50, 0-379-11147-0), number 49 in the Legal Almanac Series published by Oceana this year. This well-written, concise, 147-page book presents information on anticruelty and animal fighting statutes, laws to protect wildlife, humane slaughter laws, and regulations for transportation of animals. It first gives an overview and then pinpoints specific state and federal laws. This is definitely a useful book for reference shelves, and it should be available to anyone who handles live animals either in the laboratory or for marketing.—*H. Robert Malinowsky.*

Annals of English verse, 1770–1835

The subtitle of this 1985 addition to the Garland Reference Library of the Humanities (xiv, 709p., $76, 0-8240-8841-7) indicates what it is: *A Preliminary Survey of the Volumes Published.* In its Introduction its compiler (J. R. de J. Jackson) clearly explains its function and the intricacies of its scope—and states: "This survey is preliminary to a complete catalogue of the volumes of English verse published from 1770 to 1835. It is issued in its preliminary form for three reasons: first, it has reached a stage at which it should be of significant use to literary and social historians; second, the rate of correction and augmentation has slowed from a flood to a trickle, and comprehensive improvement seems likely to be the work of many years; and third, advice and comment that will help to reduce the imperfections of a final version may be elicited." Promotional material claims "over 10,000 citations." Titles are arranged by year, then alphabetically by title. There are Author/Title and Anonymously Issued Title Indexes. Jackson is to be congratulated on his achievement, preliminary though it be; libraries supporting advanced study of English literature will want to acquire it and will look forward to its completion—and to its eventual extension (by Jackson or by others) forward and backward in time.—*Robert M. Pierson.*

Art and architecture in the Balkans

A recent addition to the G. K. Hall series Reference Publications in Art History covers medieval architecture, painting, sculpture, minor arts, iconography, and archaeological sites in Albania, Bulgaria, and Yugoslavia. Compiled by Slobodan Ćurčić, associate professor in the Department of Art and Archeology at Princeton, *Art and Architecture in the Balkans: An Annotated Bibliography* (1984, $65) consists of more than 1,300 geographically arranged citations to monographs and journal articles. Though most of the material cited is in foreign languages, the English-language annotations and complete bibliographic information will be a boon to scholars.—*Josephine McSweeney.*

The art and history of printing

Bibliographers of the history of printing will appreciate the usefulness of Vito J. Brenni's *The Art and History of Book Printing: A Topical Bibliography* (Greenwood, $35) which brings together, in one volume, material that has heretofore been scattered. Some 1,200 unannotated entries appear in classified arrangement, and there is a final segment which includes a checklist of titles related to writing/calligraphy and typography. The work will be especially helpful for students.—*Donald G. Davis.*

Arthritis alternatives
Arthritis Alternatives (Facts On File, 1985, $14.95, 0-87196-796-3) is a fairly complete guide and directory to the treatment of arthritis for laypersons. Introductory chapters discuss the nature, types, and diagnosis of arthritis. Then follow chapters on traditional treatments (including medications and surgical options), such alternative treatments as special diets and acupuncture, and arthritis research now taking place in the U.S. The directory section consists of annotated listings of health professionals, hospitals, and clinics that specialize in arthritis; professional associations, foundations, organizations, and self-help groups; publications, including magazines, newsletters, and books; and services, including information clearinghouses, special travel organizations, and manufacturers.—*Martin Kesselman.*

Arts and sports USA
Arts and Sports USA: The Professional Attractions Guide is designed to serve the professional planning needs of group travel and tour agents, meeting planners, and special-events promoters. This comprehensive guide profiles, in its 644 pages, more than 1,800 museums, theaters, arenas, stadia, racetracks, zoos, gardens, and historic homes located all over the U.S. Details on tours, programming, discounts, ticket prices, meeting space, contacts, telephone numbers, and other information necessary for group management are formatted to facilitate comparison and evaluation of entries. Arranged alphabetically by state, entries are divided by city or sites of note within states. Although designed for professional planners, it will be of general interest to any traveler. Published by Cultural Services Inc., Bethesda, Md., and distributed by Oryx Press for $35 in paper.—*J. Linda Williams.*

The athlete's game plan for college and career
If you are an athlete or advise athletes, you need Peterson's *Athlete's Game Plan for College and Career* ($9.95). Stephen and Howard Figler have compiled a wealth of information on athletic, academic, and career success. Arranged in three parts, it covers choosing a college, winning in college athletically and academically, and how to use your college education for a career. Budding young athletes are being exploited more and more in this day of high salaries—all the more reason for this book that gives information on such topics as "the ABCs of being a student athlete," "studying and coping skills," and "fighting the dumb jock image." *The Athlete's Game Plan for College and Career* is a necessary purchase for high school and college libraries. The Board recommends it highly for students interested in pursuing athletics as a career.—*H. Robert Malinowsky.*

Audiovisual resources in food and nutrition
Oryx has released volume 2 (1979–82) of *Audiovisual Resources in Food and Nutrition*, an index prepared from cataloging records done by the U.S. Department of Agriculture's Food and Nutrition Information Center (FNIC). This volume covering 1979–82 material acquired by FNIC—volume 1 covered 1973–78—lists 754 audiovisuals including kits, models, charts, and posters. Citations are arranged alphabetically by title within each subject section, e.g., livestock products, food additives, and home economics. Entries contain accession number and FNIC call number, bibliographic information, audience level, descriptors, and an abstract. There are six Indexes: Personal Author, Corporate Author, Title, Subject, Intellectual Level, and Media. There are no cross-references in the Subject Index or among the citations themselves. This will be a useful item in any library serving nutritionists or those planning health and home economics curricula on almost any level (123p. $38.50, 0-89774-105-6).—*Pauline M. Vaillancourt.*

BBC pronouncing dictionary of British names
British names hold many traps for the unwary in their pronunciation. As a result, the BBC maintains a file of correct pronunciations of names of places and persons, often obtained by checking with the individuals bearing the name in question. The first edition of this work, edited by G. M. Miller, appeared in 1971. This new edition (Oxford, $14.95), edited by G. E. Pointon, pronunciation advisor to the BBC, is an expanded version which also indicates the geographical location of the place-names included. Entries are deliberately restricted to British names only, but there is a six-page Appendix for the Channel Islands. A handy, if not essential, purchase.—*Norman Horrocks.*

Basic reference sources
Scarecrow Press has just published a third edition of *Basic Reference Sources* by Margaret T. Taylor and Ronald R. Powell (1985, paper, $16.50, 0-8108-1721-7). Scope and purpose remain unchanged, as does the number of starred titles, except for 29 added titles. In reviewing the second edition (*RSBR*, July 1982), the Board commended its arrangement by form of reference book, its well-selected questions, and its general commentary and good Index as well designed for student self-study. This commendation also holds for the third edition.—*Frances Neel Cheney.*

Bibliography of British economic and social history and Bibliography of European economic and social history
The *Bibliography of British Economic and Social History* (compiled by W. H. Chaloner and R. C. Richardson, Manchester University Pr., 1984, 208p., $37.50), is a revised updating of the 1976 edition. This version, with 5,800 entries compared to the first edition's 4,200, retains the original's purpose of selecting the best books and articles in English on Britain's social and economic history from 1066 through 1970. Coverage of Scotland and Ireland has been expanded. The years 1300, 1500, and 1700 divide the bibliography into major sections which are subdivided by topics. Scope notes and cross-references are helpful. Unfortunately, the bibliography perpetuates the anachronistic form of citation many British scholars foolishly favor for books, listing only author, title, and date.

A new companion, *Bibliography of European Economic and Social History* (compiled by Derek H. Aldcroft and Richard Rodger, Manchester University Pr., 1984, 243p., $37.50), covers the rest of Europe from 1700 through 1939. Each country's section is organized topically. All items are in English, and selection was confined almost exclusively to books and articles. As a convenience to users, journal titles are spelled out in full rather than abbreviated, and, to the compiler's credit, book entries include price and publisher. For larger public and academic libraries.—*James R. Rettig.*

Black elected officials
A popular method of keeping up with minority progress in the U.S. is numerical analysis of elected officials. A notable example of such assessment is *Black Elected Officials: A National Roster*, written by the Joint Center for Political Studies, Washington, D.C., and published by UNIPUB for $27.50, 0-89059-033-8. Now in its thirteenth year of publication, this annual has seen a growth from listing 1,500 in 1971 to 5,700 in 1984. Obviously, as the editors point out more than once, the 1.2 percent of total elected officials this represents is a far cry from the estimated 12 percent of blacks in the total population. The publication is made useful by its alphabetical arrangement by state and then by name of person. A General Index provides access by name. Hopefully, history will render such studies obsolete, but for now it is useful.—*A. P. Marshall.*

Books and real life
Nancy Polette, an education professor, has compiled an annotated selective list of fictional works which deal with everyday problems. All are designed for intellectually gifted children and young adults. Titles are listed alphabetically by author and are described in brief summaries. Discussion questions and activities appropriate for the age group accompany the listings. *Books and Real Life* (McFarland, $15.95) will be useful in children's and young adult collections in school and public libraries.—*Pamela S. Bradigan.*

Bowker's 1985 complete sourcebook of personal computing
Microcomputer hobbyists as well as potential micro users will find that this annual sourcebook contains a great deal of up-to-date information on computer equipment and resources to help them keep adequately informed on new microcomputer developments. There are sections listing more than 750 computers as well as modems, disk drives, and printers; more than 2,000 software products and citations to reviews for many of these; and lists of computer books, magazines, consumer databases, and clubs and user groups. Also included are an introduction to personal computers, checklists of what to look for in computer hardware and software, a glossary, and an index. Unfortunately the information contained will become dated fairly quickly, so libraries could use updates on more than just an annual

basis. (paper, $19.95 plus shipping and handling, 0-8352-1931-3).—*Martin Kesselman.*

Business forms on file and Personal forms on file

When Facts On File issued, several years since, *Maps on File* (cf. *RSBR,* August 1982), it launched an interesting series: maps and other items, in looseleaf notebooks, specifically geared to the needs of would-be photocopiers. The series now includes *Historical Maps on File, The Human Body on File,* cf. *RBB,* April 15, 1984 (anatomical drawings mainly), and (most recently) *Business Forms on File* and *Personal Forms on File.* These last, both of them the work of Richard Zeldin, are to be supplemented annually. The *Business* collection provides 150 forms (including personnel record forms) and seems suited to public libraries and some special libraries and offices; the *Personal* collection—the more novel compendium—also provides 150 forms (wills, leases, adoption agreements, baby growth records, etc.) and seems suited to public libraries; it may also prove useful in some homes. Announced for fall 1984 are *Designs on File,* with "over 750 of the most frequently used patterns and designs"—geometrical figures, projections, lettering samples, etc.—and another map collection, viz., *State Maps on File.* In all cases, material may be freely copied without fear of copyright infringement—except of course for inclusion in material to be sold. For information on any or all of these titles, contact Janis Kern or Rachel Ginsburg, Facts On File, Inc., 460 Park Avenue S., New York, NY 10016.—*Robert M. Pierson.*

CP/M software directory

This list of 1,628 CP/M software packages deals with topics such as agriculture, business administration, database management, and personal and home use. CP/M (Control Program for Microcomputers) is an operating system used by many microcomputers (and, until the advent of IBM's MS-DOS, was a de facto standard for most business applications programs).

Each entry includes the title of the software package, the CP/M operating system on which the program will run, and a nonevaluative description. Additional information may include price, source programming language, RAM (random access memory) required, and other hardware or software requirements. The directory also includes Indexes by Title and Vendor, a vendor directory, glossaries, and a listing of dial-up bulletin boards for users to locate information on new CP/M programs online. Useful for most public and academic libraries, especially those that serve business-related clientele (Bowker, 1984, $24.95, 0-8352-1973-9).—*Martin Kesselman.*

The Canadian encyclopedia

Mel Hurtig, publisher, Hurtig Publishers, Ltd., 10560-105 St., Edmonton, Alta, Canada T5H 2W7, tells me that the "first comprehensive general reference work on modern Canada and a sweeping portrait of its people" will be published in September 1985. The new *Canadian Encyclopedia* in its three volumes and 2,080 pages is said to be authoritative, well illustrated, easy to use, and up-to-date. According to Hurtig, 1,000 of its 8,000 articles are brand new and have never appeared in other reference works, not even in *Encyclopedia Canadiana.* Prepublication retail price is $125 (with a 10 percent discount to libraries, schools, and other educational institutions). At publication the encyclopedia will cost $175. The material is not scheduled to go to press until January 1985. We have already requested tear sheets as soon as any are available. For further information, call Fiona Goulet, at the Edmonton address 403-426-2359 or Gordon Garner at 416-226-3640 (Toronto) or Ian Cameron at 604-669-6850 (Vancouver). In Canada only, call Hurtig toll free at 1-800-661-6464.—*Helen K. Wright.*

Caribbean business telephone directory

Now the *Caribbean Business Telephone Directory 1984–1985* is available for $35 from Caribbean Imprint Library Services, 410 W. Falmouth Highway, Box 350, West Falmouth, MA 02574. Covering select products, services, and businesses in 19 countries and island groups with limited entries for Miami and Puerto Rico, the work intends to be a marketing aid for English-speaking business people. A Business Classifications Index, under such headings as *attorneys, automobile leasing, customs brokers, guest houses,* and *pipe line contractors,* supplies the numbers needed to access the yellow pages. The yellow pages organized by these numbers and subarranged by country provide addresses, telex, and telephone numbers. The white pages arranged by country give telephone numbers and the "business classification number."—*Josephine McSweeney.*

Chaucer source and analogue criticism

Many Chaucer tales are recastings by him of the written or recorded stories of other authors; "The Knight's Tale" in *Canterbury Tales* is probably based on Boccaccio's *Teseide.* Now, a major bibliography by Lynn King Morris, published by Garland, 1985, and selling for $65 (0-8240-9031-4), enables Chaucer scholars to identify sources and analogues more easily. A selected annotated bibliography of 1,477 books and articles written during the nineteenth and twentieth centuries forms the basis of the work. Four cross-referenced Indexes refer users to specific numbered items in the bibliography. More than half of the references are to journal articles.—*Milton H. Crouch.*

Children's books of international interest

Designed to promote international understanding through children's books, this American Library Association publication, in its third edition, has enlarged its focus to include "collection development and individual reading guidance in the hope that teachers and librarians both here and abroad will use the bibliography to help children realize their place as world citizens."

More than 215 new main entries have been added to the 136 retained from the second edition. High quality titles of special interest to preschool through junior high–age youngsters have been chosen. Full bibliographic information and brief annotations describe books which "incorporate universal themes or depict the American way of life." At the time of publication of this bibliography (1984), all titles were in print.

This edition, edited by Barbara Elleman, Children's Books editor of *Booklist,* retains Virginia Haviland's insightful preface to the previous edition. It also includes a Directory of Publishers and an Index. ($7.50, 0-8389-3314-9).—*Ruth M. Hadlow.*

Children's literature from A to Z

This is "a broad general introduction to children's literature and ways of introducing it to children." There are one- to three-page articles of five types: (1) short essays on major authors and illustrators (mainly American, British, and Canadian); (2) brief notes on a representative sampling of authors and illustrators of the post–World War II era; (3) essays on widely read folktales and heroic figures; (4) essays on various genres of children's literature, e.g., Biography, Fantasy, Picture Books; and (5) discussion of the Caldecott and Newbery Awards. These are arranged in an alphabetical sequence with an Index of Titles. Following each entry is a brief, cursory suggestion on how to expand childrens' appreciation of the material.

The author teaches English at the University of Alberta; he acknowledges that he could not cover everything; however, one misses such authors as Beverly Cleary, Susan Cooper, and Shel Silverstein. The 1979 change in composition of the Caldecott Committee from one group to two is not noted.

Children's Literature from A to Z is a readable and informative guide which will be useful to parents. Librarians and teachers, however, will probably learn little from it. (McGraw-Hill, $12.95, paper, 0-07-061791-0)—*Ruth M. Hadlow.*

China trade handbook

Distributed in the U.S. by Facts On File, *The China Trade Handbook* (1984, The Adsale People, P.O. Box 20032, Hennessy Road, Hong Kong, $60, 0-8160-1166-4) provides useful information for entrepreneurs and business specialists researching trade possibilities with China. The four sections of the handbook include essential information on the Chinese economy, China's foreign trade, the government and legal system of China, as well as travel information for businesspersons in China. The discussions on setting up offices, arbitration, advertising, and buying and selling from China will be especially helpful. This paperback compendium of information will be most useful in business libraries.—*Ruth J. Person.*

Choreography by George Balanchine

Libraries which were unable to justify acquisition of the handsome Eakins Press Foundation's *Choreography by George Balanchine* ($75; see *RBB* Oct. 1, 1983) will be pleased to know that Viking Penguin has issued a reduced-format edition for $20. The latter also includes some notes on recent productions and new books on Balanchine not listed in the original edition. Since the Eakins Press edition is a fine example of book design and typography, worthy of conservation, those libraries with the original volume might still want this new version for their circulating collections or as a "working" copy.—*Stuart W. Miller.*

Chronology of culture
Several reference tools enable users to identify quickly when a particular historical event occurred. However, this work by John Paxton and Sheila Fairfield (Van Nostrand, 1984, $18.50) concentrates on cultural events with concise descriptions and is arranged in columnar form: Literature, Dance & Drama, Music, Architecture, Three Dimensional Art, and Visual Arts. The lack of a subject index lessens the work's usefulness. Editors of this work are with *The Statesman's Year-Book.* It is actually a paperbound reprint of *The Calendar of Creative Man* (Facts On File, 1980); the cut-off date is 1970.—*Arthur S. Meyers.*

The college cost book
The 1984–85 edition of *The College Cost Book* aims to take inexperienced college applicants through the steps needed to pay the bills, in part by using three students who estimate their expenses and meet them. Information on evaluating assets, the dreaded Financial Aid Form, strategies for stretching resources, and on understanding what one is accepting with aid is all included, but is not consistently organized for clarity or ease of use by students. There is a detailed Contents page but no index. Mean expenses for 1984–85 are cited at public and private two- and four-year colleges; specific expenses for 3,500 colleges occupy more than 100 of its 235 pages. A set of work sheets allows students to work their situations through. Useful, with the reservations noted, to college applicants but perhaps more useful to parents and counselors. (New York, College Entrance Examination Board, paper, $10.95, 0-87447-187-7)—*Judith H. Higgins.*

The college money handbook 1985
In this second annual handbook on the subject, 1,738 accredited four-year institutions in the U.S. and its territories are listed. Cost and aid profiles on each institution include an institutional overview and details regarding financial aid: undergraduate financial awards summaries (need and non-need scholarships—these categorized by interest), such money-saving options as off-campus housing, and forms and information needed for applying, deadlines, and college contact person. More schools are covered here than in such titles as *Financing College Education* and *College Cost Book.* The book is also easy to use. The Introduction includes a financial work sheet which ought to help readers answer their own queries on financial aid (Peterson's Guides, 1984, $12.95 paper, 0-87866-282-0).—*Frances Corcoran.*

Combined retrospective index to book reviews in humanities journals 1802–1974
Research Publications, 12 Lunar Drive, Drawer AB, Woodbridge, CT 06525, has completed publication of the ten-volume retrospective index of humanities journals begun in 1982. The first nine volumes are arranged alphabetically by author, and the last volume is a Title Index to the others. According to the managing editor, Stan Schindler, the set provides access to some 500,000 book reviews that were published in about 150 humanities journals. The materials sell for $1,165.—*Helen K. Wright.*

The complete peerage
Like the British peerages themselves, *The Complete Peerage* (6v., New York, St. Martin's, 1984, $450, 0-312-15836-X) is a family enterprise. First published between 1887 and 1898 under the editorship of George Edward Cokayne, it was revised and reissued in 12 volumes between 1910 and 1959 under the editorship of Vicary Gibbs (Cokayne's nephew) and others. These editors enriched the original with a thirteenth volume (1940) covering peerages created between 1901 and 1938. All 13 volumes retain their value as tools for the study of Britain and its distinguished families. They give "concisely and precisely so far as they have been obtainable, particulars of the parentage, birth, honors, orders, offices, public services, politics, marriage, death and burial, of every holder of a Peerage" extant, extinct, or dormant at the time of original publication. The work's title has remained constant through its various incarnations. Although in this compact reprint the original page size has been reduced by half, the print is legible even to unassisted eyes.—*James Rettig.*

Computer books and serials in print
Patterned after *Books in Print*, the above-named book (Bowker, $49.50) offers a collection of computer print material in the usual author, title, and subject formats. Domestic and foreign publications and serials are included. Using 608 Library of Congress computer-related subject headings, the titles are also divided for ease in determining use. The two major categories are computers and computer applications. The serials segment is a unique service in that it collects periodicals in given subject areas and lists them with information regarding indexing services and microform availability. If you need a reference source which covers computers from mainframes to portables and applications in the arts and sciences, then you will like this volume.—*Frances Corcoran.*

The computer data and database source book
"Access to billions of dollars worth of public data—most of it free! . . . Listings of organizations that do free research . . . how to turn a government database into a commercial database for your own profit." So proclaims the covers of *The Computer Data and Database Source Book* (Avon, $14.95). It is one of the first database directories written for personal computer users.

The work is divided into three main sections: commercial databases, a list of more than 1,000 databases currently available from commercial vendors; government databases, a similar directory of more than 200 databases offered on a free or cost-recovery basis; and public data sources, a collection of sources for publications, computer tapes, and data experts in various subject fields, including both government and commercial sources.

For the low price, this directory may be helpful to experienced database users who would like to have information about most available databases in one source. However, for small business/home computer users, too many sources are covered in too little detail to aid in selection of the best database or source. More detailed information on a more selective list of sources might have helped the book better fulfill its goals. However, the most serious drawback is the lack of any sort of subject access to the data in the first two sections. The third section will be a handy guide to source material on everything from agriculture to zinc. Although the lack of systematic access is a drawback, *The Computer Data and Database Source Book* is one of the most comprehensive and least expensive database guides.—*David A. Tyckoson.*

A concise dictionary of foreign expressions
Foreign-language expressions often baffle even the best of us. Fear not! There is now available an inexpensive ($6.95) paperback, *A Concise Dictionary of Foreign Expressions* (Rowman & Allanheld, 81 Adams Dr., Totowa, NJ 07512), that not only lists such Latin and other phrases as *Parturient montes, nascetur ridiculus mus*, but also, in its 147 pages, lists many single words, e.g., *Auflage* (edition), *gouache* (a method of painting), *piolet* (a mountaineering ice-ax), as well as a few well-known acronyms, most of which are readily identified, but we might like to know exactly what they stand for, e.g., INRI, KGB, or even RSVP. Pronunciation is given, and there are some *see* references, a few of them (contrary to usual library practice) from noun to article (Roi Soleil *see* le Roi Soleil). On the whole, a thoroughly useful book.—*Raymund F. Wood.*

The concise McGraw-Hill dictionary of modern economics
McGraw-Hill has recently published an abridged edition of their *McGraw-Hill Dictionary of Modern Economics,* third edition in paperback at a price of $19.95. Called *The Concise McGraw-Hill Dictionary of Modern Economics,* it provides the same complete definitions as the hardbound parent volume but has omitted some 250 terms, primarily from the fields of accounting and insurance, and a number of organizational entries. (One must remember, however, that the 15 organizations included are still in a separate section.) With its clear definitions, which usually also address underlying principles and possible opposing viewpoints and provide bibliographic references, this abridgment should provide good value for students and for libraries which could not afford the parent volume.—*Winifred F. Dean.*

A consumer's dictionary of food additives
Received in the *RBB* office is a revised (Crown, 1984, paper, $8.95, 0-517-55287-6) edition of Ruth Winter's *Consumer's Dictionary of Food Additives* (1978). School, public, and academic libraries will want to acquire it—and so, one hopes, will many households. Both natural ingredients (e.g., horseradish and nutmeg) and artificial ingredients (e.g., calcium chloride and sodium nitrite) are covered, and there are entries for general topics, e.g., Fixative, Flavoring Compound, and Preservative, and results, e.g., Filled Milk. The Introduction will repay careful reading: it illumines—sometimes glaringly—the additive scene. The complacent (who assume that what is good for Amalgamated Foods is good for the country) should read Winter's account of why chicken fat is so yellow and why saccharine is still on the market and should note her observations that the majority of food additives "have nothing to do with *nutritional values*" (italics hers) and that if studies show that one consumer in a million will develop cancer, "that's pretty low except, of course, if you are that one consumer."—*Robert M. Pierson.*

Cooks' books
Cooks' Books: An Affectionate Guide to the Literature of Food and Cooking has been announced for publication in January 1985 by Facts On File ($17.95 hardbound; $9.95 paper). It is chock-full of information, presented in a lively style by the compiler of *The World Book Encyclopedia of Food*, L. Patrick Coyle. He follows an anecdotal history of cookbooks with chapters on various types—classic, general, national cuisine, specific food groups, and particular processes. Helpful information on shopping and equipment and an entertaining chapter on food-related art and humor complete this suitable gift for cooks. Coyle pays proper homage to the French and provides colorful accounts of famous chefs along with a number of recipes such as fresh basil sorbet and marinated snake cooked with rice. More readable than *The Garland Recipe Index*, it is an excellent guide and a nice addition to home economics collections.—*Frances Neel Cheney.*

Copywriter's handbook
Suitable for larger and specialized reference collections, this book by Nat G. Bodian (ISI Press, 3501 Market St., Philadelphia, PA 19104, 1984; $29.95, hardcover and $19.95, paper) should be read by all acquisitions librarians—indeed, by anyone interested in how books are marketed. Its subtitle—*A Practical Guide for Advertising and Promotion of Specialized and Scholarly Books and Journals*—accurately describes its content. Of particular interest to readers of *RBB* is chapter 11, "Copy Approaches for Book Promotions to the Various Library Markets." Sensitive readers will realize that much of what Bodian says concerning advertising copy beautifully applies to the preparation of reviews and reading lists. Other interesting chapters include "Working with Words," which lists "Over 50 Other Ways to Say 'Book,'" and "Headline Writing"—a provocative de facto short course on the writing of annotations and news releases. An interesting special feature is appendix A: "Copywriter's Glossary: A Vocabulary of Advertising and Promotion."—*Robert Pierson.*

Countries and islands of the world
This second edition is a handy item for reference desks because it lists the names of countries and islands and their changes throughout the ages. References include former names, alternate names, and transliterated names with lots of cross-references. For most place-names a brief history is given, including, for example, when it was discovered, colonized, or split. Even though this guide is selective, it includes islands of the world fairly comprehensively as well as all the states and provinces within such larger countries as the U.S., the USSR, Canada, Australia, and India. Unfortunately, the provinces of China are not included (Shoe String, 1985, $16.50, 0-85157-383-6).—*Martin Kesselman.*

Country experts in the federal government
This revised edition of *Country Experts* is book three in the multipart reference set called the Briefcase Series, published by Washington Researchers (1984). Like the earlier edition and its companion volumes, it provides lists with complete addresses and telephone numbers for government analysts. Serious researchers probably will find it more appropriate and useful to have online access rather than paperbound copy. Also, the high price for the volumes in the biennial series that contain information available elsewhere may dissuade persons who would appreciate its briefcase portability. And staff changes and governmental reorganization may render this information obsolete quickly. Thus, this is an interesting but unnecessary purchase. (0-934940-26-6, $40).—*Patricia M. Hogan.*

Cubans in the United States
Cubans in the United States: A Bibliography for Research in the Social and Behavioral Sciences, 1960–1983 (Greenwood, 1984, $35, 0-313-24509-6) compiled by Lyn MacCorkle, tries to fill the need for a bibliography on the Cuban refugee movement. It cites only a portion of available titles in English and excludes creative literature and newspaper articles. There are seven topical sections, e.g., Education and Language, and Politics; entries are arranged by a code which uses the authors' names and years when the works appeared. Articles from academic journals, unpublished papers, and government documents published after 1959, as well as periodicals and books directly concerned with Cubans living in the U.S., are represented.

This is a useful addition to bibliographies on Cuban Americans, but the lack of a subject or title index and its emphasis on research materials limit its usefulness primarily to scholars or specialists.—*Patricia M. Hogan.*

Current issues
Current Issues (Arlington, Va.: Close Up Foundation, 1984– , $5) is an annual which presents discussions on ten domestic and ten foreign policy issues. Each chapter provides a general introduction to the issue, background information, key questions surrounding the issue, and arguments supporting all sides of those key questions. *Current Issues* also contains brief summaries on administrative officials, a list of Supreme Court justices, and a list of current members of Congress. The economy, education, civil rights, the Soviet Union, international trade, and nuclear proliferation are some key topics covered. *Current Issues* is a good beginning source for high school and undergraduate college students who are preparing for debates.—*Pamela S. Bradigan.*

Dark city
Films discussed in Spencer Selby's *Dark City: The Film Noir* (McFarland, 1984, $18.95, 0-89950-103-5) flourished in the postwar disillusionment of the forties and fifties. They feature subtle qualities of tone and mood, dark and seamy themes, and often have the look of glorified B movies even when they are better than that. The book begins with detailed descriptions of 25 notable films and continues with a filmography of nearly 500 films giving basic credits and one- or two-sentence descriptions. This selection includes more films than Silver and Ward's comprehensive *Film Noir: An Encyclopedic Reference to the American Style* (Overlook, 1979), but one might question some of Selby's choices; his broad view of the genre includes films like *Rebecca* and *Spellbound* as well as unquestioned choices like *Double Indemnity* and *The Killers*. There are appendixes and indexes. *Dark City* will be of value in library film collections.—*Mona McCormick.*

Data base user service
Knowledge Industry Publications has announced its Data Base User Service, produced in conjunction with the American Society of Information Science. The service includes the following: access by a variety of means to information on publicly available online databases in North America; authority to search an online file; subscriptions to the annual *Data Base Directory* and the monthly *DataBase Alert* (with a binder and cumulative indexing); and personal assistance via a toll-free hotline. Online access for subscribers is limited to $75 worth (after that, at a rate of $60 per hour, minimum charge of $7 per call). Total cost for one year is $185, $166 for ASIS members.—*Stuart W. Miller.*

Deans' list of recommended reading for prelaw and law students
Nearly 100 law schools cooperated in this second edition of *Deans' List of Recommended Reading for Prelaw and Law Students,* compiled by law librarians Julius J. Marke and Edward J. Bander (New York, Oceana, 1984. 387p. $30). Arranged under specific subjects ranging widely from *Accounting* to *Women*, its 2,330 numbered entries incorporate all of those found in the first edition plus some new ones, enough to supply serious-minded lawyers with lifetime read-

ing. Those who are pressed for time can read the very informative annotations, many of them excerpted from law reviews. The general reader will find the full biography section of interest.—*Frances Neel Cheney.*

Death and dying in the classroom

The primary purpose of this work subtitled *Readings for Reference* (Oryx, 1984, $28.50, 0-89774-137-4) is to encourage teachers to discuss these topics with students and to provide them with a variety of approaches. Eighteen articles by academicians, classroom teachers, and counselors, all reprinted from professional journals and magazines are included. Appendixes provide (1) a list of print and non-print media concerning death, geared to children and young adults; (2) a selective list of organizations which will supply information on death and dying; and (3) a 75-item questionnaire which the editor thinks could be useful with children and young adults in stimulating discussion but which some teachers may find more appropriate for older teenagers and adults. The articles give readers overviews of the emotions children express when confronted with death, and they present guidelines to help teachers assist the grieving, dying, or simply curious child. *Death and Dying in the Classroom* assembles some solid articles in a difficult teaching area and makes them easily accessible. The book and its bibliography will be useful in school libraries and education collections.—*Judith H. Higgins.*

Design on file

Using the heavy 8½-by-11 inch opaque stock and loose-leaf format of the On File series, *Design On File* presents for copying purposes approximately 750 patterns and designs on 350 leaves. The broad scope can be appreciated from the section titles: Geometry, Patterns, Projections, Diagrams, Scales, Maps, Planning, Lettering, and Human Form. A detailed contents and "browsability" make the Index almost unnecessary. Heavy use will soon result in loose pages, but lost or stolen pages can be replaced for a dollar. Although there are more comprehensive books on most sections of this compendium, *Design On File* (available from Facts On File for $75) is most appropriate for high school and college libraries and public libraries serving students.—*Josephine McSweeney.*

The dictionary of American bird names

Ernest A. Choate's *Dictionary of American Bird Names* (1975) has now been revised by Raymond A. Paynter (Harvard Common Pr., 1985, $9.95 paper, 0-87645-117-2; $17.95 cloth, 0-87645-065-6). Using the 1983 *Check-list of North American Birds* by the American Ornithologists' Union, Paynter incorporates changes and corrects errors in derivations and origins discovered since the 1975 edition while retaining the witty and authoritative comments used by Choate to describe the origin of English common names for birds of North America. Separate alphabets for common and scientific names, a biographical Appendix giving brief sketches of ornithologists, a brief Bibliography, and an English-Latin Glossary supply a valuable source for identification of bird *names*, not birds themselves. It answers such questions as, "Why is a dove called a dove?" or "Why is the Great Blue Heron called Poor Joe?"—*Frances Neel Cheney.*

The dictionary of American Catholic biography

John J. Delaney, author of the *Dictionary of the Saints* and editor of numerous works relating to the Catholic faith, has compiled this biographical directory which presents a panorama of American Catholic history through the lives of the men and women who created it. The 1,500 concise biographies cover the period from the days of the explorers to the recent past and include not only ecclesiastics but also Catholics from all walks of life who have contributed significantly to the development of American Catholicism and/or the U.S. Published by Doubleday, the book sells for $22.50.—*Stewart P. Schneider.*

A dictionary of classical reference in English poetry

Eric Smith says that *A Dictionary of Classical Reference in English Poetry* is intended as a handbook for those who lack the classical knowledge necessary to appreciate some poetry. The first part briefly identifies characters or events appearing in the works of 80 major poets, ranging in time from Chaucer to Robert Graves, most of them objects of study in standard English courses. Chaucer, Shakespeare, Milton, Spenser, Keats, and Shelley lead in the number of classical references in the appended Index to the poets. If you are reading *Paradise Lost* and come upon "Tantalus," you can find out who he was and which other poets referred to him in their poetry. A timesaving source for a nonclassical age suitable for high school, public, and academic libraries. (Totowa, N.J., Barnes & Noble, 1984, $39.50, 0-389-20430-7).—*Frances Neel Cheney.*

The dictionary of dreams

Arco has reprinted this facsimile of *The Dictionary of Dreams* by Gustavus Hindman Miller. First published in 1901 with the title *What's in a Dream?* this popular book has been reprinted many times since then, recently by Rand McNally as *Ten Thousand Dreams Interpreted.*

The A–Z list interprets and studies 10,000 subjects of dreams, e.g., flying, climbing, playing chess, wearing a wig—everything from accordions to Welsh rarebit. It emphasizes dreams which foretell the future—to dream of knitting, for example, is for a young woman an "omen of a hasty but propitious marriage." The age of the work is evident; airplanes are "flying machines," and modern dreamers will find out about the import of coal hods but not computers. Interpretations do not take into account the dream theories of psychology and psychoanalysis, and the language may seem old-fashioned, but the publishing history of this title indicates the enduring interest people have in dreams and the ready market for dream books (0-688-06394-7, $6.95).—*Margaret Power.*

A dictionary of media terms

Edmund Penney's new book (Putnam, 1984, $14.95, 0-399-12958-8) offers a list of some 2,000 terms and their definitions as used in the television and film industries. The work combines slang, technical words, jargon, and names that form the dynamic vocabulary of media and its allied disciplines. Despite the constant changes in these fields, this dictionary has managed to capture terms used in the workplace today. As such, this specialized dictionary will be helpful in any library that serves students or persons interested in nonprint media.—*Patricia M. Hogan.*

Dictionary of new information technology acronyms

Gale is distributing another acronym dictionary: *Dictionary of New Information Technology Acronyms* (London, Kogan Page, $56). It is a listing ONLY (with a few cross-references) of possible meanings of acronyms in information technology (called "IT" throughout the Introduction). Some inaccuracies and a strange assortment of inconsistencies creep in: CANYOLE for the Canadian CANOLE, AHONDA for Ad Hoc Committee on New Directions of the Research (sic) and Technical Services Division (of ALA), ALA is included, but RTSD is not; Modern Language Association is listed, but Medical Library Association is not (despite a press release that claims that the book is a "desk reference for those in . . . medicine and health"); and the American Bankers Association is listed with no explanation.

Gale's *Acronyms, Initialisms and Abbreviations Dictionary* cites many additional pertinent acronyms; it is to be preferred over *Dictionary of New Information Technology Acronyms.*—*Pauline M. Vaillancourt.*

The dictionary of retailing

Fairchild Books, noted for its long-running *Fairchild's Financial Manual of Retail Stores* and other books on fashion and the retail trade, has recently published *The Dictionary of Retailing* (0-87005-437-6, $25, 1985) by Rona Ostrow and Sweetman R. Smith, both academic librarians and retail business specialists. All facets of the retailing industry, from store organization, advertising, and accounting to personnel matters, shopping centers, and many other topics, are covered in the nearly 4,000 entries. Also included are organizations such as the Food Marketing Institute and the Footwear Council, and capsule biographies of persons who were early innovators and giants of the trade (e.g., Adam Gimbel, Herbert Marcus, and A. L. Neiman). Entries (words, phrases, abbreviations) are arranged alphabetically word by word with abbreviations listed as if they were words. Definitions are short but clear and include cross-references. This specialized dictionary, a first for its field, will be useful to many persons and in libraries.—*Winifred F. Dean.*

A dictionary of sexist quotations

This latest effort by Simon James (Barnes & Noble, 1984; $23.95) is a compilation of quotations about men and women and about what used to be called the battle of the sexes. Its title is misleading: much of the material is not what is usually termed sexist. Besides the expected depressing or amusing material on what a husband is good for and what a woman's place is, etc., there are numerous extracts from feminists, notably Mary Wollstonecraft. Quotations are grouped under just over 100 alphabetically arranged topical headings, and there are Author/Anonymous Source and Keyword Indexes. Public and academic librarians will want to consider this book for their reference and circulating collections.—*Robert M. Pierson.*

Directory of Central America organizations

The extent of U.S. involvement in Central America is indicated in the *Directory of Central America Organizations* (Austin, TX 78768, P.O. Box 2327, Central America Resource Center, 1984, paper, $8). Listed alphabetically by state along with address, telephone number, name of contact person, objectives, activities, countries, and national links, each organization in another section is then arranged according to activity: support, legal aid and sanctuary for refugees, research, travel, speakers, solidarity, direct assistance, political organizing/lobbying, community education, church liaison, human rights, etc. Citing more than 500 such groups, the compilers hope to maximize efforts at networking in regard to issues from this area.—*Richard D. Woods.*

Directory of fee based information services

The compiler of this new work, Helen P. Burwell, has produced an easy-to-use and well-designed resource. It has nearly doubled in size since Kelly Warnken compiled the previous editions (1978–79) which had the same title. It contains 334 entries which list "information brokers, freelance librarians, independent information specialists, information packagers, public and academic libraries, and others providing library and information services for a fee." Entries are arranged by state and by 17 foreign countries, none of which (except for Canada), were included in the earlier edition. Each entry gives typical directory information—name, address, telephone number, names of key individuals—plus lists of the subjects and services the firm provides and a descriptive paragraph about the company. The book concludes with four Indexes: Personnel, Companies, Subjects, and Services.

The directory has relatively little overlap with the *Encyclopedia of Information Systems and Services* from Gale, which, while vastly larger (over 2,500 entries) and more expensive ($250 for the fifth edition), only covers about one quarter of the entries which are included in this new directory. Thus, even libraries that own the Gale volume might do well to supplement it with Burwell's work, and it could be useful in many other situations as well (Burwell Enterprises, 5106 F.M. 1960 West, Suite 349, Houston, TX 77069, paper $18.95 + $2 postage and handling).—*Bruce D. Bonta.*

The directory of mail order catalogs

Catalogs for boating, clothing, foods, gifts, and handicrafts are the most numerous among the 33 categories listed in the second edition of *The Directory of Mail Order Catalogs* (Facts On File, 1984, $99, 0-939300-01-X). It gives address, telephone number, names of chief officers, and products for 5,667 companies which sell directly to consumers—some as specialized as AFTCO, which supplies upholstery and top material for vintage cars. Most of the topical groupings are further subdivided, e.g., Health and Personal Care has subheads for cosmetics, drugs, etc. A section on major catalogs of companies with more than $10,000,000 annual sales includes the familiar Sears Roebuck and big department stores like Macy's. If you want to know where to buy unusual seeds, consult the Product and Company Index. An interesting piece of social history as well as a source of current directory information that will be welcomed in almost any general reference collection.—*Frances Neel Cheney.*

Directory of short-run book printers

Subtitled *A Nationwide Directory of Book Printers Capable of Producing from 10 to 10,000 Copies of a Book, Booklet, Catalog, Manual, Journal, Directory or Other Bound Publication*, this second edition, compiled and written by John Kremer, is published by Ad-Lib, 51 ½ E. Broadway, Fairfield, IA 52556-1102. It sells for $10 (0-912411-05-8). It lists approximately 200 short-run publishers and provides specific details on more than 90 of them: minimum quantities, bindings available, terms, general comments, etc. Two are in Canada, and the remainder are spread across the U.S. Praise and criticism of the printers' work are given, and in more than a dozen cases questions are raised as to whether the firm is still in existence as a short-run printer. In addition, there are brief notes on how to seek a quotation, compare prices, and choose a printer. A handy guide for almost *any* operation issuing publications.—*Norman Horrocks.*

Dissertations in the history of education, 1970–1980

Anyone doing a computer search of *Dissertation Abstracts International* for the years 1970 to 1980 on the broad topic of the history of education will be astounded with 2,443 hits. Yet a manual search designed to overcome the limitations of the online keyword approach and the categorizations of the hard-copy *DAI*'s organizational scheme retrieved just that number. The results have been published in Edward R. Beauchamp's *Dissertations in the History of Education, 1970–1980* (Scarecrow, 1985, 259p., $22.50). Although organized into eight chapters for different regions of the world, the chapter on the U.S. accounts for nearly 1,800 dissertations. Chapter subdivisions appear in neither the Table of Contents nor the Index, an ironic note in a work intended to circumvent organizational obstacles in *DAI*. Entries include *DAI* entry numbers where lengthy abstracts will clarify a dissertation's scope and nature. The book has obvious uses for a specialized audience; it is also interesting as another example of an increasingly popular reference genre—an index to other reference works.—*James R. Rettig.*

Drug abuse and the elderly

According to author Douglas H. Ruben, elderly persons who seek relief from physical and mental ailments via chemical means make up a large proportion of today's drug abusers. Focusing on those individuals over the age of 55, Ruben's bibliography includes the topics of alcohol use and abuse, illegal and legal drugs, medication, epidemiology, drug and alcohol education, and institutionalization and drug abuse. The bibliography will be of most use in providing a historical perspective with few references since 1981; most citations are from 1960 to the present with some as early as the 1930s. Three indexes, by journal, author, and subject, are included. The bibliography is priced at $20 and is available from Scarecrow (ISBN 0-8108-1677-6).—*Martin Kesselman.*

Educators' passport to international jobs

This paperback ($9.95, 0-87866-271-5) from Peterson's Guides is written by Rebecca Anthony and Gerald Roe, career and placement specialists at The University of Iowa. It provides practical information on résumés, application forms, interviewing, packing, etc., for those seeking or embarking upon overseas jobs. However, what many educators really want to know is not included, e.g., the top employers; the average number of positions available annually; and information on insurance, benefits, salary, retirement plans, living accommodations provided by the major employers, etc. Nowhere is there information on the most desirable subject specialties or which employers are seeking teachers with specific academic backgrounds. The best chapter is concerned with résumés and application forms, "Preparing the Paperwork."—*Milton Crouch.*

Electronics ready reference manual

This compact (10 by 14cm.) handbook from McGraw-Hill ($24.50, 0-07-048723-5) contains essential electronics facts needed by engineers, technicians, students, and hobbyists. It covers everything from definitions and equations to communications and safety and presents its information in language comprehensible to those with pocket calculators and personal and mainframe computers. The publisher might well consider providing a sturdier cover to this pocket-size handbook—it certainly will be receiving heavy use. Individuals involved in electronics will want personal copies, and reference librarians will wish to provide their patrons with the information contained therein.—*H. Robert Malinowsky.*

Encyclopedia of information systems and services

Since its inception in 1971, Gale Research Company's *Encyclopedia of Information Systems and Services* (the fourth edition was reviewed in *RSBR*, May 15, 1982) has enjoyed continuous growth while remaining constant in its purpose of identifying and describing a wide variety of information services and systems. Now in its sixth edition covering 1985–86, it has grown so large that it has been split into two volumes, one for domestic organizations and an *International Volume* for foreign concerns. The latter, published late last year ($165), lists "more than 1,100 national information organizations, systems, and services . . . in approximately 65 countries."

When the 2,200-item U.S. volume is published this month, the whole will be 35 percent larger than the fifth edition (1982). The *International Volume* features the *Encyclopedia*'s usual copious variety of specialized indexes. The split offers economy to libraries which do not need the international coverage, for the U.S. volume, at $190, will cost $90 less than the fifth edition.—*James R. Rettig.*

The encyclopedia of mammals

Those wanting to augment their animal watching on television, or learn more about the endangered species, will enjoy *The Encyclopedia of Mammals,* announced for Oct. 31, 1984, publication. An impressive list of nearly 200 advisory editors and contributors from over the world, but chiefly from the U.S. and England, have aimed their more than 700 articles at the general reader. The publisher, Facts On File, points out that it will be more up-to-date than the earlier Grzimek's *Animal Life Encyclopedia,* also aimed at a general audience. This book is to be profusely illustrated with more than 1,000 full-color photographs, reflecting new methods of animal photography. (Edited by David Macdonald. 2v. $45.)—*Frances Neel Cheney.*

The end of the Beatles?

The End of the Beatles? by Harry Castleman and Walter J. Podrazik (Pierian, 1985, 553p., cloth, individuals—$29.50; institutions—$39.50, 0-87650-162-5) is the tenth volume in the Rock & Roll Reference Series. It covers the period between 1977 and 1983. Describing the "preparation, packaging and presentation" of the releases of the Beatles as a group and as individuals in those years, the work has five sections: a year-by-year chronology; releases by those connected to the Beatles (i.e., Yoko Ono, Harry Nilsson, and Julian Lennon); bootleg records; in-depth essays on specific aspects of the Beatles; and "Indexes and Instructions." The 15 indexes and the abundance of photographs contribute to the book's value. *The End of the Beatles?* belongs in most popular music reference collections.—*Laura Mason.*

Ethnicity and aging

Compiled by Edward Murguia, et al., and published by Trinity Univ. Pr. in 1984, this 132-page volume has been produced with cloth ($18) binding. It is one of a series (*Checklists in the Humanities and Education*) and is a selective list of readily accessible books and journal articles, geared toward researchers, teachers, and policymakers.

The work is made up of 1,432 numbered entries, organized by ethnic groups, subdivided by such topics as Death and Dying, Marriage and Family, Women, etc. Entries are arranged by author, then title, and include standard bibliographic data. Most entries are from the 1970s but some are from the 1980s, and several are earlier, e.g., 1953. Cross-references are sometimes provided. This is an important multicultural work that will be useful in years to come in public and academic libraries.—*Arthur S. Meyers.*

Everyday legal forms

A new volume in the useful Legal Almanac series, this title, which is available from Oceana ($7.50, 0-379-11176-4), provides sample legal forms for a variety of transactions. Included are forms for wills, dissolution petitions, warranty deeds, trusts, bills of sale, leases, and power of attorney. The Table of Contents provides adequate access to the forms, and there are cross-references to related titles in the series. *Everyday Legal Forms* will be helpful to laypersons involved in routine legal transactions; it is appropriate for public library collections.—*Pamela S. Bradigan.*

The Facts On File dictionary of fitness

With the interest in physical fitness in today's helter-skelter society, it is only natural that new jargon and buzzwords seem to appear overnight and old words take on new meanings. Terms such as *runner's toe, power rack,* and *heavy legs* along with medical terms such as *rectus femoris, hyperventilation,* and *beta-endorphin* are becoming more visible. The 158-page *Facts On File Dictionary of Fitness,* by Ardy Friedberg, defines the jargon, buzzwords, phrases, placenames, individuals, and medical terms that readers may encounter in publications or hear on the radio or television. The easy-to-understand and accepted definitions should satisfy the needs of any exercise buff, marathon runner, coach, or spectator. This dictionary is a wise investment ($14.95), if you intend to hold intelligent conversations with today's fitness-crazed individuals.—*H. Robert Malinowsky.*

The Facts On File dictionary of troublesome words

This dictionary, compiled by a copy editor of *The Times* (London), Bill Bryson, provides easily understood explanations for some of the more perplexing issues and misused words in written English. Correct meaning and use of frequently used words (e.g., *disinterested, glean,* etc.) are emphasized. The author provides examples of questionable usage (taken from the popular press), and he suggests correct usage. Arranged *A–Z,* the book is well written and should help those who have too little understanding of grammar to appreciate fully more complete discussions (and the more humorous ones) provided by H. W. Fowler, Cornelia and Bergen Evans, and Theodore Bernstein. First published in Great Britain (Penguin Books, 1984) as *The Dictionary of Troublesome Words,* the sole drawback is the limited number of entries.—*Milton H. Crouch.*

Fatherhood U.S.A.

Kramer vs. Kramer brought fatherhood to public attention. The Fatherhood Project of New York's Bank Street College of Education has carried the torch and has researched the situation. Two staff members, Debra G. Klinman and Rhiana Kohl, have put together a comprehensive directory of programs, services, and resources for fathers in *Fatherhood U.S.A.* (Garland, 1984, $14.95 paper). It covers education programs encouraging male involvement, college and university courses on fathering and male roles; support groups for fathers (including those who are single, teenage, gay, or incarcerated), programs for expectant and new fathers, and for fathers of special-needs children. Complete addresses, telephone numbers, and names of contact persons are given, and there is a Geographic Index. Space is given to fathers' rights organizations and to lists of books, newsletters, and nonprint media about fathers. *Fatherhood U.S.A.* will be useful for ready reference in public libraries and for counselors in schools, churches, and other organizations developing programs for fathers.—*Judith Higgins.*

Federal register

Congressional Information Service, Inc., is now offering a new weekly index to the *Federal Register.* The 53-page premier issue covers *Federal Register* issues dated January 3–6, 1984, and provides access by subject (policy areas, commodities, industries, occupations, chemical substances, etc.), by responsible agency, by authorizing law, and, where appropriate, by specific geographic area, organization, or individuals affected. Entries contain short annotations, references to *Federal Register* issue date and page, and an indication of issuing agency and document type (rules, proposed rules, notices, etc.). Two additional indexes by *Code of Federal Regulations* section affected and by agency docket number are supplied. Cumulative issues are planned for 5-, 15-, and 26-week intervals. Free sample copies may be obtained from CIS, P.O. Box 30056, Bethesda, MD 20814 or by calling Customer Service (toll-free) 800-638-8380; $595 for a one-year subscription. The latest issue will generally be available one week after the date of the last *Federal Register* issue covered (i.e., the following Friday).—*Vincent Jennings.*

Federal statistical directory

The 26th edition of the *Federal Statistical Directory* (1979) was the last sold by the U.S. Government Printing Office and sent to depository libraries. The 27th edition (1984) has been compiled for ICUC Press by Richard J. D'Aleo and William R. Evinger; it lists by organizational unit the name, title, and telephone number of more than 3,000 federal government officials with statistical responsibilities. The familiar arrangement has been retained (executive office of the president followed by cabinet departments, independent agencies, and agencies outside the executive branch), as has the Name Index. New features include a Subject/Agency Index and a detailed, informative Appendix entitled "Guide to Information Sources" which cites a number of key government publications important for understanding the federal data-gathering effort. 236p. paper $14.95 plus $2 postage and handling from ICUC Press, P.O. Box 1447, Springfield, VA 22151 (703) 323-8065.—*Vincent Jennings.*

A field guide to America's history

This field guide by Brownstone (Facts On File, $17.95) is an introduction to natural and manmade marks in our history. It covers everything from canals to inns and railroads to nails and cites the section of the country (but not the specific locale) where the objects can be found; it explains such operations as millstones and illustrates styles of architecture, types of agricultural implements, etc. While the volume is sketchy and will not be useful for in-depth reference questions and will not guide users to specific cities or towns, it can give novices in America's physical history a general understanding of what exists. An Index facilitates finding materials.—*Arthur S. Meyers.*

Finding co-ops
According to its publisher (Washington, D.C.–based Cooperative Information Consortium), this is the first listing of some 20,000 U.S. cooperatives and 500 cooperative associations, federations, and resource organizations. The criteria for inclusion are that a cooperative must be incorporated under state law as a cooperative or nonprofit organization and operate according to cooperative principles, i.e., controlled by members, with an open membership policy, and distribution to members of savings not otherwise reinvested in the business.

The cooperatives are grouped by broad subjects, e.g., Agriculture, Child Care, and Insurance, subdivided by state, under which names and addresses (no telephone numbers) are listed in no discernible order. The geographical listing puts all of the cooperatives (names only) by city, and there is an alphabetical listing with addresses.

While the basic arrangement is acceptable, better design work would have prevented a potentially confusing practice—the topical sections begin with a short commentary on one page, but the actual listing begins on the other.

Finding Co-ops is a handy item, particularly for public libraries emphasizing consumer aids (288p., $15.95, paper 0-916701-02-6).—*Arthur S. Meyers.*

Follies and foibles
At once entertaining and informative, *Follies and Foibles: A View of 20th Century Fads,* by Andrew Marum and Frank Parise (Facts On File, 1984; $22.95, $14.95 paper), should be considered for reference collections of libraries with a demand ("serious" or otherwise) for information on popular culture. Its scope is American enthusiasms from the turn of the century (*Stereoptican Views, Gibson Girl,* etc.) through subsequent decades (*Betty Boop, New Look, Panty Raids,* etc.). As its Foreword notes, it is on "things and activities," not on intellectual and other movements thereby manifested: still, one could wish for a *little* more depth, e.g., the note on the zoot suit fad includes no reference to associated Anglo-Chicano tensions. Its chronological approach makes *Follies and Foibles* ideal for continuous reading and "dipping"; reference use is facilitated by a topical index—and would have been helped by a more than minimal Table of Contents, i.e., a display of riches, and by a better cross-reference network. (There are indeed cross-references to headings under which related material exists, but since the arrangement is nonalphabetical one must first consult the Index. Thus, under *Fake Facial Hair for Men* is a reference to *Wigs for Women*—which could be anywhere in the chronological sequence. In the Index is, sure enough, *Wigs*—which cites the page on which *Wigs for Women* appears. Such cross-referencing is, if not, as they say, legally blind, surely roundabout.)—*Robert M. Pierson.*

The free software catalog and directory
Microcomputer aficionados will find this new guide to what's available very helpful in amassing a software library for as little monetary investment as possible. Robert Froehlich ends his introduction to *The Free Software Catalog and Directory* (Crown, paper, $9.95, 0-517-55448-8) with the admonition that "Free Software is for Everyone!" In addition to the catalog listing of free files, Froehlich provides four "directories" (i.e., indexes) to the listings: keyword, language, author, and file name. There are also bulletin board and club listings, some free program documentation, tips to help users get more from software and computers, and a guide to sources for free software. Public libraries in particular will find this a helpful addition to growing computer-related collections.—*Jennifer S. Cargill.*

Frew's daily archive
Breadth if not depth distinguishes *Frew's Daily Archive: A Calendar of Commemorations*—about 4,500 events, 2,300 birthdays, and 1,300 commemorations or holidays arranged by days of the year. Unlike *The American Book of Days,* there is no accompanying commentary. The Preface states that it is "intended to illustrate the significant affairs, the fascinating vagaries, the humor, the ironies of our planet." This it does, unrestricted as to place or time. Separate indexes to Birthdays, Commemorations, and Events provide answers to such questions as the founding date of the Anti-Cigarette League of America in 1919, Women's Equality Day on August 26, the death date of Mohammed the Conqueror on May 3, 1481, and the first publication of Fannie Farmer's cookbook on January 7, 1896. *Frew's Daily Archive* is a good ready reference for public libraries. (Jefferson, N.C., McFarland, 1984. $24.95, 0-89950-127-3)—*Frances Neel Cheney.*

Future war novels
Edited by John Newman and Michael Unsworth, this work is based on the Imaginary War Fiction collection at Colorado State University. The criterion for inclusion in this listing is that a plot involve wars "that occur in at least the nominal or immediate future among existing nations on earth or close parallels to them." Emphasis is on the realistic novel that focuses on political and military events. There are 191 novels in chronological arrangement; coverage extends from 1946 through 1983. Annotations summarize plot, setting, and characterization and include short assessments of literary quality. Various editions are noted in the bibliographical entries, but in-print status is not given. Further access is provided by Author and Title Indexes. The focus of the work is timely but narrow. Public libraries will be interested in acquiring it (Oryx, 1984, 101p., $25, 0-89774-103-X).—*Douglas G. Birdsall.*

The Garland recipe index
For a well-chosen collection of about 50 cookbooks published in the last ten years, covering basic, regional, specialty, and foreign and ethnic cooking, two indexers/cooks have compiled *The Garland Recipe Index.* Kathryn Torgeson and Sylvia Weinstein have carefully indexed recipes by name, principal food ingredients, and cooking style, with copious cross-references. Considering the eccentric indexing in some cookbooks, this unique guide to the contents of such popular titles as those of Julia Child, Craig Claiborne, Jean Hewitt, and others will be a great time-saver (New York: Garland, 1984; 314p. cloth $35).—*Frances Neel Cheney.*

Global guide to international education
David Hoopes, author of a dozen books in the international/intercultural field, has compiled a sourcebook of programs, organizations, and publications in his *Global Guide to International Education* (New York, Facts On File, 1984, $75, 0-87196-437-6). Assisted by an advisory board of six qualified educators, he has concentrated on international education (comparative education) in the U.S., limiting certain categories covered elsewhere, e.g., traditional language and literature programs, standard undergraduate international relations programs with political science orientation, study-abroad programs, and others—all of which limitations are fully set forth in the Introduction. Its three major sections, each subdivided, cover general sources, those focusing on particular world regions, and those focusing on specific countries (150 altogether), the latter revealing how many more programs there are for the USSR and Japan than for Iran and Iraq. Purposes, services, and publications of a large number of organizations are described, giving name of contact. Also briefly described are publishers and individual books and journals. Indexes to organizations, publications, and topics are appended, with topics ranging from names of countries or languages to grants (how to obtain them). Unlike some educational directories, it is relatively up-to-date. "Just before going to press we asked virtually every organization, academic program and publisher . . . to make sure that the data we had was as accurate and up-to-date as possible." The response was very good—a fact which will make the sourcebook especially useful in education collections.—*Frances Neel Cheney.*

Great romantic ruins of England and Wales
Anglophiles and students of English history and literature will be delighted to know that another book of the "Treasures of Britain" type has been published. Entitled *Great Romantic Ruins of England and Wales* (Crown, 1984; hardcover $25), its emphasis is on the words *romantic* and *ruins.* The text, describing the history of each structure, is excellent, and the color photographs, many of them double page, are superb. Each entry ends with directions, present owner, and parking instructions.

Tintern Abbey, Harlech Castle, and Newstead Abbey are all here, and from Roman times or earlier there is Bath, Stonehenge, and

Hadrian's Wall. But don't look for Melrose (it is in Scotland), or Fotheringay (not enough ruins left to photograph), or Salisbury or Winchester (not yet in ruins). The same is true of Windsor Castle, which is likewise excluded.

It is to be hoped that companion volumes covering Scotland and Ireland will also be published. Meanwhile, enjoy!—*Raymund F. Wood.*

Growing up with science
Subtitled *The Illustrated Encyclopedia of Invention,* this beautifully illustrated 25-volume set will be welcomed by parents, teachers, and librarians who work with children of elementary and junior high school age. Written by experts who have written science and technology books for many years, the first 22 volumes cover, in alphabetical arrangement, scientific discoveries and techniques, structures, devices, and natural phenomena. Volume 23 is devoted to inventions of all sorts, and the next volume will discuss outstanding scientists and inventors. The last volume features 40 science projects, a Glossary, and an Index. *Growing Up with Science* is available to schools and libraries from Marshall Cavendish for $199. The Board will review the material in depth in a forthcoming issue.—*Helen K. Wright.*

Guide to colleges in New England
This volume in the Peterson's Regional Guide to Colleges series covers Connecticut, Maine, Massachusetts, New Hampshire, Rhode Island, and Vermont, focusing on four-year public and private colleges and two-year private colleges. Information is presented in the standard Peterson-guide format, which allows for easy comparison of the colleges listed. The college profiles, arranged geographically by state, provide an introductory paragraph followed by academic information; student body status; costs and aid; application requirements; admissions picture; and who to contact for further information. Some include data on campus life, campus visits, interviewing, and admissions philosophy. All profile information was submitted by college admissions directors.

An alphabetical Index to the colleges is included; three directories, which permit identification of colleges according to their major fields of study (almost 400 listed) and degrees; athletic programs and scholarships; and ROTC programs complete the work. For high school, public, and college libraries, particularly those in the northeastern U.S. ($6.95, paper, 0-87866-274-X).—*J. Linda Williams.*

Guide to innovation resources and planning for the smaller business
The National Technical Information Service is offering for $13.50 the paperbound *Guide to Innovation Resources and Planning for the Smaller Business* (PB84-176304) prepared by the Office of Productivity, Technology and Innovation, U.S. Department of Commerce. Intended to help smaller technology-based companies translate ideas into new products and processes and be innovative, this is chiefly a directory of some but not all federal, state, and local government and private sector agencies and organizations interested in new technologies or providing venture capital. It also includes a case study and appendixes giving "America's 50 Hi-Tech Highways" (reprinted from an issue of *Venture*), federal offices serving small and disadvantaged businesses, and a brief bibliography, chiefly U.S. government documents. The aim is to help correct the belief that we in the U.S. "are being outmanaged and outproduced." For general reference collections.—*Frances Neel Cheney.*

Guide to the use of four standard reference works
Gale Research, Book Tower, Detroit, MI 48226, 1-800-521-0707 toll-free, has produced a 64-page *Guide to the Use of Four Standard Reference Works: Contemporary Authors, Contemporary Literary Criticism, Something About the Author,* and *Dictionary of Literary Biography.* Copies are free to teachers and their students. The booklet introduces users to each work, describes entries, and presents sample questions that can be answered using the publication, and it should be a godsend to users of these works.—*Helen K. Wright.*

The Guinness book of Olympics facts and feats
Stan Greenberg, sports statistician and former sports editor of *The Guinness Book of Records,* has brought together information on the Games from their modern re-creation in 1896 through the summer of 1980 in *The Guinness Book of Olympics Facts and Feats* (Sterling, 1984, $19.95 cloth; $12.95 paper). After an overview of each Olympics, both Summer and Winter, he deals with each sport in turn. In addition to giving details of the medal winners and related statistics, Greenberg also provides brief narrative comments. Sports no longer included in the Olympics and those which now are demonstrated at the Olympics are also described. Illustrations appear throughout the text. There are also many tabulations of medal winners and records as well as much comparative information of the type now associated with Guinness compilations.—*Norman Horrocks.*

Halliwell's filmgoer's companion
The seventh edition of *Halliwell's Filmgoer's Companion,* first published in hardcover in 1980, is now available in paperback (New York: Scribner, $10.95). Identical to the hardback edition, the paper version has a much smaller typeface and it lacks illustrations that readers have come to expect in the *Companion.* Libraries unable to afford the hardcover will welcome this inexpensive version. By adding the paperback to the circulating collection, libraries can satisfy browsers, movie buffs, or trivia fans.—*Patricia M. Hogan.*

Handbook of Latin American studies
The most continuous and comprehensive reference book on Latin America, the *Handbook of Latin American Studies* (Univ. of Texas Pr., $65) is now in its forty-fourth volume. Since volume 43 concentrated on the social sciences, the present work (following a practice established in 1964) covers only the humanities. Editor Dolores Moyano Martin of the Hispanic Division of the Library of Congress, with the collaboration of more than 60 scholars, provides a state-of-the-art essay on each of seven disciplines of the humanities along with 7,762 briefly annotated entries on books and articles. The list of more than 700 journals suggests the scope of the field. Retrieval of these items is through Subject and Author Indexes. Indispensable for any library serving those with a research interest in Latin America.—*Richard D. Woods.*

Health and medicine series
Crossroad Publishing Company and Project Ten of the Lutheran General Medical Center of Park Ridge, Illinois, are producing a very authoritatively written group of books on health and medicine in the various religions. The series intends to show how the beliefs and practices of the various faith traditions shape and are shaped by encounters with issues in health and medicine. Three volumes are available now: *Health and Medicine in the Lutheran Tradition* by Martin E. Marty ($14.95, 0-8245-0613-8); *Health and Medicine in the Catholic Tradition* by Richard A. McCormick ($15.95, 0-8245-0661-8); and *Health and Medicine In the Reformed Tradition* by Kenneth L. Vaux ($14.95, 0-8245-0612-X). At least seven other titles are planned, including ones on the Jewish, Islamic, Mormon, and Hindu traditions. Each volume is complete with extensive documentation.—*Helen K. Wright.*

Helpful hints for better living
Thrifty housewives may be familiar with some but not all of the cost cutters described in *Helpful Hints for Better Living: How to Live Better for Less.* The authors, Hap Hatton and Laura Torbet, cover the waterfront, from food shopping hints to how to make your pantyhose last longer by putting them in the deep freeze before wearing them. Tips on removing stains (from blood to wine), travel (use the bus), growing your own food and making your own bread, wine, and clothes are obviously aimed at women who stay home with their families, but a bit hectic for the woman with a job outside. Many briefly annotated sources of further information are given. This tool will be useful both as a circulating item and a reference work (New York, Facts On File, 1984, 231p., cloth $15.95).—*Frances Neel Cheney.*

The Hispanic almanac
The most valuable section of *The Hispanic Almanac* (New York, Hispanic Policy Development Project, 1984, $49.95 to libraries, community groups, and nonprofit organizations; $97.65 to corporations), "The Top 20 Hispanic Market Profiles," focuses mainly on Mexicans, Puerto Ricans, and Cubans within 20 U.S. metropolitan areas and provides much data on socioeconomic status, population and growth, age and distribution, income, educational status, use of Spanish language, area of dominant influence, and accuracy of local

census. Tables have source citations for further reference. Complementary data with comparative statistics may be found under accompanying sections covering origins, a national socioeconomic profile, election patterns, etc. Valuable for any library or organization providing services to Hispanics or perceiving them as a potential market.—*Richard D. Woods.*

Hispanic first names
Libraries serving a Hispanic-American clientele and/or supporting programs in Latin American studies and linguistics will want to acquire Richard D. Woods' *Hispanic First Names: A Comprehensive Dictionary of 250 Years of Mexican-American Usage* (Greenwood, Aug. 1984, $35). Entries cite English equivalents, etymologies, diminutives, variants, etc. A "Glossary" consists of cross-references from English equivalents, e.g., "William *see* Guillermo." An Appendix provides data on frequency of use. There is also an excellent Bibliography. Woods' previous publications include *Latin America in English—Language Reference Books, Reference Materials on Latin America in English,* and (of particular interest in the present context) *Spanish Surnames in the Southwestern United States.—Robert M. Pierson.*

A Hispanic heritage, series II
Isabel Schon has written the second series of her work, *A Hispanic Heritage,* which is "a guide to juvenile books about Hispanic people and cultures." The work lists 218 books for students in grades K–12, which are arranged into chapters on Latin America, 16 individual Central and South American countries, and Spain. Most of the titles appear under Cuba, Latin America, Mexico, Puerto Rico, and Spain. In-print books in English published since 1979 in the U.S. are arranged alphabetically by author within the chapters, and noteworthy books are marked with an asterisk. Suggested grade levels are given for each title, and each entry is subjectively annotated. An alphabetically arranged bibliography of listed titles precedes the Author Index, Subject Index (including references and cross-references), and the Title Index. *A Hispanic Heritage, Series II* (Scarecrow, 1985, 153p., cloth $13.50, 0-8108-1727-6) will be worthwhile for those public or school libraries wishing to stress Hispanic heritage in their juvenile collections.—*Laura Mason.*

A historical catalogue of scientists and scientific books
Using 26 major reference sources, Robert Mortimer Gascoigne has compiled this impressive list of 1,175 pages citing 13,300 persons from earliest times to the close of the nineteenth century. Only persons important in the development of science and for whom biographical information is available in reference books are included.

Chronologically arranged in three parts, it has four indexes: main, selected titles, dictionaries and encyclopaedias, and bibliographies and book catalogues. Although expensive ($150), *A Historical Catalogue of Scientists and Scientific Books* (Garland, 1984, 0-8240-8959-6) is a must for any history of science collection.—*H. Robert Malinowsky.*

Hollywood and American history
Subtitled, *A Filmography of Over 250 Motion Pictures Depicting U.S. History,* this book, written by Michael R. Pitts and published in 1984 by McFarland, sells for $24.95 (0-89950-132-X). It resembles other film lists in that it provides numbered entries listed under title, and it cites production company, date of release, running time, whether in black and white or color, cast, and gives a summary/critique. Pitts broadly interprets the term *history* to encompass the accounts of gangsters as well as war heroes. And many accounts, rather than being factual, reflect the way events were interpreted to the public at the time the film was made. There is an Index to Subjects, Names, and Titles. *Hollywood and American History* will engage the attention of film, history, and culture students. Its major value may be as a catalog of the manner Hollywood depicted history in fact, fantasy, and the mixture of these elements.—*Patricia M. Hogan.*

The Hollywood novel and other novels about film, 1912–1982
Nancy Brooker-Bowers, in her fully annotated bibliography *The Hollywood Novel and Other Novels about Film* (New York, Garland, 1985, $40, 0-8240-9007-1), provides a chronological view of 694 titles published in English over a 70-year period. Augmenting Carolyn See's 1963 dissertation, its contents range widely from the very influential *Merton of the Movies* and Nathanael West's disturbing *The Day of the Locust* to 35 potboilers by Victor Appleton of Tom Swift fame. Author and Title Indexes include such well-known names as F. Scott Fitzgerald, Evelyn Waugh, and Aldous Huxley, but the majority will never make an *Oxford Companion*. Cogent synopses and a good historical introduction recommend it to any film collection.—*Frances Neel Cheney.*

The Holocaust
More an eclectic listing of source material on the Holocaust than the "Annotated Bibliography and Resource Guide" it purports to be, this publication covers books, journal articles, films, music, art, and multimedia kits on the history and literature of the Nazi genocide. It also offers lists on traveling exhibits, archives and research institutes, memorials and landmarks in the U.S. and Canada, high school curricula, teacher development plans, survivor groups, speakers, and funding sources for programs on the Holocaust. In addition, it contains material which can be used in memorial services marking the tragedy. Based largely on existing bibliographies and organized very loosely with inconsistent annotations (some evaluative, some descriptive, many citations are unannotated), the compilation is not comprehensive, and it does not employ verifiable criteria in its selectivity. The strongest "bibliographic" chapters deal with Holocaust fiction, AV materials, and books for "young people" (down to age 8, though the book's preface states 15 and up). Updates are planned; presumably they will include a restructuring of the book, the utilization of selective criteria, and a clearer focus, as well as the addition of an index. Some church/synagogue libraries and elementary and secondary school libraries and media centers should consider the paperback edition. Public libraries and academic libraries should wait for a stronger future edition. (KTAV, $16.95, paperbound, 0-88125-058-9; $29.50, hardcover, 0-88125-057-0).—*Jack Forman.*

Home book of quotations
The tenth (1967) edition of that old standard, *The Home Book of Quotations, Classical and Modern,* by Burton Stevenson, has just been reissued and is available from Dodd, Mead for $34.95. Arranged by topic (from *Ability* to *Zephyr*) and including Author and Word Indexes, this immense (2,816 crowded pages) and lamentably squat volume is, despite its age, still useful. Libraries whose copies of the tenth edition are in shreds and patches will want to acquire this reissue—as will libraries, should there be any, that lack it altogether. An eleventh edition, with better coverage of twentieth-century material and improved format (e.g., larger and fewer pages and crisper typography), must surely belong on any list of needed reference tools.—*Robert M. Pierson.*

Horror and science fiction films III
Donald C. Willis, indefatigable recorder of *Horror and Science Fiction Films,* has now completed the third volume of the series (Scarecrow Press, $25, 0-8108-1723-3), covering releases over the world, from the end of 1981 through December 1982, with some retrospective coverage, especially from the 1950s, e.g., the classic *Wild Women of Wongo*. Lists of memorable features, shorts, and performances preface the main body which gives very full production information, and for many of the films, a very informal commentary. Examples: "A man's guts pop out" or, "pitched at the simpers-and-jealous-pouts level." It seems that in these days, every little medium has a bibliography all its own. For film collections and addicts.—*Frances Neel Cheney.*

How to manage
New from Facts On File is Ray Wild's *How to Manage* (1985, $17.95, 0-8160-0026-3). An unusual work—suitable for browsing and of possible reference value in public and academic libraries and in the office or staff collections of practicing managers—it records the views of more than 100 experts on a variety of management topics. Contributors include such well-known figures as Warren Bennis, Koji Kobayashi, and Peter Drucker; topical headings include Management Objectives and Responsibilities; Management Skills and Abilities and Their Development; Management Philosophies; Managing People; Policy and Planning; and Entrepreneurs, Innovation, and Change—to cite but a few. Public libraries may wish to circulate *How to Manage*; business libraries may well decide to keep two copies—one for reference and one for circulation.—*Robert M. Pierson.*

IBM software directory

PC Telemart's database has been combined with Bowker's to form an extensive resource for mini- and microcomputers. One of the first by-products (other titles include directories for CP/M and Apple), this is the paperback *IBM Software Directory* (Bowker, $24.95). The three tables of contents serve as indexes with a master list of all sections; a software list by category and subject; and an alphabetical title list. The work describes more than 3,000 software packages run on or compatible with IBM and which use the PC DOS operating system. A vendor cross-reference list and a list of 600 IBM PC users' groups complete the volume. Entries include memory or RAM, type of operating system, and price. While the *Whole Earth Software Catalog* (see below) selects the best products, this directory offers a more comprehensive listing and information for users, sellers, and developers to evaluate products themselves. On the other hand, the *Datapro/McGraw-Hill Guide to IBM PC Software* is similar and costs only $19.95 (cf. *RBB*, Dec. 1, 1984).—*Patricia M. Hogan.*

The illustrated discography of surf music, 1961-1965

A revised second edition of the 1978 title of the same name, this edition, compiled by John Blair, covers instrumental and vocal recordings by groups and individuals and is volume 15 in Pierian Press' Rock & Roll Reference Series. The amply illustrated volume has four sections: Singles, Albums, Appendixes and a bibliography, and Indexes to personal and group names, to record labels and numbers, and to song and album titles. *The Illustrated Discography of Surf Music* (Pierian, 1985, 166p., cloth, individuals—$19.95; institutions—$29.50, 0-87650-174-9) will be an asset in any music or pop-culture collection.—*Laura Mason.*

The illustrated encyclopedia of metal toys

Written by two toy experts from Sotheby's, this copiously illustrated volume is aimed at toy collectors, particularly novices or would-be collectors. It presents "an overall survey of the kind of material that may come his or her way." Roughly, it covers the last 120 years and includes only metal toys. The criteria on which items were selected for inclusion "were, basically, their probable availability to the 'average' collector in Europe and the United States." A few rare and valuable examples are shown, particularly among the toy ships.

Following the introduction, toys are considered by kinds: mechanical novelties, railroad, automotive, ships and boats, airplanes, soldiers and military, farms and animals. Items discussed are shown in full color, accompanied by identifying captions. A short section considers British and European catalogs and other printed materials from toymakers 1900–80. After this, international toy manufacturers' trademarks are shown.

Illustrated Encyclopedia of Metal Toys is delightful to browse in, and it will be a good addition to collectibles collections. (Crown, $19.95, 0-517-55399-6).—*Ruth M. Hadlow.*

Integrating women's studies into the curriculum

Integrating Women's Studies into the Curriculum: An Annotated Bibliography (Greenwood, $29.95, 0-313-24482-0) is an annotated resource guide for schools and colleges that are integrating knowledge about women into their curricula. The sources have been selected to help identify biases and exclusions and to introduce new perspectives for research and teaching.

Seven sections of the book cover sources in the traditional disciplines, ranging from literary studies to science and social science perspectives. A section is devoted to quantitative reasoning. Two general chapters include bibliographic studies and resource guides, and issues and perspectives on the topic. The book focuses on 1976 to 1983 productions, but earlier works sometimes are included.

Teachers and students interested in women's roles and activities in specific fields should find this guide helpful. Also, for those who want a guide to scholars' views on women's studies, the bibliography will provide a starting point for research.—*Jane A. Rosenberg.*

International acronyms, initialisms and abbreviations dictionary

As a companion volume to Gale Research Company's well-known *Acronyms, Initialisms and Abbreviations Dictionary (AIAD)*, *International Acronyms, Initialisms and Abbreviations Dictionary (IAIAD)* now appears in a softcover, *preliminary* edition with about 35,000 entries in 318 pages. Distributed free to libraries which order the promised "First Edition," the final version is promised for February 1985; it will have about 750 pages and more than 80,000 entries, will sell for $140, and will presumably be hardbound. The stated purpose of this preliminary edition is to "make the [already] collected material accessible as quickly as possible," and to permit the publisher to benefit by comments or suggestions made by users. A full evaluation of the completed work will be made by the Board upon publication in 1985.—*Raymund F. Wood.*

International development resource books

The complete 20-volume set ($881.75/set; $45 to $59.95 per volume) of a Greenwood series on issues confronting international development in the Third World is available. All volumes except the first were prepared under the auspices of the Center for International Development, University of Maryland, and the World Academy of Development and Cooperation (Washington). (The first number was prepared under the auspices of the Center for Advanced Study of International Development, Michigan State University.) The volumes address such topics as industrialization and development (no.1); energy policy (no.4); health, food, and nutrition (no.6); disarmament (no.17); and a modernization perspective on developing South Asia (no.18), Latin America (no.19), and Africa (no.20). Each volume follows a consistent four-part format. Part I—the largest portion—consists of readings on current issues and trends, analytical methods, strategies and policies, and country studies. Part II, Statistical Information, provides both a bibliography of data sources and statistical data on the topic of the volume. Part III is an annotated bibliography of the literature (e.g., books, journal articles, reports, documents, directories, bibliographic subject index). Part IV is a directory of information sources divided into four sections: United Nations information sources, bibliography of bibliographies, periodicals, and research institutions. While each volume is indexed, there is no index to the entire set.

Considering that each volume devotes more space to readings than to what is strictly reference information—statistical, bibliographic, directory—libraries may well decide to let individual volumes or the set circulate rather than restrict them to a reference center.—*Wiley J. Williams.*

Iran media index

Compiled by Hamid Naficy, a writer on Iranian film and producer-director of television at UCLA, *Iran Media Index* (Greenwood, $45, 0-313-23895-2) is a comprehensive, descriptively annotated index of films, filmstrips, and television news produced in English-speaking countries (mostly the U.S.) in this century through 1981. It contains 3,539 entries. Holdings of the major archives and networks are included. Arrangement is alphabetical by title within 125 topical sections; the Television News section is chronologically arranged. Each entry has basic identifying information, running time, producer, distributor, holdings location, and a brief, scrupulously objective annotation. The work has a comprehensive, accurate, 21-page Title Index and an Index of Producers, Holders, and Distributors which includes addresses, telephone numbers, and contact persons.

Through reduced type size in the Index and proper and judicious use of abbreviations, the compiler has brought together a massive amount of information in a compact but legible format. Users in large public, academic, and special libraries will find it invaluable and other public and secondary school libraries may find it useful for program and curriculum planning. A work of distinction.—*Arthur S. Meyers.*

Japan directory of professional associations

The Japan Publications Guide Service, CPO Box 971, Tokyo, Japan 100-91, has produced *Japan Directory of Professional Associations* (4-900178-03-9). The producers refer to it as "the most complete directory of associations in Japan published in English." It lists almost 4,000 organizations under more than 100 subject categories. The work sells for $150 and is updated until 1987 by *JDPA Update* ($100).—*Helen K. Wright.*

The Ku Klux Klan

Periods of intensified racism in the U.S. have prevented the full growth and development of harmony in a land noted for racial dissimilarities. Lenwood G. Davis and Janet L. Sims-Wood have documented the existence of this phenomenon and the country's response in their exhaustive publication, *The Ku Klux Klan: A Bibliography* (Greenwood, $49.95). Access to important materials is simplified dramatically in this well-arranged volume. Beginning with "Major

Works, Books and Pamphlets," the work identifies dissertations, theses, official Klan documents and publications, and government documents. Even speeches and records of Klan spokespersons are included to round out the available information.

Almost any library which is concerned with U.S. history (particularly those which specialize in social and historical phenomena) can benefit from this volume.—*A. P. Marshall.*

Law, medicine, and health care

James T. Ziegenfuss, Jr., has compiled a comprehensive bibliography of more than 3,500 citations dealing with the interdisciplinary areas of law and medicine. Subjects covered include ethical concerns in general, as well as specific citations to abortion and sterilization, patient's rights, consent to medical and surgical procedures, physician and nurse liability (malpractice), and scientific experts and testimony. Of particular interest is a geographical list of law firms with practices specializing in the law, medicine, and health-care field taken from the *Martindale Hubble Law Directory* (Facts On File, $45; 0-87196-828-2).—*Martin Kesselman.*

The law of inheritance in all fifty states

Eugene M. Wypyski, member of the New York Bar, has updated his *Law of Inheritance in All Fifty States* in a fourth edition published by Oceana (1984, 0-379-11106-3, $7.50). Number 33 in Oceana's Legal Almanac Series, it describes and tabulates in concise form the current salient features of the laws of descent and distribution, citing statute references. Ten chapters cover such pertinent topics as rights of a surviving spouse, of children and descendants, of parents and of aliens, with a final chapter on estate administration. The clarity of the text makes it comprehensible to laypersons as well as lawyers. Since death and inheritance taxes affect almost every person sooner or later, Wypyski's manual will be a handy guide in both public and law libraries.—*Frances Neel Cheney.*

Leading consultants in computer software and custom programming

The second annual edition of this guide hopes to provide micro-, mini-, and mainframe computer users with a comprehensive guide to 7,000 experienced consultants and firms which create, improve, specify, and modify software. It was compiled with the support and endorsement of the Independent Computer Consultants Association and comes from J. Dick Publishing, Lake Bluff, Ill., 290p. 28cm. paper $75; 0-943692-08-3 ISBN; 0742-5988 ISSN. In addition to name, address, telephone number, etc., each entry provides information on the number of active consultants employed, years of consulting experience, specialties, and types and categories of computers with which they work. An alphabetic keyword Index permits users to select consultants according to software or hardware application, programming languages, and exact specialties. *Leading Consultants in Computer Software and Custom Programming* will be a useful tool for persons consulting business, medical, industrial, legal, scientific, or education libraries. However, such a work needs to be updated often, and users should be aware of that fact when they are using it.—*Lucille M. Wert.*

Library of nations

Time-Life Books' newest series, *Library of Nations,* has been launched with China, a 160-page volume of seven picture essays. Following an introductory overview, the first section features a farm family's daily routine and emphasizes that some old ways persist amid radical changes; the second part explores the four regions of this vast country; the third features a college student's life; the fourth gives a brief history of China, including an illustrated chronology and a portion devoted to the civil war (1945–49); the fifth concerns itself with the Cultural Revolution; the sixth is devoted to a look at China's basic economic structure; the seventh documents the life of a Chinese government executive.

There are numerous soft-toned color photographs throughout, some black-and-white ones, and several charts and diagrams displaying such data as births and deaths, industrial gains, and political structure. A Bibliography of both books and periodical articles and an Index conclude the volume. On the front endpapers is a relief map of China; the back endpapers carry a full-color political map.

Following China in the *Library of Nations* series will be books on the Soviet Union, the U.S., France, West Germany, the Arabian Peninsula, Mexico, Japan, and other countries.

This is an interestingly written, informative, up-to-date introduction to modern China for junior high and up. Junior and senior high school students doing reports on China may want to use a general encyclopedia for quick, accessible facts, but this book, with its emphasis on people, offers good supplementary material. If the volumes to come follow a similar pattern, they, too, will offer useful supplementary reading.—*Ruth M. Hadlow.*

Literary criticism index

This index to bibliographies and checklists cites sources of criticism of particular authors. Compiled by academic librarians Alan R. Weiner and Spencer Means, who hope *LCI* helps their peers make the most of existing bibliographic tools, this 686-page work is published by Scarecrow and sells for $49.50. Arrangement is alphabetical by author with general material listed first, then individual titles and any collaborative works. Entries give a symbol and page number for each source, with the key in the front of the book. *LCI* will be an extremely helpful source in libraries with the 86 sources listed (most published by Gale, Swallow, Scarecrow, Shoe String, and AHM), with the unavoidable disadvantages of an index that is *twice* removed from the information sought. Universal in scope.—*A. Virginia Witucke.*

Literature searching in science, technology, and agriculture

In spite of the title, this 174-page work compiled by Eileen Pritchard and Paula R. Scott, and published by Greenwood, 1984 ($29.95), is a how-to-do-it guide for library research in science and technology. Its purpose is to provide an overview of the basic library tools for persons doing research for the first time—college students and nonscientists. The Preface also states that it will be useful to library personnel unfamiliar with scientific materials, although it in fact lacks the depth required by most librarians. Divided into chapters arranged in the order of steps an individual would follow in conducting a literature search, this work begins with chapters on surveying types of literature, formulating a search strategy, and finding books in a library. It ends with chapters on locating literature through computer retrieval, finding specialized reference sources, and bibliographic style. Throughout are illustrative examples showing catalog cards, entries from abstracting and indexing tools, online search strategies, etc. There are also charts of such items as manual search strategies for both novices and experienced searchers.

The Appendixes (abstracts and indexes, journals, databases and their sources, and sources of review articles) are arranged alphabetically by subject discipline then by titles. While *Literature Searching in Science, Technology, and Agriculture* is a book primarily for beginners, many of the books cited will only be found in research libraries.—*Lucille M. Wert.*

The marching band handbook

Much of what is included in *The Marching Band Handbook* (McFarland, $18.95, 0-89950-105-2), giving the who and where of marching competitions, indoor guard, drum and bugle corps, military bands, parades, baton twirling, music selection and sources, instruments, judging, clinics, fund-raising, publicity and public relations, travel arrangements, and trophies, is probably familiar to even the beginning band director. Some well-known companies involved in fund-raising have been omitted. Interviews with band directors and performers are included. An optional purchase.—*Judith H. Higgins.*

Media and microcomputers in the library

This update of a 1978 ERIC document, *Media in the Library: A Selected, Annotated Bibliography,* is written by Evelyn H. Daniel (ED 168590); it lists 579 sources, all published since 1978, and none are carried over from the first edition. All references are to printed sources on nonprint media—none are references to the media themselves. The body of the work consists of six chapters on specific formats: audio, film, slides and photographs, toys, video, and computers. The work also cites sources of general information and material on media selection for school library media centers; a final section discusses copyright and the future of technology.

With the exception of the chapter on toys (which has only two references), each chapter includes a selection of the most useful recent publications on that particular medium's format. The only change in scope since the previous edition is the addition of a chapter on computers. Although there are many other bibliographies on the use of computers in libraries that go into greater depth than this one, it will be useful to beginning computer users. The chapters on selection, organization, and use of media should be a valuable resource for most media librarians. A worthwhile addition in any media center.—*David A. Tyckoson.*

Medical meanings
Medical Meanings: A Glossary of Word Origins by William S. Haubrich, M.D., is the first work on the etymology of medical terms since the second edition of Henry Alan Skinner's *The Origin of Medical Terms* was published in 1961. Arranged in dictionary format, the etymologies and definitions of more than 1,000 medical terms are included, often accompanied by historical and anecdotal perspectives. Users of this book will learn that chicken pox never had anything to do with fowl, but was so named by William Heberden to distinguish the illness from the much more serious smallpox, or that the phrase "under the weather" has been attributed to seamen who sought shelter below deck during a storm. Index; Harcourt Brace Jovanovich, $19.95 and $8.95 (ISBN: 0-15-658572-3).—*Martin Kesselman.*

Memorable film characters
A fascinating one-volume reference source that identifies and describes the key characters (and their performers) from some of the more memorable films between 1915 and 1983, this work covers mostly American films (all genres). More than 1,500 characters (listed alphabetically) are identified by name, brief description, title of movie, release date, and name(s) of person portraying the role. Film and Actor Indexes provide alternative access. A very selective Bibliography is also included. As the primary purpose is to identify characters, a series character is only mentioned once and not necessarily from the first performance. Remakes or new issues are not listed unless they too were deemed memorable.

Whether you are looking for the name of the performer who portrayed a role, the name of the character, or the title of the film the character or performer was in, this source will provide the answer and much browsing pleasure for anyone interested in film. Nostalgia buffs, crossword puzzle solvers, and especially players of the silver screen edition of Trivial Pursuit will love it; libraries with standard film sources may wish to pass (Greenwood, $29.95, 0-313-23977-0).—*J. Linda Williams.*

Microcomputer software buyer's guide
The ubiquitous microcomputer is fast becoming a standard machine in library offices. The problem, of course, is the availability of a plethora of brand names and models of these computers and a corresponding bewildering array of application software. Since it is virtually impossible for average software buyers to examine and evaluate personally the available packages in order to make purchasing decisions, the *Microcomputer Software Buyer's Guide* (McGraw-Hill, 422p. paper, $19.95, 0-07-068967-9) will be practical. It reviews selected, popular spreadsheets, word-processing, database management, and integrated software packages. Well written and relatively detailed, each review is signed, and some products are reviewed more than once. The *Guide* includes a Glossary and an Index (which could be better). Of course, it goes without saying that a guide such as this one, while good, should be supplemented by perusal of current issues of periodicals such as *Byte* and *InfoWorld* for reviews on more recent products.—*Rao Aluri.*

Money A to Z
Public libraries needing another financial handbook for laypersons may want to acquire *Money A to Z: A Consumer's Guide to the Language of Personal Finance* by Don and Joan German ($15.95 from Facts On File). In the first section, 700 alphabetical entries ranging from a few lines to several pages are both clearly defined and readable. Many contain a "Consumer Tip" section. Technical terms (e.g., *assigned risk; Clifford Trust*), laws (e.g., Equal Credit Opportunity Act; Uniform Gifts to Minors Act), acronyms (e.g., ERISA, NASDAQ), and items of general interest (e.g., *bankruptcy, personal; real estate investment trust; will*) are covered. Section 2 provides an overview of aspects of "Financial Planning" (e.g., bank accounts, borrowing, home financing, and life insurance) along with lists of references to entries in section 1. The book's popular tone and lack of depth make it more appropriate for circulating than reference collections.—*Josephine McSweeney.*

Motorcycles in magazines, 1895-1983
For researchers who need to locate that hard-to-find information about motorcycles published in magazines, Richard D. Christensen has developed a very useful reference work—*Motorcycles in Magazines, 1895-1983* (Scarecrow, 1985, $19.50, 0-8108-1756-X). It is arranged in three parts: general interest and popular technical magazines; automotive magazines, 1950-83; and *Cycle* magazine from 1978-83. Complete bibliographic citations are given for each article, and there is a brief description of coverage. Most of the citations are to American publications. In addition to a general Index, there are an Index to Competition Reports and a detailed Index to Motorcycle Tests, Impressions, Descriptions, and Model Announcements. High school, technical trade, and public libraries will find *Motorcycles in Magazines* useful.—*H. Robert Malinowsky.*

Musicals! A directory of musical properties available for production
Here is help for the amateur theater company wondering what musical to do next. Compiler Richard Chigley Lynch examined the recent catalogs of the ten major licensing agents who, with few exceptions, control available properties. The resulting 400 musicals are arranged alphabetically by title, and entries include date of the New York production, playwright, composer, lyricist, and a descriptive paragraph drawn from reviews, catalogs, record liners, and personal recollection. Also noted is the availability of librettos, condensations, appearances in anthologies, scores, and recordings. Although many libraries and theater groups have agent catalogs, *Musicals!* should be a useful, one-stop compilation of shows available for production. An Index has entries for composer, lyricist, and librettist, and appendixes provide a directory of licensing agents and music publishers. Available from the American Library Association at $19.50 (200 pages, LC 84-468, ISBN 0-8389-0404-1).—*Douglas Birdsall.*

Mutual fund sourcebook
With investments high on everyone's list of priorities these days, a new quarterly publication may be of interest. The premier issue of *Mutual Fund Sourcebook: A Quarterly Survey of Mutual Funds* was published in fall 1984 by Mutual Fund Sourcebook, Inc. (53 W. Jackson Blvd., Chicago, IL 60604, $39.50). While the publication does not give advice on investing, it does describe more than 400 equity mutual funds, providing for each investment criteria, performance statistics from the past ten years (when applicable), portfolio holdings, and data concerning operations. A separate listing of more than 500 money market/fixed income funds gives advisers' names and net assets. In addition to an alphabetical index, there is an Index by Investment Objective—11 categories such as Aggressive Growth Funds, Income Funds, etc. General statistics on mutual fund activity and a couple of articles round out the issue. Other features are planned for the future, and performance and portfolio sections will be updated quarterly from filings with the SEC, share-holder reports, etc. The annual subscription price is $110.—*Winifred F. Dean.*

NTIS tech notes
Responsible for alerting industry and government to any federally developed technology that has a potential for commercial or practical use, the National Technical Information Service issues the monthly *NTIS Tech Notes*. This publication announces new processes, equipment, materials, and software. On an annual basis, the issues are summarized and indexed in the *Federal Technology Catalog: Summaries of Practical Technology*. Users can browse through the summaries, arranged under 24 broad subject groupings, and decide whether or not any are worth pursuing. Order forms are provided so that the complete tech note can be obtained. *NTIS Tech Notes* can also be accessed on the online NTIS bibliographic database. The 1982 catalog is now available for $19.50 and the 1983 for $23.50 from NTIS, U.S. Department of Commerce, 5285 Port Royal Rd., Springfield, VA 22161.—*H. Robert Malinowsky.*

National Geographic index 1947-1983
The new emulative *National Geographic Index 1947-1983*, $13.95 (Washington, The National Geographic Society, 1984) is a splendid reference tool in addition to being handsome and easy to use. More than 25,000 entries for subjects, titles, authors, and photographers unlock the contents of 445 issues of the magazine. Full information (title, author, photographer, painter, pagination, and date of issue)

is provided in each entry, and often descriptive contents are given. *See* and *see also* references are numerous. Books, maps, map supplements, and television specials are indicated by color codes. The work includes readable essays with photographs and data on exploration. Information on the Society and its work precede the index.—*Josephine McSweeney.*

The new encyclopaedia Britannica

With the just-released 1985 revision of the massively restructured fifteenth edition (1974), *Encyclopaedia Britannica*, our oldest and most prestigious English-language encyclopedia, seems to have hit the jackpot. Returning to the original concept of an encyclopedia as a work containing information on all branches of knowledge which is, in itself, a complete system of learning, *Britannica* has reorganized its alphabetically arranged ready-reference *Micropaedia* of some 60,000 articles and 250,000 cross-references, its topically arranged *Macropaedia* of 681 long, scholarly articles on broad subjects, and its *Propaedia* comprising 15,000 topics expounding on the ten-part circle of knowledge. And, with its new two-volume comprehensive Index, finding what one needs ought to be a pleasure. This publishing monument has been executed under the direction of Mortimer J. Adler, philosopher, educator, and editor, who chairs the *EB* Board of Editors, Philip W. Goetz, editor in chief, and Margaret Sutton, executive editor. *Reference Books Bulletin*'s best minds are busy analyzing the new work, and in due course, you will find our verdict in these pages. Meanwhile, Hail Britannica!—*Helen K. Wright.*

The new state of the world atlas

The New State of the World Atlas by Michael Kidron and Ronald Segal, an updated edition of the innovative thematic atlas that first appeared in 1981, is now available from Simon & Schuster. The maps continue to be grouped in 12 broad categories: the system of sovereign states; armaments; natural resources; economy; government; language and religion; business; labor; social indicators; environment; manifestations of economic instability; and popular resistance and minorities. Some gaps in data, in particular with respect to China, have been filled, and a notable new feature is a three-page list of data sources following the section of notes to the individual maps (explanatory text of from half a page to two pages). New maps have been created on financial and scientific power, on forms of government rule, on endangered species and unprotected land, and on ecological, gay, and minority consciousness. Some of the original topics, such as unemployment, have been completely reworked; the high design standards have been maintained. Paper $10.95 (0-671-50664-1). This is an excellent source of information on an array of current events–type topics.—*Vincent Jennings.*

No uncertain terms

No Uncertain Terms, by M. and D. K. Dittrick, is a charming and instructive paperback from Facts On File (1984, $6.95). Its function is to distinguish words that are readily confused, e.g., *spire* and *steeple*; *hue, shade, tone*, and *tint*; and *marsh, bog*, and *swamp*. From the reference point of view there are two drawbacks: arrangement of entries is apparently random, and there are only 60 entries—which means (as the Board has so often pointed out in reporting on other highly selective tools) low predictability as to inclusion. Still, selection is good and explanations are clear and informative. Circulating collections will want to acquire this work, and reference librarians should note it in their query files.—*Robert M. Pierson.*

The official encyclopedia of bridge

The American Contract Bridge League has published its fourth edition of *The Official Encyclopedia of Bridge*, edited by Henry G. Francis (New York: Crown, 1984, $24.95). Originally published in 1964, this is the first revision since 1976. For ease in use, the encyclopedia is divided into four major sections, the first being General Information containing A–Z entries on technical aspects, history, procedures, national organizations, and terminology of bridge. It has been extensively revised, reflecting the many changes in methods and theory over the past eight years. The other three parts cover biographies now including 2,500 bridge notables; Tournament Results, containing all North American and important international tournaments; and a Bibliography, a 21-page detailed listing of significant books on bridge presented in 17 subject areas.

An easy-to-use source with many cross-references, it indeed lives up to its stated purpose, "to provide an official and authoritative answer to any question a reader might ask about the game of contract bridge and its leading players."—*J. Linda Williams.*

Official publications of Western Europe

This first volume of a series of guides to government publications covers Denmark, Finland, France, Ireland, Italy, Luxembourg, The Netherlands, Spain, and Turkey. It was produced by Mansell in London and is distributed in the U.S. by Wilson at $56. A second volume is in preparation for the other countries of Western Europe. After a brief introduction to the acquisition of foreign official publications, each country is treated in an individual essay. Written by different authors, the essays vary somewhat in their depth of coverage—inevitable when the amount of material published is so much greater for some countries than others. This is a useful conspectus with helpful bibliographies for each country and indexes by organizations, titles, and subjects.—*Norman Horrocks.*

Omni online database directory

Written by Mike Edelhart and Owen Davies, this directory has just been published by Macmillan at a price ($10.95 paperback, $19.95 hardback) that will make it attractive to many people with personal computers. Written in an easy-to-read style, the book has introductory chapters for home computer owners which explain what databases are, how to choose appropriate equipment that will allow searching of dial-up online databases, how actually to use the databases, and the costs of searching. The directory itself provides information about the contents, access, suppliers, and, often most interesting, an evaluative paragraph headed "user's comment," about more than 1,000 databases. The book concludes with lengthy statements about the major vendors, the two large home computer vendors (Source and CompuServe), and directories of services and telecommunications. This book may influence a lot of home computer hobbyists to become end-user database searchers.—*Bruce D. Bonta.*

Opera and concert singers

Persons looking for biographical writings about vocal artists of the past four centuries will find Andrew Farkas' recently issued *Opera and Concert Singers: An Annotated International Bibliography of Books and Pamphlets* (Garland, $50, 0-8240-9001-2) a valuable resource. Nearly 800 artists are covered, and the 1,850 titles listed incorporate all known writings by the artists including their autobiographies and biographical works. Comprising works in 29 languages, English-language translations are listed when available, and English-language annotations are provided for most entries. Although the annotations are mostly descriptive, critical comments are included in a few instances, and most fulfill the author's intention "to allow for pleasant and informative reading." For in-depth music or biographical collections.—*Stewart P. Schneider.*

Our food, air and water

An exceedingly timely addition to Facts On File's series Editorials On File Books is *Our Food, Air and Water: How Safe Are They?* (1984, $22.95, 0-87196-967-X). Like other titles in this series, it is excerpted from the standard continuation *Editorials On File*. (These topical compilations focus upon particular concerns: libraries which subscribe to the parent title should seriously consider this and similar compilations, possibly for their reference collections, certainly for their circulating collections; libraries that do not receive the parent set will find the compilations, acquired selectively or en bloc, useful additions to their reference collections.)

Our Food, Air and Water arranges reproductions of editorials under the headings Food, Air, Water, and Land, each subdivided, e.g., under Air such subheadings as *Asbestos, Passive Smoking*, and *Clean Air Act*. Each section has a brief overview. Within subheadings, editorials are displayed scrapbook fashion, presumably according to size and shape, resulting less in conventional reference-book patterns than in mélanges or montages fascinating to contemplate and/or stimulating to the imagination. One recalls what Herrick said about "delight in disorder." For the serious-minded, a brief Subject Index supplements the classified arrangement: perhaps the publisher should consider, for this series, author (e.g., newspaper title plus date) indexing, with or without topical indicators. All in all, a potentially useful overview of controversies and a useful supplement to tools, e.g., *Facts On File* itself, which emphasize events as opposed to public reaction to them as expressed in editorials.—*Robert M. Pierson.*

The Oxford guide to word games

This book by Tony Augarde (Oxford, 1984, $12.95, 0-19-214144-9) "chronicles," states its dust jacket, "the endless variety of word games that have evolved in different times and places, tells how they began and how they're played, and describes the many variations that have proliferated over the years." Public and academic librarians should consider this book for circulating and reference collections; though not set up for ready reference, it is full of information, and its Index will help one locate specific data. Chapter titles include "Riddles," "Enigmas," "Acrostics," "Crosswords," "Palindromes," "Spoonerisms," and "Puns," to cite but a few. Word games are presented less as pastimes than as historical phenomena; the result is to game books what histories of cuisine are to cookbooks—and is something to treasure. As Will Weng, quoted on the dust jacket, says, "Tony Augarde has done his homework beyond the call of duty."—*Robert M. Pierson.*

The oxter English dictionary

No, not *Oxford—Oxter*, a dialectal word meaning "armpit," where, gracefully tucked, this book may be carried. An entertaining production of possible reference value in school, public, and academic libraries, it lists and defines (with documentation from modern authors) words claimed to be so rare as to be unlikely to be found in standard desk dictionaries. Not that all are truly rare: *deliquesce, ductile, glutinous, gnomic, ungulate,* and *widdershins* I supposed—perhaps wrongly—already to be in the vocabulary of all "great readers"; but many entries are indeed baffling: *callipygian*, for example, and *delphinet, febrifuge, iridal, pollskepped, tup,* and *vellication*, to cite but a few. The book's "after matter," as a student of mine once called the front matter's opposite, includes interesting comments from authors quoted as well as a list of sources cited. G. S. Saussy III compiled this book; its publisher is Facts On File; and it retails for $14.95 (0-87196-962-9).—*Robert M. Pierson.*

People's handbook of allergies and allergens

Allergies and allergens affect more than 35 million Americans and can be annoying, uncomfortable, and sometimes disabling or even life threatening. In order to help individual sufferers understand more about their afflictions, Ruth Winger has put together *People's Handbook of Allergies and Allergens* (Contemporary Books, $7.95). Its 138 pages are devoted almost entirely to an alphabetical listing of allergies, allergens, and related terms with brief definitions or descriptions. Also of interest to the sufferer are several Appendixes on a food diary to help uncover food allergies; clues to the cause of allergic contact dermatitis; a geographically arranged pollen alert for common trees, grasses, and weeds; and a list of potential food allergens. This very useful handbook should be of interest to individuals, and almost any public, school, or hospital library will want it.—*H. Robert Malinowsky.*

People's Republic of China year-book 1983

Detailed information on the year 1982 in mainland China is available in the *People's Republic of China Year-Book 1983;* formerly *China Official Annual Report,* this third edition is the first under the new title. Divided into sections such as General Introduction, Chronology of Events, Politics, Culture-Education-Health, Names in the News, etc., the information is provided in narrative format supplemented with tables, charts, and maps. There are black-and-white illustrations throughout and several special multipage sections of full-color photographs. If your interests pertain to China in 1982, they should be addressed here: the constitution adopted on Dec. 4, 1982, the statement made on International Women's Day that "China has 34 million working women," new census counts, descriptions, and color photos of each of China's 56 nationalities, the words and music of the national anthem, etc. The major drawback to use as a reference book is the lack of a detailed index; all articles must be found by using the relatively broad Table of Contents, which while including some subheadings does not pinpoint specifics which may be scattered through several sections. Nevertheless, this presents an excellent, broad picture of the PRC from its own viewpoint. Published by the Beijing Xinhua Publishing House with the cooperation of Hong Kong's Evergreen Publishing Co., it is distributed in the U.S. by Prentice-Hall for $125.—*Winifred F. Dean.*

Peterson's college database

Peterson's Guides (609-924-5338) and BRS are offering online information on 3,000 two- and four-year colleges in the U.S. and Canada. The database provides up-to-date profiles of the location, size and composition of student body, majors offered, costs and financial aid, and, for many colleges, data on campus life, facilities, student government, and admissions requirements. Peterson's expects to offer the same shortly via Dow Jones News/Retrieval Service, DIALOG Information Retrieval Service, and CompuServe.—*Helen K. Wright.*

Peterson's competitive colleges

Peterson's, the company which produced *Peterson's Guide to Colleges* for separate geographical areas, has come up with a timesaving third edition of *Peterson's Competitive Colleges* (Peterson's Guides, Department 4704, P.O. Box 2123, Princeton, NJ 08540, $7.95 plus $1.25 shipping). This guide devotes a page to each of 302 colleges which practice admissions selectivity. Each easy-to-scan page lists such objective information as enrollment, special programs, profile of undergraduates, data on the freshman class, majors, athletics, and application requirements. Specialized schools which may be small but are also selective, e.g., College of the Atlantic and St. Louis College of Pharmacy, are listed, as well as the more famous. There is a Geographic Index. Other indexes list, e.g., colleges costing $4,000 or less in 1983/84, colleges with the most financial-aid recipients, and colleges requiring that students take a computer course. Brief information is given on highly selective arts colleges and conservatories. *Peterson's Competitive Colleges* is neat, tidy, and a godsend to harried counselors and students.—*Judith H. Higgins.*

Peterson's guide to colleges in the Midwest

Peterson's introduces a series similar to its *Travel Guides to Colleges* in format but without the maps and travel information and with additional information aimed at students. Twelve midwestern states are covered, and only public and private colleges which grant a bachelor's degree or accredited private nonprofit colleges that award an associate degree are included. Costs are for the 1983–84 academic year; other statistics are from 1982–83. There are lengthy directories of majors and degrees, athletic programs, scholarships, ROTC programs, and introductory chapters on selecting colleges and on state and federal financial-aid programs. Almost half of the pages are devoted to profiles of colleges by state; each entry gives a brief description of the school, academic information, student body statistics, costs and aid, application requirements, admissions picture (rated noncompetitive to most difficult), and an address and telephone number for information. Similar guides to New England, New York, and Middle Atlantic colleges are available at $6.95 each. 266p. (0-87866-228-6 ISBN; 0742-4949 ISSN).—*Judith Higgins.*

Philip Roth

A recent title in the Scarecrow Author Bibliographies series is a second edition of Bernard F. Rodgers' *Philip Roth: A Bibliography,* $27.50, which brings the 1974 listing up-to-date. During the past decade, seven more novels by Roth have been published (an eighth, *The Anatomy Lesson,* appeared too late to be included here). Controversies over the work of an author who "has intrigued (or frustrated) some of the finest critics and reviewers of our time" obviously have not abated; the new edition contains twice the number of primary sources, and fully four times as many secondary entries as the old.

After examining Roth's own collection of foreign editions of his works and his review files, Rodgers has added all editions plus local and regional newspaper reviews, and news and feature articles. Also newly included are juvenilia, published letters to the editor, and information on unpublished works in the Roth Collection at the Library of Congress. Those who would study the author of *Portnoy's Complaint* and *Goodbye Columbus*—and one of the major voices in contemporary fiction—now have a comprehensive base for their inquiries.—*Jane A. Rosenberg.*

Pictorial history of the Jewish people

David C. Gross, editor of *Jewish Week* has updated Nathan Ausubel's *Pictorial History of the Jewish People,* first published in 1953, published this year by Crown (ISBN 0-517-55283-3, $19.95). More than 100 pages have been added; these give annual reviews of the last 30 years of Jewish life. Recurring topics include anti-Semitism, Israel's foreign relations, intermarriage, and brief obituaries of prominent Jews, e.g., Herbert Lehman and Martin Buber. More than 1,200 well-selected illustrations and a detailed Index enhance the reference value of this readable account of the "struggle for survival" of the Jewish people.—*Frances Neel Cheney.*

The president
Much more a supplementary text than a reference work, *The President: Preacher, Teacher, Salesman: Selected Presidential Speeches, 1933–1983* (World Eagle, Inc., 64 Washburn Ave., Wellesley, MA 02181, $9.95 plus $1.50 shipping, 0-9608014-4-8) well illustrates how U.S. presidents use speeches to achieve policy ends. Excerpts from 37 speeches—many familiar, others less so—are used as examples in sections on the president as moral leader and the president as public educator on domestic and foreign issues. Each speech is preceded by a background paragraph or page and questions for the student and is followed by graphics showing the political, social, and economic conditions of the time, and more questions and comments by the editor, who chairs the History and Social Sciences Department at Phillips Academy/Andover. Not without bias or errata (the tiny corrigenda slip will doubtless be ignored or lost), its topicality will appeal to both social studies teachers and reference librarians.—*Judith H. Higgins.*

Presidential also-rans and running mates, 1788–1980
Once every four years there is increased interest in past presidential elections. This book, compiled by Leslie H. Southwick and published by McFarland in 722 pages for $49.95, 0-89950-109-5, will be an excellent source of trivia for election followers. The 51 chapters cover the 49 quadrennial presidential elections from 1788/89 to 1980, the 1861 Confederate election, and the selection of vice presidents in 1973 and 1974. For each election, there is a summary of the election, a list of biographical data on the losing candidates, and narrative sketches of the also-rans (one each for the losing presidential and vice-presidential candidates), and a Bibliography. Appendixes, a brief, general Bibliography, and an Index conclude the book.

Aside from persons preparing for Trivial Pursuit tournaments, this book will be useful for American history and political science students.—*Jennifer Cargill.*

Psychiatric glossary
The trade edition of the American Psychiatric Association's *Psychiatric Glossary* is now available at $7.95 in paperback—a 142-page work for laypersons. This monument, first released in 1957 for professionals, has had five editions. The *Glossary* contains terms and "prominent names and schools of psychiatry" and numerous cross-references. There are seven extensive tables on topics of particular interest such as commonly abused drugs, drugs used in psychiatry, and legal terms. *Psychiatric Glossary* is a worthwhile addition for any library that does not already have the initial 1980 hardbound version as well as for the home, for which it is intended.—*Pauline M. Vaillancourt.*

Race and ethnic relations
The quickening pace of change in ethnic and racial relations in the U.S., particularly since 1960, gave rise to the need for an annotated bibliography on the subject. Graham C. Kinloch now provides coverage in 250 pages: *Race and Ethnic Relations* (Garland, 1984, $40, 0-8240-8971-5). Searches in approximately 120 social science journals and many relevant texts covering the general spectrum of the social sciences yielded 1,068 entries, mostly from the 1960s and 1970s. These are divided into four major sections: (I) General Bibliographies and Research Trends (18 items); (II) Theory and Methodology (154 items); (III) Race and Ethnic Relations in the United States (696 items); and (IV) Race and Ethnic Relations in Other Societies (198 items). Author and Subject Indexes enhance the usefulness of the volume. Valuable to college students as well as those doing more in-depth research.—*A. P. Marshall.*

Rare halos, mirages, anomalous rainbows
That "the atmosphere plays many curious optical tricks" is evident in the bibliography *Rare Halos, Mirages, Anomalous Rainbows and Related Electromagnetic Phenomena.* Scientific literature of the past 150 years is fully listed, often with excerpts, being mainly the "testimony of mariners, explorers, and those who frequent the remote, open places of the world." A Place-of-Event Index reveals the worldwide scope, with Great Britain and the U.S. predominant, while the Time-of-Event Index extends from 1597 to Sept. 12, 1983. The Source Index has a large number of citations to *English Mechanics, Marine Observer,* and *Nature.* Description, possible explanation of each phenomenon, and black-and-white drawings precede the citations. (Comp. by William R. Corliss. P.O. Box 107, Glen Arm, Md., Sourcebook Project, 1984. 238p. $12.95.)—*Frances Neel Cheney.*

The record producers file
This listing of more than 20,000 albums is available from Sterling in both hardcover ($17.95, 0-7137-1429-8) and paperback ($9.95, 0-7137-1430-1). It reflects the enhanced prestige and power of record producers during the period since 1962. The editor, Bert Muirhead, is well known in record-collecting circles and manages a collector-oriented record store in Scotland. In preparing this work, he checked some 65,000 albums. Fans and those in the music and record business in the U.S. and the U.K. will find entries that cite artist(s), album name, record company, and release date. The volume concludes with tables on the producers' chart successes and an Index. *The Record Producers File* supplements *New Rock Record* and other discographies. Libraries will want both circulating and reference copies.—*Patricia M. Hogan.*

Research guide to musicology
From ALA comes this fourth and last item in its series Sources of Information in the Humanities: *Research Guide to Musicology,* by James W. Pruett and Thomas P. Slavens (1985, $30, 0-8384-0331-2). Like its predecessors, it is in two parts: bibliographical essays (by, in this case, Pruett) and an annotated list of basic reference sources in the field (by, as before, Slavens). Researchers will perhaps be more drawn to Pruett's chapters; reference librarians, to Slavens' bibliography. But reference librarians, particularly those not expert in music, will want to study Pruett's chapters, which will offer insights into how musicologists think, i.e., into what one's patrons are up to—something which general introductions to music history and theory are less likely to do, except incidentally and indirectly. (For a note on the third volume in this series, *Research Guide to Philosophy,* see the Sept. 1, 1984, *RBB* issue.)—*Robert M. Pierson.*

Running
The Olympics brought to press numerous books on sports and individual athletes. Many are picture books but others are reference books. *Running: A Guide to the Literature* by Bob Wischinia and Marty Post (Garland, 1983) is one that is well done. It includes 335 annotated entries on English-language materials; the work covers books (including fiction) and pamphlets, training books, biographies, historical reference works, and medical manuals from the 1950s to early 1983. Also listed are running periodicals, associations, Olympic champions, and world record holders. Libraries of all types and sizes should find this a very useful book at $18.—*H. Robert Malinowsky.*

Science books for children
This annotated bibliography reflects some of the best of science trade book publishing for children, preschool through junior high, from 1973 through 1983. Only a small percentage of the approximately 650 titles is no longer in print. Some subject areas have more titles than others. This, the compiler says, is a "reflection of publishing trends and not the selector's bias." Full bibliographic information is given for each title; annotations are both descriptive and evaluative. *Science Books for Children* promises to be a helpful resource for school and public libraries. It is published by the American Library Association and sells for $15 in paper (0-8389-3312-2).—*Ruth M. Hadlow.*

Sean O'Casey and his critics
E. H. Mikhail has updated and expanded his earlier bibliography in *Sean O'Casey and His Critics: An Annotated Bibliography, 1916–1982* (Scarecrow, 1985, $25, 0-8108-1747-0). About 4,500 entries published chiefly before 1983 cite a number of bibliographies and indexes but not Lowery's 1983 annotated index to O'Casey's autobiographies. Reviews of individual works are followed by criticism in books and journals, with separate sections on films, dissertations, manuscripts, and recordings—all fully indexed. The number of German, Russian, and other foreign citations as well as those to the *O'Casey Annual* are evidence of the continued interest in the work of this colorful dramatist whose *Plough and the Stars* caused a riot when it opened at the Abbey Theatre.—*Frances Neel Cheney.*

Sheldon's retail and Phelon's resident buyers 100th annual edition
Sheldon's Retail Directory celebrates its centennial with another of its annual catalogs, listing over 3,000 stores, half of them large independent department stores, the rest being large home furnishings

and women's specialty stores in the U.S. and Canada, arranged by state or province. Names of stores, personnel, and types of merchandise are given for each. Section 2, Phelon's Resident Buyers and Merchandise Brokers, alphabetical by firm's name, supplies address and telephone number for such firms as Carr Specialties, which buys large and half-size apparel for more than 60 women's specialty stores, all of which are identified. An Index to stores gives location. The complete file is an excellent source for the history of retailing as well as an up-to-date directory of this multi-billion-dollar industry. The 101st annual edition is available from the publisher (Sharon, Conn., Grey House Publishing, 1984, $90).—*Frances Neel Cheney.*

Solar census

From AATEC Publications (P.O. Box 48107, Ann Arbor, MI 48107) comes *Solar Census: Photovoltaics Edition* (paperbound, $14.95; distributed by Kampmann and Co., Inc., New York). It lists "manufacturers, suppliers, designers, R&S, education and information sources." Entries, listed alphabetically, give directory data and brief profiles, and there are Contact Name, Place, and Topical Indexes. Overlap with H. W. Wilson's 1983 *Solar Energy Directory* (cf. *RBB*, Dec. 1, 1984) is less than one might expect; public and special libraries aspiring to comprehensive coverage of the solar energy situation will want to consider this publication—as will many individual engineers and home builders. Annotations are pertinent; indexing is thorough; and the Table of Contents is remarkably informative (and therefore worth imitating).—*Robert M. Pierson.*

State maps on file

Facts On File is offering a new set in its series of loose-leaf map collections designed for photocopying: *State Maps on File*, some 1,500 maps organized by region into seven volumes. Based on surveys of school curriculum needs in each state, the black-and-white maps present a variety of kinds of information—political, physical, economic, demographic, and historical. Updates are planned at approximately four-year intervals. The maps are printed on heavy stock, which prevents show through. Each of the seven buckram-bound binders contains its own Index and sells for $55; the full seven-volume set is available for $250.—*Vincent Jennings.*

State policy data book, 1984

In this loose-leaf annual (1984–   ), to be updated quarterly, data are limited to noncopyrighted sources (copyright sources are to be added later) identified by organizations, not by publication titles. Perusal of the approximately 30 sources in a tabbed Notes section reveals heavy reliance in the 200-plus tables on federal agencies—Bureaus of the Census, Economic Analysis, Labor Statistics, etc.—supplemented by a few well-known nongovernmental sources (American Medical Association, Tax Foundation, etc.). Nowhere is there mention of such redoubtable, comprehensive sources or indexes to data as *Book of the States, Statistical Abstract of the U.S.* and supplements, *DataMap, American Statistics Index, Statistical Reference Index,* and *Statistics Sources.* As thus far published, there is little that is unique to *State Policy Data Book.* The publisher (State Policy Research, 3516 S. Wakefield St., Arlington, VA 22206) offers this title separately at $85 or as part of a full-service subscription ($360) to 24 issues a year of *State Policy Reports,* which are similar in coverage to the Council of State Governments' quarterly *State Government* and monthly *State Government News.*—*Wiley J. Williams.*

State political action legislation and regulations

This directory (Westport, Conn., Quorum Books, 1984) is a successor to the Interstate Bureau of Regulations' former loose-leaf service, *Political Action Register.* This new directory concerns political action committees (PACs)—sources of political propaganda and funding. PAC registration and financial reporting are required by the Federal Election Campaign Act (1971), and the primary feature of this new directory is its compilation of state statutes governing PAC groups. Also included for each state are existing state regulations, an index to statutes and regulations, and a listing of PAC groups. A Master PAC Listing and a Master Index complete the volume. The directory provides no financial data for individual groups, and special interests are not identified unless indicated by name. Utah, Hawaii, and Nevada are the only states without statutory laws concerning these groups. An interesting note in the Introduction informs readers that a listing of PAC organizations in Minnesota is not included as state law prohibits the use of information copied from reports and statements filed with the state's Ethical Practice Board from being sold or utilized for commercial purposes.

The directory complements Marvin Weinberger's *The PAC Directory* (Cambridge, Mass.: Ballinger, 1982), a good source for funding information, and Edward Roeder's *PACs Americana* (Washington, D.C.: Sunshine Service, 1981), a well-organized listing of PAC groups. All are desirable if comprehensive coverage is sought.—*Milton H. Crouch.*

Subject compilations of state laws, 1979–1983

This 1984 Greenwood Press title, by Cheryl Nyberg and Carol Boast, continues *Subject Compilations of State Laws* (covering 1960 to mid-1979) by Lynn Foster and Carol Boast (Greenwood, 1981, see *RSBR*, March 1, 1982). The two-part arrangement and the bibliographic style of Foster/Boast have been retained. Part I updates the state statutory research guide and adds a research guide to state administrative regulations. Part II is a subject-arranged, annotated bibliography of more than 1,400 compilations of state laws followed by an Author Index and a Publisher Directory and Index. Nyberg is an assistant professor of library administration and assistant law librarian, documents/reference, and Boast is professor of library administration and assistant law librarian, head of reference; both are at the University of Illinois at Champaign. This update will be extremely useful—alongside the 1960–79 compilation—in law libraries and in other libraries with extensive collections in state laws and administrative regulations ($55, 0-313-23335-7).—*Wiley J. Williams.*

Symbol sourcebook

That much-admired collection by Henry Dreyfuss, *Symbol Sourcebook: An Authoritative Guide to International Symbols* (McGraw, 1972), is now available in paperback from Van Nostrand Reinhold at $20.95—considerably less than the hardcover edition, still available from McGraw at $59.95. Libraries lacking Dreyfuss may prefer the hardcover version, but artists, industrial designers, and students of communication will surely welcome the paperback. Dreyfuss first groups signs and symbols under broad headings, e.g., Medicine, Physics, and Traffic; then he, in effect, regroups them by shape (students of indexing will want to see how he does this); and he concludes with a section on color. Front matter features a Table of Contents in no fewer than 18 languages and stimulating essays (in English) by various hands, and end matter includes a good (if somewhat dated) Bibliography and a well-constructed Index.—*Robert M. Pierson.*

TV trivia teasers

For those who enjoy pursuing trivia, here are 1,004 questions and answers relating to television entertainment. Numbered consecutively, the questions are organized into four categories: comedy, mystery and adventure, general, and movies on television. Scattered throughout the book are an additional 86 "photo teasers" for identification—publicity glossies of TV stars and would-be stars. A 40-page Index consists chiefly of personal names, series, and film titles. The Index is excellent, and it is handy for quickly finding specific questions and answers. The author is W. Wilson Casey, who writes "TV Teasers," a syndicated newspaper column. Published in paperback by Greenfield Books, a division of Pierian Press; 260 pages, $9.50, LC 84-81219, ISBN 0-87650-164-1.—*Douglas G. Birdsall.*

Taft corporate giving directory, 1985 edition

In its sixth edition, this companion volume (0-914756-75-3) to *Taft Foundation Directory* provides comprehensive profiles and analyses of more than 500 major American corporate philanthropic programs. These programs presumably represent the largest donors in corporate philanthropy: about half of the companies listed donate $1 million or more. The directory's unique feature is the inclusion of brief biographical information of corporate and foundation officers—information accessed through three indexes (by name, place of birth, and alma mater). Other indexes are by headquarters state, type of grant, type of recipient, operating location, and sponsoring company. The directory and two monthly newsletters—*Corporate Giving Watch* and *Corporate Giving Profiles* (formerly *Corporate Updates*)—make up the *Taft Corporate Information System,* which together with the *Taft Foundation Information System* constitutes Taft's grants information management system, *BASIC II.* Subscription rates: *Taft Corporate Information System* (the directory and 12 issues each of the two newsletters), $347; the directory alone, $267;

newsletters alone, $127. (Note: Two similar titles are *Corporate 500: The Directory of Corporate Philanthropy* [3d ed., 1984, $245; San Francisco: Public Management Institute] and *Corporate Foundation Profiles* [3d ed., 1983, $50, New York: Foundation Center]. Neither provides biographical data.)—*Wiley J. Williams.*

Taft Foundation reporter, 1985 edition

American fund-raising does not lack for a variety of directories. On the one hand, *Annual Register of Grant Support* (Marquis Who's Who), *Directory of Research Grants* (Oryx), *Foundation Directory* (Foundation Center), and *The Grants Register* (St. Martin's) are examples of useful general directories giving brief descriptions of giving interests, sponsor's name, telephone number, and address, application procedures and deadlines, etc. On the other hand, the annual *Taft Foundation Reporter* (1971– , Taft Corporation, 5125 MacArthur Blvd., NW, Washington, DC 20016, 0-914756-21-4) features 500 in-depth profiles (including a list of sample grants) and analyses of major American private foundations "chosen for inclusion on the basis of several criteria: level of assets, total annual grants, geographic focus and location, and particular areas of interest.... Each foundation profiled generally has assets valued at more than $500,000 or awards more than $100,000 in grants annually." The brief biographical information on foundation officers and directors—a unique feature of this publication—is retrievable through the alphabetical Index to Individuals by Name. There is also an Index to Individuals by Alma Mater and an Index to Individuals by State of Birth. Three other more traditional indexes—fields of interest, foundations by state, and type of grants (e.g., conference/seminar, general support, publication, research/study)—have been retained. *Taft Foundation Reporter* is the major component of the *Taft Foundation Information System*, which also includes 12 monthly issues each of *Foundation Updates* and *Foundation Giving Watch* (news items on foundations and events affecting them). Subscription rates: *Taft Foundation Information System* (includes the *Reporter* and 12 issues each of *Foundation Updates* and *Foundation Giving Watch*), $347. The *Reporter* alone is $267; the newsletters alone cost $110. Readers should be aware that the Foundation Center's *Source Book Profiles* is an annual subscription service ($250) offering a detailed description of the 1,000 largest foundations, analyzing giving patterns by subject area, type of support, and type of recipient. The service operates on a two-year publishing cycle, with each one-year series covering 500 foundations. Each quarterly installment includes about 125 new profiles as well as information on changes in address, telephone, personnel, or program, and a revised, cumulative set of indexes—by name, subject interest, type of grants awarded, and city and state location or concentration of giving.—*Wiley J. Williams.*

Tennis

The U.S. Professional Tennis Association, the organization of America's top certified tennis instructors and coaches, has prepared an "official handbook" which will be useful for any tennis enthusiast. With chapters written by some of the best players and teachers of all time (Jack Kramer, Rod Laver, Fred Stolle, etc.), one finds here a brief history of professional tennis and tips on every part of the game from basic strokes to specialty shots and winning strategies, along with information on nutrition, fitness and injury prevention, evaluating yourself as a player, organizing tournaments, coaching, and court maintenance. Also included are the official 1984 rules and decisions, the Association's Code, and a Glossary. Clearly illustrated with more than 200 color photographs, drawings, and diagrams, *Tennis: A Professional Guide* will be useful in any sports collection (Kodansha International, 1984, dist. in the U.S. by Harper, $25, 0-87011-682-7).—*Winifred F. Dean.*

Tests

Testifying to the proliferation of its subject matter, a *Supplement* including data on an additional 500 tests has already been published for *Tests: A Comprehensive Reference for Assessments in Psychology, Education, and Business* (cf. *RBB*, Dec. 1, 1984). While most are new, a few older tests which were not in the original volume appear in this supplement. An added feature is an Appendix of Test Illustrations showing samples from 70 tests listed in either volume; reference is given from the sample to the entry describing the test, but nothing in the main entry refers to the sample. Indexes here are cumulative and include all tests in both volumes. Published by Test Corporation of America, *Tests: Supplement* is available from the distributor, Gale Research, for $65.—*Winifred F. Dean.*

Trivial conquest

Trivial Conquest by Lisa Merkin and Eric Frankel (Avon Books, 1984, paper, $9.95, 0-380-89492-0) identifies itself as "The smart reference source for 'Trivial Pursuit: The Board Game.' " The authors, aided by staff and researchers at Avon as well as by their own experience as players, have provided in dictionary format answers to questions that appear in the game and possible questions that may be suggested by answers given in the game. Part dictionary, gazetteer, and encyclopedia, this trivia paperback should delight game players and trivia fans. A note to readers suggests ways to find sports rules, fictional characters, and other information that is gathered in the book. And the compilers welcome suggestions or notice of discrepancies. Copies of *Trivial Conquest* should probably be in both reference and in circulating collections of public libraries to satisfy both Trivial Pursuit players and fans of unusual facts.—*Patricia M. Hogan.*

The twentieth century

This new chronology (World Almanac Publications, cloth bound, $24.95 ISBN 0-911818-63-4) is a "natural" for school, public, and academic libraries. It traces world history from January 1, 1900, through November 24, 1983, by briefly summarizing significant events (under date). Its emphasis is on political history, with the sciences and the arts mainly but not entirely relegated to "Other Events of (year)." Many boxed paragraphs ("sidebars") discuss, briefly and interestingly, careers, trends, and other matters that cry for something other than fragmentary coverage. An Index concludes the 512-page volume: it is good, but it could be more nearly comprehensive and would be easier to use if it cited dates as well as pages; in any case, use of the Index is essential if one's starting point is a person, place, or event rather than a date.—*Robert M. Pierson.*

The typEncyclopedia

The typewritten world is evolving into the typographic world, and those who work with electronic copy preparation and printing need a guide to good visual typography. Subtitled *A User's Guide to Better Typography*, this 1984 Bowker work has 188 pages and sells for $24.95 (0-8352-1925-9). It is a quick reference to 113 terms arranged alphabetically from *accents* and *agate* to *x-height* and *zero*. Many other terms are accessible through the index. A typical entry includes a definition, various rules of thumb or axioms of good design, and a copious use of examples and illustrations. Appendix material consists of a Type Cross-Reference, which links basic typeface designs with the various names given to them by manufacturers, and 264 type specimens. Author Frank J. Romano is copublisher of *TypeWorld*, the newspaper of the typesetting community. Intended for those who buy, specify, or set type, libraries will want to consider this title for both reference and circulating collections.—*Douglas Birdsall.*

Union list of film periodicals

Anna Brady and Richard Wall, members of the reference/bibliography staff, Queens College, City University of New York, have completed an important new bibliography: *Union List of Film Periodicals, Holdings of Selected American Collections* (Greenwood, 1984, $35). The film periodical holdings of 35 libraries (many located in New York and California) were reviewed by the editors, and their union listing provides both subject and title access to an estimated 2,000 periodicals (with a Geographical Index). The description of each title includes complete title, country of publication, language, ISSN, first publication date, former and subsequent titles if applicable, and explanatory notes where appropriate. Brady provides an exemplary introduction to the work, explaining use and methodology. Interlibrary loan librarians who must identify and locate copies of these periodical titles—once considered to be ephemeral and not always included in other union listings—will welcome this union listing. However, the printing, apparently photo-offset from dot matrix copy, is unattractive and broken letters abound. The work deserved better production.—*Milton H. Crouch.*

Van Nostrand Reinhold encyclopedia of chemistry

It has been 11 years since the *VNR Encyclopedia of Chemistry* has been revised. Van Nostrand has a reputation for producing excellent, one-volume encyclopedias, and this new one is a very good example. According to its editors, about 80 percent of the text of the approximately 1,300 entries is completely new. An Index aids users in locating information about topics with no main entry. This is a well-designed encyclopedia; the pages lie flat when open; the book uses very few photographs but has numerous well-drawn schematics, diagrams, and charts. Entries were written by experts in the field; most longer entries have additional references for further reading. Editor in chief, Douglas M. Considine, should be proud of this fourth edition which, at a price of $89.50, should be on the reference shelf of all science-technology, large public, and academic libraries.—*H. Robert Malinowsky.*

The video encyclopedia
Focusing on the needs of home-video equipment enthusiasts, Larry Langman's *Video Encyclopedia* (New York: Garland, 1983) defines video vocabulary, describes equipment, profiles pioneer developers of video, and explains the scientific concepts underlying how and why video works. Extensive cross-references among the brief A–Z articles and occasional line drawings help make this popular and rapidly expanding field intelligible to neophytes and others. It is unfortunate that newcomers to video will be confused by one contradiction, possibly a typographical error, which they are likely to encounter early on: the article on Beta Format says the loading system uses 14 inches of tape whereas the article on M-load says it uses 24 inches. A minor error in an otherwise credible and authoritative guide to a booming field.—*James Rettig.*

Want's federal-state court directory
A new annual published by WANT, 1511 K St., NW, Washington, DC 20005, and selling for $12.95, ISBN 0-942008-15-4, this directory (as the title implies) is divided into two major sections. The federal section lists federal court judges and clerks, circuit executives, U.S. attorneys and magistrates, and federal district counties. The state section is most incomplete, giving a one-page organization chart of the court system for each state and the names and addresses of only three officers: chief justice, court administrator, and attorney general. This annual faces stiff competition. A more current directory for the federal system is the *United States Court Directory* (Washington, D.C., GPO, 1978–), issued twice a year, March and September, a federal depository item and available for $9.50. Several serial publications (although all are expensive) give better coverage of state court systems: *Shepard's Lawyers-Reference Manual* (Colorado Springs, Shepard's, Inc., 1983–) and *United States Lawyer's Reference Directory* (Dallas, Tex., Legal Directories, 1977–).

All in all, *Want's* is hardly a first-choice judicial directory.—*Milton H. Crouch.*

Washington 84
Edited by Craig Colgate, Jr., for Columbia Books of Washington, D.C., this first annual edition of selective information collected through May 1984 sells for $40 (paper): ISBN 0-910416-50-8 and ISSN 0083-7393. *Washington 84: A Columbia Guide to Key Institutions and People in the City* covers "over 3,000 governmental, commercial, religious, labor, medical, legal, social and community organizations" of D.C. as well as Virginia and Maryland suburbs. Emphasis is not on the federal government but on the "public and private institutions of the metropolitan area and the people who lead them." The 17 chapters are indexed by organization and also include more than 18,000 individuals affiliated with them.—*Sharon McFarland.*

What flower is that?
Crown Publishers is distributing an extremely reasonably priced, handsome reprint of a 1969 Australian imprint: *What Flower Is That?* Stirling Macoboy, the author/photographer of 14 garden books, has photographed (in beautiful color) 1,000 plants and flowers of the world emphasizing those which flourish in the Southern Hemisphere. Everything from familiar sunflowers to the less-often-seen South African nutmeg bushes is arrayed under scientific name with a Common Name Index. A brief accompanying text supplies habitat and growing instructions for each. The charming photographs make it a pleasant book for browsing, as well as source of popular reference. ($12.95, 0-517-44738-X).—*Frances Neel Cheney.*

What indoor plant is that?
Librarians and individuals familiar with Stirling Macoboy's *What Flower Is That?* (described in these pages Feb. 15, 1985) may be even more pleased by his survey of houseplants. It too is a reprint, available from Crown Publishers, of an Australian imprint ($9.98, 0-517-44737-1).

Introductory chapters discuss a variety of topics, and the bulk of the volume is a "Picture Dictionary," with readable text and splendid photographs. There is an Index to alternate names, followed by a classified index (called Botanical Relatives) grouping species by family. Despite the implication of its title, this book does not function as an identification tool—unless readers are content to browse until they spot pictures of plants whose identities have puzzled them—or unless they have guessed enough to be able to work from the Botanical Relatives display (suspecting, for example, that a mystery plant with long parallel-veined leaves is one of the Liliaceae).—*Robert M. Pierson.*

What's in print
A new bibliography of articles which appeared in over 70 microcomputer magazines from 1981 to 1983 has been published with the rather odd title *What's in Print: The Subject Guide to Microcomputer Magazines* (Blue Ridge Summit, Pa., Tab Books, 1984, $14.95 paperback). The 26,000+ references in the work are divided into 17 major sections consisting primarily of the major brands of hardware. These are further divided into numerous subsections, such as ATARI—Interfacing or TRS-80—Programming Ideas. Some of the subsections list an overwhelmingly large number of references (e.g., APPLE—Reviews includes 1,200 articles arranged in alphabetical order).

This work may prove useful for libraries with collections of microcomputer magazines, or with patrons who enjoy browsing through lengthy lists of computer articles. It may be of less use in libraries that collect such magazines since it does not provide the page numbers for any of its references—a distinct drawback for interlibrary loan purposes.—*Bruce D. Bonta.*

Whole earth software catalog
The *Whole Earth Software Catalog* (Quantum Press/Doubleday, $17.50), the latest in the Whole Earth series, identifies and describes comparatively the best personal computer software programs. Three hundred sixty-two of the 1,900 programs in the producer's software library are recommended in this book. The catalog is scheduled to appear annually; it will be updated quarterly by the *Whole Earth Software Review*. Programs are grouped into ten topical sections from games to learning telecommunications. The illustrations are mainly photographs of black-and-white video displays with some color graphics. This useful volume should achieve the success of the earlier Whole Earth titles.

Both circulating and reference copies should be added to satisfy the interest in this subject.—*Patricia M. Hogan.*

Who's who in frontier science and technology
Another title has been added to the already long-distinguished list of biographical reference works published by Chicago-based Marquis Who's Who. This one, *Who's Who in Frontier Science and Technology*, 1st ed., 1984–85 ($84.50 + $3.50 for handling), is "based on involvement in research or other work at the frontiers of science." It includes some 16,500 scientists and technologists working in the traditional fields of research as well as the fields of advanced technology. Alphabetically arranged by name of scientist, it presents the usual who's who information with an Index by fields and subspecialties. Although there will be overlap with such works as *American Men and Women of Science*, this work is more specialized and up-to-date and somewhat cheaper in price. *Who's Who in Frontier Science and Technology* is a worthy acquisition for most science-technology collections.—*H. Robert Malinowsky.*

Who's who in Wagner
Macmillan announced September 28, 1984, publication of a delightful reference source on the composer Richard Wagner, *Who's Who in Wagner: An A–Z Look at His Life and Work* ($14.95, cloth). The generally brief entries list "all Wagner operas, all the characters, the main symbolic themes and ideas, together with a full biographical survey of the key people in Wagner's life as well as latter-day Wagnerians. The emphasis is as much on interpretation as on information." The latter comment is particularly interesting as it reveals author Phillip Hodson's preference for distinguishing between Wagner the composer and Wagner the man with not a few unpleasant warts. For instance, Hodson believes that the Nazis' use of Wagner for their own purposes should not taint the operas themselves, although he gives a lucid account of Wagner's anti-Semitism and concludes that "Wagner's personal ideology had more in com-

mon with the spirit of *Mein Kampf* than many Wagnerians would care to admit." "Latter-day Wagnerians" includes brief entries on contemporary singers and stage directors as well as a few unexpected items: the entry for Anthony Burgess quotes this author as believing that all of the operas could be improved by cutting them by half.

Although not actually a scholarly work, this compendium will be a handy reference in academic as well as public library music collections.—*Stuart W. Miller.*

Winning money for college

A guide to 55 privately sponsored merit scholarship programs each based on specific performance or accomplishment in a particular field, this work is arranged alphabetically by the name of the awarding organization (Peterson's Guides, 1984, 209p., paper $7.95, 0-87866-261-8). Each listing gives the name of the program, its focus, eligibility and entry requirements, value and number of awards, deadline and the name and address of the sponsor or administrator, and a short essay giving a detailed description of the scholarship, specific rules and procedures, helpful hints in applying, and in some cases, a sample winning entry or test. Some are restricted geographically or by type of applicant, e.g., to women or minority groups, to Boy Scout Explorers, etc. Scholarships range from the familiar (National Merit) to the less known (U.S. Senate Youth Program); the value and number of scholarships in each program vary widely.

Modestly priced, *Winning Money for College* will be useful to the busy guidance counselor and to ambitious high school students.—*Judith H. Higgins.*

Women and deviance

This timely, annotated bibliography, subtitled *Issues in Social Conflict and Change,* appears when women as victims, their gender roles, and social problems are so visible in the media. There are many citations to publications, which record how women are controlled by institutions and how they in turn react to this control. Such issues involving women as abortion, drugs, and alcohol are also subjects of materials cited.

Educators, social workers, and laypersons will find *Women and Deviance* a valuable guide to recent literature.—*Jennifer Cargill.*

Women filmmakers

Subtitle: *A Critical Reception,* written by Louise Heck-Rabi, published by Scarecrow Press, June 1984, and selling for $27.50, this book is a salute to eleven filmmakers from Alice Guy-Blache to Agnes Varda. The author selected women who have made several films or who have made a memorable entry into the field. The accounts of each person include quotes from critical reviews of the director and/or her films. Filmography and notes complete each report. The Index interfiles personal names, production companies, and film titles.

While this volume reflects the author's personal judgment and in format is not designed for reference work, it could be a resource for articles on the growing numbers of recognized women filmmakers. Academic and large public libraries should consider adding this to their circulating collections and might use it to answer some reference requests.—*Patricia M. Hogan.*

Women in development

The fact that women are beginning to look up from their neighborhoods and to address larger issues of international politics and economics is strikingly presented in *Women in Development: A Resource Guide for Organization and Action,* by ISIS International Women's Information and Communication Service (Philadelphia: New Society Publishers, 1984; $39.95 cloth, $14.95 paper). This large-format book, generously illustrated with black-and-white photographs and drawings, offers essays on relationships between women and multinationals, rural development, health, education and communication, and migration and tourism. Each overview is followed by a resources section listing organizations, books and pamphlets, bibliographies, etc. While *Women in Development* is not an in-depth study, it intends "to be a guide to recent thinking and literature about women and development and to the feminist critique of these." The Foreword, by the Boston Women's Health Book Collective, describes it as a resource for understanding "the inescapable connections between our work here in the West and the struggles of women and people everywhere in the third world." It is an important contribution to women's studies programs.—*Mona McCormick.*

Word processors and the writing process

It was almost inevitable that there would be an annotated bibliography entitled *Word Processors and the Writing Process* (Greenwood, 1984, $29 cloth). Writers who use a word processor (or hope to do so) will find this compilation helpful. It identifies articles that are how-to as well as technical papers and even a dissertation or two. There is also a list of relevant journals as well as a handy glossary for novices. While not an exhaustive work, *Word Processors and the Writing Process* will prove helpful to the increasing number of people who find they cannot even write personal letters without using a word processor.—*Jennifer S. Cargill.*

World economic survey 1984 and supplement

Narratives and tables present a portrait of world economic conditions, showing recent trends and future prospects in this paperbound UN publication. Much of the information on the current, uneven economic difficulties facing the world today are known in general, but this ongoing serial provides an authoritative source of specific data, useful mainly to advanced students and specialists (United Nations E.84.II.C.1, $12; E.84.II.C.2, $7, supp.).—*Arthur S. Meyers.*

World human rights guide

This concise handbook (New York, Pica, 1984) on rights and freedoms in 107 countries shows the extent to which their laws and practices protect ordinary citizens and minority or other groups. Data (current as of April 1983) for 75 of the nations were gathered through questionnaires sent to authoritative and official sources and are presented in a standard form, enabling clear comparisons. Briefer summary information is provided for 32 other countries for which there are few data or which have populations less than two million.

The more complete country data include the usual categories, as stated in the UN International Covenant on Civil and Political Rights, but also such areas as extreme punishments for certain crimes and extensive government controls over individual life. The guide recognizes differences between cultures and religions and between rich and poor nations and does not cover such topics as freedom from hunger or whether a better life for the poor existed under a previous government. A less expensive and handier reference tool than the roughly equivalent yearbook *Freedom in the World,* an annual from Greenwood, *World Human Rights Guide* needs to be updated if it is to remain useful.—*Arthur Meyers.*

World of science

The first six volumes of Facts On File's 25-volume series called *The World of Science,* specially written for the 9–14 age group, are available. The volumes are entitled *How Everyday Things Work, Insects and Their Relatives, Astronomy, Your Body, Weather and Its Work,* and *Mathematics.*—*Helen K. Wright.*

The year in soaps

If you are curious to know why Tristan Rogers (Robert Scorpio in "General Hospital") uses Australian colloquialisms, or want to refresh your memory on the amorous episodes in "All My Children," Rod Townley can help you. His *The Year in Soaps* gives casts, story lines, and brief biographies of performers in 13 daytime shows appearing in 1983 on the three major networks, and is profusely illustrated with stills and glamorous photographs of the players. Soap-opera addicts will find it as engrossing as movie magazines used to be (New York, Crown, 1984; 250p. paper, $8.95).—*Frances Neel Cheney.*

The yellow book

The National Education Association Educational Computer Service's *Yellow Book* (Garland, 1985, $12.95 paper, 0-8240-8900-6; $18.95 hardcover, 0-8240-6999-4) is presented as a "parent's guide to teacher-tested educational software." It reviews 272 software programs for home users. All the programs are educational in nature. The NEA Educational Computer Service is jointly sponsored by the National Education Association, which handles the reviews; Cordatum, described as a high technology consulting firm (and apparently a supplier of the materials), supplying for this publication "technical and adminstrative assistance"; and the National Foundation for the Improvement of Education, which provides liaison. Separate sections evaluate preschool, elementary, secondary, and postsecondary programs. *The Yellow Book* will be useful in both school and public library collections.—*Jeanette Mitchell.*

INDEX TO SUBJECTS IN REVIEWS AND NOTES

Abstracting
  Indexing and abstracting 1977–1981 73
Administrative agencies
  Government programs and projects directory 65
  U.S. government directories, 1970–1981 109
Adolescent psychology
  Research on adolescence for youth services 101
Adolescent psychopathology
  Young people with problems 118
Adolescent psychotherapy
  Young people with problems 118
Advertising
  Advertising slogans of America 23
  Book marketing handbook 33
  Standard directory of advertisers 105
  Standard directory of advertising agencies 105
Aeronautics
  Jane's 1983–1984 aviation review 76
  Who's Who in aviation and aerospace 114
Aerospace industries
  Who's who in aviation and aerospace 114
Africa
  African political facts since 1945 23
Afro-American arts
  The Harlem renaissance 69
Afro-Americans
  Black access 32
  Black-Jewish relations in the United States, 1752–1984 32
  Ethnic genealogy 58
  A pictorial history of Blackamericans 94
Aged
  The challenge of aging 36
  Handbook on the aged in the United States 68
  National continuing care directory 86
Aging
  Aging 23
  The challenge of aging 36
Agricultural research
  Agricultural research centres 23
Airplanes
  Jane's 1983–84 aviation review 76
America
  New Iberian world 89
American drama
  American drama criticism 25
American fiction
  Crime fiction, 1749–1980 42

Critical survey of long fiction 43
Encyclopedia of frontier and western fiction 55
Novel verdicts 90
American literature
  American writers before 1800 27
  The Cambridge guide to English literature 36
  The Oxford companion to American literature 92
American periodicals
  Index to poetry in popular periodicals, 1955–1959 73
American poetry
  Index to poetry in popular periodicals, 1955–1959 73
  The schoolroom poets 102
Animals
  Dictionary of animals 46
Antiques
  Pop culture mania 94
Apple computer
  Datapro/McGraw-Hill guide to CP/M software; IBM PC software; Apple software 45
Archaeology
  The Facts On File dictionary of archaeology 60
  Larousse encyclopedia of archaeology 78
Architecture
  Architecture 28
  A guide to the architecture of London 68
Arid regions
  Research guide to the arid land of the world 101
Armoured vehicles, Military
  Wheeled armoured fighting vehicles in service 113
Arms race
  The atomic papers 29
Aromatic plants
  Herbs 69
Art
  Fine and applied arts terms index 63
  Illustrated dictionary of art terms 71
Art, Anglo-Saxon
  Insular art 74
Art, Celtic
  Insular art 74
Art, Latin American
  Handbook of Latin American art 68
  Modern Latin American art 84
Art, Modern
  Contemporary artists 41
  Modern Latin American art 84

Artists
  From museums, galleries, and studios 64
  Twentieth-century culture 109
Asian Americans
  Ethnic genealogy 58
Associations, institutions, etc.
  Community resources directory 38
  Encyclopedia of associations 54
  Information America 73
  World guide to abbreviations of organizations 117
Astrology
  The new compleat astrologer 88
Astronautics
  Jane's 1983–84 aviation review 76
  Jane's spaceflight directory 76
Astronomers
  The biographical dictionary of scientists 32
Astronomy
  Earth and astronomical sciences research centres 52
  The science universe series 102
Atlases
  Historical maps on file 70
  Kister's atlas buying guide 76
  The Prentice-Hall university atlas 96
  Rand McNally contemporary world atlas 98
  Rand McNally family world atlas 98
  Reader's Digest wide world atlas 98
Atomic weapons
  Nuclear weapons data book 90
Atomic weapons and disarmament
  The atomic papers 29
Atoms
  The science universe series 102
Audio-visual equipment
  BKSTS dictionary of audio-visual terms 29
  Dictionary of library and educational technology 48
Audio-visual materials
  Bilingual educational publications in print, 1983 31
  The elementary school library collection 52
Authors
  Contemporary authors 42
  Twentieth-century author biographies master index 109
Authors, American
  American writers before 1800 27
  Encyclopedia of frontier and western fiction 55
Authors, English
  British writers 34

Authorship
  Style manuals of the English-speaking world 106

Banks and banking
  Banker's desk reference, 1983 29
  Encyclopedia of banking and finance 54
  The MEED Middle East financial directory, 1983 80
  Statistical information on the financial services industry 105
Bathrooms
  Better Homes and Gardens all about your house 30
Behavioral assessment
  Psychware 97
Bible, N.T.
  The Bible book 30
Bibliography
  Black access 32
  Choices 36
  Fantasy for children 61
  First editions 63
  The good book guide for business 65
  Harrod's librarian's glossary of terms used in librarianship, documentation and the book crafts and reference book 69
  Self-help 103
Bibliotherapy
  Young people with problems 118
Billy the Kid
  Billy the Kid 31
Biography
  A dictionary of eponyms 47
  The dictionary of historic nicknames 48
  Thinkers of the twentieth century 108
  Twentieth-century culture 109
Biologists
  The biographical dictionary of scientists 32
Biology
  The science universe series 102
  Victorian science and religion 110
Book collecting
  First editions 63
  Rare books, 1983–84 99
Book industries and trade
  American book trade directory 24
  Book marketing handbook 33
  The book publishing annual 33
  Harrod's librarian's glossary of terms used in librarianship, documentation and the book crafts and reference book 69
Books on microfilm
  An index to microform collections 72
Booksellers and bookselling
  American book trade directory 24
Botany
  The Facts On File dictionary of botany 60
Brand name products
  Made in America 83
Business
  Business information applications and sources 34
  Business mini-micro software directory 35
  Business organizations and agencies directory 35
  Business publications index and abstracts 35

  Dictionary of business and economics 47
  The good book guide for business 65
  Information sourcebook for marketers and strategic planners 34
  MBA's dictionary 80
  Tests 107
Businessmen
  Dictionary of business biography 47

CP/M (computer operating system)
  Datapro/McGraw-Hill guide to CP/M software; IBM PC software; Apple software 45
Canada
  Canadian almanac & directory, 1984 36
  The corpus administrative index 42
  Social reform and reaction in America 104
Canadian fiction
  Modern English-Canadian prose 84
Canadian literature
  The Oxford companion to Canadian literature 92
Canadian prose literature
  Modern English-Canadian prose 84
Career changes
  The encyclopedia of second careers 57
Catalogs, Union
  Native American periodicals and newspapers, 1828–1982 87
Charities
  Foundations 63
  Social welfare in America 104
Chemistry
  CRC handbook of chemistry and physics 36
  McGraw-Hill dictionary of chemistry 81
  The science universe series 102
Chemists
  The biographical dictionary of scientists 32
Chess
  The literature of chess 79
Chicago school of sociology
  Evaluating Chicago sociology 60
Child psychopathology
  Young people with problems 118
Child psychotherapy
  Young people with problems 118
Children's literature
  Choices 36
  The elementary school library collection 52
  A multimedia approach to children's literature 85
Children's periodicals, American
  Children's periodicals of the United States 36
Children's poetry
  Index to poetry for children and young people, 1976–1981 72
Children's stories
  Fantasy for children 61
  More notes from a different drummer 85
Children's stories, American
  A reference guide to fantasy for children 100
Children's stories, English
  A reference guide to modern fantasy for children 100
China
  Cultural atlas of China 44

Christian biography
  Encyclopedia of religion in the South 57
Christianity
  Encyclopedia of religion in the South 57
Cities and towns
  Urban development in the Third World 110
City planning
  Urban development in the Third World 110
Civil rights
  Freedom in the world 64
Civilization, Ancient
  Peoples and places of the past 93
Civilization, Islamic
  Guide to Islam 67
Civilization, Medieval
  Dictionary of medieval civilization 48
  Peoples and places of the past 93
Climatic normals
  Climate normals for the U.S. 37
Collectibles
  Pop culture mania 94
College costs
  The college money handbook 38
College students
  Tools in the learning trade 108
Color
  The science universe series 102
Comedy programs
  Television comedy series 106
Commerce
  Consumer sourcebook 41
  Lambert's world of trade, finance & economic development 77
Communication
  Communications and society 38
  The science universe series 102
Community colleges
  American community, technical, and junior colleges 24
Community development
  Community resources directory 38
Computer graphics
  Computer graphics marketplace 1983–84 40
Computer programs
  Datapro/McGraw-Hill guide to CP/M software; IBM PC software; Apple software 45
Computer service industry
  Computer graphics marketplace 1983–84 40
  The directory of software publishers 50
  Online database search services 91
Computer software industry
  Business mini-micro software directory 35
Computer terminals
  Terminals and printers buyer's guide 107
Computers
  An annotated bibliography of the history of data processing 28
  The computer information series 40
  Computer publishers and publications 40
  Computers and information processing world index 40
  Dictionary of computing 47
  McGraw-Hill encyclopedia of electronics and computers 81
  The Prentice-Hall standard glossary of computer terminology 96

Index to subjects in reviews and notes   145

The science universe series 102
Consultants
  Gevers international consultants 65
Consumer education
  Made in America 83
  Reader's Digest consumer adviser 99
Consumer protection
  The consumer protection manual 41
Consumer satisfaction
  Consumer sourcebook 41
Contract bridge
  Bridge 33
Copyright
  Jailhouse rock 76
Corporations
  America's corporate families and
    international affiliates, 1983 28
  Corporate America 42
  Foundations 63
  Ward's directory of 51,000 largest U.S.
    corporations 111
Correspondence schools and courses
  The Macmillan guide to
    correspondence study 82
Courts in literature
  Novel verdicts 90
Crime and criminals
  Crime fiction, 1749–1980 42
  Encyclopedia of crime and justice 55
Criminal justice, Administration of
  Encyclopedia of crime and justice 55
Criticism
  Literature criticism from 1400 to
    1800 79
Cuban literature
  Cuban literature 44

Data base management
  Online database search services
    directory 91
Decorative arts
  Fine and applied arts terms index 63
Democratic Party (U.S.)
  The Democratic and Republican
    parties in America 45
Design
  The Facts On File dictionary of design
    and designers 60
Detective and mystery plays
  Crime fiction, 1749–1980 42
Detective and mystery stories
  Crime fiction, 1749–1980 42
  Mystery, detective, and espionage
    magazines 86
Development banks
  Lambert's world of trade, finance &
    economic development 77
Diagnosis
  Do-it-yourself medical testing 51
Dictionaries
  Dictionary of historical terms 48
  The dictionary of modern economics
    48
Diet
  Human food uses 71
Directories
  International bibliography of special
    directories 74
Disco music
  Find that tune 62
Dissertations, Academic
  Melville dissertations, 1924–1980 84
Do-it-yourself work
  Reader's Digest 101 do-it-yourself
    projects 99
Documentary television programs

U.S. television network news 110
Doors
  Better Homes and Gardens all about
    your house 30
Drama
  The Crown guide to the world's great
    plays 44
  A guide to reference and bibliography
    for theatre research 68
  The Oxford companion to American
    theatre 92
Drawing
  Encyclopaedia of drawing 53
Drug abuse
  A dictionary of drug abuse terms and
    terminology 47
  Drug use and abuse 51
Drugs
  The encyclopedia of drug abuse 55
  Drugs and sex 51
Dwellings
  Better Homes and Gardens all about
    your house 30
  The home how-to sourcebook 70
  Who lived where 113

Earth sciences
  Earth and astronomical sciences
    research centres 52
  McGraw-Hill dictionary of earth
    sciences 81
Economic assistance, American
  U.S. nonprofit organizations in
    development assistance abroad
    110
Economic history
  The good book guide for business 65
Economic indicators
  The new book of world rankings 88
Economics
  Dictionary of business and econmics
    47
  The dictionary of modern economics
    48
  Worldmark encyclopedia of the
    nations 118
Education
  American universities and colleges
    26
  Guide to nonsexist teaching activities
    (K–12) 67
  Peterson's annual guides/
    undergraduate study 93
Education, Bilingual
  Bilingual-bicultural education 31
  Bilingual educational publications in
    print, 1983 31
Education, Higher
  A subject bibliography of the history of
    American higher education 106
Education, Secondary
  Research on adolescence for youth
    services 101
Educational tests and measurements
  Psychware 97
  Tests 107
  Tests in print III 107
Egypt
  Historical dictionary of Egypt 70
Election districts
  Politics in America 94
Elections
  The American electorate 25
Electronic data processing
  An annotated bibliography of the
    history of data processing 29

Dictionary of computing 47
Dictionary of computing and new
  information technology 47
The Prentice-Hall standard glossary of
  computer terminology 96
Electronics
  McGraw-Hill encyclopedia of
    electronics and computers 81
Emotions in literature
  More notes from a different
    drummer 85
Encyclopedias and dictionaries
  Knowledge encyclopedia 77
Endowments
  Foundations 63
  The international foundation
    directory 75
Engineering
  Directory of federal technology
    resources 1984 49
  McGraw-Hill dictionary of
    engineering 81
  Scientific and technical books and
    serials in print, 1984 102
English fiction
  Crime fiction, 1749–1980 42
  Critical survey of long fiction 43
  Novel verdicts 90
English language
  A dictionary of eponyms 47
  I stand corrected 71
  Idioms and phrases index 71
  Lite English 79
  Macmillan dictionary for students 82
  The Macquarie dictionary 83
  Prefixes and other word-initial
    elements of English 95
  The private lives of English words 97
  The Random House thesaurus 99
  Secretarial word finder 103
  Webster's new twentieth-century
    dictionary of the English language
    unabridged 111
  Webster's II new Riverside university
    dictionary 112
  The wordtree 116
English language in Australia
  The Macquarie dictionary 83
English literature
  British literary magazines: the
    Augustan Age and the Age of
    Johnson, 1698–1788 33
  British literary magazines: the
    romantic age, 1789–1836 33
  British writers 34
  The Cambridge guide to English
    literature 36
English periodicals
  British literary magazines: the
    Augustan Age and the Age of
    Johnson, 1698–1788 33
  British literary magazines: the
    romantic age, 1789–1836 33
Entertainers
  Who was who on screen 113
Entomology
  Entomology 58
Environmental protection
  Encyclopedia of community planning
    and environmental management 54
Eponyms
  A dictionary of eponyms 47
Eskimo newspapers
  American Indian and Alaska native
    newspapers and periodicals,
    1826–1924 25

Eskimo periodicals
  American Indian and Alaska native newspapers and periodicals, 1826–1924 25
Ethics
  Foundations of moral education 4
Ethics, Medical
  Medical science and the law 84
Ethnic groups
  Ethnic information sources of the United States 59
Euratom
  Common Market digest 38
Europe
  An encyclopaedia of Napoleon's Europe 53
  Historical dictionary of Napoleonic France, 1799–1815 70
European coal and steel community
  Common Market digest 38
European economic community
  Common Market digest 38
European literature
  European writers 59
Evolution and religion
  Victorian science and religion 111
Examinations
  Tests in print III 107

Fairs
  A guide to fairs and festivals in the United States 66
Family
  American family history 25
Family life education
  Education-for-health 52
Fantastic fiction
  Fantasy for children 61
Fantastic fiction, American
  A reference guide to modern fantasy for children 100
Fantastic fiction, English
  A reference guide to modern fantasy for children 100
Fantastic films
  Science fiction, horror and fantasy film and television credits 102
Fantastic television programs
  Science fiction, horror and fantasy film and television credits 102
Federal government
  Directory of federal technology resources 1984 49
Festivals
  Festivals sourcebook 61
  A guide to fairs and festivals in the United States 66
Fiction
  Fiction 1876–1983 61
Finance
  Banker's desk reference, 1983 29
  Encyclopedia of banking and finance 54
  The money encyclopedia 85
  Statistical information on the financial services industry 105
  Words of Wall Street 116
Finance, Personal
  Money management information source book 85
Financial institutions
  The MEED Middle East financial directory, 1983 80
  The money encyclopedia 85
  Statistical information on the financial services industry 105

Fitzgerald, F. Scott, 1896–1940
  The critical reputation of F. Scott Fitzgerald 42
Flower gardening
  Simon and Schuster's guide to garden flowers 104
Flowering woody plants
  Simon and Schuster's guide to garden flowers 104
Flowers
  Simon and Schuster's guide to garden flowers 104
Folklore
  Native American folklore, 1879–1979 87
  Women and folklore 115
Food
  Directory of food and nutrition information services and resources 50
  Gary Null's nutrition sourcebook for the '80s 64
Food habits
  Human food uses 71
Force and energy
  The science universe series 102
Forest conservation
  Encyclopedia of American forest and conservation history 53
Forests and forestry
  Encyclopedia of American forest and conservation history 53
France
  An encyclopaedia of Napoleon's Europe 53
  Historical dictionary of Napoleonic France, 1799–1815 70
Frankenstein films
  The Frankenstein catalog 64
Franklin, Benjamin, 1706–1790
  Benjamin Franklin, 1721–1906 30
Frontier and pioneer life
  The frontier experience 64
Frontier and pioneer life in literature
  Encyclopedia of frontier and western fiction 55

Gazetteers
  Encyclopedia of historic places 55
Generative organs
  Drugs and sex 51
Geography
  Lands and peoples 78
  Worldmark encyclopedia of the nations 118
Geography, Ancient
  Historical maps on file 70
Geography, Historical
  The Times atlas of world history 108
Geology
  Victorian science and religion 111
Geophysics
  The science universe series 102
Gods
  Ye gods 118
Gothic revival (Literature)
  Crime fiction, 1749–1980 42
Government agencies
  Consumer sourcebook 41
Government financial institutions
  Lambert's world of trade, finance & economic development 77
Government publicity
  Information America 73
Government, Resistance to
  Political dissent 94

Great Britain
  Late Georgian and Regency England, 1760–1837 78

Handicapped in literature
  More notes from a different drummer 85
Handicraft
  Reader's Digest 101 do-it-yourself projects 99
Harlem Renaissance
  The Harlem renaissance 69
Healers
  Dictionary of American medical biography 46
Health education
  Education-for-health 52
Herbs
  Herbs 69
High interest-low vocabulary books
  Choices 36
Hispanic Americans
  Ethnic genealogy 58
Historians
  Biographical dictionary of Latin American historians and historiography 31
Historic buildings
  The historic preservation yearbook 69
  Who lived where 113
Historical museums
  Who lived where 113
History
  Dictionary of historical terms 48
  Encyclopedia of historic places 55
  Worldmark encyclopedia of the nations 118
History, Local
  The American counties 24
History, Modern
  Day by Day 45
Hockey
  The hockey encyclopedia 70
Holding companies
  America's corporate families and international affiliates, 1983 28
Horror films
  Science fiction, horror and fantasy film and television credits 102
Horror television programs
  Science fiction, horror and fantasy film and television credits 102
Hotlines (Counseling)
  Telephone services directory 106
House construction
  The home how-to sourcebook 70
Humanities
  Grants in the humanities 65

IBM personal computer
  Datapro/McGraw-Hill guide to CP/M software; IBM PC software; Apple software 45
Ibsen, Henrik, 1828–1906
  An Ibsen companion 71
Illustration of books
  Book illustrators of the twentieth century 32
Illustrators
  American popular illustration 26
  Book illustrators of the twentieth century 32

Indexing
: Indexing and abstracting 1977–1981 73
Indian newspapers
: American Indian and Alaska native newspapers and periodicals, 1826–1924 25
: Native American periodicals and newspapers, 1828–1982 87
Indian periodicals
: American Indian and Alaska native newspapers and periodicals, 1826–1924 25
: Native American periodicals and newspapers, 1828–1982 87
Indians of North America
: Ethnic genealogy 58
: Indians of North America 73
: Native American folklore, 1879–1979 87
: Native American periodicals and newspapers, 1828–1982 87
Indochina
: The wars in Vietnam, Cambodia, and Laos, 1945–1982 111
Industrial management
: Business information applications and sources 34
: Information sourcebook for marketers and strategic planners 34
: MBA's dictionary 80
Industrial safety
: Encyclopedia of occupational health and safety 56
Information science
: The ALA glossary of library and information science 23
: Computers and information processing world index 40
: Harrod's librarian's glossary of terms used in librarianship, documentation and the book crafts and reference book 69
: Reference sources in library and information services 100
Information services
: Consumer sourcebook 41
: Information America 73
: Telephone services directory 106
Information storage and retrieval systems
: Directory of online databases 50
: Information sourcebook for marketers and strategic planners 34
Intercultural education
: Bilingual-bicultural education 31
Interior decoration
: Better Homes and Gardens all about your house 30
Inter-library loans
: Interlibrary loan policies directory 74
International agencies
: International organizations 75
International business enterprises
: America's corporate families and international affiliates, 1983 28
Inventions
: Growing up with science 66
Investments
: Words of Wall Street 116
Iran
: Encyclopaedia Iranica 52
Islam
: Guide to Islam 67

Jazz music
: The essential jazz records 58

Jews
: Atlas of the Jewish world 28
Judaism
: Atlas of the Jewish world 28
Judges in literature
: Novel verdicts 90
Junior colleges
: American community, technical, and junior colleges 24
Jurisprudence
: Medical science and the law 84

Keats, John, 1795–1821
: Keats's major odes 76
Kitchens
: Better Homes and Gardens all about your house 30

Labor and laboring classes
: American working class history 27
: Biographical dictionary of American labor 31
: The labor almanac 77
Labor policy
: The labor almanac 77
Laboratories
: Directory of federal technology resources 1984 49
Land use
: Encyclopedia of community planning and environmental management 54
Large type books
: Large type books in print, 1984 78
Latin America
: Biographical dictionary of Latin American historians and historiography 31
: Indexed journals 73
: Latin America, 1979–1983 78
: Latin American politics 79
: Modern Latin American art 84
: New Iberian world 89
Latin American periodicals
: Indexed journals 73
Law
: A concise dictionary of law 41
: Index to legal essays 72
: MBA's dictionary 80
Lawyers in literature
: Novel verdicts 90
Lexicography
: Dictionaries 45
Librarians
: American library directory 25
: Who's who in special libraries 1983–1984 114
Libraries
: American library directory 25
: Automation in libraries 29
: Finding answers in science and technology 62
: Interlibrary loan policies directory 74
: Libraries in American periodicals before 1876 79
Libraries, Children's
: Choices 36
: A multimedia approach to children's literature 85
Libraries, Special
: World guide to special libraries 117
Libraries, University and college
: Self-help 103
: The vocational-technical core collection 111

Library materials
: Information America 73
Library science
: The ALA glossary of library and information science 23
: Harrod's librarian's glossary of terms used in librarianship, documentation and the book crafts and reference book 69
: Libraries in American periodicals before 1876 79
: Reference sources in library and information services 100
Life (Biology)
: The science universe series 102
Life care communities
: National continuing care directory 86
Life skills
: Self-help 103
Light
: The science universe series 102
Literature
: British literary magazines: the Augustan Age and the Age of Johnson, 1698–1788 33
: British literary magazines: the romantic age, 1789–1836 33
Little magazines
: The international directory of little magazines and small presses 74
Little presses
: The international directory of little magazines and small presses 74
London (England)
: A guide to the architecture of London 68
Love stories
: Words of love 116

Machinery
: The science universe series 102
Magazine illustration
: American popular illustration 26
Mail-order business
: The fifty billion dollar directory 62
Mammals
: The encyclopedia of mammals 56
Management
: The good book guide for business 65
Management information systems
: Information sourcebook for marketers and strategic planners 34
Manufacturers
: Ward's directory of 51,000 largest U.S. corporations 111
Maps
: Rand McNally atlas of the United States 98
Martial arts
: The Overlook martial arts dictionary 91
Mass media
: Communications and society 38
Mass media and youth
: Research on adolescence for youth services 101
Medical ethics
: Medical science and the law 84
Medical laws and legislation
: Medical science and the law 84
Medical research
: Medical research centres 84
Medicinal plants
: Herbs 69

Medicine
　Dictionary of American medical
　　biography 46
　MASA 80
Medicine, Industrial
　Encyclopedia of occupational health
　　and safety 56
Medicine, Popular
　A dictionary of symptoms 49
Melville, Herman, 1819–1891
　Melville dissertations, 1924–1980 84
Memorandums
　Send me a memo 103
Mensuration
　The science universe series 102
Mental health education
　Education-for-health 52
Mentally handicapped in literature
　More notes from a different
　　drummer 85
Metropolitan Opera (New York, NY)
　The Metropolitan Opera on record 84
Microcards
　Guide to microforms in print
　　incorporating international
　　microforms in print, 1983 67
Microforms
　Guide to microforms in print
　　incorporating international
　　microforms in print, 1983 67
　An index to microform collections 72
Minorities
　Demography of racial and ethnic
　　minorities in the United States 45
　Directory of financial aids for
　　minorities, 1984–1985 49
　Ethnic informaton sources of the
　　United States 59
Minority groups
　Ethnic information sources of the
　　United States 59
Money
　The money encyclopedia 85
Monsters in literature
　The Frankenstein catalog 64
Moral development
　Foundations of moral education 64
Morris, William, 1834–1896
　William Morris in private press and
　　limited editions 114
Mottoes
　A dictionary of mottoes 49
Moving-picture actors and actresses
　Who was who on screen 113
Moving-picture producers and directors
　Film directors 62
Moving-pictures
　The films of the seventies 62
　A guide to critical reviews 66
　The New York Times encyclopedia of
　　film, 1896–1979 90
　Selected film criticism 103
Municipal engineering
　Encyclopedia of community planning
　　and environmental management 54
Music
　A dictionary of American composers
　　46
　The encyclopedic discography of Victor
　　recordings 58
　Guide to musical America 67
　Music psychology index, v. 3 86
　Perspectives of new music 93
Music and society
　Year by year in the rock era 118
Music, Influence of

　Year by year in the rock era 118
Music, Popular (Songs, etc.)
　Bibliography of discographies 30
　The great song thesaurus 65
　Popular music 95
　Popular music 95
Musical instruments
　The new Grove dictionary of musical
　　instruments 89
Musical reviews, comedies, etc.
　The collector's guide to the American
　　musical theatre 37
Musicians
　Who's who in American music 113
Mythology
　A dictionary of pictorial subjects from
　　classical literature 49
　Ye gods 118

Napoleon I, Emperor of the French,
　1769–1821
　An encyclopaedia of Napoleon's
　　Europe 53
Navies
　Combat fleets of the world, 1984/85
　　38
　Conway's all the world's fighting ships
　　1947–1982 42
Neurology
　International encyclopedia of
　　psychiatry, psychology,
　　psychoanalysis, and neurology 75
New Zealand
　Bateman New Zealand encyclopedia
　　29
Nicknames
　The dictionary of historic nicknames
　　48
Non-formal education
　Directory of United States traditional
　　and alternative colleges and
　　universities 50
Novelists, American
　Critical survey of long fiction 43
Novelists, English
　Critical survey of long fiction 43
Nuclear power
　The atomic papers 29
Nuclear warfare
　The atomic papers 29
Nutrition
　Directory of food and nutrition
　　information services and
　　resources 50
　Gary Null's nutrition sourcebook for
　　the '80s. 64

Occult sciences
　Encyclopedia of occultism &
　　parapsychology 56
Oceanography
　The Times atlas of the oceans 108
Odes
　Keats's major odes 76
Office equipment and supplies
　Office automation and word processing
　　buying guide 91
Office practice
　Dictionary of computing and new
　　information technology 47
　Office automation and word processing
　　buying guide 91
O'Neill, Eugene, 1888–1953
　The Eugene O'Neill companion 59
On-line bibliographic searching
　Directory of online databases 50

Online database search services
　directory 91
On-line data processing
　Online database search services
　　directory 91
Opera de Paris
　Paris Opera 93
Operas
　The complete Gilbert and Sullivan
　　opera guide 39
　The Metropolitan Opera on record 84
Organizations
　Consumer sourcebook 41
Outer space
　The science universe series 92
Outlaws
　Billy the Kid 31
Outline maps
　Historical maps on file 70
Out-of-print books
　Books out of print, 1980–1983 33

Peace
　The atomic papers 29
Periodicals
　Guide to industry special issues 67
　Ulrich's international periodicals
　　directory 109
Personnel management
　Psychware 97
Perspectives of new music
　Perspectives of new music 93
Philosophy
　Research guide to philosophy 101
Philosophy, Modern
　Thinkers of the twentieth century
　　108
Photographers
　Macmillan biographical encyclopedia
　　of photographic artists and
　　innovators 82
Photography
　International Center of Photography
　　encyclopedia of photography 74
Physical measurements
　Quantities and units of
　　measurement 98
　The science universe series 102
Physically handicapped in literature
　More notes from a different
　　drummer 85
Physicists
　The biographical dictionary of
　　scientists 32
Physics
　CRC handbook of chemistry and
　　physics 36
　Quantities and units of
　　measurement 98
Plants, Ornamental
　The complete handbook of garden
　　plants 39
Poetry
　Critical survey of poetry 44
　International index to recorded
　　poetry 75
Poets
　Critical survey of poetry 44
Political science
　Encyclopedia of American political
　　history 53
　Worldmark encyclopedia of the
　　nations 118
Power (Mechanics)
　The science universe series 102
Power resources

Energy research guide 58
The science universe series 102
World directory of energy
 information 117
Presidents
 The American presidency 26
 The American presidency 26
 The complete book of U.S. presidents
  39
 The presidential-congressional
  political dictionary 96
 The presidents 96
Presley, Elvis, 1935–1977
 Jailhouse rock 76
Printers
 William Morris in private press and
  limited editions 114
Printers (Data processing systems)
 Terminals and printers buyer's
  guide 107
Printing
 William Morris in private press and
  limited editions 114
Printmakers
 Print index 97
Prints
 Print index 97
Professions
 The national job bank 86
Psychiatry
 International encyclopedia of
  psychiatry, psychology,
  psychoanalysis, and neurology 75
Psychical research
 Encyclopedia of occultism &
  parapsychology 56
Psychoanalysis
 International encyclopedia of
  psychiatry, psychology,
  psychoanalysis, and neurology 75
Psychodiagnostics
 Psychware 97
Psychological tests
 Tests 107
Psychologists
 Biographical dictionary of
  psychology 32
Psychology
 Biographical dictionary of
  psychology 32
 Encyclopedia of psychology 57
 International encyclopedia of
  psychiatry, psychology,
  psychoanalysis, and neurology 75
Psychology and literature
 Psychocriticism 97
Psychology, Pathological
 A reference companion to the history
  of abnormal psychology 99
Psychotropic drugs
 Drug use and abuse 51
 Drugs and sex 51
Public health personnel
 Dictionary of American medical
  biography 46
Public libraries
 Self-help 103
Public opinion polls
 Index to international public opinion,
  1982–1983 72
 Surveys, polls, censuses, and forecasts
  directory 106
Public relations
 O'Dwyer's directory of public relations
  firms, 1983 91
Public welfare

Social welfare in America 104
Publishers and publishing
 American book trade directory 24
 The book publishing annual 33
 Computer publishers and
  publications 40
 Computers and information processing
  world index 40
 Information America 73
 Publishers directory, 1984–85 97

Quality of life
 The new book of world rankings 88
Quotations, English
 The quotable woman 98
Quotations, maxims, etc.
 America the quotable 24

Rare books
 Rare books, 1983–84 99
Recreation rooms
 Better Homes and Gardens all about
  your house 30
Reference books
 A guide to reference and bibliography
  for theatre research 68
 A guide to reference books for small
  and medium-sized libraries,
  1970–1982 68
 Indians of North America 73
 Reference sources for small and
  medium-sized libraries 100
 Reference sources in library and
  information services 100
 Tools in the learning trade 108
 Where to find what 113
Reference services (Libraries)
 Where to find what 113
Regional planning
 Encyclopedia of community planning
  and environmental management
  54
Religion and science
 Victorian science and religion 111
Religions
 The Facts On File dictionary of
  religions 60
Republican Party (U.S.)
 The Democratic and Republican
  parties in America 45
Research
 Where to find what 113
Research grants
 Grants in the humanities 65
Retirement communities
 National continuing care directory 86
Rivers
 Rolling rivers 101
Rock music
 Find that tune 62
 New rock record 89
 Year by year in the rock era 118
Room layout (Dwellings)
 Better Homes and Gardens all about
  your house 30

Scholars
 Twentieth-century culture 109
School discipline
 Discipline in our schools 51
School libraries
 The elementary school library
  collection 52
Schools
 Peterson's annual guides/undergraduate
  study 93

Science
 A bibliography of the philosophy of
  science, 1945–1981 30
 Finding answers in science and
  technology 62
 Growing up with science 66
 McGraw-Hill concise encyclopedia of
  science & technology 80
 McGraw-Hill dictionary of
  engineering 81
 McGraw-Hill dictionary of science and
  engineering 81
 The new book of popular science 87
 Scientific and technical books and
  serials in print, 1984 102
Science, Ancient
 Album of science 24
Science, Medieval
 Album of science 24
Science fiction, American
 Women of the future 116
Science fiction, English
 Women of the future 116
Science fiction films
 Science fiction, horror and fantasy
  film and television credits 102
Science fiction television programs
 Science fiction, horror and fantasy
  film and television credits 102
Scientific illustration
 Album of science 24
Scientists
 Twentieth-century culture 109
 Who's who in science in Europe 114
Scrabble (Games)
 The complete word game dictionary
  40
Secretaries
 Secretarial word finder 103
Securities
 Words of Wall Street 116
Self-examination, Medical
 Do-it-yourself medical testing 51
Self-help techniques
 Self-help 103
Sex
 Human sexuality 71
Sex discrimination in education
 Guide to nonsexist teaching activities
  (K–12) 67
Sex role
 Guide to nonsexist teaching activities
  (K–12) 67
Sexism
 Guide to nonsexist teaching activities
  (K–12) 67
Shakespeare, William, 1564–1616
 Shakespearean criticism 104
Shelley, Mary Wollstonecraft,
  1797–1851
 The Frankenstein catalog 64
Short stories
 Twentieth-century short story
  explication 109
Slogans
 Advertising slogans of America 23
Slow learning children, Books for
 Choices 36
Social indicators
 The new book of world rankings
  88
Social sciences
 Opposing viewpoints sources 91
Social security
 The complete social security
  handbook 39

Social service
  Community resources directory 38
  Foundations 63
Social surveys
  Surveys, polls, censuses, and forecasts directory 106
Societies
  Ethnic information sources of the United States 59
Sociology
  Evaluating Chicago sociology 60
Solar energy
  Better Homes and Gardens all about your house 30
  The solar energy directory 105
Solar houses
  Better Homes and Gardens all about your house 30
Soul music
  Find that tune 62
Sound recordings
  The encyclopedic discography of Victor recordings 58
Southern states
  Encyclopedia of religion in the South 57
Southwest, New
  Billy the Kid 31
Soviet Union
  Companion to Russian history 38
Space (Architecture)
  Better Homes and Gardens all about your house 30
Spanish language
  Revistas 101
Spanish literature
  Spanish literature, 1500–1700 105
Special librarians
  Who's who in special libraries, 1983–1984 114
Special Libraries Association
  Who's who in special libraries, 1983–1984 114
Spy stories
  Mystery, detective, and espionage magazines 86
Spy stories, American
  The cold war file 37
Spy stories, English
  The cold war file 37
Statistical services
  Statistics sources 105
Statistics
  DataMap 44
  The new book of world rankings 88
  Statistics sources 105
Student aid
  The college money handbook 38
Study, Method of
  Tools in the learning trade 108
Subsidiary corporations
  America's corporate families and international affiliates, 1983 28
Sullivan, Arthur, Sir, 1842–1900, Operas
  The complete Gilbert and Sullivan opera guide 39
Superstition
  Knock on wood 77
Symphonies
  The great symphonies 66
Symphony
  The great symphonies 66
Symptomatology
  A dictionary of symptoms 49

Teaching
  Bilingual educational publications in print, 1983 31
  Guide to nonsexist teaching activities (K–12) 67
  A multimedia approach to children's literature 85
Technical assistance, American
  U.S. nonprofit organizations in development assistance abroad 110
Technical education
  American community, technical, and junior colleges 24
  The vocational-technical core collection 111
Technology
  Finding answers in science and technology 62
  Growing up with science 66
  McGraw-Hill concise encyclopedia of science & technology 80
  McGraw-Hill dictionary of science and engineering 81
  The new book of popular science 87
  Scientific and technical books and serials in print, 1984 102
Telecommunications
  Dictionary of computing and new information technology 47
Television broadcasting
  Prime-time television 96
Television broadcasting of news
  U.S. television network news 110
Television personalities
  Who's who in television and cable 114
Tennyson, Alfred Tennyson, Baron, 1809–1892
  Tennyson 107
Theater
  American drama criticism 25
  Broadway bound 34
  The Crown guide to the world's great plays 44
  A guide to critical reviews 66
  A guide to reference and bibliography for theatre research 68
  The London stage, 1920–1929 80
  The Oxford companion to American theatre 92
  The Oxford companion to the theatre 93
Theology
  The Westminster dictionary of Christian theology 112
Trade-unions
  Biographical dictionary of American labor 31
  The labor almanac 77
Transportation
  The science universe series 102

United Nations
  Worldmark encyclopedia of the nations 118
U.S.
  American popular culture 25
  American popular illustration 26
  The American presidency 26
  The American presidency 26
  Business organizations and agencies directory 35
  Demography of racial and ethnic minorities in the United States 45

Dictionary of American military biography 46
Encyclopedia of American political history 53
Ethnic genealogy 58
Fiction 1876–1983 61
Government programs and projects directory 65
Index to America, v. 3 72
The national job bank 86
Population information in nineteenth century census volumes 95
The presidential-congressional political dictionary 96
The presidents 96
Scribner desk dictionary of American history 103
Social reform and reaction in America 104
Social welfare in America 104
Surveys, polls, censuses, and forecasts directory 106
U.S. government directories, 1970–1981 109
U.S. industrial outlook 1985 110
Who lived where 113
Year by year in the rock era 118
U.S. Congress
  Politics in America 94
  The presidential-congressional political dictionary 96
U.S. Environmental Protection Agency
  EPA index 51
Units
  Quantities and units of measurement 98
Universities
  Peterson's annual guides/undergraduate study 93
Universities and colleges
  American universities and colleges 26
  Directory of United States traditional and alternative colleges and universities 50
  The financing of American higher education 62
  Peterson's annual guides/undergraduate study 93
Urbanization
  Urban development in the Third World 110

Vehicles, Military
  World directory of modern military vehicles 117
Victor Talking Machine Company
  The encyclopedic discography of Victor recordings 58
Video display terminals
  Terminals and printers buyer's guide 107
Vietnamese Conflict, 1961–1975
  The wars in Vietnam, Cambodia, and Laos, 1945–1982 111
Vision
  The science universe series 102
Vocabulary
  1000 most important words 91
  1000 most practical words 91
  The wordtree 116
Vocational education
  The vocational-technical core collection 111

Vocational guidance
  Materials for occupational education 83
  The national job bank 86
  Psychware 97
Voluntarism
  Community resources directory 38
Voting
  The American electorate 25

Walls
  Better Homes and Gardens all about your house 30
Warships
  Combat fleets of the world, 1984/85 38
  Conway's all the world's fighting ships 1947–1982 42
Watergate Affair, 1972–
  Watergate 111
Weights and measures
  Quantities and units of measurement 98
West (U.S.)
  The frontier experience 64
West (U.S.) in literature
  Encyclopedia of frontier and western fiction 55
Western stories
  Encyclopedia of frontier and western fiction 55
Windows
  Better Homes and Gardens all about your house 30
Women
  The Europa biographical dictionary of British women 59
  The quotable woman 98
  Women and folklore 115
  Women and sexuality in America 115
  Women in China 115
  Women in Western European history 115
  Women of the future 116
Women composers
  International discography of women composers 75
Women musicians
  The musical woman 86
  Women composers, conductors, and musicians of the twentieth century 115

Women novelists
  Women novelists, 1891–1920 115
Word games
  The complete word game dictionary 40
Word processors
  Office automation and word processing buying guide 91
World politics
  World view, 1984 117
World politics in literature
  The cold war file 37
World War, 1914–1918
  The Marshall Cavendish illustrated encyclopedia of World War I 83

Youth
  Research on adolescence for youth services 101

Zoology
  The encyclopedia of North American wildlife 56
  Macmillan illustrated animal encyclopedia 82

INDEX TO TYPE OF MATERIAL

ALMANACS
   Animal rights and the law 122
   Canadian almanac & directory 36
   The Hispanic almanac 131

ANNUALS
   The book publishing annual 33
   Current issues 126
   The historic preservation yearbook 69
   Jane's 1983–84 aviation review 76
   People's Republic of China year-book 137
   State policy data book, 1984 139
   U.S. industrial outlook 110
   Washington 84 141
   World view, 1984 117
   Year by year in the rock era 118
   The year in soaps 142

ATLASES
   Atlas of the Jewish world 28
   Cultural atlas of China 44
   Kister's atlas buying guide 76
   Peoples and places of the past 93
   The Prentice-Hall university atlas 96
   Rand McNally atlas of the United States 98
   Rand McNally contemporary world atlas 98
   Rand McNally family world atlas 98
   Reader's Digest wide world atlas 98
   The Times atlas of the oceans 108
   The Times atlas of world history 108

BIBLIOGRAPHIES
   Abstracts and indexes in science and technology 121
   African books in print 121
   Aging 23
   American and British poetry 121
   American education, 1622–1860 122
   The American electorate 25
   American Indian novelists 122
   American popular culture 26
   American popular illustration 26
   The American presidency 26
   American working class history 27
   Anglo-Saxon and Anglo-Scandinavian Art 122
   An annotated bibliography of the history of data processing 28
   Any-book 119
   Architecture 28
   Art and architecture in the Balkans 122
   The art and history of printing 122
   The atomic papers 29
   Automation in libraries 29

Basic reference sources 123
Benjamin Franklin, 1721–1906 30
The Bible book 30
Bibliography of British economic and social history 123
Bibliography of discographies 30
Bibliography of European economic and social history 123
A bibliography of the philosophy of science, 1945–1981 30
Bilingual-bicultural education 31
Bilingual educational publications in print 31
Billy the Kid 31
Biographical reference sources 1
Black access 32
Black-Jewish relations in the United States, 1752–1984 32
Books and real life 123
Books out of print, 1980–1983 33
Bridge 33
Business information applications and sources 34
Business publications index and abstracts 35
The challenge of aging 36
Children's books of international interest 124
Children's home reference library 3
Choices 36
Communications and society 38
Computer books and serials in print 125
Computer publishers and publications 40
Contemporary artists 41
Cooks' books 126
Corporate America 42
Crime fiction, 1749–1980 42
The critical reputation of F. Scott Fitzgerald 43
Cuban literature 44
Cubans in the United States 126
Deans' list of recommended reading for prelaw and law students 126
Death and dying in the classroom 127
The Democratic and Republican parties in America 45
Demography of racial and ethnic minorities in the United States 45
A dictionary of American composers 46
Discipline in our schools 51
Dissertations in the history of education, 1970–1980 128
Drug abuse and the elderly 128
Drugs and sex 51
EPA index 51

Education-for-health 52
The elementary school library collection 52
Energy research guide 58
Entomology 58
Ethnicity and aging 129
Evaluating Chicago sociology 60
Fantasy for children 61
Fatherhood U.S.A. 129
Fiction 1876–1983 61
The financing of American higher education 62
First editions 63
Foundations of moral education 64
The frontier experience 64
Future war novels 130
The Garland recipe index 130
General consumer health reference books 5
The good book guide for business 65
Guide to industry special issues 67
Guide to Islam 67
Guide to nonsexist teaching activities (K–12) 67
A guide to reference and bibliography for theatre research 68
A guide to reference books for small and medium-sized libraries, 1970–1982 68
Handbook of Latin American art 68
Herbs 69
A Hispanic heritage 132
Historical maps on file 70
The Hollywood novel and other novels about film, 1912–1982 132
The Holocaust 132
Home reference books for junior and senior high school students 7
Horror and science fiction films III 132
Human food uses 71
Human sexuality 71
Index to legal essays 72
Indexing and abstracting, 1977–1981 73
Indians of North America 73
Information sourcebook for marketers and strategic planners 34
Insular art 74
Integrating women's studies into the curriculum 133
International bibliography of special directories 74
Keat's major odes 76
The Ku Klux Klan 133
Large type books in print 78
Late Georgian and Regency England, 1760–1837 78
Latin America, 1979–1983 78

Latin American politics 79
Law, medicine, and health care 134
Libraries in American periodicals before 1876 79
The literature of chess 79
Materials for occupational education 83
Media and microcomputers in the library 134
Melville dissertations, 1924–1980 84
Modern English-Canadian prose 84
Modern Latin American art 84
Money management information source book 85
More notes from a different drummer 85
Motorcycles in magazines, 1895–1983 135
A multimedia approach to children's literature 85
Native American folklore, 1879–1979 87
Native American periodicals and newspapers, 1828–1982 87
The new state of the world atlas 136
Novel verdicts 90
Opera and concert singers 136
Philip Roth 137
Popular music 95
Psychocriticism 97
Race and ethnic relations 138
Rare books, 1983–84 99
Rare halos, mirages, anomalous rainbows 138
Reference sources for small and medium-sized libraries 100
Reference sources in library and information services 100
Research guide to musicology 138
Research guide to the arid land of the world 101
Research on adolescence for youth services 101
Revistas 101
Running 138
The schoolroom poets 102
Science and technology reference sources for high school and undergraduate libraries 15
Science books for children 138
Scientific and technical books and serials in print, 1984 102
Sean O'Casey and his critics 138
Self-help 103
Social reform and reaction in America 104
Social welfare in America 104
Spanish literature, 1500–1700 105
State maps on file 139
Statistics sources 105
Style manuals of the English-speaking world 106
A subject bibliography of the history of American higher education 106
Television comedy series 106
Tennyson 107
Tests 107
Tests in print III 107
Twentieth-century short story explication 109
Union list of film periodicals 140
U.S. television network news 110
Urban development in the Third World 110
Victorian science and religion 110
The vocational-technical core collection 111
The wars in Vietnam, Cambodia and Laos, 1945–1982 111
Watergate 111
What's in print 141
Where to find what 113
William Morris in private press and limited editions 114
Women and deviance 142
Women and folklore 115
Women and sexuality in America 115
Women in China 115
Women in Western European history 115
Women of the future 116
Words of love 116
Young people with problems 118

CATALOGS
American eccentrics 122
Annals of English verse, 1770–1835 122
Education-for-health 52
The Frankenstein catalog 64
The free software catalog and directory 130
Guide to microforms in print 67
A historical catalogue of scientists and scientific books 132
The illustrated encyclopedia of metal toys 133
NTIS tech notes 135
Psychware 97
The record producers file 138
Terminals and printers buyer's guide 107
Wheeled armoured fighting vehicles in service 113
Whole earth software catalog 141

CHRONOLOGIES
Album of science 24
Chronology of culture 125
Day by day 45
The twentieth century 140

CRITICISM
American drama criticism 25
American writers before 1800 27
British writers 34
Chaucer source and analogue criticism 124
The cold war file 37
The complete Gilbert and Sullivan opera guide 39
Critical survey of long fiction 43
Critical survey of poetry 44
European writers 59
Frew's daily archive 130
Guide to musical America 67
Literature criticism from 1400 to 1800 79
Selected film criticism 103
Shakespearean criticism 104

DATABASES
Marquis who's who 119

DICTIONARIES
The ALA glossary of library and information science 23
Advertising slogans of America 23
BBC pronouncing dictionary of British names 123
BKSTS dictionary of audio-visual terms 29
The Cambridge guide to English literature 36
Companion to Russian history 38
The complete word game dictionary 40
A concise dictionary of foreign expressions 125
A concise dictionary of law 41
The concise McGraw-Hill dictionary of modern economics 125
A consumer's dictionary of food additives 126
Dictionaries 45
The dictionary of American bird names 127
Dictionary of animals 46
Dictionary of business and economics 47
Dictionary of computing 47
Dictionary of computing and new information technology 47
The dictionary of dreams 127
A dictionary of drug abuse terms and terminology 47
A dictionary of eponyms 47
The dictionary of historic nicknames 48
Dictionary of historical terms 48
Dictionary of library and educational technology 48
A dictionary of media terms 127
Dictionary of medieval civilization 48
The dictionary of modern economics 48
A dictionary of mottoes 49
Dictionary of new information technology acronyms 27
A dictionary of pictorial subjects from classical literature 49
The dictionary of retailing 127
A dictionary of sexist quotations 127
A dictionary of symptoms 49
An encyclopaedia of Napoleon's Europe 53
Encyclopedia of American forest and conservation history 53
Encyclopedia of banking and finance 54
Encyclopedia of community planning and environmental management 54
The encyclopedia of drug abuse 55
Encyclopedia of occultism & parapsychology 56
Encyclopedia of religion in the South 57
The Facts On File dictionary of archaeology 60
The Facts On File dictionary of botany 60
The Facts On File dictionary of design and designers 60
The Facts On File dictionary of fitness 129
The Facts On File dictionary of religions 60
The Facts On File dictionary of troublesome words 129
The films of the seventies 62
The Harlem renaissance 69
Harrod's librarian's glossary of terms 69
Hispanic first names 132
Historical dictionary of Egypt 70
Historical dictionary of Napoleonic France, 1799–1815 70

Index to type of material 155

The hockey encyclopedia 70
Idioms and phrases index 71
Illustrated dictionary of art terms 71
International acronyms, initialisms and abbreviations dictionary 133
International Center of Photography encyclopedia of photography 74
Knock on wood 77
Lite English 79
MASA 80
MBA's dictionary 80
McGraw-Hill concise encyclopedia of science & technology 80
McGraw-Hill dictionary of chemistry 81
McGraw-Hill dictionary of earth sciences 81
McGraw-Hill dictionary of engineering 81
McGraw-Hill dictionary of science and engineering 81
Macmillan dictionary for students 82
The Macquarie dictionary 83
Medical meanings 135
The money encyclopedia 85
The new Grove dictionary of musical instruments 89
No uncertain terms 136
1,000 most important words 91
1,000 most practical words 91
The Overlook martial arts dictionary 91
The Oxford companion to Canadian literature 92
The Oxford companion to the theatre 93
The oxter English dictionary 137
Prefixes and other word-initial elements of English 95
The Prentice-Hall standard glossary of computer terminology 96
The presidential-congressional political dictionary 96
The private lives of English words 97
Psychiatric glossary 138
Quantities and units of measurement 98
The Random House thesaurus 99
A reference guide to modern fantasy for children 100
Science fiction, horror and fantasy film and television credits 102
Scribner desk dictionary of American history 103
The TypEncyclopedia 140
Webster's new twentieth century dictionary of the English language unabridged 111
Webster's II new Riverside university dictionary 112
The Westminster dictionary of Christian theology 112
What indoor plant is that? 141
Words of Wall Street 116
The wordtree 116
World guide to abbreviations of organizations 117
Ye gods 118

DIRECTORIES
Address book 121
Agricultural research centres 23
American book trade directory 24
American community, technical, and junior colleges 24
American library directory 25

American universities and colleges 26
America's corporate families and international affiliates, 1983 28
America's meeting places 122
Biographical dictionary of American labor 31
Biographical dictionary of Latin American historians and historiography 31
Biographical dictionary of psychology 32
The biographical dictionary of scientists 32
Black elected officials 123
Book illustrators of the twentieth century 32
Business mini-micro software directory 35
Business organizations and agencies directory 35
CP/M software directory 124
Caribbean business telephone directory 124
Children's periodicals of the United States 36
The college money handbook 38
Combat fleets of the world, 1984/85 38
Community resources directory 38
The complete peerage 125
Computer graphics marketplace 1983–84 40
Consumer sourcebook 41
Contemporary authors 42
The corpus administrative index 42
Country experts in the federal government 126
Data pro/McGraw-Hill guide to CP/M software 45
The dictionary of American Catholic biography 127
A dictionary of American composers 46
Dictionary of American medical biography 46
Dictionary of American military biography 46
Dictionary of business biography 47
Directory of Central America organizations 128
Directory of federal technology resources 1984 49
Directory of fee based information services 128
Directory of financial aids for minorities 1984–1985 49
Directory of food and nutrition information services and resources 50
The directory of mail order catalogs 128
Directory of online databases 50
Directory of short-run book printers 128
The directory of software publishers 50
Directory of United States traditional and alternative colleges and universities 50
Earth and astronomical sciences research centres 52
Educators' passport to international jobs 128
Encyclopedia of associations 54
Ethnic information sources of the United States 59

The Europa biographical dictionary of British women 59
Federal statistical directory 129
The fifty billion dollar directory 62
Film directors 62
Gevers international consultants 65
Global guide to international education 130
Government programs and projects directory 65
Grants in the humanities 65
Great romantic ruins of England and Wales 130
Guide to colleges in New England 131
Guide to fairs and festivals in the United States 66
IBM software directory 133
Information America 73
Interlibrary loan policies directory 74
The international directory of little magazines and small presses 74
The international foundation directory 75
International organizations 75
Jane's spaceflight directory 76
Japan directory of professional associations 133
Lambert's world of trade, finance & economic development 77
Leading consultants in computer software and custom programming 134
The MEED Middle East financial directory 1983 80
Macmillan biographical encyclopedia of photographic artists and innovators 82
The Macmillan guide to correspondence study 82
Medical research centres 84
Musicals 135
National continuing care directory 86
O'Dwyer's directory of public relations firms, 1983 91
Omni online database directory 136
Online database search services directory 91
Peterson's annual guides/undergraduate study 93
Peterson's competitive colleges 137
Peterson's guide to colleges in the Midwest 137
Publishers directory, 1984–85 97
Sheldon's retail and Phelon's resident buyers' 100th annual edition 138
Solar census 139
The solar energy directory 105
Standard directory of advertisers, 1983 105
State political action legislation and regulations 139
Surveys, polls, censuses, and forecasts directory 106
Taft corporate giving directory, 1985 139
Taft foundation reporter, 1985 140
Telephone services directory 106
Thinkers of the twentieth century 108
Twentieth-century culture 109
Ulrich's international periodicals directory 109
U.S. government directories, 1970–1981 109

Index to type of material

U.S. nonprofit organizations in development assistance abroad 110
Want's federal-state court directory 141
Ward's directory of 51,000 largest U.S. corporations 111
Who lived where 113
Who was who on screen 113
Who's who in American music 113
Who's who in aviation and aerospace 114
Who's who in frontier science and technology 141
Who's who in science in Europe 114
Who's who in special libraries, 1983–84 114
Who's who in television and cable 114
Winning money for college 142
World directory of energy information 117
World guide to special libraries 117
The yellow book 142

DISCOGRAPHIES
The collector's guide to the American musical theatre 37
The encyclopedic discography of Victor recordings 58
The essential jazz records 58
The illustrated discography of surf music, 1961–1965 133
International discography of women composers 75
International index to recorded poetry 75
Jailhouse rock 76
The Metropolitan Opera on record 84
New rock record 89
Popular music 95

ENCYCLOPEDIAS
1984 Annual encyclopedia roundup 10
Bateman New Zealand encyclopedia 29
The Canadian encyclopedia 124
Encyclopaedia Iranica 52
Encyclopaedia of drawing 53
Encyclopedia of American political history 53
Encyclopedia of crime and justice 55
Encyclopedia of frontier and western fiction 55
Encyclopedia of information systems and services 128
The encyclopedia of mammals 56
The encyclopedia of North American wildlife 56
Encyclopedia of psychology 57
Growing up with science 66
International encyclopedia of psychiatry, psychology, psychoanalysis and neurology 75
Knowledge encyclopedia 77
McGraw-Hill encyclopedia of electronics and computers 81
Macmillan illustrated animal encyclopedia 82
The Marshall Cavendish illustrated encyclopedia of World War I 83
Mystery, detective and espionage magazines 86
The new encyclopaedia Britannica 136

The New York Times encyclopedia of film, 1896–1979 90
The official encyclopedia of bridge 136
Prime-time television 96
The science universe series 102
Van Nostrand Reinhold encyclopedia of chemistry 140
The video encyclopedia 141
Worldmark encyclopedia of the nations 118

FILMOGRAPHIES
Dark city 126
From museums, galleries and studios 64
Hollywood and American history 132

GAZETTEERS
Encyclopedia of historic places 55

GUIDEBOOKS
ABC's of nature 121
American Indian and Alaska native newspapers and periodicals, 1826–1924 25
British literary magazines 33
Children's literature from A to Z 124
Countries and islands of the world 126
The Crown guide to the world's great plays 44
The great symphonies 66
Guide to innovation resources and planning for the smaller business 131
A guide to the architecture of London 68
Guide to the use of four standard reference works 131
Made in America 83
Microcomputer software buyer's guide 135
Simon and Schuster's guide to garden flowers 104
Symbol sourcebook 139
Tools in the learning trade 108
What flower is that 141

HANDBOOKS
African political facts since 1945 23
The American counties 24
American family history 25
Arthritis alternatives 123
Arts and sports USA 123
The athlete's game plan for college and career 123
Banker's desk reference 29
Better Homes and Gardens all about your house 30
Book marketing handbook 33
Bowker's 1985 complete sourcebook of personal computing 123
Broadway bound 34
Business forms on file 124
CRC handbook of chemistry and physics 36
China trade handbook 124
Climate normals for the U.S. 37
The college cost book 125
The college money handbook 1985 125
Common Market digest 38
The complete book of U.S. presidents 39
The complete handbook of garden plants 39

The complete social security handbook 39
The consumer protection manual 41
Copywriter's handbook 126
A dictionary of classical reference in English poetry 127
Do-it-yourself medical testing 51
Electronics ready reference manual 128
The encyclopedia of mammals 56
The end of the Beatles 129
Ethnic genealogy 58
European writers 59
A field guide to America's history 129
Finding answers in science and technology 62
Finding co-ops 130
Foundations 63
Freedom in the world 64
Halliwell's filmgoer's companion 131
Handbook of Latin American studies 131
Handbook on the aged in the United States 68
Health and medicine series 131
Helpful hints for better living 131
Home book of quotations 132
How to manage 132
I stand corrected 71
An Ibsen companion 71
The labor almanac 77
Lands and peoples 78
Larousse encyclopedia of archaeology 78
The law of inheritance in all fifty states 134
Library of nations 134
The marching band handbook 134
Medical science and the law 84
Memorable film characters 135
Money A to Z 135
The musical woman 86
The national job bank 86
The new book of popular science 87
The new compleat astrologer 88
Nuclear weapons databook 90
Office automation and word processing buying guide 91
Official publications of Western Europe 136
Our food, air, and water 136
The Oxford companion to American literature 92
The Oxford companion to American theatre 92
The Oxford guide to word games 137
People's handbook of allergies and allergens 137
Personal forms on file 124
Pictorial history of the Jewish people 137
Political dissent 94
Politics in America 94
Pop culture mania 94
The president 138
The presidents 96
The quotable woman 98
Reader's Digest consumer adviser 99
Rolling rivers 101
Secretarial word finder 103
Send me a memo 103
Subject compilations of state laws, 1979–1983 139
TV trivia teasers 139
Tennis 140
Trivial conquest 140

Word processors and the writing process 142
World directory of modern military vehicles 117
World economic survey 1984 142
World human rights guide 142
World of science 142

INDEXES
Adult video index '84 121
Audiovisual resources in food and nutrition 123
Combined retrospective index to book reviews in humanities journals, 1802–1974 125
The computer information series 40
Computers and information processing world index 40
DataMap 44
Dissertations in the history of education, 1970–1980 128
Federal register 129
Find that tune 62
Fine and applied arts terms index 63
The great song thesaurus 65
A guide to critical reviews 66
Index to America 72
Index to international public opinion, 1982–1983 72
An index to microform collections 72
Index to poetry for children and young people, 1976–1981 72
Index to poetry in popular periodicals, 1955–1959 73
Indexed journals 73
Iran media index 133
Literary criticism index 134
Music psychology index 86
National Geographic index 1947–1983 135
News bank 120
Perspectives of new music 93
Population information in nineteenth century census volumes 95
Print index 97
Twentieth-century author biographies master index 109
Women novelists, 1891–1920 115

SOURCEBOOKS
America the quotable 24
American landmark legislation 122
Choreography by George Balanchine 124
The computer data and database source book 125
Conway's all the world's fighting ships, 1947–1982 42
Design on file 127
Drug use and abuse 51
The encyclopedia of second careers 57
The Eugene O'Neill companion 59
Everyday legal forms 129
Festivals sourcebook 61
Follies and foibles 130
Gary Null's nutrition sourcebook for the '80s 64
The Guinness book of Olympics facts and feats 131
The home how-to sourcebook 70
International development resource books 133
Literature searching in science, technology, and agriculture 134
The London stage, 1920–1929 80
Mutual fund sourcebook 135
The new book of American rankings 87
The new book of world rankings 88
New Iberian world 89
Opposing viewpoints sources 91
Paris Opera 93
A pictorial history of Blackamericans 94
Presidential also-rans and running mates, 1788–1980 138
Reader's Digest 101 do-it-yourself projects 99
A reference companion to the history of abnormal psychology 99
Research guide to philosophy 101
Statistical information on the financial services industry 105
Tests supplement 140
Who's who in Wagner 141
Women composers, conductors, and musicians of the twentieth century 115
Women filmmakers 142
Women in development 142

Ref Z 1035.1 S922 1984/85

FEB 2 5 1986